00 044 $4

California

Nancy May

John W. Caughey

with
Norris Hundley, jr.

Prentice-Hall, Inc., Englewood Cliffs, New Jersey 07632

FOURTH EDITION

California

History of
a Remarkable State

Library of Congress Cataloging in Publication Data

CAUGHEY, JOHN WALTON (date)
 California, history of a remarkable state.

 Rev. ed. of: California, a remarkable
state's life history. 3rd ed. 1970.
   Bibliography: p.
   Includes index.
   1. California—History. I. Hundley, Norris.
II. Title.
F861.C34 1982   979.4   81–23467
ISBN 0–13–1124 74–9   AACR2

Editorial/production supervision by Joan L. Lee
Cover design by Judith Winthrop
Manufacturing buyer: Edmund W. Leone

Jacket photograph by Edward Weston
© 1981 Center for Creative Photography
University of Arizona
Arizona Board of Regents
Used by permission.

Quotation from John Steinbeck, *Grapes of
Wrath*, reprinted by permission of Viking Penguin
Inc. Photograph of Upton Sinclair in 1934 repro-
duced by permission of *The Huntington Library,
San Marino, California.*

Prentice-Hall International, Inc., *London*
Prentice-Hall of Australia Pty. Limited, *Sydney*
Prentice-Hall of Canada, Ltd., *Toronto*
Prentice-Hall of India Private Limited, *New Delhi*
Prentice-Hall of Japan, Inc., *Tokyo*
Prentice-Hall of Southeast Asia Pte. Ltd., *Singapore*
Whitehall Books Limited, *Wellington, New Zealand*

To LaRee

Contents

Overview

On three sides California is marked off by arbitrary lines. The Spanish and American negotiators of the Florida treaty in 1819 drew the northern boundary. A diplomat trying to end the Texas-caused War with Mexico platted the southern boundary in 1846. The jointed eastern boundary was invented in the California constitutional convention in 1849 as a compromise between the small-state proposal of the Sierra Nevada and the large-state preference for the crest of the Rockies. Yet California as thus created makes sense.

For the Indian period anthropologists see six culture areas or ways of life in the expanse of "the original 48 states," one of them stretching into Mexico and three into Canada. California is the only state to have a culture area of its own, and within it a sixth of the Indians between Mexico and Canada.

Geographers catalog a wide range of elevations, precipitations, microclimates, minerals, vegetation, and the like in the state. Perhaps most notably it alone in the United States is favored with a Mediterranean climate which, with irrigation, permits extraordinary crop production.

Though discovered much earlier, Spanish occupation of California was delayed almost to the time of the American Revolution. Spain and then Mexico sent few colonists to this distant province. By 1846 when the American flag went up, the population other than un-controlled Indians numbered no more than 15,000, but the Spanish-Mexican heritage is out of all proportion to that number. As recently as 1930 three-fourths of the standard college texts dwelt on California's pre-American years, and for another generation the standard fourth-grade study was of the Indians, the missions, and the ranchos.

With discovery of gold California exploded into tremendous activity and developments in trade, transportation, politics, agriculture, lumbering, industry, commerce, and culture. The stress later shifted to wheat, railroads, health-seekers, and a real estate boom. At the turn of the century the orange, irrigation, tourists, port development, and the Pacific Electric flourished, and ahead lay capitalization on movie-making, the automobile, the retired, oil, and an influx of new residents not even halted by the Great Depression.

The pattern became clear that every generation requires a new history with new characters, new activities, new problems, and new responses, and with an approximate doubling of the population. That happened again during World War II and then on more majestic scale in the postwar extravaganza, 25 years in which the population rose from less than 10 million to more than 20 million and things material far more than doubled.

The material history of California has been likened to a multiple-decker ice cream cone with a generous gold-caramel dip, then a larger one for the 1870s and 80s, then ever-larger dips of still other flavors up to 1968, after which for the first time a smaller topping is in order.

There had been faith but never a guaranty that exponential growth would go on forever, not only supporting times over more Californians but covering up many mistakes. The recent past is certainly a change-up but not entirely a halt, though environmental considerations suggest that a halt would be in order.

On such order is the multilayered, frequently mutating history of California which we have tried to capture. Despite the enormous changes continuities are stubbornly persistent and, we hope, are caught in this rear-view mirror. Distinctive though California has been, its history is a remarkable sampling of the American experience.

This book owes much to the vast company of researchers and writers in this field, to insights from colleagues and students, to the ever-continuing discourse in the journals and elsewhere, and to the artists who captured or created many of the illustrations. Joan Lee, to whom we are deeply indebted, supervised production of this fourth edition.

John Caughey
Norris Hundley, jr.

California

Maps

California

CHAPTER 1

Cave Painting, Tassajara
Inspiration for Robinson Jeffers' Poem "Hands"

L. S. Slevin

Between the land of California and those who first discovered and settled it there came into being as perfect a symbiosis between the People and Nature as the world has known, the people taking in moderation, respectfully and knowledgeably, the people containing the population of their own species within numbers the natural garden could support. The conquerors wrested from its owners a land undespoiled: no tool heavier than a woman's wooden digging stick had broken the earth's protecting crust.

Theodora Kroeber
*Drawn from Life: California Indians
in Pen and Brush* (Ballena Press 1977)

The First Californians

The history of California has a tentative beginning with a Spanish discovery voyage just 50 years after Columbus began the process of discovering the New World of America. Four other voyages were made to this coast in the next 60 years. The first Spanish outpost that endured was established half a dozen years before the outbreak of the revolution that launched the United States as a nation. These dates, 1542 and 1769, mark the arrival of the first writer and the beginning of continuous record keeping, the familiar sources on which historians mainly rely.

In contrast the story of the inhabitants of California reaches back thousands of years, and the Indians have better claim than the Spaniards to be called the first Californians. Furthermore, for many years after 1542 they continued to be the only residents. Until 1849, when an avalanche of gold-seekers poured in, the Indians constituted the most numerous population and for another quarter century they were the largest racial minority.

Prehistory

Human skeletal remains found at Agoura and Mugu in the Santa Monica Mountains have been identified as 6,000 to 7,000 years old. More ancient are carved bones of animals long extinct, part of the salvage from the tar pits at La Brea in Los Angeles. Microscopic tests establish that the carving was done when the bones were "green" and the radiocarbon dating reads 15,500 years. Other finds may push the horizon back a bit more.

On the basis of archaeological evidence, anatomical characteristics, and culture traits and complexes, anthropologists have established that the original populating of America was over a bridge of land or ice from northeastern Asia to Alaska. In fairly short order, descendants of these pioneers spread throughout North and South America. Isolation and adaptation to contrasting environments then began to produce distinguishable physical types and ways of life. The California Indians and their culture at the time of white contact were products of this background, together with several waves of migration from other parts of Indian America.

Piecing together what has been learned from Indian artifacts and remains, testimony of surviving Indians, recorded descriptions from earliest contacts to the present, and analysis of Indian adaptations to the way of life imposed by the whites, anthropologists have little to report on year-to-year or even generation-to-generation development in Indian California. They cannot offer a prehistory at all approaching the sequential beauty and complexity of history, but they can describe, in detail, Indian life as it was at the coming of the whites. And that is precisely the information most useful to an understanding of what followed.

In California, as throughout Indian America, the way of life differed from tribe to tribe and even from village to village. One description will not do for all, but north of Mexico and south of Canada there were areas in which group descriptions were possible, such as for the corn-raising, lodge-dwelling, birchbark-canoe Indians of the Northeastern Woodlands, the buffalo hunters of the Plains, and the wood-carving, fishing Indians of the Northwest Coast. Anthropologists see this California unit as one of a half dozen such culture areas in the 48-state rectangle cornered at Bar Harbor, Miami, San Diego, and Seattle.

The Indians living in the desert southeastern quarter of California are seen as marginal members of the Southwestern culture area climaxed by the Pueblo Indians. A much larger number lived in the coastal and northern part of the state, including the Central Valley and the Sierra foothills. Their culture pattern calls for a description of its own.

As the Spaniards recognized at once, these Californians differed sharply from the city-dwelling, maize-growing, gold-working, highly organized Aztecs. Nowhere in California were there palisaded towns and vast cornfields such as De Soto saw in Alabama or multistory apartment houses such as Coronado found in New Mexico. The Spanish missionaries, when they began their work, complained that they had to teach the California natives almost everything. The overland pioneers from the United States also saw these Indians as many steps below the Iroquois or the Civilized Tribes of the Southeast, and much less formidable than the mounted warriors of the Plains.

The Californians, with the exception of some along the lower Colorado River, did not practice agriculture or make pottery. They used no metals, had no domesticated animals other than the dog, did not read or write, and placed little emphasis on organized warfare, government, or religion. Yet by hunting and fishing and especially by gathering edible plants, they had assured themselves a reliable food supply. They excelled in certain skills, notably basket weaving and boat building. They had an oral literature of tradition and wisdom, and their social customs yielded substantial satisfactions. Thus seen, they are promoted several grades above the level assigned by Spanish and American pioneers.

Numbers and Groups

As to the initial number of California Indians we have estimates rather than a count. In the 1870s, when no more than 25,000 survived, Stephen Powers envisioned 700,000 at the time of first contact. The first scientific calculation came half a century later. A. L. Kroeber, drawing on his cyclopedic knowledge of the lifestyles and dietary habits of these Indians, the food supply, and testimony of early observers, reduced the figure to 130,000, not much above the capacity of the Rose Bowl and miniscule compared to the millions Cortés had found in southern Mexico.

Another half century later, Sherbourne Cook and other scientists accepted Kroeber's estimates for the quarter of the state south and east of the Tehachapi, increased it moderately for the south central coast, but trebled it or more for the San Joaquin and Sacramento Valleys and for the coastal strip from Monterey north. They arrived at a total of 310,000.

Their revisionism is slight for the area Spain actually occupied, where the missions functioned, and where a number of early counts were made. The modern revisionists also posit times over more Indians in the West Indies, southern Mexico, and the present United States. All agree that in this nation's Indian period California had about a sixth of the population. Relatively that is a greater concentration than modern California can claim. By the 1980 census it had only a tenth of the nation's residents.

The Indians of California are identified by tribes, several dozen in number, and they often are described tribe by tribe. The thousand or more rancherías (villages) in which they lived had considerably more cohesion. These Indians also are identifiable by the languages they spoke, some 135 in number, and on analysis classified as representing half a dozen linguistic families.

The Penutian family with such tribes as the Miwok, Maidu, Yokuts, and Costano, held the central part of the state from Mt. Shasta to the southern San Joaquin Valley

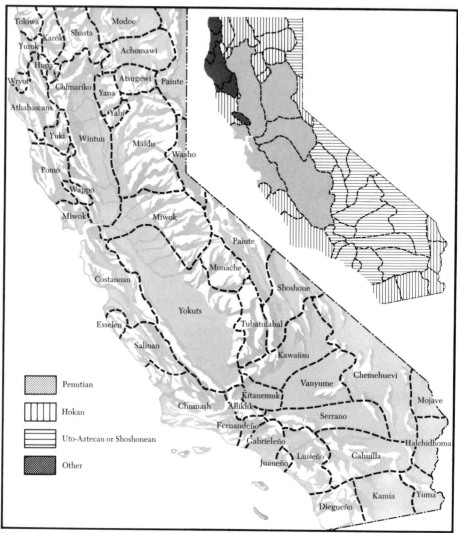

Indian Tribes and Languages

Legend:
- Penutian
- Hokan
- Uto-Aztecan or Shoshonean
- Other

and from the Golden Gate to the Sierra foothills.

The Pomo of Sonoma, Lake, and Mendocino counties were of the Hokan family, as were the Karok, Shastan, and Yana capping the Sacramento Valley, the Washo and Chumash, and further to the south, the Diegueño, Cocopa, Yuma, and Mojave.

The Shoshonean contingent included the Paiute and Mono, the Chemehuevi, Cahuilla, and Serrano, the Luiseño, Juaneño, and Gabrielino. More distant members of this linguistic family were the Comanche and the Aztecs. Language is one indicator that these Shoshoneans were relatively late arrivals in California.

Far to the north were the Yuki with a speech of their own, the Oregon-affiliated Modoc, the Algonkian-speaking Wiyot and Yarok, and a few Athabascan speakers.

Material Culture

Throughout California the fundamental garment was a two-piece apron of buckskin, shredded bark, or other plant fibers, worn with the smaller apron in front. The back piece extended to the thighs and might meet the front apron at the sides. For females this double apron was universal; even girl babies only a few days old were so attired. The manly fashion was to go naked. In cold weather men and women wrapped themselves in blankets, preferably of otter skins though more often of rabbit skins or deerskin. The central and northern Californians had moccasins but normally went barefoot. Skin leggings and oval snowshoes had more restricted distribution. South of the Tehachapi sandals replaced moccasins but again were not worn constantly. Basketry caps were common in the north and south but not in central California. Southern women used them as a pad for the pack straps; in the north they were fashionable as a regular item of female attire.

Buildings varied widely. Some were covered with brush, others with thatch, bark, or earth. Conical and dome shapes were favored except in the northwest where the rectangular pattern of the neighboring woodworking experts was followed. Some houses were partly dug out. Most were one-family dwellings and, except in the northwest, all were rude huts.

Sweat houses rather than residences were the most characteristic structures. Throughout central California sweat houses were small and conical, covered with earth to conserve heat, and reserved for men. After kindling an open fire inside the sweat house (temescal), three or four men would enter and lounge on the floor to escape the smoke. When they were perspiring freely, they rushed out and plunged into a nearby stream or lake. For certain disorders, such as rheumatic complaints, this treatment was beneficial, but when applied to new maladies, such as measles and smallpox introduced by the whites, it was disastrous. Yet therapeutic use was at most incidental; the sweat house was really a daily masculine social habit. In northwestern California the temescales were larger and served as clubs where the men assembled to discuss affairs of state. In some villages it was customary for the men to spend the night at the temescal and only the women and children slept in the ordinary houses.

Most of the Californians had no better boats than tule balsas, bundles of reeds hurriedly tied together for ferrying a river or made with greater care and propelled by poles or paddles on lakes and bays. Dugouts, carved from cedar logs, were employed in the northwestern rivers and bays and on the ocean. By sewing planks together the Chumash and Gabrielino made seaworthy boats described as trim, light, and capacious. They even paddled these boats back and forth to the Channel Islands.

The most common archaeological specimen in California is the stone grinding bowl or mortar. The Indians had many other implements of stone, bone, shell, and wood, some of them less enduring. These implements included simple bows and arrows in the south and sinew-backed bows in the north, arrows with flint or obsidian points, harpoons, spears, awls and arrow straighteners, rattles and whistles, bull roarers, and flutes, and in the south a throwing stick for rabbit hunting. Pottery was much less emphasized and limited to the region of strongest Southwestern influence.

Shields and protective armor were almost unknown. Bows and arrows, spears, and clubs were used, but in actual fighting the Californians exhibited a more primitive tendency to let fly any stones that might be lying about. Warfare was uncommon. One village might attack a neighboring one to avenge a visitation of disease supposedly caused by the neighbors, but the fighting usually stopped before many lives were lost. There was very little discipline or strategy, though Stanislau and Modoc Jack later won recognition as highly capable leaders. Scalps were sometimes taken, but scalping as a means of winning renown and scalp dances to claim public honors were not California traits.

Hunting and fishing were done mainly with nets and traps. Although fish and game were sometimes speared, the Channel Indians did most of their fishing with hook and line. Large game was generally avoided. Coyotes and eagles had mythological connections that secured them a reverent regard. Bears were looked upon as semihuman and the flesh of the dog was abhorred as poisonous. Along with the total lack of agriculture, these taboos seriously restricted the food list. Yet an adequate food supply was characteristic rather than exceptional. Acorns were the staple, with herbs and grass seeds next in importance, followed by fish, shellfish, rabbits, and other small game. Snakes, angleworms, grasshop-

Indian Mortar Holes, Yosemite National Park   *Ansel Adams,* This Is the American Earth

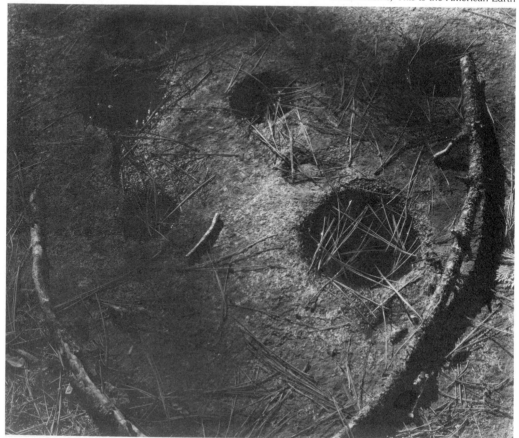

pers, honey, snails, and grubs were relished but their use was by no means universal.

Throughout much of the area oak groves dotted the landscape and provided large and regular crops of acorns. Acorns could readily be stored and, being richly nutritious, were eminently suitable for human consumption, provided that the tannic acid could be removed.

The clever extraction process represents one of the greatest California achievements. Since food preparation was women's work, the leaching procedure was probably a woman's invention, as were other refinements and improvements. Taking a few handfuls of acorns from the basketry granary, she removed the husks and pulverized the nut meats, using a stone pestle on a bedrock mortar or in a bottomless basket on a rock slab or stone bowl. The flour was then winnowed by tossing in a shallow basket. Meanwhile, water had been heated by dropping hot stones into a basket of water. The meal was spread out on a sand pile and leached with eight or ten doses of hot water. When the water ran off clear, revealing that the tannic acid was gone, the meal was gathered up and cooked in water, again heated by plunging hot stones into the basket. Acorn meal swells up like cornstarch, forming a gruel or pudding, which was eaten either plain or flavored with berries, nuts, or meat.

Although ingenious, the acorn process was most laborious and time consuming. Like manna, prepared acorn meal would keep only a short time; the California women therefore were almost constantly employed in some part of the process. Once developed, the process became firmly established. Grinding was extended to other foods, such as buckeye berries and rabbit meat, a special boon to toothless old people.

Basketry was the handicraft in which the Californians excelled. They used baskets for all conceivable purposes—for hats, for storage granaries, for containers of all sorts, and for cooking vessels. In some instances cooking baskets were caulked with pitch or tar, but others were woven so compactly as to be watertight. These baskets could withstand stone boiling provided the cook stirred and kept the hot stone from resting too long against the side or bottom. The basketmakers commanded several techniques of weaving and many methods of decorating in geometric or pictorial designs or by application of shell mosaics, beads, or feathers. Museum collections provide vivid exhibits of this California skill. The most skilled weavers enjoyed proving their craftsmanship by fabricating tiny thimble-sized baskets, perfect in almost microscopic detail, and remarkable demonstrations of virtuosity. Basketry too was women's work.

Social and Religious Practices

In almost all these tribes the largest political unit was the ranchería. In most villages the chieftainship was hereditary and not military. Some chiefs were women, some had an assistant chief, some had specified assistants to act as messengers, some were accorded deference, but none had much power.

Most of the tribes south of San Francisco were split into two parts with descent traced along the father's side and with marriage partners to be selected from the other. Marriage was characteristically arranged by purchase, though in the south often only on a token basis. Several tribes had kinship taboos, such as against conversing with one's mother-in-law. The Yana had separate dialects for men and women. Cremation was standard in most of California. In the northwest the Indians held slaves and placed great emphasis on wealth, though they lacked the associated symbolism of the property-minded Kwakiutl and Haida. Other Californians were less mercenary but prized strings of dentalium shells or clamshell

Chumash Baskets Presented to the Malaspina Expedition at Monterey in 1791

Museo de América, Madrid

beads and cylinders of magnesite or shell.

From the pioneers, both Spanish and American, later Californians inherited a low appraisal of the California Indians, often spoken of in contempt as Digger Indians, a canard that anthropologists protested as inappropriate and uncalled for. Certain modern writers lapse into the old attitude and, in addition, picture these Indians as wallowing in vermin, filth, and stench. To these writers it seems irrelevant that the Spanish and American frontiersmen went a long time between baths and changes of clothes. Allowance should be made for liberal exposure of the Indians to one cleansing element, the air. The temescal also was an effective cleanser. Early visitors report many rancherías where everyone bathed daily and speak of fastidiousness and cleanliness.

The Californians had a variety of games calling for strength or dexterity, among them contests roughly similar to shinny, lacrosse, football, double ball, and the hoop and pole game. They were addicted to gambling, betting heavily on athletic contests and on guessing games such as the hand game (similar to up-jinks) and the throwing of marked sticks (similar to dice). The Californians by all accounts played the hand game zealously and passionately, appointing someone to keep up the fire and to sing, an accompaniment that doubtless helped the players to keep poker faces. Psychologically, poker and the hand game are very similar. In Indian California there was no frowning on the game or on the betting that went with it.

Shamans, women as well as men, cured through songs or by removing the "disease object," usually by pretended sucking. In much of California, the shamans' power to cure was believed to rest upon having within their own bodies disease objects which would have caused a nonshaman immense pain. There also were specialists: weather shamans who engaged in rainmaking, rattlesnake shamans who handled snakebite cases, and grizzly bear shamans who either changed into bears or masqueraded in bearskins, thereby gaining extraordinary powers, which, it was hoped, they would use for the good of the tribe.

Ceremonials were few but some were highly developed. A girls' adolescence ceremony was universal and was taken as the occasion for liberal preachments on the advisability of good behavior for the benefit of the entire community. Southern and Sierra tribes also had an annual mourning ceremony. Other ceremonies occasionally encountered included semiconfinement of the father at time of childbirth, New Year observances, boys' puberty rites, the first salmon rites, and the ant ordeal.

More distinctive were the initiation rituals of the Kuksu cult in central California and of the toloache, or Jimsonweed, cult in the south. Embracing every man in the villages involved, these societies had developed complicated and impressive ceremonies of initiation. The Kuksu rituals were built around impersonated spirits, with elaborate costumes, regalia, and disguises representing the mythical characters. In the toloache cult the ceremonial began with the administration of the powerful drug, which stupefied for one or more nights and, in some instances, killed. The visions seen during this period of narcosis were of lifelong sanctity. Then followed several nights of dancing and a period of fasting. Much instruction was included, partly by song and partly by means of ground painting.

These Indians had a profusion of legendary stories, many of which represented high achievement in speculation on fundamental philosophical problems: explanations of the creation, the origin of death, and the problem of good and evil. The characters were animals. The coyote was a favorite, an arrogant, mischievous trickster, sometimes a benefactor of mankind, at other times bringing disaster or embarrassment. Apart from their mythology these often humorous tales make good reading or good listening, and, like the Old Testament of the Hebrews, they shed much light on the mundane habits of the people who passed them on to posterity.

Adjustment to Environment

In California nature gave the Indians a rich variety of environments, a land of many and great contrasts, often in close juxtaposition. The mighty Sierra Nevada, more than 400 miles in length, is the longest and boldest mountain range in the United States. Its Mt. Whitney (14,494 feet in elevation) and fifty others tower over 13,000 feet. This range was created by the raising of a great block of the earth's crust, with faults and subsidence at the eastern edge and tilting toward the west. There are passes of varying difficulty at elevations of 7,000 to 10,000 feet.

The Cascades to the north are more recent and volcanic in origin. Mt. Shasta (14,162) has the classic beauty of a volcanic cone, and Mt. Lassen was active as recently as 1914. The northwestern corner of the state is a jumble of nonvolcanic mountains, the Klamaths, with some peaks approaching 10,000 feet. The Coast Ranges reach southward as parallel fingers set at a slight eastward angle from the coast. Along the Eel there are peaks of 7,000 to 8,000 feet; near San Francisco Bay the mountains are not above 3,000 to 4,000 feet; the Santa Lucia range is higher; and Mt. Pinos reaches 9,214 feet.

From Mt. Pinos the Tehachapis extend east and northeast to meet the Sierra, while the mountain axis of southern California, culminating in the San Gabriel and San Bernardino Mountains, stretches eastward. From the San Bernardinos one short jump southward is Mount San Jacinto, outpost of the Peninsular Range, which extends into Lower California.

These mountains and other stray peaks and ranges in the deserts occupy a good half of the surface area of the state. By intercepting and storing moisture carried in by winds from the Pacific, the mountains perform a highly valuable service. They have other uses, but never have anything like half of California's residents lived in the mountains.

Another third of the state—the Colorado and Mojave deserts, the arid Carrisa Plain, the overwet valley of the Eel, and the frosty and thin-soiled Volcanic Plateau in the northeast—has obvious drawbacks. The Indians shunned the highest mountains, the thickest forests, and the deserts except where there were oases. They much preferred the flat land of plains and valleys, the rolling hills where grass and trees interspersed, and the coastal spots where fish could be had.

In order to make the most of the foods to be gathered, many of the Indians shifted their base with the seasons, camping on the plain in the spring when grass and certain bulbs were tender, pursuing game into the hills or mountains in summer, coming down to the oak groves for the acorn harvest, and going to another site for the winter camp. Other Indians were on the coast for a season of fishing, elsewhere when grass seeds were most abundant, and in the desert at harvest time for mesquite beans and agave.

Despite such shifting about, the California Indians were evidently not great travelers. Few if any, one gathers, could have passed an examination on the geography from one end of the state to the other or from the mountains to the sea. Yet from most localities, it is possible without traveling far to reach a place that is much warmer or cooler, wetter or drier, with more fog or more sunshine. In general the Indians chose the sites where the climate was benign. They paid the climate the further compliment of wearing little or no unnecessary clothing and chose to live where light shelter was enough.

Along the Colorado, the American Nile, where all they had to do was scatter seeds where the river overflowed, the Yumas and their neighbors had crops to harvest. Since they merely planted and harvested but did not cultivate, perhaps that was not real farming, yet the concept of agriculture came that close to the rest of the California tribesmen. They resisted it, in part because their gathering techniques and the acorn process were satisfactory, and in part because to have tied themselves down to localized planting and cultivating would have interfered with the larger harvesting of the natural crops.

These Indians lacked the technological means that would have permitted them to use many resources that the land had in store: gold, silver, tungsten, the power of falling water, oil (except in the brea used to caulk boats and baskets), San Francisco Bay (except as a clam and oyster flat), the climate as an inducement to tourists, and real estate as a medium of speculation. In terms of the technology available to them they had a most satisfactory inventory of what was edible or poisonous, what fibers were suitable for basket making, what stones would chip sharp for knives and arrowheads, how to outwit fish and game, and where to be in each of the many harvest seasons.

Short of what we call science they had extensive knowledge as naturalists. Their mode of life, furthermore, put little or no strain on the natural resources. Kroeber's population estimates have as one base his calculation of the carrying power of a given area with its foodstuffs and other necessities. He assumes that population would tend to rise to this carrying power. He emphasizes, however, that the Californians seldom experienced famine or starvation, another way of saying that they did not overtax the natural supply. A modern conservationist would say that their behavior was exemplary.

Appraisal

Such, in brief, was the culture of the California Indians when the white man arrived. Their subsequent experiences at mission and rancho, in the gold fields, on the reservation and off, as early town and farm laborers, and as participants on the modern scene are threads in the general history of the state since 1769 and are handled in that fashion in the chapters that follow.

Since modern California has moved so rapidly, the question arises why the Indian life was so static as well as primitive. If this criticism implies that these Indians should have invented a printing press, steam engine, or atomic bomb, it asks the impossible. Such achievements could come only after certain plateaus in science had been reached. The first Californians were far from that eligibility, and they were a conservative people with built-in resistance to change. As they saw it, their way of life was good. Later, many Indians looked back on the prewhite period as a happier day of peace, leisure, enough to eat, and good times.

Whatever else it may signify, this conservatism does not mean that these Indians were innately stupid as some have alleged. The life of Ishi of the Yahi, "the last wild Indian," exemplifies a high capacity to adjust to radically different circumstances.

Ishi

Ishi grew to manhood in an enclave of wild hill country east of Marysville. With an old uncle, his mother, and his sister, the last remnant of their tribe, he followed the ancient practices near ranches and towns and the railroad but with almost complete avoidance of the new

Ishi Fashioning a Harpoon

Robert H. Lowie Museum of Anthropology,
University of California, Berkeley

Californians. Fleeing from a party of surveyors, his little group split. He never saw the old
man or his sister again, and his mother soon
died. In 1911, almost starving, he came down
to Marysville where, for safekeeping, he was
put in jail. A newspaper story alerted University of California anthropologists, one of
whom came to see this derelict. After reading
off a long list of Indian words the visitor came
at last to a word Ishi recognized. With that
breakthrough he gradually won Ishi's confidence. He took him to live at the anthropological museum in San Francisco where he was
initiated into the intricacies of the white man's
way of life.

Ishi responded by becoming a most valuable informant on the Yahi language and on
many elements of Indian culture. One of his
new associates, T. T. Waterman, rated Ishi the
man of all others he most admired. His story
has been told and retold, most effectively by
Theodora Kroeber in *Ishi in Two Worlds* and
Ishi, Last of His Tribe.

Other Indians, less dramatically, have
demonstrated similar capacity to adapt to
what is considered a much more sophisticated
civilization. The clear implication is that their
native capacity is substantially the same as that
claimed by other Californians. The twentieth
century instance of Ishi reduces the time gap

between today's most modern culture and that of the Stone Age people who were the only Californians as recently as 1768. Expanding knowledge of the full picture of life in prehistoric California also suggested that in many particulars the arrangements then achieved were much to be admired. Not least was the continence in handing the land on to each succeeding generation as beautiful and habitable as before.

CHAPTER 2

**Drake's Beach, Point Reyes National Seashore, in
the Vicinity of Drake and Cermeno Landings**

Philip Hyde

1492 to 1768

Know ye that on the right hand of the Indies there is an island called California. . . .

Garcí Ordóñez de Montalvo
Las sergas de Esplandián (about 1510)

Explorers and Empire Builders

California was discovered in the course of the greatest addition ever made to geographical knowledge. Columbus began it in 1492 by sailing due west from the Canaries to what he called the West Indies. That was half the distance from Spain to California. He and his contemporaries soon located all the other Caribbean islands and ran the entire circle of that sea. Within a quarter century the coast was mapped from Nova Scotia down to Patagonia. Obviously a tremendous land mass blocked Columbus's intended sailing route to the Indies, though at Panama Balboa crossed to another ocean which he named the South Sea. So far no one had been made rich by America.

At the strait named after him Magellan in 1519 entered the Pacific Ocean. He sailed across it all the way to the Philippine Islands and one of his ships two years later completed the voyage around the world.

In those same years Hernando Cortés marched inland and seized the Aztec empire with its great wealth in gold and silver. Other Spaniards were inspired to attempt comparable conquests. In Central America a small amount of wealth was found, more in the highlands of present Colombia, and in the Inca empire even more than Cortés had found in Mexico. In the great valleys of the Orinoco and the Amazon, in Chile, Argentina, and north of Mexico in the southern third or more of the United States, the would-be conquerors learned much about geography but found little or no negotiable wealth. They had spied out half of North America and much more of South America. Meanwhile mariners ran from the Strait of Magellan to about the Oregon line. By the fiftieth anniversary of the discovery of America, the northwesternmost of these explorers approached, named, and reached California.

The Lure of the Northwest

Cortés was the pioneer of the west coast exploration. Though most that was necessary for shipbuilding had to be packed across from Veracruz, Cortés had two ships ready to send out in 1532 and two more the next year. None returned, but survivors reported an island rich in pearls. Because of his reputation as a treasure finder, volunteers were numerous for his expedition in 1535. At Santa Cruz Island the land was arid, the sea crossing difficult, and the pearls disappointing. After 23 men died of starvation, he abandoned the pearl fishery.

Almost at once Cortes' interest was revived by the news of the arrival of Alvar Núñez Cabeza de Vaca at Culiacán, then the northwestern outpost of New Spain. Shipwrecked on the Texas coast, six years a slave, trader, and medicine man among the Indians, Cabeza with black Estevánico had hiked west and northwest to the far side of the continent. He had marvels to describe, but the most alluring was that he had heard of wondrous cities farther north. These, the Spaniards assumed, must be the Seven Cities famous in Old World legend as Christain oases stranded far out in heathendom.

Cortés claimed the right to investigate this new attraction. But the recently arrived Viceroy of New Spain was under instructions to reduce Cortés' power. Rather than allow him to carry out a conquest of another Mexico, the viceroy turned to Francisco Coronado.

Blocked on land, Cortés was able to send out one more fleet. Francisco de Ulloa sailed up the coast on the chance that the Seven Cities might be within striking distance by sea. He went far enough to be convinced that the strait was a gulf and the island a peninsula. Rounding its tip, he went on to explore its outer shore.

Meanwhile Hernando de Alarcón, sent up the gulf, crossed the bar and entered the Colorado River, which he named because of its color. Hoping to encounter Coronado or some of his men, he traveled upriver for some days, then turned back. A detachment under Melchor Díaz arrived too late. There is no certification that either of these parties set foot within the present state of California. To both some of California's southeasternmost mountains almost certainly were visible.

In 1541 the viceroy sent Francisco de Bolaños to try to make contact with Coronado and the Seven Cities. He confined his work to the area near the tip of Ulloa's peninsula, which minimizes him as an explorer, but he is the most likely candidate for the honor of having named California. In the narrative of the next explorer in 1542, Cortés' island of Santa Cruz is referred to as California. The usage is casual, as though it were a name already established and familiar. The time of naming must have been after Ulloa and before Cabrillo. Bolaños was then the principal leader in the field, and other place names such as Cabo San Lucas are his.

For a long time the derivation of the name was a matter of wildest speculation. Now it is convincingly traced to one of the most popular pieces of early sixteenth century fiction, *Las sergas de Esplandián (The Deeds of Esplandián)*, by Ordóñez de Montalvo. *Esplandián* was a fantastic thriller. Among other wild adventures it relates how the Christians at Constantinople were opposed by a force of Amazons led by Queen Calafía of the island of California. The island was described as being "at the right hand of the Indies" and very close to the Terrestrial Paradise, an Amazon island abounding in gold and infested with many griffins. The known familiarity of Cortés' men with the Montalvo romance establishes the derivation of the name.

The state of California not only has this literary derivation for its name, it also has the distinction of having been named before it was discovered.

First Visit to the Coast of California

By the time of Bolaños' return, the viceroy was disillusioned about the Seven Cities. He ordered Juan Rodríguez Cabrillo to sail along the coast toward Cathay and to look for the western entrance to the Strait of Anian, the much talked-about water route from the North Atlantic to the Pacific.

Cabrillo gave the coast only a cursory examination up to Cabo del Engaño. Continuing northward, he passed the future international boundary and became the first authenticated visitor to Alta California. On September 28, 1542, he discovered San Diego Bay, and behind Point Loma his two tiny ships lay sheltered during a three-day storm. "They discovered a port, enclosed and very good," reads the account of this voyage.

They were at Santa Catalina and San Clemente islands on October 7 and 8, named San Pedro Bay, the Bay of Smokes, the reference being to brushfires set by the Indians, and went on to Town of Canoes, where possession was again taken in the name of the king. Repeatedly, the Indians made signs of other Spaniards to the east. Cabrillo followed the coast very closely as far as Point Concepción, stopping at several places.

Encountering stiff northwest winds beyond the point, he returned temporarily to San Miguel Island and there had the misfortune to break an arm, or, as other accounts have it, a leg. Although the break was most painful and did not heal properly, Cabrillo shortly took advantage of a southwester to explore more of the coast. Just how far north he went is uncertain. He made no landings and much of the

California as an Island

Section of a Map by Joannes Blaeu, 1648

time had to stand well out to sea. He did, however, become well acquainted with a Baia de los Pinos (according to the description, Monterey Bay), and he observed some other parts of the coast both north and south of this bay. Stormy weather finally forced him back to San Miguel Island, where the old injury brought about his death on January 3, 1543.

On his deathbed Cabrillo instructed his second in command to continue the northward exploration. Bartolomé Ferrelo made a sincere effort, but stormy weather still interfered, and he was unable to land anywhere north of Point Concepción.

In Alta California they had found no more wealth than Coronado had in New Mexico and Kansas. Although the Indians of southern California were numerous and friendly, they were not wealthy enough to invite Spanish exploitation. The bay at San Diego, though excellent, was of little or no practical use until some excuse for occupying Alta California should arise. Even the recognition of southern California as a "land of endless summers" did not rouse Spanish interest in this distant region. The best news, perhaps, was that the Strait of Anian, if it existed at all, must strike the Pacific so far north that its discovery by other Europeans would not seriously menace Spain's hold upon Mexico and South America.

The Manila Galleon

After Cabrillo, interest in exploration northwestward lagged. Discovery of fabulous silver deposits focused interest on a mining frontier close at hand and an activity that would continue for centuries. In the sixties, however, at the same time that he ordered a naval station built at San Agustín on the Florida coast, Philip II ordered expansion to the Philippine Islands. In 1564 Miguel López de Legazpi sailed from Mexico to establish a foothold at Manila.

The task remained to open a return route across the Pacific. How to do it had been reasoned out. It would be by the formula used by Columbus for the return voyage across the Atlantic—to make a northing to the latitude of the prevailing westerlies, ride them across the ocean, and then turn southerly to the home port.

Fray Andrés Urdaneta had been designated to test this theory and discover such a route. Early in 1565 he set sail in a 500-ton ship on this slightly modified great-circle course. It was favored by ocean currents as well as winds, but the distance was great. The voyage took 129 days; 16 of the crew died before reaching port and four after, in addition to four Filipinos.

The glory of this first eastward crossing of the Pacific was slightly tarnished by the antics of Alonso de Arellano. On the outward voyage he deserted in a 40-ton patache, sailed on to the Philippines, and then, in advance of Urdaneta, back to Mexico. There is no question that he reached the home port first, but the authorities saw him as a deserter rather than a discoverer.

The sailing course became popular at once. Trade at first was unrestricted and many merchants engaged in it. Silks, wax, china-ware, spices, and other eastern staples were the principal items involved. When merchants in Spain protested that they were losing the market of New Spain, the king obliged them in 1593 by restricting the Mexican-Philippine trade to a single 500-ton vessel each year, with a cargo not to exceed 250,000 pesos in value and not to include any silks, and with the privilege of exporting reserved to citizens of Manila. The restrictions lessened the volume but made the trade more profitable for those who could participate.

Annually, until almost the very end of the Spanish colonial period, the Manila galleon skirted California from Cape Mendocino or Monterey past the tip of Baja California. Landings were infrequent and usually the coast was not sighted north of Cenizas Island, but for two centuries it was the only coming of Spaniards into the vicinity of California.

Drake at Nova Albion

In the English-speaking world the 200-odd sailings of the Manila galleon have been eclipsed by a single stop-over by Francis

Drake in 1579 in the course of the first English circumnavigation of the globe.

As the first freebooter to the Pacific, Drake entered on what had been a Spanish lake. He could pillage unfortified towns and capture unarmed ships, chief of which was the Panama-bound treasure galleon. With literally tons of silver and gold, his remaining problem was to get the treasure safely home. Continuing round the world seemed more prudent than trying to return by way of the Strait of Magellan.

Captured sailing instructions indicated that he should wait a few months for the right season. He elected to do this north of the Spanish settlements. Chance took him to a bay in Marin County. There he repaired his ship, exchanged presents and pleasantries with the natives, ventured inland a few miles, took possession in the name of his queen, and named this land Nova Albion (New England).

Californians have magnified these actions out of all proportion and popular writing has made much of his alleged dream of founding an English colony on this coast.

In 1937 a plate of brass discovered in Marin County was unveiled with a flourish to the California Historical Society and extolled as the one Drake nailed to a post when he took possession of Nova Albion. Certain experts on history, language, and hieroglyphics expressed doubt. E Clampus Vitus, the fraternity of western history buffs, made merry over it in an ornate booklet, Ye Preposterous Plate of Brasse. An electrochemist, asked to examine the plate, pronounced it not only sixteenth-century brass but Drake's very own, greater certitude than could rightfully be expected of his science.

Criticism and even skepticism waned. Then in 1977 another metallurgist rejected the plate as sixteenth-century British brass. The likelihood, however, is that Drake's plate would have been Spanish brass. As Lawrence Kinnaird sagely observed, proof or disproof is yet to be established. The Bancroft Library still exhibits Drake's plate, which some now call the Shinn plate after its finder, but alongside it the Bancroft summarizes evidence and analysis challenging its authenticity.

The four hundredth anniversary of Drake's California visit stirred scholarly debate especially as to the site. A dozen or more nominations were made and in particular four Marin County bays, Bodega, Drake's, Bolinas, and San Quentin. The last of these is the most radical suggestion because it is well inside the Golden Gate and, if that is where Drake was, another puzzle arises: How is it possible that San Francisco Bay escaped discovery and mention until 190 years later?

Historically it seems to be of no consequence which of these bays was Drake's anchorage. Pure intellectual curiosity, however, was enough to produce a great deal of individual and group research, analysis, argument and counter-argument. The California Historical Society tried to orchestrate the discussion by posing twenty questions. Out of these came more talk and writing, which Warren L. Hanna systematized in his Lost Harbor, a neat summary of what is known about Drake's visit.

Spain was disturbed by Drake's freebooting in the Pacific. To prevent a recurrence, the galleons were armed, larger naval forces were maintained, and some of the coastal towns were better garrisoned. His excursion to California on the other hand, aroused no Spanish concern. It is difficult to say just when the Spaniards learned that he had been there, but they seem to have estimated correctly that he had found no compelling attraction for English colonization. Subsequent Spanish activity on the coast apparently had no connection with his visit.

Seeking a Port of Call

Eight years after Drake, galleon commander Pedro de Unamuno was ordered to reconnoiter for a California port of call. He went ashore at Morro Bay, took possession, ventured inland, and was surprised by the Indians. A Spaniard who had taken off his coat of mail and a Filipino were killed.

The next effort was by Sebastián Rodríguez Cermeño in 1595. This time a storm caught the galleon at anchor under Point Reyes. It foundered and everything aboard was lost. Cermeño and his men completed assembling an open launch which had been brought for the purpose of searching for a port of call. They set down a much more detailed description of the place and the Indians than had Drake. Archaeological evidence also confirms the identification of their anchorage as at what is now called Drake's Bay. To the anguish of his 70 men, Cermeño hove to on dark nights so as not to miss seeing segments of the coast and in other ways lengthened the voyage, though they were on starvation rations. At San Martín Island they were saved by finding a large fish stranded on the rocks, which nourished them for seven days. Their expedition was a heroic experience and ordeal. It was also the last use of a richly laden Manila galleon for the dangerous work of exploration.

At century's end the viceroy contracted with Sebastián Vizcaíno to sail up the coast and find a port for the galleon. On the way back he would have permission to search for pearls in Baja California. With his fleet Vizcaíno proceeded slowly up the coast applying new names as he went. Among them are San Diego, Catalina, Buenaventura, Santa Bárbara, Point Concepción, Point of Pines, Carmel, and Monterey. In Father Ascención he had a diarist more voluble than Cabrillo, but there is substantial similarity in their descriptions of this part of California. In his enthusiasm Asunción mentions "golden pyrites, . . . a sure sign that there must be gold in the mountains," and another substance which he called amber. The Indians were numerous and friendly and offered water, fish, and jicama roots.

Beyond Point Concepción, although he tarried to chart San Luis Obispo Bay, Vizcaíno's next stop was at Cabrillo's Bay of Pines, which Vizcaíno renamed after Viceroy Monterey. Vizcaíno described it as "the best port that could be desired, for besides being sheltered from all the winds, it has many pines for masts and yards, and live oaks and white oaks, and water in great quantity, all near the shore." He spoke of the land as being thick with Indians and very fertile, the "climate and the quality of the soil resembling Castile," and the port commodious, "sheltered from all winds," and at the ideal latitude to provide "protection and security for the ships coming from the Philippines."

Since discovery of a port for the use of the galleons had been Vizcaíno's assignment, his enthusiastic description of the Port of Monterey was the most impressive feature of his report. In fact until more than a century and a half later, the excellence of Monterey was accepted as the central fact about Alta California and was the chief motivating force attracting revived Spanish interest in the region.

Farther north they came to Cermeño's anchorage, which the chief pilot recognized. They talked of going ashore to look for the silk and wax left there after the wreck but did not do so. Bearing on up the coast, near snowy mountains, the pilot thought they were close to Cape Mendocino. Heavy seas, in which Vizcaíno was thrown from his bunk and broke his ribs, and fog and stormy weather forced them to turn back.

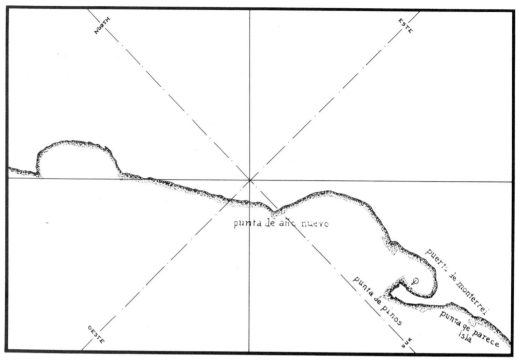

**The Port of Monterey as Drawn and Reported by the
Vizcaino Expedition**

The voyage south was rapid. Vizcaíno made additional observations but did not stop, doubting the ability of his men to lift the anchor. At long last they reached Mazatlán.

Pleased with the report and in particular with the finding of so excellent a port, the viceroy rewarded Vizcaíno with appointment as commander of the next Manila galleon. Unfortunately a new viceroy took over, cancelled the galleon assignment, and blocked any establishment of a port of call. It could be argued that by the time the mainland was sighted, the voyage from Manila was almost over. Nevertheless, the glamor Vizcaíno bestowed on the Port of Monterey endured for generations.

Empire Builders

Alongside the explorations of the hundred and more years from Columbus to Vizcaíno, Spain established an empire in America and an imperial system.

For a dozen years the only occupied place was Santo Domingo on the island of Española. Then towns were planted on the other larger islands and at Darién. With the conquests of the Aztecs and Incas, the center of gravity shifted to the mainland. There was a rush from the islands, and from Spain, and in short order Spanish occupation spread over southern Mexico, Central America, and into what would become half a dozen South

American provinces and ultimately nations.

In the next half century silver strikes northwest of the Aztec capital and in Upper Peru (Bolivia) made compact additions that were highly and continuously productive. The king claimed everything that the wide-ranging explorers had seen and more. Garrisons were established at San Agustín and Manila and, at century's end, an island of settlement was created far out in Indian country on the upper Rio Grande in New Mexico.

In New World history the seventeenth and most of the eighteenth centuries seem to belong to the English and French and incidentally to the Dutch, Danes, Swedes, and Russians. Alta California, strange to say, went absolutely silent. Not a shred of history is recorded, not a single episode in the 166 years after Vizcaíno's departure. Nevertheless, Spain was then adding to its North American holdings an area at least equivalent to the French and English occupations. Included were the provinces of Florida, Louisiana, Texas, Coahuila, Chihuahua, New Mexico, Sinaloa, Sonora, Pimería, and Baja California. One sector of this growth reached toward California.

In and for this growth Spain developed a method of frontier advance and administration in sharp contrast to England's and France's and different from that of the era of the wide-ranging and self-financed conquistadores. It carried forward the central features of royal control and Roman Catholicism. True to the Spanish tradition it emphasized the town as the unit of new settlement and the prime agency of local government. As a matter of royal policy and of practicality, reliance was put on government-directed and government-paid participants.

Three frontier institutions took shape: The presidio was a garrisoned fort not unlike the army posts of the American West. The mission was a self-sufficient station where Indians were assembled to live and work together under the direction of a missionary or two who would Christianize and ready them to live and function as regular subjects of the king. The pueblo was an agricultural town established when and where royal policy dictated. In varying combinations these three agencies carried out the later frontier advance.

Black Robes at Work

From 1591 to 1768 the northwestward arm of the frontier of New Spain depended heavily on missionaries of the Jesuit Order. Beginning in Sinaloa and advancing along both sides of the Sierra Madre of Mexico into Chihuahua, Sonora, the land of the Pimas, and Baja California, these Jesuits established hundreds of missions.

The tribes involved included some of the most warlike—the Mayo, Yaqui, Seri, and Apache. Spanish arms as represented at the presidios were necessary, though the ratio of missions to presidios was several to one. The civilian element also was important, sometimes coming spontaneously as in the succession of mining rushes, but also in the settlers recruited for pueblos as they were founded.

From 1687 to 1711 this northwestern frontier had the services of a remarkable missionary, Italian-born and German-educated Eusebio Francisco Kino. Sent to Mexico in 1681, he had his first field experience in Lower California and with an unsuccessful colonization attempt in 1685. After that he was sent to Pimería Alta (Upper Pima Land) in northern Sonora. He spent the rest of his life there, as his biographer puts it, as Apostle to the Pimas.

Using Mission Dolores on the San Miguel

River as his base, Kino added a score of other missions on the Altar, Magdalena, and Santa Cruz rivers. Besides ministering to three of these stations and supervising the rest, he explored beyond the Gila and the Colorado and across into Lower California. He added to and corrected geographical knowledge and made a map of Pimería which was not improved on for a century and a half. He wrote a history of his work, modestly entitling it *Celestial Favors*.

Throughout most of the seventeenth century the Indians had Baja California to themselves except intermittently when pearl fishers came. The major effort was from 1679 to 1685 when Governor Isidro Atondo of Sinaloa, accompanied by Kino, tried to establish a pearling station. After his first attempt failed, he tried again at San Bruno, where he built a fortified town and church, diverted water from the stream, and planted maize, frijoles, and garbanzos. Because the rains stopped and all the crops failed, he concentrated on the search for pearls but was unsuccessful. His experiment cost the royal treasury $250,000.

Out of the effort came negotiations with the Jesuits. If given full charge and permission to raise an endowment, they agreed to establish missions. Launched in 1697, the work was exceedingly difficult. Supply service across from the mainland was unreliable, the Indians hard to attract, and the harvests uncertain. Except for the Pious Fund they could not have continued.

Juan María Salvatierra, the first head of these missions, labored for 20 years, established five missions, and is credited with several miracles. Juan de Ugarte succeeded him and achieved better success in farming and stock raising. After his years there were revolts by the Indians, who on one occasion nearly captured a Manila galleon that had put in for water and supplies. A subsequent Indian revolt was put down only after 160 Yaqui warriors were brought over from the mainland.

Mission work was resumed and several new missions were established in the north. In the south the population declined, several missions were consolidated, and others secularized, converted into parish churches and the Indians released. Pearl fishing started again and a few settlers were welcomed. Yet at best Baja California was barely self-supporting and no real encouragement to northwestward expansion.

The End of the Jesuit Epoch

In 1767 the Spanish court decided to follow the lead of Portugal and France and expel the Jesuits. The reasons stemmed but slightly from the conduct of the missionaries in Baja California or on the Mexican mainland, though there were some complaints and also wild rumors that the missionaries were hoarding vast treasures from secret mines, pearl fisheries, and exactions from the natives.

The expulsion of some 678 Jesuits from New Spain was thought too delicate a task for the viceroy and his staff. Instead it was entrusted to Visitador-general José de Gálvez, who was on the scene conducting an inspection and overhaul of imperial administration in the viceroyalty. So that the neophytes would not dispute the removal and the missionaries would not have time to hide or dispose of their mythical treasures, Gálvez moved secretly. For the task in Baja California, where there were 16 Jesuits to be sent off to the Vatican, he delegated the responsibility to Captain Gaspar de Portolá.

Reaching Loreto on December 17, 1767, Portolá notified the missionaries to be prepared to board ship on January 25, 1768. Although they and their charges were grief-stricken, there was no resistance. The Black Robes sailed on February 3, leaving the Indians with no guardians other than Portolá's soldiers. Fray Junípero Serra and his brother

Franciscans did not arrive until April. Meanwhile, Portolá carefully inventoried the mission property, which fell far short of expectations. Some of this property was dissipated before April, and there were further losses during a transition period in which the Franciscans had merely spiritual authority. On August 12 Gálvez placed them in full charge of the missions.

Gálvez saw need of other reforms in Baja California. He came with optimism that mining could be developed, and he tried to encourage the coming of miners and agricultural settlers. He soon realized that regeneration of the missions was the real hope of the colony. He had several missions consolidated, others abandoned, and the neophytes transferred to better situated missions. Some of his more radical proposals, such as transferring northern Indians far to the south, were not carried out. Nor were the Franciscans able to accomplish much in their five-year tenure on the peninsula. They established only one new mission, San Fernando de Velicatá.

CHAPTER 3

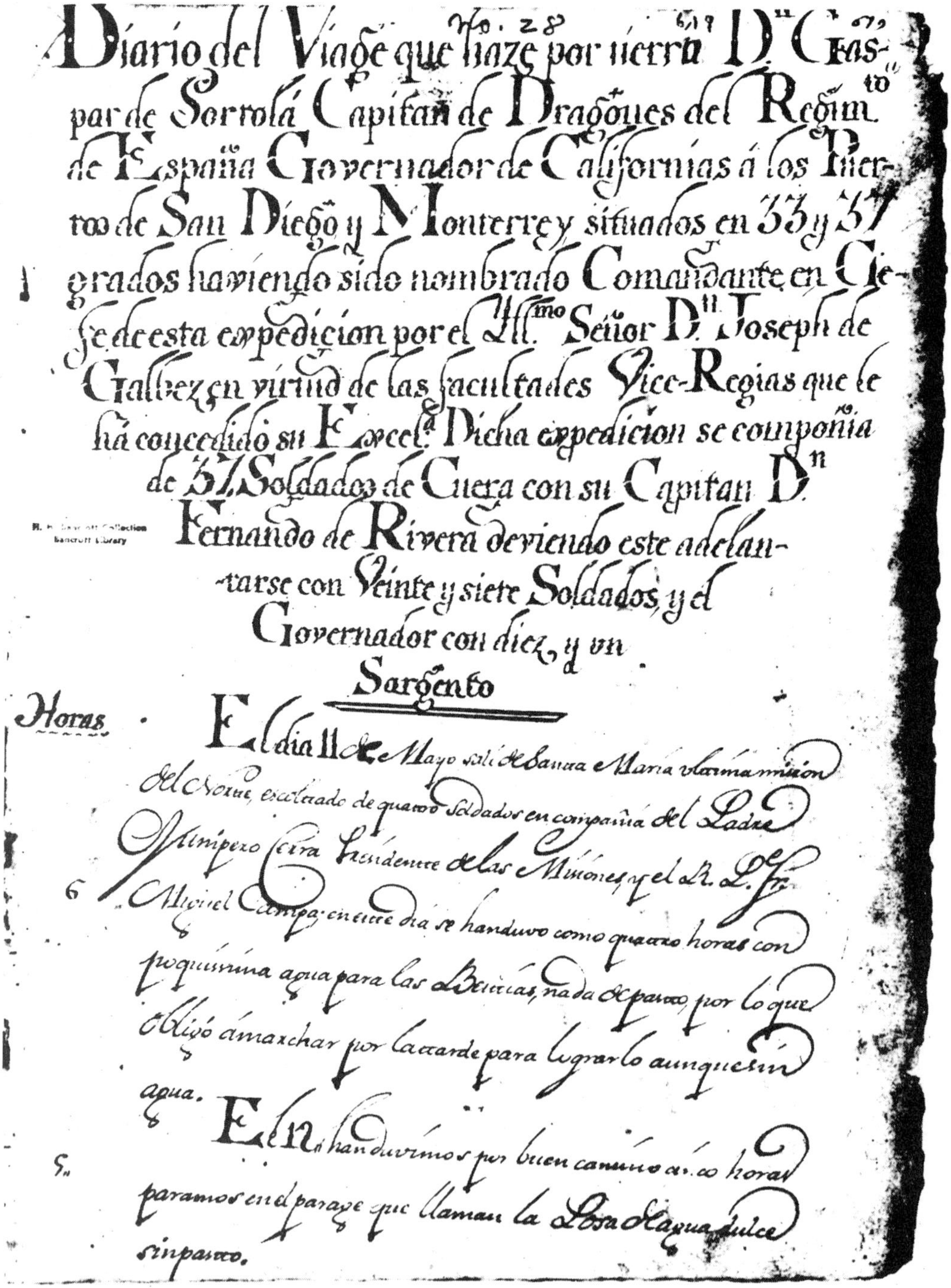

Diario del Viage que haze por tierra Dn. Gaspar de Portolá Capitan de Dragones del Regimto. de España Governador de Californias á los Puertos de San Diego y Monterrey situados en 33 y 37 grados haviendo sido nombrado Comandante en Gefe de esta expedicion por el Illmo. Señor Dn. Joseph de Galbez en virtud de las facultades Vice-Regias que le há concedido su Excela. Dicha expedicion se componia de 37 Soldados de Cuera con su Capitan Dn. Fernando de Rivera deviendo este adelantarse con Veinte y siete Soldados, y el Governador con diez, y un

Sargento

Horas

6 El dia 11 de Mayo sali de Santa Maria ultima mision del Norte, escoltado de quatro Soldados en compañia del Padre Junipero Serra Presidente de las Misiones, y el R. P. Fr. Miguel Campa: en este dia se anduvo como quatro horas con poquissima agua para las Bestias, nada de pasto, por lo que obligó á marchar por la tarde para lograrlo aunque sin agua.

5 El 12. anduvimos por buen camino cinco horas paramos en el parage que llaman la Poza de agua dulce sin pasto.

Opening Page of Portolá's Diary

The departure from San Diego having been fixed for the 14th of July [1769], the governor ordered out six soldiers and a corporal to explore the country for the distance of the first two days' marches. These soldiers left on the morning of the 12th, and returned on the afternoon of the following day with the information that they had found a watering-place sufficient for the men and horses at a distance of six or seven leagues.

Miguel Costansó
Diary

A Spanish Outpost

Imperial Ferment

At the time of the expulsion of the Jesuits there was little reason to suspect that the frontier was about to leapfrog to San Diego and Monterey. The then northwesternmost provinces, Sonora and Baja California, were not bursting at the seams.

Imperial policy was in flux. The decisive outcome of the Seven Years War led to the partition of French America. Britain took the St. Lawrence Valley, west to the Canadian Rockies, and the eastern half of the Mississippi Valley. Spain, also a loser, had to surrender the Floridas in order to ransom Havana. But it picked up the island of New Orleans and the western half of French Louisiana, thereby holding the British half a continent away from California.

Imperial reform was in vogue. Portugal expelled the Jesuits and liberalized trade for Portuguese America. In British America George III and his ministers sought increased revenue and more effective royal control. Their steps, such as the Stamp Act and the tax on tea, are remembered less as reform measures than as irritations leading to the American Revolution.

In Spain a much more able monarch, Charles III, carried out similar, more extensive, and much more fruitful reforms. He redeployed garrisons, set up Buenos Aires as capital of a new viceroyalty, appointed a commandant general for the northern frontier, and overhauled the revenue system of the empire. Adapting a French device, he appointed intendants, officials specifically charged with stimulating economic development. He also opened additional ports to trade with Spain and France. In the epoch of these reforms Spanish America prospered.

As part of this program Charles had sent Gálvez to inspect the viceroyalty of New Spain, empowering him to carry out changes deemed advisable. Besides expelling the Jesuits, Gálvez struck at graft in the customhouse, established the tobacco monopoly, and improved collection of other royal revenues, particularly of Indian tribute.

En route to the recently developed west coast port of San Blas, Gálvez received word from the viceroy of reports by the Spanish ambassador to Russia of Russian penetrations along the northwest coast of America. On the chance that the Russians might intend to occupy the Port of Monterey, the viceroy suggested a voyage of reconnaissance. Using the

José de Gálvez, Visitador-General

L. Alamán, Disertaciones sobre la historia de la República mexicana

Russian menace as an excuse, Gálvez adroitly magnified the viceroy's request into an order to occupy Alta California.

On to California

In May, 1768, Gálvez sailed for Baja California. He found only a skeleton group of Spaniards and fewer than 8,000 Indians at the missions. He instituted certain reforms and for a time was optimistic about mining and pearl fishing, but little was achieved. Organizing the expeditions for Alta California became his preoccupation in the months that followed. Not until the following May did he return to the mainland. That he devoted a year of his time as visitador-general to marshaling men and materials for the expeditions to California indicates the importance he attached to this advance of the frontier.

Gálvez did not hesitate to draw upon the meager resources of Baja California. He drafted the Franciscans for missionaries in the new field and requisitioned much that was needed from the peninsula missions. He commandeered the San Carlos and the San Antonio. From the mainland he assigned officers and soldiers.

When the San Carlos arrived, it had to be careened and reloaded. Gálvez directed the work personally, frequently lending a hand, and by January 9, 1769, this 200-ton ship with Vicente Vilá as captain was ready to sail. Lieutenant Pedro Fages and 25 Catalan soldiers were on board, along with cosmographer Miguel Costansó, the sailors, a baker, two blacksmiths, seed, agricultural implements, altar furniture, and other materials for the new settlements. Although the San Antonio was in better shape, Gálvez had it thoroughly overhauled also before sending it out under Juan Pérez on February 15. Less is known about the personnel and cargo aboard

the San Antonio, but Pérez came to be the ranking mariner along the California coast.

Captain Fernando de Rivera y Moncada commanded the first land division. He had 25 "leather-jacket soldiers," so called because of their sleeveless jackets of tough leather, protection against most Indian missiles. They also carried bullhide shields and wore heavy leather chaps fastened to the pommels of their saddles. They were as much cowboys as soldiers, and Fray Juan Crespi called them "the finest horsemen in the world." This party included three muleteers and 40 mission Indians from Baja California with tools for roadwork, who were counted on to help pacify the Indians farther north. Crespi was chaplain and diarist. Needing pasturage for his 400 animals, Rivera moved up to Velicatá, at that time the limit of Spanish control. He set out for San Diego on March 24.

The second land expedition consisted of Captain Gaspar de Portolá as officer in charge of the entire project, Fray Junípero Serra as head of the missionaries, Sergeant José Francisco de Ortega, 10 or 12 soldiers and servants, and 44 Christian Indians. On May 15 Portolá and his men took the trail for San Diego, the appointed rendezvous with Rivera and the ships. Gálvez equipped a third vessel, the San José, which sailed on June 16, but it was lost with all on board.

Misinformed as to the latitude of the bay, Pérez sailed too far north. He first took the San Antonio to the Santa Barbara Channel and then dropped down to San Diego Bay where he anchored after 54 days' sail. The San Carlos, which had started a month earlier, was 110 days on the way and did not arrive until April 29. Her crew was so wracked by scurvy that Pérez' men had to come to lower the boats. For a fortnight the chief work was caring for the sick and burying the dead.

The land parties fared much better. Rivera's men had to make a number of dry camps along the arid peninsula but were drenched in a couple of rainstorms. For most of the distance they were breaking a new trail over rough and mountainous terrain. The natives along the way showed some hostility but there was no fighting. Portolá and Serra had fewer cattle to bring over the trail, traveled during better weather, and much of the way followed the route Rivera had tested. They reached San Diego in six weeks.

By July 1 these four divisions were united. Possession was formally taken, a presidio was founded, and on July 16 Serra founded the mission of San Diego de Alcalá.

Of perhaps 300 men who had set out from La Paz and Velicatá, only 126 now remained. In addition to those lost on the *San José*, 93 had perished on the other two vessels. Only a score of the Indian auxiliaries were left; a few had died en route, the rest had deserted. Almost half of the 126 survivors were unfit for service. Such was the physical toll upon this first band of California pioneers.

Portolá's March through the Land

Because the Port of Monterey, the real objective, was still to be attained, Portolá prepared to march north. He sent Pérez and eight men in the *San Antonio* to get supplies and reinforcements from San Blas. The *San Carlos* was left at anchor in the bay for want of a crew, and Serra and a few others were left to care for the half hundred invalids. As Portolá worded it, he then "went on by land to Monterey with that small company of persons, or rather say skeletons, who had been spared by scurvy, hunger, and thirst."

Sergeant Ortega and the scouts constituted the vanguard. Next rode Portolá, Fages, the six Catalans who were fit for service, Costansó, missionaries Crespi and Gómez, and the Indian auxiliaries. The 100-mule pack train followed, and Rivera and the remaining soldier-cowboys, driving the *caballada*, brought up the rear. Through southern California travel was easy and pleasant. The numerous natives encountered were friendly, though often embarrassingly inquisitive. Pasture was abundant and water easily obtained. A sharp earthquake at the Santa Ana River crossing suggested the name Río de los Temblores. According to Crespi, the earthquake "lasted about half as long as an Ave María, and about ten minutes later it was repeated, though not violently." Other shocks were noticed until the Los Angeles River was crossed.

At the river they were impressed by the favorable conditions for irrigating, a year-round flow where the stream left the narrows and good land on both sides to which water could easily be diverted. They marveled at the tar pits, met rancherías of Indians gathering grass seeds, were blocked at the Palisades from proceeding along the coast, but went over Sepulveda Pass. At Encino Lake they were greeted by more than 200 Indians, continued northward across the valley, over a pass to the Santa Clara River, and followed it to the ocean. Their route ran along the Santa Barbara Channel, into the Santa Ynez Valley, past San Luis Obispo and Morro Bays to Ragged Point, where the coast became impassable.

The Sierra de Santa Lucía was a formidable obstacle. For a week they tarried at its base while Ortega and his scouts sought a pass. "The mountains," wrote Crespi, "are inaccessible not only for men but also for goats and deer." Finally, a way was found, and men and mules scrambled up only to be greeted at the summit by the sad prospect of mountainous country as far as the eye could see. Through this rough terrain they laboriously threaded their way. The fatigue of the long

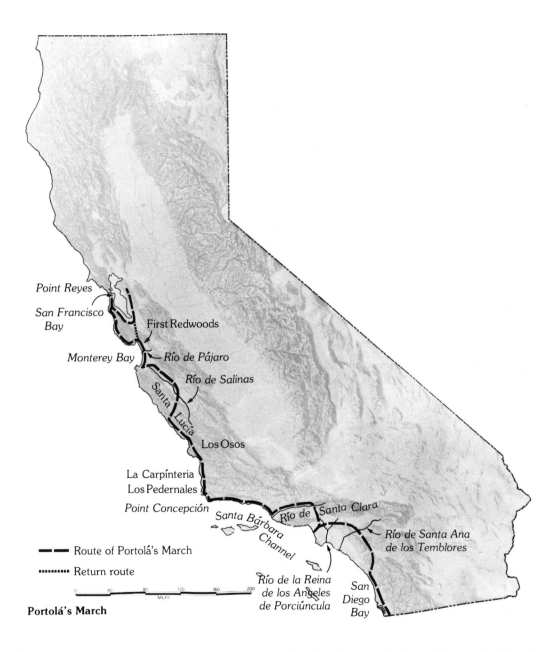

Portolá's March

Point Reyes

San Francisco
Bay

First Redwoods

Monterey Bay — Río de Pájaro

Río de Salinas

Santa Lucía

Los Osos

La Carpínteria
Los Pedernales

Point Concepción   Santa Bárbara   Río de Santa Clara
Channel

Río de Santa Ana
de los Temblores

Río de la Reina
de los Angeles
de Porciúncula

San
Diego
Bay

journey was particularly felt at this stage, and scurvy broke out.

After the mountains the Salinas Valley was a relief. The company descended this valley for six days and eagerly approached the Port of Monterey. Portolá recognized Vizcaíno's landmarks—the Point of Pines, the Carmel River, the magnificent sweep of the bay shore—but he was bewildered not to see the fine harbor. He expected the whole bay to be landlocked. Actually, its mouth is more than 20 miles wide. As Robert Louis Stevenson

Torrey Pines, A Threatened Species

Marc Myton

described it, the bay is like a giant fishhook, curving down from the north with the Point of Pines as the barb and the port the small area behind this barb. When later put to use, this anchorage proved safe and reliable. Reconnoitering it on horseback, Portolá could not see its full merits; in fact, he did not recognize it. Nonplussed, he concluded that the real Port of Monterey must be farther on and that this spot merely happened to coincide as to landmarks.

Resuming the northward march, they discovered giant redwoods, to which they gave the name palo colorado. From Half Moon Bay, a few days later, they could see the Farallones, Point Reyes, and Drake's Bay (to the Spaniards, Bahía del San Francisco, or Cermeño's Bay). These places were recognized

unmistakably for they had been often and well described. It was obvious that they had passed Monterey, but before turning back to confirm its identification Portolá determined to explore a little farther. Gálvez had ordered that the third Alta California mission, that in St. Francis' honor, should be established at the Bay of San Francisco (Drake's Bay). Since they were only a few miles from the spot, Portolá decided to visit that small indentation before retracing his steps.

Ortega was sent to blaze a trail to Point Reyes. Meanwhile, hunters, climbing the hills east of Half Moon Bay, were the first white men to see San Francisco Bay. They returned to camp to describe the great quiet harbor just over the hills. Hot upon their heels came Ortega with word that the trail to Point Reyes was blocked by the entrance to this bay. Crespi wrote in his diary: "It is a very large and fine harbor, such that not only all the navy of our most Catholic Majesty but those of all Europe could take shelter in it." Portolá, however, entered in his journal on the day of the discovery that "they had found nothing." To him the bay was an obstacle to further advance northward.

Advised by the Indians that a large ship, perhaps the San José or San Antonio, was anchored two days' march to the north, Portolá endeavored to get around the arms of the bay. His farthest point north, however, was in the neighborhood of Hayward. On the way south Monterey was definitely identified and Vizcaíno's Port branded a hallucination. Portolá's band plodded wearily to San Diego, during the final 12 days butchering and roasting one of the weak old mules each evening, and at last entered Serra's camp "smelling frightfully of mules."

Talk of Abandonment

The outlook for California was now most discouraging. The "Estuary of San Francisco Bay" (now known as San Francisco Bay) blocked the way to the site for St. Francis's mission. Monterey seemingly had no harbor. The San Diego Indians, repulsing the overtures of the missionaries, had attacked the camp and stripped garments from some of the invalids. More men had succumbed to disease. Portolá's men returned exhausted from their journey. Supplies were very low; for several months the colony subsisted chiefly on geese, fish, and such food as the Indians would trade for the soldiers' clothing. So acute was the crisis that on February 10, 1770, Portolá sent Rivera and 40 men back to Baja

California with instructions to get all the supplies the peninsula missions could spare and to drive up the cattle that had been left at Velicatá. In the meantime their absence would reduce the number to be fed at San Diego.

For another six weeks privations were severe and abandonment of the colony hung in the balance. Contemporary records do not mention it but in his Life of Serra, published 17 years later, Fray Francisco Palóu states that Portolá set March 20 as the date for leaving unless a supply ship should appear sooner and that Serra and Crespi announced that they would stay and hold out to the last breath. The friars started a novena (a nine-day season of prayer), and one day before the fateful twentieth the San Antonio appeared. The critical situation was not exaggerated; San Diego could not have been held much longer except for the supplies on the San Antonio. Portolá's men "got very particular consolation out of the corn, flour, and rice which it brought."

In praising Serra, Palóu cast unwarranted reflections upon Portolá. The captain was less entranced with California, but he had not given up. To his wise and courageous leadership in this initial crisis much credit is due for preserving the Spanish hold on Alta California.

Over Pérez' protests Portolá sent the San Antonio on to Monterey, while he marched north again with the 16 able soldiers. He repeated the ceremony of taking possession and on June 3, 1770, formally established a presidio and the mission of San Carlos. Then, in accordance with his instructions, he invested Fages with the government of Alta California and sailed with Costansó and Pérez for Mexico.

News of the occupation of Monterey was hurried to Viceroy Croix, who in special compliment to Gálvez ordered the church bells rung and flags flown to signalize the 300-league advance of the frontier to the famed Monterey.

A Precarious Start

In Alta California celebration of victory seemed premature. In the summer of 1770 the only stations held were San Diego, a long jump from Velicatá, and Monterey, another long jump northwestward. Each had a presidio and a mission, but both were in the early stages of development. They were surrounded by many thousands of Indians, some of whom had shown hostility. For the presidial garrisons and the mission guards there were, all told, 43 soldiers.

The return of Rivera and his pack train from the peninsula was a valuable reinforcement, but that was partly nullified by his pique at having been passed over for the California command. Hearing that Fages had been given this office, Rivera refused to budge beyond San Diego.

The most crucial problem was that of supply. At Jamestown, Quebec, Plymouth, and elsewhere on the Atlantic seaboard, the early colonists characteristically faced a starving period. Because modern California is so phenomenally productive, it may appear that the Spanish pioneers should have had no worries. Living off the country had proved difficult, however, for Portolá and his men as they made the return journey from Monterey, and at San Diego early in 1770 starvation was imminent. Living off the Indians was difficult too. Although they are praised by anthropologists for the adequacy of their food getting, their food list was one that the Spaniards could not readily adopt, assuming there was an actual surplus.

As soon as they could, the missionaries made small plantings of corn, beans, and wheat. In 1770 and 1771 late spring rains were sufficient to produce a yield. In 1772 more normal conditions prevailed, and it be-

The First Published Picture of a Grizzly

Louis Choris, Voyage pittoresque autour du monde, *1822*

came clear that fields and gardens would have to be irrigated.

Meanwhile, food had to be imported. No further exactions could be made on Baja California. Sustenance had to come by the sea route from Mexico. In 1772 the ships were late and came only as far as San Diego. To relieve what otherwise would have been a famine, Fages organized a famous bear hunt in the San Luis Obispo vicinity. Bear meat was the staple until a pack train came north with beans and flour.

Beyond what was required for sustaining the soldiers and missionaries, food was vital for attracting Indians to come and live at the missions. Any shortage in supply translated itself into a dearth of new converts as well as a departure of disillusioned neophytes.

The military were plagued by desertions. Soldiers, wearied or bored by their duties, often decamped. Fleeing all the way to Mexico was out of the question, and maintaining themselves in the Indian country was dangerous as well as difficult. Deserters usually were recaptured or came back, but this absenteeism reduced the effectiveness of the troops.

Misconduct of the soldiers, especially toward the Indian women, was another complaint. An Indian uprising at San Gabriel in 1771 was the direct result of the lassoing and mistreatment of an Indian woman. Elsewhere, Indian resistance was similarly invited. The missionaries could protest, but only the military could punish.

A sharper discord arose over the founding of new missions. In 1771 the *San Antonio* brought ten Franciscans, two as replacements for their brothers at San Diego who had asked to be retired, the other eight available for assignment at new missions. Serra had the approximate locations in mind. On July 14 he

had the pleasure of launching Mission San Antonio de Padua in an oak-dotted valley in the Santa Lucías, some 25 leagues south of Monterey. On November 8 missionaries and soldiers moved up from San Diego to the base of the Sierra Madre and founded Mission San Gabriel Arcangel. On September 1, 1772, Serra added a fifth mission, San Luís Obispo de Tolosa.

Serra had missionaries available for still another mission which he proposed to locate among the Chumash on the Santa Barbara Channel. No step could be taken without Fages' approval and assignment of a military guard. As to the proposed Mission San Buenaventura, Fages demurred on the sound ground that soldiers were not available. Serra also had urged missions in the San Francisco Bay area but had met with the same rebuff. The plain fact was that Spain had provided enough missionaries for six or eight missions but not enough soldiers. By 1773 Fages had 61 soldiers for the two presidios and five missions.

Meanwhile, there was work to be done in moving Mission San Diego to a more favorable site and Mission San Carlos from Monterey to the alluvial lands on the Carmel River. In each instance the prime consideration was the better prospects for crop production.

In pleading for additional missions, Serra could not cite much progress at the existing stations. Mission San Gabriel operated more than a year before a single conversion was accomplished, and the first baptism at Mission San Carlos had to compensate for six months' labor. By the end of 1773 not quite 500 Indians had been baptized, not a very large number in comparison with other missionary fields; and of these converts almost all were women and children. The record was so uninspiring that the father-superior of the College

Junípero Serra

Statue in the Capitol, Washington, D.C.

of San Fernando, from which the California Franciscans were drawn, seriously considered recommending closing these missions. The viceroy, late in 1772, warned the authorities in Spain that abandonment of Alta California might be necessary. Planned improvements at San Blas were canceled, and less of an effort was made to send supplies.

Serra Intercedes

At San Diego in September of 1772 Serra did his best to persuade Fages to cooperate in the establishment of Mission San Buenaventura. When Fages refused, Serra took the extraordinary course of going to Mexico to appeal over Fages' head to the viceroy. For one of his frail health, this action was heroic.

Serra sailed on October 20, arrived at San Blas on November 4 and, although waylaid by illness, reached Mexico on February 6, 1773. Early in March he was granted an audience by Viceroy Antonio María Bucareli y Ursúa.

In a petition with 32 numbered points, Serra put in writing his recommendations. He itemized improvements needed in allowances and delivery of supplies, urged that a land route be opened from Sonora, requested blacksmiths and carpenters, and the assignment to each mission of six peons (non-Indian laborers). He proposed enlarging the mission escorts to 10 soldiers, and, for two projected missions, to 20 and 15 respectively. Protesting past interferences with the mission programs, he asked that certain specified powers of decision be given to the missionaries. He even went so far as to ask that Fages be removed, and nominated as his replacement Sergeant

Ortega, who had served ably as Portolá's scout.

After consulting his council, Bucareli acted but did not grant Serra's every wish. The mission guards, for instance, were not expanded, nor was a complement of six peons provided. The viceroy did improve the service of supply, ordered the opening of an overland trail, provided for reinforcements, issued a *Reglamento*, or governing code, for the province, and recalled Commandant Fages.

Bucareli Supports

When Serra returned to California the omens seemed favorable. The missionary contingent numbered more than a score. Missions San Carlos and San Antonio were beginning to prosper. A new commandant, Rivera, would govern, and, most encouraging, Viceroy Bucareli was now actively supporting the province.

In his instructions to Rivera, Bucareli emphasized that, since the settlements were destined to become great cities, sites should be selected accordingly and the land parcelled carefully. Aware of the strategic importance of San Francisco Bay, he ordered careful examination of that region with a view to its early occupation.

As instructed, Rivera enlisted married recruits in Sinaloa and took them and their families, all told 51 persons, including the first women and children to go to the new province. They came by way of Loreto and Velicatá.

Bucareli also greatly improved the service of the supply ships. In 1774 he sent out an extra vessel, which arrived just in time to avert a serious famine. Merely to keep the service in operation was difficult. Because of the climate most supplies had to be loaded and shipped out promptly. The voyage was always long and had such a bad reputation that sailors commonly had to be shanghaied. Yet Bucareli not only maintained but improved the supply service by sea.

Further exploration of the coast was motivated by concern about the British even more than the Russians. In 1773–74 Pérez went as far north as 55° latitude. In the *San Carlos*, Juan Manuel de Ayala made the first entrance into San Francisco Bay in 1775. That same year Bruno de Hezeta discovered the Columbia River and Juan Francisco de Bodega sailed as far north as 58° but saw nothing of the Russians. Because of these voyages, Spain could claim priority in the exploration of most of the coast from the Columbia well into Alaska.

Bucareli's greatest contribution to California unquestionably was in bringing about the opening of a land route from Sonora.

Opening an Overland Route

At Tubac in southern Arizona, Captain Juan Bautista de Anza had heard in 1769 from Pima neighbors that white men were going up and down the California coast. That clearly was a report on Portolá's expedition. These prompt tidings by way of the Yumas convinced Anza that a land route to California must be feasible. He volunteered to lead such an expedition.

Bucareli inquired of Costansó, Portolá's cosmographer, who assured that the expedition would release the California soldiers from "perpetual and involuntary celibacy." On other grounds, Serra, then in Mexico, added his endorsement. Bucareli referred the question to a junta and, when it agreed unanimously, he issued the necessary orders.

An Apache raid on Anza's horse herd delayed the start, but by late December, 1773, he set out with some 20 soldiers, a dozen helpers, and 200 animals. At Caborca he picked up as guide Sebastián Tarabal, a runaway from Mission San Gabriel. Another member of the party, Francisco Garcés, a Franciscan, had travelled beyond the Colorado. Beyond Caborca they came to Camino del Diablo, a 200-mile stretch where they had to depend on water holes or tanks, and where several dry camps had to be made.

At the Colorado crossing Anza took pains to win the friendship of the Yumas. He greeted their chief, Salvador Palma, with appropriate formality. After an exchange of speeches, around Palma's neck Anza hung a red ribbon with a medal on which was a likeness of Charles III, symbol of Palma's authority under that great monarch. All night the friendly and inquisitive Indians stayed around the camp, "making sleep impossible, and life generally miserable."

In the morning Anza forded the Gila, the tall Yumas carrying the baggage across on their heads. The next day they assisted again in the crossing of the Colorado, carrying Garcés across on their shoulders.

Beyond the Colorado, Anza's problem was trail breaking. The Yumas warned against a northwest or west course. Moving down to the Cajuenche village of Santa Olaya, he struck out into the sand dunes. The first day they made 20 miles, after which the guides turned back. On the third day, they lost the trail in drifting sand, and horses and mules began to give out. The only thing to do was to retreat. A

dozen animals died, and the rest were so worn down that Anza despaired of moving everything to California.

Summoning Palma, he left much of the baggage, the cattle, and the jaded pack and saddle animals in his care. The head muleteer and two soldiers volunteered to remain and watch over this property. While the horses and mules recuperated, the soldiers relaxed by dancing with the Cajuenches to the tune of a soldier's violin. "They seemed so attached to it, that they gave up their own pastimes, and in their stead learned the customs of our men, particularly the women, who constantly wished to be dancing the seguidillas which the soldiers taught them, and in whose steps they became proficient."

On March 2 Anza set out again, this time with only ten pack mules and with his men mounted on the "least bad" horses. They circled farther south around the sand dunes, made a dry camp and a 40-mile march to water and pasture, went on to another dry camp, and came to more hard going. Finally they reached a camp that Tarabal recognized.

Their route now led through Borrego Valley to good forage at San Gregorio, up Coyote Canyon to the Royal Pass of San Carlos, to Cahuilla Valley, "most beautiful green and flower-strewn prairies, and snow-covered mountains with pines, oaks, and other trees which grow in cold countries." By way of San Jacinto and Alessandro valleys they had easy going to the Santa Ana, and two pleasant days brought them to San Gabriel. They had broken trail from Sonora to California.

In the spring of 1774 Spanish Alta California could not take care of 25 visitors. Anza sent to San Diego for supplies and mounts so that he could go on to Monterey. From there he intended to return by a more inland route. Neither sort of help was forthcoming. Consequently he had to send Garcés and most of the soldiers back to the Yumas to wait for him there.

Anza went on to Monterey, where he consulted with Palou about a chain of missions along the Anza trail and about mail service over it from Mexico to Monterey. Returning to San Gabriel in a nine-day ride, Anza hurried on to Santa Olaya. Palma's Yumas rafted him across the Colorado. He continued by way of the Gila to Tubac and, after a time, was allowed to go to Mexico to report to Bucareli.

CHAPTER 4

Desert Near Borrego Springs   *Philip Hyde*

No other service could be so important as the encouragement of sowing, planting, and stockraising at the three presidios and also to give the pueblo settlers all possible assistance in their farming and stockraising so that a few sites may produce what is necessary to make these new establishments self-supporting.

Neve to the Viceroy
June 7, 1777

Spain's Hold
Established

Anza's Second Expedition

Anza's first expedition had been a notable feat of exploration, complementing Portolá's march and the North Pacific voyages. Bucareli commissioned him to go a second time over the trail, this time with a substantial reinforcement. To open the first stations in 1769 Gálvez had sent some 300 men, of whom less than half reached California and not all of them stayed on. In his second trip Anza would bring 240 men, women, and children and livestock to match. The earlier increments were for garrison and missionary duty. Those of 1775–76 would have the added roles of populating and stocking the province. With still another reinforcement in 1781, they put the province on a durable basis.

The soldiers and settlers destined for San Francisco Bay were to be recruited in Sinaloa where there were many families "submerged in poverty." They were to be outfitted at government expense. Equipment included carbines, cartridge belts, leather jackets, saddles, bridles, pack saddles, blankets, and all the necessary provisions for the journey.

This expedition included 3 missionaries; 3 officers; 20 veteran soldiers; 20 recruits; wives, children, and relatives totaling 165 persons; and some 30 muleteers and other helpers. They moved out with 695 horses and mules and 355 cattle. The cavalcade was equivalent to a ranch on the move.

Through the diarists of the expedition, particularly Fray Pedro Font, and their translator, Herbert Eugene Bolton, we have knowledge of innumerable episodes of the trek. A woman died in childbirth at the first camp beyond Tubac. The infant and two others born along the way came over the trail safely. At the Gila, Pimas presented Anza with two fresh

Apache scalps. At one town on the Gila, Anza shook hands with 1,100 Indians. On the king's birthday he issued each soldier a pint of aguardiente.

For Chief Palma, Bucareli had sent a gorgeous outfit consisting of shirt and trousers, a jacket with a yellow front, blue cape with gold braid, and a black velvet cap. Yuma hospitality featured a gift of 3,000 melons. Getting 241 persons across the Colorado was a problem. One rider floundered off course and a little girl riding with him was swept away. Men stationed below the ford for just such an emergency rescued the little girl. Font, suffering from ague, crossed with a Yuma on each side holding him on his horse. Garcés crossed on the shoulders of three braves, "two at his head and one at his feet, he lying stretched out face up as though he were dead."

A cabin was prepared and supplies set aside for the two Franciscans and the seven Indian servants who were to tarry with the Yumas.

This time Anza made the desert crossing in three relays so that the water holes could refill. They had to endure dry camps and camps without firewood, a hardship because the weather was unusually cold. Snow and cold continued in the Borrego Valley and at the Royal Pass of San Carlos.

On Christmas Eve, just below Coyote Canyon, another child was born. On New Year's Day they crossed the Santa Ana, and a few nights later were at San Gabriel with the entire complement of people but a substantial shrinkage in the number of horses and cattle.

They arrived at a time of crisis. The mission Indians at San Diego had just risen in rebellion, killing one of the missionaries and two soldiers. Anza and Font and 17 soldiers joined Governor Rivera in a journey to San Diego to punish the offenders. In their absence five muleteers deserted and headed for Sonora with 25 horses. Lieutenant José Moraga pursued, overtook them just short of Santa Olaya, and brought them back with most of the horses and a few head of cattle lost in a stampede in the earlier crossing.

The Founding of San Francisco

On February 21, 1776, Anza and half the party started for Monterey; the rest would follow with the cattle. Four weeks later they reunited at Monterey. Anza's orders were to take them on to San Francisco but, contrary to expectations, a precise site had not been selected. In the seven years since the Portolá discovery there had been several visits: by Fages in 1772, Rivera and Palou in 1774, and Juan Manuel de Ayalla in 1775. Ayalla spent a month exploring the various arms of the bay and another 11 days trying to sail out its mouth. He also made a good map of the bay, which he described as "not one port, but many with a single entrance."

Encouraged by the padres, Anza went north to reconnoiter. He and Font were most enthusiastic about the setting. "The port of San Francisco," wrote Font, "is a marvel of nature, and might well be called the harbor of harbors." In all his travels he had seen no site that pleased him as much. Anza chose Fort Point as the site for the presidio and Arroyo de los Dolores for the mission. He also rounded the southern arm of the bay and followed the east bay all the way to Carquinez Straits and Antioch.

Anza had hoped to conduct the colonists personally to San Francisco, but Rivera's obstructions made that impossible. In mid-April, after turning the settlers over to José Moraga's command, he started for Sonora. As one further service to California, he carried two pairs of cats destined for mousing at San Gabriel and San Diego. Below Monterey he met Rivera, half-crazed with anger that the San Francisco project was moving forward despite his disapproval. Rivera had ridden all the way from San Diego to confer with Anza, but he was in such a rage that he rode on to Monterey after only the most perfunctory salutations. Almost immediately he was riding south again to overtake Anza at San Luis Obispo, but the captain declined to have any discussion with him except in writing. In a smouldering rage Rivera waited for an hour and then posted off to San Gabriel, where it became his turn to deny Anza an audience.

Anza camped near the mission. Some letters but no spoken words passed back and forth, and after three days he departed for Mexico without having come to any agreement with the governor about the move to San Francisco. An order from the viceroy, however, reached California soon after Anza left, and Rivera had no alternative but to comply. Lieutenant Moraga and Palou led the soldiers and settlers to the chosen site, founded the presidio on September 17, 1776, and dedicated the mission on October 9. But this imperial outpost clearly owed most to Bucareli, who had sponsored the entire project, and to Anza, who had opened the trail and conducted the colonists to California.

With San Francisco as an added station Spanish California began to gain its ultimate proportions. The cattle Anza brought were the principal progenitors of the vast herds of later decades. Along with the much smaller group of families brought by Rivera in 1774 and those who would come in 1781, the Anza contingent would be the chief reliance for populating and perpetuating the Spanish presence.

Pueblos Recommended;
San Jose Founded

Although Portolá, Fages, and Rivera are customarily thought of as governors, technically they were commandants, subordinate to the governor stationed at Loreto who had jurisdiction over both Californias. In 1776 in recognition of the increased importance of Alta California, Bucareli instructed Felipe de Neve to transfer the governing authority to Monterey.

Neve traveled north in 1777, continued up the Portolá trail to Monterey and, for good measure, on to San Francisco and back to Monterey. He thus began his governorship with a careful inspection of the entire province, seeing the three presidios and the eight missions. Mission San Juan Capistrano, opened temporarily on October 30, 1775, had been reestablished on November 1, 1776, and Mission Santa Clara de Asís had been founded on January 12, 1777.

Neve realized that what California needed most was adequate on-the-scene food production. As he traveled, he took stock of the achievements at the occupied places and carefully examined the agricultural potential at other localities along the way. His residence in Baja California had prepared him to under-

Northern California Foothills   *Ansel Adams*

stand that, with rainless summers, irrigation was a necessity. In appraising crop-raising capacity, he therefore looked for two requisites: an adequate year-round flow of water and arable land to which this water could be brought by gravity flow.

On June 6, 1777, Neve described to Bucareli the seasonal pattern of rainfall and the meager and uncertain harvests since 1770. Wherever a planting had been attempted, he mentioned it, but he saw little prospect that farming would flourish at the presidios and, as of 1777, the missions still produced less than their own requirements.

What the province needed, wrote Neve, was a few pueblos—country towns of farmers and stock raisers. Thus far, Alta California had none. Specifically he asked for 50 or 60 farmer families to establish two pueblos. As the most advantageous locations he recommended sites on the Porciúncula River (Los Angeles) near Mission San Gabriel and on the Guadalupe near Mission Santa Clara.

At the presidio of San Francisco, Neve found four soldier-settlers brought by Anza, the widow of another, and a vaquero, and at Monterey nine other soldiers, practiced farmers, who could be spared for the establishment of the northern pueblo. Without waiting for approval, Neve took the responsibility of moving these 15 and their families, a total of 68 persons, to the bank of the Guadalupe, three quarters of a league from Mission Santa Clara. There on November 29 the pueblo San José de Guadalupe was founded.

Near the plaza, future center of the pueblo, each settler was assigned a building site, lands for cultivation, and cattle. Because the dam and zanja would be adequate to irrigate a spacious meadow, an extra apportionment of lands for cultivation was made, with still other lots reserved for new residents. The pueblo would have *ejidos* (commons), grazing land, and woods.

By April, 1778, when Neve could forward a report, lack of oxen to pull the plows had limited the planting to no more than six *fanegas* (hundredweights) of maize and the same amount of beans. Also, a freshet washed out the dam. Within a few years, however, he hoped that the pueblo would supply grain to the presidios of Monterey and San Francisco. On July 15 Bucareli approved the founding of California's first pueblo.

Shortly thereafter jurisdiction over the northern frontier, California included, was transferred to the commandant of the frontier provinces. Bucareli could look back on five years of significant strengthening of California by improved shipments of supplies, the opening of an overland trail, the great reinforcement through the second Anza expedition, the advance to San Francisco, and Neve's good start as governor.

Neve Asks for More Settlers

When Gálvez, as the newly appointed Minister of the Indies, persuaded Charles III to set up the frontier commandancy, he nominated Teodoro de Croix for the appointment.

Facing more pressing emergencies in the eastern part of his domain, Croix left much initiative to Neve. On July 1, 1779, Neve issued a *Reglamento* which served as the fundamental code, some call it the constitution, for the rest of the Spanish period. It also contained plans and itemized expenditures for an additional presidio, pueblo, and missions.

Neve notified Serra that his patent to confirm neophytes needed Croix's approval. Though "pretending obedience," Serra went right on confirming. Neve withdrew the friars' privilege of franking letters, insisted on a permit from the governor before any friar could retire from the province, and cut down on their use of military escorts. In the *Reglamento*

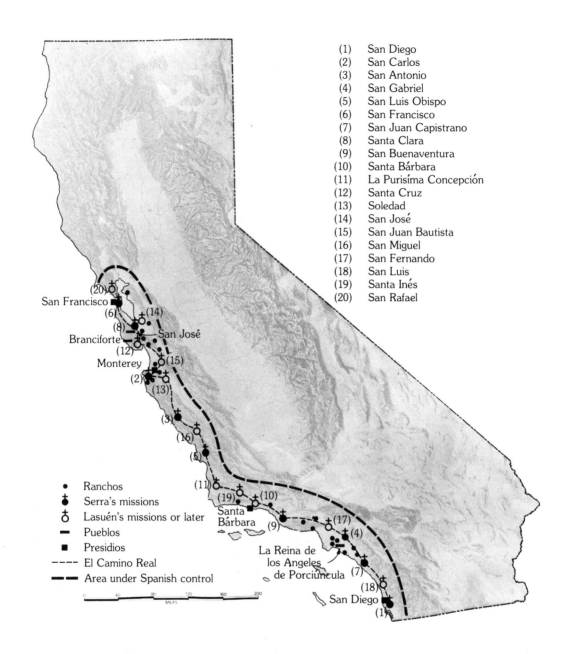

(1)	San Diego
(2)	San Carlos
(3)	San Antonio
(4)	San Gabriel
(5)	San Luis Obispo
(6)	San Francisco
(7)	San Juan Capistrano
(8)	Santa Clara
(9)	San Buenaventura
(10)	Santa Bárbara
(11)	La Purisíma Concepción
(12)	Santa Cruz
(13)	Soledad
(14)	San José
(15)	San Juan Bautista
(16)	San Miguel
(17)	San Fernando
(18)	San Luis
(19)	Santa Inés
(20)	San Rafael

(20)
San Francisco
(6)
(8)
Branciforte
(12)
Monterey
(2)
(13)
(14)
San José
(15)
(3)
(16)
(5)
(11)
(19)   (10)
Santa
Bárbara
(9)
(17)
(4)
La Reina de
los Angeles
de Porciuncula   (7)
(18)
San Diego
(1)

- • Ranchos
- ♠ Serra's missions
- ♀ Lasuén's missions or later
- — Pueblos
- ■ Presidios
- - - - El Camino Real
- ▬ ▬ Area under Spanish control

0   40   80   120   160   200
MILES

Spain's California

he specified that *pobladores*, the pueblo settlers, were not to be assigned to work at the missions. When the pueblo of San José was accused of encroaching on the land and water supply of Mission Santa Clara, Neve rejected the charge. He also urged single-friar missions but could not compel such assignments.

Late in 1779 Croix approved the proposal of a pueblo and a presidio and missions for the Santa Barbara Channel and sent Rivera to recruit 24 married settlers and their families; 34 married soldiers and their families; and 25 unmarried soldiers, to take the place in Sonora of a like number of Anza's veterans who would thus be released for California service.

Rivera could hold out liberal inducements. The settlers would be granted lands in California and could count on 10 pesos a month for three years plus a daily allowance for rations. Complete outfits, including everything from saddles and shoes to hair ribbons, would be issued to them in advance. Pack and riding animals would be provided, and at the new pueblo each colonist would be started off with two cows, two oxen, two horses, three mares, one mule, two ewes, and two she-goats, in addition to the necessary tools and implements.

Despite the generous subsidy offered, recruiting proved difficult. Rivera began his canvassing in February, 1780. Not till May 30 did he enlist the first poblador and by August 1 he had only seven. Soldiers were easier to persuade, 45 having enlisted by the latter date. By the end of the year, the full quota of 59 soldiers had been reached, but only 14 settlers were enrolled. With this number Rivera decided to stop.

Throughout these months of recruiting Rivera had been contracting for horses, mules, and cattle (some 960 head) and for other necessary supplies. Escorted by 17 soldiers, the pobladores—now only 12 because

two had deserted—set out for Guaymas, to be ferried across to Loreto. On the peninsula, smallpox eliminated another poblador; thus only 11 families, totaling 44 persons, actually arrived. With the other 42 soldiers, some 30 of whom were accompanied by their families, Rivera set out for the Yuma crossing.

The Yuma Massacre

In the autumn of 1780 Croix had ordered an advance to this crossing of the Colorado, a key point on the overland route to California. Gálvez' plan of 1768 had called for it; the Yumas had requested it in 1773; and Anza had prepared for it in 1776 by conducting Palma and a delegation of chiefs all the way to Mexico City. But in 1780, when Croix finally acted, it was by an unorthodox and parsimonious method. He sent missionaries, soldiers, and soldiers' families, but, instead of establishing missions or presidio or pueblo, he substituted two military towns with churches to which in theory the Indians would come and be made Christians. It was a setup that did much less for the Indians and in which the customary missionary control was lacking.

With no diary preserved, the details of Rivera's march are not known. Apparently he reached the Colorado without undue difficulty. There he was met by Sergeant Juan José Robles and five or six soldiers of the Monterey company. For the desert crossing the California-bound company would have guides.

Because many animals were exhausted, Rivera decided to tarry among the Yumas with part of the stock and the unmarried soldiers. Those with families he sent on. Although it was midsummer, they made their way over this more difficult part of the Anza trail and on to Mission San Gabriel.

Although the Yumas had urged Anza to

stay with them, they were restive under the kind of colonization Croix provided. Neither the missionaries nor the soldiers achieved effective control, while the Spaniards and their stock interfered with Yuma food gathering.

On July 17, in almost simultaneous attacks, the Yumas fell on Croix's two outposts on the west side of the river. The next day they surprised Rivera and his soldiers. Women and children were spared, but every man was killed—four missionaries, Rivera, and more than 30 soldiers.

A small force sent by Neve to investigate was driven off. Other expeditions from Sonora rescued or ransomed the captured women and children but did not reestablish the outposts or punish the Yumas. With sufficient escort it was still possible to travel the Anza trail, but in actuality this supply route to California was a casualty.

Founding the Pueblo of Los Angeles

By mid-August, 1781, the founding settlers for Los Angeles—11 families, 44 persons—had arrived. Because of smallpox in Baja California they were encamped some distance from Mission San Gabriel.

The site for the pueblo had been foreordained by the discoverors in 1769 and by Neve in his reconnaissance in 1777. It was to be a short distance below where the river Nuestra Señora de la Reina de los Angeles de Porciúncula emerged from the narrows between the Santa Monica and San Gabriel mountains. With the *toma* (dam site) and the course of the zanja in mind, a plaza would be located, with *solares* (building sites) around it, and *suertes* (planting lots) in an adjacent tract.

On August 26 Neve issued instructions on the locating of these fundamentals. Some of the preliminary work may have been done in

advance, and there are suggestions that some of the pobladores had already made camp on the site.

The founding date is official. A census on November 19, 1781, mentions it as September 4 and the formal confirmation of titles to solares and suertes occurred on that date in 1786. No recording of the founding ceremonies has come to light.

That vacuum invited early twentieth century writers to panoply the founding with pomp and ceremony befitting the start of the largest city in western America. A procession is described headed by Governor Neve, the padres from Mission San Gabriel, an escort of soldiers, the pobladores, and the mission Indians trooping along. A Mass and oratory are attributed and other details such as Neve marking off the four square leagues of *terminos* (pueblo lands) and within them *propios* (revenue lands), *ejidos* (common lands), *abrevados* (grazing lands), and *montes* (woodlands). The presence of the governor, padres, and neophytes is most unlikely and in all likelihood the beginnings were as unpretentious as those at San José.

The first ceremony was five years later when Sergeant José Dario Argüello came over from the presidio of Santa Barbara to confirm titles to solares and suertes, record each poblador's brand, and indicate propios, ejidos, and montes.

Much more effectively than the missions and the presidios, the pueblos were a step forward in the civilian settlement of California. Yet judging from the comments made about them, these pueblos were not an immediate or an unmixed blessing to the colony. The Los Angeles pobladores had been recruited from the most poverty-stricken in Sinaloa. They were cosmopolitan. The quartermaster accounts identify each as Spaniard, Indian, Negro, mestizo, or mulatto, and one as chino, which some scholars read as a refinement of mestizo, while others read it as meaning a Filipino or Chinese from Manila. Most of the pobladores were illiterate; at the account closing in 1786 all signed with a cross. Two decades later one of the missionaries complained that the townfolk were a set of idlers, addicted to cards, song, and seduction of the Indian women, and that all labor at the pueblo was performed by Indians. By 1800, however, Los Angeles was second only to the mission San Gabriel in agricultural production.

In the spring of 1782 Neve ordered the advance to the Santa Barbara Channel. Mission San Buenaventura was launched on March 31 and the presidio of Santa Barbara, three weeks later. Neve was ready to proceed with two more missions. Word came, however, that the viceroy and the College of San Fernando had disagreed on whether the mis-

sionaries should have the customary control of the temporalities or should operate on Croix's Colorado pattern. News of this deadlock did not reach California in time to prevent the establishment of San Buenaventura and the presidio, but the other two missions were not added until four or five years later—Santa Barbara on December 4, 1786, and La Purísima Concepción on December 8, 1787.

Late in 1782, Teodoro de Croix having been promoted to viceroy of Peru, Neve was named commandant general of the frontier provinces. He left California the better by his *Reglamento*, two pueblos, a ninth mission, and a fourth presidio. The reinforcements he had urged had consolidated the Spanish hold, and the farming and stock raising which he promoted were on the verge of ending any further dependence on food shipments from Mexico.

CHAPTER 5

**Visit of la Pérouse at the Mission of
San Carlos, Carmel**

Voyage de la Pérouse, *1797*

The Spaniards have, at a great expense and considerable industry, removed every obstacle out of the way of an invading enemy; they have stocked the country with such multitudes of cattle, horses, and other useful animals, that they have no longer the power to remove or destroy them; they have taught the Indians many of the useful arts and accustomed them to agriculture and civilization; and they have spread a number of defenceless inhabitants over the country, whom they never could induce to act as enemies to those who should treat them well; by securing to them the enjoyment of liberty, property, and a free trade, which would almost instantaneously quadruple the value of their actual possessions; in a word, they have done everything that could be done to render California an object worthy the attention of the great maritime powers; they have placed it in a situation to want nothing but a good government to rise rapidly to wealth and importance.

William Shaler
Journal (1804)

Local Annals

A Holding Operation

Through the first dozen years of the Spanish period California faced an endless succession of crises. Whether by sea, up the peninsula, or over the Anza trail, the road to California was hard. Especially at the outset the toll of lives was high. The Indians, though not aggressively warlike, showed meager interest in conversion and on occasion rose in rebellion. The land itself was refractory, resisting through these dozen years the efforts of presidios, missions, and pueblos to make it yield crops sufficient to sustain the few hundred agents of empire, the soldiers, missionaries, and settlers, and the neophytes.

The remaining 40 years of the Spanish period had a different character. As livestock multiplied and the people at missions and pueblos learned how to make their plantings productive, the threat of food shortage disappeared. The royal treasury continued to pay wages, salaries, and stipends but seldom made a special outlay. No imperial officer exerted himself particularly on behalf of the province. When the Franciscans on the scene proposed a second chain of missions in the interior, authorization was not given, and the contour of Spanish California continued to be the coastal belt from San Diego to San Francisco. For imperial defense, as in the time of Gálvez and Bucareli, Spain wanted her flag flown over California yet was content with a holding operation, seeing no profit in any active effort to build up the colony. California thus was destined for a placid and unprogressive epoch, rustic, untroubled, and, as some see it in retrospect, idyllic and romantic.

Serra and Lasuén

At this stage the annals record the departure of many who had been conspicuous in the earlier work. Several, of course, were already gone. Portolá left in 1770. Gálvez' direct connection terminated at about the same time. Pérez, dean of the ship captains, died in 1775, Anza left in 1776, and Bucareli died three years later. Garcés and Rivera fell in the Yuma Massacre. Crespi, diarist of so much of the early exploration, died in 1782. Later in that year Neve was promoted to the commandancy of the Provincias Internas, in which he died in 1784.

On August 28, 1784, death had overtaken the first father-president of the California missions. Serra's closest companion, Francisco Palóu, had already applied for retirement because of his infirmities. Temporarily, Palóu assumed charge of the mission work, but in 1785 he left for the College of San Fernando, where two years later he issued the first California biography, *Relación histórica de la vida . . . del venerable Padre Fray Junípero Serra*.

Palóu's *Life of Serra* is by a confessedly enthusiastic admirer. Its imputations of miracles and its appropriation for Serra of credit partly due Portolá and others are defects, but out of Palóu's love and zeal emerges a portrayal which has beatified this brave and unselfish man in the hearts of Californians if not in the official list of the church.

A native of Mallorca, Serra entered the Franciscan order at 16 and, after schooling, gained a reputation as an effective preacher. In 1749 at 36 he was sent to America. For ten years he labored in the Sierra Gorda missions of what is now Tamaulipas. In 1768 he was put in charge of the missions of Baja California. The last 15 years of his life were devoted to Alta California.

Such is Serra's fame that many have assumed he had full charge of Alta California. In fact, his authority was only over the missionaries. In personal matters he was as humble, meek, and self-effacing as the founder of his order, the gentle St. Francis of Assisi. Yet when mission welfare was at stake, he was spirited and stubborn, quick to make vigorous protest to the viceroy and the court, where often though not always he, rather than the governor, was upheld. Although his combativeness is a principal basis for his recognition, his admirers concede that he was a more tempestuous and pugnacious champion of the missions than was necessary.

Another basis for his fame was his willingness to exhaust himself in the service to which he was committed. He was most constant in his devotions; for instance, during his trip to Mexico, in spite of grave illness, he insisted on spending hours on his knees in the cold chapels. Like many of his contemporaries, he believed that pain and discomfort purified the spirit. Besides refusing comforts, he inflicted self-torture. While journeying from Veracruz to Mexico at the outset of his missionary career, he deliberately exposed himself to insects, with the result that he was lame forever after. On the expedition up the peninsula with Portolá, his sore leg plagued him, at length so seriously as to threaten holding up the expedition. He steadfastly refused any treatment but finally relented to the extent of allowing one of the muleteers to apply a salve of herbs and tallow intended for use on the animals.

Serra's most distinguished successor, Fray Fermín Francisco de Lasuén, is by comparison most obscure. Yet in solid achievement his presidency compares favorably. During his 18 years of control, from 1785 to 1803, the number of missions doubled and the number of Christian Indians approached 20,000.

Lasuén's mission founding began with those Neve and Serra had planned for the Chumash, Santa Barbara, and Purísima Concepción in 1786 and 1787. In 1791 he added two others in the vicinity of Monterey—Santa Cruz and Soledad. Then in 1797–98 came five others: San José de Guadalupe, San Juan Bautista, San Miguel Arcangel, San Fernando Rey de España, and San Luís Rey de Francia. Some of these came to be among the most noteworthy. Each was at a site favorable for agriculture and among Indians not yet touched by earlier missions.

Along with numerical growth Lasuén brought about an economic transformation. In Serra's time a rather slender beginning had been made in stock raising and farming. Under Lasuén these activities were furthered, and the introduction of a number of industries made the missions diversified establishments rather than mere agricultural centers. Lasuén brought in a score of artisans from Mexico and set them working at their trades and helping instruct the Indians in the work of carpenters, masons, smiths, and the like. The new style in mission architecture exemplifies the change; hitherto the buildings had been unpretentious, thatch-covered structures; now tile and stone came into general use along with timber and adobe. New missions were constructed, and Serra's nine were rebuilt, all in what is now known as the mission style.

Like his predecessor, Lasuén had difficulties with the governors. When it was proposed that new missions be established with only a single missionary, Lasuén, who had had five years of such experience at Borja in Baja California, was adamant that no such unsatisfactory stations should be opened. Nor would he agree that the missionaries should relinquish all temporal control over the neophytes, allow them to live in their own villages, and have them come to the missions merely for religious instruction. Lasuén was as firm in this stand as Serra had been, but he conducted his disputes amiably.

Although an older man, Lasuén was robust and enjoyed the vigorous longevity for which Californians were noted. He traveled widely and frequently from his headquarters at San

Carlos, notably in 1797 when, at 76, he presided over the inauguration of four new missions and visited all the others.

Fages' Second Term

Of the later Spanish governors, Fages was the most colorful. The central feature of his second administration was the continuation of the contest with the missionaries. In 1785 he entered a formal protest with the viceroy who, through the Audiencia of Mexico City, laid it before the College of San Fernando. The guardian of the college, none other than Francisco Palóu, responded with an elaborate defense of the actions of the friars and preferred countercharges against Fages. The case was then laid before the commandant-general of the Provincias Internas. The latter asked Lasuén for a detailed opinion on the issues involved, but, because the Provincias Internas had been returned to the direct supervision of the viceroy, he contented himself with ordering the agents of state and church in California each to observe the proper jurisdictional limits and to work in harmony. The temperaments of Lasuén and Fages made this accommodation possible.

Fages' second administration was enlivened by the presence of his spirited wife, Doña Eulalia de Callis. Only by enlisting the aid of Neve did Fages persuade Doña Eulalia to join him in California. Finally she came as far as Loreto, where her husband met her and escorted her to Monterey. The journey has been likened to a royal progress because of the enthusiastic receptions en route by friars, soldiers, settlers, and Indians for the first lady of California, a pageant which provided the frame for Walter Nordhoff's novel *The Journey of the Flame*. Traveling through the Californias, Doña Eulalia gave presents from her own and her husband's wardrobe, especially

to the naked Indians, until Don Pedro made clear that there would be no opportunity to purchase such things in Alta California.

After a short residence at Monterey, Doña Eulalia had had enough of California. She tried to persuade her husband to send her and their two children back to Mexico. When he refused she exerted pressures, first excluding him from her rooms and then denouncing him for infidelity, broadcasting threats that she would sue for divorce. After a sojourn at Mission San Carlos, during which the friars were scandalized by her tantrums, Doña Eulalia began divorce proceedings, which were heard before the acting commandant-general at Chihuahua and then transferred to the Bishop of Sonora. Before a decision was reached, Don Pedro effected a reconciliation. A month later, in October, 1785, he had the embarrassing task of trying to intercept a letter in which his wife had petitioned the audiencia to remove her husband from office because of ill health. In 1790 Doña Eulalia won her point by less direct action. She persuaded her husband to ask to be retired, and, when a favorable answer was received late in the year, she and the children sailed at once for San Blas.

Rancho Grants

In 1773 Bucareli authorized grants of land to persons living at a mission or presidio. One such grant was made to Manuel Butron of the Monterey garrison in 1775. It was for a small plot of 140 *varas* (Spanish yards) and, for lack of use, it reverted. Without land assignments some of the soldiers ran a few cattle.

In 1784 Juan José Domínguez, a retired soldier at San Diego, Corporal José María Verdugo of the military escort at Mission San Gabriel, and Manuel Pérez Nieto, another soldier at San Diego, applied for grants. Each had horses and cattle. Domínguez asked for a tract on the coastal plain south of the pueblo of Los Angeles; Verdugo, for a pie-shaped area rising from a point near the pueblo's *saca de agua* (the dam for drawing off water to be used at lower levels); and Nieto, for a tract on the San Gabriel southward from Mission San Gabriel.

Fages responded favorably, with the proviso that there be no encroachment on the pueblo or the mission. The grant to Nieto specified that he was "to sleep at the Pueblo," that is, to maintain his residence there rather than on the land granted. Presumably that was expected also of Domínguez, while Verdugo would continue at San Gabriel.

None of these grants contained even an estimate of its size, land being in superabundant supply. The Domínguez Rancho, later regranted as Rancho San Pedro and Rancho Palos Verdes, amounted to 74,000 acres in all. Verdugo's San Rafael was later measured at 36,000 acres. Nieto's grant had an extent of 33 square leagues, or more than 150,000 acres.

Domínguez immediately put 200 head of cattle on his grant but did not go to live there until 1800. He was under some criticism for neglecting his stock and letting his horses multiply to the point of being a nuisance. Verdugo stocked his rancho but did not retire to it until 1797. Nieto made the transition somewhat sooner, but by 1800 his headquarters was a small satellite of the pueblo of Los Angeles.

Inasmuch as these were the first grants of their kind in California, Fages' action was taken under review by the legal adviser of the commandant-general, Pablo Galindo y Navarro. Turning to the *Laws of the Indies*, Galindo found permission for grants of land, provided certain conditions were observed. They must not encroach on lands belonging to a pueblo, and their use must not result in any injury to mission, pueblo, or Indian village. The grantee must build a house and stock his rancho with at least 2,000 head of cattle. Grazing lands, though included in such a grant, must continue to be enjoyed in common rather than exclusively. The rights thus assigned were contingent on use rather than having the quality of title in fee simple.

Fages' action did not start a rush. In the rest of the Spanish period, some 30 grants were made, some small, others baronial in extent. Among the more significant were Luís Peralta's San Antonio (1820), covering most of present-day Berkeley, Oakland, and Alameda; José María Soberanes' Buena Vista (1795), near Monterey; the Ortegas' El Refugio (1795), west of Santa Barbara; the Picos' Simi (1795); and José Antonio Yorba's Santiago de Santa Ana (1810). Half the Spanish rancho grants were in the vicinity of the pueblo of Los Angeles. At the close of the Spanish period half the rancho grants had reverted because they were not put or kept in use. At that date also the number of residents on all the ranchos did not equal the population of the pueblo of Los Angeles. Nevertheless, the device of land grants as encouragement for rancho development was a useful precedent.

Famous Visitors

In 1786 California was visited by the first non-Spanish ship since Drake's *Golden Hind* more than two centuries earlier. The following decades witnessed an increasing international interest in the North Pacific, one consequence of which was a whole series of English, American, Russian, and French contacts. Of these nations France gained the least advantage in the North Pacific, but it was a Frenchman, Comte de Lapérouse, who initiated these visits to Spanish California. In the course of a round-the-world reconnaissance for his government, he stopped for ten days in September, 1786, at Monterey, where he was entertained by Fages, Lasuén, and the provincials as lavishly as circumstances permitted.

The expedition went on to the Philippines, Kamchatka, and Australia and then disappeared. Fortunately for the historical record, the earlier records of the expedition, including the stay in California, had been sent home and were published in four volumes in Paris in 1797. The unknown fate of the gallant explorers enhanced interest in the Lapérouse account. Years later wreckage discovered on a reef of Vanikoro in the Santa Cruz Islands confirmed the disastrous end of this French voyage.

Lapérouse's observations on California, as printed in his posthumous *Voyage autour du monde*, were perspicacious and, for the most part, sympathetic. The Spaniards, he thought, would not develop the province rapidly; and indeed, except for furs, he did not detect any promising source of wealth. The persons whom Lapérouse met, Lasuén in particular, fare well in his book, but the mission system does not. His verdict was that the missions were making only slight progress toward converting the Indians into civilized, industrious, profit-minded persons.

Some five years later, almost to the day, a Spanish round-the-world scientific expedition put in at Monterey for a 12-day stay in September, 1791. Fages having retired and his successor not yet having arrived, a subordinate and Lasuén did the honors. For a long time this visit by Alejandro Malaspina had small place in California's written history. Its auspices being Spanish, it lacked the cosmopolitan piquancy of the visit by Lapérouse. Nor did its ships sail out into mystery and tragedy. Completing his mission, Malaspina reported at court, was promoted, and began arranging and editing the findings of his voyage. But, on the objection that he was becoming too friendly with ladies of the court, he soon was banished. The result was a 90-year delay in the publication of any account of the voyage. The book issued in 1885, although a weighty tome, was fragmentary on the California interlude.

Recent research located voluminous scattered records of the Malaspina visit. These visitors were lyrical about the beauty and the varied resources of Monterey. On the age-old question of the suitability of Monterey as a port for the Manila galleon, Malaspina was emphatically negative. He saw it fog-shrouded, rock-girt, and exposed. His ships needed cannon fire from the presidio to guide them in. They lost three anchors in the process and spent several days in laborious and fruitless dragging for them. Relying mostly on what he was told by Lasuén, Malaspina reported favorably on the missionary effort.

The scientists and naturalists of the expedition made observations to determine latitude and longitude, gathered information on Indian culture, collected descriptions and specimens of flora and fauna, fish and birds. Artists sketched or painted scenes and specimens. A complete inventory of all that was done does not exist, but clearly it was a more thorough cataloguing than Lapérouse and his men achieved. Donald Cutter's *Malaspina in California* (1960) for the first time gives due credit to this inspection and reproduces highly informative drawings, paintings, and maps.

In 1778–79 the famous British navigator, James Cook, had sailed into the North Pacific, discovered the Hawaiian Islands, reconnoitered the northwest coast of America, and, for the furs that were plentiful on that coast, discovered a most rewarding market in China. A detailed report of this voyage was published in 1784 and circulated widely. Its information about the transactions in furs led to a flurry of commercial voyages under many flags. Spain, alert to protect her northwestern claims, sent a naval officer in 1789 to check on the British, Russian, and American activity in this north-

Indians in Balsa, San Francisco Bay   Georg Heinrich Langsdorff, *1812*

ern extension of California. This officer acted with what may have been an excess of zeal. While not interfering with American ships, he took possession of a British trading post, or fort, at Nootka, Vancouver Island, seized two British vessels, and held one ship captain prisoner. Britain demanded satisfaction for these insults and compensation for damages due her traders. Spain had to accede, and in 1790 the first Nootka treaty took shape.

To see that the treaty was carried into effect, Britain sent George Vancouver to the Pacific. At Nootka he and the Spanish commander could not agree upon an interpretation of the treaty, which they referred back to Europe for clarification. Vancouver proceeded to engage in extensive exploration and mapmaking, adequately represented in his three-volume narrative, *A Voyage of Discovery*, published in London in 1798.

In the course of his work Vancouver made three visits to California. He was the first foreign visitor to San Francisco Bay in November, 1792. Then followed a 50-day sojourn at Monterey. After a trip to Hawaii, he returned to San Francisco on October 19, 1793. Gov-

ernor José Joaquin Arrillaga, in the meantime, had ordered strict enforcement of the regulations with regard to foreign visitors. Vancouver got what he considered a very cool reception. At Santa Barbara and San Diego the regulations were more hospitably disregarded. Vancouver's final visit to Monterey, in November, 1794, coincided with the arrival of a new governor. The British were welcomed into the festivities. Vancouver had much greater opportunity than Lapérouse to observe California. His comments are prolix. Except toward Arrillaga he was generous in praise of the personalities he had encountered, but he agreed with Lapérouse's judgment that the province did not hold promise of rapid development under Spanish rule.

Borica and Branciforte

In November, 1794, the government of California was taken over by an urbane, convivial, and witty Basque, Diego de Borica. Quickly becoming enamored of California, Borica liberally sprinkled his letters with tributes to its pleasant and healthful climate, the good provender that was available at Monterey, the high spirits that life in the province seemed to engender, and the "astounding fecundity" of Spaniards and natives. California, he asserted, "is the most peaceful and quiet country in the world; one lives better here than in the most cultured court of Europe."

Borica became governor when, for the first time, California seemed exposed to invasion. The controversy with Britain over Nootka flared again, and the increased activity of British fur hunters along the northwest coast compounded the exposure. In addition, a state of war existed between Spain and France. The California presidios had not been geared to meet anything more powerful than Indian attack. A first step was to bring up reinforcements and more respectable artillery. These were requested and, early in 1796, some 75 Catalan volunteers, commanded by Pedro de Alberni, arrived and were portioned out to the presidios. Repairs were made and additional guns were mounted.

Rumors of an imminent British attack followed the French scare, and Borica issued elaborate instructions on how the Californians should flee inland. In 1800 rumor of a forthcoming Russian attack occasioned the usual precautionary orders, but the provincials refused to be alarmed. "An invasion from Kamchatka," Bancroft observes, "seems to have had no terrors for the Californians after their success escaping from the fleets of Great Britain."

As governor, Borica took a personal interest in development of irrigation, encouragement of hemp and flax culture, a rather futile effort to stimulate sheep raising, and launching of the mission industries. Thanks to his active interest, schools were opened for the children of the soldiers and the settlers. Borica not only arranged for teachers and schoolrooms, as in the public granary at San José,

but also planned the curriculum and required that reports and copybooks be sent to him frequently for inspection.

Persuaded that California needed a second line of defense, Viceroy Branciforte authorized recruitment of settlers to found another town in the neighborhood of San Francisco. On receipt of this word Borica sent engineer Alberto de Córdoba and Alberni to select a proper site for the new town. Their reports stated emphatically that the Alameda was impossible because of a meager supply of water which, in addition, lay in a bed far below the land to be irrigated. San Francisco was worse. They saw no land suitable for cultivation within seven or eight leagues of the presidio. Wood was scarce, pasture lacking, and water in very poor supply. Besides, the locale (shades of Candlestick Park) was plagued by unruly winds.

The place to establish an agricultural town, Córdoba and Alberni agreed, was near Mission Santa Cruz, 30 leagues from San Francisco and from Monterey, 22 if by land and 12 if by sea. Borica adopted their recommendations and accepted their justifications. The site, he reported, was wonderfully favored with fertile soil, water for irrigation, abundant pasture, wood and timber, extraordinary opportunity for fishing, and a good landing. So that these settlers might start farming immediately, Borica proposed that the government construct their houses for them.

The settlers recruited for this town, Villa de Branciforte, fell far short of Borica's hopes. He had requested "poor but honorable colonists . . . of pure blood." Most of those who came were convicts. A few proved vicious and incorrigible; many of the others, though more unfortunate than hardened in crime, were feeble, diseased, or unskilled. On July 17, 1797, Gabriel Moraga supervised the launching of the villa with nine convict colonists and eight others. They were joined by four retired soldiers who brought some 200 head of horses and cattle. Another 19 convicts arrived at Monterey early in 1798. Although most were assigned elsewhere, six eventually came to Branciforte.

The start was inauspicious. A report in 1801 says that the colonists were poor workers. The Franciscans objected strenuously to the settlement as an encroachment and a disturbance to the mission. In part because of these protests, the government financing was cut back, and the town was not granted enough arable land. Borica proposed a radical remedy: let Mission Santa Cruz be closed and its Indians transferred to Missions San Juan Bautista and Santa Clara. That might have saved Branciforte, but it did not

happen. Population reached a peak of 16 families and 101 persons in 1802 but declined to 31 persons in 1804. In 1815 there were 53, but the villa disintegrated and did not survive even in name.

Sea Otter Hunting

By the 1790s an international competition in trade was developing in the North Pacific. The Russians, after a centuries-long advance eastward across Siberia, were as far as southern Alaska. British fur trappers had crossed Canada to the shores of the Pacific. British and American ships were beginning feverish activity in the China trade and were starting

Sea Otter   *Allan Brooks, University of California Press*

to scour the Pacific for goods in demand in China. On the northwest coast the Americans prevailed in this rivalry and soon were in close collaboration with the Russians in extending this fur gathering southward into the most favored habitat of the sea otter, the California coast down as far as the twenty-eighth parallel.

The first American ship to enter a California port was the *Otter*, captained by Ebenezer Dorr, which put in at Monterey in 1796 for wood and water. The *Eliza* made a similar stop at San Francisco in 1799 and the *Betsey* at San Diego in 1800. Dorr took advantage of the hospitality to put ashore ten men and a woman, fugitives from Botany Bay. Although these former convicts proved good workers, Governor Borica, as the law required, forwarded them to New Spain.

These ships were representative of a larger number engaged in sea otter hunting at the Santa Barbara Channel Islands and along the rockier parts of the California coast. Occasionally an otter might be clubbed on shore. Furs could also be had from the Indians. The standard technique was to go first to Russian America, take on board a number of Aleut hunters with their kayaks, and have them do the hunting with harpoon and line off the California coast. The otter hunters began to use some of California's unoccupied bays as places to careen their ships, remove barnacles, and repair before going on to Alaska, China, or New England. Avalon Bay at Catalina was much favored for these purposes. They also opened a small-scale trade with the Californians, bartering New England goods for beef, grain, and furs. Since Spanish law forbade such trade, California officials had to take a stand against it, but it was such a boon to the isolated province that many officials closed their eyes or even connived in the trade.

Occasionally a Yankee captain fell afoul of the authorities. In 1803 the commandant at San Diego confiscated several hundred otter skins and part of the cargo of the *Alexander*. A few days later the *Lelia Byrd* (so named in the literature but probably a misreading of *Delia Byrd*), with William Shaler as captain, entered port. Its mate, Richard Cleveland, recorded an opinion that the commandant would have liked to sell his stock of a thousand otter skins but, having just penalized the captain of the *Alexander*, could not do so. Three men sent ashore at night to buy furs were arrested. Captain Shaler promptly sent another detachment ashore with drawn pistols to rescue these men. He then raised sail, unlimbered his six three-pounders on the starboard side, and sailed out within musket shot of the battery of eight nine-pounders at the entrance to the bay. For three quarters of an hour the engagement was brisk, but with no serious damage on either side.

Less fortunate was George Washington Eayrs of the *Mercury*. In 1812 he was near Point Concepción, taking on water and getting oak timbers for repairs, when an armed longboat from the *Flora*, one of the Peruvian ships that had come to California that year, demanded his surrender. The *Flora* took the *Mercury* to Santa Barbara. There its cargo was confiscated, and for the next two years Eayrs was detained at Santa Barbara and San Diego. His protests, models of forceful rhetoric and irregular spelling, availed him little. It is significant that he was put out of business by a Peruvian competitor rather than by a California official, for most of the latter were sympathetic toward commerce with the fur ships.

In the period of the Wars of Independence after 1810, with the suspension of regular shipments from San Blas and prolonged failure to meet payrolls, trade with the Boston ships found a new excuse. It increased in volume and in openness and came to be highly convenient for the Californians.

Sea otter pelts were the first California commodity to find its way to an outside market. Most of these furs were taken by what the Spanish officials regarded as poaching and without any economic benefit to the province. The rest went out as contraband, in exchange for goods much wanted by the Californians and for which after 1810 there was no real substitute.

To calculate the volume of this trade is not much easier than to compile figures for the number of otter and seal pelts taken. Some estimates are available. In 1801, 18,000 otter furs are said to have been marketed in China. Within half a dozen years the annual average was nearer 15,000, and at the end of the decade it was about 10,000. Many of these furs came from the northwest coast. Otter hunting was pursued so relentlessly that after 1820 not enough of these remarkable animals were left to justify further hunting voyages. A few pelts were occasionally obtained in the next two or three decades, but that was all. Thereafter the sea otter became exceedingly scarce. In recent years, under protection, they have staged a comeback and can be seen again, playing in the sea, swimming incredible distances underwater and surfacing to recline at ease and dine on mussels or sea urchins.

The fur seal was present in much larger numbers. Furs of this animal bulked large in the cargoes carried to China. The islands of southern Chile yielded millions of these furs, and California was not far behind. Particularly at the Farallones the sealing was excellent. This business was also carried on without any thought of conservation, with the result that by about 1820 the fur seal was almost exterminated from southern waters. Thus an end came to the voyages of the Boston fur ships to California. Their epoch was brief, but it had given to the Californians their first taste of foreign commerce and to Americans their first contact with the inviting land of California.

The Coming of the Russians

In the winter of 1805–06 scurvy and starvation threatened the Russian trading post at Sitka. Nikolai Rezanov arranged temporary relief by purchasing the American ship *Juno* and its cargo. To develop a more permanent source of supplies he decided on a voyage to Spanish California. The Hawaiian Islands might have been a more logical choice had supplies been the only objective, but Rezanov was also interested in developing fur trade along the California coast.

Sailing from Sitka on March 8, 1806, he reached San Francisco on April 5. At first the Russians and Spaniards had great difficulty in communicating. The first conversations were between engineer Langsdorff and Father Uría in Latin. Later a priest who could speak French came up from Santa Clara.

Rezanov soon discovered that Spanish law forbade any traffic with foreigners and that the California officials were not inclined to permit trade. A battle of wits ensued in which he tried to conceal the dire straits at Sitka, apparently on the assumption that the Californians would be more apt to permit a nonessential commerce than one which would be the salvation of Russian America and the guaranty of its permanence. Both Luís Argüello, the commander at San Francisco, and Governor Arrillaga came to realize, however, that the Russians were in a critical situation.

Rezanov did not prevail until he enlisted the aid of Concepción Argüello, the beautiful daughter of the San Francisco commander. Their romance is one of the most famous and

Maison des colonies de l'Amerique Russe

Duflot de Mofras, Exploration, *1844*

most touching in all California history. She was the acknowledged belle of the province; he, as dashing and polished a gentleman as had ever visited California. "I imperceptibly," Rezanov says, "created in her an impatience to hear something serious from me on the subject." She quickly accepted his proposal; her father and the padres, though more obdurate because Rezanov was of the Greek Orthodox faith, finally gave in.

Because of his obvious ulterior motives, the genuineness of Rezanov's love has been questioned. His fiancée's influence upon her father and, through him, upon the governor won permission for the desired trade. From the missions Rezanov secured a full cargo of foodstuffs and on May 21 sailed to relieve Sitka. The trade permit, however, was for this one occasion only.

From Sitka, Rezanov returned to Kam-chatka and started across Siberia to report to the czar and, presumably, to seek permission to marry his California love. But at Yakutsk he was stricken with what proved to be a fatal illness and consequently did not have the opportunity to prove that his intentions were honorable. Of Doña Concepción's sincerity there is not the slightest doubt. Year upon year she remained true to her lover, at first confidently anticipating his return, then taking refuge in the robes of a nun. Not until 35 years later, when Sir George Simpson visited California, did she learn of her lover's fate. Her faithfulness has been extolled in poem, novel, and story. To the Californians of her day the tragic sadness of her blighted romance was somewhat eclipsed by her kindliness, and it may be that she found consolation in the cherished memory of that spring when she was sixteen.

During the Wars of Independence

In the Spanish-American Wars of Independence, which raged from 1808 into the 1820s, California, as might have been expected, played the role of innocent bystander. The newest English colonies, Canada and the Floridas, had not joined the American Revolution. California, the youngest Spanish colony, was so effectively isolated from Mexico that Hidalgo's Grito de Dolores, which reverberated through most of Mexico, did not find an echo in this province.

Breakdown of supply service and lack of remittances from Mexico made Californians aware of the war. In Bucareli's day such a stoppage would have meant starvation; now it merely meant inconvenience. Missions and pueblos had large enough herds and crops to supply the entire population adequately. Even though the missions were induced to enter upon the unprofitable business of cashing presidial requisitions, the presidial soldiers were the worst off. Except to the soldiers, however, the deprivation was chiefly in luxury goods, and several expedients minimized this distress.

Two Peruvian ships, the *Flora* and the *Tagle*, arrived in 1813 with cloth and other goods which were bartered for tallow and hides. In the cargo of the *Mercury* was $16,000 in coin, which was confiscated for the royal treasury. The governor prudently retained this coin in the provincial treasury and sent a draft to Mexico.

Another trade possibility was with the new Russian establishment at Fort Ross, just north of Bodega Bay. In 1812 Ivan Kuskoff arrived there with 80 Russians and 50 Aleuts to set up a base for fur gathering. Governor Arrillaga was meticulous in refusing official approval to trade with these interlopers, but Argüello admitted $14,000 worth of Russian goods at San Francisco in 1813, and trade continued. In 1815 when Pablo Vicente de Solá arrived as governor, he interrupted the trade with Fort Ross. He had Eliot de Castro and Boris Tarakanof arrested and sent to Mexico on the very ship that had brought him north. It did not take him long, however, to see that California must have some sort of foreign trade, and in the following month he authorized barter for $7,000 worth of goods from a British vessel.

The main relief was provided by American ships. The Boston fur ships offered no facilities for the transmission of reports and orders to and from New Spain, and consequently a degree of autonomy was thrust upon Californians. Officials had to make decisions that once would have been referred to Mexico City.

In 1818 the war was brought home to the Californians by the appearance at Monterey of two Buenos Aires privateers operating in the revolutionary cause. An American ship had brought a few weeks' warning that these ships were en route from Hawaii, and Solá took energetic though none too effective measures to stiffen the defenses.

On November 21 an improvised shore battery embarrassed the *Santa Rosa* and prevented a direct landing at Monterey. From the *Argentina*, however, Commander Hippolyte de Bouchard landed at Point Pinos, forcing Solá to retreat as far as present-day Salinas with the provincial archives.

Bouchard's men, under the loosest sort of discipline, spent a busy week provisioning their ships and plundering the town. They ranged the streets and broke into dwellings as well as storehouses in search of money or other valuables. In their looting they wantonly destroyed much that they found, laid waste gardens and orchards, and fired the town.

Their next stop was at Refugio, where they burned Ortega's ranch building. The Californians, under Sergeant Carlos Antonio Carrillo, lassoed three of Bouchard's men and carried them off to Santa Barbara. Possession of the prisoners saved that town, because Bouchard agreed to do no harm if the men were given up. Anticipating a descent upon their mission, the Buenaventurans retreated inland, while the Angelenos for once rejoiced that their pueblo was 20 miles from the coast. San Juan Capistrano bore the brunt for southern California, partly because the commander defied the pirate-patriots. Bouchard's men

came ashore, pillaged and burned, got drunk, and sailed away the next morning. San Diego polished its defenses and packed its women and children off to Pala, but Bouchard passed on by, and the War of Independence was over as far as California was concerned.

When news of Bouchard's attack reached Mexico, the viceroy was much alarmed. He immediately ordered two transports sent to California with reinforcements and, even after receiving Solá's report of the departure of the insurgents, he allowed the order to stand. In the late summer of 1819, 100 good cavalrymen arrived from Mazatlán under Captain Pablo de Portilla and an equal number of infantrymen from San Blas under Captain

Asistencia de Pala   *David Packwood*

José Antonio de Navarrete. These infantry-men Solá described as vicious, quarrelsome vagabonds without religion, drunkards, gamblers, thieves, lepers—in short, to sum it up in a vigorous California phrase, *cholos.* Solá complained bitterly that they only added to his troubles. Yet each of the presidios had a larger garrison by approximately 50 men.

Two years later the Mexican revolutionaries finally won independence from Spain. The news would not reach California until early in 1822, but by this remote action the province had ceased to be a possession of the king of Spain.

The province at the time included some 20,000 Indians at the 20 missions strung out in a meandering line from San Diego to San Rafael. In the interior were several times that many uncontrolled Indians. The *gente de razón* (the civilized) are estimated at 3,300, of whom perhaps one fourth were men. Some of these people lived on the 15 or 20 ranchos. A few lived at or near the missions. A larger number is accounted for at the four presidios. The population of San José is put at 240, and that of Los Angeles at 650, second only to Monterey with 700. The sum was a Spanish occupation which as planned was token, but which had preserved Spanish title to the region and had implanted Spanish institutions and ways that would continue and expand.

CHAPTER 6

Arcade, Mission San Fernando

Now all is gone. These Southern California Missions, built of adobe, when once unroofed melt away in the rains as quickly as Christianized Indians also disappear.

Walter Nordhoff
Journey of the Flame

A Mexican Province

Adjusting to Independence

Early in 1822 word reached California that Spanish control in North America had ended and that an independent Mexican nation was being organized. Governor Pablo Vicente de Solá, his associates, and the soldiers at Monterey immediately swore allegiance to the new regime. Electors from the four presidios and the pueblo of Los Angeles met and chose Solá as deputy and Luís Argüello as alternate.

An American ship soon brought the design of the new flag and a report that Agustín Iturbide, one of the generals in the long War of Independence, had taken over as emperor. An agent of the new regime soon arrived. He insisted that California must have a *diputación* (provincial legislature) and that California's *jefe político* (governor) must be American-born rather than a Spaniard. He pressed hard on that issue and by one vote the *diputación* chose Argüello. On Solá's departure, early in 1823, he became governor.

The principal issue in 1823 was Fray José Altimira's petition to remove Mission San Francisco to a more healthful location in the Sonoma Valley. The ultimate decision was not to abandon San Francisco but to establish a new mission at that site.

In November, 1823, California learned that it once more was part of a republic rather than an imperial monarchy. Agustín I (Iturbide) had been forced to abdicate and the *Cortes* (congress) was at work on a republican constitution.

In February, 1824, after a soldier flogged an Indian at Mission Santa Inés, the Indians rebelled and set fire to the mission. When troops arrived from Santa Barbara, this revolt was soon put down. But the unrest had spread to Purísima Concepción where the Indians attacked the mission guard, killing two guards and two white visitors. For a month they held control.

Hearing what had happened, the Indians at Mission Santa Barbara seized the weapons of the guards and took charge, but after a half-day battle presidial troops recaptured the mission. Most of the Indians escaped to the hills, but others were killed during and after the fighting.

From Monterey the governor sent an army of a hundred men. Training a four-pound cannon on Mission Purísima, they forced its surrender. A series of campaigns reaching as far inland as the tulares brought back most of the Santa Barbarans.

Early in 1825 California learned that the Constitution of 1824 was in force. Patterned on that of the United States, it provided for a federal republic in which California's role would be more analogous to that of a territory than a state. After Argüello, for instance, the norm was that California governors were appointed by the authorities in Mexico rather than elected in the province. Conservatives, particularly the friars, were none too pleased with the shift to a republican form of government. But because the change had come by gradual transition, opportunity to resist had been muted.

Politics by Revolution

In all parts of Spanish America the first years of independence were turbulent because the colonial experience had offered little preparation for freedom. There was much talk about such abstractions as democracy, class equality, and constitutionality, but provincialism, personal ambition, and shows of force were more common. California's position outside

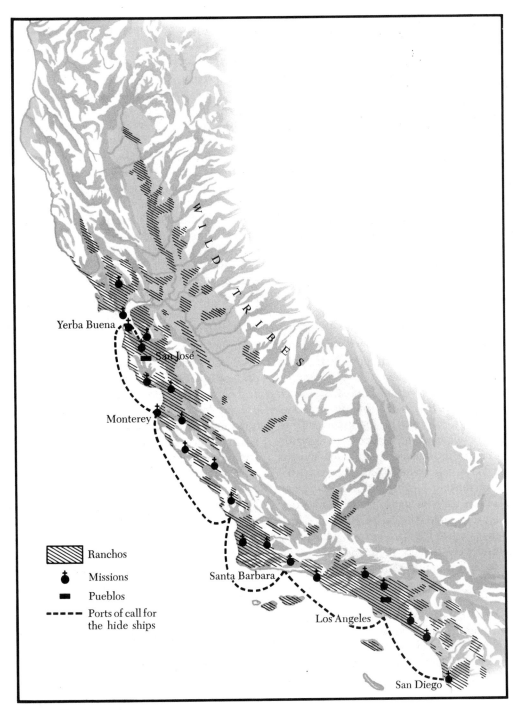

Yerba Buena

San José

Monterey

WILD TRIBES

Ranchos

Missions

Pueblos

— — — Ports of call for
the hide ships

Santa Barbara

Los Angeles

San Diego

Mexican Province

the theater of combat in the struggle for independence softened militarism. Unrest in the early national decades was usually expressed by parading, maneuvering, and bombastic talk rather than in actual fighting and bloodshed.

Revolution as a political method was first used against Governor José María Echeandía, a Mexican appointee who arrived in 1825. Out of concern for his health he decided to govern from San Diego. That choice and the inability to pay the presidial troops led to a soldiers' revolt in Monterey in 1828 headed by a ranchero and former convict, Joaquín Solís. The presidios of San Francisco and Santa Barbara supported the uprising.

Moving north to Santa Barbara, Echeandía confronted the rebels. There were feints and threats, but the battle was mainly of words, after which Solís fell back to Monterey. Echeandía followed, managed to capture Solís and several other ringleaders, and shipped them off to Mexico.

Echeandía received little praise for his work as governor. When American fur trappers entered from the east, he made it clear that they were not welcome in Mexican California. In 1826 he proclaimed that certain Indians could leave the missions and receive assistance in making a living on their own. Few applied. In 1828 he announced that by Mexican law all Spaniards must leave. Several missionaries asked to be relieved, but their requests were denied; they were needed in California. Echeandía did find that Monterey was a habitable place and governed from there for a year.

In 1830 when Manuel Victoria came to replace him, Echeandía would not go to San Diego to hand over the reins. He would not even go to Santa Barbara. Within a few months after Victoria reached Monterey and

took charge, a revolution against him arose in Los Angeles. José Antonio Carrillo, Juan Bandini, Pío Pico, and Abel Stearns were leading spirits. They persuaded Echeandía to head it, and San Diego and Los Angeles were quickly taken. The two forces met at Cahuenga. Victoria asked the regular soldiers to come over to his side. When they did not do so, he ordered a volley fired, which was returned with no damage. As he and Romualdo Pacheco rode forward, José María Avila met the challenge. Brandishing his sword, he charged Pacheco, whose lance was at the ready. They passed without contact, but Avila drew a pistol and shot Pacheco dead. Avila next attacked Victoria. Others joined the melee. In its course Avila was killed and Victoria wounded. When the joust was over, Victoria agreed to withdraw to Mexico.

Next it was the northern Californians' turn to mount a revolution. On the whole they had preferred Victoria. They rallied military support for Agustín Zamorano, formerly secretary and of more enduring fame as California's first printer. Zamorano sent an armed force south, but after a battle of words a truce left Echeandía in control as far north as San Gabriel and Zamorano over the rest of the province.

Foreign Trade Welcomed

Independence also opened California to foreign trade. As in the Spanish period, ships on a variety of missions made occasional stops in California and some trade resulted. The visit in 1841 by the United States Exploring Expedition is one instance. From the 1820s on, whalers showed active interest in North Pacific whaling grounds. Many of them put in at Monterey or the Bay of San Francisco for wood, water, and foodstuffs.

In 1829 a party of traders from the sister Mexican province of New Mexico came to Los Angeles offering silver, blankets, and American goods for horses, mules, and China silks. Over a route circling north of the Grand Canyon this traffic continued.

From its regional headquarters on the Columbia the Hudson's Bay Company sent fur-gathering brigades into northern California. It also opened commerce with the Californians and for a time stationed a resident agent in San Francisco.

A far more important trade centered on the cowhide, the commodity that California could offer in greatest abundance. The ships carrying on this trade came expressly to California, brought goods to exchange for a full cargo, and constituted Mexican California's chief contact with the outside world.

Small quantities of tallow had gone to San Blas in 1810. The *Flora* and *Tagle* from Lima took larger amounts as well as soap and a few hides in 1813, but the real start of the hide trade came with the opening of the Mexican period.

First to arrive were two representatives of John Begg and Company, an English house. These men, Hugh McCulloch and William E. P. Hartnell, operated subsequently as a California partnership which in Spanish transliteration as "Macala and Arnel" is often mentioned in the early annals. Bringing a small stock of goods from Lima, they opened negotiations for a long-term monopoly of California trade. Father Payeras, prefect of the missions which would supply the bulk of provincial products, was a canny bargainer. In the three-year contract finally drafted, the English firm agreed to take all hides offered at $1 each and at least 25,000 arrobas of tallow at $2 an arroba (25 pounds). Prices of suet, lard, and soap were set at $3, $4, and $16 a hundred,

pickled beef at $4, and wheat at $3 a *fanega* (1.6 bushels). Horns, wine, furs, and other products were listed but without fixed price. The English thus had an early advantage in the conduct of California trade. Hartnell remained as resident agent.

Within a month the first American hide trader arrived, William A. Gale, a veteran dealer in seal and otter furs, who had persuaded a number of Boston merchants to join him in sending the *Sachem* to California with a cargo of goods. Gale came as supercargo. The McCulloch-Hartnell contract made it impossible to get a full cargo of hides, yet some of the missions evaded the agreement and thus the voyage was moderately successful. The

Richard Henry Dana

Title Insurance and Trust Company, Los Angeles

Sachem returned, other vessels were sent out, and Gale was soon, to all intents and purposes, resident agent for the Boston firm of Bryant and Sturgis. At the expiration of the Hartnell contract the English advantage disappeared, and thereafter more than half of the trade was carried on by New Englanders.

From the early twenties until the gold rush the trading methods were the same, with the exception that, when the missions were secularized, most though not all of the business was transferred to the ranchos. The ships came stocked with every conceivable commodity that the Californians might want, from toothbrushes to millstones. They were, as Richard Henry Dana described them, "floating department stores." Mexican law regularized the trade. Upon payment of port duties at Monterey, ranging usually from 5,000 to 15,000 pesos depending on the amount of cargo, a ship was authorized to trade anywhere in California until its cargo of hides and tallow was completed.

Some captains carried on their trade entirely within the law. Others resorted to bribery and still others to transferring of goods from a non-duty-paying vessel or to caching part of a cargo at one of the islands before putting the ship through customs at Monterey. Just how much smuggling went on is not easily determined but, although there were frequently 20 or 30 ships engaged in the trade, the annual revenue from port duties seldom exceeded $75,000.

Ship agents went ashore and visited missions and ranchos to arrange for the purchase of hides and tallow. As the sole source of "civilized" articles they were welcome visitors and received a special measure of the hospitality for which friar and ranchero were famous. There was a strong element of incongruity, however, in the picture of these enterprising Yankees transacting the business of the Californians. Creaking carretas dumped the hides at the beach or sometimes on the mesa above the beach. It was up to the hide droghers (the sailors and their Kanaka helpers) to get them aboard. Unfortunately for the sailors, where the hides were the most abundant the harbor was the worst; the ships frequently anchored three miles offshore at San Pedro and the sailors had a long row in addition to the customary work of wading through the surf with hides balanced on their heads.

Thanks to the twin advantages that subsequently found expression in the nickname "Baynclimate," San Diego became the principal depot for the hide business. It had the one good port in southern California, and the weather was ideal for the curing that the hides required prior to the long voyage around the Horn. Some of the sailors, together with the ubiquitous Kanakas, were detailed to complete the cleaning of the hides, the Californians being none too meticulous in scraping off all the flesh. Salt and sunshine had their roles in the process, after which the hides were stored in warehouses until the time came to load a ship for the return voyage. Usually captains were two or three years in making up their cargoes.

Some of the hide and tallow men remained in California. Alfred Robinson came in the course of an ordinary voyage, stayed an extra year to act as resident agent for his company, then married into the Noriega de la Guerra family and became a permanent resident of Santa Barbara. In time there were resident traders up and down the coast, such as William Leidesdorf in San Francisco, Thomas Larkin in Monterey, and Abel Stearns and Henry Dalton in Los Angeles. They gained acceptance among the Californians and soon were among the most influential.

The hide trade spread information about California. Ship captains, supercargos, and

Hide Houses at San Diego

William Meyers, 1843, The Bancroft Library

sailors took back reports on life in California and the resources of the province. Robinson's *Life in California* ranks first among the descriptions of the land, the people, the times, and the trade, but was far surpassed in popularity by Dana's *Two Years Before the Mast*, which almost overnight became a literary classic. An outstanding travel book, the first sea tale written from the viewpoint of the ordinary seaman, and a vivid description of Mexican California, it became the most widely read book pertaining to California.

Any account which mentioned merely the immediate satisfaction of California wants, the revenue to the provincial treasury, the marketing of tallow in Mexico, Peru, and Chile, and the foreign market provided for New England manufactures would underestimate the significance of the hide trade. Its transparent consequence was the economic annexation of Mexican California to the United States.

Along with that impact the hide trade took up where Shaler and the other Boston fur men had left off and familarized New Englanders with California and its potentialities. The new awareness led New Englanders to swell the American colony in this Mexican province, to endorse the annexation program of the Tennesseean James K. Polk, and to participate in large numbers in the gold rush. The hide trade had made California an outpost of New England.

Figueroa and Secularization

For two and a half years beginning in January, 1833, California was blessed with a governor far above the Mexican average, José de Figueroa, Aztecan mestizo, a veteran of the Sonora frontier, and a competent executive. After granting amnesty to all concerned in the

Zamorano revolt, Figueroa took up the problem of California's northern defenses.

He sent Mariano Guadalupe Vallejo to the north bay region to locate sites for settlements to serve as buffers against the Russians of Fort Ross and the British on the Columbia. After visiting Fort Ross, Vallejo reported that it was a fur-gathering base rather than a fortification, had a personnel of 300 of whom 70 were Russians, who were having moderate success in farming and stock raising. Vallejo chose sites for countercolonization but warned that the Indians had been antagonized by the attempts to compel them to live at the missions. With a handful of colonists Vallejo established settlements at Petaluma and Santa Rosa and subsequently at Sonoma.

Figueroa's attention was soon engrossed in the assigned task of secularizing the missions and in dealing with an ambitious colonization project. Secularization meant converting the missions into parish churches, releasing the neophytes from complete supervision by the friars, and releasing much of the mission lands for other use. Such action had long been contemplated. Spain's original plan had been to secularize after ten years of mission operation, but because the instruction of the natives and the build-up of a body of settlers to assist in the second stage of civilizing and assimilation went slower than expected, the mission period was prolonged.

When Figueroa came to California the intention was to continue the missions. Indeed, he brought ten Franciscans from the College of Zacatecas to reinforce the Fernandinos. What he saw and what he learned from the missionaries led him to recommend against immediate secularization. The Mexican Congress, however, voted immediate and total secularization, and Figueroa had no option but to obey.

The plan Figueroa worked out called for distributing half the mission property to the Indians, which could not be sold or conveyed. Secular administrators were appointed, some of whom proved conscientious, others greedy or inattentive. The quality of their work declined abruptly when Figueroa was no longer there to supervise. The mission experience clearly had not prepared many of the Indians to manage properties of their own and, with most of the Indians departed, the missionaries could not readily demonstrate need or ability to use the lands and the remaining stock. A substantial beginning in breakup of the mission properties occurred in Figueroa's three-stage program from 1834 to 1836. The pace accelerated in 1844 when Governor Manuel Micheltorena found in the threatened war with the United States a need to order disposal of the remaining mission properties. By 1846 only Mission Santa Barbara continued under Franciscan control.

The other side of the coin was that, because of secularization, in the midthirties and more especially in the forties there was substantial and then phenomenal strengthening of the privately held ranchos.

The Padrés-Híjar Colonists

About the time Figueroa began his governorship, events in Mexico took a peculiar turn. The elected president, Antonia López de Santa Anna, chose to retire to his estate and turn the governing over to Vice President Valentín Gómez Farías. With a reform-minded Congress, Gómez Farías evolved a broad plan designed to bolster California against the Russians, break the mission land monopoly, allow the Indians an opportunity to be integrated into the provincial populace, and stimulate colonization from Mexico and by foreigners. The Congress enacted a much less detailed measure authorizing the executive branch to act, with key expenses to be drawn from the Pious Fund.

Gómez Farías selected José María Padrés, a soldier of some experience in California, and José María Híjar to head the operation, Padrés as military commandant in Alta California and Híjar as governor of Alta California and director of colonization in both Californias. Some 300 persons were recruited in Mexico City with promise that they would be outfitted, conducted to California, and provided with land and all that was necessary to set them up as colonists. The colonists left the capital in April, 1834, and on August 1 sailed from San Blas on the *Natalia* and the *Morelos*. They went, however, under a cloud. Santa Anna had come out of retirement, issued an antireformist pronunciamento, placed the vice president under arrest, and barred the members of Congress from their meeting place. By special courier over the Anza trail he sent word to Figueroa that Híjar's appointment as governor was revoked.

In normal circumstances Californians would have welcomed this largest of all contingents of colonizers, among whom were a score of qualified teachers and many skilled artisans. But old California hands saw them as rivals for the mission stock and the Indian labor who would encroach upon the mission lands about to be distributed. Figueroa, though concerned about the Indians and the productivity of the mission properties, resented the threat to his authority and was morbidly suspicious of the whole Padrés-Híjar project. He sent Padrés and half the colonists to a site near Santa Rosa but left the *Morelos* passengers stranded in southern California. He quarreled peevishly with Híjar over the colonization program and, when excuse offered, arrested the leaders and several others on charges of conspiracy to revolt and

shipped them off to Mexico. Figueroa then spent several weeks writing a polemic attacking Padrés and Híjar and, their allegedly nefarious scheme. He had this printed under the title *Manifesto*.

Except for Bancroft, California historians have been uniformly critical of the Padrés-Híjar colonization project, seeing it as a grab for mission land, Indian labor, and power, and deriding the colonists as too effete, possessed of the wrong skills, and unsuited for the rough frontier. The principal modern researcher on this topic, C. Alan Hutchinson, asserts that these colonists were precisely the sort that California officials had been asking for and would continue to request and that the plan had merit in the transition it offered for the mission lands and the Indians released from mission protection. Hutchinson sees Híjar as deserving of a more cordial reception than Figueroa gave him and Figueroa's *Manifesto* as a piece of special pleading unworthy of "the most capable governor" of the Mexican period. The reformist plan failed, but California was considerably strengthened by the additional colonists.

Further Political Turmoil

Political annals for the province after the death of Figueroa are a compound of vacillation between home rule and government from Mexico and of neighborly quarreling among the Californians, mingled with general resentment against the governors from Mexico. Figueroa's temporary successor, José de Castro, was followed shortly by Nicolás Gutiérrez, who proclaimed a Mexican decree elevating Los Angeles to the rank of city and designating it the official capital of California. This legislation, however, was dependent on the finding of free quarters for the seat of government.

Although Los Angeles had two or three appropriate buildings, their owners did not volunteer to make them available, and no group of citizens rallied to force them to do so. The capital, therefore, remained at Monterey.

Gutiérrez, in turn, was replaced by Mariano Chico, a Mexican appointee thus rewarded for his support of the reactionary movement calling itself Centralism. Chico held the office only three months but in that time came to be the most unpopular governor of the Mexican period and perhaps longer. His official actions and pronouncements as recorded do not justify such a rating, but the Californians turned against him, forcing his abdication and departure.

When Chico landed at Santa Barbara en route to Monterey to begin his governorship, the principal news reported to him was from Los Angeles and concerned the work of California's first vigilance committee. A vaquero, Gervasio Alipas, had alienated the affections of the wife of a well-liked citizen, Domingo Felix. Felix asked the alcalde to bring about a reconciliation, which was done. It seemed successful, but as the Felixes rode home to their rancho, Alipas intercepted them, stabbed the husband, and then he and Doña María dragged the body with a reata to a ravine and hastily covered it with earth and leaves. The body was soon discovered and the two brazen suspects were arrested.

Popular indignation led some fifty citizens to take action. As they alleged, several other killings had gone unpunished and the law itself authorized no civil court in the province to assign the death penalty. Organizing as a *junta defénsora de la seguridad pública*, these citizens called on the ayuntamiento to surrender the prisoners; sent to San Fernando asking the padre to come and minister "to a dying Indian"; seized the prisoners, and with due

formality shot them. The regular authorities had protested every step by this vigilance committee, but now accepted the proposal that the committee assist for a few more days in maintaining order.

Chico vigorously rebuked these vigilantes, only to find that it was difficult, if not impossible, to prevail against the nearly unanimous community sanction. He also quarreled with the head of the missions and ordered one prominent citizen, Abel Stearns, into exile. Fifty years later historian Bancroft found that the old Californians to a man denounced Chico as a reprobate.

Against the provisional government of Gutiérrez, whom Chico left in charge, a revolt was raised by a dashing young Californian, Juan Bautista Alvarado. A native of Monterey, a protégé of Solá, a product of California's schooling, and a friend or relative of every prominent paisano of northern California, Alvarado had many followers. He also enlisted the help of Isaac Graham and his American riflemen. Gutiérrez' surrender was easily secured. Southern California's recognition of the new government proved a more difficult prize, but through show of force, skillful maneuvering, and judicious compromise Alvarado at last got the nominal support of the southern Californians.

At the outset of his administration Alvarado had the *diputación* declare California "a free and sovereign state," so to remain until Mexico returned to the liberal federal constitution of 1824. The capital was also restored to Monterey, though, in deference to the feelings of southern Californians, the south was organized as a canton under a local *jefe político*, virtually a subgovernor. Alvarado also promised noninterference with private religious practices. In the maneuvering for general support of his government these plans were greatly modified. The assertion of independence became merely a claim for self-government, and the absolute orthodoxy of the province was reaffirmed.

By 1842 Alvarado had tired of politics. His earlier troubles with the southern Californians had been followed by a difference of opinion with his uncle, Mariano Guadalupe Vallejo, the military commandant. Consequently Alvarado welcomed the arrival of a Mexican appointee, Manuel Micheltorena, who was to take over the reins of government, both political and military. Micheltorena's stay was brief. The 300 soldiers who had come with him were an insufferable nuisance, most of them exconvicts and branded as *cholos*. Although Sutter and some other foreigners rallied to his support, a revolution engineered by Alvarado and Castro culminated in another famous battle at Cahuenga Pass, on February 20 and 21, 1845, in which on one side a horse was killed and on the other a mule wounded. The battle proved decisive. Micheltorena agreed to take his *cholos* out of the province, and political and military government passed to Californians Pío Pico and José Castro. Thereafter, Mexico's hold on California was nebulous.

Pastoral California

This period of political turmoil witnessed not only the decline of the missions but also the rise of the ranchos. In the earliest years Spain, although preferring that settlers reside in the pueblos or near the presidios, made generous grants to prospective rancheros. Two features of these land grants contrast sharply with the system of American California: they conveyed a right conditional on use rather than an absolute title and they involved very extensive acreage. Both features, however, were in accord with Spanish custom, and the second represented a far better understanding of a cattleman's needs in a semiarid land than the United States government has yet achieved. A homestead comprising a quarter section or even a full section makes a ridiculous ranch holding.

Although a few earlier grants had enduring importance, the great majority of "Spanish" grants date from the Mexican period. A score or so were made in the first decade of independence. A boom came with secularization of the missions, which opened some of the best land for private use and provided cattle for stocking new ranchos. The hide trade, then in full swing, stimulated cattle raising, and the gradual increase in population meant additional manpower.

By 1845 as Mexican control of California came into greater jeopardy, the governors were authorized to use land grants as compensation for services rendered or bills owed and to sell lands to raise money for defense of the province. Such purchases were only a small fraction of the total. To the end of the Mexican period, land was superabundant and private holdings came by application to pueblo authorities for town lots and fields or to the governor for rancho lands. In all, more than 800 grants were made, adding up to approximately ten million acres. They were spread along the coastal belt from San Diego to Sonoma, with the exception of Big Sur, and included a much lighter sprinkling in the Delta and Sacramento Valley.

With the rise of the ranchos, pastoral California reached its romantic zenith. Cattle roamed over a thousand hills. Horses became so numerous that they were hunted down to save pasturage for the cattle. Hides and tallow were bartered to Yankee and British traders for all the attractive gewgaws of a more sophis-

Diseño, Rancho San Miguelito de Trinidad, near Monterey

The Bancroft Library

ticated civilization. And the outlanders—English and Yankee traders, Russian fur hunters, Hawaiian hide droghers, Rocky Mountain trappers, and American settlers—though they presaged the end of Mexican control, lent a cosmopolitan touch. Even those two inescapables, death and taxes, seemed to have been stayed, the latter being indirect and therefore unnoticed, while the former at least was long postponed.

The bizarre amusements are an index to the spirit of the times. Grizzly bear hunting with lasso and mustang was a royal sport, demanded, prosaically enough, by the necessity of protecting the cattle herds against these marauders. Similarly, wild horse hunting was both a diversion and a necessary task, especially in seasons of drought when the grass had to be preserved for the cattle and sheep.

Likewise, the rodeo, in addition to being a gala occasion when the men of an entire district convened, was essential to the adjustment of individual ownership of livestock and the unfenced and communal range. Bull and bear fights, with the odds approximately even, had no utilitarian value but were natural in view of the frequency with which the vaqueros had to measure the mettle of these ferocious beasts.

Vaqueros escaped much of the drudgery faced by the cowboys of the American West. They had no fences to ride. Cattle were raised chiefly for their hides and tallow, and consequently there was less concern about their condition. Because California cattle were turned loose and received practically no attention except at branding and butchering time, the vaqueros were spared most of the doctoring and the veterinary work of the cowboy's routine. Even the butchering (*matanzas*) was done from horseback, by means of dexterous thrusts of the knife. Removal of the hides and rendering of the tallow remained the only unadulterated toil, and it was delegated to Indian laborers.

The ranchero's resplendent attire gives a clue to the desultory nature of his labor—gold or silver embroidered deerskin shoes; velvet or satin breeches, slashed at the knee, gold-braided and silver-buttoned; velvet or silk vest with wide sash of red satin; dark cloth jacket embroidered in gold and silver; wide flat-topped sombrero with cord of silver or gold. The ordinary vaquero was less gaudily outfitted but this was his pattern. The women not only dressed in more sedate fashion but are credited with being more industrious. Since large families were the rule, cooking and housework were substantial tasks. In addition, these matrons indulged in a prodigious amount of lace making and embroidery. Many women rode and hunted but picnics and dances were the favorite diversions. Dances celebrated every event—weddings, births, political changes, and religious festivals. The elders were privileged to open the festivities; later on the younger people had their turn at the *contradanza, jarrabe,* and fandango.

These romantic Californians are also renowned for their openhandedness especially

Early California Fiesta

A. F. Harmer, Los Angeles County Museum of Natural History

in the provision of meals, lodgings, and riding animals. Tradition has it that these were available without stint to any wayfarer. The mission fathers, as Alfred Robinson relates, might permit a contribution to the saints; rancheros were above accepting pay for their hospitality, and some are said to have placed a supply of money in their guest rooms in which visitors might dip as they needed.

Spanish and Mexican Heritage

Although it may appear to the casual observer that the brusk Americans wiped the slate clean and supplanted the older manner of life with a civilization in which Spanish, Mexican, and California elements found no place, this judgment is superficial. Land titles are merely one factor resting on an older base. Place names by the hundreds have survived; highways such as el Camino Real follow the old trails; the modern vocabulary is enriched by scores of words carried over from the Spanish; numerous fiestas, rodeos, and other celebrations hark back to these days. Certain trends in architecture and furniture, especially in southern California, modify and embellish but also perpetuate features of the Mexican period. Descendants of the old families have been outnumbered by sons of the gold rush, and they in turn by the more recent avalanche of people, yet these scions of the Arcadian age have attained a position of respect far out of proportion to their small number.

Another important part of this heritage has been in history, folklore, and appeal to the imagination. The historical record is rich in nondocumentary materials, of which the chain of missions is the best known but by no means the sole example. Besides the still unpublished treasures with which the archives of Spain, Mexico, and California abound, there is a vast literature of which the Cabrillo and Vizcaíno diaries, the Costansó and Font journals, the Venegas and Palóu histories, and the descriptions by Dana, Robinson, and Colton are merely the outstanding examples. Authoritative historical studies have followed, and a legion of more popular interpreters, including Bret Harte, Lummis, Atherton, Jackson, James, Austin, and White, have found themes and settings for medleys of fact and fiction in the glamorous pre-American period. These writers, along with the Mission Play and the Serra legend, are smitten by the charm of the days of the dons.

Through California's Mexican quarter century the Mexican flag flew overhead, Mexican officials were in the ascendancy, and nine tenths of the *gente de razón* were Mexican. The language was Mexico's and so were the cuisine and most of the architecture and dress. The available body of description of this society supports this categorizing but published biographies do not. The lives of Vallejo and Zamorano stand on one side but are overwhelmed by the lives of Davis, Hartnell, Stearns, Reid, Dalton, Marsh, Sutter, Larkin, Smith, Pattie, Walker, Nidever, Bidwell, Belden, Wilson, Rowland, and company. These Anglos, to be sure, represent the wave of the future—and historians constantly look ahead—but they do not cancel the reality of that substantial part of California's historical timespan which was Mexican.

Nevertheless, the significance of the Mexican period often goes unnoticed. Certain writers dismiss it as nothing more than an interregnum between the Spanish and American regimes. The old Californians are partly responsible, for out of their dislike for the Mexican governors and their *cholo* troops came a tendency to shun the very word "Mexican." Yet without the transition provided by the Mexican period, the change from Spanish colony to American state would have been uncomfortably abrupt. It was most fortunate that the work of secularization, the introduction of such concepts as republicanism, constitutionalism, and representation, the initial contacts with non-Spaniards, and economic annexation to New England could take place while California was a Mexican province.

CHAPTER 7

Covered Wagon Train   *Andrew P. Hill, California State Library, Sacramento*

You have undoubtedly heard that there are English and American settlements in California; but it is not the case. There are from 3 to 600 foreigners here, principally English and American, but they do not live in settlements by themselves; they are scattered throughout the whole Spanish population, and most of them have Spanish wives, and in fine they live in every respect like the Spaniards.

John Bidwell
A Journey to California, 1841

Trappers and Settlers

Two waves of overland advance penetrated to Mexican California. The first party of beaver trappers came in 1826 and the first covered wagon party (albeit without the wagons) in 1841. That was the sequence throughout most of the American West but almost always with a much longer interval between the two.

French fur trade, relying mainly on Indians to do the actual hunting or trapping, had spread across the Mississippi and to the Canadian Rockies. On the upper Missouri River, Spaniards and Americans were trading before the coming of Lewis and Clark. In 1822 William Ashley, at the head of 100 men from Missouri, gave the business a new twist by assigning these Americans and some French and Indian veterans of the earlier trade to do the actual trapping. These men quickly scoured the beaver streams of the Rocky Mountains from Montana to New Mexico and passed on ever westward. The heyday of this activity lasted only through the 1830s. It reached California in 1826.

Jedediah Smith, Pathfinder

Jedediah Smith participated in Ashley's 1822 campaign up the Missouri. His feats of daring and bravery in conflict with Indian and grizzly bear won him a reputation for the traits dearest to the mountain men. His explorations helped shift trapping southwestward into the Rockies and toward Great Salt Lake. This transfer created need for a new base, a rendezvous, at which trappers could make delivery of a season's catch of furs without having to go all the way to St. Louis. It became increasingly common for them to remain in the beaver country for three or four years.

Another change came in 1826, when Ashley sold the Rocky Mountain Fur Company to Smith, David Jackson, and William Sublette. At the Jackson's Hole rendezvous that year these men determined to attempt a further expansion southwestward in search of untrapped beaver streams and, if possible, to open a new marketing outlet through California. Smith, 27, was the logical choice for leader. The territory into which he was about to plunge was very nearly the least known part of North America. Exploration had swirled all around it—the Spaniards far to the south and on the California coast; Zebulon Pike on the eastern flank of the southern Rockies; Lewis and Clark, the Astorians, the Nor'westers, and Ashley's men in the Northwest—but in the area from Great Salt Lake west and southwest to the Sierra Nevada no one had traveled.

Accompanied by 17 men Smith left Salt Lake in August, 1826. He went southward past Utah Lake and up the Sevier River. He turned southwestward past a range of mountains, then south again across the Beaver to the lower course of the Virgin River, which he followed to the Colorado or, as he called it, the Seedskeeder. At the Mojave villages he remained 15 days, recruiting men and horses. Then with two Indian guides and fresh horses obtained from the Mojaves he went into the desert to the Mojave River, which he aptly called the Inconstant. Following this stream, or its bed, into the San Bernardino Mountains, he crossed at or near Cajon Pass, and in November arrived at Mission San Gabriel.

The friars extended a generous welcome, supplying the Americans with beef, cornmeal, wine, and 64 yards of cloth with which to replace their tattered shirts. In 1774 the arrival of Anza's party had taxed the province's food supply so severely that half the soldiers had to be immediately sent back to the Yumas. A half century later there was no such shortage of foodstuffs. A single mission could set an abundant table for a score of unexpected guests even though they tarried six weeks.

Harrison G. Rogers, Smith's lieutenant and the principal chronicler of the expedition, paid his respects to the prosperity of the mission. It had more than 1,000 Indians. Some 30,000 head of cattle bore the mission brand, and there were horses, sheep, and swine by the thousands. There were grain fields, vineyards, and orchards of apples, peaches, oranges, and figs. Skilled workers produced cloth, blankets, and soap, and a water-driven gristmill and a distillery were in operation. Rogers mentioned all this and more; he was captivated, too, by the favorable location and the attractive appearance of this mission community. His highest praise, however, was reserved for the jovial friars who were gracious and generous hosts to the Smith party. He was particularly drawn to José Bernardo Sánchez. In fact, he was prepared to list "Old Father Sanchus" as his "greatest friend," and in every respect "worthy of being called a Christian."

Arriving at San Diego to see the governor, Smith found that he was looked at as an unauthorized interloper. He had been in Mexican territory ever since crossing the 42d parallel, north of Salt Lake. A hide ship captain interceded for him, but even after a present of eight fine beaver skins the governor would not grant permission to traverse California to the Russian post at Bodega. Smith was told to leave the way he had entered.

With new horses and supplies he crossed Cajón Pass but then turned north across the Tehachapi into the San Joaquin Valley. He tried to cross at "Mount Joseph," seemingly his name for the entire Sierra. After four

horses died he retreated to the valley, where he left most of his men to trap beaver. On May 20 he and two companions tackled the Sierra again. They encountered snowfields four to eight feet deep, but in eight days struggled across. Theirs is the first recorded crossing of the Sierra.

Working their way eastward across Nevada's sand, rocks, and mountains was even more exhausting, but after 20 days they sighted Salt Lake. Snake Indians told them where their fellow trappers were, and they went on to the rendezvous.

Ten days later Smith was off for California again with 18 men. This time as he was rafting across the Colorado the Mojaves attacked and killed ten of his men. Traveling by night he and the others reached Mission San Gabriel and a much less cordial reception. They moved north to rejoin the men of the first expedition and, after rebuff at Mission San Jose, headed for Oregon. All went reasonably well except for hard going through the heavily forested northwest coastal region until they reached the Umpqua River. There the Indians attacked and only Smith and two others were able to escape to Fort Vancouver on the Columbia. The Hudson's Bay Company factor, John McLoughlin, sent men to recover the lost property. Deducting a charge of $4 a head for horses lost and $5 a month for his men's services, McLoughlin gave Smith a draft for $3,200 as the value of his pelts. He also assisted Smith to rejoin his partners in the Rockies.

Smith subsequently went to St. Louis and then started west in a caravan headed for Santa Fe. On that well-traveled route he carelessly walked into an Indian ambush, was shot in the back, and killed. His most noteworthy achievements were in opening three routes: Salt Lake to California, across the Sierra, and California to Oregon.

James Ohio Pattie

In 1825 James Ohio Pattie set out from New Mexico to trap along the Gila, the "Helay" in his orthography. Because this was new territory he and his companions found beaver plentiful and accumulated a good quantity of furs. An Indian attack, however, resulted in the loss of most of the pelts and they returned to Santa Fe almost emptyhanded.

Pattie went back the next year with another group. The Papagos attacked, but the Yumas proved friendly and a lively trade was carried on with them. Entering Mojave territory, the trappers were greeted with a night attack, a shower of arrows that killed two men and wounded two more. Pattie's bedfellow was one of those killed; two arrows struck his own hunting shirt, and 16 pinned his blanket to the ground. The most provoking thing, to judge from Pattie's laconic account, was that the Mojaves fled before the trappers could fire a shot in return. "We extinguished our fires," he wrote, "and slept no more that night."

By a circuitous route reaching as far as the Yellowstone, they returned to Santa Fe where the governor charged them with trapping without a passport and confiscated their furs.

Undaunted, Pattie went again to the Gila. The party found beaver plentiful but lost their horses to the Yumas. They made a dugout canoe and set out for the Mexican city they expected to find at the head of the gulf. As they neared the uninhabited mouth of the river, their geographical notions were roughly corrected. The only recourse seemed to be to bury their furs and go overland to California. Actually they emerged at a mission in Baja California but were sent on as prisoners to San Diego.

A year or more later, when a smallpox epidemic struck, the governor released Pattie to use a supply of vaccine he providentially had and vaccinate the Californians—officials, soldiers, settlers, padres, and mission Indians. Pattie toured the province and ministered to 22,000 persons. The Russians paid him $100 for similar services at Fort Ross.

When the governor set the condition that he could be paid only in land and only if he would profess the Catholic faith, Pattie refused. He went to Mexico to protest to the viceroy, then home to Tennessee. He is said to have returned in the gold rush but there is no record of his experiences. His fame rests on his fur trapping, his opening of the Gila route, his incarceration, and his prophylactic peregrination. His fame is solidified by the remarkable narrative that he composed on these adventures which was published in 1831.

Other Mountain Men

In 1831 David Jackson entered California with five pack loads of silver pesos to buy 2,000 mules and horses for the Santa Fe caravans. He could get only 700 and the Mojaves ran off more than half of his herd.

Jackson's partner Ewing Young trapped along the Gila, then turned to sea otter hunting along the coast and an excursion all the way to Klamath Lake before returning to the Gila and New Mexico. In 1834 Young came again to Los Angeles, secured a herd of horses, and drove them all the way to the Columbia. Three years later he purchased 500 head of California cattle and drove them to the Willamette Valley. His route was considerably more serviceable than Smith's. Young stayed on in Oregon.

In 1833 Joseph Reddeford Walker led 60 men to explore west of Salt Lake. Reaching a river which he called the Barren and which was successively renamed Mary's, Ogden, and Humboldt, he followed westward to its sink, across 40 miles of desert to Walker Lake and up one of its tributaries and across to a tributary of the Tuolomne.

Looking down from precipitous heights, he and his men were the first to gaze upon the majestic grandeur of Yosemite Valley. Their journal entries were matter-of-fact; indeed they were more concerned about finding a way to get down with their horses to the game-filled San Joaquin Valley. As a wonder of nature the giant sequoias brought more of a response. Trapper Zenas Leonard commented on them as "incredibly large," 16 to 18 fathoms around at the height of a man's head.

Half a dozen of Walker's men preferred to stay in California, among them George Nidever of subsequent fame as a grizzly bear hunter, a crack shot, and a long-time resident of Santa Barbara.

The next spring Walker left the San Joaquin by a wide and easy pass, turned northward up the length of Owens Valley, then northeastward over rough country to the Humboldt River, and back to his starting point in the Rockies. Of his numerous discoveries—the Humboldt, Walker Lake, the Yosemite, the sequoias, Walker Pass, and Owens Valley—the greatest historical significance attaches to the route he pioneered to California by way of the Humboldt and a central Sierra crossing.

Many other fur men who reached California could be mentioned. For several their trapping is overshadowed by their later activities. J. J. Warner and Isaac Williams are better known as California ranchers, Thomas Fitzpatrick and James Clyman as guides for the pioneer settlers, Fitzpatrick and Kit Carson as guides for Frémont and for the military during the war with Mexico and in subsequent Indian campaigns.

These functions may seem diverse, but they rest on the superior knowledge of the West acquired by the mountain men. In the search for beaver they penetrated every park and valley in the Rocky Mountain area, every potential trapping spot in the Great Basin, and all the beaver streams in the California mountains and foothills. In so doing they blazed and mastered the major transcontinental routes to California; they became the experts on the Rocky Mountain and Intermountain West, the most competent guides for all others who wished to venture into this vast area, and the disseminators of information about it and about the Mexican province of California which lay beyond. Thus, they were stimulators of interest as well as invaluable guides for the westward migrations which followed.

Thanks to the prodigies performed by Hubert Howe Bancroft in accumulating information about the early Californians, it is possible to compile trustworthy statistics on the number of foreign arrivals year by year, to identify a surprisingly large number by name, and to trace the career of practically every individual who figured at all prominently in the affairs of the province. Up to 1840 Bancroft identifies 600 or more. Some died or departed, but as of 1840 he calculates only 380 remaining. Of these about 50 had come by the overland routes, the rest in the various forms of seaborne commerce. Because of old age, infirmities, or inaction many were inconspicuous, but others constituted "an influential and highly respected element of the population, largely controlling the commercial industry of the country."

Many of the foreigners found it advantageous and pleasant to become Californians. If they married it was to Californians. They learned and used the Spanish language, Hispanicized their names, accommodated to the Catholic church, and conformed to the mores of their adopted land.

John Gilroy, a Scotch sailor set ashore in 1816, appears as the first foreign resident in California. Better known is Joseph Chapman, one of Bouchard's men captured at Monterey in 1818. He built gristmills at several of the missions and even a schooner. At the end of the Spanish period there may have been six or eight other resident foreigners.

William E. P. Hartnell readily adapted, a process made easier by his previous residence on the west coast of South America. Two years after his arrival he was baptized, and a year later he married María Teresa de la Guerra, who, in the course of the years, bore 20 sons and five daughters. In 1834 he received patent to Rancho Patrocinio del Alisal, about 20 miles inland from Monterey. As a ranchero he had average success. By 1849 he had 8,000 head of cattle and several thousand horses and sheep. His cultivated fields, or *milpas*, were tilled indifferently, and the vineyard was also the victim of neglect, but the vegetable garden, with a year-round production of vegetables and berries of many kinds, left nothing to be desired.

Hartnell held various governmental posts: collector of taxes and customs, court clerk, interpreter (he used Spanish, French, and German as freely as his native English), surveyor, and county assessor. From 1833 to 1836 he was the agent for the Russian American Fur Company. At about the same time he opened a school known as the Seminario de San José in which his own children were often in the majority. His most important commission was as visitador-general of the secularized missions in 1839–40. On this hopeless task he worked faithfully and heroically.

Another of California's adopted sons famous for his large family was William Goodwin Dana. Almost immediately upon his arrival from Boston in 1826, he fell in love with Josefa Carrillo. He was not allowed to contract the marriage until the preliminaries of his baptism and naturalization were fulfilled, processes which wasted the better part of two years and delayed the wedding until his intended bride's sixteenth year. Besides his 21 children, Dana's achievements included service as appraiser, captain of the port, and alcalde of Santa Barbara. In the American period he was prefect and county treasurer. He is listed as a trader, soapmaker, physician, and architect, and for a time as the holder of a special license for sea otter hunting, but his livelihood was drawn principally from Rancho Nipomo, granted him in 1837.

Abel Stearns, after three years in Mexico, came to California in 1829 and soon became the leading trader at Los Angeles. Often accused of smuggling, he had several difficulties with the authorities. On the other hand, as the husband of Arcadia Bandini and a most capable assistant in the management of the Bandini properties, he ingratiated himself with the Californians. He acquired several ranchos and at his death left holdings of more than 200 square miles.

Thomas O. Larkin was an exception in several particulars. He married an American widow who came out on the same ship in 1832. He mastered Spanish but was not entirely simpático with the Mexican regime. He was in trade but not a ranchero though later an investor in real estate. He is well known as first American consul and secret agent for President Polk.

John Marsh, a Harvard graduate, came via New Mexico in 1836, practiced medicine briefly in Los Angeles, then was granted a rancho near Mt. Diablo. He capitalized on Indian labor, supplemented his income by doctoring, and spent his spare time urging acquaintances in the States to come to California. He was notoriously disagreeable and stingy, yet his biographer gives him much of the credit for stirring American interest in California.

John A. Sutter reached California by way

Sutter's Fort

Joseph Revere, A Tour of Duty, *1849*

of Indiana, St. Louis, the Santa Fe Trail, the Rocky Mountains, the Columbia, the Sandwich Islands, and Alaska. His ambition was to develop a feudal colony. In 1840 Governor Alvarado approved a land grant in the unoccupied Sacramento Valley. Sutter began as a ranchero, different only in that he employed Kanakas, Americans, and other foreigners as well as Indians and Californians. In fact, he had a compunction to find work for every foreigner who came along.

In 1841 he bought out the Russians at Fort Ross, acquiring among other things horses, cattle, a launch, a threshing floor, and 40 assorted cannon. With this artillery he was able to fortify his New Helvetia, an adobe fortress mounting 12 guns and with an armed garrison and sentries. Thus Sutter was secure not only against Indian attack but against interference by the Mexican authorities. Yet

for the most part he kept on very good terms with them.

In addition to the cattle ranch Sutter engaged in extensive fur trade and trapping, planted a large acreage in wheat, constructed an irrigation system, built a mill, a distillery, and a tannery, set some of his Indian employees to blanket weaving, and ran his launch regularly to San Francisco Bay. His debt to the Russian American Fur Company was one incentive for this feverish activity; another was his feeling of obligation to find or make work for any foreigners who came and asked for it. "Hospitable, visionary, improvident land baron of the Sacramento," Sutter has been well called. The unbounded hospitality that he extended to American immigrants is the real key to his greatness. It made his fort the mecca of the overland pilgrimages. He set weary travelers on their feet as

McLoughlin did in Oregon. He sent relief parties as far east as Reno to assist the faltering steps of the less sturdy pioneers. The military accouterments and strategic location of his fort made impossible any Mexican exclusion of American immigrants.

A Migration of Settlers

By 1840 the American frontier of settlement faced the broad treeless plains regarded as unsuitable for white habitation and therefore called the Great American Desert. Beckoning past it to the Far West were the trails broken by the mountain men, the trade route to Santa Fe, and the paths of fur men and missionaries to Oregon. Because the United States laid claim to Oregon, the interest aroused by these civilians was fanned by flag-waving editors and congressional debates. California could not compete with Oregon in this hold on the attention of the American people. The migration figures for the early forties are in the ratio of eight or ten to Oregon as against one to California. But California gained a secondary advantage from the Oregon publicity.

Dana, Pattie, a visiting author named Thomas Jefferson Farnham, and letter writers like Marsh gave California some direct advertising. At a meeting in Platte County, Missouri, in the fall of 1840, trapper Antoine Robidoux rhapsodized on the salubrious climate. To an ague-wracked inquirer, he answered that the chills were unkown in California except for one fellow who had carried the disease in his system from Missouri. His affliction, Robidoux affirmed, was such a curiosity that "the people of Monterey went 18 miles into the country to see him shake."

Then and there the Western Emigration Society was organized. More than 500 signed a pledge to meet the next spring at Sapling Grove, just beyond Independence on the Missouri, prepared to journey to California. During the winter the Platte County merchants, fearful of losing so many customers, circulated discouraging reports about California. They made particularly good use of a clipping from a New York paper in which Farnham recanted all the praise of California that had gone into his volume on western travels. His first impression had been good, but, when he visited Monterey a second time and without cause was lodged in jail, he had a complete reversal. Sabotaged, the Western Emigration Society dwindled from 500 would-be emigrants to a single person, young John Bidwell, recently a schoolmaster. At Sapling Grove he was soon joined, however, by 68 others who had not promised but now proposed to go.

John Bidwell

California State Library

The Bidwell-Bartleson Party

This group organized and selected as captain John Bartleson, perhaps the least qualified member of the entire party. He is remembered chiefly for his blunders, selfishness, and ineffectual leadership, especially over the latter part of the journey. Bidwell looms far more important, partly because he was the one member who had signed the original agreement, partly because he subsequently became one of California's leading citizens, partly because the best contemporary description of the journey is from his pen, but mostly because of his informal assumption of command when the real difficulties were encountered. Historians speak of the Bidwell-Bartleson party or, more simply, of the Bidwell party.

Although many of the group had resided near the frontier of settlement in Missouri, none had an accurate understanding of the country through which they proposed to pass. Bidwell tells how "an intelligent man" with whom he had boarded showed him a standard map that depicted a large lake in the vicinity of Great Salt Lake having two outlets, each appearing as large as the Mississippi and emptying into the Pacific. Bidwell's friend advised him to take along tools for canoe making so that, if the country proved too rough for their wagons, they could reach California by water. Since this is a fair example of the Bidwell party's advance knowledge of the West, their great good fortune in falling in with a small band of fur trappers and missionaries who were bound for Oregon is apparent.

Father De Smet of the latter group was a regular globe-trotter and well versed in northwestern travel. Thomas Fitzpatrick, leader of the trappers, was one of the best of the mountain men. From Sapling Grove to Soda Springs in the southern part of present Idaho, these expert guides smoothed the way for the California-bound emigrants. The route followed would soon be known as the Oregon Trail. From Sapling Grove it led northwestward across a rolling prairie to the Platte, along this stream to the Forks, past Fort Laramie on the North Platte to Independence Rock and the Sweetwater, through South Pass to the Sandy and the Green, and across a divide to Bear Valley with its Steamboat and Soda Springs.

Thus far the pioneers had smooth going though enlivened with many a stirring incident. Young Nicholas Dawson acquired the nickname "Cheyenne" by venturing out to hunt and shortly rejoining the train "without mule, gun or pistol and lacking most of his clothes." He reported that thousands of Indians had despoiled him and were about to attack the train. A band of Cheyennes returned Dawson's belongings, professed friendship, and explained that they had disarmed the frightened hunter to prevent his shooting at them in his excitement. Another member of the party died of an accidentally self-inflicted gunshot wound. Four others turned back. But there was nothing particularly hazardous or difficult in this much of the journey. Later parties likewise found it comparatively easy to negotiate this first half of the trail to Oregon or California.

Beyond Soda Springs the Bidwell party faced an unknown trail. Half the group decided to forego the joys of California and continue with their guides to Oregon. The other 32 struck out southwestward to open their own trail to California. They asked directions from the Hudson's Bay Company men at Fort Hall, but none had traveled the route. All they were told was not to go too far north, lest they get into rough terrain where many fur men had died, and not to go too far south, lest they get into a very arid country where they probably would die—sound advice but not very illuminating. Undaunted, the pioneers moved out.

Soon after leaving Bear Valley, they found it necessary to abandon their wagons and much of their baggage and pack the basic essentials on their horses, mules, and oxen. At making and fastening packs they were greenhorns. The result was great confusion, though soon they and their animals came to a working understanding. Eventually they reached the south branch of the Humboldt. Over alkaline flats, finding little grass or game, they went on to Humboldt Sink. Bartleson and eight of the best mounted men deserted the rest and pushed on ahead toward California. Bidwell and the others struggled across the desert to Carson River and the Balm, which was their grateful name for the Walker. Here the Bartleson deserters straggled into camp, none the better off for having gone ahead so selfishly.

After the last oxen had been killed and the meat jerked, the men began the ascent of the Sierra. They were three weeks in finding a pass and making their way across by the Walker and Stanislaus. Fortunately the winter set in late, and, though they did not get over the divide until the very last of October, they escaped being snowed in. Their supplies, however, were virtually exhausted, and the grass and game of the San Joaquin Valley were most welcome. Bidwell wrote with great feeling about their first California feast, a fat coyote of which his share was only "the lights and the windpipe." Unappetizing as this may sound, Bidwell thought it a welcome change from mule meat. He cooked the morsel on the coals and "greedily devoured it."

A little farther on they came to better hunting, "elk tracks by the thousands" and "hundreds of antelope in view." Many of the party despondently reckoned 500 miles still to

go and another mountain range (the Coast Ranges looming to westward) to cross before reaching California. But the end of their six-month journey was at hand. They soon reached the ranch of John Marsh near Mt. Diablo and had their California geography set straight.

In the reminiscences of his mellower years "Cheyenne" Dawson wrote very warmly of Marsh and the hospitality he extended to these wayfarers. Bidwell concurred in the more general opinion that their host was a skinflint. Marsh charged what Bidwell considered an exorbitant price for a bullock and a small hog, the emigrants paying in lead, powder, and knives. To this price was added a fee of $3 apiece for getting them passports from the provincial authorities. Worst of all, Marsh complained bitterly about the heavy expense these emigrants were occasioning him, whereupon Bidwell was convinced that they had fallen in with "the meanest man in California."

In fairness it should be pointed out that the emigrants had made the mistake of butchering a bullock that had been broken to the yoke. And since the California authorities had repeatedly taken a stand against the entrance of Americans by the overland route and more recently had shown an anti-American spirit in the Graham affair, it was not easy for Marsh to persuade Vallejo to issue passports for the party. Furthermore, it was merely by oversight that a passport was not secured for Bidwell. His three days without food in the flea-infested jail at San José undoubtedly sharpened his pen against Marsh.

Nevertheless, the significance of the Bidwell party does not lie in these personal issues or even in the trying difficulties encountered along the way. It lies rather in the fact that the party was the entering wedge for the new type of migration to California. The group soon scattered. A number of the men went to work

Contra Costa Hills   *Rondal Partridge*

for Sutter at New Helvetia; most of the others, including Benjamin Kelsey's wife and daughter, the first American woman and child to come overland, settled in the northern part of the province. Flood tide in the flow of Americans into California was not to come until the gold rush and the boom of the eighties, but the arrival of these pioneers marked the start of a steady current of migration.

Other Immigrants

A second party of 25 reached southern California that same season. Included were Isaac Given and Albert Toomes, who, missing connections with the Bidwell party near Sapling Grove, had elected to follow the Santa Fé Trail with one of the trading caravans. Because New Mexico at that time was in a state of alarm over an expected invasion from Texas, a number of American residents decided that the prudent thing to do was to move on to California. Given and Toomes joined this party under the leadership of William Workman and John Rowland. They left Abiquiu in September, followed the usual trade route, the Old Spanish Trail, across the Colorado, through southern Utah and Nevada, and over the Mojave Desert and Cajón Pass to Los Angeles, where they arrived two months later. The party drove along a flock of sheep for food and

93

traveled much of the distance in company with the annual band of traders from New Mexico. A dozen of these Americans intended to settle in California, and a few others actually did so, including Benjamin D. Wilson, who wanted to go on to China but could not make connections with a ship. Workman, Rowland, and Wilson became rancheros and prominent figures in southern California.

From Oregon a few other Americans moved to California in 1841, among them Joel P. Walker, brother of the famous fur trapper, Joseph Reddeford Walker. Joel Walker came with the land party of Wilkes's United States Exploring Expedition. He brought with him his wife and five children. Two other Oregonians brought their families. Their coming, though less spectacular than that of the Bidwell and Workman-Rowland parties, was not necessarily less significant.

In 1842 there was a temporary backwash in the tide of American migration to California. No parties came westward; instead, nine or ten men of the Bidwell party, led by Joseph B. Chiles and Charles Hopper, ascended the San Joaquin Valley, crossed Walker Pass, and by the way of the Old Spanish Trail went on to Santa Fe and Missouri. Nevertheless, these men contributed to the advertisement of California as a land highly suitable for American settlement. Many others joined in the same work. Marsh's correspondence included a 19-page letter to Commodore Jones expounding "some of the most interesting facts relative to California." Captain Henry A. Pierce dispatched a similar letter to Honolulu, and eastern papers printed his comments on the designs on California of the Hudson's Bay Company. Rowland went back to New Mexico to get his family, while Bidwell forwarded copy to a printer friend in Missouri for a 32-page pamphlet on his journey to California. Publicity of this sort, coupled with increasing volume of migration to Oregon and con-

tinued hard times in the Midwest, led to more migration in succeeding years.

The first immigrants of 1843 were recruited by Lansford W. Hastings, mostly from a party of 160 persons which he had led to Oregon the year before. Late in May be started south with some 25 armed men and their families, a total of 53 persons. Beyond Rogue River they met a band of cattle drivers accompanied by a few disillusioned California settlers. A third of Hastings' party turned back; the remaining 35 proceeded by way of Shasta River to California.

On the way they had much unnecessary trouble with Indians. According to one informant, two or three of the party were continually taking potshots at Indians; and Hastings tells of one occasion when he did the same thing. Between Stony Creek and Colusa, on the upper Sacramento, a pitched battle took place and 20 or 30 natives were killed. In the lower Sacramento Valley and the north bay region these Indian fighters settled down, but first, two of the party, George Davis and a certain Miss Sumner, crossed over to New Helvetia and had Sutter marry them.

Joseph B. Chiles, veteran of the Bidwell expedition, organized the second party of 1843. In Missouri he gathered about 50 persons and led them over the standard trail to Fort Hall. There, because of shortness of provisions, it was decided that Chiles should go on with about ten men to Fort Boise and strike directly for California. He did so, getting in safely by a new route along the Malheur and Pit rivers, though there are intimations of fighting with the Indians and of one of his men having to be extricated from a bear trap.

The rest of Chiles' party was conducted by Joseph Reddeford Walker over the route he had explored a decade earlier. With comparatively little difficulty they took their wagons down the Humboldt Valley, across the desert to Walker Lake, and then "with infinite hardships'' across the divide to Owens Valley. There they buried some of their belongings, burned the wagons, and packed into the California settlements by way of Walker Pass. Chiles had been expected to come to their relief in the upper San Joaquin Valley. He did not come, or at least, did not meet them, and their worst hardships were in getting across the valley and over the next range of mountains to the Salinas Valley and Gilroy's rancho.

In 1844 a party of 36 put in its appearance from Oregon. Included were several members of the Kelsey family who had been shuttling back and forth between California and Oregon. More notable was the Stevens-Murphy party from Missouri by the regular route along the Platte and the Humboldt. At the foot of the Sierra this party split. The Murphys and a few others crossed by way of Lake Tahoe and the headwaters of the American River. Three men attempted to winter at Donner Lake, and one, Moses Schallenberger, stayed there till spring. The main body of the party pushed on into California by Truckee River and Pass, the first to utilize this subsequently favorite route and the first to get their wagons into California.

At least 250 persons came over the trails in 1845, the movement to California having been stimulated by reports carried back from earlier settlers, by the showmanship of the government explorer John Charles Frémont, and by the strenuous efforts of Lansford W. Hastings, who returned to the States in 1844 to foment American migration to California. Green McMahon and James Clyman brought in 43 persons from Oregon, among them James Marshall, who was to be the discoverer of California's gold. The Swasey-Todd train came by the Truckee route. From St. Louis, Solomon Sublette brought 15 men, described as the best equipped of any who made the journey. The Grigsby-Ide party, also by Truckee, numbered more than 100 members, and Hastings conducted a much smaller party

across the Sierra just before the winter snows closed the passes. There may have been still another party not recorded.

The Donner Tragedy

In 1846 Elder Sam Brannan headed a party of 200 Mormons who moved to California by the sea route around Cape Horn. Overland pioneers that same year considerably exceeded that figure. The majority reached California safely. Notwithstanding such excellent trail records as Edwin Bryant's *What I Saw in California* and J. Q. Thornton's *Oregon and California* in 1848, these companies are usually lost sight of in the stark tragedy that overtook the Donner party.

In the vicinity of Fort Bridger, Hastings met the westward caravan in 1846 and tried to induce those California-bound to take a cutoff south of Great Salt Lake. Guided by James M. Hudspeth, Bryant's packtrain party followed this route without accident. Hastings personally guided a wagon party which reached the Humboldt after considerable difficulty. The Donner party, coming a trifle later, attempted the cutoff, got lost, and wasted valuable time and strength clearing a road for their wagons. Loss of oxen here and in crossing the Great Salt Desert necessitated abandonment of essential supplies, and, when they finally reached the Humboldt, they were both destitute and far behind schedule. William McCutcheon and Charles Stanton were sent ahead for supplies, and Stanton returned with two California Indians and five muleloads of beef and flour sent by Sutter.

An unusually early snow plunged the distraught group into panic. No leader rose in this crisis to insist on energetic cooperation to get over the Divide or on careful preparations for a winter in camp. Instead, the party strung out along the trail and was trapped early in

Camp at Donner Lake, November, 1846, based on a description by one who was there

Thompson and West, History of Nevada County

November by ten feet of snow. Shelter was inadequate, firewood had not been gathered, and most of the cattle had been lost in the storm. Inevitable tragedy followed, with starvation and cold and death at Donner Lake. The "forlorn-hope" party tried to escape on makeshift snowshoes to Sutter's Fort, but only seven of the 15 got through, and they had subsisted upon the flesh of their dead companions and had shot their two Indian guides for the same purpose. Four rescue parties were necessary to extricate the others. Only 45 of the 79 who had been snowed in escaped and their sufferings beggar description, even though some of the shocking things said about their actions are probably untrue. The ordeal also called forth many acts of high courage and unselfishness by, among others, Tamsen Donner, Virginia Reed, William Eddy, William McCutcheon, and James F. Reed. It was the worst western tragedy since the Yuma Massacre.

Agents in the Epic of American Expansion

Although the pioneers of 1846 and the smaller parties which came over the trails in the next two years shared many of the experiences of those who had come earlier, in one respect they belong in a different category. They found the American flag waving over California, for the outbreak of the War with Mexico had afforded the opportunity to terminate the Mexican regime and to claim the province for the United States. The military completed this step, but the pioneer settlers of the early forties had laid the foundation, and there is good reason to believe that, without any assistance from the military, the infiltration of settlers—the process whereby Texas and Oregon had been acquired—would soon have achieved the same result in California. Viewed in this light the pioneers of 1841 through 1845

Diary of Patrick Breen, February 25 and 26, 1847, a Member of the Ill-fated Donner Party

The Bancroft Library

appear not as mere curiosities, objects of interest because of their early appearance in California, but as effective agents in the epic of American expansion.

Nevertheless, the vast majority of the pioneer settlers came to California because they envisioned an opportunity for a better livelihood. Most did not scruple about professing the Catholic religion or applying for Mexican citizenship. Paradoxically, a large number of the pioneer settlers did not stay but drifted on to Oregon or returned to the States. Consequently the "foreign colony" in the province was increased from 380 in 1840 to only about 680 at the end of 1845, which suggests that much significance was still attached to the older settlers who antedated the covered wagon. To these pioneers, however, goes the credit for setting in motion the first conscious migration to California and for bringing the province within the scope of the westward-moving American frontier.

CHAPTER 8

Customhouse at Monterey

William R. Hutton

I declare to the inhabitants of California that altho' I come in arms with a powerful force, I do not come among them as enemy to California: but on the contrary I come as their best friend, as henceforward California will be a portion of the United States.

Commodore John D. Sloat
July 7, 1846

American Takeover

Interest in Annexation

In the 1830s American officials began to show interest in annexing California. The rising number of American residents and the profits in the hide trade were factors. So were the expansionist spirit of Manifest Destiny, Mexico's weak hold which set up a prospect of transfer to Britain or some other power, and the strategic value of San Francisco Bay.

Anthony Butler, while minister to Mexico, blighted chances for a purchase by flaunting his opinion that half a million dollars judiciously applied would obtain any portion of Mexico desired. But he whetted President Andrew Jackson's interest by asserting that the United States should have not just Texas but "the whole of that tract or territory known as New Mexico, and higher and lower California, an empire in itself, a paradise in climate, . . . rich in minerals and affording a water route to the Pacific through the Arkansas and Colorado rivers."

Encouraged by a report from William A. Slacum, Jackson tried to arrange a purchase. In 1837, when General Santa Anna was in Washington, Jackson tried to persuade him that Mexico's boundary should run along the Rio Grande and the 37th parallel, which passes through Four Corners in the Navajo country and enters the Pacific at Santa Cruz.

In Martin Van Buren's presidency the Graham affair and the arrest of 40 American riflemen in the Pajaro Valley and their banishment to Mexico led to assigning more American naval forces to the Pacific.

John Tyler's minister to Mexico, Waddy Thompson, praised California as "the richest, the most beautiful, and the healthiest country in the world" and potentially "the granary of the Pacific." He too was intrigued by the gateway at the headwaters of the Arkansas and by the California ports and their advantage to American whalers.

Daniel Webster, as secretary of state, tried to negotiate a three-way treaty with Mexico and Britain by which the United States would pay off American and British holders of Mexican bonds, Britain would gain clear title from the Columbia River to Alaska, and the United States would receive Texas and California. It appears unlikely that any of the three nations would have ratified such a treaty. A circumstance beyond Webster's control intervened.

The ap Catesby Jones Incident

In 1842 at Callao, Peru, Commodore Thomas ap Catesby Jones as commander of the American naval forces in the Pacific received a dispatch that indicated to him that the United States and Mexico were at war. Following his general instructions he set sail at once for California to take possession before Mexico could hand California over to the British for safekeeping.

Arriving at Monterey on October 19, 1842, Jones seized the town. The defenses were in disrepair and no fighting was necessary. The next day Jones learned of later dispatches which persuaded him that it was all a mistake. He apologized, restored Monterey undamaged, and sailed south to San Pedro. A carriage took him to Abel Stearns' home in Los Angeles, where he and his staff were wined and dined with Governor Micheltorena—and presented with a well-padded bill for the damages done.

The Californians let the Monterey incident pass as a joke, though a rather humiliating one. In Mexico there was deeper indignation. Minister Thompson was forced to admit that it had become "wholly out of the question to do anything as to California."

In 1839 Alexander Forbes, British vice-consul at Tepic, published a *History of California*, the first work in English with such a title. In it he outlined a plan for British creditors to write off $50 million in Mexican bonds and take over California. Some readers assumed that the plan was in operation. Actually the British government was not ready to take such aggressive action, but semiofficial statements to the contrary continued. Duff Green in 1844 and Wilson Shannon in 1845 reported from Mexico that "the mortgage on the Californias" was about to be foreclosed.

Anglophobia took a further upward turn with the inauguration of James K. Polk as president. A native of Tennessee, nurtured in Jacksonian democracy, and elected on a platform stressing a firm stand against Britain in Oregon and Texas, Polk believed the worst about British designs on California. His agents furnished evidence of Britain's aggressive attitude. William S. Parrott wrote from Mexico, "Great Britain has greatly increased her Naval Forces in the Pacific, the object of which as stated is to take possession of and hold Upper California, in case of war between the United States and Mexico."

Parrott also reported that a young Irish priest named Eugene McNamara proposed to serve Catholicism and his countrymen and "to put an obstacle in the way for further usurpations on the part of an irreligious and anti-Catholic nation." His plan of bringing 10,000 Irish colonists to a California grant of 3,000 square leagues was not immediately approved, but early in 1846 he chose a location embracing most of the eastern half of the San Joaquin Valley. The provincial assembly at Los Angeles approved his request on July 6,

and Governor Pico made the grant at Santa Barbara a week or so later. Because of the raising of the American flag on July 7, Pico seems to have predated the grant as of July 4, thus making it illegal in that it was made prior to the action of the assembly. Furthermore, the grant grossly exceeded the legal maximum of 11 square leagues, but the scheme alarmed Americans in California and in Washington.

Of greater influence on Polk's policy was a Larkin letter of July 10, 1845, reporting that British merchants were financing an impending Mexican reinforcement of California and appointment of British and French salaried consuls in the province. Neither nation had sufficient commercial contact in the province to justify such an appointment. Larkin was sure that the British appointee was a secret agent for Larkin's "Colossus of the North," the Hudson's Bay Company.

Polk's Aggressive Policies

Before his inauguration one of Polk's campaign promises was fulfilled. The outgoing administration and Congress attended to the annexation of Texas, although as to boundaries problems of interpretation would remain. On another campaign promise Polk moved promptly by insisting on negotiation of a new treaty with Britain to end joint occupation of Oregon and clear an American title.

Polk reasserted the Monroe Doctrine in clearer and more vigorous language: "The people of this continent alone have the right to decide their destiny." He served notice against the establishment of any European colony or dominion anywhere in North America. The importance he attached to this principle is suggested in his assertion after the War with Mexico that the fact that California "has become a part of the Union and cannot be subject to a European power constitutes ample indemnity for the past."

As for California, Polk was determined that it be acquired. He was a Manifest Destinarian and saw direct benefits to the United States. As early as September, 1845, Washington observers were predicting peaceful acquisition. Polk attempted purchase, authorizing an offer of $40 million but to no avail.

Polk gave Larkin secret instructions to persuade the Californians to resist any transfer to Britain or France and on the contrary to break with Mexico and accept the protection of the United States. That was not the "Texas game," to be played by Americans insinuating themselves into the province. In addition to acculturated Californians such as Abel Stearns, Jacob Leese, and J. J. Warner, Larkin turned to Mariano G. Vallejo who favored annexation and General José Castro who confided his agreement.

Polk also had assistance from a government explorer already in the field who was doing a remarkable job of publicizing the Far West and particularly the approaches to California.

Frémont's Adventures

In 1841 California was visited by a most elaborate exploring expedition, a fleet commanded by Charles Wilkes and assigned to explore the Pacific in the interest of the American whaling industry. After extended observations in the Northwest, Wilkes sent a detachment overland to California and sailed south to join forces at San Francisco Bay, which was explored in detail. Monterey also was visited. The wealth of data gathered was drawn on for a five-volume report which, however, was embalmed in a limited edition in 1844.

Another explorer, John C. Frémont,

John C. Frémont

through his *Reports* was doing a remarkable job of publicizing the Far West and especially the approaches to California. Gifted with magnetism and bravado, Frémont went from one electrifying experience to another. As son-in-law of Senator Thomas H. Benton of Missouri he had a powerful friend. Assisted by his wife he had a very attractive literary style. It is easy to understand how he became the best-known westerner, how he was chosen by the Republican party as its first presidential nominee, and how enthusiastic biographers came to do him excessive homage as "A Man Unafraid," "The Pathfinder," and "The West's Greatest Adventurer."

His first expedition, in 1842, reached only to South Pass and the Rockies. On the second, in 1843–44, he went west by Bent's Fort, South Pass, and the Oregon Trail to The Dalles, south along the eastern side of the Cascades and Sierra Nevada, and across the

Sierra by way of Carson Pass in the dead of winter. After recuperating for a month at Sutter's Fort and purchasing fresh horses and supplies, he moved up the San Joaquin Valley, crossed Tehachapi Pass, followed the Old Spanish Trail into southern Utah, and returned to the States by way of Sevier River, Utah Lake, the headwaters of the Grand and the Arkansas, and Bent's Fort.

This was a notable journey even though most of it was over beaten trails except as Frémont turned aside to examine wonders of nature. And it was a personal achievement even though he relied heavily on his fur-trapper guides, Thomas Fitzpatrick, Kit Carson, and Joseph Walker. This journey illustrates the enigmatic nature of Frémont's career. Riddles persist despite the efforts of eminent historians from Bancroft and Royce to Nevins and De Voto to solve them. Why, for example, did Frémont include a howitzer in the equipment of this supposedly purely scientific expedition? Did he really believe that the Buenaventura River existed? Was the wretched condition of his horses sufficient explanation for his decision to make a mid-winter crossing of the Sierra into California?

These and other questions may always baffle, but there exists no doubt that the principal importance of the journey was in fanning interest in the West. From November, 1843, until the next July, while Frémont traveled from the Columbia to the Kansas, no word of his whereabouts reached the States. There were allusions to the "lost expedition," and national concern was felt for its safety comparable to contemporary anxiety over some unreported flier or polar expedition. The circumstance awakened interest; appearance of his volume clinched it. Thousands of copies were struck off by government and private presses, and it became the principal popular source of information about the West.

In the spring of 1845, shortly after Polk's inauguration, Frémont was on the trail again with a party of 62 men. His route was over the regular trail to Salt Lake and by the Humboldt Valley to Walker Lake. There, with winter fast approaching, he decided to take 15 men across to Sutter's Fort while the main party took the more roundabout way by Walker Pass. A rendezvous was appointed at the "River of the Lake" just west of Walker Pass, but, failing to find the place, Frémont went on to Yerba Buena and Monterey and eventually was joined by his men in the Santa Clara Valley. Through Consul Larkin he obtained permission for his "scientific" party to spend the rest of the winter in California on condition that they remain back from the coast. The appearance of the entire party at Salinas convinced the provincial authorities that the American leader was acting in bad faith. A blustering correspondence passed back and forth, reaching a climax in Castro's order that Frémont depart at once. For three days Frémont remained in his fortified camp atop Hawk's Peak, then retired toward Oregon "slowly and growlingly."

In the Klamath Lake region he was overtaken by Lieutenant Archibald Gillespie, who, in the guise of a convalescent merchant, had hurried to California by way of Veracruz, Mazatlán, and Hawaii as a special messenger for President Polk. The dispatch that he delivered verbally to Larkin was the one described above. Its contents have long been known to historians. What message he delivered to Frémont has been the subject of much controversy. Presumably he related the substance of the dispatch to Larkin, though Frémont later expressed doubt and disbelief that Larkin had been commissioned as Polk's confidential agent. Gillespie delivered a packet of letters from Senator Benton, but their significance is minimized because of the Senator's slight connection with the Polk administration and because it was only an afterthought of the Department of State to send them by Gillespie.

The sending of a special messenger was decided upon perhaps ten days after the Larkin instructions were formulated, and Gillespie was privately instructed by Polk and Secretary of the Navy Bancroft and again privately by the President. It is possible, therefore, as some writers suggest, that Gillespie brought Frémont a message that went considerably beyond the Larkin instructions. If, on the other hand, there were no secret instructions, the fact that Gillespie had traveled a dangerous 500 miles to overtake him was ample justification for Frémont's turning back to California. He was in no way hesitant that this was the thing to do, but there was another duty to discharge first, to retaliate against the Klamaths for killing two or three of his men. Vengeance was swift and ample and apparently sweet.

By the latter part of May, Frémont was camped at Marysville Buttes on the Sacramento. His purpose was not transparent. To his wife and his father-in-law he wrote that he was on the point of returning to Missouri. He also announced that intent to Captain Montgomery of the *Portsmouth*, though qualified

Early California Home

by the remark that emergencies might arise to detain him.

The emergency arose almost immediately; thus we cannot be sure of the genuineness of Frémont's intention. Opinions of his subsequent conduct vary. One suggestion is that he was fulfilling Polk's guarded orders to bring on hostilities in California which would perhaps lead to war with Mexico and certainly to the annexation of California. Yet his actions seem to indicate that his first endeavor was to avoid any hostilities which would jeopardize Polk's reiterated preference for peaceful acquisition.

Flag of the Bear

Excited American settlers began to come to Frémont's camp. For some months they had been kept on edge by rumors of war. The Graham incident, the Hawk's Peak affair, and Castro's recommendation that the Mexican government buy out Captain Sutter, presumably as a preliminary to forbidding further American immigration, contributed to make these frontiersmen uneasy. It was also rumored that the Californians were inciting the Indians to attack the Americans, and Frémont's experience with the Klamaths seemed a case in point. The presence of his armed force served as a rallying point for these alarmed and disaffected settlers. Yet Frémont at first would not join them against the California officials. He even dissuaded Carson and others from resigning from the service to join with the settlers. Forty-five years later Frémont claimed that he "knew the hour had come" before he turned back from the Klamath region, but his actions at Marysville indicate that he was not yet ready to join in the violence and thereby ruin all chances of conciliating the native population and winning them over to the United States. He was not above suggesting lines of procedure to the settlers and thus had a measure of direct responsibility for what unfolded.

A band of settlers "who had nothing to lose" launched the revolt on June 10 by seizing a herd of horses belonging to Castro. The Californians supposed this to be an act of robbery rather than rebellion. Four days later a similar group descended upon Sonoma and surrounded the house of Mariano Vallejo. "Almost the whole party," according to one of its members, "was dressed in leather huntingshirts, many of them very greasy; taking the whole party together, they were about as rough a looking set of men as one could well imagine." Vallejo's wife urged that he flee out the back door, but instead he opened the front door and asked the business of the intruders. He soon discovered that he was to consider himself a prisoner and then, through his son-in-law, Jacob Leese, negotiations proceeded but in ludicrous fashion.

Ezekiel Merritt, Robert Semple, and William Knight entered as commissioners to arrange with Vallejo, Salvador Vallejo, and Victor Prudon the terms of surrender. After a long wait the Bear Flaggers sent John Grigsby to expedite the procedure and after another long pause they sent in William B. Ide. The latter found the preceding emissaries befuddled by Vallejo's aguardiente. Ide declined Vallejo's "potent hospitality," and the negotiations were speedily finished. There was a written guaranty of protection for noncombatants. There was talk of paroling the prisoners but, instead, the Vallejos, Prudon, and Leese were sent to Frémont's camp and on to Sutter's Fort. The violence to Vallejo was an unfortunate mistake on the part of the Bear Flaggers, both in the way that it was mismanaged and because Vallejo had been a firm advocate of American acquisition.

The Bear Flaggers went on to construct their flag, a grizzly bear passant and a lone star on a field of white, bordered at the bottom by a broad red stripe, and beneath the bear the caption, "California Republic." William B. Ide proclaimed that the aim of the movement was to set up a "Republican Government" in place of the "Military Despotism" which had seized the mission property, oppressed the people, and made enormous exactions on imports. He promised that the new government would guarantee civil and religious liberty, would detect and punish crime, would encourage industry, virtue, and literature, and would leave unshackled "Commerce, Agriculture, and Mechanism." In conclusion he summed up his political credo, saying "that a Government to be prosperous and happifying in its tendency must originate with its people . . . that its Citizens are its Guardians, its officers are its Servants, and its Glory their reward." In style and in ideology Ide's proclamation is at variance with the usual picture of the Bear Flaggers as uncouth ruffians.

Near San Rafael the Bear Flaggers fought their one battle, the practically bloodless "Battle of Olompali" in which one or two Californians were killed and a number of horses captured. Soon after, moved by the capture and execution (and some add mutilation) of two Americans on their way to the Fitch rancho on the Russian River for a barrel of powder, Frémont announced his support. His 60 men joined, as did the other settlers of the vicinity. There was maneuvering back and forth in the north bay region, and Castro cleverly extricated his small force from the Marin peninsula, but a few days later official news of the Mexican War arrived and the Bear Flag movement had no further necessity. The charge is made, in fact, that it never had any excuse, that it occasioned unnecessary violence, engendered ill will, ended all hopes of peaceful annexation, and neither saved the province from British seizure nor hastened American acquisition. It was, however, an interrupted movement that did not run its full course. Had the Mexican War postponed its intrusion, the Bear Flaggers might easily have extended their sway over northern California at least in a Texas-like preliminary to annexation to the United States.

The War with Mexico

The causes of the Mexican War pertain largely to Texas and to the question of title to all of Texas, not merely the strip between the Nueces and Rio Grande. Another factor was Polk's ambition to add California and other southwestern territory to the national domain. His efforts to purchase this area had failed. The method of peaceful persuasion upon the Californians through the confidential agency of Larkin was not given time enough to operate, nor was the Bear Flag Revolt, which Polk did not start but probably would have approved. The method of conquest remained.

The war was really fought and won south of the Rio Grande and in the Valley of Mexico, but Polk was careful to see that the coveted territories were occupied. The ap Jones drama was reenacted, this time by a less impetuous hero. Commodore John D. Sloat, commander of the Pacific fleet, had standing instructions that virtually duplicated Jones'. As soon as he was assured that war had broken out he sailed to Monterey to forestall any possible intervention by Admiral George Seymour of the British Navy. Although Sloat entered port on July 2, he delayed announcing the war or taking possession until the seventh. Just why he held off is not clear, though his instructions were to preserve if possible the goodwill of the inhabitants. To spur him into action required Larkin's persuasion, urging by his officers, apprehension that the British were coming, and realization that the Bear Flaggers must be forestalled in acquiring control of the province. On the ninth there were flag raisings at San Francisco and Sonoma and two days later at Sutter's Fort.

Sloat's proclamation may be criticized for casting the entire blame for the war upon Mexico and exaggerating Zachary Taylor's initial success against General Arista. It is significant, however, for the conciliatory tone which Sloat maintained and for the point-blank assertion that the United States would retain possession. He went on to promise the Californians full privileges of citizenship, freedom "to worship the creator in a way most congenial to each one's sense of duty," freedom from revolution, and the right to import from the United States free of duty and all foreign goods at one quarter of the duty Mexico imposed. He predicted that under the American flag the province was bound to "improve more rapidly than any other on the continent of America."

On July 23 Sloat resigned his command to Commodore Robert F. Stockton, and a more vigorous policy ensued. The Bear Flag men were enlisted as volunteers in the United States Army, with Frémont as major and Gillespie as captain. Stockton determined to extend the conquest into southern California. He also issued a bombastic and inflammatory proclamation full of threats against the California leaders. On August 13 he entered Los Angeles and on the seventeenth proclaimed: "The Flag of the United States is now flying from every commanding position in the Territory, and California is entirely free from Mexican dominion." So far, so good; but again with unnecessary harshness he went on to decree martial law, to forbid the carrying of arms, and to establish a strict ten o'clock curfew.

Revolt and Reconquest

In southern California, as in the north, the Californians offered no resistance to the forces of the United States, and the change was altogether peaceful. But Stockton erred in the tone of his proclamation. He also made the mistake of leaving Gillespie in command with an inadequate garrison, and Gillespie unwisely issued tactless regulations further restraining the Angeleños from certain harmless and accustomed enjoyments. On September 23 Gillespie was made aware of the extent of American unpopularity. Sérbulo Varela and other semioutlaws, filled "with patriotism and perhaps with wine," made a disturbing though innocuous attack on the American barracks, and, when Gillespie sought to arrest these disturbers, he found most of the populace against him.

The first major engagement was at Chino Rancho where B. D. Wilson and a score of Americans were forced to surrender. Heartened by this victory, the Californians tightened their siege upon Gillespie's force, which had taken refuge on Fort Hill back of the plaza. Gillespie managed to get a messenger, Juan Flaco (Lean John) Brown, off to Stockton. After a narrow escape from the Angeleños, Brown rode madly to Monterey and on to San Francisco. He covered the 500 miles in five days, but Gillespie could not hold out even this long and surrendered. He was allowed to take his men to San Pedro on condition that they embark immediately.

Before the ship sailed, the relief party from San Francisco appeared, and Gillespie's men landed to assist in the recapture of Los Angeles. The ensuing Battle of the Old Woman's Gun was a decisive California victory. On October 8 the Americans marched inland 15 miles to Domínguez Rancho. California horsemen hovered about but the principal obstacles were heat, dust, and thirst. The next day José Carrillo's men resisted further advance. They were indifferently armed with carbines and homemade willow lances but excellently mounted and had a four-pound swivel gun that they used with telling effect. A woman had secreted the gun at the time of Stockton's entrance; now it was lashed to the front half of a wagon's running gear. Ignacio Aguilar fired it with a lighted cigarette, and reatas whipped it out of the Americans' grasp and back into position. The Americans wore themselves out in futile efforts to capture the gun; the Californians were "content to let the gun do the fighting," which it did so well that the invaders fell back to San Pedro. It was a victory for California horsemen, powder made at San Gabriel, and a salute-firing cannon from the plaza.

Two other forces were converging on the Angeleños. Frémont, with more than 300 men, was marching south from Monterey, and General Stephen W. Kearny was headed west from Fort Leavenworth. Kearny's march was part of Polk's general plan of occupying the Mexican areas whose cession was desired. New Mexico was the first objective; Kearny gained control over that province without serious difficulty. Leaving the greater part of his command as a garrison at Santa Fé, he set out with 300 dragoons by the Gila route for California. On the Rio Grande below Socorro he met Kit Carson on his way to Washington with dispatches from Stockton. When Carson, who

had left the settlements prior to the Los Angeles outburst, showed him Stockton's official statement that American control was already established, Kearny decided to send most of his men back to Santa Fe, but he induced Carson to guide him to the coast.

The desert crossing involved severe hardships. Then, before his men and animals had recovered their strength, Kearny found himself opposed by a large force of Californians under Andrés Pico. At San Pascual the Californians retreated before an American attack, but, as soon as the pursuers were strung out, Pico's men turned and attacked. Sixteen or eighteen Americans were killed and as many wounded while the Californians had only a few minor wounds. The survivors were still at bay before the California horsemen. Kit Carson and Lieutenant Edward F. Beale slipped through to San Diego, Stockton sent out 200 marines and soldiers, and with their help Kearny got in to San Diego on December 12.

Kearny reported San Pascual as an American victory. He had come off in possession of the battlefield, though with practically all the casualties. He could find, however, feeble excuse for bringing on the battle. Even had he won a decisive victory, the California revolt would have remained virtually as strong. He must answer for sending his men into battle on worn out mules and half-broken horses, with their powder wet and with no weapons but clubbed guns and rusted swords against skilled and well-mounted lancers. Clearly the Californians were underrated, yet Pico appears to have planned the battle and the tactics most vaguely and, when reinforcements arrived, he disappeared.

Weeks passed before Kearny and Stockton were ready to move on Los Angeles. January 8 found them at the upper ford of the San Gabriel, with a California force under

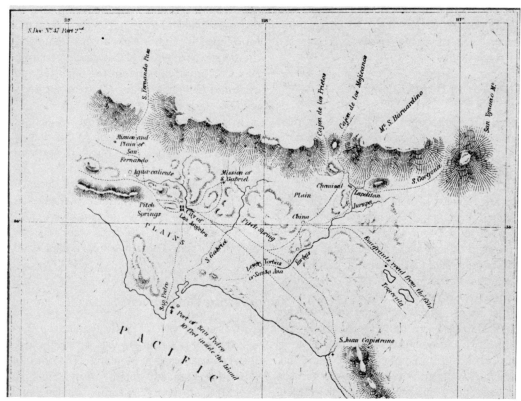

The Los Angeles Plains   *Topographical sketch by E. O. C. Ord, 1849*

José María Flores commanding the opposite bank. The Californians were advantageously posted, but dissensions and bickerings within their ranks had dissipated most of the enthusiasm evidenced at Chino, Los Angeles, and San Pascual. Their powder also was poor and consequently their artillery fire, which otherwise would have been withering, did not hinder the Americans from crossing the river. At Los Angeles River the next day the performance was repeated, again with almost no casualties on either side.

Los Angeles surrendered to Kearny and Stockton on January 10. Flores turned his authority over to Andrés Pico and left for Sonora. Rather than surrender to Kearny and Stockton, Pico preferred to capitulate to Frémont, now as far south as San Fernando. Frémont's pardon of Jesús Pico, another leader in the revolt and a parole violator, doubtless had much to do with Andrés Pico's choice. Justifying Pico's hopes, the Cahuenga Capitulation on January 13, 1847, ended the revolt without the least semblance of vindictiveness. No punishments were threatened or provided; conciliation was its pervading spirit.

Like the Bear Flag Revolt this southern California uprising may appear a fruitless and unnecessary outburst. But its causation was clear and it at least demonstrated the gallantry, the dash, and the valor of the Californians.

The War in Baja California

After this spirited action in Alta California, American attention was directed to the peninsula. On March 29, 1847, Captain Montgomery of the *Portsmouth* raised the American flag at San José del Cabo and on April 13 did the same at La Paz. In each instance he exacted a pledge of neutrality and invited all who wished to become American citizens. The American officers were as emphatic as they had been in Alta California that the province would be retained permanently by the United States, yet Commodore William Shubrick was more intent upon blockading the mainland ports than upon ensuring the complete submission of the peninsulares. In July Colonel Burton and 115 men of the New York volunteers arrived from Santa Barbara to garrison La Paz, and in November, Shubrick left Lieutenant Heywood and 24 men to hold San José.

Several weeks earlier Captain Manuel Pineda had crossed the gulf from Guaymas to Mulege and begun preparations to oust the invaders. Waiting prudently until the American naval vessels had left, he launched attacks on the American barracks at La Paz on November 16 and on San José on the nineteenth. At La Paz the investment continued until the arrival of the *Cyane* on December 8, with the sharpest fighting occurring on November 17, 27, and 28. San José was temporarily relieved by two American whalers on November 21, and additional marines and sailors brought Heywood's force up to 46 men. In January Pineda renewed the attack. By February 10 he had possession of the town; two days later Heywood was in distress for lack of food and water, but on the fourteenth the *Cyane* came to the rescue and the siege was lifted. In March, reinforced from Alta California, Burton took the offensive and captured Pineda and several other opposition leaders.

In February, 1848, terms of peace had been negotiated at the village of Guadalupe Hidalgo near Mexico City. Mexico's northern boundary would be at the Rio Grande and the Gila and beween Alta and Baja California. The return of the peninsula to Mexico is understandable. Few Americans were resident there, known resources were meager, and Polk's stated objectives had not included it.

Military Government

As was customary for newly acquired territories, military government was set up the day the flag was raised at Monterey. The office of governor changed rapidly from Sloat to Stockton, Frémont, Kearny, Mason, and Riley. General Persifer F. Smith could have claimed the title during Mason's last six weeks but preferred to concentrate on command of the Army's Pacific Division. Even so, the average tenure in this office was about six months.

Except perhaps for Frémont the occupants saw their role as temporary caretaker until Congress provided civil self-government. Sloat promptly substituted American for Mexican import duties, but wherever decision making could be deferred the tendency was to postpone. The major decision, and it was made early, was to continue local government as institutionalized under Mexico. Essentially that meant alcalde rule. Most Mexican Californians, though a few repatriated after the southern California revolt, accommodated to the new regime.

It was newly arrived Americans who most bitterly protested government by the military. Asserting that the Constitution followed the flag, they demanded immediate civil government. Curiously the one element of civil government that did exist, alcalde rule, struck them as particularly un-American. Seemingly it mattered not that most of the appointed alcaldes were Anglo-Americans, among them Walter Colton, former chaplain on the *Savannah* and best known for the revealing diary he faithfully kept on his work as alcalde at Monterey; and Stephen J. Field, alcalde at Yubaville, who went on to become the first Californian on the nation's Supreme Court.

The nub of the complaint was that the office violated the Anglo-American fetish of separation of powers. A writer in the *California Star* complained that alcaldes exercised "authority far greater than any officer in our republic—the president not excepted. . . . The grand autocrat of the Russians . . . is the only man in Christendom I know of who equals him."

A month after the Cahuenga Capitulation the *California Star* urged formation of a constitutional convention, and in January, 1848, "Pacific" complained in that same paper, "we have had no government at all . . . unless the inefficient mongrel military rule . . . be termed such."

With the cession of California the arguments against military government gained added weight. In the spring of 1848 Congress approved territorial government for Oregon, but an amendment to do the same for California and New Mexico was rejected on the ground that "native-born Oregon should not be unequally yoked with territories peopled by Mexicans and half-Indian Californians."

Congress and the White House hesitated to act, for one reason because of the strong sectional jealousy about adding states or prospective states that would break the balance of slave states and free states. The Mexican Cession was not suitable for slavery, but within the confines of the nation it was about the only area that seemed available.

By the time Californians learned that the cession was a reality, they also had more exciting news of gold along the streams of the Sierra foothills. That became the overriding interest throughout the summer and fall of 1848. Goldseekers flocked to the diggings and came by the hundreds from Mexico, Chile, Hawaii, and Oregon. The seasonal rains of winter interrupted mining, and many of these forty-eighters retreated to San Francisco, where some of them reflected on Washington's delay in extending civil government. On February 12, 1849, a resolution was passed calling for a better organized town government, and months later a similar resolution called for election of delegates to a constitutional convention to assemble on the first Monday in August. Meetings at San Jose, Sacramento, Santa Cruz, and Monterey endorsed this plan.

Organizing a State

When he became governor, General Bennett Riley concluded that it would be more proper for a convention to gather at his invitation. Accordingly, as soon as he learned that Congress had adjourned without acting for California, he issued a call for a convention to meet at Monterey on September 1. The elections were held and early in September the delegates gathered.

Riley's proclamation authorized San Diego, Santa Barbara, and San Luis Obispo to send two delegates each; Los Angeles, Sonoma, Sacramento, and San Joaquin, four each; and Monterey, San Jose, and San Francisco, five each. Taking advantage of an option to send larger delegations if that seemed appropriate, the northern districts increased Riley's allotment by 11, which enlarged the convention to 48.

The convention proceeded to frame a state rather than a territorial government. Because of the gold rush California had received such a great influx of population that it could skip the territorial stage. Forty-niners, however, did not dominate the convention. Not more than a dozen of the 48 members had come in the rush. The others were "old-timers": a few native Californians, such as Vallejo, Carrillo, and De la Guerra; some Americans of long residence, such as Stearns and Larkin; others like Semple, who had come with the overland immigrants in the forties; and Mexican War veterans, of whom Halleck is representative. These old-timers who were to be California's Founding Fathers were not old; only four had passed 50, thirty were not yet 40, and nine were still in their 20s.

The most debated question was where to locate the eastern boundary. A large-state faction urged the Rockies; the small-state faction, the Sierra. Six or eight compromise lines were proposed, and the convention repeatedly switched its approval from one to another. From the debates it is evident that the territory west of the Sierra and that fronting on the Colorado was what really mattered. Beyond that, the prime consideration was to get a line that Congress would approve promptly. Exclusion of the Mormon district around Salt Lake seemed advisable because the Mormons were not represented in the convention and preferred to remain apart. Another argument of the small-state advocates was that the national government should be left responsible for protecting and relieving emigrant parties in the intermountain desert basin. The present line was the eventual compromise.

The work of the convention was greatly simplified because of the availability of other state constitutions. Chief reliance was on Iowa's, the most recent constitution in the West, and on New York's newly revised frame of government, but the influence of six or eight others can be detected.

Several circumstances tended to impair the reputation of this first California constitution. It was suspect because it had been drawn up in the wild and boisterous West and by a body irregularly convened. The disgracefully low standards of political conduct in California in the following decade also reflected unfavorably upon the constitution's standing. Furthermore, within 30 years the state discarded it in favor of a new one. On the other hand, it is worth noting that the work of the Monterey convention was approved almost without dissent when submitted to popular vote. Congress criticized the procedure followed but made no complaint about the constitution. Moreover, political scientists agree that this first constitution was a superior document. It was a simple statement of fundamental principles and procedures, not cluttered with a multitude of technical provisions really legislative in character.

A most striking tribute to the excellence of this constitution of '49 is that it was a principal inspiration and model for the Argentinian constitution of 1853. Comparison of the two documents reveals their similarities. We have also the testimony of Juan Bautista Alberdi, father of the constitution of 1853. Acknowledging his indebtedness, Alberdi had this to say of the California document: "Without universities, without academies or law colleges, the newly-organized people of California have drawn up a constitution full of foresight, of common sense and of opportunity."

Statehood was not approved by Congress until almost a year later. The constitution, some Congressmen charged, had been "concocted" by President Taylor through Governor Riley. Others objected that the Californians were a grab bag of adventurers who could not be trusted to operate a state government; furthermore, they were ill-mannered upstarts who had not waited for an enabling act as the signal to draw up a frame of government. Such a dangerous show of disregard for Congress should be rebuked as an example to the rest of the West.

The real reasons for the delay, however, lay elsewhere. They concerned the overlapping claims of Texas, New Mexico, Deseret, and California, reflected party jealousies and disputes between the President and Congress, and were inherent in the disagreement between the North and slave-holding South. Only through the exercise of Henry Clay's suave peacemaking could these issues be compromised. In the end the national government approved what the West had done and on September 9, 1850, California took her place in the family of states. Her elected representatives were waiting in the wings, ready to be seated.

CHAPTER 9

The Mill at Coloma   *William R. Hutton, 1849*

My messenger sent to the mines has returned with specimens of the gold; he dismounted in a sea of upturned faces. As he drew forth the yellow lumps from his pockets, and passed them around among the eager crowd, the doubts, which had lingered till now, fled. . . . The blacksmith dropped his hammer, the carpenter his plane, the mason his trowel, the farmer his sickle, the baker his loaf, and the tapster his bottle. All were off for the mines, some on horses, some on carts, and some on crutches, and one went in a litter.

Walter Colton, Alcalde of Monterey
June 20, 1848

The Discovery

When the Spaniards came to California, they were the world's most famous treasure finders and producers of precious metals. With this reputation, one of the ironies of history is that they did not discover California's gold. Some of the forty-niners rationalized on the basis of the alleged depravity of the natives and the Catholic religion of the Spaniards. The latter, according to this theory, would have used the California gold "to keep the world in darkness and to extend the dominions of popery," whereas the prevailingly Protestant Americans would put it to a better use. This argument was not entirely convincing, not even to the forty-niners; as one of them, after speculating on the point, went on to say of his fellows, "But still the majority, perhaps nine-tenths, are seeking it for wicked purposes," an observation heartily endorsed by many witnesses of the gold rush.

Without invoking the intervention of a divine and Protestant Providence, it is understandable that the Spaniards did not make the discovery. Those who came were soldiers, settlers, and missionaries. In Mexico, as in most of Spanish America, mining had been for silver more than for gold, and, since the days when Columbus and his companions washed the gravels of Espanola, placer mining had been of slight importance. Also, the Spanish mineral discoveries were usually deposits which the Indians were already working, and the California Indians had not taken this preliminary step. The Spaniards, furthermore, occupied only the coastal strip. Even when ranchos were extended inland, contact with the mother lode area was infrequent and superficial.

To be sure, California had yielded small amounts of gold prior to 1848, the most famous and most important find being that by

Francisco López in San Feliciano Cañon in 1842. Several score prospectors followed López into the mountains back of Mission San Fernando and took out varying amounts. From these placers came the first California gold presented to the United States mint, some 20 ounces forwarded by Alfred Robinson for Abel Stearns. These placers also influenced Deputy Manuel Castañares to report to the Mexican government in 1844 that mining promised to be one of the most profitable industries of the province. These southern deposits, however, did not live up to expectations. Interest in them was local and short-lived, and it remained for James Wilson Marshall to make effective discovery of California's fabulous wealth in gold.

On January 24, 1848, while constructing a sawmill at Coloma on the American River, Marshall chanced to notice flecks of yellow along the tailrace. The tailrace had cut across a bend in the river and was to all intents and purposes a rough sluice through a bar such as the Argonauts learned to look for. Marshall gathered samples of this "color," enough by the next day to make three ounces. On the fourth day he rode off to Sutter's Fort to confer with his employer, the potentate of the Sacramento Valley. Behind locked doors the two men examined the contents of Marshall's pouch and applied every test that their ingenuity or the *American Encyclopaedia* could suggest. By all accounts Marshall, an excitable young man, was worked up over the discovery, doubtless in large degree because some of the men at the mill had insinuated that he was crazy. Sutter records that his own sleep was disturbed that night by thoughts of the disruption of his ventures which excitement about gold might cause. Yet many accounts read entirely too much drama and foreknowledge into the conference of Marshall and Sutter. As of that time the magnitude of the

Jim Marshall
Britton & Rey broadside

discovery was not yet discernible.

Sutter, worried about keeping his laborers, went up to Coloma and persuaded the men to promise to continue at their task for six weeks. Gold prospects in the vicinity, nevertheless, suggested the advisability of acquiring title. Accordingly, he called together the Coloma Indians and dickered with them for a three–year lease of the 10 or 12 leagues of land surrounding the mill. The consideration was some shirts, hats, handkerchiefs, and flour, "and other articles of no great value." Next he dispatched Charles Bennett, one of the mill hands, to Monterey to get Colonel R. B. Mason to validate his title to the land.

Throughout these first weeks Sutter's course was inconsistent. He sought to minimize the importance of the discovery yet rushed to get title. He bound Bennett to secrecy yet sent with him six ounces of gold. He made Marshall's men promise to work for six weeks yet allowed them to prospect on

Sundays. He attempted to isolate Coloma from New Helvetia but sent teamsters back and forth to the mill. He was noncommunicative to his employees but as early as February 10 was writing to Vallejo at nearby Sonoma: "I have made a discovery of a gold mine, which, according to experiments we have made, is extraordinarily rich."

To keep such a secret was impossible; it escaped through numerous leaks. At Benicia on his way to Monterey, Bennett could not resist trumping a rumor of coal near Mount Diablo by displaying his sample of a mineral "that will beat coal." At San Francisco and at Monterey he again showed the gold. At Coloma one of the Wimmer boys babbled of gold to a teamster, and his mother, to prove the boy was not a liar, brought forth some of the metal. The teamster in turn, ordering a bottle of whiskey at Smith and Brannan's store at Sutter's Fort, offered gold dust in payment. In February, Henry Bigler shared the secret with three of his Mormon friends who, as Bancroft put it, "united with them three others to help them keep it." So it went, and before long word of the discovery had permeated much of northern California.

Although the secret escaped, California was not immediately gripped with a furor for mining. The first newspaper mention of the discovery was a perfunctory notice tucked away on the second page of the San Francisco *Californian* of March 15. Three days later the *California Star* made an equally noncommittal statement and on March 25 reported that enough gold had been mined to make it "an article of traffic" at New Helvetia. In its next issue, on April 1, the *Star* ran a long installment of V. J. Fourgeaud's "The Prospects of California." He mentioned gold but bracketed the American River diggings with the old placero a few miles from the Ciudad de los Angeles and dwelt primarily on agricultural and commercial resources. On May 6 Editor E. C. Kemble, after a jaunt through the inte-

117

rior, made only this staccato report: "Great country, fine climate; visit this great valley, we would advise all who have not yet done so. See it now. Full-flowing streams, mighty timber, large crops, luxuriant clover, fragrant flowers, gold and silver."

A few venturesome individuals stole off to Coloma, but not until the latter part of May did the gold fever really become virulent. Then it was Sam Brannan's quinine bottle full of the precious dust and his infectious shout of "Gold! Gold! Gold from the American River!" that started the rush. Alcalde Walter Colton described the excitement at Monterey on June 20. Everyone, except one old codger who insisted it was "some Yankee invention, got up to reconcile the people to the change of flag," admitted that the specimens of gold were genuine. Monterey was quickly depopulated. An American woman who had opened a boardinghouse rushed off before her lodgers had a chance to pay their bills, and Colton was left to govern "a community of women," a gang of prisoners, and here and there a soldier. By July for lack of a servant he, Governor Mason, and Lieutenant Lanman of the *Warren* were their own cooks.

Other parts of California soon felt the effect of the gold excitement. San Jose was largely deserted; places as far south as Santa Barbara and Los Angeles contributed their quota of prospectors; rancheros and farmers hustled off to diggings; army pay of $7 a month was not enough to keep men in the ranks; and ships which put in at San Francisco were quickly stripped of their crews and often of their officers as well. The immediate consequences were frequently grotesque. San Francisco and Monterey were on the way toward becoming ghost towns. Business, except in picks, pans, shovels, and mining outfits, was at a standstill, labor was not to be had, construction stopped, and real estate tumbled to give-away prices. A San Jose stablekeeper was urged by his brothers, already in the

mines, to burn his barn if he could not otherwise dispose of it. On the other hand, mining equipment rose to fantastic prices and transportation to the mines was at a premium. Horses could still be had for about $15, but every small vessel on the bay was eagerly sought out, and Semple's ferry at Benicia did a tremendous business.

The Season of '48

Meanwhile, the field of mining operations spread rapidly from the initial point at Coloma. Henry Bigler and other employees at the mill discovered better diggings downstream, and friends of theirs dug the first gold at Mormon Bar. Upstream, Marshall discovered Live Oak Bar where Indians were soon set to work mining. On March 8 Isaac Humphrey, an experienced Georgia miner, began prospecting at Coloma and the next day had a rocker in operation. Later in the month John Bidwell visited Coloma, observed the alluvial deposits in which the gold was found, and was reminded of similar formations near his rancho at Chico. He soon had his Indian retainers at work at Bidwell Bar on the Feather River. P. B. Reading was inspired to put Indians to work far to the north at placers along Clear Creek and the Trinity. Soon other placers were being worked along Feather River. Here seven men from Monterey, assisted by 50 Indians, took out 273 pounds of gold in seven weeks. On the Yuba, principal tributary of the Feather, gold was still more abundant. The first five prospectors there made $75,000 in three months, and other miners were said to have averaged $60 to $100 a day.

Prospecting was also extended to the tributaries of the American River. John Sinclair was the pioneer at its forks, a Mormon group began work at Spanish Diggings on the middle tributary, an Irishman opened the Yankee

Jim, and a party sent out by Charles M. Weber, after visiting the Stanislaus and the Mokelumne, mined the first gold at Weberville on the south branch of the American. One of the best strikes in this vicinity was at Dry Diggings, subsequently rechristened Hangtown and still later Placerville. Here the daily yield in the summer of 1848 was said to be from three ounces to five pounds per man, and that summer, as Bancroft aptly observes, "the 300 Hangtown men were the happiest in the universe."

Such were the northern diggings. Except for Reading's placers far to the north it was a fairly compact district on the American and the Feather rivers and on their several tributaries, such as the Yuba, Bear, and Weber. The miners were principally Americans from the northern ranchos and towns, deserters from Mason's command, sailors from every vessel that anchored at San Francisco, and Indians native to the gold region.

Indians were the pioneers in the southern

Miner

From a Contemporary Lettersheet

diggings. Weber's company was partly responsible. Twenty-five Stanislaus Indians were taken to Weber Creek, given a short course in mining methods, and sent back to their native haunts with the promise of a ready market for any gold they might gather. They brought in such quantities of coarse gold (one nugget is said to have weighed 80½ ounces) that they convinced their white friends that they had found "the place where all the gold came from." The Weber group led a rush to the Stanislaus and was soon joined by others from the north, a large contingent of southern Californians, and many prospectors from Sonora.

Phenomenal success greeted some of these gold seekers. At Knight's Ferry on the Stanislaus three men with no better equipment than pick and knife averaged $200 to $300 a day each. On the Tuolumne, Antonio Coronel took out 45 ounces the first day; another found a 12-ounce nugget; another secured 52 pounds in eight days; and a Sonoran spent a short day cleaning out a pocket with a horn spoon and piled a tray with so much clean gold that he could hardly lift it. Few miners fared that well but the average return seems to have been approximately an ounce a day.

Shallow mining was characteristic of 1848. Prospectors overran practically the entire area that was to be worked in the next decade but confined themselves to scratching the surface. With pan and rocker they washed the gravel convenient to the streams, and at dry diggings such as Auburn, Hangtown, and Sonora they creviced with pick, knife, and horn spoon and carried the pay dirt to water or winnowed it by dry washing. Scarcity of silver coin resulted in a very low price for gold, $6 to $8 an ounce being common, while abundance of gold and shortage of supplies, particularly toward the end of the season, bred high prices for all commodities. Outrageous prices were typical: flour, $800 a barrel; whiskey, $100 a gallon;

Gold District of California

James Wyld, London, 1849

hire of a rocker, $150 a day. Even the forty-niners were less extravagant.

Although the miners were beyond the effective reach of the law, the season of '48 was remarkably free of crime. The accounts all mention the safety with which equipment, supplies, and gold were left lying around unguarded. Nor was there much claim jumping. The forty-eighters, drawn largely from California, continued as friends and neighbors. Honest toil was yielding fabulous returns and the mining region was not yet crowded. The few thousand miners of '48 were spread over the same area occupied by several times that number in the following years. A measure of credit should go to Mason for his action invalidating the Mexican system of denouncing mining claims. Had a few individuals attempted to file on the best diggings, friction would have developed. Already the miners were showing themselves capable of working out their own code of mining regulations and of punishing such crimes as were committed. Only two hangings are on record for 1848. That one victim was French and the other Spanish suggests that race prejudice was already in evidence.

The mining population for 1848 has been grossly overestimated by some writers. In May there were only a few hundred at work, by July 3,000 or 4,000, and Colton's estimate of 50,000 at the end of the season must be scaled down to 8,000 or 10,000. California contributed the majority but the contagion spread rapidly over the Pacific area. Oregon sent some 1,500 prospectors, and Hawaii and Mexico sent perhaps 2,500.

The Rush of the Forty-Niners

Gradually the excitement spread to the States and Europe. By August and September, California letters telling of the gold discovery had been printed in various eastern papers. The first reports, however, were met with polite or raucous incredulity, and months passed before the nation began to believe. Finally attention was riveted by the arrival of official messengers from California. The Navy sent E. F. Beale by way of Hawaii, Peru, Panama, and Jamaica, and Governor Mason sent Lt. Lucien Loeser by way of Mazatlán, Veracruz, and New Orleans with his report and a tea caddy containing $3,000 worth of gold. In his message to Congress on December 5, Polk took official notice of the discovery, and his words became the signal for a stampede.

The news came opportunely in the midst of postwar adjustment. The War with Mexico was not a great upheaval, but thousands of soldiers had been recently mustered out, many had not yet found peacetime employment, and others were dissatisfied with a humdrum existence and longed for new adventures. For them California gold mining had a compelling appeal. Farmers, shopkeepers, clerks, physicians, and politicians also caught this "yellow fever," not to mention "the briefless lawyer, the starving student, the quack, the idler, the harlot, the gambler, the henpecked husband, the disgraced."

California could be reached by three principal routes, Cape Horn, Panama, or overland. For New Englanders the sea route was the natural one, both from habit and for convenience. Ships were numerous, seafaring men even more so, and, thanks to the otter trade, the hide trade, and whaling, there were many men expert in the voyage to California. Astute shipowners withdrew their vessels from other commerce, some 71 from whaling, for example. They fitted these vessels to carry Argonauts to California and then, after the crews had deserted at San Francisco, wondered how to get their ships home. Other New Englanders formed joint-stock companies, bought vessels, provisioned them, selected ship officers, and sailed to California. One such group was the Boston and California Mining Company whose members were exhorted by President Edward Everett of Harvard to go to California "with the Bible in one hand and your New England civilization in the other and make your mark on the people and country." In nine months 549 vessels arrived at San Francisco, many from Europe, South America, Mexico, and Hawaii but most from the Atlantic seaboard.

Although travelers by sea vied with Panama men and overlanders in calling their particular path the worst, the Cape Horn route probably offered the easiest journey. It may, indeed, have been too easy, for many passengers were so softened by four to eight months of inaction as to be unfit for the hard labor in the diggings. It was something of a white-collar route, favored by gamblers, politicians, saloonkeepers, and prostitutes, as well as by Bible-bearing Yankees. Every forty-niner by sea visited San Francisco before proceeding to the mines, and many went no farther. The sea route also made a material contribution in bulky machinery, furniture, and foodstuffs which could not have come overland. Included in the cargoes was a choice assortment of patent mining machinery destined for un-Christian burial on the flats below San Francisco. By accident some shovels and picks were included along with pianos, printing presses, and other appliances.

Providentially, just at the time that gold fever became virulent on the East Coast, bi-monthly steamer service from New York and New Orleans to Chagres and monthly service from Panama to Oregon was launched. The federal government had contracted for it to provide naval officers experience under steam. The greater benefit would be to Argonauts intent on reaching California as quickly as possible. From the tentative schedule it appeared that the journey might be made in 30 days.

To cross the isthmus travelers had to depend on native boatmen and muleteers, and on the Pacific side there was woeful shortage of ships. Stray sailing ships were pressed into service but an impatient horde was left stranded. A cartoon history of the gold rush follows this route to the mines and back and at Panama finds one identifiable original companion still waiting for passage to San Francisco.

While the Argonauts waited, insects, tropical heat, poor food, and bad water plagued them. Yellow fever brought death. Some of the more enterprising, notably Collis P. Huntington, traded and prospered. But whether one crossed at Panama, Nicaragua, Tehuantepec, or central Mexico, the problem of finding transportation up the coast remained. As rapidly as possible, the Pacific Mail brought out more steamers via the Straits of Magellan and improved its service.

Almost 40,000 forty-niners followed these water and land-and-water routes. For most residents of the Mississippi Valley, however, the overland trails were nearer at hand and less forbidding. Editors in Texas, Arkansas, and Missouri vied in praising the routes from Corpus Christi through Mexico, across Texas to El Paso, from Fort Smith to El Paso, or over the Santa Fé Trail and on by the Gila or the Old Spanish Trail. These southern trails had the advantage of passing through a number of settled points in Mexico, on the Rio Grande, and in southern California where it would be possible to rest and reprovision. They were not subject to closure by winter snows; in fact, winter was probably the ideal season for crossing the southern desert into California. Opened by Spanish explorers and restless beaver trappers, these southern trails had been broadened and improved by the caravans of Santa Fé traders and by American military forces during the recent war. They attracted some 10,000 to 15,000 forty-niners, most of whom got through safely, however much they may have grumbled at delays and difficulties.

From Missouri north the consensus of opinion recommended the Platte – South Pass – Humboldt itinerary, which had been broken by the fur men, favored by the pioneer settlers, used in part by the Oregon missionaries and settlers and by the Mormons in their hegira to Salt Lake, and advertised by Frémont. Some 25,000 to 35,000 persons swarmed over this most direct route and made it known as the California Trail.

Although the major overland trails had been well worked out before 1849, few competent guides were available at the starting points along the Missouri, and reliable information was not available in print. Guidebooks were shortly produced to point the way and advise as to methods, yet it is a curious commentary that the best one was written by a St. Louis newspaperman, Joseph E. Ware, who had never been west of Missouri. Most of the forty-niners, lacking even such a guide, had to learn by experience the procedure of crossing the plains, the desert, and the mountains. According to a typical gold seeker, "There were few, if any, who possessed a definite knowledge of the road and, as a consequence, there was great suffering."

In outward appearance the migration of 1849 duplicated those of earlier years. The same prairie schooners and the same sorts of

Overland to the Diggings

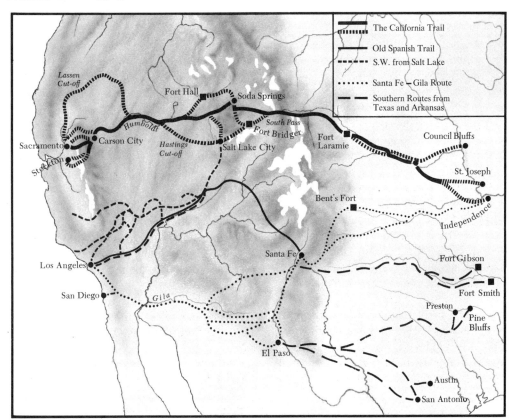

teams were used, though the proportion of families to single men was somewhat less than in the earlier migration of agriculturists. In 1849, nevertheless, many of the gold seekers carried the fundamental farming equipment with them. By reason of its very magnitude, however, this movement was basically different. In an earlier period the chief dangers had been from Indian attacks or from losing the way. Gold seekers on their way to California found the Indians harmless except for depredations on livestock along the Humboldt, and, as for getting lost, the only ones to go astray did so voluntarily.

Shortcuts lured the emigrants repeatedly, usually with unfortunate results. One such experience was on the shortcut or detour southwest from Salt Lake. Late season emigrants were advised to take that roundabout route rather than risk being snowed in like the Donner party. When Jefferson Hunt agreed to go as guide, enough forty-niners to make a 107-wagon train accepted the proposition. En route another Mormon overtook them and enticed most of them to turn off on a shortcut more directly westward. They soon ran into very rough country, broke up into many small groups, some shifting to packing and others struggling on with their wagons. A few returned to Salt Lake, or went back to Hunt's trail and straggled on into Los Angeles.

Others wandered into a below-sea-level desert basin which they named Death Valley. A dozen or more lost their lives not far from this spot. One small group, the Bennett-Arcane party, pitched camp in the valley and waited while two young teamsters pushed on to San Fernando, obtained a mule and two horses and a small quantity of food, and courageously went back into the desert to bring out the imperiled men, women, and children. Lewis Manly's *Death Valley in '49*, a gold rush classic, is a reminiscent account by a hero in this rescue.

Lassen's Cut-off, from the Humboldt

across Black Rock Desert to a northern pass, Pit River, and the upper Sacramento, lured a dozen or more wagon trains. The most voluminous of all gold rush diarists, J. Goldsborough Bruff, wintered and almost starved in the mountains on this route. Although Sublette's Cut-off was an improvement, the usual result was that voiced by Alonzo Delano concerning the Lassen Cut-off. "Instead of avoiding the desert, instead of the promised water, grass and a better road, we were in fact upon a more dreary and wider waste, without either grass or water, and with a harder road before us. . . . We had been inveigled there by false reports and misrepresentations."

Diaries and journals make much of the great concourse of people on the trail, of how each night's camp was made within sight of other campfires, of how the migration resembled a large city on the move. Delano gives this picture of the great trek: "For miles, to the extent of vision, an animated mass of beings broke upon our view. Long trains of wagons with their white covers were moving slowly along, a multitude of horsemen were prancing on the road, companies of men were traveling on foot, and although the scene was not a gorgeous one, yet the display of banners from many wagons, and the multitude of armed men, looked as if a mighty army was on its march."

Exhaustion of the grass supply and ravages of cholera, the two most serious problems facing the forty-niners, were products of the crowded trail. At many camp sites where caravans had found luxuriant pasturage the grass was cropped clean by the cattle of the earliest forty-niners and later parties found none. Then there were certain mendacious individuals who fired the grass as a deliberate hindrance to those behind, apparently hoping to reduce competition in the diggings. Nightly detours or side trips of two or three or four miles became the rule for the hindmost parties. From the Missouri to the Rockies the

Death Valley *David Packwood*

ravages of cholera were frightful. Cholera struck suddenly. Some died after two or three hours of violent chills and fever; others lingered between life and death for days or weeks. Medical attention was seldom available, and relatives were rarely on hand to care for the afflicted. Supposed friends occasionally abandoned their companions, but in other instances utter strangers went out of their way to minister to those in distress.

Fortunately the cholera did not cross the Continental Divide; mountain fever took its place as the principal ailment and then it too was left behind. But the road became worse. The Platte Crossing, the alkaline lakes, Sublette's Cut-off with its 35 miles without water, the Green River Crossing—these earlier crises paled before the Humboldt. In its valley the forty-niners, excepting those who had circled south of Great Salt Lake, had their first real taste of desert travel. It was hot and dusty. The landscape was cheerless and devoid of vegetation except for a little grass and a few small willows at the immediate margin of the river.

As the grass along the south bank was exhausted, many of the later travelers had to cross the stream nightly to gather grass for their cattle, and these discomforts and annoyances made the Humboldt the butt of their grumbling, as numerous diaries attest. Argonaut John Steele called it "the neighborhood of the rich man's hell"; versifying his salute, Horace Belknap started off in this vein, "Meanest and muddiest, filthiest stream, most cordially I hate you;" and the average Argonaut would have been ready to endorse Horace Greeley's observation, "Here famine sits enthroned, and waves his sceptre over a dominion expressly made for him."

The Humboldt Valley had its shortcomings, yet as an attenuated oasis stretching most of the way across the Nevada desert it made possible the use of this overland route. Unfortunately, the river terminated in the "Sink," beyond which lay 40 miles of unrelieved desert before reaching the Carson River or the Truckee. Because men and animals were weakened and worn out by the rigors of the long trail, the desert crossing was even more difficult. Milus Gay, one of the more restrained diarists, described it in these terms: "Continuing across the Desert got across to Carsonville on Carson River about 4 p.m. 12 or 15 miles of the latter part of the Journey being sandy was very hard on our cattle the distance across is perhaps about 40 miles—Such destruction of property as I saw across the Desert I have never seen I should think I passed the carcases of 1200 head of cattle and horses and a great many waggons—Harneses—cooking utensils—tools water casks &c. &c. at a moderate estimate the amount I would think the property cost in the U.S. $50,000. We also see many men on the point of starvation begging for bread. We stopped an hour in this wagon and tented ville. bought 2 lb Beef for which we paid $1—and eat it all for supper. went up some 3 or 4 miles and encamped Grass scarce 〰 (N. B. Water 8 miles from C[arson] R[iver] sold for $1 gallon.)

After tarrying briefly to recruit their cattle on the lush grasses at the eastern base of the Sierra, the emigrants hurried on. Several routes were available but there was not much choice. That by the Truckee and Donner Pass was in some respects the easiest but in ill-repute because of the Donner tragedy. The Truckee could be followed to Henness Pass and the Yuba, or the Carson to either Johnson's Pass or Carson Pass and Placerville on the American, or the Walker to Sonora Pass and the Stanislaus. By any route the rocky fords and steep ascent made it hard pulling for man and beast. Some wagons and much baggage were taken no farther. Adding to the difficulty, winter set in earlier than usual but, thanks to the energetic measures of relief directed by Major Rucker of the United States Army, duplication of the Donner tragedy was averted.

The migration of 1850 was a repetition differing only in detail. The number was as great, the cholera was worse, ferry service was now available at a dozen rivers along the way, and the regular trail along the Humboldt was under water as the result of most unusual rains. The desert took its accustomed toll, and California relief agencies, this time managed by William Waldo of Sacramento, again saved thousands from impending disaster in the Sierra.

In the Diggings

These overlanders plunged immediately into mining. They imitated the old-timers' use of pick and shovel, pan and cradle. Even when the more efficient long tom and sluice were introduced, they found gold mining back breaking. One moved as much dirt as a ditch digger, frequently standing in icy water and under a broiling sun. There was excitement, of course, and any day might bring a rich prize, but the excitement was a temptation to overwork and to neglect such prosaic tasks as cooking. The miner's home was an uncomfortable tent or shanty and his clothing was nondescript and often inadequate protection against the elements.

The rewards, furthermore, were not only uncertain but on the average unsatisfactory. The "pound diggings" of 1848 were succeeded by the "ounce diggings" of 1849 and 1850, and thereafter came a further decline. The statistics are incomplete and conflicting, but it has been calculated that the mean return after 1850 was about $2 a day per man. Apart from the few who struck it tremendously rich, the wisest forty-niners were those who turned to saloonkeeping, merchandising, hauling, farming, or dishwashing, where the compensation was not only more certain but higher.

Frank Marryat offers this eyewitness description of an active camp: "A turn of the road presented a scene of mining life, as perfect in its details as it was novel in its features. Immediately beneath us the swift river glided tranquilly, though foaming still from the great battle which a few yards higher up, it had fought with a mass of black obstructing rocks. On the banks was a village of canvas that the winter rains had bleached to perfection and round it the miners were at work at every point. Many were waist deep in the water, toiling in bands to construct a race and dam to turn the river's course; others were entrenched in holes, like grave diggers, working down to the "bedrock." Some were on the brink of the stream washing out "prospects" from tin pans or wooden "batteaus"; and others worked in company with the long tom,

Sunday Morning in the Mines *Charles Nahl, Crocker Art Museum, Sacramento*

by means of water sluices artfully conveyed from the river. Many were coyote-ing in subterranean holes, from which from time to time their heads popped out, like those of squirrels to take a look at the world; and a few with drills, dissatisfied with nature's work, were preparing to remove large rocks with gunpowder. All was life, merriment, vigour and determination, as this part of the earth was being turned inside out to see what it was made of. . . .

"Small patches of garden surrounded the village which bore so palpably the stamp of cheerfulness and happy industry, that I was disappointed on learning that its name was 'Murderers' Bar.' "

A glance at the miners' amusements reveals that the favorites were drinking, gambling, and dancing, with certain men delegated for women's parts. Dissipation and roistering, however, were less prevalent than is sometimes represented. Horse racing, cockfights, and practical jokes were frequent. Evenings were devoted to conversation and song, some of the ballads being only less distinctive than those in the cowboy's repertory. Sundays were largely given over to frolic (and washing and baking), but many of the miners set an example of rectitude with debating societies or even religious services. The theater also came to the mines. There was a regular circuit from Rabbit Creek to Mariposa, played by such celebrities as Lotta Crabtree, Lola Montez, Katherine Sinclair, and Edwin Booth.

Women in a Man's World

Men *alone* were the personnel in the sea otter traffic, the hide trade, and the coming of the trappers to California. That Thomas O. Larkin met his wife on one of the hide ships was a rare exception. Men also were a majority in the covered wagon companies, but there were families, and women such as Tamsen Donner and Margaret Reed provided actual basis for the heroic statue of the Pioneer Woman which symbolizes this migration.

The masculine imbalance intensified with the arrival of Stevenson's regiment and the other military increments. Then came the forty-niners, in many companies completely comprised of men and boys. In the mining camps, too, the rarity of women is recorded in the kerchief insignia for square dance partners, the excitement stirred by news of "a woman in camp," and the homesickness mentioned in so many letters for home cooking, clean clothes, mother, wife, or sweetheart, and usually in that order.

Here too there were notable women participants—Mother Bennett and Mrs. Brier in the Death Valley contingent, Sarah Royce with her brood on the trail and at Grass Valley, and Dame Shirley, the acutely observant correspondent from Rich Bar.

Few though they were, these women lit up the pages. Without them the historical fictionists would have been hard pressed for the makings of a plot.

The Urban Forty-Niner

The effects of the gold rush spread far beyond the mining camps. As on most mining frontiers, many who came to prospect never washed a pan of gravel, others experimented only briefly in the diggings before turning to farming, merchandising, transportation, and other familiar work. Some were not physically equal to the hard life in the mines; many became disgusted with their luck and gave up. Enough miners were deserting the diggings to afford William Harlan a profitable business buying their implements for a song and reselling them to greenhorns at California prices. Some of these disappointed ones returned to the States, but vast numbers remained in the West, the majority in California and particularly in San Francisco. The urban forty-niner developed as great a significance as his red-shirted brother of the placers.

When gold was discovered, San Francisco was a village boasting two hotels, two nearly completed wharves, and 812 persons. Early in the summer of 1848 the population shrank almost to zero; everyone had gone to the mines, and the town was dead. It revived rapidly under the impetus of hundreds of thousands of dollars in gold pouring in from the diggings. The miners wanted supplies, and San Franciscans assumed the twin responsibilities of providing goods and an outlet for the miners' gold. Although business flourished during the last months of 1848, the next year saw the real boom with 40,000 Argonauts avalanching upon the town.

No amount of stretching and crowding would make facilities planned for 800 accommodate the sudden throng. Hotels and lodging houses put 10 or 20 men in a room and charged exorbitant prices. Rents skyrocketed to $40,000 a year for the El Dorado gambling saloon tent and $3,000 a month for a small store. Other prices jumped correspondingly. A meal cost $3 or more, drinks 25¢ and 50¢, and coppers and small coins were virtually unknown. Wages went up in proportion. Unskilled labor commanded $10 to $12 a day.

Excitement charged the atmosphere. Everyone was in a hurry. Loans were for a month rather than a year. An abnormal fraction of the population was in the streets or the gambling saloons, adding to the bustle. Gambling itself was rapid-fire, for the tables were crowded and others were anxious to make their bets. The regal splendor of the fifties was not yet attained, but plate glass mirrors, prism chandeliers, ornate bars, and lascivious paintings had already arrived.

Whereas San Francisco had at least a municipal existence prior to the gold rush, several other communities owed their origin to it. Grass Valley, Auburn, Placerville, Columbia, and Sonora were born and flourished mightily but then with the mining eclipse went into as sudden a decline. Sacramento and Stockton also came suddenly into existence on the flood of gold but demonstrated commercial, industrial, and political reasons for continued existence after the passing of the mining era.

The rise of San Francisco and these satellite cities was only one consequence of the gold rush. Others included the drastic alteration of the price structure in California and to a lesser extent in the world at large. Commerce, agriculture, lumbering, and countless other pursuits were greatly stimulated in northern California and up and down the Pacific coast. New arguments and incentives were created for transportation development. California's population multiplied many times over. Additional foreign strains intensified its cosmopolitan character, while the predominance of Argonauts from the States greatly accelerated the change from Mexican to American society. The worldwide interest in California, so abruptly created, reduced the intellectual as well as the physical isolation of the province. Most important, perhaps, were the psychological consequences, the unrestrained and masculine society of gold rush California, the willingness to believe that the fabulous could be realized, and a fortification of the historical heritage as a unifying factor for all Californians. Gold, without question, exerted a powerful influence on the state's history.

CHAPTER 10

LOMBARD, NORTH POINT and GREENWICH DOCKS,
SAN FRANCISCO.
SHIPS GREAT REPUBLIC, HURRICANE AND ZENOBIA DISCHARGING.

San Francisco Waterfront

The Bancroft Library

On the evening of Saturday, the 13th of August, 1859; the superb steamship Golden Gate; *gay with crowds of passengers, and lighting the sea for miles around with the glare of her signal lights of red, green, and white, and brilliant with lighted saloons and staterooms; bound up from the Isthmus of Panama, neared the entrance to San Francisco, the centre of a world-wide commerce.*

Richard Henry Dana
"Twenty-Four Years After"

Mushrooming Economy

Most of the Argonauts came to make their fortune and then return to civilization in the States, Europe, Sonora, or wherever they had come from. Many held to that purpose, but a larger number became Californians. By the end of 1849 population reached 100,000, in 1852 the state counted 224,435, and in 1860 the official census showed 380,015. This sudden increase in a province that for generations had lain practically dormant produced far-reaching change. The state shortly acquired a new political framework, a new social structure, and a new economy.

The Persistence of Mining

Most gold rushes are short-lived, but in California for years gold mining continued to be fundamental to the economy. As late as 1863 mining employed more of the state's workers than any other pursuit. Production also held up. The peak came early in the fifties followed by a gradual tapering off. In the first decade and a half, however, the average annual output was $50 million. After 1865 production levelled off at about one third of this amount. Although in recent years other minerals, particularly petroleum, have far overshadowed gold, to the end of the century gold was the unchallenged leader in the state's mining industry.

Techniques improved. The prospector held to the pan, but the cradle gave way to the long tom and in turn to the sluice, the essential apparatus in gold washing.

The hydraulic method was the easiest way to deliver paydirt to the sluice. With a nozzled canvas hose or iron pipe delivering 50 or more feet of water pressure, half a dozen men could wash more dirt than hundreds wielding pick and shovel. The method was so cheap that it could be used profitably on dirt yielding as little as one cent to the cubic foot, which would have been considerably beneath the attention of the nonhydraulic miners. Popularity of hydraulic mining is revealed by statistics of 1854 which indicate 4,493 miles of ditches or flumes delivering water for mining operations. Hydraulickers devastated the landscape and the debris they set in motion cumulatively did great damage to agriculture and navigation and created enormous flooding.

The miners were eager to work back to the source of gold. An early theory was that some kind of volcanic eruption had spewed gold over the diggings. Logic better supported the vein theory, with the possibility of a mother vein or lode. Late in 1849 a lode in quartz was being worked on Frémont's Mariposa grant.

Gold-bearing rock had to be quarried, brought to the surface, and crushed. Mexican and Chilean mule-powered arrastras were the first reliance, later supplanted by the stamp, a battery of pile drivers with straight fall or improved by a twirling motion. The final step was a mercury-assisted separation of the gold from the crushed rock. By 1863 one third and by 1870 more than half of the gold mined was from quartz.

California provided much of the mercury. The New Almaden mine near San Jose had been opened in the Mexican period and named after the famous quicksilver mine in southwestern Spain. Under the impetus of increased demand and price the working of this mine was boosted until production reached 220,000 pounds a month. Both the mining and the reduction of the ore were fairly simple processes. The ore occurred in large and irregular masses rather than in veins. For reduction it was placed in a furnace. When heated

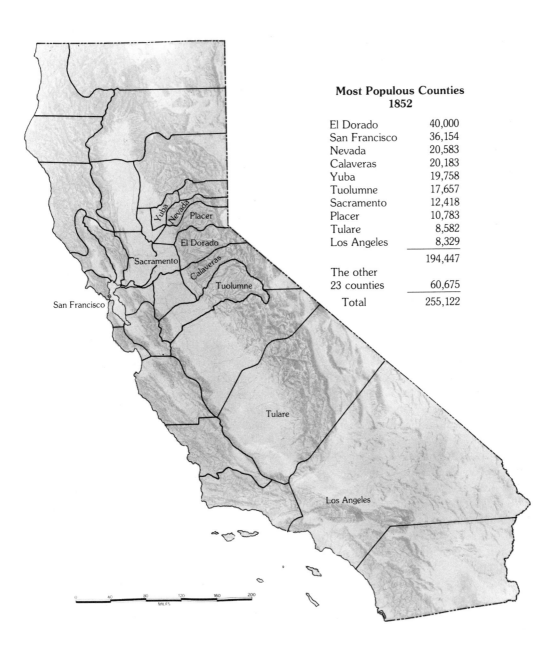

Most Populous Counties
1852

El Dorado	40,000
San Francisco	36,154
Nevada	20,583
Calaveras	20,183
Yuba	19,758
Tuolumne	17,657
Sacramento	12,418
Placer	10,783
Tulare	8,582
Los Angeles	8,329
	194,447
The other 23 counties	60,675
Total	255,122

Most Populous Counties, 1852

the mercury was driven off in gaseous form and recovered by passing through a series of condensing chambers opening into each other alternately at the top and bottom.

Trade and Freighting

Of the three quarters of a billion dollars' worth of gold, a conservative estimate of what was produced in California up to 1865, an indeterminate fraction was carried out of the state by the miners returning eastward. A much larger quantity changed hands at least once in California. The effects of this tremendous increase in purchasing power and of the accompanying spurt in the number of customers challenge the imagination. To cater to the miners' wants, stores sprang up throughout the diggings.

At the outset many stores stocked only the basic commodities, salt pork and beef, flour, and whiskey. As quickly as circumstances permitted, however, the list was extended. The storekeepers, it was generally agreed, were more likely to profit than the diggers of gold. Perhaps on that account there was a tendency to look down upon them as a class. Although John Bidwell, Charles M. Weber, Alonzo Delano, and certain other storekeepers were highly respected, the majority were not held in such high esteem. In fact, the Yankee merchant was reckoned not much above the professional gambler, another familiar figure in the diggings.

Closely associated with the storekeepers were the freighters who replenished their stocks. By wagon or pack train over abominable roads and the roughest of trails they moved a varied cargo from Sacramento and Stockton to the most remote mining camps. They took the first consignments of gold away from the diggings and by easy transition became the pioneers in mail, express, and banking services. Although superseded by railroads and trucks, the freighters were less transitory than those who made their living by hunting game for the miners or by driving up cattle and sheep to be butchered at the diggings.

San Francisco and Sacramento soon boasted wholesale and retail merchants who became the commercial czars of California. The fortunes, for instance, of Stanford, Huntington, Hopkins, and Crocker, the "Big Four" of Central Pacific fame, were laid on foundations of this sort of commerce. The stories of Collis P. Huntington's warehouse, his dealings with ship captains, and his corner on shovels amply illustrate the complexities, the uncertainties, and the ethics of this first big business in California.

At first there was no such thing as ordering goods from the East; merchants merely dealt in whatever commodities New England, New York, or foreign shippers had seen fit to send to San Francisco. The result was an unpredictable schedule of prices. Of some goods there was an oversupply, hence the San Francisco sidewalks "paved" with tierces of tobacco, sacks of flour, and in another instance with cook stoves. In contrast, a dearth of some other commodity resulted in a price that seemed exorbitant even to Californians. A frequent comment was that the spread between wholesale and retail prices was out of all proportion.

Besides the round-the-Horn shipments the movement of goods to gold rush California involved many other avenues. Wagon trains on the overland trails brought household goods, tools, and implements that were important in the aggregate. These trains and more formal drives brought horses, cattle, and sheep. Ships from Puget Sound and the Columbia delivered lumber, while the agricultural settlements in the Willamette Valley sent eggs, garden produce, and grain. Dried beef—

Freighter on the Placerville-Carson Route   *Vischer's Miscellaneous Views, 1861*

charqui or jerky—came from Chile, and diversified cargoes were sent from Hawaii and the Orient.

In 1849 California was producing few of the items required by her new population. It is said that San Francisco's soiled linen was sometimes sent to Hawaii or China for laundering. Soon, however, local producers and enterprisers came to the rescue. Existing branches of agriculture and industry were stimulated, and new branches were started to supply the gold seekers. In many instances it was found that a much broader market existed and could be developed.

Cattle and Sheep

Cattle raising was the branch of agriculture that could most readily be expanded to meet the new opportunity. Cattle which had found

no market at $5 and $6 a head brought as much as $500 at the mining camps. The price did not remain long at this fantastic figure, but in the fifties beeves often brought from $50 to $100 a head. With its Mexican ranchos California was well grounded in the cattle business. Additional herds were driven in from Texas and the Midwest, several hundred head in 1850 and as many as 40,000 a year in the middle fifties. It was a "long drive" predating the more famous one from Texas to the northern plains, and as beef cattle the California breed was somewhat improved.

Southern California rancheros suddenly became prosperous, though the easily acquired wealth was in most instances as rapidly dissipated. In the San Joaquin Valley Henry Miller began to build up the more enduring Miller and Lux ranches and fortune. From less than 300,000 head of cattle in the state in

135

1848 there was an increase to 3 million head in 1860. In the great drought of 1863–64 cattle died by the tens of thousands. The distress of the cattlemen was aggravated by the extremely high interest rates. In 1870 the official inventory showed only 630,000 head of cattle in the state.

At the missions sheep had been almost as numerous as cattle but after secularization they fell into disfavor and in 1849 there were less than 20,000 in the state. With the miners providing a market for mutton the industry revived. There were drives from Chihuahua, from New Mexico by way of the Old Spanish Trail, and from the American Midwest by way of the Salt Lake–Los Angeles route, with Kit Carson, Wilson Flint, and the Bixbys as some of the better-known participants. The peak years were 1853 and 1856 when 135,000 head and 200,000 head, respectively, were brought in. By 1860 the state had 1 million sheep yielding, however, only 2 million pounds of wool. Importation of blooded stock brought an improvement, and by 1870 the number had increased to 2.75 million and the wool clip to 11 million pounds.

A Bonanza in Wheat

Another mission activity which revived and expanded in the golden era was cultivation of small grains. After secularization the rancheros, less abundantly supplied with laborers than the friars had been, allowed grain cultivation to lapse. Sutter was sowing large fields of wheat in the Sacramento Valley on the eve of the gold discovery but he also found the labor supply inadequate. The farming of the fifties was more directly an outgrowth of Sutter's agriculture than of the earlier cultivation at the southern California missions. The local market created by the hungry gold diggers led to a "back-to-the-farm" movement. The low-

er San Joaquin and Sacramento valleys and northern California provided the lands first brought under cultivation, though subsequently the San Joaquin Valley became the center of California's wheat belt.

California soil and climate proved most congenial for wheat production. The yield per acre surpassed the midwestern average, and the dry summers prolonged the harvest season and made the wheat very dry and hard. It was unimpaired by shipment to distant markets, and flour milled from it was preferred in tropical markets. Another advantage was that ships which had been sailing from San Francisco in ballast could now take cargoes of wheat. In the late sixties the business boomed, with the acreage trebling within half a dozen years. In 1850 wheat production was estimated at 17,000 bushels. It rose to 5.9 million bushels in 1860, 16 million in 1870, and 40 million in 1890.

The characteristics of this farming were large holdings, mining of the soil with no rotation of crops, a high degree of mechanization, emphasis on export around the Horn to Liverpool, and speculative returns because of the uncontrolled variables in the cost of seed, sacks, and shipping and in price on the Liverpool market.

California's wheat frontier parallels the better publicized prairie farming frontier in the belt from Texas to Saskatchewan. It had a character of its own in more absentee ownership and in several other features. In a procession of new machinery from the Stockton gangplow to giant steam-powered combines, it ran a jump or two ahead of the midcontinent wheat belt. Rail rates meant little to the Californians, and elevator middlemen were not in the picture. The California wheat was moved in the sack from farm to flatcar or barge to the hold of the ocean transports.

The best-known entrepreneurs were Dr. Hugh J. Glenn, who had the equivalent of an old California rancho in cultivation along the Sacramento, some 55,000 acres, and Isaac Friedlander, who, besides being a major grower, was the leading ship charterer, seed and sack dealer, and handler of selling at Liverpool. Many farmers were convinced that their hard work was piling up profits primarily for Friedlander, the Grain King.

In 1873–74, through the State Grange which then had 104 locals, the disgruntled farmers tried to band together in a loose-knit cooperative pledged to ship and sell through a broker of their own. They also pledged to buy their sacks through this agent, and, because the prospects appeared good for higher prices later in the season, they agreed to hold off selling in order to take advantage of that rise.

Everything went wrong. More ships were chartered than the cooperating farmers were ready to fill, and Friedlander picked them up at reduced rates. The sack monopolists cut prices and spoiled that investment. The market did not rise and the returns were disappointing. The cooperative dissolved and Friedlander resumed his dominant position. As Rodman Paul wrote, the eulogist at Friedlander's funeral in 1878 was not far wrong when he said, "He gathered the grain crops of California in the hollow of his hand."

Wheat growing continued to expand, reaching its peak in the early nineties. It required many teams of horses or mules at planting time and harvest time. Labor demands also were seasonal and held down by the mechanization. This was a spectacular branch of agriculture, and the number of ships filled in a year rose as high as 500.

Diversity of Crops

California's suitability for a wide variety of other crops was thoroughly proven in the fifties and sixties. In 1854 B. D. Wilson wrote to his brother in Mississippi that Los Angeles County produced "every species of grain and fruits in the greatest abundance." To prove his point he listed the different fruits growing on a farm he had just purchased: grapes, oranges, pears, apricots, peaches, apples, almonds, English walnuts, cherries, figs, olives, quinces, and plums, all growing so luxuriantly that he did not know which grew best.

In his *Resources of California* a few years later John S. Hittell catalogued the state's subordinate agricultural products—oats, maize, hay, potatoes, kitchen vegetables in great variety, berries of all sorts, and fruits of the several kinds listed above. The potatoes he described as half again as large as those in the States, and he vouched for a 10-pound carrot, a 26-pound turnip, a 53-pound cabbage, a 118-pound beet, and a 260-pound squash. At the time of his writing in 1863 half the state's 2,500 orange trees were in the grove of William Wolfskill at Los Angeles.

Much of this horticulture was carried over from the mission period, but Johnny Appleseeds brought in additional stock and new varieties from the East. In California fruit trees were more precocious, practically every vegetable was in season twice as long as in the East, and San Francisco had a year-round supply of strawberries from the Santa Clara Valley. In the fifties and sixties, however, all these fruits and vegetables were limited to the California market. Consequently, they did not rival the big four in the state's agriculture—beef cattle, sheep, wheat, and barley.

Through its associated industry of wine making, grape culture offered better possibilities. As a heritage from the Franciscans, California possessed a number of plantings of "mission grapes," hardy vines and good bearers though not extraordinary in quality. This was the stock on which the earliest commercial vintners depended, notably Luis Vignes of Los Angeles. By 1842 he was doing a thriving business in supplying northern California and the coastal trade with wine and brandy.

After the gold rush created an enlarged market, others entered the business. It was profitable because vines could be brought into production more rapidly than fruit trees. There was good demand for table grapes, and the derivatives, wine and brandy, had the great advantages of being compact and relatively imperishable. The assessment records indicate 1 million bearing vines by 1855, 8 million by 1860, and nearly 28 million by 1870. In 1870 production approached 2 million gallons of wine. One fourth of the total, mostly in sweet wines, was from Los Angeles County; a sixth, mostly in dry wines, came from Sonoma County.

Meanwhile, hopes rose that the ideal industry for California would be silk raising. In 1864 the legislature offered a bounty of $250 for every planting of 500 two-year-old mulberry trees and $300 for every 100,000 salable cocoons. Under this impetus 10 million trees were set out by 1869. The leading enthusiast was Louis Prévost. He organized the California Silk Center Association, which bought 8,500 acres in the Jurupa district (later to be called Riverside) and went in for sericulture on a grand scale. Predictions were freely made that silk would become the state's most valuable product. Silkworm eggs sold for a time at $10 an ounce, and a few men profited greatly. When Prévost died and the legislature withdrew the bounty offer, agriculturists turned unanimously from this glamorous fad.

Cotton was also in style for a brief season. In Civil War days William Workman and others made a few plantings. In 1876 Matthew Keller planted 60 acres in a field just north of what is now the University of Southern California campus. He got a good crop but found no satisfactory market, the experience of other cotton planters. The ambitiousness of their plans, however, was reflected in the formation of the California Cotton Growers and Manufacturers Association, which had 10,000 acres at Bakersfield and a colony of cotton pickers imported from the South. These blacks, however, preferred other work, and, since white labor was expensive and marketing difficult, California cotton growing was postponed for another half century.

Notwithstanding these failures California agriculture was shifting from the pastoral economy of the ranchos to a stress on cultivation of the soil. The droughts of the early sixties dealt a body blow to the cattle industry and the positive success with grain and grapes confirmed the shift. By 1872 the trend had advanced to the point where there was overpowering sentiment in favor of the "no-fence law," an act which placed the responsibility for the restraint of livestock upon their owners rather than upon the planters, who formerly had to fence other people's stock out of their fruit groves, vineyards, and grain fields. B. D. Wilson's experience was characteristic. In the fifties he had run thousands of head of cattle and sheep, but in 1873 he considered a herd of 100 cattle overlarge. The new agriculture included cattle and sheep but centered on grain and grapes and other fruits.

Expanding Industry

Hand in hand with the development in mining, commerce, and agriculture, manufacturing began to flourish in the northern towns. The discovery of gold had come about as a by-product of lumbering sponsored by Sutter. The gold rush, though it wrought havoc with Sutter's affairs, returned the compliment to lumbering by creating a great demand for sawmill products. The placer miners needed quantities of planks for their sluices, flumes, and wing dams. A special 12-foot plank, 2-

inches thick, 14 inches at one end and 18 at the other, was turned out for sluice bottoms so that the sections could be fitted together without nails. Quartz miners also required timbers and planks for bracings in their shafts and tunnels. Lumber also was the favored material for building purposes, at least after San Francisco passed the canvas and paper stage. Railroad construction provided another important market, and, since barbed wire had not yet appeared on the scene, fencing called for many rails and planks as well as posts.

Mendocino and Humboldt counties had the state's largest mills and in 1860 produced the most lumber, 35 and 30 million feet respectively. Most of it was redwood, sawed from logs averaging 4½ feet in diameter. Schooners of from 150 to 300 tons transported the lumber to San Francisco. Santa Cruz County was next with 10 million feet a year, all redwood, much of it shipped to southern California. Santa Cruz lumber was distinguished also by the fact that much of it was split rather than sawed. For a skilled workman, redwood splits straight and smooth; consequently this technique was efficient for getting out fence posts, rails, rough planks, joists, beams, and shingles. More than one Argonaut found that he could make his pile more quickly and surely by splitting shingles in the Santa Cruz Mountains than by wielding pick and shovel in the diggings. Other sawmills, many of which were portable, operated in the Sierra forests turning out lumber for the miners.

The forty-niners provided an excellent market for flour. The first mills in the state were largely engaged in remilling spoiled imported flour, but as wheat raising boomed, flour milling followed suit. The flinty character of the California wheat made the local flour excellent for shipment even through the tropics, and, when the Crimean War and the Civil War handicapped older areas of flour production, the California industry was greatly stimulated. In the late sixties California flour was exported not only to the mining camps throughout the

Logging Team in the Redwoods 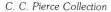 *C. C. Pierce Collection*

Rocky Mountain West but also to Japan and China, to the British Isles, and to continental Europe. By the end of the decade the state had over 200 mills, capable of milling as much as 1,000 barrels a day.

Wagon and carriage making had even wider distribution. As a Spanish and Mexican province California had gotten along without, but with the coming of the Americans the wheeled-vehicle complex was introduced. The first wagon shops were crude. Soon, however, wagon and carriage making was as universal as the automobile repair shop of later date. The most famous names connected with the business were those of John Studebaker of Placerville, of subsequent fame as an Indiana manufacturer of wagons and automobiles; George P. Kimball of Oakland, who built a quarter-million-dollar factory in 1868; and Phineas Banning of Wilmington, whose specialty was coaches of the Concord type.

The abundant supply of cowhides, coupled with the great demand for heavy boots in the mines, harness and pack saddles in the freighting business, thoroughbraces for the stages, and belting in all sorts of machine operations suggested the erection of tanneries and leather-working establishments. The first large tanneries were on the San Lorenzo River in Santa Cruz County. San Francisco soon took first place and tanneries appeared at Sacramento, Benicia, and several other northern towns. The output was mostly heavy leather goods until Civil War days when a boost was given to shoe manufacturing. In spite of relatively high wages this industry flourished until the hard times in the nineties.

Quartz mining in California, silver mining in Nevada, and excavation and tunneling for railroad construction created a heavy demand for explosives. When the Civil War made the continued importation of powder both dangerous and expensive, its manufacture was begun. The California Powder Works put up a $150,000 plant on the San Lorenzo River.

The Pacific Powder Works in Marin County was even larger. In 1868 these two mills manufactured a million kegs of blasting powder. Contra Costa County boasted half a dozen smaller plants.

Textile mills were introduced at about the same time and under similar provocation. Those designed for cotton, such as the one William H. Rector built at Oakland in 1864, did not succeed. Manufacture of grain sacks out of jute from the Orient was temporarily more profitable, but the largest and most thriving mills were those turning out woolens. Of these the best known was the Mission Woolen Mills of San Francisco. Other mills were at Marysville, Sacramento, and Santa Rosa.

Other industries of some importance included sugar refining and cigar making. The raw cane sugar came from the islands of the Pacific and from China, though a number of unsuccessful efforts were made to promote sugar cane cultivation in southern California. William T. Coleman and Claus Spreckels were the leading refiners. San Francisco was also the cigar making center with predominantly Chinese labor.

Relying on iron brought it in at low cost as ballast on wheat ships, iron working rose in importance. Farming and lumbering as well as mining and railroading in California and the adjacent West made a large market for machinery of many kinds. The Union, Neptune, and Vulcan Iron Works of San Francisco were the earliest large plants. Besides smaller products they turned out locomotives and iron riverboats.

Banking

Prior to 1848 California had only rudimentary banking as carried on by the government account keepers, the prefects of the missions, the hide and tallow traders, who extended

Locomotive Calistoga Issuing from the
Vulcan Iron Works

Vischer's Miscellaneous Views, 1863

credits, and the Army and Navy quartermasters in the period of the conquest. As gold came into production facilities for storing and transmitting it were called for, and as commerce and industry sprang up some means of handling financial transactions was required.

Merchants and saloonkeepers provided the first banking service, that of safekeeping the miners' sacks of gold. Then by easy transition they added buying and selling of gold, arranging for its transmission to the East, and making loans. The earliest banking was simply a side line to other businesses; soon, however, it became a business in itself. A number of Californians entered it, and eastern firms such as Adams and Company, Palmer, Cook and Company, and Page, Bacon and Company opened branches in the state.

The first banking was largely in the hands of inexperienced men and was entirely unregulated by the state. Remoteness from the financial centers of the world made the matter of remittance and exchange difficult and expensive. Nor were the unsettled conditions in California conducive to conservative banking practices. In consequence the early record is full of irregularities. For half a decade most banks prospered; interest rates were from 2 to 5 percent a month, and the miners did not object to a substantial charge on drafts on eastern banks.

In 1855, however, a panic gripped San Francisco which several banks could not weather. Most spectacular was the closing of Page, Bacon and Company. News of the failure of its St. Louis branch precipitated a run in San Francisco. For a week the bank met every demand but on February 23 was forced to close its doors. Other banks were affected, notably Adams and Company, whose crash

141

was rendered all the more disquieting by reason of the eleventh-hour transfer of its remaining assets to Palmer, Cook and Company. Not until the sixties did California banking fully recover from the shock of 1855. Its recovery was greatly assisted by the upsurge of local industry and agriculture and by the outpourings of the Nevada silver mines.

These early banks helped much less than might have been expected in the provision of a circulating medium of exchange. Out-of-state exchange was managed fairly well, though it was so expensive that California exporters often resorted to conversion of their receipts into commodities for shipment to San Francisco. Locally, the banks were not authorized to issue bank notes, and Californians had such an addiction to gold that it is probable such paper money would not have circulated anyway. Throughout '48 and '49 most payments were in gold dust, weighed or guessed at, a pinch passing for a dollar. Then slugs of approximately three ounces passed for $50. Even after a government mint was established in San Francisco in 1854 Mexican silver coins remained in use. In the sixties, when the rest of the nation was doing business chiefly in greenbacks, California scorned them and stuck to hard money, the favorite being the double eagle, the $20 gold piece.

The Comstock

California's financial history was profoundly affected by the opening of the silver mines of Washoe, now called Nevada. In the late fifties prospectors began to turn up mineral wealth all over the mountainous West. There were strikes in Colorado, Oregon, Idaho, along the Fraser, in Arizona and Nevada, and eventually in Alaska and the Klondike. In many of these rushes Californians predominated, particularly in Nevada and its Comstock Lode.

The detailed story of the discovery, the working of the mines, the experiments in milling, the problems of drainage, cooling, and ventilation, and life in Virginia City belongs to Nevada history. The discovery late in 1859 produced an eastward rush from California. These former gold seekers soon found that silver mining was very different, requiring elaborate machinery and heavy investment. Within a year 37 companies were organized with stock issue in excess of $30 million, and 49 more companies appeared in 1861, though not all had footage on the Comstock Lode. From the outset San Francisco was the exchange for the Nevada companies.

Under the most favorable circumstances Comstock shares would have fluctuated wildly as the vein widened or narrowed, offering bonanza or borrasca, or because of floods, cave-ins, and fires.

For four years the strategically located companies paid well. Managers and investors put millions into excavation, timbering, hoists, and pumps, and hundreds of thousands into a mill. Then in 1864 several mines ran into borrasca and only Gould & Curry produced satisfactorily. Most of the mines had to levy stock assessments and mill owners had to borrow until quantity production returned.

William Ralston's Bank of California was the principal lender and it soon foreclosed on most of the mills. With D. O. Mills and a couple of other bank officers Ralston organized as a separate venture the Union Mill and Mining Company to operate these mills. He could then insist that the richest ore be delivered to the Union mills. This monopoly would pay off most handsomely if there was another bonanza.

Adolph Sutro, a young mill owner who was subsequently to be mayor of San Francisco and a generous benefactor of that city, proposed a tunnel tapping the lode at about the 2,000-foot level which would ventilate the mines, carry off excess water by gravity flow, and correspondingly save on ore-hoisting expense. Sound from an engineering standpoint, Sutro's tunnel would have had the side effect of making the bank's mills and hoisting machinery obsolete. The bank refused to cooperate and for more than a decade blocked the tunnel.

A fire in the Yellowjacket mine enabled Sutro to win support from the miners. Two members of the bank ring, John P. Jones and Alvinza Hayward, found new ore bodies in the Crown Point and organized their own mill company. Two other mining men, John W. Mackay and James Fair, and two San Francisco saloonkeepers, James C. Flood and William S. O'Brien, acquired four mines. A small bonanza on one of them permitted capture of two well placed but nonproducing mines, the Virginia and the California. A stock assessment on these mines raised money for exploration and in March, 1873, Fair uncovered a rich vein 54 feet wide. Dan DeQuille, the most reputable mining reporter in Nevada, appraised the ore in sight at $116,748,000. The director of the mint said $300 million.

With this mine pouring out unprecedented treasure, the Crown Point doing well, and English money available for Sutro's tunnel, Virginia City prospered as never before. Speculation outran the actual production, but the market, mainly on margin, was vulnerable. A rumor that the vein was pinching out dropped the market value of Consolidated Virginia and California $24 million within a week.

The market recovered with another round of margin purchasing only to crash again in the summer of 1875. This time the book loss was over $60 million and this time the Bank of California went down in the crash.

Several members of the bank ring salvaged their personal fortunes. Ralston did not. Ousted as cashier, he walked to North Beach for his customary swim and, by accident or design, drowned. An audit of his books showed unsecured liabilities in excess of $4.5 million. The temptation is to condemn Ralston as a predatory economic royalist. He had taken the lead, however, in many enterprises of great civic importance. The Palace Hotel, his estate at Belmont, and the Bank of California had been his principal monuments, but steamship lines, the Spring Valley Water Company, the Lone Mountain Cemetery, the University of California, and so many other projects had benefited from his promotion that a biographer chose the title "The Man Who Built San Francisco."

On the ruins of Ralston's bank the bonanza kings erected the Nevada Bank of San Francisco and assembled a Comstock monopoly more complete than its predecessor's. In another few years, however, the bonanza was exhausted, and Virginia City soon dwindled to ghostlike proportions. California fortunes based on the Comstock, such as those of Mackay, Fair, Flood, O'Brien, Sharon, Mills, Jones, Sutro, and Hearst, were prominent in subsequent chapters of the nation's and particularly of California's history. To San Franciscans, however, the Comstock is above all memorable for the two decades of great excitement and the glorious opportunity for speculative investment that it afforded. In popular fancy it dwarfed such enterprises as wheat ranching, flour milling, carriage making, and lumbering.

CHAPTER 11

Monterey in 1849

Joseph Revere, A Tour of Duty

What we have here to do is to understand what forces worked for and against order in this community of irresponsible strangers.

Josiah Royce
California

Politics and Land Titles

State Government in Operation

California's admission to statehood is widely heralded and celebrated. It is not so well known that the impatient Californians had not waited for formal admission to start operating their state government. After approval of the constitution at the election in November, 1849, the first legislature assembled in December, and on the twentieth of that month Peter H. Burnett was sworn in as the first civil governor. The wheels of government creaked not so much because they were new as because money raising was practically impossible so long as ultimate recognition of the state government was uncertain. In this intermediate stage, of course, California had no representation in Congress. Consequently, admission to the Union meant much to the state. It dispelled the specter of military government, regularized the state government which was already operating, seated California's senators and congressmen in Washington, and set a seal of approval upon a state constitution which was a lasting monument to the good sense and wisdom of the Californians of '49.

Although this first constitution demonstrated the political capacity of the Californians, their day-to-day citizenship was more nearly of the caliber predicted by the congressional pessimists who had hesitated to entrust state government to these gold-mad westerners. Inexperience was one obstacle to good government. A contributing factor was inattention induced by the absorbing and highly profitable nature of private enterprise. In the conduct of state government the result of this crass neglect was a record of gross abuse.

The legislature of 1849 faced a peculiar handicap in that the delay of admission left all its acts in a position of dubious legality. This first legislature enacted a code of laws and chose the first United States senators, but it is better known as the "Legislature of a Thousand Drinks" in remembrance of Senator Thomas J. Green's constant advocacy of adjournment for liquid refreshment. The legislature of 1851, it pleased a San Francisco journalist to observe, was "an infamous, ignorant, drunken, rowdy, perjured and traitorous body of men."

In the Mexican period the capital had been shifted from Monterey to San Diego, Santa Barbara, or Los Angeles at the caprice of the governor. As the American period began, one of the major issues was where to bring the capital to rest. The military governors had stationed themselves at Monterey. There likewise the constitutional convention assembled, but the sudden importance of the mining area seemed to dictate removal to some point nearer the center of population. Local aspirations influenced the decision. For the first legislative session San Jose was designated. The question then arose whether to continue there, return to Monterey, go to New York of the Pacific, a budding metropolis on Carquinez Straits, or cross the straits to a site tendered by Mariano Guadalupe Vallejo. By offering 156 acres of land and a contribution of $370,000 to the building fund, Vallejo prevailed.

In 1852, however, when the legislature convened at Vallejo, it found none of the promised conveniences and shortly took ship for Sacramento. The merchants of that town having thoughtfully chartered a riverboat for the purpose, the legislature moved, lock, stock, and gavel. The next year it tried Benicia but in 1854 returned permanently to Sacramento. As long as gold mining dominated the economy this site was convenient, but with the shift of population to southern California the argument lost weight. Certainly the removal from Monterey meant the abandonment of a distinctive geographical environment, rich in historical associations, for one with climatic handicaps reminiscent of the midwestern states.

Gwin versus Broderick

Throughout the fifties California was heavily Democratic. The governorship fell only once to the opposition, and the United States Senate seats, regarded as much higher political prizes, were reserved exclusively for Democrats. Within the party, however, a bitter rivalry developed. Leadership was in the hands of two astute politicians, each of whom had come to California with a determination to dominate the politics of this new commonwealth. The bitterness of their spirited contest fortunately has seldom been surpassed in the subsequent political experience of the state.

First on the scene was William M. Gwin of Tennessee and Mississippi, well-educated, magnetic, a veteran of Jacksonian politics, and a protégé of the Polk regime. His leadership was particularly acceptable to those from the South and his faction was often spoken of as the Chivalry or Chiv Democrats. At the convention at Monterey, Gwin had impressed as a most capable and experienced political leader. He encountered little opposition in his candidacy for the first full-term seat in the United States Senate, Frémont being chosen for the other place.

David C. Broderick, who was to enter the lists against Gwin, had brief experience in Tammany-Hall politicking in New York City. Within a few months after his arrival in San Francisco he had made himself sufficiently known to be elected to the first legislature and there had the honor of defeating a bill to forbid the entrance of free blacks. In the next legislature he unsuccessfully opposed a stringent fugitive slave law. In 1851 and 1856 he was an open critic of the illegal actions of the San Francisco vigilance committees. A likable young Irish-American, he became the leader of the anti-Chivalry faction.

Although the federal patronage was beyond his grasp, Broderick quickly built up a personal following through the state patronage, the municipal machines at San Francisco and Sacramento, and control of the party conventions. By 1854 his control of the legislature had reached the point where he thought it safe to call for the choice of a successor to Gwin in the Senate, though normally the vote would not have been taken until the following year. This proposal was narrowly defeated, but only after most bitter and abusive debate. The breach widened, and in 1856 the Know Nothings, who in California were more anti-foreign than anti-Catholic, were able to take advantage of it to elect J. Neely Johnson governor.

In 1857, when the senatorial question was finally brought to a vote, Broderick was able to dictate the terms. He got himself elected to succeed John B. Weller, whose term was to expire that year. The other place went to Gwin but only after he had agreed to place the federal patronage in Broderick's hands. Gwin gave evidence of a sincere intention of going through with his part of this hard bargain, but President James Buchanan would have nothing to do with Broderick, who had vigorously opposed his policy regarding Kansas. Colleagues in the Senate likewise failed to warm to him with the result that Broderick returned to California in 1859 very much embittered and, because of his loss of the patronage, with fewer supporters in the state than when he had left.

Broderick plunged immediately into strenuous campaigning, featuring angry tirades against Gwin and his associates. There were responses in kind, including a rebuke volunteered by Justice David S. Terry of the state supreme court, who had been a testy member of the Law and Order faction at the time of the Second San Francisco Vigilance Committee. A scathing reply prompted a friend of Terry's to challenge Broderick to a duel.

Resort to "the field of honor" was so common in this era that the framers of the constitution in 1849 felt impelled to decree in Article 11, Section 2, that any citizen participating in a duel would be excluded from voting or holding office. Dueling continued with at least a couple of hundred encounters in the 1850s. Broderick had participated in one in 1852. He scorned the challenge by Terry's friend, who happened to be a noncitizen, but immediately after the election when Terry's second delivered formal demand for "satisfaction," Broderick promptly accepted.

Friends interposed with a writ on the morning of September 12, 1859, but early the next morning the two men met at close range at a spot near Lake Merced just across the line into San Mateo County. Broderick was an expert marksman, but Terry had practiced with the chosen pistols and knew their hairtrigger set. When the signal was given, Broderick's pistol fired prematurely, with the ball striking the ground a short distance in front of him. Terry's carefully aimed shot went true to its mark.

Public opinion turned against Terry and reacted against Gwin. As a martyr Broderick gained stature. The formalized shoot-out at Lake Merced discredited dueling more effectively than had the constitutional provision. The immediate political consequence was a deeper split in Democratic ranks, and in 1860 the state's votes in the electoral college went to the Republican candidate, Abraham Lincoln.

Movements for State Division and for a Pacific Republic

Throughout the fifties a strong undercurrent of feeling ran in favor of division of the state. The southern delegates had raised the question at the constitutional convention because they thought territorial government more suited to the needs of their section, and as state government went into operation their worst expectations were realized. The southern counties were given much less than their due share of representation in the legislature, legislation was selfishly or thoughtlessly directed for the exclusive benefit of the mining counties, and taxation rested most heavily upon the nonmining cow counties. In 1852 Governor McDougal admitted that the six cow counties with a population of 6,000 paid $42,000 in property taxes and $4,000 in poll taxes, while the north with 120,000 residents paid only $21,000 and $3,500, respectively. Los Angeles newspapers protested in similar vein and fumed over the inadequate representation of the south. Even the San Francisco *Daily Alta* protested that the majority of representatives from the mining counties acted as though "no bond of connection or sympathy existed between their interests and those of the commercial cities and other sources of wealth of our infant state."

Southern Californians began to advocate state division. In 1851 a Convention to Divide the State of California was called to meet at Los Angeles. The men who summoned it asserted that state government had proved a "splendid failure" and that Los Angeles in particular was tasting the bitter fruits in political neglect, paralyzed commerce, insupportable taxation, and the complete lack of protection against Indian depredations. Separation, "friendly and peaceful but still complete," they claimed to be an imperative necessity. Other efforts followed, and in 1859 Andrés Pico secured legislative approval for the incorporation of the counties from San Luis Obispo south as the Territory of Colorado. A two-thirds vote of approval in the counties affected was assured, but, before congressional approval could be gained, the Civil War broke out and blocked the step completely.

Discriminations against southern California continued far into the twentieth century. Superficially there was annoyance with such terms as non-American, backward, rustic, disloyal, and "cow counties," and in San Francisco's appropriation of the expression "the City." Taxation for many decades bore more heavily on the south, and appropriations for highway construction, education, and many other functions favored the north. Southern Californians furthermore were consistently underrepresented in Sacramento and in Washington. Although the census of 1920 revealed that the population majority had passed to the south, reapportionment of the Assembly and House seats did not take effect until 1933, and not until 1967, by intervention of the Supreme Court, was the principle of one man, one vote applied to the state senate.

Of the remaining political issues of the fifties the one of broadest potentialities was doubtless the recurrent suggestion of a Pacific Republic. Back in the Mexican period there had been a tendency toward independence, which the Revolution of 1836 put largely into effect. Certain early Americans in the province, Lansford W. Hastings in particular, also dreamed of a western independence. The Bear Flag movement, had it been allowed to run its full course, might have led to such a result. For a decade and a half thereafter the scheme was proposed as often as California had a real or fancied grievance. When military government was prolonged and statehood denied, the idea came to the fore. During the days of the Second Vigilance Committee, when there seemed to be a possibility of federal interference, a "strong undercurrent of secession" animated the vigilantes. They made no public announcement to that effect because such a statement would have justified the interposition of national arms, but later several of the leaders admitted that it had been so. Whenever the Californians felt that they deserved better mail service, more protection against the Indians, a transcontinental railroad, or additional ports of entry, their dissatisfaction with Washington was apt to inspire visions of a Pacific Republic.

Lincoln's election raised the question in earnest. Although a free state, California had been consistently Democratic and in 1858 had endorsed Buchanan's Kansas policy. California was isolated. Its population was drawn mostly from the North, but a substantial minority was of southern extraction. Should any Californian be called upon to fight against the "land of his nativity"? Governor John B. Weller advised escape from the dilemma of choosing between the North and South by founding on the shores of the Pacific "a mighty republic, which may in the end prove the greatest of all." Other officials agreed, particularly Congressman John C. Burch, who became its leading advocate.

California's gold and her population, comprised of "the most enterprizing and energetic of the country," were counted on to secure the new nation favorable reception into the family of nations. Advantages were also foreseen in the rivalry of North and South for California's trade. On the other hand western population was small, Oregon and Utah could not be counted on for financial support, the bulk of trade had been with northern states, and the national government had been spending millions for California's benefit. Sober second thought discouraged westward secession.

The Civil War

The choice of supporting North or South remained. The legislature passed loyal resolutions, while Governor John G. Downey repudiated Lincoln's policy. "I do not believe," he said, "that an aggressive war should be waged on any section of the Confederacy, nor do I believe that this Union can be preserved by a coercive policy." Loyalty demonstrations answered pro-South appeals and men rallied to both sides. The plain truth was that California was a border state, fairly evenly divided between Union and secession sentiment.

Although a divided Democratic vote in 1860 had allowed the Republicans to carry the state for Lincoln, they had polled only three-eighths of the vote. Loyalty was not absolutely proved, and the state election of 1861 was looked upon as a significant test. The "Secesh" faction redoubled its efforts; Union sympathizers organized the Home Guard and made a systematic effort to swing the state to Leland Stanford, the Republican candidate. Helped by the firing on Fort Sumter, the death of proslavery Stephen A. Douglas, and especially the oratory of a Unitarian clergyman, Thomas Starr King, the Republican and Union ticket carried the election.

Far from being silenced the Secesh faction continued its protests in press and pulpit, poem and harangue. Sometimes the criticism was direct, with the Union Army assailed as "a whining running army, that has disgraced our flag, lowered our cause and dishonored Republican chivalry," or with Lincoln called an "unprincipled demagogue," an "illiterate backwoodsman," and a "narrow-minded bigot." At other times there was more subtle reference to "Mr. Lincoln" and "President Davis." On Thanksgiving Day, 1862, the *Visalia Equal Rights Expositor* "prayed": "O Lord we thank thee for letting the rebels wallop us at the battle of Pittsburg Landing— for letting them smite us hip and thigh, even unto the destruction of 9,600 of our good loyal soldiers, and 463 of our officers; and for giving speed to their legs through the awful swamps of Chicahominy; and, O Lord, most especially do we thank thee for the licking they gave us at Bull Run the second, and assisting our flight from that fatal field; and, O Lord, never while we live will we forget Antietam, where we had 200,000 and they only 70,000—if they, O Lord, had a happened to a had as many men as we, we'd a been a done gone in—and that friendly creek between us, the mountains that kept our men from running. . . ."

General George Wright responded to the most vicious of these attacks by excluding half a dozen papers from the mails. When this and other forms of persuasion failed to moderate the editors of the *Expositor*, soldiers without consulting their officers broke into the newspaper office, broke the press, and pitched type, paper, and ink into the street. Rev. William Scott in San Francisco had the temerity to insist before his presbytery that Jefferson Davis was no more a traitor than George Washington had been. Berated by the press and threatened by a mob, Scott was forced to resign his pulpit and leave the state, although he later returned to his pastorate.

Southern sympathizers in California made one effort to strike for the Confederacy. Under the pretext of a commercial venture to Manzanillo, they loaded a quantity of ammunition and arms on the schooner *Chapman*, intending to intercept a Pacific Mail steamer, convert it into a privateer, and ravage Union shipping in the Pacific. Federal authorities got wind of the plot, seized the *Chapman* before she passed the Golden Gate, and interned the men involved.

Since Confederate sentiment was so strong, the federal government hesitated to draw many loyal volunteers out of California. Of the 16,000 who were enlisted, a few did garrison duty along western trails but the majority remained in the state. The "California Hundred" and the "California Battalion," recruited in the East, were attached to the Second Massachusetts Cavalry and participated in more than 50 engagements. The next nearest approach to active service was when the California Column under General James Carleton marched through Yuma and Tucson to the Rio Grande to repel the Confederate invasion of New Mexico. The invaders had already fallen back, and the principal consequence of the march was that a number of deserters started a mining rush to Bill

Thomas Starr King

California State Library   Sacramento

Williams Fork. Overall, gold shipments rather than fighting men were California's greatest contribution to the northern cause.

Although California was not in the heat of the conflict, several of her citizens gained great fame for their war work. For one there was Leland Stanford, the war governor. A more popular figure was Colonel E. D. Baker, a great orator and one of the most prominent members of the California bar. Shortly before the war he had gone to Oregon where he was promptly elected to the United States Senate. His speeches did much to strengthen the Republican cause in California and to bring about the election of Stanford, and in the Senate he was one of Lincoln's most valued supporters. Upon the outbreak of hostilities he resigned his place in the Senate to serve brilliantly in the northern army and to die at Ball's Bluff.

The Reverend Myron C. Briggs of the Methodists was another favorite patriotic orator slightly less famous than his Unitarian colleague, Thomas Starr King. King had been a very popular lecturer on nature topics. He spoke for Lincoln in 1860 and for Stanford in 1861, but his greater fame rests upon his eloquent solicitation for the Sanitary Commission, the Civil War precursor of the Red Cross. Largely through his efforts California contributed $1,233,831.31, more than one fourth of the entire amount received by the Commission. For humanitarian as well as patriotic reasons, therefore, Thomas Starr King was considered second only to Junípero Serra among California heroes.

For a decade after the end of the war Californians were more alive to national issues and the problems of Reconstruction than to local politics. No arresting questions arose comparable to the contest between Gwin and Broderick or to the crucial election of 1861. The Civil War had laid to rest several of the issues of the fifties such as the questions of state division and of a western secession. Others, such as the location of the capital, had died a natural death or had gone into protracted hibernation. The problem of governmental inefficiency and corruption held over but was not considered particularly pressing. Attack upon it was delayed until the late seventies when it was caught up in a wave of more general unrest and discontent.

Challenge to Land Ownership

In the Spanish period a couple of dozen land grants had been made to individuals and each of the pueblos was assured its lands. In the Mexican period many more grants were made, including lands formerly used by some of the missions and in the last years a few grants that were as compensation. In addition there were towns both Indian and white that could enter claims.

The military governors represented, and the Treaty of Guadalupe Hidalgo more explicitly guaranteed, that titles to property that would have held good under Mexico would be honored by the United States. It turned out that there were more than 800 such claims, some for only a few acres but others in excess of 100,000 acres. These claims covered practically all the cultivated land in the state, vast expanses of land grazed by cattle and horses, plus additional land not visibly in use.

The earlier experience of Americans had not prepared them to understand the propriety of large landholdings so customary in California. For cattle raising as it had been conducted in the province and as it was later to be conducted on the Great Plains, holdings of up to 11 square leagues (50,000 acres) were not excessive. Land was abundant; several acres were required to graze a cow, and a man could own many head of cattle and still not be rich. Few Americans could comprehend. Furthermore, most of the grants were vague as to boundaries or seemed irregular in other particulars. It was argued that they should be reduced to the American norm before confirmation. Another proposal was that ratification of all these titles would leave none of California for the Americans, whereas Manifest Destiny was usually expected to confer individual advantage as well as national aggrandizement.

Before any decision was reached, the entire issue was complicated by the great gold rush. The broad holdings of the Mexican grantees now appeared fabulously and inexcusably rich. The inrushing tide of Americans increased the pressure upon California's land supply thus jeopardizing the older titles. Prejudice against all things Mexican appeared. In the Sacramento squatter riots, for instance, the mood was to eradicate all preconquest titles without any formalities. That scheme was defeated but squatterism remained a strong force.

In 1851 Congress faced up to the problem. It had the benefit of two reports, one by Captain H. W. Halleck and the other by William Carey Jones. Halleck saw imperfections in most of the Mexican titles which would give the United States an entering wedge for breaking them. Jones, after a careful examination of the California archives and consultation with Mexican and American officials in the province, reported that most of the titles were valid and that the few which were fraudulent could easily be detected. An official survey, he said, would be sufficient preliminary to confirmation of most of the grants.

Jones' proposals were echoed in the Senate by Thomas Hart Benton and Frémont. Benton stoutly opposed the creation of a special tribunal to pass on land titles. Such a step, he insisted, would be a violation of the recent treaty. He wanted confirmation made very simple with the district court's findings

final for values not exceeding $5,000. Fré-
mont proposed a commission from which
only the claimant could take an appeal.

Gwin countered with a bill to eliminate the
restrictions on appeal by the United States. He
argued plausibly that there was precedent in
the Louisiana claims and that the courts could
be counted on to decide justly, but neither he
nor anyone else answered Benton's protest
that the prolonging of litigation would spell
confiscation rather than confirmation. Clearly
the Senators were more in sympathy with the
squatters than with the grantees. They suspected many of the grants to be fraudulent
and most of them excessive in size and pic-
tured every California rancho as a prospective
gold mine. Gwin's bill was enacted by the

Senate with but a few negative votes on February 6, 1851, and by the House without
debate on March 3.

The Course of Litigation

In accordance with this act a board of three
commissioners was installed in San Francisco
in January, 1852. Every claimant of land was
required to appear before it within two years
to present proof of title. The commission is the
least denunciated feature of American land
policy in California. The several commissioners were honest and conscientious men
though totally unfamiliar with local usage and
with the Spanish and Mexican land system.
They went as far as legal-minded persons

Diseño of Rancho Parage de la Laguna de Temécula　　　　　　　*The Bancroft Library*

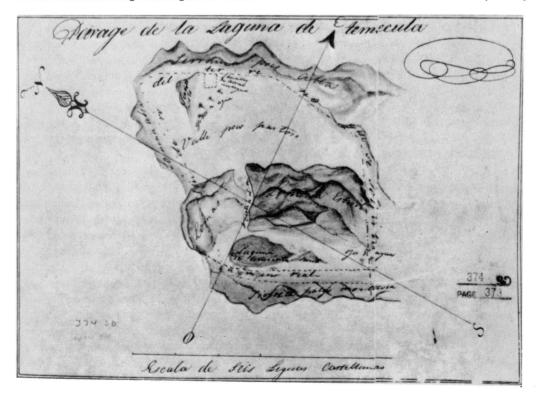

might have been expected to go in simplifying the hearings and the taking of testimony from the nonlegal-minded Californians.

Even so, it was no easy matter for many grant holders to marshal the necessary proof for presentation. Their expenses were much increased because the commission, except for a short session at Los Angeles in the fall of 1852, held all its meetings at San Francisco. The commission acted fairly expeditiously on the 813 claims presented; by the date of its final adjournment on March 1, 1856, it had confirmed 521, rejected 273, and discontinued 19. The worst feature was one prescribed by the law, that claimants had the burden of proof. Their claims were reckoned faulty or fraudulent until positive proof to the contrary was brought forward.

Some 132 claimants appealed to the district court and through introduction of new evidence 98 won reversals. The government attorneys entered 417 appeals, succeeding in only five. These attorneys also refused to content themselves with test cases. More than ninety cases were carried to the Supreme Court, in all instances with cost of transcripts charged to the claimants. A few of these cases were remanded for retrial. Even without that the process was drawn out and costly.

In the first few instances a deputy of the surveyor general made and forwarded the survey to the commissioner of the land office in Washington who, if all seemed in order, issued the final patent. By a law of 1859, however, every survey had to go to the district court and, as before, its decision was subject to appeal. That set up a second round of three times and places at which a claim could be rejected. Not surprisingly most titles remained unsettled for at least 15 years.

Many of the claimants found that the confirmation and patent of their titles gave only an empty victory. For some it was a matter of their property having been eaten up by the heavy expenses of the protracted litigation.

For others the real difficulty was that squatters refused to get off even though the land case had been decided in favor of the grant holder. The squatter spirit is in evidence in a proposal of Gwin's in 1852 to allow squatters to "homestead" 80 acres on Mexican grants, the grantees to be allowed a like number of acres from the public land. A state law four years later required grant holders to pay for improvements which squatters might have made or to sell at the appraised value of the land. This law was declared unconstitutional in 1857.

Barbecues to celebrate the defeat of Pico's Moquelumne claim in 1876 and of Berreyesa's Milpitas claim in 1877 may be considered proper manifestations of squatter feeling, but not the improper six-month imprisonment of Domingo Peralta by militant squatters in the East Bay area or the defiance of the sheriff who had come to evict them by a thousand armed squatters near Santa Clara in 1861.

Certain patterns appeared in the evaluations. Archival proof that the grant had been made was preferred but testimony of witnesses was considered.

Although Governor Pico and the diputación had been still at large and still functioning, it became a fiction agreed upon that the Mexican regime ended on the day Sloat took possession. That set up temptation to predate certain claims. The Palmer grant to Point Lobos, for example, was rejected upon proof that Pico had not been in Los Angeles on the date that showed on the grant.

Practically all the Mexican grants had been conditioned on occupancy and putting to use, usually within a year. The initial impulse was to insist on literal fulfillment, but as to Frémont's Mariposa grant the Supreme Court in 1856 brushed aside this Mexican technicality and from that time on the test of occupancy and use went by the board. Curiously that meant that a set of claims such as Frémont's, which would not have held up by Mexican standards, had the stamp of American approval and of ownership in fee simple.

A Mexican statute prohibited grants to foreigners within ten miles of the coast. The courts recognized that that law had not been enforced. The limitation to 11 square leagues was more scrupulously enforced. Hartnell had received two grants, one of 5, the other of 11 leagues. The second was trimmed down to 6. Overlapping grants and floating grants in a specified locality but not pinned down posed problems not always solvable by the surveyors.

Seeming injustices occurred. P. B. Reading's grant was invalidated on the ground that Mexico would have revoked it because of his participation in the Bear Flag Revolt. Vallejo's claim to the Soscol was rejected because Governor Micheltorena had made it in partial satisfaction of bills for supplying the provincial garrison. Serrano's claim to the Temescal would have been approved on the basis of long-term occupancy but the document shown was a temporary permit of 1819, and the court ruled that it ruined his claim to permanent title.

A multimillion dollar injustice seems to have been done to the British company which had bought the Castillero mercury mining right at New Almadén. The district court upheld that claim, and there seems to be no question that Mexican law was in support, but the surveyor placed this mine in another land grant. Under Mexican law that would have made no difference; these rancho grants did not confer mineral rights. Applying American law, the Supreme Court handed this rich mine to another claimant.

In February, 1853, a French trader, José Limantour, astounded the residents of San Francisco by filing a claim to four square leagues including the better part of that fair city. The decade-old grant had never been heard of, but the documents and testimony seemed to be in order and the land commis-

sion gave its approval to the claim in 1856.

San Francisco was immediately in turmoil, and excited lot holders rushed to pay tribute by paying handsomely for quitclaims. William Carey Jones denounced the claim as fraudulent. Henry W. Halleck insisted that the grant would be invalidated because it included practically all the pueblo lands. John S. Hittell, on the other hand, gave his opinion that the claim was valid and that the squatters' only recourse was to deal with Limantour.

Two years later in Judge Hoffman's court the fraud was laid bare. Documents, it was proved, had been antedated, signatures had been forged, witnesses had committed perjury, and finally the seals on the Limantour grants were demonstrated to be counterfeit. Limantour not only abandoned his claim but prudently fled the country.

Several other fraudulent claims were exposed though none so grandiose. A smaller number escaped detection until after the titles had been patented. The courts refused the government's request to reopen these cases, certainly a tempering of justice with practical wisdom. A patent, however, did not protect against third parties. In 1870 a litigant named Majors was awarded one third of the Rancho Refugio near Santa Cruz, though it had previously been patented to a certain Bolcof. Majors proved that the original grant had been to the Castro sisters, one of whom he had married, but that in the earlier trials the document had been presented with Bolcof's name fraudulently substituted for theirs.

Mission and Pueblo Lands

A special set of claims concerned the mission lands. In their original status under Spain and Mexico the missions had been granted no lands. The system was merely that the government refrained from granting to anyone else such lands as were needed by the neophytes.

After secularization parts of the mission tracts had been granted to individuals, both Indian and white, and these grants were handled by the land commission exactly as any other Mexican grants to individuals.

In a special category, however, fell some 17 claims based on sales by Governor Pico in 1845 and 1846. Differing from the regular colonization grants to which conditions of residence and improvements were normally attached, these sales were regarded as emergency measures partially necessitated by the crisis in provincial affairs. The validity of these titles was at least doubtful. Sales had been private rather than at auction; a communication from Mexico City, dated November, 1845, had ordered suspension of such sales; and a subsequent order giving Pico and Castro "ample powers" for the defense of the province had not arrived until after most had been consummated. Eight titles were confirmed. The rest, including those of greatest intrinsic value, at San Francisco, San Gabriel, and Santa Barbara, were finally blocked by a Supreme Court ruling.

Through its archbishop the Catholic Church entered a claim for a league of land at each mission, but, since no semblance of a grant could be produced, these titles were refused. The courts did confirm title to the actual mission sites, the cemeteries and gardens attached thereto, the Santa Inés College tract, and La Laguna at San Luis Obispo.

The Act of 1851 gave due recognition to the Spanish-Mexican practice whereby a town was entitled to four leagues of land. San Jose and Los Angeles as pueblos and Branciforte as a villa were obviously eligible; the pueblos subjoined to the presidios at San Diego, Santa Barbara, Monterey, and San Francisco could present a strong case for inclusion; and a number of Indian villages located at secularized missions were also qualified. Branciforte

and several villages of the third class, including Las Flores, San Dieguito, San Pasqual, San Juan de Argüello, and San Juan de Castro, presented no claims. The post-Mexican towns of Sonora and Sacramento presented claims which were promptly thrown out, and the commission and courts were left with eight or ten claims of respectable antiquity. Several of these had complicating factors.

Los Angeles asked for a tract four leagues square, 16 rather than four square leagues. The most astute scholar on this topic, Neal Harlow, on the basis of the Pueblo lands as administered and as understood by the residents, finds that a tract far larger than four square leagues was indicated. Early in the adjudication, however, in order to get clear title to four square leagues the city relinquished its claim to a larger area.

At San Jose the tract claimed was interspersed with parts of ranchos and other private grants, a condition that prevailed elsewhere as well. Litigation delayed confirmation of most of these titles until the sixties and the issuance of patents until the seventies or eighties.

The great contest, meanwhile, involved San Francisco. Government attorneys in fighting the claim charged that San Francisco had never been a pueblo. They insisted that Kearny had had no authority to relinquish the United States' claim to beach and water lots or even to ordinary town lots. They pointed out irregularities in the sale of lots by the town council and by a justice of the peace. Uncertainty was at its height in the late fifties when Limantour's claim was still pending, when parts of the city were being claimed as parts of other grants, and when a claim under Pico's sale of the mission lands had not yet been invalidated.

Meanwhile San Franciscans could not be sure whether their title to lots should derive from the pueblo, from Limantour or some other "ranchero," from the purchase of the mission lands, or directly from the United States. Under such circumstances the difficulty of conveying title to town lots can well be imagined.

Various attempts were made to cut the Gordian knot. In 1851 the state legislature ceded water lots to the city. In 1855, by the Van Ness Ordinance, the city legalized lot holdings as of 1851. The legislature approved in 1858, and in a test case two years later the state supreme court upheld the pueblo title. Congress made the ordinance effective against any possible federal title, and in 1867 the pueblo title was finally confirmed. The matter of survey remained, and not until 1884 were attendant difficulties sufficiently ironed out so that the patent could be issued.

In Bancroft's opinion the United States' system of dealing with the California land claims "was thoroughly bad in almost every respect" and "merits only condemnation." Josiah Royce stigmatized it as "legalized meanness." John S. Hittell's verdict was that it was outright "persecution." That the grant holders were unjustly treated is an accepted fact.

There are lawyers and historians who brush aside all such criticisms on the basis that "the claimants had their day in court." So they did, at least those who could afford it and could wait that long.

The damage, however, was by no means confined to the claimants. All Californians suffered, the squatters included, for throughout the long period of litigation, lasting until after the Civil War, no land title in the state was secure. It was impossible for a settler, whether businessman or agriculturist, to get certain title to any real property. All enterprise was thus subjected to an extra hazard. Since real estate was a doubtful collateral, interest rates were kept abnormally high, successful forty-niners hesitated to send for their families, and many

of the most substantial men who had come in the gold rush reluctantly left the state. In 1863 Hittell estimated that California's population was a million persons less than it would have been had the question of land titles been settled promptly, fairly, and generously. The figure may be too large, but, excepting the land lawyers and money lenders, it appears that every class in California would have been much better off.

Mineral Rights

A companion evil, one for which the Californians were largely responsible, was the delay in providing for private ownership of mines. In the first years of gold washing, the entire mother lode country was reckoned public domain and the individual ownership of a mining claim was purely usufructuary.

By the midfifties the drawbacks came to outweigh the advantages. Because of the impossibility of acquiring permanent title, miners were discouraged from installing expensive and efficient equipment. Like the ranch owners with clouded titles, they found it impossible to borrow money at reasonable rates. Consequently they had no incentive to build adequate or respectable houses, and they wasted inordinate time and energy in moving about from one digging to another.

But the roving habit was strong, and, since the system seemed to embody freedom, it was praised, though perhaps inaccurately, as a safeguard against monopoly. It did render the miners largely untaxable, which, despite the hardship on the tax-ridden cow counties, undoubtedly was a boon to the miners. As an unsettling factor, however, the practice was subject to most of the criticism leveled against the delay in providing sound titles to the state's urban and agricultural lands.

CHAPTER 12

The Hanging of James Stuart   *From a contemporary print*

Their majesties the mob, with that beautiful consistency which usually distinguishes those august individuals, insisted upon shooting poor Harry—for, said they, and the reasoning is remarkably conclusive and clear, "a man so hardened as to raise his hand against his own life, will never hesitate to murder another!"

Louise Amelia Knapp Smith Clappe
Dame Shirley Letters

The Vigilante Habit

Law and Justice
in the Diggings

The bold, impetuous, swashbuckling temper of the Californians of the golden era is apparent in their approach to the problems of economic development and state politics. It is observable also in their attack upon the problems of law and justice.

In the diggings a peculiar situation existed. Gold seekers poured in so rapidly that regular agencies of government could not keep pace. The season of 1848 caught California in transition from Mexican to American administration, with a military governor stationed at Monterey but nothing more than makeshift alcalde government at the scattered towns. Because these conditions persisted through the next year, the men in the mining camps were left pretty much to their own resources both as to law making and law enforcement.

Taking matters into their own hands, the miners devised a system of claim law beautiful in its logic and simplicity. Some indebtedness is traced to the lead miners of Iowa and more to Spanish colonial and European precedents which the California miners freely adapted. Although specifics varied from camp to camp, the essentials were that each miner was entitled to one claim of specified size and that the only way to perpetuate title was to work the claim. Absentee and speculative owners thus had no place in the miners' society, nor was anyone allowed to enclose natural resources or to place them out of the reach of labor, which was recognized as the prime agency in wealth production.

Each camp, gulch, or section of a river had its own way of applying these principles. Local practices varied on the size of claim, how it was to be marked, what frequency of working was required, how disputes were to be resolved, and what power should reside in the camp alcalde, recorder, arbitrator, or chairman. Unsettled disputes would come before a general meeting of the camp.

As mining advanced from the washing of surface gravels to stream diversion for working the bed of a river, to hydraulic washing, and following a vein of quartz far beneath the surface, the codes had to be elaborated. There were also attempts at standardization at the county level, with Nevada County's quartz laws providing a much used example, and at the state level. What is sometimes called "the California common law on mining" spread to near-by Nevada and many other western territories and states and gained national recognition and acceptance in the western half of the nation.

In 1848 and 1849 the setup was less refined. "The beginning," as E. Douglas Branch observes, "was a signboard on a California gravel bar: CLAIME NOTISE,—Jim Brown of Missoury takes this ground; jumpers will be shot."

Claim law was an everyday necessity in the diggings. Throughout 1848 there was very little occasion for anything more, but later intermittent need for criminal law arose, and the extralegal democracy of the forty-niners was extended to meet these emergencies.

Dry Diggings near Coloma provided the first memorable instance. In January, 1849, five men were caught red-handed in an attempt to rob a Mexican gambler. Courts, jails, and authorities being far away, the alternatives seemed to be to turn them loose or to set up a local substitute for court machinery. The miners chose the latter option. A jury of 12 was formed and its verdict of 39 lashes duly executed. Then new charges were brought against three of the culprits for crimes committed during the preceding fall on the Stanislaus. Hanging was the popular verdict. E. Gould Buffum, a miner on the scene, entered a vigorous protest but the mob was not to be dissuaded. Three corpses soon dangled from a convenient oak, and Dry Diggings was ready for its new name, Hangtown.

As occasion arose other mining communities followed the Hangtown example until, as Bancroft put it, the quiet oaks were "tasselled with the carcasses of the wicked." Again, procedure varied from camp to camp but, in general, suspected thieves or murderers were brought before a miners' meeting, testimony was heard, a jury returned the verdict or in smaller camps the decision was reached by an open vote of all assembled, and the group promptly executed the sentence. Since imprisonment was out of the question, hanging, banishment from the camp, ear cropping, and whipping were the customary penalties. A typical account of miners' justice is recorded in Milus Gay's diary: "I was called up last night 11 or 12 o'clock to assist in taking and trying a man for stealing money—George Gillin late of Ioway—Took him up to Dry Town—went into the "Southern House" I was appointed Judge—selected 12 men for Jury tried him—found him guilty—sentenced him to 39 lashes on the bare back—blind folded. Tryal occupyed the night—Jury rendered their verdict about sun up—took him out—tied him up and applyed the lash—required him to leave by 3 p.m."

Some writers insist that miners' justice was no justice at all, with the innocent suffering as often as the guilty and with only the most haphazard correlation between crime and punishment. Bret Harte, for example, recounts the apocryphal tale of the jury that was told its verdict had better be right because the defendant had already been hanged. Yet until

very recently the consensus of opinion has been that the miners administered justice admirably in civil cases and remarkably well in criminal cases. That result has been attributed to the Anglo-Saxon genius for spontaneous self-government, a genius balanced at the time only by the gross corruption in the municipal government of San Francisco.

The miners' justice savored of lynch law, not only in retrospect but also to many contemporary observers, to Buffum at Dry Diggings in 1849, and to residents of Hangtown who saw that as an opprobrious name and changed it to Placerville. David P. Barstow, a witness of the execution of Juanita at Downieville in 1851, characterized the participants as "the hungriest, craziest, wildest mob" he had ever seen and insisted that "the hanging of the woman was murder." "Since that time," he continued, "I have no sympathy with or confidence in mobs; I prefer the law for redress of grievances."

In the first couple of years, even within 40 to 50 miles of regular justice, no machinery existed for bringing mining camp suspects to trial there. There were no marshals to conduct the accused and the witnesses to that distant bar and no funds to meet the costs. To the miners it seemed impractical to release their suspects, some of whom were caught red-handed, to a remote and uncertain jurisprudence.

Regular justice, even in 1849, was even less available for the overland parties en route to California. Months out on the trail, these travelers were beyond the reach of any court. When confronted by an act of violence, their alternatives were to improvise a court or to let clear instances of assault, robbery, or murder go unpunished.

On the Sweetwater on June 20, 1849, a man named Williams shot and killed a teamster who had repeatedly threatened his life.

Williams went to several wagon train camps and offered to stand trial but none would act. On July 3 a man named Brown killed one of his messmates. The volunteer posse sent in pursuit did not catch Brown but brought back Williams, and at Green River Ferry the next day an open-air court was convened. Partly because the participants were deeply involved in a "spirited" celebration of the Fourth of July, the trial did not get beyond vigorous debate on a challenge of jurisdiction, after which it broke up. Williams took the cue and left, by inference cleared of the murder charge.

Later in the summer on the southern trail near the Gila two young men from Arkansas quarreled and fought. They were pulled apart but one boy drew a knife and made one fatal lunge. The men of the train immediately picked a judge and jury and the entire company confirmed the verdict. The next morning 12 rifles were handed out, six loaded with blanks and six with powder and ball. Over the grave they posted a brief statement of what they had done.

As to these trail incidents and to a number of the earliest in the mines, it can be maintained that at the time there was no law, and the only valid comparison must be with the anarchy that would have prevailed except for the functioning of an extralegal court.

This justification of lynch law decreased in validity as regular courts and sheriffs appeared on the scene. Often, however, there was a preference for direct action even after the orthodox machinery was available. Many of the forty-niners enjoyed the excitement of taking the law into their own hands. On other occasions local chauvinism entered in, as in 1857 when the prospectors at Grass Valley preferred to try their own culprits rather than turn them over to the county authorities at the rival town of Marysville.

Politics also figured, as in the hanging of Hamilton McCauley at Napa in 1851. He had been convicted in regular court for the murder of the municipal judge, but fellow Chivalry Democrats brought persuasion to bear upon Governor McDougal and procured a reprieve to be delivered by the sheriff from the rival town, Benicia. The Napans got wind of the sheriff's coming and delayed him on the road just long enough for the prisoner to be properly hanged, thus serving the ends both of party politics and of town pride.

The San Francisco Committees

Related and yet distinct from these rustic manifestations were the famous popular tribunals of San Francisco. As early as 1849 the ineffectiveness of police, prosecutors, and courts led to the appearance of the Hounds, or Regulators. Ostensibly a volunteer police organization, this group of young men was actually a gang preying chiefly upon the weak and inoffensive. Few Americans suffered but foreigners were victimized. Not until the Hounds perpetrated a particularly atrocious raid upon Little Chile were San Franciscans sufficiently aroused. Led by Sam Brannan the citizens took a day off, gathered at the Plaza, contributed money for the rehabilitation of the Chileños, and ordered the arrest of the leading Regulators. Banishment and other penalties were decreed for several of these "Sydney Ducks," others fled before the wrath of the citizens, and the gang was broken up.

Early in 1851, after a brutal assault and robbery of merchant C. J. Jansen, two Sydney Ducks were arrested as suspects, one of them identified by the victim and taken to be the notorious criminal James Stuart, known as English Jim. Angry citizens led by Sam Brannan seized these two men and were about to string them up, but another merchant, William T. Coleman, protested that first they should have a trial. A people's court was hastily set up. The principal suspect insisted that he was Thomas Berdue, not English Jim. This doubt, compounded by some question about Jansen's ability to recognize his assailant, led to a divided jury, whereupon the two suspects were given back to the sheriff. Berdue, or Stuart, was tried in regular court, found guilty, and sentenced to 14 years in prison. He thereupon was forwarded to Marysville to stand trial for murder in the mines.

A continuing crime wave, together with the belief that arsonists had set some of the San Francisco fires, 6 within 18 months, revived the vigilante group. Another Sydney Duck, John Jenkins, was caught in the act of stealing a small safe. The vigilantes assembled at once, tried him that very night, and immediately took him to the plaza and hanged him. When some of their number were identified at the inquest, the committee published its membership roll. It went on to arrest other suspects, hold trials, and assess penalties.

Among the suspects brought in to vigilante headquarters was another man alleged to be English Jim. When confronted with this charge, he at first denied it, then confessed and went on to recite a long list of crimes he had committed. Convinced after a time that he was the man they should have tried two months earlier, the committee came to a guilty verdict and in broad daylight marched the real English Jim to the end of the Market Street Pier, a site in full public view though easy to protect against any attempted rescue, and proceeded with the hanging. Meanwhile, two vigilantes were hurrying to Marysville, arriving after Berdue's conviction for an English Jim murder but before sentence was pronounced and carried out. The San Francisco committee

tried 90 suspects, hanged two others, whipped one, banished 28, and handed 15 over to the regular authorities.

The provocation had been great, with crime rampant, the regular courts weak and unreliable, and the citizens of San Francisco most inattentive to civic responsibilities. The summary actions of the vigilance committee were said to have been more of a lesson to the criminal element than 50 regular hangings.

That estimate, however, must be drastically revised downward because the cure was only temporary. Robbery and arson declined for a time, but within a few years new abuses developed. Municipal offices fell into the hands of unprincipled persons. Scandals occurred in connection with public works contracts, local government expenses shot up, and elections were brazenly manipulated. The courts were also notoriously corrupt. They tolerated and connived at the sharp practices of criminal lawyers to such an extent that it was practically impossible to get a conviction for murder no matter how clear the evidence. The Chivalry Democrats reaped political profit from this sad state of affairs, but it was the apathy of businessmen and of the people generally that made its existence possible.

When the panic of 1855 redirected attention to governmental problems, the editor of the *Bulletin*, the dynamic James King of William, launched a vigorous campaign for better government. Seeing himself as "a moral gadfly" and "the conscience of San Francisco," he was in vituperation and invective another John Randolph of Roanoke. He systematically exposed the iniquities of Palmer, Cook and Company, one of the leading financial houses of the city, and castigated the courts, leading lawyers, and the sheriff's office. He mentioned men by name, specified their misdeeds, and called upon the citizens to demand legal steps toward reform.

Among others he antagonized James P. Casey, a county supervisor. Because King had broadcast that he was a former inmate of Sing Sing and had refused to give any space in the *Bulletin* to a denial or rebuttal, Casey challenged the editor to a duel. When King declined, he threatened to shoot him on sight. At least a score of like threats had been made by others pilloried in the *Bulletin*, and King apparently took this one no more seriously. But fired up by his cronies, Casey intercepted King as he left his office and shot him down.

King had not been in all respects admirable. One of the most reputable attorneys then practicing in the San Francisco bar insisted that he was a notorious broken down money dealer, that his paper was small and scurrilous, and that its leading columns were devoted to daily abuse without much regard to facts. This attorney further asserted that King refused to publish evidence disproving his charge against Casey, that he declined the latter's challenge to a duel, that he provoked a street fight, and that he was warned to draw and defend himself and had his cocked pistol half drawn when Casey fired. Had the latter withheld his fire one second longer, according to this informant, the fracas would have been called a fair fight rather than an assassination. As it was, Casey lifted the somewhat unworthy James King of William to martyrdom.

Public indignation ran high and Casey was put in the county jail for safekeeping. He had abundant confidence in the courts, and well he might, for Charles E. Cora had just escaped conviction for the murder of a United States marshal. Many San Franciscans had no confidence that the courts would administer justice to Casey. A mob swarmed around the jail, but the mayor, police, and militia succeeded in quieting it. Mass meetings followed, but the matter might have been dropped except for an advertisement in the morning papers calling a meeting of the vigilance committee.

Fundamentally the committee faced the same problem as in 1851, but, whereas the legal government then had been marked principally by inefficiency and weakness, it was now characterized by corruption and abuse of authority. City and county officials, the forces of the police and the sheriff, the powerful political machine, the leading newspapers, a majority of the bar, and a substantial number of sober citizens stood for "Law and Order," then as now an appealing phrase. They opposed illegal action by the vigilantes. Furthermore, since the corrupt officials might be able to get state or national troops to suppress an insurrection, the second vigilance committee had to move cautiously. The leadership of such men as William T. Coleman and Clancy Dempster proved of inestimable value.

Solemnity, secrecy, and deliberateness marked the committee's work. Because of the strong opposition, the committee could not afford to take an overt step until its membership had risen to several thousand trustworthy men, its military equipment and discipline had been brought to a satisfactory stage, and a definite plan of action had matured. To many the delay seemed interminable, but actually only three days had been required for the preparations.

On Sunday, May 18, some 3,000 armed men surrounded the jail, a cannon was brought to bear upon the door, and a mounted horseman rapped on the window and handed the jailer a note demanding Casey's surrender. Thereupon two carriages drove up, and Casey was brought out and carried off to the vigilante headquarters. On a second trip Cora was taken. The trials of these men were not hedged about by legal technicalities but otherwise they were fair. Just before sentence was passed, word came that James King of William had died, but the outcome of the trial was already certain. Both men were condemned to die. On Thursday, at the first stroke of the bell signaling the start of King's funeral procession, the platforms under the two men were dropped.

Casey and Cora were only the symbols of what the vigilantes were striking at. The committee worked on down through its blacklist, banishing from the city men it identified as thugs, robbers, murderers, and other criminals and turning certain offenders over to the regular courts, which, significantly enough, promptly sentenced them though previously convictions had been rare. Besides these obvious criminals the committee banished a dozen hitherto respected characters, such as Judge Edward McGowan, who had no police records but were regarded as undesirable citizens.

Governor J. Neely Johnson vacillated, but his sympathies were chiefly with the Law and Order faction. General William Tecumseh Sherman sided against the vigilantes and later belabored them in his *Memoirs*. Judge David S. Terry left the bench in Sacramento to rush to the assistance of the so-called Chivalry. Other men, less famous but more substantial, cast their lot with the opponents of the vigilantes. Their stand was that even if conditions in San Francisco were as bad as represented the proper remedy would have been to bring the pressure of public opinion to bear on the officials in office or to wait less than two years until the next regular election provided an opportunity for legal reform. In theory and in practice there is much to be said for the Law and Order distrust of extralegal procedures.

The second vigilance committee, however, avoided the worst pitfalls in its path and rapidly gained strength. The vigorous but dignified punishment of Casey and Cora lent confidence; revelations of the iniquities of the political machine helped as did blunders by the opposition. Terry ended whatever chances the Law and Order party may have had when he plunged a knife into one of the vigilantes, thereby exemplifying the illegal tendencies of the Law and Order faction. He was taken prisoner and indicted before the committee on a number of counts including four other attacks upon citizens.

The committee was convinced that Terry deserved punishment, but it was a ticklish problem to attempt to impose a sentence upon a supreme court justice. After 25 days' deliberation—his victim in the meantime having recovered—it was decided to acquit. Although Terry was not punished, the incident discredited the opposition.

State interference had shown its impotence before Fort Gunnybags, the vigilante headquarters, and the federal authorities, especially General Wool in command of the military department of California, had declined to provide men or arms to suppress the committee. Its work done, the committee displayed its strength in a mammoth parade of 6,000 armed men, held a public reception at Fort Gunnybags, and adjourned sine die.

Vigilante action, especially as symbolized by San Francisco's second committee, has come down in popular tradition as a noble example of community action. The majority of eastern editors at the time, while granting that the provocation was great, refused to admit that tribunals operating outside the law were justified and branded them as "pregnant with lamentable and disastrous consequences." The New York *Courier and Enquirer*, however, said, "Our admiration is commanded no more by the promptness and decision of their action than by the dignity and decorum which seems to have accompanied it." The New Orleans *Delta* affirmed that "the people of San Francisco acted well," and the *Boston Journal* and the New York *Sunday Times*

Fort Gunnybags

endorsed the summary proceedings and the peremptory justice "which the venality of the courts had made necessary." With the exception of the *Herald*, most San Francisco papers, in step with the thinking of the business community, endorsed the work of the committee.

Historians improved on these phrases. Bancroft hailed the 1856 committee as "the greatest popular tribunal the world has ever witnessed." Theodore H. Hittell, in more labored prose, saluted it as "one of the purest and best intentioned bodies of men ever assembled in San Francisco" and its work as "the most remarkable municipal reform ever known in this country." In the volume on the forty-niners which he wrote for Yale's *Chroni-*

cles of America series Stewart Edward White said that "the effect was the same as though four hundred had been executed." Robert Glass Cleland in 1922 concluded a generally favorable treatment with the slightly guarded comment that "few today will deny that San Francisco profited from this over-riding of law to save law."

In 1964 in his book on the 1851 committee George Stewart quotes with approval Richard Henry Dana's judgment with more special reference to the committee of 1856 in which Dana says that San Francisco was "rescued and handed back to soberness, morality and good government, by that peculiar invention of Anglo-Saxon Republican American, the solemn, awe-inspiring Vigilance Committee of the most grave and responsible citizens, the last resort of the thinking and the good, taken to only when vice, fraud, and ruffianism have intrenched themselves behind the forms of law, suffrage, and ballot, and there is no hope but in organized force, whose action must be instant and thorough, or its state will be worse than before."

Several twentieth-century historians arrived at a judgment considerably more critical. In 1950 in his *A Self-Governing Dominion* William H. Ellison charged that the committee of 1856 failed in its administration of justice, disregarded the safeguards for the rights of individuals, was a menace to organized society, and "shockingly demonstrated the ease with which lawlessness in the form of mob or extralegal action" may arise.

At the centennial of San Francisco's Great Committee, a paper taking its title from Dame Shirley's phrase "Their Majesties the Mob" analyzed vigilantism as practiced on the frontier and flourishing again in the 1950s. Some episodes were almost exact replicas of the old-time impromptu trials and executions. Others were in the context of racism or of McCarthyism. In 1960 a book with the same title expanded the analysis and the examples and concluded that whatever the temptation to escape the technicalities of legal justice by substituting direct action, the wiser course is to handle all such cases through the regular courts. *Their Majesties the Mob*, thus, is a brief for due process.

Rustic Vigilance

Although in San Francisco the immediate sequel to vigilante action was less commission of crime and more prompt and vigorous functioning of regular justice, throughout the rest of the state, not to mention other parts of the West, the much more prominent result was a stimulation of vigilante action in imitation of that in the metropolis. Vigilante action became so common that it was the accepted order of the day. In some instances it was kept at the high plane of dignity and dispassion attributed to the committee of 1856, but in other instances it sank to the lowest level of mob vengeance and lynch law. The excuse given, as in San Francisco, was that the regular courts were totally ineffective, or that the cleansing of San Francisco had shunted habitual criminals to the provinces, or that horse stealing and cattle stealing must be stopped. Again judgments differ as to the adequacy of these excuses. Undeniably the arm of the law was of much more rudimentary development in most parts of the back country than in urban San Francisco.

In 1851 there was reason to believe that a statewide criminal ring existed. The burning of Stockton on May 6, just two days after the great San Francisco fire, was an incendiary attempt at jail delivery. Sacramento, Marysville, Nevada City, and other communities seemed to be caught in the same toils. Accordingly there were proposals for a statewide organization under the sponsorship of the San Francisco committee. Some correspondence was exchanged both in 1851 and in 1856, chiefly warnings as to the whereabouts and past records of known criminals. The Sacramento committee used the constitution of its Bay City counterpart. This spirit of cooperation strengthened the position of local committees and helped forestall any effective state interference in San Francisco in 1856, but the metropolitan leaders wisely refused to assume any responsibility for possible excesses by local bodies beyond the limits of their control.

Their fears proved well founded, for in the smaller communities the vigilante movement ran the entire gamut from fair and temperate trial to the most degenerate and revolting forms of mob violence. A few random illustrations will suffice.

At Weaverville in the early fall of 1852 Michael Grant was charged with murdering a Missourian named Holt. Arrested by the sheriff, he was taken in hand by the miners, who appointed judge and jury and attorneys for prosecution and defense. Fairly tried and convicted, Grant was allowed a ten-day stay of execution and the ministrations of a clergyman, after which he was solemnly hanged.

At Visalia in 1858 vigilantes brought pressure to bear upon William C. Deputy in an attempt to force him to restore properties fraudulently taken from his nephew. The pressure was by marching the old man out to a tree, adjusting a rope around his neck, and swinging him. After three or four trips skyward he agreed to the demands of the vigilantes and was returned to the jail. In the morning a lawyer and a notary called and took the necessary depositions after which the sheriff turned his prisoner loose.

Sonora had one of the most active committees. In the summer of 1851 it disposed of a case almost every day, usually by laying on 50, 75, or even 150 lashes but sometimes by branding horse thieves with the appropriate initials.

In Los Angeles lynch law frequently supplanted regular justice. In rationalization it is asserted that Los Angeles was one of those proverbially tough cow towns with cowboys, teamsters from the Salt Lake freighting line, desperados expelled by the San Francisco vigilantes, Latin bad men like Tiburcio Vásquez and Juan Flores, and Indians crazed with the poisonous liquor dispensed in "Nigger Alley." The press lashed out against the mounting crime wave—44 homicides in 15 months and not a conviction in 1851.

By 1854, though doubtless with appropriate exaggeration, the rate was quoted at a murder a day. The courts proving inadequate, lynch law was invoked.

Although responsible persons usually condemned the resort to lynch law, a vigilance committee was formed on July 13, 1851, by official action of the mayor and city council of Los Angeles. Among its more famous actions were the hanging of two alleged Mexican murderers in August, 1852, and a few months later, the hanging of three others charged with the murder of Major General J. H. Bean. Five years later proof came to light that one of these young men had been innocent.

In January, 1855, Mayor Stephen C. Foster of Los Angeles resigned his high office to take active part in lynching Dave Brown. The "good work" done, he was promptly re-elected mayor. This particular lynching, besides being personally directed by the mayor, was outstanding because a full report of it was printed in the Southern Californian some hours before the actual hanging. This anachronism occurred because the enterprising editor of this sheet wanted to feature the story in his issue for the ten o'clock San Francisco steamer. At three, when the hanging actually occurred, the vigilantes had, so to speak, a full printed script for their performance, complete even to a last-minute confession by the murderer. The chief divergence from the printed program was that Brown objected angrily to being hanged by "a lot of Greasers." In deference to his wishes the Mexican-American volunteers stepped aside and let an Anglo American crew haul on the rope.

Thus was justice served at Los Angeles. The ranger company, in other words the vigilantes, in 1854 and 1855 brought about 22 executions "in accordance with the the law or without the law, whichever was most convenient." Two years later some 200 men turned out to avenge the slaying of Sheriff James R. Barton by the Flores gang. Not counting those killed in the process of apprehension, 11 members of this gang were hanged at the jail. As late as 1863 a single month witnessed seven lynchings.

These popular tribunals of town and country have only a fraction of the fame enjoyed by the two great committees of San Francisco. In nicety of organization and in dramatics they were far inferior. Few of them would be held up as high examples of good citizenship triumphing over difficulties occasioned by corrupt and venal officials. They were, nevertheless, close kin to the vigilance of San Francisco and belong in every general picture of extralegal justice in California. In fact, they perhaps should have the principal attention, for in number of hangings these rural tribunals exceeded San Francisco's two committees by at least twenty to one. In the year 1855 alone there were 19 vigilante hangings for murder, 24 for theft, and four for minor crimes, a total of 47, not one of which took place in San Francisco.

Southward
the Course of Empire

Californians of the fifties expressed their lofty disdain for the due process of criminal law through the vigilance movement. Their corresponding disregard for international law was revealed in numerous filibustering expeditions. California was merely the starting point for these expeditions directed toward Sonora, Baja California, Hawaii, or Central America. The operations lay outside the state and none of these forays succeeded, yet this activity sheds light on the state of mind of many Californians of the day.

The United States had just taken long strides westward with the annexation of Texas in 1845, present-day Oregon, Washington, and Idaho in 1846, and the Mexican cession in 1848. Manifest Destiny, as Americans were repeatedly told, had decreed all this. Many Americans and Californians were reluctant to believe that only that much expansion had been ordained.

Baja California and Sonora were remote from and neglected by Mexico's central government, and Sonora lay open to Apache inroads. Hawaii's native government was decrepit, her commercial ties were with the United States, and her foreign colony was largely American. Central America's faltering governments and the popularity of the Panama and Nicaragua routes to California came within the scope of American interest. California's volatile and adventurous population made it the inevitable rallying point and, as in most matters, San Francisco led.

Answering invitations to assist in Indian control and in a revolution, Joseph C. Morehead sought recruits. As quartermaster he drew on funds and supplies left over from the Yuma campaign of 1850 and purchased the bark *Josephine*. In June, 1851, he sent 200 men to La Paz. They engaged merely in trade and soon dispersed. A larger party was moving through Los Angeles toward the Gila and the Sonora frontier. It likewise broke up. After stopover at San Diego, where most of his men deserted, Morehead sailed to Mazatlán. The authorities searched the ship but found no arms or ammunition. These filibusters proved entirely innocuous.

In the *Game Cock* in 1851 Sam Brannan took out a band of armed men intent on liberating Hawaii only to find that no such help was wanted.

San Francisco's French were numerous because of the famous lotteries in which the winners received free passage to the land of gold. Some became prominent as merchants, importers, hotel and restaurant keepers, gamblers, and bankers. Others were unemployed or underemployed and therefore ready recruits for adventure such as filibustering.

At the head of such a group Charles Pindray sailed to Guaymas in November, 1851, and then moved to an assigned tract near one of Kino's old missions. The colony was intended as an agricultural venture, an outpost against the Apaches, and a base for mining. The Apaches ran off their stock, and when Pindray went to protest lack of Mexican support a dispute arose and he was killed. The colony soon disintegrated as did a smaller French outpost attempted near Tucson.

Count Gaston de Raousset-Boulbon did the next enlisting in San Francisco. Invited by Mexican officials, he led an expedition in 1852 via Guaymas to the Sonora frontier. Disputes with the authorities led to hostilities in which he brilliantly captured Hermosillo with 240 men pitted against 1,000. But when he was incapacitated by dysentery his men surrendered to another general.

Safely back in San Francisco, Raousset resumed recruiting. He went to Mexico City and conferred with Santa Anna but without achieving an agreement. Continued recruiting resulted in the Mexican and French consuls being taken to court on charges of violating American antifilibustering laws. Americans, however, seemed to be immune to conviction on such charges.

By the summer of 1854 Raousset was at Guaymas with another expedition. Fighting broke out and the French were decisively defeated. Raousset's execution 30 days later was the coup de grâce to French filibustering from California.

Meanwhile, William Walker was openly recruiting volunteers in California. After his offer of "assistance" to Sonora was rebuffed, he sailed with 45 men to La Paz, seized the governor of Baja California, and issued a bombastic proclamation as president of the Republic of Baja California. Hostilities forced his retreat to Ensenada. After a farcical attempt to march around the head of the gulf to conquer Sonora, he scurried back into the United States. His filibustering had embarrassed the negotiation of the Gadsden Treaty and contributed to the exclusion of Baja California from that purchase.

A year later Walker embarked with 58 Californians for Nicaragua. After much adventure and some good fortune he became the master of this republic only to incur the wrath of the Cornelius Vanderbilt transportation interests. After a series of humiliations he faced a firing squad at Truxillo, Honduras, in 1860.

Less deserved and more tragic was the fate of the Stockton lawyer and state senator, Henry A. Crabb. Interested in Sonora because of his wife's properties there, he took some 50 colonists to the province in 1856. A local revolutionist urged him to recruit a larger force of Californians to assist in an uprising and prepare the way for annexation to the United States. He did so, but at the Sonora frontier encountered opposition by the revolutionist who had suggested the scheme. Having already achieved his purpose, this insurgent now wanted no entrance of filibusters. Crabb pushed on as far as Caborca where, partly by treachery, he was induced to surrender. The next morning the 59 prisoners were taken out in batches and butchered.

The United States government protested only perfunctorily, which hints that Crabb's fate was deserved. On the contrary it appears that his expedition was more colonizing than filibustering.

Others might talk about further southwestward expansion of the United States but

Crabb was the last of the California filibusters. The actual expeditions are less significant than the restless, adventurous, and imperialistic attitude of the Californians, which made them ready to enlist in such enterprises, ready to condone actions which violated the statutes, and as jurymen unwilling to convict leaders like Walker who were brought to trial for violation of the antifilibustering law. To a degree the West was a law unto itself and did not yet realize that Manifest Destiny had run its complete course.

CHAPTER 13

Mojave Mother and Children

*A. L. Kroeber, Lowie Museum of Anthropology,
University of California, Berkeley*

The California valley cannot grace her annals with a single Indian war bordering on respectability. It can boast, however, a hundred or two of as brutal butcherings, on the part of our honest miners and brave pioneers, as any area of equal extent in our republic.

Hubert Howe Bancroft
History of California

A White Man's Country

"Wars" and Massacres

The first Indian policy in California was introduced in 1769 by the Spaniards. Its underlying principles were that the Indian should be preserved, civilized and trained, and used as the basic element in the permanent population. In coastal and southern California, mission, presidio, and pueblo had carried this process well along toward realization, at least to the degree that most of the labor at mission, town, and rancho was performed by "domesticated" Indians.

The earliest arrivals from the United States accepted this attitude and soon came to regard the California native as a useful and acceptable element in the local population. Sutter, Bidwell, and others even extended the practice into the Sacramento Valley, and the mining season of 1848 witnessed something of the sort in the gold area, where the two races worked side by side and for the most part without friction in the extraction of the precious metal.

After secularization of the missions, however, the Indian policy derived from Spain lost its vital features. The Indians already civilized or "domesticated" might continue so, though many reverted to their ancestral customs, but no effective agency was at work for the training of additional Indians. Besides that decline, grave abuses developed in the treatment of many former mission Indians. Walter Colton tells of the problems created by the former neophytes at Monterey. The year-by-year records of Los Angeles for the late forties and fifties mention the Indians reduced to starvation, beggary, and petty crime, their hopeless addiction to drink, of Indians rounded up like cattle for the work season, and of the Monday slave mart at which their services for the week were auctioned off to cover the fines for weekend drunkenness. This shameful practice was matched by callous indifference to the killing of an Indian. The prevailing attitude seemed to be that such an act was by no means a crime.

In retrospect this misuse of unfortunates may seem the darkest phase of local Indian history, but most southern Californians of the day were more alarmed by the depredations by Indians from the mountainous and desert interior. Such thievery had occurred during the Spanish and Mexican periods. Renegades from the missions and a growing taste for horse meat and beef aggravated the practice, and at the same time the greatly improved market for ranch products magnified the value of the losses. To the local military and to the federal and state authorities southern rancheros clamored loudly for protection and for punitive expeditions against these marauders.

With the gold rush the great central valley, the Sierra foothills, and northern California were suddenly overrun by headstrong Argonauts engulfing whole tribes and dispossessing others of their hunting and food-gathering lands. These gold seekers had had no opportunity to absorb the Spanish philosophy of race relationships. Most of them had been nurtured on the contrary Anglo-American principle that the Indian should be made to give way before the advancing tide of white settlement, a principle alternately practiced through wars of extermination and treaties for Indian removal. On the overland routes to California difficulties with the Pawnees and the Humboldt Valley natives inflamed hatred of Indians, and many miners transferred this hate to the California natives. The whites are charged with the first violence, though the mere entrance of miners into certain districts roused the Indians to resistance. Thereafter retaliation flowed in both directions, often without any discrimination between the original offenders and the innocent. For the operations that followed, the name "wars" is sometimes employed. It is a sordid and disgraceful chapter, seldom stressed in local histories.

The first of the so-called wars occurred in the spring of 1848. Outrages attributed to former members of the New York Volunteers led to retaliation by the natives of the Coloma district, whereupon the miners organized parties for Indian hunting. McKay's party is credited with killing 30 at one rancheria and capturing seven men and 40 women, while Greenwood's party at another village killed 20 and captured others, of whom six were sentenced to run before a firing squad. Only one escaped. For the rest of the year hostilities were avoided but in 1849 they broke out again, particularly on the Yuba and in the Kings River region, where the natives were charged with a number of atrocities such as flaying intruders alive. The Yumas also inflicted insults and damages upon immigrants passing through their territory. In the Clear Lake country two settlers met a well-deserved death at the hands of the Indians and were promptly avenged by a force under Captain Nathaniel Lyon which killed 175 Indians.

Indian depredations continued, often provoked by inconsiderate whites, and had cumulative effect in a series of campaigns in 1850. Regulars and militia after several pitched battles brought the Yubas to terms in May. Yet opportunities for friction were numerous and the peace did not last. When hostilities spread up and down the valley, the governor authorized Sheriff Rogers of El Dorado County to lead 200 volunteers into action. This time most of the Indians managed to elude Rogers. Those who put up a fight gave good account of themselves with their arrows. All the damage the posse could do was limited to the destruction of huts, acorn stores, and the like, and its exploits were reckoned far from brilliant. Campaigns in the San Joaquin foothills had similar results.

From Los Angeles, meanwhile, a company was raised to punish the Yumas for killing 11 Americans who had operated a Colorado River ferry. The campaign won little popular support, the general opinion being that the ferrymen were murderers and robbers who had deserved their fate. By conscripting from emigrant trains, Joseph C. Morehead got together 125 men. He found the Indians quiet but prodded them into a fight in which a score were killed. The expense account of this campaign ran to $76,588.

In 1851 the Yumas and the Luiseños gave southern California a more serious scare. The Luiseño chief claimed that 3,000 warriors would attack. But regulars and volunteers were gathered at Los Angeles and San Diego, and the obstreperous chief was seized by the Cahuillas and handed over for execution. Major H. P. Heintzelman made war on the Yumas and at length captured and executed their chief.

The most famous campaign of 1851 was that of the Mariposa Battalion under James D. Savage. After strenuous efforts the people of several hostile and semihostile rancherías were rounded up, but by a clever ruse Chief Tenieya and 350 Yosemites and Chowchillas gave their captors the slip, making a second campaign necessary. To recapture the chief the whites resorted to trickery. Exciting though the campaign was, the Mariposa Battalion's greatest achievement was the effective discovery of Yosemite Valley. Walker's fur men had looked down on the valley 17 years earlier, but not until these Indian hunters of 1851 came along was its majestic beauty hailed and appreciated.

The northern fringe of the state was the next scene of conflict. Oregon was in the throes of a war bloodier than any California had witnessed. The Klamaths showed a disposition to follow the example of their northern neighbors but were held fairly well in check by army posts established at Humboldt, Reading Valley, and Scott Valley. Then in 1852 the Shastas went on the warpath, and the contagion spread to the Pit River Indians and the Modocs. The latter were held responsible for a midnight onslaught on an immigration train on its way to California. Nearby miners organized to strike back. Negotiations were opened. Both sides suspected treachery, but the whites struck first, slaughtering some 40 Modocs in what is known as Ben Wright's Massacre.

The melancholy narrative continues: Oregon's Rogue River War kept on disturbing the northern California tribes. The Shastas went on a rampage in 1853, and other tribes committed depredations. Regulars and volunteers retaliated upon the lower Klamaths in 1854 and 1855, forcing them to accept reservation life. The fighting in Siskiyou County was more drawn out. Even the mission Indians of southern California provided a war scare in 1857 but were placated by the appointment of agents, supposedly to provide for them. To hostilities in the San Joaquin Valley, General Kibbe responded in 1858–59 by campaigning in the Coast Ranges along its western edge, where he killed more than 100 natives and rounded up several times that many for the reservations.

Similarly on Mad River and Eel River in the north, cattle stealing was the excuse for campaigns in which more than 200 Indians were slaughtered. The grand jury entered a courageous protest against these atrocities, but the prevailing sentiment was clearly indicated by the fact that Francis Bret Harte was practically run out of Humboldt County for sharply criticizing the massacre in his paper, the Union *Northern Californian*. The Hoopas held out obstinately for five years, and were rewarded with an excellent reservation in the lower Trinity Valley.

T. T. Waterman, the anthropologist who spent the most time with Ishi, the last of the Yahi, searched for information on the decline of that tribe. Disease played a role, but there also were massacres.

In one recorded incident in 1865 a party of whites in search of scalps (the whites did the scalping in California then) discovered a band of Yahi encamped—men, women, and children. Before daybreak the whites closed in on them from two sides. When the firing started the Indians avoiding one group ran into the other. An informant who visited the scene later told Waterman that he found 43 skeletons.

Six years later another party of whites cornered a small band of Yahi in a cave, poured in rifle fire, and then went in to finish off the children with a revolver. Soon thereafter the tribe, reduced to a few individuals, disappeared almost completely from sight.

Owens Valley had its massacres. As advancing settlements cut down on their forage grounds, the natives were forced into cattle stealing. The settlers struck back in 1862 and again in 1865. In January of that year more than 40 Indians were killed at one rancheria. The next month 100 or more were driven into the brackish waters of Owens Lake, where the whites "saw to it that they perished." That was the last major engagement that far south, though in 1866 the owner of Rancho San Pascual was killed by Indian arrows within the limits of present Pasadena.

The Modoc War

Farther north the stage was already being set for the dramatic climax of California Indian fighting, the Modoc War. In 1864 the Modocs had been forced to agree to move to a reservation in Oregon. They found their lot miserable because they were thrown in with a larger number of Klamaths. After a short taste of reservation life Captain Jack (Chief Kientepoos) led his people back to their old haunts on Lost River. In 1869 he was persuaded to give the reservation another chance, but in the spring the 200 Modocs decamped once more in favor of their homeland. Again overtures were made to persuade them to return to the reservation but, the Indians proving adamant, the army was called to round up Captain Jack's band.

Warned of the advancing column, the Modocs took refuge in the impenetrable lava beds near Tule Lake. Captain Jack had only 50 fighting men equipped with muzzle-loading rifles and a few revolvers and encumbered with at least 150 women and children. Arrayed against them were 400 well-armed soldiers, 225 of them regulars, supported by a battery of howitzers. Colonel Frank Wheaton came to the natural conclusion that the quickest way to end the war was by an immediate attack in force. The attack was made on January 17, 1873. The Americans advanced bravely enough. They saw no Modocs, but from howitzers and rifles they poured a heavy fire into the lava beds. The Modocs answered with careful shots from their places of concealment, killing nine and wounding 30

before the Americans fell back. Wheaton sent for four more howitzers and 410 more men. Other attempts to dislodge the Modocs were no more successful; in fact, because of captured rifles and ammunition the Indians were stronger than at the outset.

In such circumstances the Americans turned to a renewal of negotiations. Late in March, Captain Jack was persuaded to come out to a peace conference. He soon found that the only terms offered were absolute submission, this in spite of the fact that the Modocs had by no means been vanquished. His moderate proposals, such as a mutual surrender of thieves and murderers, were brushed aside as naive. The American commander, General E. R. S. Canby, would not concede the Modocs a reservation anywhere except among the overbearing Oregon Klamaths.

Captain Jack seems to have had no illusions of success but agreed to consult with his tribesmen. They opposed his plan of working for peace and, by taunting him as a "fish-hearted woman," won him over to a plot to kill the American leaders at the next peace conference. The commissioners were warned by a Modoc woman, Winema or Tobey, but they proceeded with the conference on April 11. At Captain Jack's signal the Modocs whipped out revolvers and knives and even rifles. Canby and the missionary, Eleazer Thomas, were killed and Indian agent A. B. Mecham was wounded.

The Modoc leaders got away to the lava beds. More soldiers were brought up and battle was joined again. Another attempt to storm the Modoc position was as disastrous as had been the assault in January. But with supplies running low the Indians had given up hope of attaining any favorable terms from their opponents. Split into smaller groups they fled from their haven in the lava beds. One band was captured and its leader, Hooker Jim, offered to help take his former chief.

At length, accompanied by three forlorn followers, Captain Jack came out and surrendered. With the loss of five men, two of whom were killed while trying to open an unexploded howitzer shell, he had been able to hold off a far superior force for over three months. The Americans, meanwhile, had lost 8 officers, 39 privates, 16 volunteers, 2 Indian scouts, and 18 civilians, besides numerous wounded. The war cost half a million dollars, whereas the Modocs would have been satisfied with a 2,000-acre reservation, worth at the most $20,000, or even with the worthless lava bed area.

Besides having the best of the fighting, Captain Jack seems to have advanced the more reasonable arguments and proposals in the conferences held. His captors, however, were not swayed by any sentimental admiration. They tried him for his violation of the code of the whites, and in company with Black Jim and Boston Charley he was hanged at Fort Klamath.

Introducing the Reservation System

Throughout these years of warfare the United States government had employed its customary peaceful devices to solve the Indian problem in California. The first agents, Sutter, Vallejo, and J. D. Hunter, were named as adjuncts of the military by Kearny in 1847. Two years later they were followed by Subagent Adam Johnston, whose responsibility was to the newly created Department of the Interior. That same year California Indian affairs were given cursory examination by an emissary extraordinary of the Department of State, the cavalier Thomas Butler King. Far more important was the arrival in January, 1851, of three commissioner agents, Redick McKee, G. W. Barbour, and O. M. Wozencraft. These men found that the militia had just been called out for an Indian campaign in Mariposa County and that the legislature had set up a "war chest" of $500,000.

The three commissioners plunged immediately into negotiations with the Central Valley and Sierra foothill tribes. Their basic theory was that the tribes whose lands had been taken over by the miners should be assigned tracts on the floor of the valley and suitably indemnified with beef, blankets, and other supplies. The theory was that to feed the Indians for a year would be cheaper than to fight them for a week. Eighteen treaties were negotiated, calling for the settling of some 139 tribes or villages on reservations adding up to about one fourteenth of the total area of the state. The program was endorsed by Edward F. Beale, newly appointed superintendent of the California Indians, but the Senate promptly rejected all 18 treaties. The Senate may have been aghast that the three commissioners with $50,000 appropriated for their expenses had laid out more than $700,000. It certainly was moved by the vehement protest lodged by California's representatives that the treaties deeded to the red men some of the best land in the state.

The summary rejection of the treaties encouraged further encroachment upon the Indian lands and necessitated new expedients and strategies by the superintendent. This officer, the spirited young lieutenant who had made the perilous trip to San Diego to get relief for Kearny after the battle of San Pascual, was equal to the occasion. He arrived on the scene in mid-September, 1852. Six weeks later he proposed a new program calling for a

A Costanoan Woman's Grinding Bowl in White Quartz,
Uncovered by Roadbuilders in 1976

system of military posts "for the convenience and protection of the Indians." At each post there would be a resident agent vested with disciplinary authority and responsibility for instruction of the natives.

The reservations thus created would have exactly defined limits. The Indians would be required to stay on the reservation and be taught civilized pursuits, such as farming and the simpler trades which would enable them to be self-supporting. This plan suggests a revival of the Spanish mission, shorn only of its religious aspects. It was not the old-style "reservation" system through which the United States had been shunting the Indians out of the way of the juggernaut of white settlement.

On the basis of the blueprint drafted by Beale and his southern California subagent, B. D. Wilson, the new-style reservation system was inaugurated in California. From there, with slight modifications, it was taken to Oregon, Kansas, Nebraska, and New Mexico and became the kingpin of the United States' Indian policy. It became so much the standard that few persons would guess that its first use

was as recent as the 1850s or that its place of origin was Beale's California.

Although Beale and Wilson are to be credited with devising and introducing the policy which the nation adopted, immediate results in California were far from brilliant. In the fall of 1853 they launched the first reservation at Tejon. The neighboring Indians were not easily persuaded to come in and experiment with the new life, but the superintendent's boundless energy and optimism, together with the loyal support of Wilson and other assistants, overcame the initial reluctance.

The next June, Beale could report 2,500 Indians on this reservation and a first harvest of 42,000 bushels of wheat and 10,000 bushels of barley. Already, however, Beale was in disfavor in Washington where political opponents had been after his scalp. They found a talking point in the irregularity of his financial accounts, and, although subsequent investigation absolved him of all blame, this attack led to his dismissal.

The next superintendent, Thomas J. Henley, expressed himself as fully in sympathy with Beale's program. He established four more reservations: at Fresno, at Nome Lackee near Tehama in the northwestern extremity of the Sacramento Valley, at Klamath River, and at Cape Mendocino. He even found a way of circumventing the legal limitation of the reservations to five by setting up "farms" that were reservations in disguise. Unfortunately, however, the increase in reservations seems to have appealed to Henley primarily because of the multiplication of the lucrative positions at his disposal. Most of his appointees were not of the high caliber of Beale's, and they were soon joined by their chief in cheating the government and the Indians.

An official investigation in 1858 by J. Ross Browne disclosed the grossest mismanagement; for example, Indian supplies had been issued to laborers at a private sawmill, and other supplies had been bought at inflated prices through a store in which Henley had an interest. Consequently there was a new superintendent in 1859, a sharp reduction in the appropriation, discharge of many persons who had in theory been working for the Indians, and abandonment of most of the farms and reservations.

Tejon was abandoned in 1863. At the end of the decade only three stations were left, Hoopa and Round Valley in the north and Tule farm in the San Joaquin Valley. In 1870 these were transferred from army to Methodist supervision, a change that seemed to be for the better. The relocation of Tule farm in 1873, however, was to a site which could support only about one fourth of the agency population.

In 1870 there was a halfhearted attempt to provide a reservation for the mission Indians of the south. The Pala and San Pascual valleys were set aside for their occupancy, but white settlers of the vicinity took the announcement as an invitation to rush in and occupy this land.

A resolute agent might have prevailed against these squatters, and a tribe like the Klamath probably would not have given in without a fight. These mission Indians, however, had repeatedly been imposed upon. They seemed aware of the futility of resistance. Their resignation in the face of injustice was at length rewarded with sturdy championing of their cause by Helen Hunt Jackson, Charles F. Lummis, and others, but not until much later was their lot improved.

Decline in Number

Although early census figures on the number of "wild" Indians in California are not helpful, it is clear that in the third quarter of the nineteenth century the number of them and of domesticated Indians was alarmingly and shamefully reduced. Wars and massacres contributed as did the expansion of white settlements and industries, which diminished the food resources of the natives. The reservation system or its abuses bore heavily on many tribes. Also, the government kept only those promises that suited its convenience. And finally disease, respiratory and venereal, took a heavy toll. By 1875 not more than one fourth as many natives remained as had occupied the state a quarter of a century earlier.

The crushing of the natives in numbers and in spirit is sometimes credited with freeing the state from Indian "troubles" in the years thereafter, yet this result seems due primarily to the still more rapid increase of the white population. Reduced to so insignificant a minority, the Indians had no choice but to accept the white man's regulations.

In the main the present generation takes the side of the Indian. For a long span of years Californians have been in perfect safety from

Indian attack or depredation. Anthropological studies have played up the aboriginal virtues and attainments. The Indian was the underdog, and the land, all freely admit, was originally his.

In the early American period, however, even this justice was denied the California native. The Treaty of Guadalupe Hidalgo, it was held, had transferred full title to the land from Mexico to the United States government and therefore no further formalities or compensations were thought necessary for extinguishing Indian title. This legalistic argument is a clue to the attitude then current. Rather than idealized as at present, the Indian was feared and despised. That state of mind explains but does not excuse the heartless liquidation of so many of the California Indians.

Discriminations against Other Races

Race prejudice showed against other groups. Vicente Pérez Rosales, a distinguished Chileño, on one occasion rescued some of his countrymen from discriminatory abuse by giving the impression that they were Frenchmen. The French themselves often ran into difficulty in the diggings, though the principal incident, the so-called French Revolution, passed off without a pitched battle. Australians in San Francisco were particular targets of the vigilantes in 1851. It was, however, against Indians, blacks, Mexicans, and Chinese that the white claim to superiority was most glaring.

By the fall of 1849, when the constitutional convention assembled, the miners had made clear that they wanted no competition from slave gangs. Relatively few southerners had brought slaves, which meant that the threat

was remote. A related contingency pressed the issue of making California a free state. Only thus was there prospect that the Congress would approve statehood. The convention went further and tried to ward off any suggestion of future division which might have produced a slave territory or state in southern California. Many who were against slavery were as adamant against admitting free blacks. This proposition was debated at length before being set aside.

The antislavery provision in the constitution lacked teeth against the holding of slaves brought earlier into the state and was weakened further by a state fugitive slave law enacted in 1852. Masters asserting intention of taking slaves back to a slave state thereby had some color of protection. The most famous case on this issue reached the California Supreme Court in 1858. Justices Peter H. Burnett, who had been the first elected governor, and David S. Terry recognized that the master was not legally entitled to possess Archy Lee as a slave. But, since this was the first case and would be a hardship to the owner, they were "not disposed to rigidly enforce the rule." They returned the slave to his owner.

The owner promptly started for Mississippi. In San Francisco he was intercepted by a new court action which hinged on the fugitive slave issue, and by court order Archy Lee was set free. Perhaps as a carry-over of the condescension toward blacks, this case comes down in history not as *Lee vs. Stovall* but as *ex parte Archy*.

Meanwhile, the first legislature had barred testimony by a black against a white in criminal litigation, and the second legislature had extended the ban to civil cases. Prominent blacks such as William Yates, Mifflin Gibbs, and Jonas H. Townsend petitioned the legis-

182

lature to rescind these actions and won support from such notables as Edward D. Baker,
David Broderick, and J. Neely Johnson. In
1863, stimulated by the war for the Union, the
legislature authorized black and Indian testimony, though not testimony by Chinese.

Discriminations against blacks continued.
In 1870 a black couple in San Francisco
objected to the practice of school segregation.
They tried to enroll their child in the school
nearest their residence and were refused
admission. They went to court for an order to
the principal of the school to admit their child,
but were rebuffed in the decision in *Ward vs.
Flood* in which the court fully accepted the
rationale of separate but equal.

Discriminations against Mexicans are much
better known, in part because there were so
many more of them. Yankee newcomers held
themselves superior, demonstrated, so they
said, by the victory in the War with Mexico.
Old-line Californians as well as gold seekers
from Mexico were forced out of the better
diggings. This discrimination was legalized in
the Foreign Miners Tax of 1850, aimed more
against Mexicans than anyone else. The prejudice was made more explicit in the Anti-
Greaser Act of 1855, ameliorated only slightly
the next year by deleting the word "greaser,"
though retaining the impact. Vigilantism, as
indicated, was also carried out prejudicially
against Mexicans and other "foreigners."

These pressures caused resentment, again
by the Mexicans, who found a way to express
it in banditry. The legendary hero here was
Joaquín Murieta, in Walter Noble Burns'
phrase, the Robin Hood of Eldorado, who
took it upon himself to avenge the slights and
cruelties to his countrymen. His deeds of
brigandage were rivaled by those of Juan
Flores in the fifties and Tiburcio Vásquez in the
sixties and seventies.

Murieta so terrorized the southern mines
and the San Joaquin that the legislature commissioned a posse headed by former Texas
ranger Harry S. Love to run him down. Love
and his men returned with a head they said
was Joaquín's and collected the reward, plus a
$5,000 bonus added by the legislature. Muri-
eta lived on in legend, claimed by Chile as well
as Mexico, painted in heroic pose by Charles
Nahl, and acclaimed in a best seller, *The Life
and Adventures of Joaquín Murieta* (1854),
by John Rollin Ridge, perhaps the more sympathetic because he was a Cherokee.

Many of the Mexican forty-niners went
back to Mexico and some Mexican Californians also repatriated. In northern California
the old-timers almost immediately became a
minority; in southern California they were not
outnumbered for another twenty years. Their
relative share of California wealth fell off as
they were shunted out of the diggings, lost
their titles by the Land Act or the cost of litigation, and had difficulty competing with the
more aggressive newcomers. Yet many of this
group accommodated to the new regime and
assimilated into the new society.

The first Chinese to come to California
were given a place of honor at San Francisco's
celebration of admission to statehood. In the
diggings, however, the hardy miners acted on
the assumption that Providence as well as the
Mexican War had made California a white
man's country. They had no intention of letting Chinese stake out claims and compete on
equal footing. Chinese swarmed to the area.
By 1852 there were 25,000 in the state, making them the largest minority, and most of
them were in the mines. For the state one
person in ten was Chinese; in some of the
mining counties, three out of ten.

In 1852 Senator George B. Tingley introduced a measure to authorize contract labor

Joaquín Murieta

on a ten-year basis, supervised by the state. The assembly approved, but the senate, alert to what this would mean in the mines, defeated the bill. When Governor John Bigler urged a law to check the tide of Asiatic immigration, Rev. William Speer, a former missionary, spoke up in praise of the Chinese, but others bore down on them as morally depraved transients and a menace to the state's tranquillity. The legislature responded with a renewal of the foreign miners' tax with full expectation that its principal application would be to the Chinese. There were evasions and peculations by some of the collectors, but from that date, 1852, through the sixties nearly a quarter of the state's re-

Young Aristocrats

Arnold Genthe

ceipts would be obtained from this source.

In 1854 the state government added another thrust. In *People vs. Hall* the state supreme court extended the constitutional ban on testimony against a white by an Indian to exclude the Chinese as well. The reasoning was that "Indian" was a generic term intended to cover all nonwhites, to which the justices added what was then the quaint notion that Indians and Chinese were of the same "Mongolian" branch of humankind.

The Chinese endured these and other discriminations. In the sixties the building of the Pacific Railroad improved the market for Chinese labor and, though thousands were imported, little friction resulted. Chinese also proved themselves in agricultural labor. They began the process of establishing a welcome as launderers, houseboys, cooks, and vegetable growers and peddlers. Yet in these first decades there was a foretaste of greater discrimination to come.

CHAPTER 14

**Ballard's Little Red Schoolhouse in Use
Continuously since 1883**

King Merrill

Between 1848, when James W. Marshall discovered gold at Coloma, and 1869, when San Francisco celebrated the building of a railroad that ended its isolation, a people lived through a condensed version of the world's economic and cultural growth. To this phenomenon the writers of El Dorado owe their distinction and western literature its absorbing interest.

Franklin Walker
San Francisco's Literary Frontier

Cultural Awakening

Church and School

The gold rush stimulated a cultural awakening. The Spaniards had made California a Christian land, and to them, of course, Christian meant Roman Catholic. Protestant services and churches date from the gold rush. Several denominations sent missionaries to California, the American armed forces brought chaplains, and the forty-niners included a goodly number of clergymen. One observer, doubtless exaggerating, put the preachers at one in ten.

San Francisco as in all else took the lead. In November, 1848, a conclave of its citizens invited Rev. Timothy Dwight Hunt to be city chaplain on a nondenominational basis. Thirteen months later there were 12 bona fide ministers established in their work, and by the midfifties San Francisco could boast 32 churches ranging from African Methodist to Welsh Presbyterian.

The pioneer period is better represented by William Taylor's street preaching in San Francisco or by the circuit rider in the diggings who persuaded a saloonkeeper to clear a space before the bar for a Sunday morning discourse. Except in the suddenness with which organized churches took shape, California's experience was that of the West in general. Many of her pioneers had no interest in churches. Others out of homesickness or conviction wanted the solace of religion and tried to achieve as close a reproduction as possible of their accustomed church.

How well they succeeded is another matter. Sarah Royce, perhaps with excess of charity, remarks on the "fixed attention," the "intense earnestness," and the "reverence, devotion, and glow of intelligence" characterizing the congregation she observed in San Francisco. On his visit in 1859 Dana met a Harvard man, a regular churchgoer in New England, who could not even direct him to Bishop W. Ingraham Kip's church. Once he located it, Dana found a congregation "precisely like one you would meet in New York, Philadelphia, or Boston."

Although it was said of San Francisco at the time that being a religious man was considered "not exactly a crime but only a misfortune," men of outstanding talent labored in its churches. Episcopalian Bishop Kip, Catholic Archbishop Joseph S. Alemany, Presbyterian William A. Scott, and Unitarians Thomas Starr King and Horatio Stebbins were leading and influential citizens.

Notwithstanding some lapses, as at San Luis Rey, the massive architecture of the missions well suited the land. The church buildings of the early American period, of all shapes and styles or of no style at all, disfigured the scene more often than adorned it.

Formal education in California began with the Franciscan missions. For pupils other than Indians Bancroft lists 55 schools of the Spanish and Mexican periods. Except for W. E. P. Hartnell's Colegio de San José all were elementary and most functioned only briefly. It is understandable that, when it could be afforded, boys were sent away to Honolulu, Valparaiso, or even to Paris for their elementary schooling. In 1847 several American-type schools were opened, the first at Santa Clara. On April 3, 1848, San Francisco pioneered with a public school taught by Thomas Douglas, formerly of the Young Chief's School in Honolulu. By the end of May, when four of the five trustees and all but eight of the pupils had been carried away by the gold fever, schoolmaster Douglas closed his classroom and took himself off to the mines.

The upsurge of population, wealth, and, more gradually, of stability contributed by the gold rush gave momentum to the demand for schools. Several of the missionary pastors engaged in teaching as well as in preaching, and under other private auspices schools were opened. In the American culture pattern public responsibility to provide for instruction was recognized. The state consitution called for a school, operating at least three months every year, in each district in the state. The legislature in 1851 passed an implementing act, later improved and broadened.

The first state superintendent of schools, John C. Marvin, was elected in 1851. He worked diligently for a system of public schools which would be free, secular, compulsory, state financed, and relevant for Californians by including geology and mineralogy and stressing Spanish and French rather than Latin and Greek. The legislature moved gradually in the direction Marvin recommended, and within two years public schools were opened in 47 counties. In 1862 the office of

John C. Swett

California State Library

state superintendent was filled by a dedicated, energetic, and persuasive apostle of education, a young San Francisco teacher, John C. Swett.

Twice reelected, Swett had a total of five years in which to make his imprint on the state school system. His achievements included a rewriting of the school law in 1866 and completion of the transition to a free public school system. He has been hailed as the Horace Mann of California and the father of this state's public school system. Swept out of office in the Democratic landslide of 1867, Swett went back to the ranks of teacher and principal in San Francisco. In 1890, upon challenging Blind Boss Buckley's patronage school appointments, he was forced to resign.

California's first kindergarten opened in San Francisco in 1863, and its most famous one, the Silver Street kindergarten in Tar Flat, a slum as tough as the Barbary Coast, was opened by Kate Douglas Wiggins, later a very successful children's writer. Meanwhile, a number of academies and seminaries approximately of high school level had been started, and in 1856 San Francisco pioneered with the first public high school.

The University of Santa Clara traces its origins back to the College of Santa Clara and to classes conducted in 1851. The University of the Pacific, through a college, traces back to 1851, and the University of California, through the private College of California which it later absorbed, goes back to 1855.

In 1868, encouraged by the federal subsidy offered through the Morrill Land Grant Act, the legislature chartered the University of California as a state institution. It enrolled its first students in Oakland in 1869 and the next year took the radical step of admitting women students. In 1872 it gained distinction through the appointment of Daniel Coit Gilman as president and the following year shifted to its campus in Berkeley. From the start the university had some excellent men on its faculty, including John and Joseph LeConte, professors of physics and geology, and Ezra S. Carr, professor of agriculture and horticulture.

It was not, however, a university in today's sense, associating several collegiate programs or offering advanced work. In 1874 a controversy came to a head over whether the stress should be on agriculture and mechanic arts with instruction in carpentry, blacksmithing, and other practical fields or on a more comprehensive and liberal program of instruction. The general education advocates prevailed, but before the year was out President Gilman decided that he would find a more congenial climate of opinion in the East and resigned to go to Johns Hopkins, where he developed the first genuine graduate school in the United States.

Theater

The theater was a culture form that could respond buoyantly to the stimulation of gold. Although there had been amateur performances such as those by the men of Stevenson's regiment, bored by garrison duty at Monterey, the first professional to take a turn apparently was Stephen Massett from England. In June, 1849, he put on a one-man show in San Francisco. In a rich baritone he sang several of his own compositions; in falsetto he mimicked an operatic diva. Next came a series of monologues in Yankee dialect, climaxed by a seven-voice rendition of a New England town meeting. Massett was followed by a minstrel show at the Bella Union, its run cut short when one of the "bones" was killed. Later in 1849, in a large tent at Clay and Kearny, Joseph Rowe presided over a circus featuring nine acrobats and equestrians and a posing horse.

At Sacramento the Eagle Theater company opened with *The Bandit Chief; or, The Forest Spectre*. Plays such as *The Wife, Dead Shot, Othello, Batchelor Buttons, William Tell, Rent Day,* and *Charles II* were also in the repertoire. In January, 1850, this company brought legitimate theater to San Francisco. Although the manager of the troupe lost the first week's receipts at monte, the popular response encouraged other impresarios to provide similar entertainment. Rowe built a platform across one end of this tent and substituted actors for acrobats. As an annex to the Parker House saloon and gambling hall Tom Maguire opened a theater which he called the Jenny Lind. When this theater burned he built a second Jenny Lind and, when it burned, a third which the city fathers bought for a city hall. With $50,000 raised by popular subscription Dr. David Robinson built the Adelphi. He was responsible also for the American Theater and had a share in Bryant Minstrels, later converted into San Francisco Hall and still later into Maguire's Opera House.

The ebullience of the audience often made playing the San Francisco stage an exciting experience. Making the circuit of the mining camps was even more of a test. Traveling by stagecoach or on horseback, putting up at primitive hotels, living on rough fare, and performing in makeshift theaters, the troupers had to rise above circumstances. A play, often sharply curtailed, was the feature of each performance. To it the artists added solos, dances, readings, impersonations, and skits, a combination of legitimate theater and vaudeville.

The mining camp playgoers were exacting. As in San Francisco, when lines were cut, forgotten, or muffed, they stamped and hooted. On the other hand, if a performance caught their fancy, they showered the stage with coins, nuggets, and bags of gold dust.

The theater faced competition from cockfights, bull-and-bear fights, and other bizarre amusements. The saloon and the gambling

Lola Montez

UCLA Library

Lotta Crabtree

The Bancroft Library

hall were more potent counterattractions. Borrowing from the theater, the larger of these establishments added musicians, dancers, variety acts, and minstrel acts. Headline talent came to the Gold Coast. Representing the minstrels were Ed Christy, end man Eph Horn, soft-shoe dancer Dan Bryant, and banjo virtuoso Thomas F. Briggs. Singers Elisa Biscaccianti and Kate Hayes joined the trek. So did a host of noble actors, including the Booths, the Chapmans, Edwin Forrest, Catherine Sinclair, and such personalities as Lola Montez, Adah Isaacs Menken, and Mathilda Heron.

The paragon of the gold rush theater was Lotta Crabtree. Her debut was at a tiny log theater in Rabbit Creek. In long-tailed green coat, knee breeches, and tall hat, she bounced onstage and danced a vigorous Irish jig and reel. After encores she reappeared in a white dress with round neck and puffed sleeves and sang a plaintive ballad. The hardened miners went wild, showering the stage with coins, nuggets, and a 50-dollar slug. Brown-eyed,

red-haired Lotta, all of eight years old but looking no more than six, was their darling.

Tutored by her ambitious mother and other willing helpers, Lotta made a rapid tour of the camps. She learned new songs and steps. A black minstrel taught her to do a soft-shoe breakdown. Lola Montez introduced her to Spanish dancing and Jake Wallace taught her how to make a banjo ring. From others she picked up buck-and-wing and new bits of pantomime. Thus equipped she could put on a whole show in the style of Stephen Massett. With barrel-top numbers at auctions, variety billings in the mines and in San Francisco, bits in the regular plays, and specialties between acts, Lotta had a busy childhood. In one little vibrant bundle of energy she represented the things the Californians of this generation most prized: humor and pathos, high skill and lower buffoonery, mastery of the traditional forms and indulgence in pyrotechnics.

Less spectacularly the gold rush encouraged the pictorial arts. In illustrated books,

191

canvases, and illustrated letterheads this record is partly preserved. Delano's drawings, Charles Nahl's group scenes, J. W. Audubon's travel sketches, J. Goldsborough Bruff's sketches, the paintings of W. S. Jewett and Thomas Hill, and Edward Vischer's lithograph prints are examples.

Journalism

California writing began long before the golden era. The classics include Palóu's *Life of Serra*, Font's *Complete Diary*, Shaler's *Description*, Pattie's *Personal Narrative*, Robinson's *Life in California*, Bryant's *What I Saw in California*, and Frémont's *Report*. Most of these books are distinguished for content more than for style, yet they are usually pronounced readable, and one of their company, Dana's *Two Years Before the Mast*, besides being widely circulated, is frequently used in academic courses as a model of style in English composition.

Palóu's and Font's writings were works of Christian duty, but these writers, like the others, were inspired by a conviction that the existing California experiences of which they had direct knowledge were eminently worth recording and would be read with interest in Mexico and Spain or in the States. The same is true of the trail journals, ocean logs, and miners' diaries of '49. The first book printed in the province, Figueroa's 16-page code of laws (1834), though intended for local use, was hardly literature; nor was the arithmetic book, *Tablas por los niños que empiezen a contar*, printed two years later.

The outset of the American period was marked by an increased demand for reading matter, a demand that was met after a fashion by the shin-plaster journals started by Semple and Colton at Monterey and by Brannan and Kemble at San Francisco. With the gold rush the demand multiplied. It was evidenced by the long queues at the San Francisco post office, the special fees readily collectible for delivery of letters at the mines, the popular excitement whenever a steamer entered the Golden Gate, and the high prices paid for eastern newspapers which were part of the incidental baggage of the Argonauts. Fifteen hundred copies of Greeley's *Tribune*, brought by a fellow passenger of Bayard Taylor, sold within two hours for a dollar apiece.

The first repercussion of the gold excitement in the summer of 1848, drawing away editors and compositors as well as subscribers and advertisers, was the suspension of publication of the pioneer weeklies, the *Californian* and the *California Star*. The secondary effect was the creation of a much larger field for journalism. Reviving their moribund sheets, the editors decided on January 4, 1849, to pool their resources in a new venture, the subsequently famous *Alta California*. In May the *Placer Times* blossomed at Sacramento, followed shortly by a motley assortment of papers scattered through the bay region and the mining towns. Included for a short time in the fall of 1850 was the *Illustrated Times*, which lived up to its name by featuring woodcuts. Also of short duration was the allegedly humorous *Hombre* of 1851, a pioneer in its field. Reflecting California's cosmopolitan character, the press quickly became multilingual. In 1850 the first French paper appeared, in 1852 one in German, two years later the first Spanish journals, and shortly after one in Chinese. Eventually there were publications in practically all languages, including the Scandinavian.

Quantitatively, California journalism scaled heights that without the gold rush would not have been attained for decades. For many years the state could boast a per capita circulation exceeding even that of New York. As for quality praise must be more niggardly. The presses, type, and paper available were uniformly inferior, composition and presswork were indifferent, and proofreading was an undeveloped art. Most of the sheets were blatantly partisan and reflected the malodorous state of local politics. News coverage was haphazard, editors depended largely on their shears, and much that was printed seemed to have no other justification than that it filled space. The most hopeful sign was a tendency to escape some of the inhibitions of eastern journalists.

San Francisco naturally enough had the lion's share of these early newspapers, yet some of the most influential journals were not of the city. Two examples stand out, the Sacramento *Union* and the Virginia City *Territorial Enterprise*. In the fifties the Sacramento *Union* was of moderate significance. It had the advantage, however, of being near the seat of state government and the greater advantage of honest, patriotic, and high-minded management. Its proprietors aimed to be fearless champions of the common people and to the best of their ability they adhered to that policy.

The *Union*'s proprietors wielded a remarkable influence and employed and subsidized a notable staff of writers, among them Mark Twain. It was a "travel grant" from the *Union* that made possible his jaunt to the Sandwich Islands, which in turn led to his career as a platform lecturer, his world tour, and the travel book *Innocents Abroad*.

The *Territorial Enterprise* issued from Washoe, later labeled Nevada, but the society which it vocalized was part and parcel of the California culture area, and it is no violence to the facts to include it in a discussion of the state's early journalism. In addition, the *Enterprise* had special ties with California. Joseph T. Goodman, its editor and guiding genius, was a graduate of California's *Golden Era*, as was Rollin M. Daggett, whose principal fame is as cofounder of that magazine. Mark Twain heads the list of those who reached California publishers by way of the Nevada paper which

Mark Twain
California State Library

he immortalized so satisfactorily in *Roughing It*.

The journal flourished in the lush environment of sagebrush and alkali, nurtured on the white gold of the fabulous Comstock. The Washoe community was, if possible, more masculine and more unrestrained than the camps of the forty-niners. Journalism in this unreal setting was free to follow any path of hyperbole or to perpetrate any outlandish hoax and under no obligation to print a story just because it was news. With what gusto the "sagebrush school" embraced this opportunity can be seen in the books of Mark Twain and Dan De Quille (William Wright) or, better still, in the broken files of the *Territorial Enterprise*.

From Golden Era to Overland Monthly

Most early California newspapers contained a few literary pieces, which were received with enough favor to suggest in 1852 the issuance of a weekly paper largely devoted to such

193

materials. This journal, the *Golden Era*, included ordinary news but its distinction lies in its emphasis on literature. It flourished for almost half a century and was read more widely than any of its competitors. This very popularity made the journal suspect.

Superior and condescending critics have often remarked that the *Era* catered to low tastes, specifically to those of California's rustics and miners. The accusation may be true. Attired in miner's boots and flannel shirt, co-editor Daggett did tour the diggings soliciting subscriptions. The editors furthermore chose to emphasize California themes. To start the paper off, Daggett had written up an adventure he encountered on the overland trail from the States, and his partner, J. Macdonough Foard, had drawn similarly on his recollections of Cape Horn. To the end the *Era* dealt mainly with matters within the comprehension or even the experience of a majority of Californians. Only in dramatic criticism did it take on airs.

For all its popularity the *Era* did not produce the best articles. Contributors, having acquired a reputation through its columns, were quick to desert to more pretentious journals. Thus surprisingly little of the prose and poetry that it printed was judged worthy of inclusion in the collected works of Mark Twain, Bret Harte, and the rest. With one or two exceptions, however, the entire galaxy of early California writers found their initial opportunity in the *Era*. Alonzo Delano's pen name, Old Block, was a frequent signature during the fifties, as were also Caxton (William A. Rhodes) and Yellow Bird (John R. Ridge).

In the sixties the new editor, Colonel Joe Lawrence, was even more indefatigable in casting the net for local writers. Mark Twain, fresh from his triumphs with the *Territorial Enterprise*, contributed enough sketches to make a small volume. Bret Harte entered "by the backdoor" as compositor and before

long contributed "M'liss," archetype of the California short story. Ina Coolbrith, Joaquin Miller, Charles Warren Stoddard, and Charles Henry Webb, better known to his readers as Inigo, are representative of others who got their start with the miners' favorite. So notable a roster is ample justification for the *Era's* policy of being popular and unpretentious.

Competitors were numerous but for the most part shortlived. One of these was the *Pioneer*, launched as a monthly in January, 1854, and kept afloat only two years. In the first issue, probably to emphasize the contrast to the *Golden Era*, Ferdinand C. Ewer announced that the new magazine would be devoted to literature, politics, science, belles lettres, poetry, and "the more flowery paths of Literature." The contributions of California writers, he predicted, would make the magazine a credit to "the noble State in which it had its origin." The promise was realized in fair degree.

The fame of the *Pioneer* really rests on certain prose contributions. Early issues contained a serial, "California in 1851," now known as the *Shirley Letters* and hailed as one of the most accurate, penetrating, and charming descriptions of life in the diggings. Another outstanding contributor was Stephen Massett. His column, signed James Pipes of Pipesville, contained many a sparkling gem.

Ewer's greatest triumph was to entice George H. Derby to contribute. Beginning in June, 1854, nine successive issues contained Derby's humorous sketches under the pseudonym John Phoenix, the more remarkable because they were composed in the somnolent repose of San Diego. Eastern journals hailed the *Pioneer* as "a capital periodical ... freighted with good things," and the Boston *Post* said, "we prize it like a nugget of gold for its many excellences." These journals paid the *Pioneer* the more obvious

John P. Squibob

George H. Derby. Phoenixiana

compliment of copying its material wholesale, especially the John Phoenix sketches. In spite of such wide and favorable notice and notwithstanding its fine roster of writers, the *Pioneer* could not continue beyond its second year.

Next in the field was Hutchings' *California Magazine*, begun in 1856. A much quoted item is his "The Miner's Ten Commandments." His favorite theme is illustrated by his "In the Heart of the Sierra," an impassioned tribute to the beauty and grandeur of the Yosemite Valley. He is often regarded as the first of the California nature enthusiasts.

The *Hesperian*, founded in 1858, gained distinction by falling into the hands of Mrs. F. H. Day. She improved the quality of illustrations, introduced a juvenile department, and gave the magazine something of a homey tone, yet managed to retain a measure of masculine interest.

The *Californian*, established in 1864, ran for only three years, but its quality was so high and its contributors so distinguished that it deserves more than passing interest. Editor Charles Henry Webb had left the *Era* with the avowed intention of producing a more "high-toned" magazine. Assisted by such literati as Stoddard, Coolbrith, and Twain, he succeeded in this laudable purpose only to find the market totally inadequate.

California's literary tradition culminated in the *Overland Monthly*, launched in July, 1868, and terminating its first series in 1875. Revived in 1883, the *Overland* survived various vicissitudes but did not duplicate the achievements of the initial series. Origin of the magazine is credited to the publisher, Anton Roman, and to him goes a further plaudit for vesting absolute editorial control in Francis Bret Harte. It was Bret Harte's editorial genius, and often his pen, that gave the *Overland* its high repute.

As the vehicle in which the best of his stories and poems appeared, the *Overland* was an important chapter in Bret Harte's personal development yet no more so than in the literary evolution of the West. In its heyday this journal drew the writings of practically every promising local author and by its high standards challenged them to improve.

Also significant was the stress on the potentialities of the West. Its subtitle proclaimed that the *Overland* was "devoted to the development of the country," a pledge redeemed in a number of ways. Besides a quota of enthusiastic descriptive pieces the early numbers contained items such as "High Noon of the Empire," "The Tropical Fruits of California," "Art Beginnings on the Pacific Slope," and "Farming Facts for California Immigrants," all frankly promotional.

Even more noteworthy was the deter-

Bret Harte

California State Library

kin." Yet to catalog the subjects tells only half the story. Much of this writing had a vibrancy, a freshness, a western flavor difficult to analyze but unmistakably recognizable. It was this quality which won the *Overland* a warm reception on the Atlantic Coast as well as on the Pacific.

Books along with magazines made their appearance. Included were such compendia as *The Annals of San Francisco*, by Soulé, Gihon, and Nisbet (1855); *The Resources of California*, by John S. Hittell (1863); *The Natural Wealth of California*, by Titus Fey Cronise (1868); and two anthologies of western poetry. Two thrillers were far more widely read: Ridge's *Joaquín Murieta* and Royal B. Stratton's *Captivity of the Oatman Girls*. Treatises on philosophy and political economy are conspicuously absent, and history has no better representatives than Frost and Dwinelle. Thus nonfiction was at the level of simple reporting and narration rather than of contemplative inquiry.

mined effort to give the *Overland* an unmistakably western flavor. The *Atlantic Monthly* is often cited as its model and inspiration; the *Overland*, however, was not a mere imitation of the Boston monthly but rather its Pacific counterpart, differing from it as West from East. A glance at the contents of the first volume reveals a few contributions, such as the Reverend E. C. Bissell's "Egotizing" or T. H. Rearden's "Favoring Female Conventualism," which were environmentally footloose.

A much larger number would have seemed outlandish in the *Atlantic*. They are by no means confined to California but range broadly over the American West and the Pacific area, illustrating the expansive outlook of the *Overland* and of Californians. Random examples are: "Portland-on-Wallamett," "The Apache Race," "A Ride on the Texas Frontier," "The French in Mexico," "Carthagena," "Lima," "Hawaiian Civilization," "Japanese Holy Places," and "In Nan-

The Galaxy of Writers

Many of the writers of this early period have been judged worthy of no more than passing attention. The majority of the poets, in particular, may be dismissed with the remark that their outpourings were indifferent in quality and contributed little to American letters. Quantity was not lacking. The wares of these poets may be sampled in the files of the early magazines and newspapers and in anthologies such as *Poetry of the Pacific*, assembled in 1865 by May Wentworth, and *Outcroppings*, sponsored the following year by Bret Harte. The modern reader is apt to close these volumes with little reluctance. As to early acclaim Bret Harte and Joaquin Miller were the leaders together with Coolbrith, Stoddard, and Pollock.

In the field of prose the quality was somewhat higher. In the fifties, for example, there was the miners' particular favorite, Alonzo Delano, who wrote under the name of Old Block, contributing to many papers and journals and illustrating many of his pieces with appropriate caricatures. It was inevitable that Delano's fame should decline with the passing of the forty-niner generation, for much of his writing was dated and presupposed familiarity with the diggings. Furthermore, Delano's readers in the fifties were under the spell of his personal magnetism: his nose, California's largest, and his integrity, demonstrated so forcefully in the panic of 1855 when he undertook to pay off the obligations of his bankrupt employer. The most durable of his books is his narrative of 1849, *Life on the Plains and Among the Diggings*.

Of greater fame and doubtless of greater stature was George H. Derby of the Topographical Engineers. He came to California in 1849 with an excellent military record and left half a dozen years later with the reputation of being the nation's favorite humorist. More important were the hilarious sketches he published in the *Alta California* under the name Squibob and then in the *Pioneer* under the name John Phoenix which were reproduced in journals far and near. In 1856 a hastily assembled collection was brought out as a book, *Phoenixiana*, which soon ran through 34 editions. Some of his choicest bits can be appreciated today only by antiquarians immersed in the nicer details of late gold rush California, yet even the most modern reader will find that his wit has not lost all its savor.

It was in the West that Mark Twain found himself and it was there that he had his first practice in writing and as platform lecturer. Western themes were his first stock in trade, and western readers were his first, his most loyal, and his most consistent supporters.

Bret Harte's debt to California was even greater. Not only were California journals his first medium of publication, but in gold rush California he found the setting for all that was meritorious in his writing. He had a mastery of expression, but for all its excellence his style availed him little except when he was exploiting the unique background of California in its golden era.

Joaquin Miller also became a world celebrity through strictly western writing. Playing up outward manifestations of the West in a bid for attention, he paraded in London society attired in miner's boots and red flannel shirt. The genuineness of his westernism, nonetheless, is beyond dispute. He wrote with the fervor of sincerity. He did not desert California and it was constantly recurrent as the theme of his poetry. He made slips in grammar, his poorer poems detract from his best, and his paean to the West is not distinctive. Nevertheless Miller still stands above the other California poets of his day.

To single out Delano, Derby, Twain, Bret Harte, and Miller may obscure the picture of the broader ranks of California writers. That they were many is an elementary fact; that they produced an astonishing quantity of creditable literature is also admitted. An explanation must include comment on the caliber of the individuals brought to California in 1849, allowance for the early material prosperity, recognition of the stimulation afforded by the majesty of nature in the West, and allusion to the isolation which dictated western publishing instead of the mere purchase of eastern goods. These early Californians also had a high estimate of their own importance. They were the pioneers who had reached continent's end; overnight they were erecting a magnificent state; their gold was a decisive factor in preserving the Union. California writers, steeped in this feeling, were sure they had something important to write about.

CHAPTER 15

POST OFFICE, SAN FRANCISCO, CALIFORNIA.

A FAITHFUL REPRESENTATION OF THE CROWDS DAILY APPLYING AT THAT OFFICE FOR LETTERS AND NEWSPAPERS.

San Francisco Post Office

Library of Congress

As a motion picture man once told me: We don't want to present the stage-coach as it was. We must show it as the people think it was. Or else they won't believe us.

William and George Hugh Banning
Six Horses

Steamboats and Stages

In the drowsy calm of the pastoral period California had made no transportation demands which could not be met by a saddled horse, an ox-drawn carreta, or the irregular sailings of the trading vessels. The Argonauts wanted more modern means of getting about, for which they were ready to pay. The result was a revolution in communications within the state and a speedy provision of land and sea connections with other parts of the world, particularly the eastern states.

On Inland and Coastal Waters

Commissioned by fellow miners, Alexander Todd came down to the San Francisco post office to carry up their mail at an ounce a letter. Bill Ballou cut the price to a quarter ounce and carried a thimble as measuring cup. With only 34 post offices in the state by June, 1851, private mail carrying expanded and soon merged with a reverse flow of gold delivery. Adams and Company opened a San Francisco office in 1849 and Wells, Fargo in 1852. Their express carrying was supplemented throughout the interior by many smaller outfits.

Carrying passengers was another opportunity. The first artery was the river line to Sacramento, plied by a miscellany of small craft propelled by sail and oar. A few round-the-Horn ships were worked up to Sacramento. By the late summer of 1849 sidewheelers were in commission, soon joined by the 400-ton *McKim* and the *Senator*, said to have netted her owners $60,000 a month. Within a year fifty steamers large and small were operating on the bay and the inland waterways. The *New World*, built for excur-

Sacramento from the River   *The Bancroft Library*

sion duty on the Hudson, was boarded up and sent around the Horn. On the San Francisco–Sacramento run she cut the *Senator*'s time from ten to six hours.

Competitive rate wars, lowering the Sacramento fare from $25 or $30 to $1, led to organization of the California Steam Navigation Company in 1854, capitalized at $2,500,000. Stabilizing fares at $10 for cabin, $7 for deck, and $6 to $8 for a ton of freight, the company made comfortable profits. Would-be competitors were forced out or bought out. The company also gained control of several coastal routes: to Humboldt Bay, to San Diego and way points, to the Columbia, and in 1867 to Alaska.

Disasters were common. The waters were not thoroughly chartered, many vessels were faulty, steamboat inspections were lax, and the passion for racing led to boiler explosions. The first half dozen years saw a score of such accidents with up to 50 people killed. The Californians delighted in impromptu races and the more steam carried the better they liked it.

At an early date steamships became the chief connection of San Diego, Los Angeles,

Santa Barbara, San Luis Obispo, and Santa Cruz to the San Francisco metropolis. At these towns steamer day became a major feature on the calendar, and for several decades these ships provided the most favored transportation. Schooners and steamships were soon plying the wilder coast north of San Francisco, accepting passengers and general cargo, but chiefly loading lumber at Eureka and less sheltered ports. This connection with the outside world was dominant past the end of the nineteenth century.

From San Pedro stages ran to Los Angeles. They were the way to reach Yosemite and many other points in the state. Wagon freighting also became a very active business, to and from the ports, ranchos, mines, forts, and Indian reservations, from Los Angeles to San Bernardino and back, and all the way to Salt Lake.

By the sixties a number of shortline railroads had been built where proven traffic already was available. The Los Angeles–San Pedro route, realizing Phineas Banning's scheme, was ready for service in 1869. Six years later the Los Angeles and Independence Railroad, which looked across Cajon Pass to

Los Angeles and San Pedro Train, 1870 *UCLA Library*

mines on the Nevada border, laid tracks to the Santa Monica waterfront and gave Los Angeles a second access to shipping.

Staging

In the autumn of 1849 John Whistman, with an old French omnibus and a mixed team of mustangs and mules, offered a ride from San Francisco to San Jose, the fare, two ounces. A competing line appeared. In the autumn of 1850 two experienced stage operators, Warren F. Hall and Jared B. Crandall, bought out Whistman and extended service to Monterey. Their lyric advertising emphasized "no more charming drive" and the skill of their drivers, "Professors Dillon and Crandall." Professor Crandall's most famous drive was in the fall of 1850. With Governor Burnett on the box beside him, he raced toward the state capital in San Jose to beat the rival stage and delivered the news of California's admission to statehood.

Meanwhile, at Sacramento young James Birch had come on the scene with a ranch wagon and four fractious mustangs, offering a 30-mile ride to Mormon Island at a fare of two ounces. Enthusiastic response attracted others to the business. Lines multiplied and extended to the major camps in the northern diggings, even as far as Shasta. By the fall of 1851 the San Francisco papers were ready to admit that Sacramento had become the hub of the stage lines. The daily stages included six to Marysville, two to Coloma, and one each to Nevada City, Placerville, Auburn, Stockton, and Drytown-Jackson. The daily haul on the Marysville run averaged 70 passengers each way. Fares had been reduced from the original dollar a mile, but they were still enough to make the business highly profitable.

Rivalries and the price structure stimulated rapid improvements in horse flesh and rolling stock. American horses replaced the native cowponies. Matched leaders and wheelers ordered from Kentucky and Ohio cost as much as $4,000 a span. The first Concord appeared in San Francisco in June, 1850, creating a sensation and nostalgia in the editor of the *Alta*. Manufactured by Abbott, Downing of Concord, New Hampshire, these coaches were freighted around the Horn or caravaned overland.

By the midfifties the California lines boasted newer and better equipment than anywhere else. On a conventional running gear with a pair of C-shaped springs anchored to each axle, thoroughbraces (manifold leather straps) were stretched to cradle the egg-shaped body of the Concord. This suspension allowed the body to swing fore and aft. However much the passengers were inconvenienced, the device was an effective shock absorber for the teams, and to spare the horses was the ruling purpose.

Nine or ten passengers could be squeezed in, and about as many on top. Boots at front and back carried mail and baggage. The Concord weighed less than most "light" automobiles. Delivered in California they cost $1,200 to $1,500. Although driven at great speed— 10, 12, or even 15 miles per hour over unconscionably rough roads—they seldom needed repairs.

The driver or "whip," as he preferred to be called, was one of the heroic figures of the West. His wizardry in piloting a stage on a night run or careening down a mountain road and his exploits in foiling hold-ups and Indian attacks made him a legend. And indeed, to manipulate whip and brake and play upon the six reins so that each horse was individually controlled called for a virtuoso.

Schedules up to 60 miles in 6 hours and record runs of 160 miles in 13 hours were unsurpassed except perhaps by England's Royal Mail, with its advantage of macadamized post roads.

In 1854, the year of the consolidation of the

riverboats, five-sixths of the state's stage lines were joined in the California Stage Company. Two young New Englanders, James Birch and Frank Stevens, headed the company. The new company, capitalized at $1 million, advertised regular service on lines totaling 1,500 miles and "the most extensive and complete line of stages in THE WORLD." Two years later, with 3,000 miles of stage lines in regular operation, not to mention the large fleet of steamboats plying the inland waters, the state could boast excellent facilities for handling intrastate passengers, mail, and express.

The Panama Steamers

With California's sudden flourishing, improved facilities for those who needed to go back or forth were a necessity. The Panama steamers were the most promising for passengers. The Pacific Mail tried to build up its fleet, but for several years its ships were crowded. That circumstance prompted "Commodore" Cornelius Vanderbilt of the Hudson River boats and ferries to promote a competing line using the Nicaragua crossing.

Nevertheless hazards were real; these ships were subject to wreck, fire, and foundering. The Pacific Mail lost the $300,000 *Tennessee* off San Francisco in 1853. The Vanderbilt line lost five vessels. The crowning disaster came in 1857, some 400 miles below Point Hatteras when the palatial *Central America* spread her seams and foundered, carrying to a watery grave more than $2 million in gold and 400 men.

Notwithstanding the hazards the Panama route came to be the favored path between California and the States. Completion in 1855 of the Panama railroad, alleged to have cost a yellow fever victim per tie, reduced the transit schedule from three or four days to four hours. The larger steamers put into service also reduced the running time, especially on the

Pacific, and by 1866 the schedule had been pared from 33 or 34 days to 21. The fare fluctuated wildly, but in the later years it was usually less than half the original rate of $450 for first class and $225 for steerage.

Government officials, politicians, businessmen, and men of means were almost unanimous in their choice of the Panama route. It was the choice also of the miners who, having struck it rich, wanted to return home. Much California mail was carried by way of Panama even after the opening of the overland stage line and was delivered as expeditiously. Express was also carried, and the shipments of California gold, which in Civil War days assumed such significance, were all by way of Panama. Perhaps the best indication of the importance of the steamship line is that the surplus of westbound over eastbound passengers accounted for a fifth of California's population increase in the fifties and for a half in the next decade.

The Clipper Ships

Gold Rush California called forth the glamorous climax for the American merchant marine, the California clippers, tall ships, graceful and powerful, the greyhounds of the sea. The Argonauts who rounded South America bought, hired, or commissioned so many sailing vessels, very few of them ever to return, that a boom in Yankee shipbuilding was inevitable. Then, because the gold findings were much more than a flash in the pan, California for years was ready to pay high charges for rapid shipment of many kinds of freight.

A young naval officer, Matthew F. Maury, had just completed a tabulation of ship logs of all seasons at all parts of the Seven Seas. From the data on winds and currents he was in position to chart the most favorable round-the-Horn track. It was not a great circle course or a land-hugging route. Instead it called for working far to the east in the Atlantic, then southwestward toward the Horn. There it might be necessary to sail much more to the south in order to work sufficiently to the west. Then farther north another seeming detour far to the west was prescribed for gaining the latitude of the Golden Gate. This course cut travel time by several weeks.

Yankee ship designers and builders made a comparable contribution. Owners had insisted on capacity and sturdiness more than speed. Now unleashed, the builders could turn to a hull shape that would cut through the water, a larger size, more sails, and captains instructed to drive the ships hard. From Boston or New York to San Francisco the forty-niners often were at sea six to eight months. McKay's *Flying Cloud* in 1851 came through in 89 days and 21 hours, and three years later trimmed that record by another 13 hours.

Throughout the fifties clipper after clipper came within ten or a dozen days of that record. In 1851 almost every ship paid for itself out of the freight charges on one run. The banner year was 1853. The number of sailings tailed off rapidly in the late fifties. By 1860 many of these fine ships had been idled, some too weakened to be driven hard, and others not able to compete with slower but more capacious ships on runs where speed was not necessary or profitable. Clippers had figured in the China trade, but their prime glory was rushing freight to the gold-inflated California market.

Pacific Railroad Surveys

Despite the magnificence of the clippers and the industriousness of the splashing steamships, Californians thought their state was entitled to an overland connection. Orators insisted that the federal government had the manifest duty to forge a transcontinental link, which meant a railroad. Easterners joined in, though on different grounds: national defense, national solidarity, and opportunity in the Pacific.

Less than a score of years earlier the first trains had begun operations near Baltimore. By 1850 the steam horse had become commonplace east of the Mississippi and north of the Ohio. The total track mileage, 9,818, was impressive, but practically all was accounted for by short lines of local initiative and construction, built to handle a traffic already in existence.

To throw a line across 2,000 miles of unoccupied plains and mountains to the Pacific was beyond the resources of any magnates then in the business, and, with the small prospect for traffic, it was not a proposition attractive to private enterprise. The advocates of a Pacific railroad ignored the economic realities, just as they underestimated the difficulties of actual construction.

Sectional squabbling over location of its eastern terminus held up authorization. The steamship companies lobbied against such bills, many easterners were unconvinced that the federal government should embark on so grandiose an internal improvement, and the exact technique of federal aid was not immediately agreed upon. Nevertheless, had there been unanimity on the route it seems probable that construction would have been begun in the early fifties. The federal government's first step toward establishing an overland connection with California was to appropriate $150,000 in 1853 for the survey of the several feasible Pacific railroad routes.

The surveys, conducted by the army, resulted in the accumulation of a vast quantity of topographical, ethnological, botanical, geological, zoological, and climatic information, impressively stored up in the ponderous tomes of the *Reports*. The surveys thus are of considerable geographic and academic interest, though, beyond the assertion that there were a half-dozen possible railroad routes to the Pacific, their practical utility was slight. Sectional bickerings prevented congressional action until 1862, at which time the politics of war determined the choice of route, and before actual construction took place a more thorough plotting proved necessary.

The Overland Stage

In the meantime Californians renewed their clamor for overland communications and at the end of the decade were rewarded with stage line, pony express, and telegraph. Although the telegraph was something of permanent utility, overland mail and pony express functioned only briefly. The latter shortened the interval for communications between California and the States, though, as demonstrated, improvements on the Panama line soon reduced its schedule to approximately the equivalent of the transcontinental stage. Toward the movement of passengers the pony express contributed nothing and the overland a negligible amount. On the score of practical utility, then, they deserve only a fraction of the attention which their spectacularity has won them in popular works and scholarly history. Their true significance is that they gave practical demonstration of the possibility of through service on the overland routes, and by their very shortcomings helped evoke the railroad.

For the stage line there were antecedents in certain mail contracts, such as one in 1850 to a "camping-out" company which freighted the mail from Independence to Santa Fé and another in 1851 for a line from Independence to Salt Lake City. Birch's flourishing California Stage Company was much better supplied with the wherewithal to provide rapid through service.

Californians, like the easterners, wasted much energy in bickering about the choice of route. Persuaded that Johnson's Pass was the best Sierra crossing, the state appropriated funds for road building, and in 1857 the intrepid Crandall inaugurated stage service across the Sierra from Placerville to Washoe.

Meanwhile, 75,000 California voters had petitioned Congress to construct a military wagon road to California by way of Salt Lake. This colossal document, the largest thus far laid on the Congressional doorstep, led to one appropriation of $200,000 for roadwork along the southern route and another of $300,000 for the Salt Lake line, but with the western terminus fixed far to the north of Johnson's Pass.

Hot on the heels of that appropriation, Postmaster General Aaron Brown of Tennessee was authorized to contract for six years at $600,000 a year for semiweekly service on a 25-day schedule from the Mississippi to San Francisco. He could be expected to choose the circuitous southern route. It was also freely predicted, despite the bid of an eastern coalition headed by John Butterfield, that the award would go to California's James Birch, hailed by the New York press as "a gentleman of large capital and much experience, and more competent, perhaps, than any other single man in the United States to execute this great mail contract."

In an apparent preliminary to the larger contract, Brown awarded Birch a $150,000 contract for monthly mail stages from San Antonio to San Diego. This line "from nowhere to nowhere," partly by relays and partly by camping out (hence its nickname, "the Jackass"), defies explanation except as a subsidiary of the larger overland. It went into operation late in 1857, giving Birch the honor of operating the first transcontinental stage line. By Presidential intervention, however, the greater opportunity was deflected from him into the hands of Butterfield and his

The Overland Mail

Theodore R. Davis, Harper's Weekly, *February 8, 1868*
Library of Congress

associates. Birch had little time to ponder on the strange ways of statesmen, for that very fall, still in his twenties, he perished at sea in the wreck of the *Central America*.

The task confronting Butterfield was in 12 months to man, stock, and equip 2,800 miles of stage line. For efficiency he divided the line at El Paso into an eastern and a western section, each consisting of four divisions 300 to 400 miles in length. West of El Paso the line was manned by Californians and stocked with California equipment.

Preparations were completed on the appointed day, September 17, 1858, and stages set out simultaneously from Tipton, Missouri, the railhead west of St. Louis, and from San Francisco. Each completed the run with more than a day to spare, the eastbound coach to be greeted by a congratulatory telegram from President Buchanan and the westbound to encounter exuberant enthusiasm at San Francisco. As the *Bulletin* described the event: "At a quarter after four o'clock the coach turned from Market into Montgomery Street. The driver blew his horn and cracked his whip; at which the horses, four in number, almost seemed to partake of his enthusiasm, and dashed ahead at a clattering pace, and the dust flew from the glowing wheels. At the same time a shout was raised, that ran with the rapidity of an electric flash along Montgomery Street, which throughout its length was crowded by an excited populace. As the coach dashed along through the crowds, the hats of the spectators were whirled in the air and the hurrah was repeated from a thousand throats, responsive to which, the driver, the lion of the occasion, doffed his weatherbeaten old slouch, and in uncovered dignity, like the victor of an old Olympic race, guided his foaming steeds toward the Post Office."

With no stopovers except to change horses, with no pretense at facilities for sleeping, and with not much preparation for meals en route, traveling the overland was hard work. For one passenger it brought on insanity, and another pair got on each other's nerves enough to provoke a duel. Others, inured to western hardships, pronounced the ride a thrill and a pleasure. But with emphasis on the mail rather than the passengers the overland ran on, occasionally disturbed by floods, or Indian attacks on the stations, and a few times requiring more than the allotted 25 days though usually getting through with two or three days to spare.

Northern California never really warmed to the Butterfield line principally because of the conviction that a faster schedule was easily possible on the central route. Crandall's stages were demonstrating the feasibility of the Sierra crossing. In 1858 the Postmaster General loosened the federal purse strings slightly to contract with John M. Hockaday for weekly mail from Independence to Salt Lake City and with George Chorpenning for carriage on to Placerville. Commencing a few weeks prior to Butterfield's line, the central route combine brought the mail through regularly, winter as well as summer, and often in less than the 38 days which the schedule allowed. The administration, however, was careful not to build this line up into a dangerous rival of the favored southern line.

In December, 1858, the government's preference was brought into the open in connection with the President's annual message to Congress. Advance copies were promised to the Tehuantepec steamer, the Butterfield line, and the Hockaday line, but to the latter's dismay no copy was forthcoming. Thus handicapped the race went not to the swift but to the favorite. The week's head start enabled the Butterfield messenger to win, but Hockaday and Chorpenning's elapsed time of 17 days and 12 hours was quicker by more than two days. Northern Californians, none too cordial toward Buchanan's southerners to start with, were all the more convinced of the superiority of the central route.

Postmaster General Brown, though limiting the Central Overland to a niggardly $320,000 subvention, was ready to lay out funds for still other lines to California. He let a contract for a monthly stage along the thirty-fifth parallel from Kansas City to Stockton, another for a stage from Neosho, Missouri, to Albuquerque, and a third for steamers from New Orleans to Tehuantepec and on to San Francisco. The San Antonio–San Diego, also established in 1858, was enlarged to a semi-monthly line. Brown's death early in the following spring brought in an economy-minded successor, who saved a million dollars a year by eliminating several of these lines and curtailing all the others with the conspicuous exception of the Butterfield.

Deprived of their mail contracts, Hockaday and Chorpenning found themselves in trouble. Hockaday sold out to the reigning entrepreneurs of Plains freighting, Russell, Majors, and Waddell. Their stages, known as the Leavenworth and Pike's Peak Express, and then as the Central Overland California and Pike's Peak Express, did a good business

to the Colorado mines and Salt Lake City, even though the cancellation of Chorpenning's contract left no through service to California.

The Pony Express and the Close of an Era

When a new menace appeared in the form of competitors on the Colorado run, William Russell decided to gamble. He announced to Senator Gwin that the COC & PPE would establish a pony express on a ten-day schedule. His partners were skeptical but considered their firm pledged to the venture, and on April 3, 1860, this most dramatic of transcontinental mails went into action. "Away across the endless dead level of prairie a black speck appears in the sky. . . . In a second or two it becomes a horse and rider, rising and falling, rising and falling—sweeping toward us nearer and nearer, and the flutter of hoofs come faintly to the ear—another instant and a whoop and hurrah . . . a wave of the rider's

The Overland Mail, Pony, and Telegraph   *UCLA Library*

hand, but no reply, and a man and horse burst past our excited faces, and go sweeping away like a belated fragment of storm."

Mark Twain's magic pen thus captured the spell of this miracle of horseflesh and horsemanship. Practical details fade into insignificance: the half-ounce letters in oilskin pouches, the boy jockeys, unarmed and depending on their ponies' speed to escape Indian ambushes, the 75 relays, the $5 postage, and the disappointingly small volume of westbound letters.

As publicity for the central route the Pony Express might have been successful. Popular fancy was captivated, but, before Congress attacked the problem of revamping the California mails, Lincoln had been elected, South Carolina had seceded, her sister states, Texas included, had followed, Fort Sumter had been fired upon, and the Civil War was under way. The Butterfield route was abandoned and its stock hustled northward to the Salt Lake line.

Although the ponies ran a little longer, gladdening California with news little more than a week old, even that service was outmoded on October 26, 1861, by the completion of the Pacific telegraph. In actuality the ponies' contribution was to expedite communications in the 19 months immediately preceding the telegraph and, more strikingly, to become the symbol of all the gallant efforts of the prerailroad era to provide the transcontinental link.

The day of the Concord was not over. In 1861 subsidies were shifted to improve service for Denver, the metroplis of Colorado mining, and Salt Lake City, the Mormon metropolis. The first run was accomplished in 17 days and, despite Indian hostility, the severe winter of 1861, and floods in the following spring, the stages kept rolling.

Financially, however, Russell, Majors, and Waddell were at the end of their resources and in March, 1862, had to surrender to a new magnate, the expansive Ben Holladay. Holladay was accused of having all the vices of the unprincipled, domineering, coarse, and ruthless tycoons who were then riding the crest of big business' sudden rise. He was not in the tradition of staging, knew little of its niceties as a craft, took no pride in the qualities of Concords or matched wheelers, and was a demanding taskmaster rather than an inspiring leader. On the other hand he had an astounding ability to get things done and had adequate finances. In the four years of his control western staging attained its largest scale. He had 3,300 miles of regular lines in operation and enjoyed a reputation, attested by Mark Twain, of getting the mail through. In 1866, on the eve of eclipse by the transcontinental railroad, he gave further proof of financial genius by selling out at a good price to Wells, Fargo and Company.

Most published accounts of prerailroad communication concentrate on the most dramatic ventures, such as Butterfield's Overland Mail, Russell's Pony Express, the army's experiment in the fifties with a camel caravan, or John A. "Snowshoe" Thompson's ski trips across the Sierra with a pack of mail on his back. Some of the phases usually neglected seem to be of comparable significance, particularly the development of communications within the state by steamboat and stage, California's contribution to overland staging, and the continued dependence on the Panama steamers. Pony and stage sometimes outraced steamer and often monopolized public attention, but it took a doughtier foe to wrest away the bulk of the business in passengers, express, and even mail. Steamer patronage was well maintained, the peak being reached in 1868. The next year the joining of the rails at Promontory terminated a colorful and significant epoch and reduced both steamers and stages to roles subordinate to that of the new hero, the puffing locomotive.

CHAPTER 16

Through to the Pacific

Lithograph by Currier & Ives, 1870

Let the great line be adorned with this crowning honor, the colossal statue of the great Columbus, whose design it accomplishes; hewn from the granite mass or a peak of the Rocky Mountains, overlooking the road; the mountain itself the pedestal; and the statue a part of the mountain; pointing with outreached arm to the western horizon, and saying to the flying passenger, "There is the east! There is India!"

Senator Thomas Hart Benton

Rails over the Sierra

Asa Whitney's Dream

First proposed with any seriousness by Asa Whitney in 1845, a transcontinental railroad was for a number of years a most visionary scheme. Gradually its advocates gained a more sympathetic hearing. The gold rush added incentive and shifted the destination from Oregon to California. The surveys of the early fifties pronounced several routes feasible; overland stages and pony express popularized the idea; and the sectional crisis emphasized the necessity of binding the Far West to the nation. Notwithstanding the formidable difficulties encountered, Whitney's dream was realized in 1869, just 24 years later.

Throughout, hopes were pinned on the entire Pacific area which the railroad would unlock: Oregon and British Columbia, the Russian holdings on the North Pacific, the islands of the South Seas, the Japan whose door Perry was even then opening, ancient China, and the India of Columbus. Significantly, it was always called the Pacific railroad.

The prospect for such a railroad was dimmed by the sheer magnitude of the project, two thousand or more miles over treeless plains and desert and with forbidding mountain ranges to surmount. Most of the way was uninhabited except for Indians. Few of the advocates had concrete ideas on how to engineer or finance such a road, much less how to build it.

Theodore D. Judah

The first to rescue the Pacific railroad from the limbo of hazy generalities and to discuss it in terms that would impress engineers and bankers was a young construction engineer, Theodore D. Judah. Before 1854 he assisted in rebuilding a section of the Erie Canal and helped build the bridge at Vergennes, Vermont, and various New England and New York railroads, including the Niagara Gorge Railroad.

At 28 he was brought to California to build the Sacramento Valley Railroad to Folsom, 22 miles distant, and then perhaps to Shasta or even to Oregon. Rails were laid expeditiously to Folsom, at a cost only slightly in excess of his original estimate. Since a day was cut from the time required for freighting to the mines, the road was immediately profitable. Stage lines also transferred their depot to Folsom.

This railroad was California's earliest. On a handcar over its first 400 feet of track, Judah enjoyed the first railroad ride in the state. Logically, other sections of track might have been added, but at this point Judah became disturbed by the company's heavy interest charges. He severed his connections and track laying stopped.

Judah's miscellaneous employments in the next few years were overshadowed by his preoccupation with the idea of a Pacific railroad. When commissioned to chart a wagon route across the Sierra, he made his report primarily an argument for the railroad. With a one-horse wagon equipped with barometer, compass, and odometer, he made no less than 22 reconnaissances of Sierra passes and approaches, finally selecting the Dutch Flat route, which the Central Pacific eventually used. Selection of this route was one of his major contributions to the ultimate railroad. Meanwhile, he was even more active in advocating the idea; because of his incessant harping on it, people called him "Crazy Judah."

Besides pushing his hobby in California, where he gradually built up a following of

Theodore D. Judah
The Bancroft Library

converts, Judah made several bids for support in Washington. He was there in 1856 and again in 1857, urging his favorite project upon congressmen, senators, and others. The nature of his proposal is well summarized in a pamphlet that he had printed on the occasion of his second visit, *A Practical Plan for Building the Pacific Railroad.*

Judah began with a devastating criticism of the government surveys of 1853 to 1855. He argued that most of the botanical and zoological information which the military surveys had amassed was irrelevant and that prospective builders needed to know more about actual grades and alignments, requirements for tunnels, fills, and bridges, and availability of fuel, timber, and building stone. He urged Congress to appropriate $200,000 for such an "actual and reliable survey," which he represented as necessary if private capital was to be induced to take up the project. Seeing a model in the way that squatter sovereignty had taken the question of slavery extension out of the halls of Congress, he proposed that the choice of route be left to the capitalists and thereby

removed from politics. Sound though most of these arguments were, Congress in 1857 adopted none of the legislation proposed.

Two years later Judah had partial success in another quarter. The California legislature was persuaded to call a Pacific Railroad Convention, which met at San Francisco on September 20, 1859, with a hundred delegates in attendance and John Bidwell presiding. An oratorical rather than a legislative body, the convention achieved unified western recommendations regarding the transcontinental railroad.

As its most active member Judah was the natural choice to convey the convention's proposals to Congress. He sailed on October 20 in company with California's new congressman, John C. Burch who quickly became a convert. Other California and Oregon representatives gave support as did Congressman John A. Logan of Illinois, who procured a room in the Capitol for Judah's more effective lobbying. There Judah set up a Pacific Railroad Museum filled with maps, surveys, reports, and other materials calculated to sell the idea of the railroad. Notwithstanding the persuasiveness of his exhibit and his speeches, the time was not yet ripe for federal action. When Judah sailed for the Pacific Coast, he had yet to realize his hopes.

Organizing the Central Pacific

Back in California, Judah was off at once to the high Sierra to spend the entire summer in search of the best route. By the time winter snows drove him down to the inhabited lowlands his fieldwork had removed from his mind any uncertainties about the feasibility of a trans-Sierra railroad. He drew up articles of association for a company to build what he

christened the Central Pacific Railroad of
California.

Before such a company could be incorporated, state law required that its stock be
subscribed to the amount of $1,000 for each
mile of trackage proposed, in this instance
$115,000. Judah and a few Dutch Flat asso-
ciates were good for $46,500. It was with
optimism, therefore, that he left for San Francisco to raise the remainder. For a time
prospects seemed rosy, but the metropolitan
financiers proved too coldly calculating and
the Central Pacific had to go begging to
Sacramento.

After many conferences and conversations
had failed, a meeting was called in a small
room over the Sacramento hardware store
owned by Mark Hopkins and Collis P. Huntington. Those in attendance included Judah,
Dr. Daniel W. Strong, druggist; James Bailey,
jeweler; Cornelius Cole, lawyer; B. F. Leete,
surveyor; the Robinson brothers; Lucius A.
Booth; Leland Stanford, wholesale grocer;
Charles Crocker, dry goods merchant; and
the hosts of the evening. Stanford was shortly
to be the Republican candidate for governor
and he and Cole later went to the United
States Senate. At the time of the meeting,
however, none of those present had more
than a local reputation, none had previous
experience in large-scale construction or
financial enterprises, and their combined
resources would not have paid for even as
much of a railroad as the Sacramento Valley
line to Folsom. This certainly was not the most
promising personnel for the heroic venture of
spanning the Sierra.

Judah mentioned the plan for a transcontinental railroad in which the Central Pacific
was to be a unit, but he built his plea on
arguments which small town merchants
would comprehend. Eventually the railroad
would come, but for the present all that was
necessary was to charter the company and run

the survey over the mountains to the state line.
With that accomplished, the company would
be in excellent position to get federal, state,
and local government subsidies. More to the
point, it would control the lucrative traffic to
and from Washoe. Even with a wagon road,
Judah subtly pointed out, the Washoe market
would be theirs. Thus persuaded, these
tradesmen entered upon the speculation that
was to bring four of their number fame and
wealth beyond their wildest expectations.

They ventured, but conservatively. At the
meeting at which that minimum subscription
for incorporation was reached, Huntington
took no stock, and only after further appeal
from Judah did he agree to lend a hand. He
then promised to get six men to pay for the
projected instrumental survey across the
mountains, a valuable contribution but one
for which the six struck a hard bargain. Judah
put at the disposal of the company practically
without compensation his fund of knowledge
about railroad building, the Dutch Flat route,
and lobbying in Washington. The six merchants, Stanford, Huntington, Bailey, Hopkins, Booth, and Crocker, who took only
800 of the original 85,000 shares, were rewarded with the positions, respectively, of
president, vice-president, secretary, treasurer,
and directors of the company. There is a
poetic injustice that control should have
passed from the hands of Chief Engineer
Judah to these men, but, putting sentiment
aside, the enlistment of them into the enterprise was unquestionably one of Judah's
major contributions to the railroad.

Work on the survey began at once. Judah
was greatly heartened to have at least a portion of the load lifted from his shoulders. The
vast majority of Sacramentans, however,
were most skeptical that the Central Pacific
Company would surmount the Sierra by rail.
Even with the $1,000-a-mile requirement,
railroad planning was a favorite California

pastime, although usually with abortive result. Judah's project, more fantastic than the average, seemed most unlikely to succeed, for, as the survey progressed and demonstrated that a trans-Sierra railroad was an engineering possibility, the obstacles to be overcome were brought more clearly to view.

Never before had a railroad attempted to

scale so formidable a barrier, an abrupt rise of 7,000 feet in 20 miles, with rugged mountainsides, deep canyons, dangerous slide areas, hard granite almost everywhere a cut or tunnel was indicated, and winter snowfalls of as much as 30 feet. Judah never minimized these difficulties, but he stressed the magnitude of the Nevada traffic and the resources,

Route and Profile of the Pacific Railway   *W. F. Rae. Westward by Rail*

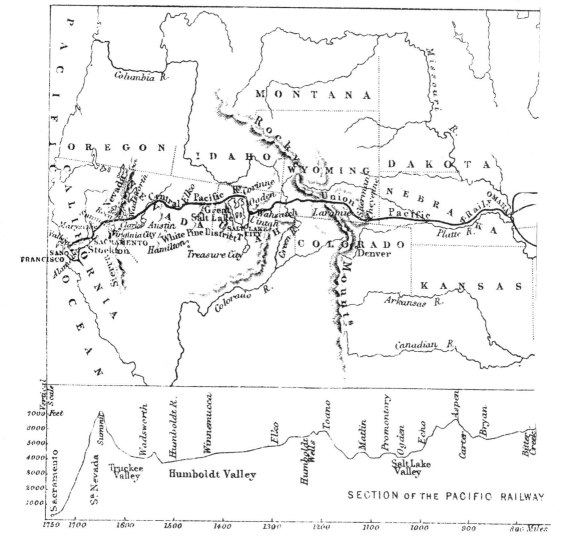

such as timber, that the road would open up.

Next on Judah's program was another jaunt to Washington. Sailing with a new congressman, Aaron Sargent, Judah persuaded him to sponsor the Pacific Railroad bill and to see to it that Judah was named clerk of the special committee to which it was referred. He already was clerk of the corresponding Senate committee and soon had similar opportunity with the House's committee on railroads.

The bill that emerged specified that the unit from Sacramento to the state line would be built by the Central Pacific Company. The road was to extend from the Missouri River to Sacramento. In addition to the 400-foot right-of-way, the companies were to receive the odd-numbered sections within ten miles of the line, that is, ten for each mile of track. Most important, the federal government agreed to advance, in 30-year 6 percent bonds for each mile of track laid, $16,000 to the mountains, $48,000 in the Rockies and the Sierra, and $32,000 on the intermountain section.

Returning to the coast, Judah found that his partners' intention was to build primarily for the subsidy. Survey beyond the mountains could be postponed, and any other way to cut expenses met their favor. Judah insisted that as chief engineer, indeed as the only competent engineer, he should have the final decision on construction matters. The partners responded by excluding him from company meetings. They called on him to pay up the 10 percent deposit on his stock, though his initial services to the company had been accepted in lieu of such payment.

The last straw was his refusal to certify to the federal authorities that the line entered the mountains some 20 miles sooner than was actually the case. By enlisting the support of the state geologist, Professor J. D. Whitney, the partners "moved the Sierra into the middle of the valley" and profited thereby to the tune of $640,000, but Judah would not be a party to the deception.

The parting of the ways was now at hand. In October, 1863, Judah sailed for New York. He had accepted $100,000 for his interest in the Central Pacific and had taken options to buy out Stanford, Huntington, Hopkins, and Crocker at $100,000 each. His plan apparently was to persuade eastern capitalists, perhaps the Vanderbilt interests, to buy out his shortsighted antagonists. Fate overruled. Contracting yellow fever at Panama, Judah was brought ashore at New York a very sick man, and on November 2, four months short of his thirty-eighth birthday, he died.

Thus the Central Pacific Railroad was left in the hands of the Californians who were soon to be ticketed the Big Four. They were content to let Judah pass into oblivion. For a decade he had been the most active promoter of the Pacific railroad. The Dutch Flat route, the Central Pacific Company, and the Pacific Railroad Act were monuments to his competence as engineer, promoter, and lobbyist. His former partners did not so much as name a whistle stop in his honor, nor did they share any of the profits of the enterprise with his widow.

The Big Four at Work

The four men whose sway over the company was now complete are among the most famous in California's history. They had much in common. Each came to California in the gold rush. Each turned quickly from gold mining to the more profitable and less speculative avenues of trade. All were conspicuous by their abundance of energy and their capacity for sustained effort. Huntington and Crocker, in particular, had given early indication of indomitable will. Crocker later indulged in periods of lethargy and Stanford was chided by Huntington for laziness, but the four were unremitting drivers of themselves as well as of those who worked for them. If in the pursuit of wealth and power they showed few scruples about the methods to be employed, their thought patterns were those of their generation.

Stanford became the titular head, the public relations chief in California, and the spokesman of the company in seeking subventions from the state and the counties. Huntington stepped into Judah's place as contact man with the national government and became the purchasing agent and the chief money raiser in the East. Hopkins' role as office man was the least conspicuous, but as the balance wheel he restrained his rasher partners from steps that would have jeopardized the company. Crocker superintended construction and could complacently assert that, whatever the others had accomplished, he had built the road.

One of Judah's criticisms of his partners had been over the way in which construction contracts were handled. The first, to grade 32 miles of roadbed, was let at an inflated figure to the Charles Crocker Company, owned by the Big Four. To the disadvantage of the numerous smaller stockholders in the railroad company, the executives voted themselves construction contracts that soon made them multimillionaires.

Forty miles of track had to be laid before the federal subsidy was collectable. With materials at inflated prices because of the Civil War, with round-the-Horn shipping commanding emergency rates, and with the war and Nevada silver competing in the California labor mart, the Big Four found it very difficult to complete this first unit. Their own resources were inadequate, for they were still men of very moderate means, and investors were not expressing confidence by rushing forward to purchase stock. Early in 1863 Crocker was so discouraged by the outlook that he was willing to "take a clean shirt, and get out."

It was Stanford who pulled a rabbit from the hat. The state government and several interested counties were induced to buy $1.5 million worth of stock and to assume interest payment on bonds to a like amount. Without this timely assistance the Central Pacific would have had difficulty building far enough to collect the initial federal subsidy.

On July 2, 1864, the company recorded another financial triumph when President Lincoln approved an amendment to the Pacific Railroad Act doubling the land grant, permitting advance payment of certain subsidies, and extending the time limit. Most important, the government agreed to reduce the security for its loans from a first to a second mortgage.

Brightening financial skies gave new zest for road building. Construction had gone forward haltingly, and two years after work had started there were only 31 miles in operation. The next six months witnessed better progress. By midsummer of 1865, trains were running 56 miles to Illinoistown, soon to be renamed in compliment to Vice-President Schuyler Colfax. At 10 cents a mile for passengers and 15 cents a ton-mile for freight, operating revenue exceeded $1,000 a day. Central Pacific had surpassed the Union Pacific, which by the end of 1865 had only 40 miles of track jutting westward over the open prairie from Omaha. At the rate of construction thus far attained and with no allowance for the greater difficulties ahead, it would have required 40 years to join the rails.

For the labor needed Crocker first relied upon California whites—Irish, Americans, Germans, and those of other nationalities. The wage scale had to be high and, worse yet, a majority of the recruits seemed to look upon

Secrettown Trestle, Sierra Nevada, 1867

railroad work as merely a convenient dodge for getting a free ride toward the Nevada mines. In spite of all that could be done the labor turnover was excessive. In desperation the Big Four considered heroic cures. One proposal was to bring up several thousand Mexicans, a solution of the labor problem to which southwestern railroads later turned for maintenance work and southern California agriculturists for crop harvesting. But Mexicans did not build the Central Pacific, nor did the 5,000 captured Confederate soldiers whom the federal government was requested to provide. The solution was found nearer at hand.

Crocker had the inspiration to try the Chinese. In the mines and in the northern towns they were already familiar. Because of the small stature of the Chinese, most of Crocker's associates were skeptical that they would be equal to the heavy work required, but the initial experiment with 50 Celestials proved that Oriental stamina was a more than adequate substitute for Occidental brawn. Thereafter, the Chinese contingent was steadily increased. California supplied 2,000 in April, 1865; by the end of the season the number had increased to 6,000 and by 1869 a peak of 15,000 was reached. The Chinese never threatened to strike as had the Irish-Americans. They were tireless. Pick, shovel, and wheelbarrow were no mystery to them, and they soon became adept with drill, blasting powder, and the other fairly simple equipment with which the line across the Sierra was to be carved.

In San Francisco labor leaders frowned on the importation of shiploads of "coolies." In the sixties violence was threatened but not actually visited upon the hapless immigrants. At the railhead, moreover, the expected opposition did not materialize. The construction crew was being enlarged so rapidly that most of the whites could be promoted to work as teamsters, powdermen, or gang foremen, and there was little objection to the Chinese taking over the backbreaking tasks.

Just beyond Colfax the railroad confronted a practically vertical granite cliff 1,000 feet high. Cape Horn was its name, and rounding Cape Horn became the problem of the year. Lowered by ropes from above, Chinese chiselers chipped out a narrow ledge, which after herculean effort was widened to accommodate the tracks. A most spectacular achievement, it gave passengers the tingling sensation of being suspended in midair.

Cape Horn, for all its difficulty, was child's play compared with the problem of holing through the quarter-mile Summit Tunnel. The hard granite of the upper ridges defied the hand drills and black powder on which the tunnelers had relied. Crocker put crews of Chinese to work at both portals and sank a shaft in the center so that they could peck away on four cutting surfaces. Drills and chisels dulled after a few blows, however, and the powder charges fizzled out of the drill holes. Progress was counted by inches and not until September, 1867, was the tunnel finished. In an endeavor to speed up the work Crocker began to use a new explosive, the dangerous and unpredictable nitroglycerin. He could not be persuaded, however, to experiment with the newly invented steam drill. Although his partners fumed and Stanford sent a drill up to the railhead, Crocker stuck by his hand drills.

The Race with the Union Pacific

With a new construction engineer in charge, the Union Pacific was rapidly advancing its tracks across Nebraska. Grenville Dodge was a driver comparable to Crocker, and his Irish "paddies" were worthy rivals of "Crocker's Pets." In the race for track mileage, the collateral for the government subsidy, the Central Pacific could not wait for Summit Tunnel to be holed through. Locomotives, flatcars, and rails were hauled on huge sledges across the divide, and grading and track laying were pushed down toward the Nevada line. These measures added $2 million to expenses, but because of the prospect of the subsidy beyond the mountains it was counted good economy. The competitive urge for haste also dictated work right through the winter in spite of heavy snows and subzero temperatures, which cut efficiency to a fraction.

Clearing, grading, and track laying went forward at a snail's pace during the winter months, but the higher portion of the completed line could not be kept open. Even five locomotives could not push a snowplow through the 30-foot drifts above Cisco. Something had to be done. Snowsheds were the answer and some 37 miles of them were built at a cost of another $2 million.

By June, 1868, the road was finally completed to the state line. Ahead lay the plums for which the Big Four had been straining, the open floor of the intermountain basin, across which tracks could be laid for half the amount of the subsidy, and the traffic of the Mormons at Salt Lake. Authorized in 1866 to build beyond the state line, the Central Pacific girded itself for a final sprint. All was not smooth sailing. Prices of steel rails, locomotives, cars, and powder had not dropped as expected at the end of the Civil War. Freight rates round the Horn were still high and ships not always easy to charter. As the road pushed into Nevada the once nominal cost of ties, timber, fuel, and hay rocketed upward. And with every mile of track built, the railhead became that much more difficult and expensive of access.

Answering the demands for speed, both Dodge and Crocker whipped their construction crews into highly expert machines. Using the factory method of division of labor, they perfected their techniques so that the rails went down at the rate of three, four, and five miles a day. In a final inspired burst of superefficiency Crocker's Chinese laid ten miles in a single day.

As the two lines approached each other, the nation suddenly realized that they might not meet. Why should they? As the law stood, each road might continue on across the continent with uninterrupted enjoyment of land grants and subsidies. An alarmed Congress intervened at the eleventh hour to designate Promontory, Utah, as the place where the rails should meet.

The completion of construction afforded an irresistible temptation for dramatics. The stage was set early in May. By Saturday, the eighth, Stanford had arrived by special train ready for his histrionic role, but Vice-President Durant of the Union Pacific was delayed by washouts and by a strike occasioned by lack of money with which to pay his workmen. The celebration had to be postponed until Monday.

The people of Sacramento, with Judge Nathaniel Bennett of Sacramento as the orator of the day, went ahead with their celebration on May 8. Judge Bennett congratulated his fellow Californians that they were "composed of the right materials, derived from the proper origins. . . . In the veins of our people [he declared] flows the commingled blood of the four greatest nationalities of modern days. The impetuous daring and dash

Held Up!   *N. H. Trotter, Smithsonian Institution*

of the French, the philosophical and sturdy spirit of the German, the unflinching solidity of the English, and the light-hearted impetuosity of the Irish, have all contributed each its appropriate share.''

With never a thought to the contribution of the Chinese, Judge Bennett moved along to his peroration: "A people deducing its origins from such races, and condensing their best traits into its national life, is capable of any achievement.''

On the afternoon of May 10 Durant's special finally arrived at Promontory. With suitable flow of oratory and to the tune of music from the Twenty-first Infantry Band, the stage properties were brought forward: a laurel tie; the last rail; spikes of Comstock silver, of Arizona gold, iron, and silver, of Idaho and Montana gold and silver, and of California gold; and from California a silver sledge-hammer. At last the final gold spike was ready to be driven home with Stanford to have the honor of giving the coup de grâce. His blow missed. Durant's courtesy was equal to the occasion. He also scored a miss and left the driving for Dodge and the Central Pacific's construction engineer. Over the last rail the two locomotives touched cowcatchers. Their engineers had the first drinks of champagne and then the celebration became general.

The building of the Pacific railroad is sometimes belittled. Parts of it needed early replacement and by business standards it was premature. But the railroad was built for reasons of state and public opinion, for the Union, progress, and the development of the country. It was a national achievement and heralded a transformation of California and of the West.

CHAPTER 17

Flood's "Wedding Cake," the Menlo Park Residence
of James A. Flood

The worst railroads on the Pacific Coast are those operated by the Southern Pacific Company. The worst railroad operated by the Southern Pacific Company is the Central Pacific. It owes the government more millions of dollars than Leland Stanford has vanities; it will pay fewer cents than Collis P. Huntington has virtues. It has always been managed by rapacity tempered by incompetence. Let Leland Stanford remove his dull face from the United States Senate and exert some of his boasted "executive ability" disentangling the complexities in which his frankly brainless subordinates have involved the movement of trains.

Ambrose Bierce
San Francisco *Examiner*
July 22, 1888

Social Unrest

A Monopoly
of California Rails

California's initial enthusiasm for the Pacific railroad soon gave way to distrust and dislike. The change was an echo of the national conviction that the railroads were responsible for most of the country's economic ills, including the panic of 1873. Californians shared that opinion and had reasons of their own for holding the railroad to blame. Shopkeepers found their business thrown into confusion by the stocks of new goods brought in by the iron horse. Western publishers had to compete with a deluge of printed matter flowing in from the East, and Sacramento, though it had led in the building of the Central Pacific, found itself declining to a way station. The railroad became a monster, the Octopus. It was a target for criticisms by all those made discontented and bitter by the hard times of the seventies.

The Big Four quickly saw that their further success hinged on establishing a monopoly of California rails, particularly with regard to San Francisco Bay. They moved rapidly. The Western Pacific Railroad Company, the Big Four under another name, was chartered to build from Sacramento to San Jose, and a branch from Niles to Oakland gave virtual monopoly of the Oakland waterfront. To control another approach they absorbed the California Pacific which had a Sacramento-Vallejo franchise. Its tracks were carried to Benicia, a ferry crossed to Port Costa, and rails continued to Oakland, completing the stranglehold on the East Bay.

Through grants from the state legislature the Big Four next sought control of San Francisco's waterfront, but because of protests from the press this grant was reduced to a mere 60 acres. The newspapers also foiled an attempt to get Congress to donate Goat Island, which under its more limpid name, Yerba Buena, is now the stepping-stone for the Bay Bridge. Undaunted, the Big Four purchased the San Francisco and San Jose, acquired two lesser lines circling the southern arm of the bay, and effectively bottled up peninsular traffic.

The railroad magnates also sought to dominate the rest of California. As early as 1865 they had chartered the Southern Pacific, ostensibly as a competitor, to build down the coast to San Diego. They also gobbled up an assortment of lines in the San Joaquin Valley, constructed occasional links, and extended through service to Goshen in Tulare County.

By 1871 the Big Four's plans for the south came more clearly into the open. To the chagrin of the people of the southern coastal counties it was announced that the Southern Pacific would shift to the valley route. Public interest would have been much better served by a coast line, but along that route were some 350 privately owned ranchos, whereas the inland route passed through government land from which the railroad's magnificent bounty could be carved. Also the inland route was in easier striking distance of Needles and Yuma, gateways to the state which the Big Four wanted to control. When construction work was let to Crocker's Contract and Finance Company, little doubt remained that Southern Pacific was simply an alias for Central Pacific.

The Big Four moved to block entrance into California by competing lines. Over the Oregon Shortline, the Union Pacific was building toward Portland. With that outlet to the Pacific it would be able to route California shipments over its own lines to Portland and from there by steamer to California. To counterbalance

224

that threat and for the land grants that could be obtained, the Big Four bought the California and Oregon Railroad and began to build north from Sacramento, following closely the route outlined in the Williamson-Abbott survey of the fifties. In 1887 the tracks were joined at Ashland, staving off the competition not only of the Oregon Shortline but also of Henry Villard's Northern Pacific.

Meanwhile, the southern gateways to California were more seriously menaced, particularly by Thomas A. Scott's Texas and Pacific. Backed by the resources of the Pennsylvania Railroad, of which he was president, and extracting full benefit from the bestowal of passes, Scott was able to get Congress in 1871 to charter the Texas and Pacific to build from Texarkana along the thirty-second parallel to San Diego. Land grant subsidies promised were calculated at $68 million.

Huntington was no less active as a lobbyist. First he persuaded Congress to grant a comparable subsidy to the Southern Pacific to build from San Francisco to Yuma. Then he endeavored to get Congress to cancel the Texas Pacific franchise west of Yuma, where for many miles its tracks would have to parallel those of the Southern Pacific. The contest between Scott and Huntington expanded into a battle royal. Huntington emerged with the spoils of victory, partly because he was able to enlist support from the territorial governments of Arizona and New Mexico and partly because the Southern Pacific set a more rapid pace in actual construction.

For a time Yuma seemed to be the probable meeting place, then Tucson, then El Paso. With Scott's successor, Jay Gould, Huntington finally decided on a junction at El Paso, with a traffic agreement and a transfer of the Texas Pacific land grant to the California company. Advantageous though this arrangement was, the Southern Pacific was ambitious for a line of its own to New Orleans; it built on

Collis P. Huntington
C. C. Pierce Collection

eastward, local lines were bought up, and by the end of 1882 the goal was reached.

Another railroad, the Atlantic and Pacific, had authorization to build westward along the thirty-fifth parallel toward the California entrance at Needles. Having crossed Tehachapi Pass on the way south toward Los Angeles, the Southern Pacific could readily build eastward from Mojave to Needles, a development designed, paradoxically enough, not to open that door but to close it against a competitive railroad. By the early eighties, therefore, the Big Four had made the monopoly of California rails almost complete. In 1884 nomenclature was simplified when this entire system was effectively coordinated in a new Southern Pacific Company, incorporated under the laws of Kentucky. To Californians, however, it was still the Octopus.

Rising Resentment against the Railroad

Big business today is multiple; in modern California it is represented by banks, oil companies, utilities, industries, and manufacturers, chain stores, large department stores, metropolitan newspapers, and the like. In the late nineteenth century all other enterprises were so overshadowed by the railroad as to be reduced to the stature of small business. The railroad was the biggest landowner and the biggest employer; its owners were the richest men in the state; its influence on government was supreme. By arbitrary manipulation of freight rates it could make or break almost any merchant, industrialist, or agriculturist in the state. In part because of its very magnitude, the railroad supplanted Joaquín Murieta as public enemy number one and was blamed for everything that went wrong.

It was a period, furthermore, when many things seemed to be going wrong. California state government, never a glorious achievement of probity and efficiency, sank in the seventies to the nadir of disrepute. San Francisco officials had reverted to the roguery of the early fifties, while in Sacramento the manifestations of corruption were equally prominent. No branch of government seemed to be exempt—not the courts, the tax assessors, or the executive officers; yet it was the legislature that seemed to be guilty of the most flagrant abuses.

Among other economic abuses, one concerned land monopoly, long to continue a burning issue. Many a writer since Henry George had railed against the vast feudal estates of hundreds of thousands of acres held off the market and out of production for a speculative profit. Prospective farmers in the 1870s, as in the twentieth century, found that much of the best land was withheld, and it was the railroad's millions of acres that stood out most prominently. Water for irrigation was controlled to an even greater extent by the monopolists, thereby contributing to the building up of still larger holdings.

22 Horse Team and Combine, San Fernando Valley *UCLA Library*

Added to these factors were numerous instances when the railroads played fast and loose with prospective purchasers, raising the price after the settler had put in expensive improvements or proceeding with summary evictions. The dramatic climax came in the Mussel Slough tragedy in Tulare County in 1880, where an attempted eviction led to the killing of seven men. The railroad had the law on its side, and five settlers were sentenced to jail; but public opinion persisted that the railroad was in the wrong.

Overshadowing these complaints against the railroad was the more obvious one that its rate structure was unjust and antisocial. The railroad magnates replied that their rates were within or below the legal limit set in 1861 of 10 cents a passenger-mile and 15 cents a ton-mile and that railroad earnings were not excessive. The counterblast was that the Big Four had become very rich. Some of the practices criticized, including that of terminal rates to meet ship competition, were upheld by the Interstate Commerce Commission and the courts. Others, such as the granting of rebates to favored shippers, have been outlawed. The fundamental contention of the critics, that transportation rates should be subject to government regulation, is taken for granted today. In the California wonderland of the 1870s that formula was inverted; state government was regulated by the railroad.

With these conditions, it is natural that a popular hue and cry should have arisen for curbing the railroad. With their characteristic faculty for obscuring the issue, the reform leaders gave first attention to another only slightly related problem, the Chinese.

The Anti-Chinese Movement

In gold rush days, when the first Celestials had appeared in California, they were given a cordial reception. Chinese had positions of honor at San Francisco's celebration of admission to statehood and again a few weeks later at the memorial services for President Taylor. Never thereafter were they completely without friends in California, though some of their advocates distinguished sharply between house-boys, cooks, launderers, vegetable peddlers, and Chinatown merchants on the one hand and coolie laborers on the other.

In the diggings, however, there was less of the race tolerance that often prevailed among the white-collar whites in cosmopolitan San Francisco. The hardy miners were convinced that Providence as well as the treaty negotiators at Guadalupe Hidalgo had intended that California's mineral resources in particular were to be reserved for "Americans." Accordingly, they exerted pressure to get laws enacted, such as the Foreign Miners' License law of 1850, which would discourage mining by non-Americans, and they took many forceful measures outside the law to make foreign miners uncomfortable. Objection was not raised to Englishmen, Germans, Scandinavians, or Irish but with varying intensity fell on Frenchmen, Mexicans, other Spanish Americans, Indians, blacks, and especially the Chinese.

Conspicuously different in color, language, dress, and customs, the Chinese were looked upon as a race apart. Because of their clannishness and a great dissimilarity of their culture, they appeared destined to continue as such, while at the same time the easy accessibility of their teeming homeland held promise that their number would mount rapidly. The matter of numbers was certainly a fundamental cause for concern. By 1852 there were 25,000 Chinese in California, making them the largest minority group. For the state at large one person out of ten was Chinese, and in some of the mining counties the ratio was three out of ten. In the light of American conviction then prevailing regarding the superior privileges of the white race, it is not surprising that hostility arose toward the Orientals.

It began with local discriminatory measures, followed by the state tax on foreign miners. In 1852 Senator George B. Tingley proposed that the state authorize and supervise the contracting of Chinese labor on a ten-year basis. While admitting that California needed laborers as industrious and orderly as the Chinese, the press remonstrated. Speaking for the opposition, Senator Philip A. Roach asserted the doctrine that white labor should not be subjected to unfair competition with Orientals, who were content with an abnormally low standard of living. A modification of Tingley's bill had passed the Assembly, but public opinion welled up so vigorously that rejection by the Senate was by a vote of 18 to 2.

On the heels of this action, Governor John Bigler urged the legislature to check the tide of Asiatic immigration and prevent the exportation of gold to China. Bigler's opportunist interjection of this issue is an index to the prejudice of the California voters.

Only the federal government could legislate exclusion, but Bigler brought out into the open criticisms of the Chinese as transients, morally depraved, and a menace to the state's tranquillity. It stirred up a former missionary, Rev. William Speer, to lecture on behalf of the Chinese, but on the other hand it encouraged a wave of anti-Chinese demonstrations and violence, especially in the mining counties. By coincidence or as a consequence, immigration slackened, and in 1853 the Chinese population had decreased by three or four thousand.

In April, 1855, hard times again having called attention to the straits of white labor, a law was enacted to impose a head tax of $50 on immigrants not eligible for citizenship. Although this basis of classification later provided the most effective curb upon Asiatic immigration, the state supreme court ruled the act unconstitutional. Chinese continued to

enter the state. Popular with capitalists, employers, and well-to-do householders, their entrenchment in certain occupations came to be relatively secure. Labor, however, had a constant tendency to regard them as unwelcome competitors, and, whenever the demand for labor fell off, this intolerance manifested itself vociferously or even violently.

In the sixties the Civil War, Nevada silver, and the building of the Central Pacific improved the market for labor and, to that degree, lessened the disposition to molest the Chinese. But with the completion of the road and the laying off of entire gangs, labor's position became much less favorable. Running true to form, labor leaders heaped most of the blame on the hapless Chinese.

The following two years witnessed a new wave of repressive measures, most of them outside the law. There was mob violence at such widely separated places as Chico and San Diego with houses and laundries burned, stores looted, and an occasional Chinese killed. The bloodiest pogrom was at Los Angeles, where resistance to a police raid on the Chinese quarter ignited the fuse. "The scum and dregs" of the city, to the number of 1,000—a sizable hoodlum element for a town of only 6,000 persons—descended furiously on Chinatown, tore it to pieces, and killed at least 22 Chinese. Local editors deplored the violence and the notoriety, for this was the first time that Los Angeles had made the nation's headlines, but no serious attempt was made to bring the mob leaders to justice.

Simple economic causation, as represented by hard times and unemployment, is not a sufficient explanation of this outburst of race hatred. Hate for the Chinese had been built up over the years by charges that they were unsanitary, a disease menace, and addicted to strange vices; that most of their women were prostitutes, that their tong organization was un-American and subversive;

that they spoke an outlandish jargon, subsisted on peculiar food, and worshiped pagan gods. As the first skirmishers for an army of 400 million Celestials, they were seen as a towering Yellow Peril. Such was the California hysteria of 1871.

The hysteria was increased, furthermore, by a feeling of frustration as a result of the failure of all previous attempts to regulate immigration. By 1871 the state and its subdivisions had enacted a series of regulatory measures, which had succeeded merely in harassing the Chinese without deterring them from coming or staying. In the state and federal courts the more far-reaching of these measures had been declared void as violations of the commerce clause in the national Constitution. In the immediate postwar years three further barriers to state action were erected: the Fourteenth Amendment with its "due process" and "equal protection of the laws" clauses, the Burlingame Treaty of 1868 with its express guaranty of free migration, and the Civil Rights Act of 1870 with its prohibition of discrimination in the courts against any person and of immigration taxes upon any particular group of foreigners.

As interpreted by the courts, this trilogy of amendment, treaty, and act seemed to close the door to state regulation. Justice Stephen J. Field of the United States Circuit Court, for example, passing on the state's attempt to require shipmasters and owners to give bond so that persons brought into the state would not be likely to become public charges or prostitutes, ruled that act, for all its ingeniousness, in conflict with the Fourteenth Amendment, the Burlingame Treaty, and the Civil Rights Act. A similar fate was in store for the Lodging House Law, imposing penalties for the renting of lodgings with less than 500 cubic feet of air space for each occupant and the reenacted Queue Ordinance, requiring that every prisoner committed to the county jail have his hair cut to within an inch of his scalp. By this time the legislature was convinced that the only hope lay in national action. Consequently, it financed a lobby in Washington that arranged the appointment of a Joint Congressional Committee of Investigation, which came to San Francisco in October, 1876.

The Kearneyites

In California, meanwhile, the forces opposed to the Chinese, the railroad, the land monopoly, and the corrupt state government achieved a temporary fusion. Earlier organizations such as the Workingmen's Alliance, the Anti-Chinese Association, the Industrial Reformers, the People's Protective Alliance, and the Supreme Order of Caucasians had paved the way, while the Granger movement supplied inspiration and example. Newton Booth had won the governorship in 1871 on a platform stressing Chinese exclusion and railroad regulation, but it was not until six years later, when the full effects of the panic of 1873 were belatedly making themselves felt in California, that an effective organization was achieved.

In July, 1877, the discontented laborites of San Francisco demonstrated against the local Chinese and against the Pacific Mail Steamship Company, the principal carrier of Chinese immigrants. These demonstrations were so alarming that the conservative element quickly organized a committee of safety. William T. Coleman, of vigilante fame, was placed in charge with a war chest of $100,000 and rifles and ammunition for 1,760 men. He armed more than 1,000 men, most of them with pick handles, and undertook to patrol the city. There were clashes, some damage to property, and the loss of a few lives, but on the whole the rioting was less bloody than in the similar and practically simultaneous labor riots at Philadelphia.

By the fall of the year the San Francisco labor leaders had developed a policy of political rather than direct action. Their program was set forth in the platform of the Workingmen's party, organized on October 5. Included were demands for the eight-hour day, direct election of United States Senators, compulsory education, a better monetary system, abolition of contract labor on public works, abolition of the pardoning power of the executive, abolition of fee payments to public officials, state regulation of banks and industry, including railroads, and a more equitable taxation system. Prosaic as most of these planks would sound today, the platform was regarded in the seventies as alarmingly radical.

Still more distressing was the way in which the leaders of the Workingmen's party appealed for support and maintained their following. Their method was to gather crowds at the sandlots across from the city hall and, by inflammatory speeches, rouse the passions of their hearers. Most popular among the speakers, and thereby head of the Workingmen's party, was a young Irishman, Denis Kearney. In his youth a seaman and more recently a San Francisco drayman, Kearney had a close intellectual kinship with his audiences. A born orator, he delighted the sandlotters with fiery denunciations of the capitalists and the monopolists and their hirelings, the corrupt politicians. His speeches bristled with such catch phrases as "The Chinese must go" and "Every workingman should get a musket." For the capitalists he recommended "a little judicious hanging," and if San Francisco did not accede to his demands he threatened it with "the fate of Moscow."

Such rabid incendiarism terrified the conservative element, especially when a mob of 2,000 was harangued in the very shadow of Crocker's mansion on exclusive Nob Hill. A few days later Kearney and five of his associates were arrested and sentenced to a fortnight in jail. Emerging from prison a martyr, Kearney blithely resumed his inflammatory oratory. Nor was he quieted by a state law making it a felony to incite a riot or to advise and encourage criminal violence. He was lionized at a mammoth labor parade on Thanksgiving Day, 1877, and he dominated the first state convention of the Workingmen's party that assembled at San Francisco the following January.

In the literature of the day and in most historical writing, Kearney is depicted as a hotheaded anarchist who played upon the coarsest impulses of the rabble, yet in fairness it should be remembered that for all his vocal advocacy of terrorist measures he precipitated no riot and produced no violence; his incendiary talk was but a means of promoting political action.

In local elections in the bay region Kearney's Workingmen's party demonstrated such strength that it appeared altogether possible that it could dominate the state constitutional convention, for which an election had been called for June 19. The campaign was well contested. Democrats and Republicans, alarmed by the patent strength of the Kearneyites, sank their differences and named nonpartisan candidates. Even so, the Workingmen's party might have seated a majority had it not been that dissension arose among its leaders. The final count indicated the election of 51 Workingmen, 78 nonpartisans, 11 Republicans, 10 Democrats, and 2 Independents. The Workingmen thus had a potent minority, especially since a number of delegates not of the party were committed to Granger ideals.

The New Constitution

The convention which assembled at Sacramento in September, 1878, is often compared with its predecessor at Monterey 29 years

THE TABLES TURNED

YOU SABE HIM ? KEALNEY MUST GO !

The Tables Turned   *UCLA Library*

earlier. With 152 delegates, contrasted to 48, it was much more unwieldy. Its deliberations likewise were much more cumbersome and complicated.

The first constitution makers had to draft a frame of government for a commonwealth whose future, however golden in prospect, was still inscrutable. They also had to keep a weather eye on national politics for fear of a federal veto. The framers of the second constitution, after three decades of statehood, were free to tackle the state's problems which were primarily social: the tax base, regulations of banks, railroads, and business, and the Chinese.

The convention sat for almost half a year.

Its 30 standing committees brought in wordy and conflicting reports. Inevitably the result was a "bundle of compromises."

To equalize tax valuations in the several counties and to assess intercounty railroad property, a State Board of Equalization was created. To regulate a variety of railroad matters an elected Railroad Commission was provided. Another section of the constitution increased the accountability of bank directors and stockholders, while still another specified the eight-hour day on public works.

An anti-Chinese section authorized legislation to protect the state from "dangerous and detrimental" aliens, prohibited employment of Chinese by corporations or the state, and authorized prevention of further immigration.

Although 120 delegates approved the constitution, it was opposed by the railroad, the banks, and the Sacramento Board of Trade. The Workingmen thought its protections of organized labor too weak. Granger optimism concerning the Railroad Commission and the Board of Equalization tipped the scales, and this constitution was adopted in 1879 by less than 11,000 out of 145,000 votes.

The constitution's ban on special legislation and on appropriation of state funds to private agencies brought about improvement. The governor's pardoning power was narrowed and the judiciary was remodelled for greater efficiency and expedition. Federal judges promptly invalidated the anti-Chinese sections and the legislation enacted to implement them. The Board of Equalization and the Railroad Commission fell far short of the expectation of the farmers. The latter came to be spoken of as a state-financed publicity bureau for the railroad. To illustrate the abortive nature of the reforms a cartoonist in 1881 depicted a distraught farmer in the coils of a huge snake labeled "The New Constitution." James Bryce in his *American Commonwealth* cited the new California constitution as a "horrible example" of western democracy at work.

Chinese Exclusion

California's efforts at Chinese exclusion through local ordinance, state law, and constitutional provision failed because they ran counter to the commerce clause, the Fourteenth Amendment, the Burlingame Treaty, and the Civil Rights Act. Finally western protests were heeded. In 1878 Congress enacted the Fifteen Passengers Bill which, as its name tells, set a quota. President Rutherford B.

Hayes vetoed it, but sent a commission to China to negotiate a permit to "regulate, limit, or suspend" entrance of Chinese laborers in so far as reasonable. When Congress voted 20-year exclusion, President Chester A. Arthur vetoed it, then in 1882 signed a ten-year exclusion bill.

Partial success fanned anti-Chinese feeling. San Francisco enacted regulations on laundries that drove 200 Chinese out of that business. There also was a threat to move Chinatown to South San Francisco. On several such gambits the courts intervened. The Chinese government vigorously protested the Geary Act of 1892 which prohibited Chinese immigration for a second ten years. By treaty in 1901 and legislation in 1902 and 1904 exclusion was put on a permanent basis.

The other problems of the "discontented seventies" also proved too formidable for immediate and local settlement. The Octopus went on untrammeled, if not even abetted, by the Railroad Commission. The land monopoly had its wings only slightly clipped. Farmers discovered that the expected boon of lower taxes, lower rail rates, and lower interest rates had slipped from their grasp; nor was there immediate abatement of the nuisance of hydraulic mining. Most of these problems, the state and the nation were learning, were so large in scope that they could be met only by national regulation.

In the eighties and the nineties California followed the nationwide tendency to look to the central government for regulation of big business. Local attention, diverted by the upward trend in economic conditions, was concentrated on the expansion of agriculture, the introduction of new crops and new farming methods, the stimulation of population growth, and the fascinating pastime of speculation in real estate.

Ineffectual and barren of result though it may appear to have been, the political ferment of the seventies is not without historical significance. In the hard times of that decade the common people of California, the urban laborers and the rural small farmers, saw themselves about to be crushed between the upper millstone of big business and the nether millstone of coolie labor. That they struck out somewhat blindly and with passion is not surprising. Nor is it surprising that they accepted the leadership of a self-tutored, emotional, and flighty young Irishman.

The meagerness of immediate results was not entirely because of the local personnel. By the accident of our federal system, Chinese exclusion, though a matter of purely local importance, was the sole prerogative of the national authorities. Control of the Octopus, on the other hand, though constitutionally within the jurisdiction of state government, proved to be so herculean a task as to require national attack. In the last analysis, therefore, these Lochinvars of the West were merely expressing in higher dramatics the common national experience.

CHAPTER 18

Wolfskill's Orange Grove   *Thompson and West,* History of Los Angeles County

No such growth had ever before been seen in any part of the world, and would have been impossible anywhere except under the climate of Southern California, which has for years infatuated a certain proportion of its visitors, and will continue to infatuate them to the end of time.

T. S. Van Dyke
Millionaires of a Day

Southern California Development

The Cow Counties
in Transition

Throughout the first American decades southern California lagged behind by almost every index—population, mining, crop production, transportation, business activity, and urban growth. While central and northern California mushroomed to half a million residents, the southern counties rose from 6,000 in 1850 to 26,000 in 1860, 39,000 in 1870, and an estimated 60,000 in 1875.

Most of the newcomers were from the States. They substantially exceeded the Spanish and Mexican older residents and their standards prevailed over most of the habits of the old regime. Older elements persisted. Adobes gave way only gradually to bricks and boards, towns and plantings were served by zanjas, vineyards and winemaking went on, and cattle raising carried over methods, equipment, and vocabulary from the pastoral era.

Coastal shipping, wagon freighting, and somewhat more incidentally the stage and local railroads had become important. The rise of newspapers, schools, and churches symbolized and assisted the transition from Mexican to American. Southern California also outgrew vigilante justice, filibustering, fanatical partisanship on Civil War issues, and the distresses of uncertainty of land titles.

When at last the Southern Pacific came down the San Joaquin Valley pointed toward a gateway at Yuma or Needles, a civic issue arose on how to persuade the Big Four to bring the rails through Los Angeles instead of veering off from Tehachapi Pass to Antelope Valley. The price set by the railroad was a depot site, the Los Angeles and San Pedro Railroad, and a donation in the amount of 5 percent of the assessed valuation of the county, $602,000.

Benjamin F. Peel and former governor John G. Downey headed a vociferous opposition, but Harvey K. S. O'Melveny argued persuasively that the pueblo had to have the railroad. A torchlight procession and more oratory persuaded the voters, and the agreement was approved by vote of 1,896 to 650. In 1876 when the Tehachapi was surmounted and the San Fernando tunnel holed through, Los Angeles could celebrate the true arrival of the iron horse.

On July 4, 1876, Los Angeles celebrated the centennial of independence very much as was happening at county seat towns throughout the nation. A parade half an hour long featured a band, horsemen, carriages, floats both commercial and fraternal, marching units representing among others the Junta Patriótica de Juárez, the volunteer fire companies including one engine with 50 men at the ropes, and comic relief by half a dozen young men dressed as Indians. The parade ended at a park where 1,500 were gathered.

The band played "Hail Columbia," "America" was sung by "gentlemen from the different church choirs," Professor Saxon read the Declaration of Independence, the Poet of the Day read his Centennial Poem, and the Orator of the Day "soared to a peroration."

The Health Rush

The excellence of the southern California climate had been recognized as far back as Cabrillo. Early in the Mexican period a governor moved south for his health. The gold rush brought a sprinkling of persons more intent on regaining their health than on getting rich. Other health seekers came from time to time, a few by overland stage, more by ship or covered wagon. As early as the forties, travel by prairie schooner had been recommended as a sort of fresh air cure. In some instances it did cure; in others it proved too heroic a remedy.

For a while southern California was too remote and too rough a frontier to have much appeal as a health resort. By the seventies, however, it was less beset by hostile Indians, bandits, and desperadoes; it was outfitted with some improvements in transportation and accommodations; and it had developed a number of new pursuits in which invalids or their relatives might find employment. At the same time the medical profession was entering a phase in which change of climate was a favorite prescription. This combination of circumstances touched off a rush of health seekers which proved to be a chief dynamic for southern California development in the seventies, eighties, and nineties.

Tuberculosis of the lungs, then called consumption, was the malady that contributed most to the rush. Asthmatics and rheumatics were numerous also, and, indeed, there was hardly an illness known to man from which some sufferer did not seek relief, on doctor's orders or on his own initiative, by moving to this region. At the outset the invalids usually went to the established towns, Los Angeles, San Diego, Santa Barbara, or San Bernardino. They found fewer conveniences than they would have liked and relatively few qualified physicians. For many, however, there was a quick recovery and as often a tendency to attribute it to the mild and equable temperature and the abundance of sunshine. To spread these tidings became a duty and a pleasure. The good news encouraged other afflicted ones to migrate to this health-giving land, crowding its housing to a still greater extent.

The housing shortage could be remedied by building more hotels and houses in the old towns or by starting new towns in which such facilities might be made available. Old towns were enlarged, particularly Los Angeles, and a dozen or more new towns took shape, including Pasadena, Riverside, Sierra Madre, Altadena, Santa Monica, Palm Springs, Ojai, and Nordhoff, many of them primarily health resorts.

Realization grew that southern California had not one climate spread over its entire area but many. That gave basis for intercity rivalries in bidding for health seekers. Los Angeles and San Diego, for example, each claimed more equable temperatures and more sunny days. The fact of diversity led also to an assessment of local advantages in a great many places and to something approaching a medical climatology. Not all the claims made were valid, but some had general medical endorsement at the time, for example, that the seaside towns were advantageous for asthmatics and that the drier interior and foothill locations were better for consumptives.

The area also abounded in thermal and mineral springs. To capitalize and encourage internal and external use of these waters was the next step. Some such as the California Carlsbad developed into spas comparable to the famous watering places of Europe. A feature of this phase of health seeking was that use did not wait for analysis. Years later, when a state chemist was commissioned to run tests, he found that some of the waters so freely drunk were harmful rather than beneficial. On the other hand testimonials to the success of the water cure were not lacking.

The migration of thousands and then tens of thousands of invalids to southern California was accompanied by a migration of doctors, some of them health seekers themselves. Through their coming and through the experience gained in local practice with this bonanza of patients, a medical advance took place. It was evidenced in part by the opening of rest homes, convalescent homes, hotel-hospitals, and eventually sanitaria and hospitals specializing in tuberculosis and other maladies. Through much of the period, however, it was a matter of putting up in an ordinary hotel room, finding a room or house in town, or taking a small place in the country and depending primarily on the health-giving environment for improvement.

Along with the medical advance there was a great deal of quackery and a high susceptibility to cults and fads. There were vegetarians and fruitarians, apostles of fresh air and those who stressed indirect ventilation, advocates of complete relaxation and others who were for hard work. One tubercular attributed his cure to clearing the brush and shouldering the stones from the field where he was setting out his vineyard.

Even with the rapid population growth southern California had a limited amount of so-called light work in which convalescents could engage. They flooded the white-collar fields. A sizable number, the majority townspeople rather than farmers in the East, turned to agriculture. Vines could be set out and brought to production without backbreaking labor. Oranges and other fruit trees could be grown with only intermittent attention. There were instances of women successfully embarking on this work. But perhaps the ideal agricultural opportunity that offered itself to the invalids was bee keeping.

A few hives of Italian bees were brought to San Diego in 1857. In the seventies bee keeping spread rapidly, especially eastward to the unoccupied interior. By 1884 these apiarists achieved a production of 9 million pounds of honey and then went on to push California to first place in honey production.

Important as they were in agriculture, the health seekers were perhaps even more significant in calling attention to southern California. Before their time, and after, the slogan "California for Wealth" drew people to the

Golden State. Recognition of the region's potential as a place of retirement and as a vacation land remained in the future. Pilgrimages to Hollywood in hopes of getting into the movies also lay ahead. These and other practical talking points for boosting the region would prove effective, but they paled in comparison to the news of the healing climate. In time, promoters, realtors, and professional Californians would sound the region's praises; none, however, with so high a sense of calling as was felt by those who could hold out the promise of health.

The response was the first big rush to southern California. Gaining momentum in the seventies, this health rush was abetted by railroads and real estate speculation in the eighties. It continued in the nineties, and still goes on, though much less spectacularly, because at the turn of the century medicine found a new prescription for consumption and substituted institutional care instead of a better climate.

The census reports score the growth of southern California population to 76,000 in 1880, 221,000 in 1890, and 325,000 in 1900 but do not specify why these people came. After making exhaustive study of this great rush, John E. Baur concluded conservatively that at least a quarter of those present in 1900 had come as health seekers.

Advertising Railroad Lands

Rail connection with San Francisco and with the East by way of Sacramento was achieved in 1876. It gave southern Californians an added sense of inclusion in the nation, then celebrating the centennial of its declared independence. With banquet, oratory, editorials, and parade, the Angeleños hailed the coming of the railroad as the advent of a new era. To their chagrin they discovered that the immediate consequences of the entrance of the Southern Pacific, even with its additional lines to Needles and through Yuma to El Paso and New Orleans, were much less gratifying than had been expected. The major reason was that local economic productivity had not yet reached the point where it could take full advantage of the new facilities for rapid transit. Local citizens, however, were less aware of this condition than of another deterrent to use of the railroad, the rate schedule, which was not only high but also discriminatory in favor of San Francisco. Nevertheless, the coming of the Southern Pacific was worth much.

Although in the first decade after its entrance into the southern part of the state the Southern Pacific was not carrying a great many passengers or a great deal of freight, it was operating through another channel to advance the development of the region. For its construction activities the company had been rewarded with millions of acres of land; the company agent in 1882 set the figure at 10,445,227 acres, most of it in the southern half of the state. The railroad moguls quickly saw that sales, especially to new farmers who would live on the land, would be doubly advantageous, for in addition to the purchase price the Southern Pacific would profit by the operating revenue which the new settlers would create.

Thus animated, the railroad embarked upon real estate promotion. It set up a land office at Sacramento which professed to have a better listing of available land than any of the government offices. Jerome Madden, in charge of this office, arranged for special pictorial editions of various newspapers such as the San Francisco *Spirit of the Times*. He ran advertisements in local newspapers and in eastern newspapers and periodicals. He prepared illustrated pamphlets such as the *Southern Pacific Sketch Book*, of which 10,000 copies were printed in 1887, and these were distributed by ticket agents throughout the country. He was the author of another pamphlet, *The Lands of the Southern Pacific*, directed more especially to prospective settlers. Numerous editions beginning in 1877 were distributed through these same channels. He also enlisted or appropriated the aid of several authors of established reputation and integrated their volumes of travel and description into the campaign to sell the railroad land.

The stamp of railroad subsidy is unmistakable in Charles Nordhoff's *California for Health, Pleasure and Residence: A Book for Travellers and Settlers* (1873) and *A Guide to California the Golden State* (1883), and also in Ben C. Truman's *Homes and Happiness in the Golden State of California* (1883), I. N. Hoag's *California the Cornucopia of the World* (1884), and Madden's own *California: Its Attractions for the Invalid, Tourist, Capitalist, and Homeseeker* (1890). Equally glowing descriptions were in Benjamin F. Taylor's *Between the Gates* (1878), W. H. Bishop's *Old Mexico and Her Lost Provinces* (1883), Lindley and Widney's *California of the South* (1888), and Ludwig L. Salvatore's *Eine Blume aus dem goldenen Lande oder Los Angeles* (1878).

The California Immigrant Union and the Pacific Coast Land Bureau maintained representatives in the East and in Europe. Their publications, such as the Union's *All About California and the Inducements To Settle There* (1870) and the Bureau's *The California Guide Book*, stressed the advisability of buying railroad land. The railroad had its own agents in Chicago, New York, London, and on the continent.

For California-bound emigrants the railroad offered the emigrant car, in which sleeping and cooking facilites could be improvised. In Texas the railroad maintained emigrant houses where travelers might put up for a

The Modern Ship of the Plains

week without charge while seeking work or earning money to enable them to go on to California. The railroad ran an informal employment service; its agents would telegraph ahead to arrange for passengers to meet prospective employers, and for a fee the European agents would locate young men as "farm pupils." Interpreters offered assistance to foreign-speaking immigrants. Fares to the West were made attractively low, and attached to the "landseeker's ticket" was a nontransferable voucher which could be applied at the full cost of the ticket on an installment purchase of railroad land.

Notwithstanding its efforts to develop the country, the Southern Pacific was the target of much criticism and abuse. Its refusal of service or connections to towns which would not meet its demands for bonus and right-of-way,

its arbitrary selection of certain sections to colonize and develop while others were held off the market, and its high rates for freight and local fares were the principal causes for dissatisfaction. In the late seventies political reform and the creation of a state commission had been counted on to regulate the great monopoly. By the mideighties hopes were pinned on the appearance of a competing railroad.

The Coming of the Santa Fe

Tom Scott's Texas and Pacific had promised to be the competitor but, thwarted by Huntington, had fallen by the wayside. Through Kansas a much less pretentious road was inching southwestward, the Atchison, Topeka and

Santa Fe, chartered in 1859. Construction was not started until 1868, but within four years the rails stretched across Kansas to Dodge City where an entirely unexpected business was encountered, the hauling of Texas cattle to market. This operating revenue was a godsend to the Santa Fe, which, with a land grant of only 3 million acres, had not appeared strong enough to build all the way to Santa Fe much less to the Pacific. It disposed of much of its Kansas land to good advantage, utilizing most of the standard promotional devices and running excursion trains in June when the prairie farms were looking their best.

From its limited scope as a cattle carrier through Kansas the Santa Fe was lifted by William B. Strong, who became general manager and president. The Atlantic and Pacific franchise was purchased; tracks reached El Paso in 1881 and Guaymas, on the Gulf of California, in 1882, and another line of greater ultimate significance crossed Arizona toward Needles. Theoretically, the Southern Pacific had blocked this gateway by building its Mojave-Needles line, but, since the Santa Fe had reached Guaymas and could threaten competition by steamship to the California ports, Strong could demand concessions.

First came a lease of the line to Mojave. Then by rapid strides the Santa Fe expanded its California facilities. Crossing Cajón Pass, it reached San Bernardino in 1885. It purchased the California Southern and gained an outlet at San Diego. It acquired rights to run over Southern Pacific tracks from Mojave to San Francisco and from Colton to Los Angeles. Finally, in 1887, by building from San Bernardino to Azusa and buying the Los Angeles and San Gabriel, it got its own line into Los Angeles. Thus, some 18 years after the completion of the first transcontinental railroad, the Big Four's monopoly was finally challenged.

The resulting competition deserves much

of the credit for California's, especially southern California's, subsequent development. More spectacular was the immediate influence in producing the boom of the eighties. Other conditions were favorable, what with new vistas in agriculture, the Southern Pacific's advertising campaign in full swing, and the nation in general enjoying greater prosperity. But competitive rail rates created excitement. When the Southern Pacific refused to concede 50 percent of the southern California business and 27 percent of the northern, the Santa Fe started a rate war that saw passenger fares from Kansas City to Los Angeles brought down to five dollars and for a time even to one dollar. Freight rates came down though not in proportion. Shipments and settlements were stimulated and, for the first time, a large stream of tourists ventured into southern California. Trains on both roads had to run in sections to accommodate all who wanted to come.

The Boom Begins

The influx of so many visitors, their enthusiasm about southern California as a place in which to live, farm, and do business, and the concurrent arrival of new residents led to a sudden awareness of glorious prospects. Astute real estate promoters, many of them experienced boomers from the Midwest, capitalized on this spirit of optimism. Few of the devices employed were of local invention, but southern California proved a most congenial setting into which to transplant them.

An enterprising promoter's first step was to acquire title to a tract on which his town could be laid out. It seemed to matter little what sort of land was chosen. The site of Ballona was swamp land; Chicago Park nestled in the rocky wash of the San Gabriel; Carlton perched precariously on a steep hillside east of

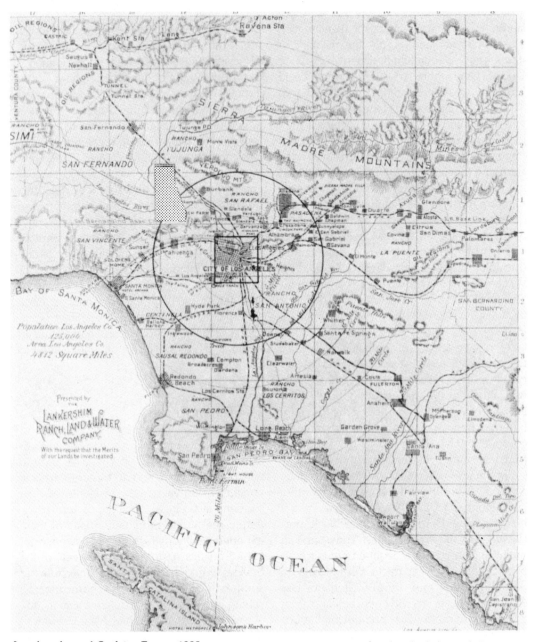

Los Angeles and Outlying Towns, 1888   *Los Angeles Lithograph Company*

Anaheim; Border City and Manchester were stranded on the far slope of the Sierra Madre, their only real asset a noble view of the Mojave Desert.

Elsewhere the subdivider ruthlessly hacked a way through orange groves. This devastation is often compared to the blight of the *Icerya purchasi*, or cottony cushion scale, which was introduced from Australia almost exactly at the time the boom began. Seemingly immune to all chemical sprays, the scale did great damage. The Wolfskill grove was one of the first devastated, and the entire citrus industry seemed threatened with ruin. The Department of Agriculture summoned the Australian ladybug to the rescue, which quickly exterminated the *Icerya*. No comparable antidote was discovered to stay the hand of the subdivider.

Choice of name was important. The Gladstone promoters circulated the report that the British prime minister was coming to erect a winter home. Lithographers and printers were called upon to produce brochures and pamphlets effulgent with roseate predictions. Slogans such as "Buy Land in Los Angeles and Wear Diamonds" were blazoned across newspaper pages and flaunted on handbills. Another standard device was to start the construction of some conspicuous building, usually a rambling frame hotel or sanatorium. When the boom was over, these monstrosities and the white corner stakes were the only surviving landmarks for several of the towns so boldly conceived.

As contributory causes of the boom these untenanted buildings pale before some of the other antics of the boomers. Sales depended less on the printed word and on buildings in construction than on ballyhoo of a more direct sort. At barbecues and free lunches, with brass bands, processions, and free excursions, through the buildup of individual sales talks

and the spellbinding of the auctioneer, they expatiated on the abundant prosperity that southern California was about to grasp.

The magnitude of the boom is indicated by several sorts of testimony. Real estate transfers recorded in the county in 1887 totaled $98,084,162, and, since many sales were on time contracts and many of the contracts were reconveyed at a substantial advance, it is a conservative estimate that the year's sales surpassed $200 million. There are statistics for the amount of subdividing that went on. From January, 1887, to July, 1889, the records indicate 60 new towns platted, with a total acreage of 79,350. Old-timers who before the boom had known everyone in town suddenly found Los Angeles filled with strange faces. The census taker in 1880 had found only 11,183 Angeleños; in the summer of 1887 six or seven times as many would have been found.

The Bubble Bursts

It was a boom replete with ridiculous features. Editors in northern California held these excited southerners up to mockery even before the real estate market broke, and as early as 1890 T. S. Van Dyke lampooned them deliciously in his volume *Millionaires of a Day*. Yet outside the locality there was much trading in southern California futures. Simon Homberg, the promoter of Border City and Manchester, marketed his lots solely in northern California, Oregon, and the East, and extracted from the gullible a cool $50,000.

Nevertheless, the boomers directed most of their fanfare toward swelling the local excitement. A measure of their success is that the record for real estate transfers in a single day rose to $664,000, to $730,000, and finally to $930,000. Those who had sold made every effort to buy in again. Philip

The Coronado Hotel   *Los Angeles County Museum of Natural History*

D. Armour of the renowned packing company is quoted: "Boom—will it break soon? There is no boom to break! This is merely the preliminary to a boom which will so outclass the present activities that its sound will be as thunder to the cracking of a hickory nut!"

For a time it appeared that Armour was right. Early in 1888, however, purchasers began to be more wary, prices were reduced and still no takers appeared, and suddenly the whole top-heavy price structure came tumbling down. Expectations were rudely shattered. A host of purchasers on contract had to forfeit their down payments. Others who had stretched their credit to buy real estate were cleaned out. Among them were a number of longtime residents who had resisted the early excitement only to succumb in the end and plunge their all on the eve of the collapse. Departing trains now had the heaviest business. Several of the communities for which the most optimistic predictions had been made became deserted villages. Carlton, Nadeau,

and Santiago were left without a single inhabitant; Chicago Park and Sunset had one resident each, the watchmen at the hotels with which the sucker list had been baited.

The setback was serious. A number of business houses were forced to the wall, local banks were shaken, and population and volume of business declined sharply. On the other hand, the catastrophe was not absolute. Even after the departure of thousands, 50,395 persons were present in Los Angeles at the time of the census of 1890, and twice that many in the county. The banks all weathered the crisis, and the largest losses were in anticipated profits. As Van Dyke has one of his characters put it: "I had half a million dollars wiped out in the crash, and what's worse, $500 of it was cash." The collapse of speculative real estate prices redirected attention to the neglected opportunities for production of wealth through agriculture and industry.

The postboom years witnessed a back-to-the-farm movement. Groves that had been blighted by *Icerya* or subdividers were re-stored to productivity, and thousands of acres of new lands were put to the plow and set out in vines or citrus. Not only did production mount but, with freight rates stabilized at a more reasonable level, the actual income for southern California was increased even further. In terms of percentages the nineties appear to have been a slack decade, yet the population increment for Los Angeles County was slightly larger than for the eighties, 68,844 as against 68,073, and for Los Angeles City it was considerably larger, 51,084 as against 39,212. The other southern counties made a more gradual recovery, but they likewise were soon participating in the general uptrend.

Selling California Oranges

By 1860 the state had only 4,000 bearing orange trees and 600 bearing lemon trees. Practically all were in southern California, with the largest concentration in William Wolfskill's Los Angeles grove. A decade later the bearing citrus trees numbered 45,000, including some extensive plantings as far north as Porterville and Oroville. The volume of production, however, was still small. In 1868 Los Angeles sent only 2,200 boxes of oranges to San Francisco, and there they had to compete with fruit from Hawaii and Sicily.

In the seventies and eighties orange growing forged to the front. Several innovations share the credit. The discovery of the agricultural possibilities of the uplands, such as those at Riverside, opened new vistas. The Riverside tract had been poor grazing land; according to the current phrase, "even the coyotes carried canteens." Louis Prevost's Silk Center had failed, but, when the colony led by J. W. North watered the land with a $50,000

canal and set out orange trees, several natural advantages came to light. The higher land proved less subject to frost, and there was no danger of tree roots reaching the water table and drowning.

A more dramatic improvement was the introduction of the navel orange. The Department of Agriculture, having received from a missionary in Brazil a dozen budded trees of a seedless variety, sent two of these trees to Mr. and Mrs. L. C. Tibbetts of Riverside. Living up to their reputation, the trees produced large seedless oranges of excellent color and fine flavor. Budwood was transferred to thousands of specimens of the older stock. So great was the demand that the Tibbetts had to enclose the trees with an extra high barbed wire fence to discourage thievery. One of the parent trees still flourishes at Riverside, and the myriad progeny, filling grove after grove, has been fundamental to the success of the California citrus industry.

In 1884 these oranges took practically every prize at the New Orleans exposition. Two years later shipments amounted to 2,250 carloads, and orange growing was southern California's most popular enterprise. In 1888 a blight on the grapevines led the Anaheim colonists to abandon viticulture in favor of oranges and English walnuts. In other localities vineyards gave way to tree planting. For the most part, however, the orange groves sprang up on lands hitherto unimproved, principally highlands that had not been considered eligible for irrigation.

Marketing was a harder nut to crack. By the close of the century there were not quite a million and a half potential orange consumers in California. If the industry was to flourish on a scale commensurate with the groves already set out, a much larger market had to be built up. The coming of the railroad and the invention of the refrigerator car opened the door for distant marketing but this took time and experience to develop.

Early experience with shipments east was discouraging. Freight charges, though moderated in the course of the rate war, were high. Delivery was not as rapid as it should have been for a somewhat perishable product. And worst of all, the growers were at the mercy of eastern commission houses and middlemen to whom the California fruit was merely an incidental matter. They did little to push its sale, and the remittances they sent were often disappointingly small. There was need for more effective management of the distribution of orange shipments, for expediting delivery, and stimulating demand. Eastern middlemen were not responsible for the fact that the orange was regarded as a luxury good, as an ornament for the Thanksgiving Day table or the Christmas stocking, yet it was clear that they could not be counted on to elevate it from an exotic curiosity to a staple.

As the solution of these two problems the orange growers resorted to a cooperative association, the California Fruit Growers' Exchange. This association brought about some improvements in production, such as in pest control and frost prevention and substitution of clipper picking for hand pulling. It also standardized packing on a much higher level of efficiency and attractiveness. Early shipments had been almost orchard run. The Exchange installed machinery for cleaning and grading the fruit and introduced techniques of wrapping, labeling, and packing. Grocers could order California oranges with more precision as to size and quality than was true of most of the goods they handled in this prepackaged era.

All these improvements influenced marketing, but the real work of the Exchange was to tackle the problem directly. The essential method was a simple one. Agents, stationed at the larger population centers in the East, kept close tabs on supply and demand in each locality. It was then a simple matter to reroute cars from an overstocked center to another that was running low. Thus the price structure was protected and at the same time prospective purchasers seldom had to be turned away.

The Exchange also set out to whet the national appetite for California oranges. Fruit trains were festooned with banners and became moving billboards. The common billboard was also pressed into service, and newspaper advertisements throughout the land sang the praises of the California orange, "Oranges for Health—California for Wealth." A test campaign in Iowa in 1905 led to marked increase in sales and encouraged the Exchange to blanket the nation with the same sort of propaganda. The word "Sunkist" was entered in the national vocabulary. To stimulate consumption and to prevent the substitution of non-California and ipso facto inferior fruit, a silver orange spoon was offered for a dozen Sunkist wrappers and a dozen pennies. The Exchange followed up this offer with still other gadgets, notably the electric juice extractor.

Francis Q. Storey, head of the Exchange during its formative years, deserves most of the credit for the astronomical rise of the association and the industry. When the sawmills which had been furnishing the boxes suddenly doubled their price, the Exchange bought itself a sawmill and a stand of timber and demonstrated its readiness to make its own boxes. Later the association modernized its sales campaign. It did not neglect the golden opportunity afforded by the discovery of vitamins and by the dictum of the pediatricians that every infant and youngster should have a daily ration of orange juice.

One of the largest concerns in the state and

a leading contributor to the material prosperity of southern California, the Exchange became a phenomenon of more than local interest. It ranks with the world's most successful cooperatives and has often elicited that sincerest form of flattery, imitation. California growers of raisins, walnuts, and avocadoes took the same course, but date growers less successfully because the smallness of domestic production handicapped the cooperative. The California Fruit Growers' Exchange—in 1952, rechristened the Sunkist Fruit Growers' Exchange—remains a model cooperative.

George Chaffey, Irrigator

Because of its multiplicity of environments and of subclimates—even within the ten-mile-long Ojai valley—California could have an almost unlimited crop list. It also could have diversity of agricultural methods: vineyards and orchards without irrigation, and other vineyards and other plantings for which irrigation was a necessity. One California specialty—sun-dried apricots, peaches, prunes, and raisins—capitalized on dry and unclouded inland summers. By the same token much of California agriculture depended on irrigation.

Governor Felipe de Neve had been the first to recognize the water imperative. It was a Canadian, George Chaffey, who came to California 103 years later who made the greatest contributions.

When Chaffey arrived in southern California in 1880, the transforming power of irrigation was most strikingly apparent at Riverside, where the poorest grazing land of Rancho Jurupa had been made a show place of citrus culture. Brief residence at Riverside convinced Chaffey of the practicability of further development through irrigation. Late in 1881 he persuaded his brother to join him in acquiring a tract of land, bringing water to it, and selling it as small farms and home sites.

On Thanksgiving Day of that year the brothers contracted for 1,000 acres of García's Rancho Cucamonga with an accompanying water right in the adjacent mountains. Subsequently the brothers added another 1,500 acres. The colony was named Etiwanda after a famous Indian chief of Michigan and Ontario. Construction of concrete pipe lines to deliver water to the upper corner of each ten-acre tract began at once, and before the end of 1882 some 1,400 acres had been sold.

The features of particular significance were: use of concrete pipes which insured against water loss, generation of electric power in conjunction with the delivery of the water, adequacy of private capital for financing the development, and, most important, addition of perpetual water rights to ownership of each acre of land by means of a mutual water company.

The problem of water law had been one of the thorniest faced by western jurisprudence. Chaffey's device of a mutual water company owning the water supply and the distributing system, and in turn owned by the landholders in the district, one share for each acre of land, proved a simple, sensible, and practical solution of a problem that had seemed insoluble.

From Etiwanda the Chaffeys went on to a larger project on the gently sloping plain at the mouth of San Antonio Canyon. The site for this colony, later named Ontario, was acquired from Rancho Cucamonga, the Kincaid ranch, holdings of Henry Hancock, and by purchase of railroad and government lands. To the skeptical it seemed that San Antonio Canyon could not furnish enough water to supply so large a tract, especially since the town of Pomona had valid claim to half the surface flow in the canyon. Chaffey, however, acting upon the Spanish adage that "the rivers of California run bottom upward," drove a tunnel into the canyon bed. Penetrating 2,850 feet, he struck a strong subterranean flow, which was conducted through a cement-lined ditch to a junction with the diverted surface water. To demonstrate the abundance of water he built a fountain near the Southern Pacific depot, which was turned on to spout high in the air whenever a train came through.

Ontario and Pomona engaged in more or less good-natured rivalry throughout these early years. Ontarians delighted in the anecdote that a circus owner had refused to take his circus to Pomona because there was not enough water there to give his elephant a drink. Chaffey was responsible for a comparable quip on Ontario. Asked by the Baptists for a church site, he replied that he had it on good Pomona Baptist authority that there was not sufficient water in Ontario to meet the requirements of Baptist ritual.

Both communities flourished. Ontario was chosen in 1903 as the model irrigation colony and was played up as such at the St. Louis World's Fair in 1904. The tribute was not only to the efficient use of water in crop production but also to the high achievement in town planning, educational provisions, home beautification, and social benefits, much of which Chaffey had planned.

In 1886, largely because of his success at Ontario, Chaffey was invited to undertake an even larger project in Australia. Mildura and Renmark were the results, both capably engineered but unprofitable because of political jealousies, inadequate transportation, and insufficient markets. When Chaffey returned to California in 1898, penniless and expecting to find himself discredited, he found on the contrary that Ontario wanted his services. Prolonged drought had reduced the water supply

alarmingly. Put under contract at $500 a month to develop additional water, Chaffey resorted to portable pumps and artesian wells with tunneled outlets, thereby saving the colony from disaster. By bringing in artesian wells on an adjacent tract he was able also to recoup his personal fortune.

At this point Chaffey was drawn into a scheme to bring Colorado River water to the Colorado Desert, a proposal advanced intermittently since as early as 1853. The river had water in abundance. Aridity, it was widely believed, was a guaranty of fertility, but the general belief had been that a white population could not endure the heat of the Colorado Desert. Chaffey's Australian experience convinced him to the contrary and, when C. R. Rockwood's California Development Company approached him as the leading irrigation engineer of the Southwest, he responded with alacrity. A six-week reconnaissance of the region led to discovery of a canal route that could be developed for an estimated $100,000, a mere pittance compared to the vast acreage that could thus be brought under cultivation.

Chaffey hastily contracted to do the work and then discovered that the company did not have either the promised option on the diversion point at Hanlon Heading or the represented right-of-way through Mexico. Bankrupt and in jeopardy of losing its charter, the company was obligated to accept $350,000 worth of land scrip at par, which was about ten times the market value. Chaffey's friends advised a break with this jumbled company, but he was determined to do the job.

Within 12 months water was being delivered to Imperial Valley, its name another reminder of Chaffey's Canadian and Australian background. In modified form his mutual water company device was also employed. By 1905 valley population had mounted to

14,000, and 120,000 acres were under cultivation. That same year, because of further
difficulties with the California Development
Company, Chaffey sold out his interests in the
valley for $100,000 and retired as engineer of
the water company.

Chaffey developed artesian water for
another flourishing colony at Whittier and had
laid plans for extending irrigation in Owens
Valley in conjunction with hydroelectric
development and an electric railway to Los
Angeles. In this last project he was foiled by
Los Angeles' own water and power designs,
and his principal monuments remain Etiwanda, Whittier, Ontario, Imperial Valley,
and, less ponderable but equally significant,
the methods which he devised for California's
material and social advancement.

CHAPTER 19

Owens River Water Entering the Aqueduct　　　　*Los Angeles Department of Water and Power*

The water [from Owens Valley] was released into the San Fernando reservoir in November, 1913, in the presence of some forty thousand spectators; as the climax of a two-day civic celebration. The one really noteworthy speech of the occasion was Mulholland's laconic remark as the foaming water roared down the spillway, "There it is, take it."

Robert Glass Cleland
From Wilderness to Empire

Broadening the Economic Base

Disaster in Imperial Valley

The immediate sequel to Chaffey's delivery of water to Imperial Valley was a blunder by his successors. Troubled by silt at Hanlon Heading, these engineers opened a new intake. At the next high water the river broke through and began to pour its full flow into the below-sea-level valley. Salton Sink changed into the Salton Sea, the railroad was forced to move its tracks, and Imperial Valley was threatened with complete inundation.

The California Development Company's resources were inadequate for damming a river 2,500 feet wide and 30 feet deep. In June, 1905, it transferred its assets and the responsibility of stopping the flood to the Southern Pacific, then an E. H. Harriman property. The railroad engineers made two abortive attempts later in the summer, and early in 1906 constructed a quarter-million-dollar dam, later washed out by the first summer flood. Appeals to President Theodore Roosevelt were fruitless because the break was below the line in Mexico; therefore, in the winter of 1906–07 the railroad tried again. A heroic 52-day drive, involving 6,000 carloads of rock and gravel and 1,200 piles and costing $1.6 million, finally closed the break and saved Imperial Valley. Yet the precarious position of the valley a few hundred feet below the level of the river denied the valley residents peace of mind until 30 years later when Boulder Dam brought the river under final control.

Taming the Sacramento

California had another river which posed perennial flood hazard. In its lower course the Sacramento ran through a wide alluvial plain of deep, rich soil. The river had greeted the forty-niners with floods that drove them to the roofs. The hydraulic miners aggravated the problem by sending down huge quantities of debris that buried good farmland and raised the riverbed many feet.

As early as 1868 farmers along the west bank of the Feather built a 17-mile levee to protect their lands. Their neighbors to the east objected that the embankment would merely shunt floodwaters onto their lands. The levee had that effect but it did not hold against recurrent floods. Piecemeal attempts to restrain the river by privately built levees were supplemented by a state program under the Drainage Act of 1880, which, however, was declared unconstitutional in 1881. Valley residents showed much more enthusiasm for a ban on hydraulic mining and were rewarded in 1884 with an injunction.

In 1893 the Caminetti Act opened a new era. It authorized a revival of hydraulic mining provided debris was controlled. More important, it set up a state agency, the California Debris Commission, in essence an authority for flood control. Under the commission's auspices Marsden Manson and C. E. Grunsky brought in an engineering report based on providing bypasses or stand-by auxiliary riverbeds. The mechanics proposed were to make the Sacramento and its tributaries run full for maximum scour but to use the bypasses to carry off quickly any excess floodwaters.

Levee construction proceeded but without shutting off the bypasses and with some levees along these auxiliary channels. The state and the federal government invested in dredging, jettying, and removing snags to give better depth and tidal scour at the mouth of the Sacramento. Much of the responsibility was still left to private leveeing, and every few years a flood demonstrated the inadequacy of these efforts.

A climax came with the mammoth flood of 1907. Up to that time it had been calculated that the Sacramento might rise from its normal flow of 6,000 to as much as 300,000 second-feet. In 1907 the engineers were astonished to learn through strategically placed gauges that the flood rate was 600,000 second-feet, in other words, equal to a hundred Sacramento Rivers at normal flow.

The California Debris Commission was now convinced that, instead of concentrating on penning in the great mass of debris along the lower Yuba, it must tackle the problem of the entire flood plain. A report was assembled. Late in 1911 Governor Hiram Johnson called a special session of the legislature which approved the Sacramento Flood Control Plan, calling for joint efforts by the state, the federal government, and private enterprise. Work began immediately, although it was not until 1917 that Congress provided funds for flood control on the Mississippi and the Sacramento. In 1928 the federal government accepted broader responsibility for flood control.

After 1911 California efforts accelerated. In 1910 protected productive acreage in the Sacramento Valley comprised 300,000 acres. By 1913 it had risen to 400,000 and by 1918 to 700,000. Levees averaged 15 feet in height, though some were higher, and as much as 30 feet wide at the top. The farming behind these levees was phenomenally productive, much of it high-value crops, fruits, vegetables, and rice. In 1911 only 160 acres were in rice. By 1915 the valley produced 720,000 sacks worth $1.5 million and

in 1916, 2.5 million sacks worth $5 million. As Robert Kelley observes, "The sea of floodwaters was replaced by a sea of waving grain."

Irrigation, often by siphoning water over the levee, was easy. Transportation to market, by short haul to river landings and by barge to San Francisco or to ship, was convenient and cheap. The intensified farming that developed broke up some extremely large landholdings and increased the number of farms. Cooperative action, state and federal aid, and decision making by government agency were fundamental to success in reclaiming the lower Sacramento and Delta area, as had also been true in Imperial Valley. The Sacramento and Delta area went on in subsequent decades to become a major fruit and bread basket in California's thriving agriculture.

Borax and Petroleum

Broadening agriculture was the keynote of the state's economic advance in this period, but substantial expansion also occurred in industry. Meat packing, the canning and preserving of fruits and vegetables, and cement manufacture were prominent on the list, together with some holdovers from the earlier economy, such as flour milling, lumbering, and foundry work. Two new industries will serve as illustrations, borax and petroleum.

Although known to the ancients—Roman arenas were sometimes cleansed with it after gladiatorial combats—borax was not discovered in the New World until 1856. The first deposits were disappointingly small, but by 1880 Nevada prospectors were agog with hopes of finding a dry lake with a thick crust of the valuable chemical. In that year Aaron and Rosie Winters, marginal ranchers at Ash Meadows to the east of Death Valley, heard about the excitement in Nevada and picked up information on the appearance and the simple flame test for the mineral. Applying the test on the salt marsh near Furnace Creek in Death Valley, Aaron shouted the immortal words; "She burns green, Rosie!"

For $20,000 the Winters sold out to William T. Coleman, former leader of the Second Vigilance Committee and the Pickhandle Brigade, and F. M. (Borax) Smith of Nevada. These two men organized the Harmony Borax Company, later changed to the Pacific Coast Borax Company, and in popular terminology, the Twenty Mule Team Company.

The difficulties confronted in the production of borax were severe and unusual. The deposit was located in a spot as forbidding as its name and generally believed to be uninhabitable for half the year. At best, work could proceed from October through May. The borax had to be extracted on the spot by boiling and crystallizing, and Death Valley had little fuel for such purposes. Greasewood, desert pine, and cedar were used; also loads of "desert hay," or sagebrush. A road had to be opened to the rails at Mojave, 165 miles distant. Most of the road was the tortuous, unimproved type customary in the mountain and desert West, but for an eight-mile stretch across the salt encrusted floor of the valley it was an improved road—improved by sledge hammer. The salt crust here was a tangle of peaks, ridges, and irregularities entirely impassable except in the six-foot swath beaten down by hammer.

For this hauling great wagons were built at Mojave with five and seven-foot wheels, ten-ton capacity, and fixed axles so that turn-ing was always by skidding. Two such wagons and a water-tank trailer made a train, pulled by two wheel horses and 18 mules and conducted on a 20-day schedule over the round trip by a driver and a swamper. The driver presided over whip and "jerk line," the single rein that stretched to the lead team. The swamper manned the brake on the second wagon, helped with the hitching and unhitching, the feeding, and the watering, and usually acted as cook. At this distance it all sounds very picturesque, but to the swampers and mule skinners of the eighties it was hard and monotonous work, and with the ever-present possibility of disaster if wagons broke down or teams gave out or if water tanks or supply stations were looted.

In the late eighties this spectacular phase of the borax industry was terminated by the discovery of colemanite, a lime and borax compound, first in the Calico Mountains near Daggett and shortly thereafter in the Funeral Mountains near Ryan. Railroad tracks penetrated to these mines, refining operations were transferred to San Francisco, and the 20-mule team rolled into limbo, leaving its reflection on the company's trademark and reechoing a half century later in a radio and then television serial presided over by a future President of the United States.

The petroleum industry may be introduced by a paraphrase of the preceding comments on borax. Although known to the California ancients, who used it both medicinally and to caulk their cooking baskets, and used by the Spaniards in roofing, petroleum's huge value waited for the American period. In the fifties there were a few attempts to distill lamp oil from the seepages in Pico Canyon, La Brea, and Carpinteria. The Drake well in Pennsylvania in 1859 did even more to stimulate wildcatting. Colonel R. B. Baker sank $65,000 on a tract near Wilshire and Hoover in Los Angeles. Phineas T. Banning, B. D. Wilson, and others formed the Los Angeles Pioneer Oil Company and sank holes 75, 100, and even 200 feet deep at Wilmington. In Humboldt County a new town was optimistically named Petrolia. Santa Rosa, Santa Clara County, and the ocean front between Santa Barbara and Ventura had their wells, but the best early results were attained at Sulphur Mountain, back of Ventura, and by tunneling rather than by well drilling.

California's big oil industry then was whaling. Shore stations operated at Monterey, Palos Verdes, and all along the coast from San Diego to Trinidad. In addition, large fleets were dispatched from San Francisco each summer to Arctic waters. The magnitude of this industry is indicated by some of the losses sustained. In 1871 an entire fleet of 33 vessels, carrying oil, bone, and ivory valued at $1.6 million, was lost in the ice fields. In 1876, 12 vessels with cargo worth $2.5 million were lost, and in 1890 six vessels out of a fleet of 52 were lost. In view of the dimensions of this industry, additional meaning attaches to the bold prediction of geologist Benjamin Silliman in 1868 that California would have more oil in its soil than in all the whales in the Pacific Ocean. As to that brash prediction the San Francisco *Bulletin* on January 8, 1866, admitted to being "a little skeptical." A decade later the state geologist expressed similar pessimism in his article on California for the *Encyclopaedia Britannica*.

The wells thus far were dug with pick and shovel or by springpole. Transportation was in barrels on wagon, freight car, or ship. The first pipeline, a two-inch pipe from Pico Canyon to Newhall, was not laid until the next decade, and the four-inch line to the sea at Ventura not until 1885. Uses also were limited. Kerosene

had to compete with whale oil and candles. Because the California oil had an asphaltum base, derivation of lubricants was difficult.

In the eighties new fields opened in the Puente Hills, at Whittier and Summerland, and by 1888 production reached 690,000 barrels. E. L. Doheny entered the oil business in 1893, bringing in a shallow well in the West Second Street field in Los Angeles. The more important finds were at Coalinga, McKittrick, Midway-Sunset, and Kern River, increasing state production to 4 million barrels in 1900.

The Harbison and Stewart Company became Union Oil. Standard Oil entered the field, Puente Oil Company enlarged to the California Petroleum Company, subsequently to be a subsidiary of Texaco. Technology advanced, in part by methods developed in California.

Even more noteworthy were new uses discovered. One was to mix the nonvolatile residue with sand to make asphalt paving blocks, foreshadowing large-scale use in highway construction. Doheny persuaded the Santa Fe Railroad to experiment with crude oil as fuel for its locomotives. It proved to be a cheaper, hotter, cleaner, and more convenient fuel. Oil-burning locomotives soon became standard equipment throughout the Southwest. Widespread industrial use followed.

Output, principally from deeper drilling in established fields, rose to 104 million barrels in 1914. Oil consumption likewise was principally in the developed pattern as fuel oil, oil for paving, illuminating oil, and lubricants.

A new consumer, the internal combustion engine, destined to be the most voracious of all, had appeared. The automobile, however, was a luxury and far from reliable, the airplane was a curiosity, and the tractor, especially on the farm, an experiment.

Doheny Discovery Well, Los Angeles

In the long run the oil industry would be blamed for the most irritating components of California smog. From the 1880s through the 1920s there were complaints that the oil fields were unsightly, the tank farms a blot on the landscape, and every refinery detectable downwind for miles. These, however, had limited impacts on the environment and seemed a tolerable price for the convenience offered by the new fuel.

In these formative years of California's oil industry, though many of the investments offered were highly speculative, the industry's contributions to the state were substantial. Among them were a new money crop worth increasing millions annually, a steadily expanding payroll, and large capital investments in wells, refineries, tank farms, and pipelines.

For the first time California had adequate power for the machinery of transportation and industry.

The Railroad Age

As for transportation the turn-of-the-century generation was predominantly the railroad age. By 1880 trackage in the state amounted to 2,195 miles. In the next decade, through the Santa Fe and Southern Pacific construction already described, it mounted to 4,356 miles. Thereafter the rate of increase tapered off and popular fancy was less captivated by the achievements of railroad builders; for another quarter century, however, activity continued. In 1901 the Southern Pacific completed its Coast Line between San Francisco and Los Angeles. Four years later Senator William A. Clark brought southern California into closer connection with the Rocky Mountain states with his San Pedro, Los Angeles and Salt Lake Railroad, which in 1921 became a part of the Union Pacific system. In 1910 the Western Pacific entered northern California by way of Feather River Canyon. These lines, together with a number of lesser projects, brought the total trackage at the outbreak of the First World War to approximately 8,000 miles, at which figure it has remained virtually constant ever since. This generation not only built California's railroads but used them to the practical exclusion of other avenues of transportation, such as waterways, highways, and air lanes.

This generation also took pleasure in the railroad, especially after the conversion to oil-burning locomotives. In many a scene the passing train was an attractive accent, its whistle a welcome sound, and its pulsating machinery a delight. As compared to the dusty wagon roads of earlier day and to the wide bands of pavement that the truck and automobile would require, the railroad was gentle. Its rails lay innocently on the roadbed, and native vegetation persisted along the right of way when virtually eliminated elsewhere. Furthermore, transportation by rail channeled travelers across the deserts and through the Sierra without giving them much chance to harm these delicate balances of land and biota.

Amplification of economic pursuits had as its corollary an increase in California population, in round numbers from 700,000 in 1875 to 3 million in 1914, which in turn created certain municipal problems. San Diego faced several such problems, especially after the crash of the real estate boom in 1887. It came to have several prominent residents of wealth, energy, and vision, such as Edward W. Scripps, but the city's regeneration was largely the work of John D. Spreckels. Spreckels kept the Santa Fe's San Diego branch operating. He took over Coronado and built it up as a tourist attraction. Organizing the Southern California Mountain Water Company, he assured the city an adequate water supply. Several business blocks, the public library at Coronado, the city traction system, and the railroad to Yuma were among his contributions, and the Panama-California Exposition of 1915 was made possible chiefly through his generosity. Other cities which had no such godfather wrestled in these years with comparable problems and worked out acceptable solutions.

Pacific Electric

At the turn of the century through the practical genius of Henry E. Huntington the Los Angeles metropolitan area acquired a most excellent system of interurban and street railways, the Pacific Electric. It grew by absorption of older electric lines and by new construction, some of which was mainly for opening new real estate subdivisions Huntington wanted to promote. Despite these ulterior purposes, the network of lines interlocked in such a way as to make the whole area readily

Santa Monica Mountains, City of Los Angeles   *Jim Tetro*

accessible. At the peak some 600 cars were in operation on more than a thousand miles of track reaching out as far as Santa Monica, San Fernando, Riverside, and Balboa. Schedules were fast and frequent and fares averaged less than three-fourths of a cent a mile.

Besides the routine work of hauling passengers and freight throughout its empire, the Pacific Electric was a great recreational asset. It ran chartered excursions for Sunday School picnics and featured day-long tours to the beaches, to Mission San Gabriel and the ostrich farm, to Long Beach, Balboa, and Santa Ana, and to the orange empire east of the city. Together with the inclined railway and trolley line up Mt. Lowe and the excursion steamer to Catalina, these tours for years channeled the

tourist view of southern California and the inspection by most residents as well. Unfortunately the Pacific Electric lines and equipment were continued without perceptible modification into the thirties, by which time the local transportation load was vastly greater, not to mention the snarls of automobile traffic. Eventually this system gave way to buses, which have never remotely approached the satisfaction given an earlier generation by the big red cars.

The Fight for a Free Harbor

In the Mexican period hide traders did their largest business with the hide providers of the

Los Angeles district in spite of its atrocious harbor. As an American city Los Angeles obviously needed better facilities. Phineas Banning, almost single-handed, extracted federal appropriations which by 1892 totalled more than half a million dollars. Deepening of the Wilmington Estuary made it possible to accommodate vessels of 18-foot draft.

The newspapers and the newly formed Chamber of Commerce began to campaign for federal appropriation for a breakwater that would provide a deep water harbor. On one occasion when Senator William P. Frye of Maine, chairman of the Senate Committee on Commerce, came to town, he was induced to visit the site. His questions were embarrassing: "Where are all the ships?" "You ask the Government to create a harbor almost out of whole cloth!" "It will cost four or five million to build, you say. Well, is your whole county worth that much?" As crowning insult he suggested moving Los Angeles to San Diego's fine harbor.

Two rival sites were offered, Redondo Beach on southern Santa Monica Bay, to which John C. Ainsworth of Portland had threaded a narrow gauge railroad, and Santa Monica, to which John P. Jones of Nevada had built a standard gauge railroad. To the casual eye Santa Monica Bay looked like open sea. There is, however, substantial protection because of the offshore islands and the indentation of the coast within the Santa Barbara Channel, and piers at Redondo and Santa Monica satisfactorily serviced loading and unloading.

The harbor boosters argued for San Pedro because of the improvements on Wilmington Estuary and because the Terminal Railroad as well as the Southern Pacific had access. Only there Los Angeles could have a free port, free, that is, from monopolistic control by the dominating Southern Pacific.

Congress authorized investigation of sites. The engineers saw possibilities at Santa Monica and Redondo as well as at San Pedro, but preferred San Pedro. The harbor lobbyists moved ahead only to be countered by Collis P. Huntington alleging that piles could not be driven into the rocky bottom at San Pedro and that the Southern Pacific would build a million dollar pier and wharf at Santa Monica.

The catch was that because of the Palisades at Santa Monica only the Southern Pacific, now the owner of Jones' railroad, would have access. The boosters for San Pedro were shaken but did not give up. Because so many Angeleños were recent arrivals they had personal contacts with many members of Congress. Their lobbying thus carried more weight than might have been expected. The Santa Fe Railroad also entered the lists in favor of a free port to which it could have access.

In 1896 the strategy of the Free Harbor League was to ask merely for $390,000 for inner harbor improvements. Out of committee came a bill providing $2,900,000 for a deep water breakwater at Santa Monica. Senator Stephen W. White of California berated this spectacle of government by special interest, that of the Southern Pacific, and debated the issue vigorously against Senator Frye. The Senate was persuaded to approve the larger appropriation but leave choice of site to another commission.

The money was appropriated and the commission reaffirmed San Pedro. In 1898 the Southern Pacific went so far as to offer to build the Santa Monica breakwater free of charge, but Representative Harry A. Cooper of Minnesota excoriated that move as an effort to buy a reversal of the will of the people. Finally in 1899 the first bargeload of rock for the breakwater was ceremoniously dropped. Los Angeles would have a harbor that would be its own rather than enmeshed by the Southern Pacific.

By the 1960s the federal government had expended more than $50 million for breakwater and dredging at this site. The Harbor Commission of the City of Los Angeles by that time had invested $126 million for improvements, and out of tideland oil revenues the City of Long Beach had exceeded that amount for improving its own harbor behind that same breakwater. Both were indebted to the impetus given by the federal support.

Tapping Owens River

Concurrently Los Angeles faced a crisis in its water supply. The Los Angeles River, with its capacious natural subterranean reservoir under San Fernando Valley, had provided enough water along with what could be had from ground sources, but for continued growth more was needed. Between 1905 and 1913 the city achieved its first "final" solution of the problem of water supply.

A dry winter in 1904 put the city fathers into a receptive mood to listen to a proposition to bring in more water. An engineer and former mayor, Fred Eaton, alert to the problem, had located a large supply of water in Owens Valley and an ancient riverbed that would greatly simplify the problem of diverting this water to the parched city some 250 miles distant.

With the necessary options in hand, Eaton broached the matter to City Engineer William Mulholland, who endorsed it wholeheartedly to the city water board. That body acted at once to acquire the site, approved Mulholland's plan for a $25 million aqueduct, and broke the news by asking the voters of the city to authorize the necessary bond issue. As an engineering venture the aqueduct was a most creditable performance. Mulholland completed it within his estimate both as to time and money, and Los Angeles benefited not only by the 400 second-feet of water delivered but also by the provision of electric power at a very moderate cost.

In other respects the results of the aqueduct were less happy. Owens Valley residents had been optimistic that the Reclamation Service would develop water for extensive irrigation. An upstream dam could have impounded sufficient water for the valley and the city. Instead, the city engineers chose the quicker and cheaper expedient of taking the water right out of the river. They were aided and abetted by the Secretary of the Interior, who stopped homesteading in the valley by declaring it forest land, and by President Theodore Roosevelt, who promptly endorsed a bill to give Los Angeles right of way for its aqueduct through Inyo, Kern, and Los Angeles counties.

All was done on the presumption that it would accomplish "the greatest good for the greatest number," yet the conviction has mounted that the planners of the aqueduct, besides devastating Owens Valley, bilked the citizens of Los Angeles in order to reap swollen profits on San Fernando real estate irrigated by the first flow of water. Certainly the first to turn a large profit were a few men with early knowledge of the project and their close associates. Over the long run the Owens Valley water was tremendously valuable to the city.

When disgruntled ranchers resorted to dynamiting and other violent action, the city had excuse to proceed still more ruthlessly in forcing the settlers out of the valley. Vehement critics, including Willie Chalfant, Morrow Mayo, and Will Rogers, tilted a lance for the settlers and stirred the city's conscience to consider belated compensation, but this did not allay the desolation of the valley, or salve all the wounds, or undo the baleful publicity that redounded to the city because of the ''rape of Owens Valley.''

CHAPTER 20

El Capitan   *Ansel Adams*

It is a habit of mine, when troubled in thought, to go for a long walk. One late afternoon I found myself at the top of Russian Hill. Around me ran the full circle of what I would be giving up if I were to leave San Francisco, a city I had grown to love and where I had made so many fine friendships. . . . It was here I belonged, in this new country which had broadened my horizons, opened my eyes to a new conception of life, and shown me a way to satisfy my desire for beauty. Having absorbed something of the American spirit of independence, I made my decisions according to my own lights. I took the first step on my career as a portrait photographer. I started in search of a studio.

Arnold Genthe

Culture
Leaders

For California in the 30 or 40 years prior to World War I the key to the social and intellectual characteristics was the fading of frontier conditions. Improvements in communication broke down the barriers of isolation. Cumulative increase in population did away with much of the roughness that had characterized gold rush days. California came closer to the national average in ratio of the sexes, proportions of age groups, occupations, and habits of thought. Distinguishing qualities existed, but, to a far greater extent, descriptions of the life of the nation became applicable to California.

One apt observation was that socially the state was divided into rural California and San Francisco. Life in small towns and in the country was the lot of the majority at the start of this generation and of a substantial number at its close, but life in rural California, for all the expansion and the innovations, was no longer pioneering. Furthermore, the hinterland was eclipsed by the metropolis.

Life in San Francisco

San Francisco had great advantages. The fortunes of the railroad builders and the kings of the Comstock added to the tribute paid by gold, agriculture, and the commerce of the Pacific slope made it a center of opulence. A picturesque setting and a vivid history were additional assets. Cosmopolitan population put San Francisco in a class with New Orleans for distinctiveness. Unchallenged as yet by any other American port on the Pacific, it had the further advantage of being on the most favored route for travelers to and from the Orient or around the world. Thus, it was a mecca for globe-trotters, counting among its more distinguished visitors former President Ulysses S. Grant, Henry Ward Beecher, Adelina Patti, King Kalakaua, Rudyard Kipling,

and Oscar Wilde. Officers of the United States Navy assigned to the San Francisco station contributed to the tone of society.

These visitors testify that San Francisco was a fascinating place. Physically its charm sprang from the conjunction of bay and mountains and the cool, gray briskness that is the typical weather.

To this noble setting buildings contributed little. Most business blocks were nondescript and most residences were unpretentious except for the ornate palaces of the plutocrats on Nob Hill, and these monstrosities, highlighted by Charlie Crocker's 30-foot spite fence and the brass fence that gave a man full-time employment as a polisher, were admired only as conspicuous proofs of great wealth. The old Palace Hotel was a showplace because of its very immensity. Cliff House overlooking Seal Rocks was also on the itinerary of every visitor, and the underground passages in Chinatown had a reputation rivaling that of the sewers of Paris, but the two man-made features most often complimented were the generous width of Market Street and the cable cars. In these the architects of the city had triumphed.

In more intimate details San Francisco made a better impression. The excellence of its restaurants was a tradition zealously upheld. Marchand's and the Poodle Dog offered an unsurpassed dollar dinner; Louis's spread a four-course dinner that stirred Will Irwin to rhapsodies, and the price was 15 cents with wine or 20 cents with coffee. The French colony supplied the leading restaurateurs. Home cooking by Chinese houseboys also attained a high standard of excellence. The best foreign schools of cooking made contributions to the California cuisine, where they were interlarded with American dishes and recipes.

Special advantages were in the profusion of fresh vegetables which the gardens of the bay region provided, the many varieties of sea foods conveniently available, the game readily obtained, and in the fruits, as luscious as they were inexpensive and abundant. Here were the ingredients for epicurean feasts and San Franciscans did their part by supplying an exacting but appreciative patronage.

Preliminary to dining, San Franciscans had the habit of strolling along the Cocktail Route. The cocktail, it was claimed, was a San Francisco invention. From the Reception Saloon at Kearney and Sutter the route led to Haquette's Palace of Art, which was practically a museum, to the Cardinal, to the Occidental Bar, to the Bank Exchange, equally famous for its marble floors, fine paintings, and Pisco Punch, to another score or so of first-class saloons, and finally to Dunne Brothers at Eddy and Market. Offering the most prodigal of free lunches, including such dishes as terrapin in a sauce of cream, butter, and sherry and Virginia baked ham cooked in champagne, the Cocktail Route's principal appeal was its provision for masculine conviviality. The habitués included, so it is claimed, every San Franciscan who mattered, and many sampled the food, drinks, and conversation at practically every station along the Route.

Since 1849 the theater had been one of the city's more prominent embellishments. In the Champagne Days, a fitting designation of the generation, San Franciscans could choose between Walter Morosco's Grand Opera House, which, under "the largest chandelier in America," specialized first in melodrama and then in opera; the Tivoli, with light and grand opera and each seat equipped with a tray on which beer was served between acts; the Bella Union; the Alcazar, with its excellent stock company; the California; the Stockwell; the Columbia, sometimes with vaudeville, sometimes with concerts, sometimes with standard

plays; the Baldwin Theater, touted as the finest outside of New York; a Chinese theater in Chinatown; the Wigwam; and perhaps most distinctive, the Orpheum, where, for half a century after its founding in 1887, vaudeville reigned as a high art. A list of the artists who performed in these always packed theaters would be a roll call of the generation's celebrities.

Of its clubs the Bohemian was the most lustrous. Organized in 1871 by a group of newspapermen including Henry George, this club was at first rigorously limited to writers, actors, musicians, painters, and sculptors. After the bars were lowered to admit prominent citizens who made no pretensions as creative artists, membership advanced to 750 and the club treasurer ceased worrying about bills and deficits. Emphasis on things artistic persisted. Its annual High Jinks, an elaborate and ambitious two-week toast to Nature, was staged in a magnificent natural amphitheater in the redwoods and became a tradition.

The pictures usually offered of San Francisco society before the Fire contain few reminders that some business was transacted in between visits to the Cocktail Route, the restaurants, the theaters, and the clubs. When the earthquake and fire wiped out many of the material elements of these Champagne Days, the effect was to give free rein to the imagination in reminiscences about "the city that was." After allowing all the bubbles to rise, what's left is a heady drink that suggests a gay, volatile, open-handed society in which Victorianism was well ventilated by gusts of robust westernism.

The Arts

California of this period seems to have been relatively sterile in such fields as architecture and sculpture and to have achieved moderately in painting and writing. In sculpture Douglas Tilden was the leader, best represented by the Donohue Fountain in San Francisco, a gigantic lever-punch operated by five muscular mechanics.

In drawings and paintings artists on some of the early ships had contributed to the pictorial history of California. William Hutton's drawings and Charles Nahl's paintings carried on that tradition at midcentury, ably assisted by artists such as W. S. Jewett and Tom Hill and by the illustrated lettersheets crafted for homesick forty-niners.

Landscape painting came very much into vogue. Thomas F. Ayres led off in painting Yosemite Valley, an example soon followed by Albert Bierstadt, William Keith, and many more. A critic in 1875 complained against these "hackneyed landscapes" which, he said, "were repainted year by year with only a cow or two introduced to give an air of originality." Ambrose Bierce threatened assault on Bierstadt for his preoccupation with Yosemite. Nevertheless, before turning to more poetic studies in lighting effects and intimate glimpses of the university campus in Berkeley, William Keith, the most prolific painter by the end of the century, had given Yosemite the full treatment. Somewhat more obscurely, Carleton Watkins in 1861 had taken the first camera into Yosemite.

The missions were another favorite subject. Edward Vischer etched and lithographed them all, Keith painted them in 1880, and so did many other artists. By this time the missions were in various stages of decay. The zeal for this particular subject had been attributed to nostalgia or more precisely as an effort by relative newcomers to establish roots in California. Because the ruins that remained were mainly the church buildings, the painters of this period inevitably failed to show the missions as thriving, shepherded, living and working communities of hundreds or thousands of neophytes.

Art was well served by associations of artists. In 1871 the San Francisco Art Association was established with Virgil Williams as its leading spirit. William L. Judson started the Arroyo Guild of Pasadena in the nineties, and William Wendt, a realistic painter specializing in the brilliantly lighted southland, was the prime mover for the Art Club of Los Angeles.

These organizations encouraged painting by widening the circle of appreciation of art and enlarging the clientele for purchase of canvases. Throughout the generation there was much talk about California as a future center of art. It was a goal, however, very much for the future, and apart from the bolder use of color California painting was dominated by the precepts laid down at Düsseldorf, Barbizon, and Paris.

The Californians of this period had the good fortune to sit for a great photographer, Arnold Genthe. He came to California as a tutor, experimented in picture taking as an avocation, and went on to make it his career. His specialty was portrait photography and, thanks in part to his practice in unobtrusive camera work in Chinatown, he succeeded remarkably well in achieving naturalness. On the morning of the earthquake, all of his possessions ruined, he went to a Montgomery Street shop to ask for a camera. The proprietor told him, "Take anything you want; it's all going to burn anyhow." From the small camera that he selected came the best pictures of this disaster.

California Novelists

Gertrude Atherton was the most prolific California novelist. Her stories were set against backgrounds as diverse as Periclean Athens, modern Austria, and pastoral California, but she is of most interest when interpreting early California in *Rezanov* or *The Splendid Idle Forties* or in her *Intimate History*.

In 1872 a transcontinental trip to view Yosemite introduced Helen Hunt Jackson to California. Nine years later when she returned she had just published *A Century of Dishonor*, a sharp attack on the Indian policies of the United States. With Abbot Kinney, founder of the California replica of Venice, she was commissioned to report on the conditions and needs of the Mission Indians. In 1884 she wrote *Ramona* which she hoped would generate the needed reforms. Still more leverage would be required, but interest in *Ramona* swept the nation. Strictly speaking Helen Hunt Jackson was not a Californian, but she found her noblest theme there.

With *McTeague* (1899) Frank Norris became America's first disciple of naturalism. His final works were *The Octopus* (1901) and *The Pit* (1903). *The Octopus* has an epic sweep in keeping with the broad valley in which it is set. Rich in action and peopled with a large cast of characters whose metamorphosis by the wheat is magnificently portrayed, it would have gone far just as a novel. But Norris deserted the amoral attitude of naturalism to pass judgment and cry out for social reforms. Whatever this may have done to the book as literature, it gave it additional significance historically by linking it directly with the reform movement which culminated in the election of 1910 and the legislature of 1911.

Many readers of Jack London see him merely as a master storyteller, vivid in his landscapes, authentic in his settings, skillful in his characterization, and infusing his tales with high adventure. *The Call of the Wild* (1903), *The Sea Wolf* (1904), and most of his later popular writings were of this stamp, but, as *The Iron Heel* (1908) and *The Revolution* (1910) show, London was a Marxian Socialist and revolutionist. Elsewhere in his publications are additional preachments on the struggle of the classes. Even more than Norris, London represents the bitter reaction against capitalism on the part of a vocal

Jack London

Arnold Genthe

minority. *Martin Eden* (1909), one of two excursions into autobiography, offers an unusual perspective on his unorthodox student days. Other titles such as *Tales of the Fish Patrol* (1905) are Californian in subject matter.

Mary Austin came with her parents to bleak years of homesteading in the parched fields near Bakersfield and the Grapevine. Then with her husband, Stafford Austin, she moved to Lone Pine, east of the Sierra, and made herself the voice for the desert that creeps across the Tehachapi into the southern end of the Owens Valley. Developing an intimacy with the land, the Indians, the Mexican vaqueros, and the Basque sheep herders, she wrote eight books and many shorter pieces about this distinctive part of California. *The Flock* (1906) is a classic on the men who followed the sheep. *Basket Woman* (1904) and shorter writings on the Indians are literary jewels. *Land of Little Rain* (1903) is sensitive nature writing illumined by a sense of oneness with the people of this stark land.

PERDRIX, MÂLE ET FEMELE, DE LA CALIFORNIE.

First Published Portrait of the California Quail

Voyage de la Pérouse, 1797

"There are still some places in the west where the quail cry 'cuidado.'"

Mary Austin

Reminiscence Glorified the Past

Not far removed from the novelists were those who committed their reminiscences to print. The principal works of this nature, by Horace Bell, William Heath Davis, and Harris Newmark, are weighted with two for the south and one for the north, though, by including Frémont's memoirs and more recently published reminiscences by Cornelius Cole, Frank A. Leach, Sarah Bixby Smith, J. A. Graves, Amelia R. Neville, and Boyle Workman, the balance is readjusted.

From a literary standpoint Bell's *Reminiscences of a Ranger* (1881) and the writings collected many years later in *On the Old West Coast* (1930) make all these others seem pedestrian. Taking advantage of the license he had enjoyed as editor of the *Los Angeles*

Porcupine and the flamboyance expected of a country lawyer, he freely embroidered on his tales. He captures the realities of the collisions and accommodations of American ways superimposed on the Spanish-Mexican and Indian society of earlier days.

Bell witnessed or participated in some of the incidents. Many of the most vivid occurred before the time of his arrival in 1852 or in the interval between 1856 and 1866 when he was off filibustering and fighting against the Confederates. Much of his reminiscing thus is secondhand rather than experienced. His empathy is clearly with the Indians and the old-line Californians.

Most of the other retrospectives were matter-of-fact in reporting what was remembered. Newmark was an exception because he jogged his memory by hiring a researcher to cull the old newspaper files. The result is a cyclopedic cascade of dated details, with accompanying commentary in kindly spirit. Though he continued toward 1913, Newmark gave three-fourths of his space to the fifties, sixties, and seventies.

Charles F. Lummis engaged in orthodox journalism as city editor of the *Los Angeles Times* but soon gave himself over to his enthusiasms, the Indians, the Spanish pioneers, and the wonders of the Southwest. His monthly, *Land of Sunshine*, later renamed *Out West*, boosted California and the Southwest with eulogies of the climate and resources and with descriptions of expanding agriculture and industry. The Southwest Museum, which put Los Angeles on the archeological map, is his monument. The house he built became a resort for ambitious artists and writers, a bohemian salon offering hospitality in the old California tradition. *The Spanish Pioneers* proclaimed his admiration for Spanish achievement and argued its significance. His *Land of Poco Tiempo* and *Little Flowers of Our Lost Romance* are excursions into the epoch of the Spanish borderlands.

Hubert Howe Bancroft
The Bancroft Library

Bancroft and Other Historians

Hubert Howe Bancroft was a most remarkable historian. He was first a San Francisco book dealer and publisher. In 1859, proud of 50 to 75 works on California that happened to be in his stock, he began adding others. The habit grew, and from sporadic forays in local shops he went on to systematic purchases in the East. Personally and through agents he searched through catalogs and stocks in London, Paris, Spain, and Italy, meanwhile broadening his interest to take in the entire Pacific slope of North America. His goal was completeness, and he made it his policy to buy every book or pamphlet that had any material

whatsoever on the history of the area. Within three years the total reached 1,000 titles, shortly 5,000, and by 1868, some 10,000.

At this point Bancroft decided to rest on his oars, but an announcement came of an auction sale of 7,000 volumes of Mexicana, the library of José María Andrade, which opened a new vista of publishing reaching back a full century earlier than Massachusetts' and with untold riches for the collector of Pacific Coast materials. He authorized his London agent to spend $5,000. The result was an addition of 3,000 volumes, printed and manuscript. Other auctions and special sales found Bancroft a discriminating but liberal bidder. The total number of titles eventually ran to 60,000.

Besides books and pamphlets Bancroft collected newspapers, the equivalent of about 5,000 volumes. He also acquired manuscripts. Some were transcripts from official archives of church and state or original documents. In the seventies he encouraged many old-timers to recite their experiences and recollections, a valuable branch of his collection. The Bancroft Library, later the property of the University of California at Berkeley, became the foundation for most of the subsequent exploration of this field.

Bancroft soon conceived a more gargantuan task, that of sifting and correlating all the information in his collection into a history of the Pacific slope. No human being could have done that all alone, and Bancroft made no pretense of doing so. He employed numerous assistants, some of whom, such as Henry Oak, Thomas Savage, and Frances Fuller Victor, became historians in their own right.

After experimenting with literal extracts from the sources, Bancroft switched to a subject index with slips citing volume and page and organized by location and then by chronology. With the aid of that index Bancroft and his staff compiled and published 39 thick volumes, a seven-and-one-half-foot shelf of books, which he entitled *The Works of H. H. Bancroft*. Seven chronological volumes and four topical volumes, the center of the set, tell in cyclopedic detail the history of California well into the 1880s, the time of publication. These 39 volumes are the prime reference in any working library on California history. More than 80 years after first publication, Walter Hebberd of Santa Barbara paid Bancroft the compliment of issuing a facsimile reprint of his seven-volume *History of California*.

Concurrently with Bancroft, Theodore H. Hittell turned aside from law practice to write a history of the state. His legal background made him particularly well qualified to deal with certain phases of California history, and he was gifted in literary style. His four volumes, published in 1885 and 1897, are a notable milestone reckoned second only to Bancroft's.

Invited by the eastern publishers of American Commonwealths to write a history of California, Josiah Royce of Harvard responded instead with *California* (1886) which probes the behavior of the American Californians from the conquest in 1846 to the second vigilance committee of San Francisco in 1856. A realistic finding of social irresponsibility, not far from Bancroft's conclusion on the pioneers, this essay gained reputation as a classic. A year later Royce published his novel, *The Feud of Oakfield Creek*, a memorial to the Mussel Slough tragedy.

George Davidson, Nestor of California geographers, wrote half a dozen important works on California's Age of Discovery. At the Santa Barbara Mission, Zephyrin Engelhardt devoted himself to study of the missions of Baja and Alta California.

The third of the state's larger histories was a by-product of the Panama-Pacific Exposition of 1915. Released under the name of its editor, Zoeth Skinner Eldredge, the first three and a half volumes were written by Clinton A. Snowden and the fifth is made up of articles by invited specialists.

Henry George and the Single Tax

In the field of political economy California was producing a greater luminary, Henry George, who has been called America's most original economist. Leaving school at 14, he sailed before the mast from Philadelphia to Australia, thence to Salem, Oregon, where he worked in a print shop, and at length to San Francisco, where he moved from one print shop or newspaper to another.

A Jeffersonian and a Democrat, George

Henry George
The Bancroft Library

was deeply concerned about the injustices of the economic order. Although endowed with abundant resources that should have made it a land of almost limitless opportunities, California in the sixties was rapidly falling into the hands of land monopolists. The swollen fortunes of the railroad builders, the tremendous land grants with which the United States subsidized them, the scandals with swamplands and fraudulent grants, the speculative profits at Oakland when it was made the terminus of the transcontinental railroad, the opulence of the Comstock fortunes—such was the atmosphere of San Francisco in the formative years of his thinking. The same general conditions were noticeable elsewhere. On a visit to New York, George was struck by the juxtaposition of highly profitable commerce and slums in which thousands lived in direst poverty.

The economic philosophy that George worked out owed little to academic economists. He was a seeker of origins, thinking, as Tom Paine had recommended, "as if he were the first man who ever thought." His cardinal principles were the inequity and iniquity of land monopoly, the viciousness of unearned increment, and the conception of the landlord as a parasite. He advocated a tax on land—that is, on rent, which he identified with unearned assets—as the panacea for the ills of society.

George has been charged with oversimplification, both in his analysis and his remedy. Not all unearned increment can be classified as rent. Nor is reason alone an adequate agent for the achievement of social reform. He was an arch-idealist, a quixotic "knight-errant from out of the newest West." In spite of the validity of these criticisms and notwithstanding that the single tax has not been adopted, George has been a most influential economist. A pioneer in analyzing exploitative capital, he attempted to bring the science of economics out of its ivory tower and make it face the problems of the common man. In this his success was only relative, yet he did much to humanize and democratize economics.

In terms of total circulation George had no California competitor. His magnum opus, *Progress and Poverty*, was rejected by all the eastern publishers. His printer friends in San Francisco had more confidence in him; they helped him set the type, make the plates, and run off an edition of 500 copies in 1879. With the chief expense of publication thus covered, D. Appelton and Company took over the book, though without enough confidence to take out an English copyright. Certain San Francisco reviewers derided the book, but the American press was warmer, and British critics on such journals as the *London Times* and the *Edinburgh Review* hailed it with the greatest enthusiasm. George also was highly successful on the lecture platform but not as the Socialist candidate for mayor of New York. Of *Progress and Poverty* a conservative estimate is that 2 million copies were printed in the first 25 years, along with at least 3 million copies of his other writings. He still is read, partly because ardent disciples still spread the gospel according to George.

Ambrose Bierce, San Francisco's Scold

Genius was equally unmistakable in caustic, perverse Ambrose Bierce. After a boyhood of poverty in Ohio and Indiana, he enlisted in the northern army, saw active service in the Civil War, came to San Francisco in 1866, and found work as a watchman at the Mint. The San Francisco press at this time was filled with boisterous comments on the passing scene from such irreverent writers as Mark Twain and Dan De Quille. Bierce was moved to try their sort of writing, first as a sideline and then

Ambrose Bierce

The Bancroft Library

instead of his work as watchman. He became a columnist in 1868.

For the next three decades, with only an occasional interlude, Bierce regaled San Franciscans with a regular column in which he impaled whatever or whoever incurred his displeasure. First it was as "Town Crier" for the *News Letter*, then as "Prattle" for the *Wasp*, and then as "Prattle" for Hearst's *Examiner*. The ideals Bierce stood for do not stir the imagination. The people, in his estimation, "were a great beast," and democracy he decried as a prelude to anarchy. He turned his siege guns on Denis Kearney and the Sandlotters, and he had equal contempt for social reformers like George who used an intellectual approach.

By the eighties, when Bierce shifted to Hearst's paper, he was still the implacable critic, but he had acquired a more appropriate adversary in the Southern Pacific and had exchanged his sledgehammer for a rapier. These should have been his most pleasant years. Certainly they were his most productive, for it was then that he wrote most of his Civil War stories, which, together with his horror stories, are the base for much of his reputation as a writer. It was also under Hearst that Bierce achieved his greatest journalistic triumph. In the nineties when the Southern Pacific brought up the Funding Bill, which would have postponed for 99 years its reckoning with the federal treasury, the young publisher sent the old misanthrope, admittedly his ace writer, to do battle for the people against the great corporation. Victory was his, and Bierce could exult that the pen was mightier than the pocketbook.

Subsequent years added little to Bierce's literary stature. He continued for a time in California, then transferred to the East. Finally in 1913, old, ill, and embittered, he crossed over into Mexico and disappeared.

Bierce's greatest genius was not in the short

story or even in the discourteous retort, but in phrasing pithy, catchy statements of eternal truths. In verse, in doggerel, in simple phrases and sentences, or in the form of short fables, he turned out these aphorisms by the hundreds. He was sufficiently cynical, competent to see beneath the surface to the essential realities, and blessed with a superiority complex that encouraged him to pass judgment. In addition, he had developed an exquisite style, structurally perfect and unerring in word choice.

Bierce might just as well have written proverbs for Solomon or sayings for Confucious as for San Francisco's champagne generation, yet it is easy to see that he was encouraged by his environment. California writers of the gold rush era had established a tradition of outspoken impertinence, and Bierce's position on Hearst's yellowing journal provided the ideal sounding board plus the necessary incentive for the grinding out of these immortal pungencies.

John Muir

National Park Service

John Muir and the Sierra Club

The late nineteenth century Californian of most enduring influence may well have been John Muir. A native of Scotland whose early years were spent in rural Wisconsin, Muir arrived in San Francisco in 1868. His immediate impulse was to escape the city. Asking the first man he met how to get to "anywhere that is wild," he was directed to the Oakland ferry. From its terminal he walked 60 miles southward to Gilroy, turned eastward, and ascended Pacheco Pass. From its summit he beheld the Sierra Nevada in its luminous majesty, in his phrase, "the Range of Light."

Walking on across the San Joaquin Valley, Muir entered the foothills and Yosemite Valley and began to inspect the surrounding wilderness. In 1869, for the express purpose of seeing more of the high country, he signed on to take a flock of 2,000 sheep to the high pastures for summer grazing. He herded as he had hiked, notebook in hand, botanizing by the way, learning about many other aspects of nature, and reading the geological record.

That summer he took a subsistence job at James M. Hutchings' station in Yosemite Valley, with time off for occasional explorations. He joined a Sierra trek with geologist Joseph LeConte and his students. Among the visiting tourists he met an English noblewoman who made him the ill concealed hero, Kenmuir, in her novel *Zanita* (short for manzanita).

For another half dozen years Muir spent most of his time in the wilds, going often on solitary rambles. He became the most knowledgable person on the Tuolumne-to-Sequoia Wilderness and the high Sierra and their most articulate champion. Decades later, Presidents Theodore Roosevelt and William H. Taft sought his guidance.

Muir came to the conclusion that Yosemite Valley was not a product of cataclysmic convulsions, as the state geologist insisted, but of glacial grinding and polishing. He persuasively argued this theory to many visitors, including LeConte. Bolstered by his subsequent discovery of living glaciers in the Sierra, Muir gained wide acceptance for this theory, which in 1934–1935 was verified by seismic explo-

rations which revealed that, underneath a thick layer of alluvial deposits, Yosemite is a U-shaped glacial valley.

Muir wrote and published voluminously in eastern and western magazines and in the New York and California newspapers. His first book, *The Mountains of California*, was published in 1894, followed in 1901 by *Our National Parks*. Some 40 years after the events, the essays describing his learning experience when he followed the sheep into the mountains were assembled as a book, *My First Summer in the Sierra* (1911). His *Yosemite* was published in 1912.

In 1892 Muir was a founder of the Sierra Club and the natural selection as its first president. An alpine club with stress on camping

Tuolomne Meadows   *Philip Hyde*

and climbing, the new organization was dedicated to the protection of the Yosemite and Sierra wilderness area. Almost immediately the club was confronted by a bill to authorize mining, lumbering, and grazing concessions in the near vicinity of Yosemite Valley. The membership was prestigious; it defeated this bill in committee. The club also prevailed in having the state reconvey Yosemite Valley to the federal government for administration as a national park.

These contests were but shadowboxing compared to the battle for Hetch Hetchy. Shortly after 1900 San Francisco saw a need for additional water supply. The Mokelumne was one source investigated, but preference went to Hetch Hetchy, a smaller and less accessible yosemite on the Tuolumne within the bounds of Yosemite National Park. The first several applications for use of this site were rejected in the courts, but in 1905 Gifford Pinchot announced that the Roosevelt administration would support the application. Pinchot saw this action as consistent with conservation by maximizing the benefits from natural resources.

When Muir and others tried to muster the forces of the Sierra Club to block this raid, some of the staunchest members sided with utilitarian conservation. By a substantial majority, however, the "nature lovers" won support for a vigorous campaign against a dam at Hetch Hetchy, which would create a reservoir that would fluctuate 240 feet each season and thereby change a beautiful valley into an eyesore.

The battle went on for years. During Taft's presidency the nature lovers staved off final approval. But Woodrow Wilson's Secretary of the Interior, Franklin K. Lane, had been city attorney of San Francisco. To him it seemed proper for the greater good of the greater number that San Francisco should have this water. By that ploy the Sierra Club lost this

nine-year battle. Muir died the next year. In 1916 Congress voted the National Park Act, intended to close the door to any repetitions of Hetch Hetchy.

Colleges and Universities

Carried over from the gold rush epoch were a number of colleges and universities, among them the state university, the College of the Pacific, several Catholic schools, a state normal school established at San Francisco in 1862, and another at San Jose dating from 1871.

In the ensuing years, a dozen or more institutions were added, the majority under denominational auspices. With a donated site in the southwestern part of Los Angeles, the University of Southern California was founded in 1879 by the Methodists. Three years later Los Angeles qualified for a branch of the San Jose state normal school, the cell from which the University of California at Los Angeles would eventually develop. In Oakland, Mills Seminary, which had been functioning for a number of years, was reinstituted as Mills College in 1885. A charter was obtained in 1887 for the Occidental Presbyterian University, later simplified to Occidental College, and a few months later the Congregationalists chartered Pomona College. In September, 1888, these institutions enrolled their first students. At the Quaker colony of Whittier there was talk of a college almost from the beginning. It materialized in 1901. In 1891 the Church of the Brethren launched Lordsburg College, later named LaVerne, and in 1909 the University of Redlands opened classes in the First Baptist Church.

Most of the schools founded in this period had the primary aim of providing a general education in liberal arts and of supplementing this program with teacher training. One exception was Amos G. Throop's school in Pasadena, which went through a succession of name changes from Throop University to Throop Polytechnic Institute, to Throop College of Technology, to California Polytechnic Institute, to California Institute of Technology.

In all these institutions the achievement of true collegiate status came only gradually. For example, the University of Southern California in 1891 had 192 students enrolled in the preparatory department and only 25 in the collegiate department. Furthermore, each college started on the most meager of financing, a few acres of ground, perhaps a hotel building in which classes could meet, some town lots that could be leased or bought, and seldom more than a few thousand dollars in pledges and cash.

Given that norm, the announcement of the Leland Stanfords late in 1885 that, as a memorial to their son, they would bestow the bulk of their fortune upon a university was electrifying. The initial conveyance was of properties appraised at $6 million, with another $1.25 million for buildings. The Stanfords promised additional gifts and bequests to bring the total to about $30 million. At the time, Columbia's productive capital was $4,680,590, Harvard's was $4,511,862, and Johns Hopkins' was $3 million. Thus the prospect was that Stanford would start as the richest of all universities.

Even this largess did not dispel skepticism that a first-rate university could be achieved. Since the peak enrollment at the University of California was only 332, experts wondered whether there would be any students at Stanford. The difficulties in getting good scholars to come to Berkeley, or to stay there, made others doubt that a competent faculty could be assembled at the new university. There was some awareness, too, that the strength of a university is in large degree a matter of spirit and tradition not acquired overnight.

The founders, however, had an inspiring model in mind—Cornell University, a happy combination of the applied sciences of engineering and agriculture and humanistic studies. They were even more fortunate in the selection of the first president, David Starr Jordan, a distinguished ichthyologist, a man of vision and initiative, forceful and compelling in expression both in writing and in speaking, at heart a poet, and an inspiring leader.

With its wealth, its dynamic head, and its fresh purpose, Stanford University was likened to a giant meteor flashing across the western firmament. Lack of students was never a problem; the 1891 opening registration was a surprising 490, and three years later 1,100 were enrolled. Stanford did not immediately outshine all other American universities. Furthermore, with the hard times following the Panic of 1893, it looked as though its wealth would evaporate. Mrs. Stanford came to the rescue, drawing on the estate left by her husband to round out the now meager income from the properties previously assigned. In the intellectual life of the West, Stanford University quickly became an active factor. President Jordan and members of the faculty took leading roles in public affairs. And the existence of the university prompted those controlling the destinies of other California schools to improve their institutions.

During the presidency of Benjamin Ide Wheeler, 1899–1919, the University of California was revitalized. Aware that personal interferences by members of the board of regents had been a handicap, he conditioned his acceptance of the position on the board's adoption of a set of rules that he held to be "absolutely essential to the existence of anything like a proper university spirit, indeed, of a university." These were that the president should be the sole organ of communication between faculty and regents, that the president should have sole initiative in appointments, removals, and matters of salary, and that, however divided in discussions during meetings, the board as a unit should support the president. The balancing factor did not have to be stated—that should the board lose confidence in the president, it could have his resignation.

Rapid increases in enrollment inspired active building. California Hall, Boalt Hall, the Hearst Mining Building, the Agriculture Building, the Doe Memorial Library, and Wheeler Hall, all rose during Wheeler's presidency.

In addition to his talent for rallying support for the university, Wheeler offered it his personal philosophy. The phrase in which he summed it up was "the abundant life." He wanted the students to avoid superficiality and refuse to narrow themselves to a single specialization but to live abundantly instead. He wanted them to prepare for a lifetime characterized by this same breadth and depth. In his day the faculty made advances in research and taught a great many practical and useful subjects. To Wheeler the things of greater importance were the kind of experiences the students could be led to have and the outlook and inspiration that they could carry away. Therein he was in step with Jordan and the more thoughtful heads of other California schools of his day.

In another generation the fields of honor in a university would be the obscure and deadly sciences and the practical professions, such as medicine and engineering. But on the California faculty in Wheeler's day it is revealing that the brightest luminaries included, and perhaps were, a professor of English and a professor of history. Charles Mills Gayley had a long and fruitful career in research and writing. His popular lectures to the public and to undergraduates were his chief glory. He developed a course on great books long before their Chicago discovery, and it soon filled the largest hall and became a campus institution.

Its only rival in popularity was H. Morse Stephens' survey of the history of the Western world. Both men mingled freely with the students; Stephens, as a bachelor living at the Faculty Club on the campus, had an advantage here. He was seldom mistaken for a profound scholar, but he had a great hold on the students which persisted with the alumni. When he died, the legislature adjourned out of respect to his memory; the Student Union building was named in his honor. Gayley and Stephens arrived independently at the pattern for their careers. Both were exemplars of the abundant life that Wheeler stressed.

CHAPTER 21

San Francisco Earthquake and Fire

Arnold Genthe

The richest thing in San Francisco was not shattered by the earthquake. Neither did it shrivel in the fire. Nor did its market value diminish. It is way above par. The spirit of the people of San Francisco today is the grandest and most practically valuable asset which the metropolis ever has possessed. . . . It was agreed by the San Francisco Real Estate Board that the calamity should be spoken of as "the great fire" and not as "the great earthquake."

San Francisco Chronicle
April 21 and 23, 1906

Political Housecleaning

State politics in 1880 was at one of those peaks of exaltation with all problems seemingly solved. The new constitution elaborated by the convention in 1879 contained, if not the summation of all human knowledge, at least a working compromise on the issues that had been central in the unrest of the seventies. Kearneyites and Grangers found satisfaction in the provisions for a state railroad commission and a board for tax equalization and in the prospect of Chinese exclusion. Conservatives were relieved that the whole program of the malcontents had not been carried into effect. With the air cleared, interest in state government flagged.

Other factors prompted the disregard of state politics. For one thing California found itself on an economic upturn. The pinch of hard times, which had contributed to urban and rural discontent in the preceding decade, was largely forgotten in the more prosperous eighties. For another, national issues absorbed much attention, what with President James. A. Garfield's assassination; Chester A. Arthur's Civil Service reforms; the "rum, Romanism and rebellion" campaign, in which Grover Cleveland squeezed in ahead of James G. Blaine, the "plumed knight"; talk about tariffs, silver purchase, interstate commerce regulation, and trustbaiting; and international incidents concerning Venezuela, Samoa, and Hawaii.

State elections, meanwhile, seemed a subordinate branch of politics. Democrats and Republicans were alternately in office, but the margin of victory was usually slight and the distinction of party objectives not much greater. Few individuals were of sufficient importance for their names to intrude upon a general history. Washington Bartlett, who was inaugurated governor in 1887 with high acclaim, died in office just a few months later. His successor built an unenviable reputation as the "Great Pardoner." The election of 1890 was supposed to hinge on the question of state division but, although the southern California candidate was elected, no steps were taken toward a split. Four years later James H. Budd won the governorship by emphasizing that he was young, a graduate of the state university, and traveled by buckboard rather than by railroad.

Combating the Southern Pacific

Gradually local issues recaptured attention. As early as 1880 the settlers at Mussel Slough near modern Hanford in Tulare County were disillusioned concerning the effectiveness of the new constitution as a check upon the Southern Pacific. They had occupied and improved the land under what they thought were bona fide offers. On various pretexts the railroad delayed conveying title and finally quoted a price far in excess of that originally contemplated. The settlers demurred and began to organize for more effective protest. When the railroad attempted to get evictions in favor of two hired purchasers, Walter J. Crow and M. J. Hart, a clash ensued. In a few moments of gunplay Hart and five settlers were killed outright or given mortal wounds. Crow hid in a wheatfield but, when he tried to climb the fence and get away, he was picked off by an unidentified settler.

Under indictment for resisting a United States officer, seven of the settlers were taken to San Francisco for trial. Five of them were convicted and sentenced to eight months in the San Jose jail. In the climate of opinion that prevailed they emerged as heroes. Several crusading novels, including Josiah Royce's

The Feud of Oakfield Creek and Norris' *The Octopus*, seized on the Mussel Slough incident as a dramatization of the burning resentment against the railroad's heartless domination.

To what extent the railroad was guilty of the many malpractices charged is difficult to say. Denunciation of big business was the national pastime, and, since it was by all odds the biggest of California's corporations, the railroad stood out as the natural target. On the other hand there was hardly an office, from the seats in the United States Senate down through the governorship and the courts to the most inconsiderable town office, in which the right man could not do the railroad a service. Suspecting the worst, critics charged freely and proved occasionally that California was governed by the Southern Pacific machine. Attacking the railroad became the touchstone of California politics.

Three times in the eighties and nineties the railroad's willingness to influence government was exposed with unmistakable candor: in the publication of the Colton Letters, in Los Angeles' fight for a free harbor, and in the defeat of the Funding Bill.

In the seventies David D. Colton had annexed himself to the Southern Pacific to the extent that its moguls were often referred to as the Big Four and a Half. As the phrase suggests, Colton never quite attained a parity with Stanford, Huntington, Crocker, and Hopkins but he did enjoy Huntington's confidence, and the latter wrote to him freely and candidly about his experiences as a lobbyist in Washington. The partners went so far as to define the conditions under which Colton might join the inner circle, but at the time of his death in 1878 they were busily engaged in squeezing him out.

His widow at first accepted a modest settlement, but, when she saw that identical securities in the Hopkins estate were valued at a much higher figure, she charged that she had been defrauded and brought suit to recover. Mrs. Colton's lawyers got little satisfaction for their client, but they contributed much to the entertainment of the railroad baiters and to the enlightenment of historians by reading into the record letter after letter in which Huntington had described with utter frankness his methods as a lobbyist. Some 600 of these letters were spread upon the court record ostensibly to demonstrate that Colton had been a key man in railroad councils. They were a devastating indictment of the railroad's chicanery.

The free harbor fight, recounted in an earlier chapter, stretched out over the better part of a decade. It produced a public indictment of the Southern Pacific's pervasive control of government. Throughout that contest the advantage seemed always to lie with the politically entrenched corporation. It was uphill for the city all the way. Indeed, Huntington frankly stated that he had some influence and that the city would be best off by going along with the railroad's preference for a deep water harbor in Santa Monica Bay.

In the end the upstart city prevailed. The railroad lost face, as it had through the release of the Colton letters, but the Southern Pacific lost no current revenue, and it entered the twentieth century firmly entrenched.

To the railroad the Funding Bill considerably overshadowed the harbor fight. It proposed that the 30-year 6 percent bonds which had secured the government's original subsidy be replaced both for principal and interest by 99-year bonds at one half of 1 percent. That would have been tantamount to cancellation, yet except for three or four impediments Huntington would probably have succeeded in putting the scheme over.

One obstacle was the determined opposition of Adolph Sutro, mayor of San Francisco. Sutro had become incensed because the street railway company, a Southern Pacific subsidiary, would not concede a five-cent fare to the gardens which he proposed to give to the city. More specifically against the Funding Bill, young William Randolph Hearst arrayed the power of his press. He sent Bierce to Washington to train his caustic pen upon Huntington and the bill. With Bierce was an expert cartoonist, Homer Davenport, who turned out a daily representation of Huntington in the act of despoiling the nation. They are credited with the defeat of funding, but assists should be scored for the Colton Letters and the free harbor fight.

At the close of the century Californians in common with other Americans had their attention diverted from local problems by Bryan's Cross of Gold speech, the blowing up of the *Maine*, Admiral Dewey at Manila Bay, Hobson at Santiago, and Roosevelt's Rough Riders at San Juan Hill. Not until 1901 did the Southern Pacific become news again. By that time Huntington, last of the Big Four, had passed on to his reward, and the Southern Pacific properties were gathered up by Edward H. Harriman and merged with the Union Pacific system, which he had just resuscitated. This concentration of more than 15,000 miles of track under one management paralleled the rise of other gigantic trusts, the United States Steel Corporation and the Northern Securities Company, against which Theodore Roosevelt's spectacular trust-busting campaign was launched. Repercussions reached California but, meanwhile, San Francisco's municipal problems held center stage.

Bosses and Graft

As of the late eighties San Francisco public job holding was firmly controlled by a saloon-keeper, Blind Boss Christopher Buckley. He operated with a certain courtliness. Story has it that when a schoolteacher applicant was advised that a prerequisite was to take five gold pieces to the boss at his saloon, Buckley picked them up and purred, "I can't imagine why a young lady like you is bringing me this present." He also was remorseless, as in the cashiering of the venerated John Swett as school principal in 1890. Buckley eventually lost out, not to reform, but to another boss.

In 1901, after bitter turmoil between organized labor and the Employers' Association, Eugene E. Schmitz was elected mayor of San Francisco as the standard-bearer of a newly organized Union Labor party. Schmitz' qualifications for office were not impressive, his previous occupation being that of theater musician, but he was reelected in 1903, and again in 1905. The admitted power behind the throne was a member of the San Francisco bar, Abe Ruef, and the Union Labor label, though still good for many votes, was something of a misnomer. Prior to the election of 1905 it was a recognized fact that the Ruef machine was in cozy intimacy with established vice and guilty of corrupt practices. The would-be reformers, however, conducted so ineffective a campaign in 1905 that Ruef not only reelected his mayor but also carried into office for the first time his full slate of supervisors.

Throughout this half decade San Francisco had been growing even more rapidly than California as a whole. The rate of increase was approximately 10 percent a year. Such growth naturally meant that public utilities would expand and that in the course of this expansion they would have to make franchise and other arrangements with the city government. Ruef's machine exacted tribute from saloons, gambling houses, bordellos, French restaurants, prize fights, and the like, but its more ambitious levies were upon telephone, gas, water, and streetcar companies. Ruef's hand in demanding a payoff was oftentimes strengthened by an aroused public opinion as to what sort of expansion would be best. Thus, in the case of the United Railroads Company, its proposal of an overhead trolley system was violently opposed by Rudolph Spreckels, James D. Phelan, and other leaders in wealth and civic pride, who insisted that for beauty and for fire protection their city should have an underground conduit system along with Washington and New York, but Ruef's machine defeated the move.

Ordeal by Earthquake and Fire

Then came San Francisco's greatest ordeal. Early on the morning of April 18, 1906, there was slippage on the San Andreas fault, and the city and other communities north and south along the fault were struck by a severe earthquake. Fire broke out and, with water mains broken and pressure practically non-existent throughout the city, the flames swept through four square miles, including most of the business district. More than 400 persons were killed and 28,000 buildings destroyed. Thousands of refugees were evacuated; other thousands camped in Golden Gate Park.

Predictions were hazarded that the city would not be rebuilt and certainly that Market Street would not flourish again, but, almost before the ruins ceased smouldering, the rebuilding work began. Two men took the lead. General Hugh S. Johnson, better known to a later generation for his place beside the blue eagle at the head of the National Industrial Recovery Administration, headed the relief work of the United States Army. E. H. Harriman of the Southern Pacific placed every resource of the railroad at the disposal of the emergency workers. Aided by $300 million in fire insurance payments, San Franciscans built their city anew, finding in the adversity a determination and a sense of civic pride which they had not known existed.

The earthquake and fire reversed the population trend in San Francisco, but the rebuilding that was necessitated presented even greater opportunities for the Ruef machine. Alleging that the earthquake had closed the cable slots, the United Railroads began substituting trolley lines on Market Street. Notwithstanding a wave of protest, the city fathers granted the company on May 21 a blanket franchise to install trolley lines throughout its system. This affront to the popular will, together with a sharp lapse in police efficiency and lavish expenditures on the part of Mayor Schmitz and the $100-a-month supervisors, led to a mass meeting at which the Ruef machine was denounced and then to an announcement by District Attorney William H. Langdon that charges of graft and malfeasance in office would be laid before the grand jury. Langdon revealed that Francis J. Heney, who had made a reputation by exposing timber frauds in Oregon, would direct the graft prosecution, that William J. Burns had been retained as investigator, and that Rudolph Spreckels had agreed to underwrite the necessary expenses.

The Graft Prosecution

The machine struck first by having acting Mayor Gallagher remove Langdon as district attorney and name Ruef in his place. Langdon, however, refused to vacate the office and Heney would not be dismissed as deputy. At the impaneling of the grand jury the presiding judge recognized the right of Langdon and Heney to proceed, and in another court they got an injunction against Ruef's attempt to take over the office of district attorney.

The grand jury was not long in bringing in five indictments each against Ruef and Schmitz for practicing extortion against the

French restaurants. Trial should have proceeded at once, but Ruef's lawyers, availing themselves of every possible stratagem, were able to delay it for three months. Meanwhile, the prosecution found proof that Ruef's henchmen, the supervisors, had taken bribes from several public service corporations.

Seventeen of the 18 supervisors signed detailed affidavits to this effect and repeated their stories before the grand jury, explaining how $200,000 in bribe money had come to them: $9,000 came from the prize fight trust, $13,350 from the Pacific Gas and Electric Company, $62,000 from the Home Telephone Company, $85,000 from the United Railroads, and the balance from the Pacific States Telephone Company and the Parkside Transit Company. The grand jury returned 65 more indictments against Ruef and a lesser number against various persons for bribery. On the extortion charge Ruef pleaded guilty, and Schmitz was convicted on the jury's first ballot.

Langdon and Heney next sought convictions of the bribe givers. They were not surprised that these men brought to court an even larger battery of legal talent than had represented Ruef and Schmitz or that these lawyers again raised all possible objections to the grand jury that had returned the indictments. These attacks were fought down successfully in court, but not the out-of-court campaign waged against the prosecution. Small newspapers in San Francisco and elsewhere in the state were subsidized to attack the prosecution. The *San Francisco Chronicle* came out with all manner of criticism; Hearst's *Examiner* systematically pilloried Langdon, Heney, Burns, Spreckels, and Phelan; and the *Los Angeles Times* savagely attacked Heney and his associates. Social distinctions were thrust upon the defendants—Patrick Calhoun of the United Railroads Company, for example, was inducted into the Olympic Club—

and discrimination both social and economic operated against the prosecution.

Although the prosecution secured a conviction against Louis Glass of the Pacific Gas and Electric Company in the first bribery case brought to trial, the tide turned rapidly. Tirey Ford, chief counsel for the United Railroads, was tried three times on three separate counts. The first jury divided; the other two returned verdicts of not guilty. That was about as close as the prosecution came to getting another bribery conviction.

At several elections the people of San Francisco recorded a vote of confidence in the prosecution. Langdon was reelected district attorney in 1907, Judge Frank H. Dunne was reelected to his office in 1909, and Judge William P. Lawlor in 1912, but the main objective of Heney, that of procuring punishment for the men of wealth who had done the bribing, could not be attained. Spreckels' expectation that the trail would lead to William F. Herrin, attorney for the Southern Pacific and boss of its political machine, also was not fulfilled. On appeal, even the conviction of Louis Glass was reversed.

For a time it appeared that Ruef would also go scot free. The higher state courts, in decisions that must be reckoned bad law, reversed the findings of the grand jury and the trial court and released both Schmitz and Ruef. The latter was immediately brought to trial on one of the bribery charges, and, when the jury divided, the process was repeated on another bribery charge. Midway in this trial prosecutor Heney was shot down in open court by a juror whom he had challenged. In jail this assailant was silenced by what may have been murder or suicide. With Heney unable to continue, Hiram Johnson and Matt Sullivan stepped into the breach and won a conviction. Ruef was sentenced to 14 years in San Quentin.

Meanwhile, the prosecution was proceeding as best it could with the trial of Patrick

Calhoun, president of the United Railroads. Calhoun's legal staff was even larger and more brilliant than that which Ruef had employed. To secure a jury, 2,370 veniremen had to be called and 922 examined, a process that took three full months. The trial itself consumed five months and eight days, after which the jury failed to agree. The prosecution began a second trial, but, before half a jury was selected, the election of 1909 intervened. Langdon declined to run again and it was Heney against Charles M. Fickert for district attorney. Fickert's election was perhaps not a valid index to San Francisco's attitude toward the graft prosecution and defense, but it was so interpreted, and thereafter no serious effort was made to secure convictions of any of the defendants. Over the protests of Judge Lawlor the second Calhoun trial was terminated and the remaining indictments were dismissed.

Striking features of the four-year program of graft prosecution had been the kidnapping of Fremont Older, outspoken partisan of the prosecution and editor of the *Bulletin*; the bombing of the house of Supervisor Gallagher, a key witness; and the courtroom shooting of prosecutor Heney. This violence, whether or not directly instigated by the graft defendants, hampered the prosecution, even though it also enhanced it somewhat in popularity. With regard to the legal procedures themselves, a more prominent feature was the hamstringing of the prosecution by the refusal of many witnesses to testify, departure of witness after witness from the state, secreting or removal of documentary evidence (including the cash book of the United Railroads), subornation of witnesses, and fixing of juries.

Yet all this pales into insignificance in comparison with the propagandist methods whereby public opinion in San Francisco was converted to sympathy for the defendants. In less than five years the determination to call to an accounting all those who had prostituted the city's government had softened into an attitude that it would be "best for business" to forget all about it. Any animosity left was directed against the prosecutors; they were held up to scorn as vicious monsters. The tactics in the courtroom, in the press, in politics, in business, and in society whereby this was accomplished have been suggested. Strangest of all was Fremont Older's sudden compassion for Abe Ruef and his agitation for a pardon after the latter had languished in San Quentin for twelve months.

Historians, also, though admitting that more penitentiary sentences would have been in order, have usually been content to gloss the conclusion over with such innocuous platitudes as the assertion that "the political atmosphere of the city was cleansed" or that there was "a renaissance of idealism." Bean's *Boss Ruef's San Francisco* stops short of that optimism. The plain fact seems to be that the political atmosphere of San Francisco remained foggy, and so important a step as the cleaning up of the Barbary Coast was left for a later administration.

The Good Government Movement

Partly out of the San Francisco example and partly by independent origin, a movement for reform in municipal government cropped up in other parts of the state. In Los Angeles the spearhead was Dr. John R. Haynes. Some years earlier he had turned from medicine to real estate with substantial profit. He also had become an ardent enthusiast for direct legislation. Almost single-handedly he saw to it that Los Angeles' new city charter, adopted in 1902, incorporated provision for the initiative, referendum, and recall. The first use of the recall seemed proper enough: to remove a councilman who had voted to award the city's legal advertising to the *Los Angeles Times* even though there was another bid $15,000 lower. Nevertheless, there were staid citizens who looked upon the experiment in thoroughgoing democracy as revolutionary and dangerous.

Direct legislation was merely one facet of the push for better government in Los Angeles, and many others in addition to Haynes took part in the work. Some of the interest in reform was traceable to the shortcomings of local officials, some to the disclosures in the muckraking literature then so popular, but much of it was in direct protest against the undisguised political control of southern California by Walter Parker of the Southern Pacific machine.

A Good Government League was organized to work for a cleanup. In 1906 a slate of reform candidates was entered in the city election. On 17 of 23 positions the reformers were successful, though they did not beat the machine candidate for mayor, A. C. Harper. A year later the *Herald* began an exposé of vice protected through purchased shares in nebulous oil and sugar companies. These engraved documents led to the mayor, set the stage for a recall election, and prompted Mayor Harper to withdraw from the race.

Other cities indulged in lesser reforms. Sacramento voted itself a new charter and employed the initiative to grant a franchise to the Western Pacific Railroad. Santa Barbara and Palo Alto adopted new charters, San Francisco adopted the recall in 1907, and in several other municipalities the trilogy of initiative, referendum, and recall was made available.

With so much reform in the air and Theodore Roosevelt chanting the same refrain nationally, it was natural that similar proposals should be made concerning the state government. Provocation was not lacking. James H. Budd had given the state a notably economical administration from 1895 to 1899, and

George C. Pardee proved his integrity and his independence of machine politics and of the great corporations during his term of office from 1903 to 1907. On the whole, however, California could not take pride in its state government. The legislature progressively and inexcusably padded its payroll. Legislative elections of United States Senators were handled on a frankly partisan basis with every indication of venality. Machine control of nominating conventions was particularly galling, notably at Santa Cruz in 1906 when the Republicans summarily shelved Pardee in favor of a more compliant tool. At this convention the most powerful boss was none other than Abe Ruef. The legislature of 1907 gave additional cause for dissatisfaction. It set a new record for wastefulness, unscrupulousness, and subservience to the machine. That gave the immediate impetus to the reform movement which culminated in 1910, but, of course, the legislature of 1907, the Santa Cruz convention of 1906, and the Senatorial deadlock of 1899 were only surface symptoms. Underneath ran a deeper current of resentment that the state was in the grasp of the machine set up by the Southern Pacific.

For many years certain Californians had been working for electoral reforms. Stuffing of the ballot box, sometimes through use of ingenious devices such as the false bottomed box in which a quantity of ballots could be stowed, was frequently charged. Other irregularities included false counting, repeat voting, marching in hired voters, and intimidating honest voters. The voter supplied his own ballot or the party did. The party ballots were distinguishable by size and color, which meant that a watcher could readily see how anyone voted. Party ballots on occasion were counterfeited to benefit a particular candidate. Party nominations, meanwhile, were manipulated through the conventions and handpicked rather than representative.

As early as 1874 the legislature authorized parties to apply in elections to their conventions the safeguards operative in general elections. Because it was merely optional, this measure had little effect. Furthermore, the safeguards referred to were feeble protections. Other legislation followed, including introduction of the Australian ballot, provided by the state and marked in private and therefore secret. In 1900 a constitutional amendment offered a direct primary for choosing convention delegates. But not until the constitutional amendment in 1908 and supplementary legislation in 1909 did it become mandatory that party nominees be chosen by popular vote.

Other reform efforts were made in the nineties and in the following decade. Public ownership of railroads and utilities was suggested, and in Fresno early in 1906 a Public Ownership Party was launched. It proved no more successful than the Iroquois Clubs organized in the Democratic party and designed to coerce that party into more progressive action. Another group of Democrats organized the Independence League and pushed Langdon for governor in 1906 but without success.

The Lincoln-Roosevelt League

The next year the Lincoln-Roosevelt League took shape. Plans were first discussed at Los Angeles by a small group assembled by Chester H. Rowell of the Fresno *Republican* and Edward A. Dickson of the Los Angeles *Express*. Formal organization with Frank R. Devlin as president was achieved in Oakland in August, 1907. The platform, in brief, called for the "emancipation of the Republican party in California" from domination by the Southern Pacific Railroad Company and allied interests, selection of delegates to the next Republican national convention pledged to Roose-velt's policies, election of a "free, honest, and capable legislature," pledging of all delegates to conventions against the "iniquitous practice of 'trading,' " direct election of United States Senators, and direct primaries for the nomination of candidates for all state and local offices.

To rouse support for this program the League depended primarily on volunteer and personal work. Half a dozen newspapers, influential but not the largest in the state, supported the League from its inception. Besides Rowell's and Dickson's papers these included the Oakland *Tribune*, the Sacramento *Bee*, and Older's San Francisco *Bulletin*. Many smaller papers joined in and an official organ, the *California Weekly*, was launched. Even a few Democratic papers such as the Los Angeles *Herald* were cordial. Reform advocates organized clubs in almost every part of the state, and speakers headed by Chester Rowell carried the campaign from one end of the state to the other.

As a first major objective the League's executive committee focused on the election of 1908 and determined to win enough seats in the legislature to enact a direct primary law. In the meantime a few trial balloons were sent up in the shape of candidates in municipal elections, and as early as September of 1907 the first of these came in a winner, Clinton L. White, who was elected mayor of Sacramento. The League gained valuable publicity at the special session of the legislature called in November of 1907, and the work of organizing and agitating went steadily forward.

In May of the following year the League sought to win control of the state convention to elect delegates to the Republican national convention. Since only a minority of the members of this convention were to be elected and the rest named by county conventions, the League was at a considerable disadvantage and did well to gain approximately 44 percent of the seats in the convention. This percentage was not enough to enable it to name the state chairman or to control the state central committee or its executive committee, but at least the League members were encouraged to continue their war against special privilege.

Seeing the handwriting on the wall, the old political bosses had allowed the legislature to put on the ballot for the election in 1908 a constitutional amendment authorizing enactment of a direct primary law. Heartily advocated by the Lincoln-Roosevelt forces, this amendment carried by a large majority. The new legislature also was sufficiently Lincoln-Roosevelt that a comprehensive measure on the subject was enacted early in 1909. Since the direct primary had been regarded as the means for gaining all other reforms, there was some talk of disbanding the League. The vast majority, however, believed that the League faced an equally important task in the election of 1910.

For that campaign Hiram W. Johnson was prevailed on to be the Lincoln-Roosevelt candidate for governor. He had built up a successful legal practice and had greatly enhanced his personal popularity by volunteer-

ing to assist in the San Francisco graft prosecution after the shooting of Heney. He put on a whirlwind campaign for the Republican nomination, traveling 20,000 miles by automobile, and this at a time when such travel was far more arduous than today. Everywhere he went Johnson reiterated his promise to "kick the Southern Pacific Railroad out of the Republican Party and out of state government." He won the nomination handily and carried with him the League candidates for almost every other nomination.

Although the Democrats had elected only one governor in the preceding 20 years, they managed to make the campaign of 1910 an interesting one. The liberal faction controlled the Democratic convention and against Johnson put up Theodore A. Bell, who had been the party's national chairman two years earlier. Bell and the Democrats could insist with a measure of accuracy that they were even more progressive than Johnson and the Lincoln-Roosevelt Republicans.

History as represented in previous platforms corroborated Bell's claim, and current intentions as represented by the platforms of

Hiram Johnson Campaigning   *The Bancroft Library*

1910 were also not unfavorable to the Democrats. There were in fact 14 major points on which the two parties made equally radical demands. These included initiative, referendum, and recall, regulation of public utilities, a nonpartisan judiciary, the Australian ballot, conservation of natural resources, segregation of first offenders in a reformatory, direct election of United States Senators, Asiatic exclusion, simplification and tightening of the administration of justice in criminal cases, government support for a Panama steamship line, government appropriations for roads, rivers, and harbors, votes for women, an income tax, and elimination of corrupt control, a euphemism for Southern Pacific machine control of politics.

With the voters it was not so much a question as to which group was sincere but which group would best be able to carry out the platform promises. By a margin of 177,191 to 154,835 the task was entrusted to Hiram Johnson and his Lincoln-Roosevelt cohorts.

Reforms Accomplished

To expedite the enactment of the many reform measures contemplated, the triumphant Republicans assembled and appointed a dozen committees to draft bills and constitutional amendments. Some legislators disapproved of this procedure, though a number of Democrats joined in. It served, at any rate, to give the legislature of 1911 a running start and went far toward enabling that body to enact, in the words of Theodore Roosevelt, "the most comprehensive program of constructive legislation ever passed at a single session of an American legislature." Even the opposition gave grudging recognition. The San Francisco *Call* continued to refer to the "Legislature of a Thousand Freaks," but the San Francisco *Chronicle* conceded that it was the most industrious legislature in the state's history and that most of the new laws were excellent.

Johnson deserves much of the credit. His inaugural address was a clarion call to progressives in both parties to fulfill the promises made. He injected a controversial note by urging that the state ballot be shortened and responsibility concentrated by instituting the appointive cabinet system for most state offices. His advocacy of making recall applicable to the governor and to all judges was also regarded as ultraradical. Under his dynamic leadership, however, the legislators set aside party jealousies. Insofar as they were constitutionally empowered, they enacted laws to carry into effect the Lincoln-Roosevelt program. To cover other points they initiated 23 constitutional amendments on which the people voted on October 11. A short session gave effect to the amendments thus adopted.

Some of these measures, such as the workmen's compensation act and the law for the regulation of weights and measures, aimed at social betterment. Most were designed, however, to insure the voters effective control of the government and thereby make impossible machine-controlled corruption such as had prevailed. The creation of a new railroad commission was in some respects the most direct blow against the old regime, yet it was only one element in a much more comprehensive attack. The Southern Pacific, incidentally, made public announcement of its retirement from the political arena.

The Lincoln-Roosevelt or Johnsonian progressives continued their success for some years. In Johnson and his handpicked successor, William D. Stephens, they held the governorship for a dozen years, and throughout most of this period they had effective control in the legislature. Nevertheless, they were unable to maintain the pace set in 1911. Some important legislation was enacted at the next session, but thereafter the Johnson and

Stephens administrations were relatively unproductive.

The main reason for this slowdown was that the Lincoln-Roosevelts had run out of ideas. By 1914 they had achieved practically complete success in translating their platform into law. Some of them envisioned other vital steps that might be taken—a few were hard at work on public ownership of utilities—but the group was not agreed on a program for further action. Nor was public opinion prepared for it. Even with the most dynamic and purposeful leadership a few years would properly have gone to consolidating the gains already made.

On top of this factor there were great distractions. In 1912 the patron saint of the League, Theodore Roosevelt, broke with the Republicans and rallied his forces as the Progressive party. Most of the California progressives went along with him. In recognition of the strength of progressivism in California, Johnson was nominated as Roosevelt's running mate on the Bull Moose ticket. Because they still had control of the Republican party organization in California, the Johnson forces were able to keep Taft off the California ballot. As a write-in candidate he ran far behind. Roosevelt and Johnson carried 11 of the state's electoral votes and Wilson picked up the other two.

Four years later, when in theory, at least, the Republican party was reunited, Johnson won the senatorship by almost 300,000 votes, but the presidential nominee, Charles Evans Hughes, ran far behind and by 3,773 votes lost the state and the presidency to Wilson. Though an eminent figure, Hughes was a man of reserve, coldness, and conservatism. He had shown no sympathy for labor and no appreciation of the achievements of the California progressives. Furthermore, when he made a campaign visit to California in August, he allowed himself to be taken completely in tow by William H.

Crocker and Francis V. Keesling, Old Guard Republicans. On the train from Oregon he slighted Chester Rowell; in San Francisco he ignored Mayor James Rolph; and in Long Beach, though under the same hotel roof with Governor Johnson, he did not see to it that a meeting was arranged.

The Long Beach affront no doubt was unintentional, but Hughes' complete neglect of the Johnson wing of the party was so consistent that it inevitably gave the impression of being calculated. After the votes had been counted, the Old Guard Republicans threw the entire blame on Johnson, charging that out of vindictiveness he had not given Hughes' candidacy genuine support. Johnson angrily retorted that the Old Guard had so misused Hughes and his California visit that the injury could not be undone. Most of the contemporary and later discussion of this election concerns what might have been. The fact most clearly established is that the Old Guard alone could not carry California. Even with the advantage of the Republican label and of Johnson on the same ticket, Hughes needed to give more convincing demonstration of agreement with Lincoln-Roosevelt-Johnsonian progressivism.

The 1916 campaign had another aftermath that illustrates a weakness among the California progressives. As a political move to appeal to the southern California voters, William D. Stephens had been persuaded to run for lieutenant governor rather than for reelection to Congress. The understanding was that if elected to the Senate Johnson would resign the governorship to Stephens. Johnson, however, made no move to do so in November or December. In January, when the legislature assembled, he continued as governor. When some of Stephens' friends protested and intimated court action, it merely threw Johnson into choleric fury. He delayed his resignation until March when a special session of

Congress was called and no alternative was left. That was one among a number of occasions when deep rifts developed within the Lincoln-Roosevelt group. Many, perhaps most, of these men were strong-minded individuals. Common cause had held them together for awhile, but this was not an amalgam that would endure the fire of Johnsonian rage and vindictiveness.

For Johnson the Lincoln-Roosevelt League was a springboard to the United States Senate. On the whole, however, the leaders in the League did not move on to public office. Roused to political action by the manifest abuses in California government, they organized, campaigned, and captured the Republican party and through it the state government. With systematic determination in the legislature of 1911 they enacted their program. Incidental additions were made in the years that followed, and by momentum the group retained control of the state government throughout the decade, gradually relinquishing leadership to regular Republicans who were less progressive or not at all. Lack of a program for continuing reform, the distractions of national politics and World War I, and a series of personal quarrels within their ranks weakened the movement, but not before it had given the state a decade of remarkably high-minded and uncorrupted government.

Lincoln-Rooseveltianism was a reform movement that captured the popular fancy with unprecedented rapidity. Here were reformers who translated their theories into practice with unusual thoroughness and efficiency. They were most astute politicians. Californians rightly took great pride in this demonstration of political acumen and statesmanship, and the nation gave it an attention not completely distracted by the fiasco of Rooseveltian progressivism or by the First World War. It stands as a high-water mark in California's record of political achievement.

CHAPTER 22

Sunrise...
Restaurant

I. INOSE, Propr.

209 East First Street
Near Los Angeles Street

Free Pudding For Dinner

Free Stewed Fruit for Supper

Nice Lunches Put Up to Order

Chicken Dinner Every Sunday 15c.

 21 Meals Ticket $2.00

BEST 10 CENT MEAL HOUSE IN THE CITY.

...MIKADO...
..Restaurant...

HIDEO MUTA, Propr.

301 Commercial Street, Los Angeles.

Meals 10 cents with Wine and Ice Cream,
... Pie or Pudding Every Day ...

Turkey or Chicken Dinner with Wine and Ice Cream,
...or Pie Every Sunday...

California was given by God to a white people, and with God's strength we want to keep it as He gave it to us.

William P. Canbu, Grand President
Native Sons of the Golden West, April, 1920

Race Prejudice and Labor Conflict

The Anti-Japanese Movement

In the period spanning the turn of the century California experienced gratifying development along almost every line. Improved transportation, expanded agriculture, and increased activity in commerce and industry yielded substantial economic growth. The traditional bulwarks of society—home, church, and school—registered noteworthy gains during the period. On the political front, too, it was an epoch of remarkable achievement. In contrast, these years were characterized by bitter class conflict. Some of it was racist; the greater part involved labor relations and had as its crux the question, "Should labor be permitted to organize?"

Prominent in this conflict was a clamor for Japanese exclusion. Until the nineties very few Japanese had come to California. In that decade immigration was at the nominal rate of about 1,000 a year, but by 1900 entrants numbered 12,626. The 1910 census showed 41,356 and the 1920 census, 71,952. Only 2 percent of the total population, this racial minority may seem too trivial to have caused much concern, but Californians worked themselves up to a high pitch of excitement. A state historian in 1922 feared that California's most difficult task would be to remain American. Many arguments used against the Chinese were raised and seemed plausible against the Japanese.

As early as 1886 when there were only 400 in the state, the slogan "The Japs Must Go" was voiced. In 1900 San Francisco was the scene of a mass meeting for similar purpose. Five years later trade union men organized the Asiatic Exclusion League and the *Chronicle* ran a series of articles advocating exclusion. Then in 1906, the San Francisco school board precipitated an international incident by announcing that Japanese students, numbering about 90, would have to go to the Chinese school. After President Roosevelt intervened this order was rescinded but only temporarily. With "separate but equal" the law of the land, the federal government could do nothing for California-born Japanese, but on behalf of those who were foreign-born the United States Attorney General brought suit. Mayor Schmitz went to Washington for a conference and a compromise was worked out.

The federal authorities, meanwhile, undertook to limit immigration of Japanese laborers. In 1907 Congress banned admission of Japanese from Canada, Mexico, or the United States' Pacific islands. Shortly thereafter Elihu Root and Ambassador Takahira drafted the Gentlemen's Agreement whereby Japan promised to grant passports only to non-laborers or to laborers who were going to join a parent, wife, or child, resume a domicile in the United States, or take possession of a previously acquired farm. The smuggling of Japanese across the Mexican border continued, and the agreement itself contained loopholes such as the permission for Japanese to come to the United States to join their spouses. Under this authorization picture brides by the thousands entered California. Californians denounced it as a subterfuge, were shocked at the high birth rate among the Japanese, and protested that the picture bride was usually another field laborer.

Much of the talk about the menace of Japanese laborers was merely window dressing. Throughout the nineties and the following decade, when they were functioning primarily as agricultural laborers, the Japanese were accepted with a minimum of distrust. They did work that white workers did not want to do and were not generally regarded as competitors. Even the San Francisco school incident did not signify a unanimous stand against the Japanese.

Shortly thereafter, by organizing and demanding higher pay, the Japanese incurred the displeasure of their employers. Increasingly they moved from farm labor to farming. In the rice districts of Glenn, Colusa, and Butte counties, in the Delta, in vineyards and orchards around Fresno and Tulare, in Los Angeles and Orange County vegetable and berry gardens, and in Imperial Valley, Japanese growers such as George Shima in the Delta, who earned fame as the "Potato King," became more numerous. By 1920 the farmland owned or leased was set at 535,000 acres, much of it the most productive land in the state. This advance into the entrepreneural class put the Japanese into competition with established producers, and, though the agitation continued against coolie labor, the drive came to be more against the Japanese capitalists.

The first major salvo of the campaign was the Alien Land Law, the Webb Act of 1913. The burden of this measure was that aliens ineligible for citizenship could not acquire farmland or lease agricultural land for more than three years. Ostensibly it applied to all aliens who could not or would not seek United States citizenship; practically its application was to the Japanese alone. The national authorities again became alarmed that the measure would jeopardize cordial relations with Japan. President Wilson sent telegrams to Governor Johnson and, while the bill was still before the legislature, dispatched Secretary of State William Jennings Bryan to Sacramento to lobby for its defeat or modification. Despite this pressure the legislature passed the bill and the governor promptly signed it.

Japanese Orange Packers   *Los Angeles Museum of Natural History*

Had the act been rigorously enforced, Japanese agriculturists would soon have been squeezed out. It developed, however, that its full rigors could be escaped through indirect leasing, incorporation, or vesting ownership in California Japanese who had aready acquired citizenship. By the end of the decade the Japanese, still constituting only 2 percent of the population, controlled more than 11 percent of the state's agricultural land.

California resolved to try again. In 1919 a more stringent land law failed to pass only because Secretary of State Robert Lansing certified that to offend Japan would endanger the peace negotiations in Paris. In 1920 the State Board of Control issued a blistering attack on Oriental immigration and an initiative which carried in every county tightened ownership restrictions. Only after an indecent interval of 40 years did the State Supreme Court find the Webb Act unconstitutional.

Regulation of immigration, of course, was a prerogative of the federal government. Californians were not reticent about proposing legislation, and beginning in 1911 various measures designed to achieve exclusion were introduced in Congress. None succeeded until 1924 when Congress had under consideration a general curb on immigration. In what must be regarded as an excess of zeal Californians had written into this bill a provision forbidding the entrance of immigrants not eligible for citizenship. Translated into practical terms this meant no Japanese.

Secretary of State Hughes urged the more diplomatic procedure of applying the same quota arrangement being set up for European nations, which would have worked out to admit only 246 Japanese a year. This counsel of tact, however, was set aside. The Japanese ambassador protested that the measure would have "grave consequences." Congress took umbrage at this "veiled threat" and passed the bill promptly, and President Calvin

Coolidge, though regretting the anti-Japanese clause, approved the bill as a whole.

Needless to say, the Japanese entrants after 1924 were few and were considerably exceeded by the number departing. The California Japanese increased to 97,456 in 1930, and declined to 93,717 in 1940. They continued to be prominent in the agricultural areas mentioned above, in flower growing, in operation of vegetable markets, as residential gardeners, and in the fishing industry, especially at San Pedro.

The California campaign for Japanese exclusion, although generating more international friction than had the earlier move against the Chinese, was not accompanied by as much violence. It produced quicker action than had the anti-Chinese drive, mainly because the United States was concerned about Japanese immigration to Hawaii and the Philippines. Most Californians in 1940 were seemingly content that Japanese immigration had ceased. The more reflective, however, could not take pride in the methods used, nor did they subscribe to the alarmist arguments of the nativists. As for assimilation, the nativists certainly had been in error. Cultural assimilation took place rapidly. By 1940 almost two-thirds of the Japanese were second generation Californians and therefore citizens, Americans in fact as well as in technicality.

Exploiting Other Recruits

With Japanese immigration forbidden and with most Japanese in California preferring to work for themselves, the state's agriculturists found a new supply of cheap labor providentially available. Raising the American flag over the Philippine Islands had made the inhabitants nationals if not citizens. In 1923 some 2,426 Filipinos were brought in, and for the rest of the decade the number mounted until the total stood at about 35,000.

At first the Filipinos were regarded as very good and docile workers. Within a few years, however, the pendulum of employer opinion swung against them. The accumulated criticism of earlier Orientals was applied, a few knifing affrays were magnified, and their association with white dance hall girls was adjudged a scandal. They were attacked, notably at Watsonville in 1930 and in the Salinas lettuce fields four years later. Exclusion was proposed and in 1935 achieved indirectly through a "free transportation" measure specifying that no Filipino who accepted free passage home could return to the continental United States. Pursuant to this law thousands were deported.

The attitude toward the Mexicans went through a similar pattern of change. Until the late teens Mexicans were of little significance in farm labor except in Imperial Valley, but as other sources of labor supply were cut off or proved inadequate, an increasing dependence was placed upon Mexicans. The year 1920 is referred to as a Mexican harvest, and throughout the twenties Mexicans were the most numerous element in California fieldwork. In the late twenties, however, Congress had under consideration bills to put Mexicans on a quota basis.

With the depression urban communities began to object more strenuously to maintaining aliens on relief through the winter so that they could work on the farms for low wages during the harvest season. Inspired by the Hoover administration's program in the early thirties to reduce unemployment by deporting aliens, Los Angeles County set in motion repatriation of Mexicans. In theory the operation was benevolent and it drew some cooperation from the Mexican government. There were objections, however, that it was damaging to trade in Los Angeles' eastside barrio and that it was counterproductive in terms of goodwill in

Latin America, which caused the Chamber of Commerce to withdraw its endorsement. After tens of thousands had been sent to Nogales and Juárez, these deportations ceased.

The next group to suffer in the vicious circle of recruitment, low wages, hard working conditions, and talk of ejection and exclusion were the Dust Bowl refugees from the Midwest. Toward these "Okies" and "Arkies" the cycle of changing attitude was almost precisely the one previously acted out with the Chinese, Japanese, and Filipinos.

While other states from British Columbia and Idaho to Arizona and Sonora felt the urge for Oriental exclusion, the experience was not nationwide or anywhere so pronounced as in California. Other local issues corresponded more closely to those of the nation, notably the one that was long the key social problem, the relationship of capital and labor.

The Right to Organize

Beginning with a printers' union in 1850, San Francisco added many labor organizations in the years that followed. These trade unions did much to stabilize wages and control working conditions, and they also achieved several items of labor legislation, including a mechanics' lien law and an eight-hour day in government work. In the troubled seventies labor's aims were unfortunately diverted to the crusade against the Chinese, but in the following decades attention was turned to more fundamental problems. Efforts centered on the waterfront, notorious for shanghaiing and other abuses.

After a waterfront strike in 1886 which failed and a brewery strike and one by the metal workers, leadership in San Francisco unionizing passed to the Coast Seamen's Union, organized in 1885 and after 1887 with Andrew Furuseth as its mainspring. In the early nineties this union contested vigorously with an Employers' Association for control of crew hiring at San Francisco and all the other ports from San Diego to Vancouver in British Columbia. The union's chances were crimped by the panic of 1893 and demolished by a bomb explosion at a nonunion boarding-house. Who set the bomb was never discovered, but public opinion jumped to a conclusion and the Seamen's Union was years in reestablishing its strength.

When the Spanish-American War and the gold rush to the Klondike provided a new basis for prosperity, labor made another effort to strengthen its position. Again the employers were equally alert. The waterfront and sea-going workers joined in the City Front Federation, soon countered by the Employers Council. On July 30, 1901, the Federation called a waterfront strike and a large number of sympathetic strikes soon followed. The employers with a war chest of $250,000 fought back. Altogether 30 assaults were reported and five men were killed. After three months the strike ended in a stalemate. The net effect, however, was advantageous to labor because of the continuing strength of the unions. San Francisco became a closed shop city, the first in the nation. At the polls, too, the Union Labor party prevailed and held control of the city government for a decade.

Meanwhile, the scene of sharpest controversy had shifted to Los Angeles. The contest began in 1890 with a walkout of typographers on four newspapers which had threatened a 20 percent wage cut. Three of the papers settled quickly, but the Los Angeles Times, commanded by the militant Harrison Gray Otis, would have nothing more to do with union printers. Nonunion men were imported, with conflict the natural consequence. Other unions expressed sympathy and Otis expanded his diatribes to include not only union printers but everything that smacked of

unionism. The unions attempted a boycott of the Times and of merchants advertising in it. Their campaign was more ingenious than effective, but against a less resourceful fighter than Otis and in a city more stable than Los Angeles it might have succeeded. Los Angeles was growing so rapidly that new subscribers and purchasers were constantly entering to take the place of those participating in the boycott, and the farming and small town people who made up a good fraction of the increase were little disposed toward unionism.

Taking advantage of the railroad strikes of 1893–94, which seriously interfered with the marketing of southern California fruit crops, Otis berated the unions for their "robber rule" and "organized despotism" and vilified merchants who stopped advertising in his paper. With others of like sentiment he organized an aggressive employers' union, the Merchants and Manufacturers Association, which soon had 6,000 dues-paying members.

The primary function of the M.&M. was to combat unionism. It obviously had extraordinary power to coerce businessmen who, forgetful of their class obligations, showed a disposition to submit to labor. Bank loans could be withheld, settlement of accounts could be delayed, orders could be diverted to other firms, and a blacklist could be employed. The structural resemblance to labor's boycott is striking, but the effectiveness was considerably greater. The M.&M. was one of the biggest guns in Otis' artillery.

Otis' pugnacious attitude was instrumental in making the Los Angeles controversy a national issue. There were other factors, such as the wage differential as compared to San Francisco's, which made that city's employers and labor leaders want Los Angeles unionized, but it was largely because of the truculence of the Times that Los Angeles became the battle front for the nation's forces for closed or open shop.

A number of strikes took place with a full complement of violence and always with the *Times* a willing participant against the strikers. In the summer of 1910 matters came to a climax with a strike of the Structural Iron Workers in which the local union was aided by a contingent from San Francisco. Strikers and strikebreakers slugged and blackjacked each other and, when the city council passed an antipicketing ordinance and the Superior Court granted injunctions against the strikers, the police entered the fray. Hundreds of pickets were arrested and sentenced to a $50 fine or 50 days in jail. When jury trials were demanded, however, most of the the strikers were acquitted, which encouraged the unions to believe that public opinion was on their side after all. The atmosphere, meanwhile, continued tense. Otis mounted a small cannon on his automobile and the *Times* surpassed itself in condemning the unions. The police reported discovery of unexploded bombs planted at the Hall of Records and the Alexandria Hotel.

The McNamara Trial

In this atmosphere of hate and recrimination Los Angeles was aroused just after one o'clock on the morning of October 1, 1910, by a series of explosions, their roar audible for ten miles. The scene of disaster was the Times Building. The explosions immediately turned the building into an inferno in which 20 men were killed and 17 injured.

From an auxiliary plant a few blocks away the survivors got out a morning edition in which the blame for the disaster was placed squarely on unionist bombs. Police and grand jury investigations as well as special reports by investigators for the mayor and the city council supported the opinion that the building had been dynamited. Labor retorted that the base-

ment showed no effect of dynamite's downward action, that broken windows were conspicuously absent, that escaping gas had overcome several persons in the building during the day, and that, because of his "criminal negligence" in maintaining a "gas-polluted fire trap," Otis should be tried for manslaughter. In Los Angeles and over the country the riddle of dynamite or gas was answered by most people according to their predilection for the *Times* and the open shop or for unionism and the closed shop.

Almost seven months later the *Times* blazoned headlines that the dynamiters had been caught and were en route to Los Angeles in custody of William J. Burns' private detectives. Still more sensational was the identity of the men seized; Ortie McManigal and J. B. McNamara, apprehended in Detroit, and J. J. McNamara of Indianapolis. McManigal and J. B. McNamara were well-known union men and J. J. McNamara was secretary of the Structural Iron Workers' Union.

The *Times* did not play up the method of the seizure of the first two in Detroit, their conveyance to Chicago and irregular extradition from Illinois, or the irregularities surrounding the extradition of J. J. McNamara from Indiana.

Union sympathizers over the nation, however, well remembered the kidnapping of three other labor leaders in 1907 and their arraignment for a dynamite murder in Idaho. Prosecuted by William E. Borah and defended by Clarence Darrow, these men had been acquitted after a sensational trial. The secret arrest of the McNamaras had all the earmarks of another "capitalist conspiracy" and was denounced as such by Samuel Gompers of the American Federation of Labor, Eugene V. Debs of the Socialist party, and numerous other national figures.

The ensuing trial was of the McNamara brothers, McManigal having turned state's evidence. It also was much more than a personal and local issue. The American Federation of Labor retained Darrow to conduct the defense, and by appropriation and private donation union labor and its adherents supplied him with a quarter of a million dollars. The prosecution had ample financial support from such organizations as the National Manufacturers' Association as well as from local interested parties.

In addition the trial had a political hookup. Job Harriman, attorney for the local labor council and an associate in the McNamaras' defense, was running for mayor of Los Angeles on the Socialist ticket. His candidacy was inextricably bound up with the insistence that the McNamaras were victims of an iniquitous conspiracy. Furthermore, victory in Los Angeles would be of inestimable value as a stimulant for the rising trend toward socialism then sweeping the country.

In October, 1911, the trial of J. B. McNamara at last got under way. Neither side seemed anxious to move it along. Darrow, according to the statement subsequently recorded in his autobiography, was convinced before the trial had started that his clients could not be saved. Delay, however, would enhance the Socialist-Labor chances in the election, while the prospect of Darrow's cross-examination of Otis and others was by no means reassuring to the prosecution. Consequently, though there was nothing on the surface to indicate it, settlement out of court seemed the best solution for both sides. Through the mediation of Lincoln Steffens a bargain was struck, and on December 1, to the stupefaction of all who were not in on the secret, the McNamara brothers appeared in court and changed their pleas to guilty. Two days later they were sentenced, J. B. to life imprisonment and J. J. to 15 years.

Why the defense took this course is not entirely clear. For socialism and for organized labor it was a most bitter blow. Instead of being swept into office as he confidently expected, Job Harriman was snowed under in the Los Angeles election. Socialist candidates elsewhere were adversely affected and the Socialist party never regained the vigor or promise that it enjoyed prior to the McNamara confession. For the next 20 or 25 years the same can almost be said of the American Federation of Labor. For socialism and for the unions conviction without confession would have been a more satisfactory outcome, for then many would have assumed that the brothers were really innocent. Darrow doubtless realized all this, but he may have believed it the only way to save his clients from the gallows. The McNamaras may have thought so too, for some most sinister rumors were being circulated, as of a Burns dictaphone installed in Darrow's office, and to this day it has not been revealed how conclusive was the proof amassed by the prosecution.

An immediate sequel was arraignment of Darrow on two charges of attempting to bribe a juror. Neither charge stood up in court.

The McNamara case still has many mysterious angles. It is impossible, for example, to reconcile the statements in the McNamara confession with the description of the planting of the bomb as elaborated in the *Times* or with the version given to the *Saturday Evening Post* 20 years later. The participants in the deal that led up to the confession, though voluble on a number of points, were close-mouthed about the most essential features and to a considerable extent carried the secret with them to their graves.

The evidence is clear, at any rate, that the bargain turned out to be more one-sided than had been expected. The prosecution made no recommendation of leniency; the judge, who had been a party to the bargain and whom Steffens had advised to speak to the defendants "as one criminal to another," instead denounced them bitterly and sentenced J. J. to 15 years instead of the expected ten. Los Angeles capitalists, furthermore, did not take the steps of which Steffens had been so confident toward establishing a peaceful understanding with labor. With the wind taken out of the sails of the labor movement the employers pushed their advantage and were able to keep Los Angeles for some years longer the stronghold of the open shop.

The IWW and the Wheatland Riot

Even before the McNamara case monopolized the headlines, the Industrial Workers of the World had invaded California. Ridiculed as the "wobblies" and attributed the slogan "I Won't Work," the IWW was well fitted to organize labor in fields thus far neglected by the trade unions. Organizers, drifting south from the lumber camps in the Northwest, found willing listeners in California mine and lumber crews and in the agricultural labor gangs. Most of the workers involved were relatively unskilled, which placed them out of bounds for the American Federation of Labor and made a union's effectiveness uncertain, but the wobblies were undaunted.

In 1910 their local at Fresno, reacting to repeated interference with IWW meetings, launched a fight for free speech. The technique was simple. The wobblies got themselves arrested singly and in groups until the jail could hold no more. Wobbly endurance and willingness to absorb punishment were pitted against the capacity of the law enforcement agencies and the patience of the community. Capacity and patience were exhausted first. Antiwobbly demonstrators burned the IWW headquarters, and the police, exasperated by the wobbly ritual of singing in jail, tried to silence them with a fire

hose. After months of strife Fresno made partial concessions.

Two years later the IWW mobilized for a similar campaign against San Diego. There were very few wobblies in the vicinity and only a few thousand in the entire state, but, summoned by grapevine and moving in by boxcar, they rapidly converged on the city to reenact the Fresno routine of getting arrested and going to jail. The San Diego police inflicted rough treatment; one of the jailed wobblies was kicked to death. With police encouragement a vigilante group rounded up several hundred wobblies, ran them through a gauntlet, and drove them away. Governor Johnson then sent an investigator to the scene, and after a time the state lent its support to the principle of free speech. These free speech fights demonstrated the fanatical devotion of the wobblies to their cause. This fanaticism in turn gave them influence, especially among unskilled labor, out of all proportion to their numbers.

A case in point was the Wheatland riot in August, 1913. On the Durst hop ranch near Wheatland 2,800 workers were camped in unspeakable filth and discomfort. Recruited by advertisements for twice as many pickers as were needed, they were paid 78 cents to a dollar a day, gouged by a company store, and detained in the camp by a 10 percent holdback on their wages. At that, conditions were not unlike those that had prevailed for years in California farm labor camps.

In the Durst camp an IWW local was formed by 30 men. On August 3 they called a meeting to demand better living conditions. As the meeting closed, a sheriff's posse accompanied by the district attorney arrived on the scene and attempted to arrest Blackie Ford, the IWW leader and spokesman. A shot in the air, fired "to sober the mob," started a riot in which the sheriff, the district attorney, and two workers were killed and many others injured. Most of the workers fled the camp.

The National Guard patrolled Wheatland for a week, while the Burns operatives combed the state for wobblies. How many were arrested no one has been able to compute because many were jailed without proper booking or were held privately by the Burns detectives. Herman Suhr, an associate of Ford's who had left the camp before the riot, was seized in Arizona, popped into a boxcar, and without formality of extradition shipped back to California. Eight months later Ford and Suhr were convicted on charges of murder and sentenced to life imprisonment. Though less famous, they are more genuine martyrs to labor's cause than the McNamara brothers could have been.

The Wheatland tragedy called attention to the plight of California's agricultural laborers. The state government was stimulated to begin regulation of labor camps. A Commission on Immigration and Housing was created and working and living conditions were somewhat improved. Another episode drawing greater public attention to the problems of the unskilled and seasonally unemployed workers was the march of Kelley's Army on Sacramento. Modeled on Coxey's Army, Kelley's 1,500 men encamped at Sacramento to demand "charitable assistance." They were greeted instead by a pickhandle brigade which drove them across the river, burned their blankets, and denied them access to the city.

Not Proved Guilty

World War I, meanwhile, was exerting new influences on labor-capital relations. In all quarters the tendency was to identify strikes with breach of patriotism. In Los Angeles, however, the war years witnessed a strengthening of unions, perhaps because business leaders had a more immediate interest in reap-

Tom Mooney in San Quentin
The Bancroft Library

ing profits than in keeping labor in check. In the north the war years were chosen as the time for a new campaign for the open shop, this time in the guise of a preparedness measure. This, in brief, was the psychological setting for San Francisco's Preparedness Day bombing on July 22, 1916, with its toll of ten lives.

Union activists Tom Mooney and Warren K. Billings were arrested and put on trial. The key testimony against them was by an Oregon rancher who volunteered that he saw a party, including the two defendants, drive up to the curb at Steuart and Market and deposit on the sidewalk a battered suitcase which contained the bomb. The defense offered testimony that Mooney and Billings were elsewhere, but the jury returned a verdict of guilty and the judge sentenced Mooney to death and Billings to life imprisonment.

Labor partisans immediately charged that Mooney had been railroaded, and at the same time more neutral analysis cast doubt on the verdict. A deluge of protest came in, including a strong suggestion from President Wilson. Governor Stephens responded by commuting the sentence to life imprisonment.

Investigative work brought to light a picture of Mooney on a rooftop some distance from the scene of the bombing with a clock registering a time that made it almost impossible for him to have planted the bomb. Police on traffic duty did not believe that any car had been permitted to make the described trip. Later it developed that the key witness had not arrived in San Francisco until after the explosion. His was perjured testimony, the only doubt being whether it was prearranged.

Motions by counsel for reversal and for a new trial were refused. Even after the jury and the trial judge publicly retracted their decisions and two of the three prosecuting attorneys recommended pardon, such action did not occur. For 22 years Mooney stayed in jail and his case continued to be American labor's leading cause célèbre.

Finally in January, 1939, when Culbert L. Olson took office as governor, Mooney was granted an unconditional pardon. Billings presumably was no more guilty than Mooney, but as a second offender he was not eligible for pardon. Nine months later by commutation of sentence he also was released.

The evidence has long since convinced historians that Mooney had not been proved guilty as charged. That conclusion was made all the more explicit a half century after the event in Richard H. Frost's meticulously researched *The Mooney Case* (1968).

As to Mooney, the hardhearted have insisted that he was worth more to the labor cause in San Quentin than out. Be that as it may, his detention there long after it was clear that he had been convicted on perjured testimony was certainly damaging to the antiunion cause. Those of that persuasion might better have exerted their influence for his release.

Criminal Syndicalism and the Decline of the Unions

Immediately after World War I the American people entered a period of particular hysteria. The tensions of the war were partly responsible. Resort to dynamiting as a means of persuasion toward unionism was another factor, as was the IWW's practice of sabotage, and by easy extension all Socialists were assumed to be anarchists and nihilists. With the Russian Revolution of 1917 engineered by men presumed to be of the same stripe, social conflict in America acquired an international overtone which suggested that world upheaval was the menace to be feared. The infamous Palmer raids and the unseating of the Socialist members of the New York legislature are two well-known consequences. California fell in with the hysteria with her accustomed vigor and, as might have been predicted in terms of prior episodes of social conflict, aimed retaliation primarily against unionism.

As modus operandi, the state legislature in 1919 enacted a criminal syndicalism law similar to the one with which Idaho had led the way two years earlier. The act defined criminal syndicalism in dragnet fashion as "any doctrine or precept advocating, teaching or aiding and abetting the commission of crime, sabotage . . . , or unlawful acts of force or violence or unlawful methods of terrorism as a means of accomplishing a change in industrial ownership or control, or effecting any political change."

In terms of the act, guilt attached equally to doing the deed, advocating it, or belonging to an organization that advocated it. Penalty was set at imprisonment for one to 14 years. The California act bore general resemblance to those legislated by 21 other states, mostly western, and by Alaska and Hawaii. Elsewhere the acts soon became dead letters but in California there was rigorous enforcement. In the first five years 531 persons were arrested, 264 were brought to trial, and 164 were convicted.

The most widely noted criminal syndicalism prosecution was of a respected philanthropist, Anita Whitney. In 1919 when the Socialist party local of which she was a member broke off and joined the Communist Labor party, she went as a delegate to a state convention in Oakland. At the convention, open to reporters and the public, she took a strong stand against revolutionary unionism and in favor of working for reform through the ballot. The state convention, however, voted a preference for the radical method. It also gave pro forma approval to the national convention's program, which in passing included endorsement of the IWW. Three weeks later Whitney was arrested for violation of the criminal syndicalism law.

In the protracted trial the bulk of the evidence adduced concerned alleged atrocities committed by the IWW. On the basis of her attendance at the state convention of the Communist Labor party, which approved the national convention's program and thereby endorsed the IWW, she was convicted of the felony of association with a group which advocated, taught, or aided and abetted criminal syndicalism.

Appeals ran until 1927 when the United States Supreme Court by a split decision upheld the conviction. Foiled on that front, Counsel John Francis Neylan urged Governor C. C. Young to issue a pardon. Impressed by this appeal and by the dissenting opinion of Justice Louis Brandeis and convinced that

Anita Whitney, "lifelong friend of the unfortunate," was "not in any true sense a criminal," the governor decided that "to condemn her to a felon's cell" was "absolutely unthinkable." He issued the pardon.

Practicing idealists from the upper strata could be caught in the coils of the criminal syndicalism act. Members of various unions and left-wing political groups also were jeopardized. Its most frequent targets, however, were the IWW members. They constituted the bulk of the persons arrested, tried, and convicted. In the free speech fights, on charges of sabotage and on other charges, the wobblies had seen a great deal of the courts prior to the enactment of this law and on the whole had little confidence in them. They seldom carried their disdain so far as the 53 "Silent Defendants." Indicted earlier in 1919 for mass trial at Sacramento, they declined to attempt any defense.

Many a wobbly, however, pleaded his own case and, even when there was counsel, the main batteries of legal talent were always with the prosecution. In these trials it became almost impossible to present defense witnesses, whereas the prosecution again and again relied on Elbert Coutts, W. E. Townsend, and John Dymond, professional witnesses. Furthermore, in the temper of the times mere membership in the IWW or association with it was regarded as felonious. Ease of obtaining convictions undoubtedly explains the frequency with which this particular charge was brought.

In 1923 when the IWW called a waterfront strike at San Pedro, the immediate response was to invoke the criminal syndicalism law against the strike leaders. Attempts to suppress the strike by direct action followed. There were wholesale arrests; one haul was variously estimated at 700 to 1,200 men taken off to stockades in Griffith Park.

Resentment against the IWW continued, in

fact, mounted. In March, 1924, the Ku Klux Klan demonstrated against it. Other incidents followed, including a sacking of the IWW headquarters, a vigilante assault on a benefit party in which a number of children were beaten and tortured, and a tarring and feathering of several of the leaders. After 1924 the IWW ceased to be a power at San Pedro though its influence lived on in other waterfront and maritime unions. Its hold on farm and forest laborers also declined rapidly, partly because of pressures from without and partly because of dissensions within.

About the same time public opinion took a turn against the criminal syndicalism statute. The president of the State Bar Association, the president of Stanford University, Max Radin of the University of California Law School, and other responsible citizens urged its repeal. It was not removed from the statute books, but after 1924 actions under it ceased for the time being. It was not revived until the late sixties and then survived only on appeal. The major reason may well have been that the IWW was no longer the threat it once had seemed to be.

Throughout the twenties the general tenor of labor-capital relations was one of greatly diminished strength for unionism. Following the defeat of a waterfront strike in 1919 and a building trades strike in 1921, San Francisco was more open shop than closed. In Los Angeles unionism declined at about the same rate and some of the accompanying features eclipsed the plain fact. The pretentious label "American plan" supplanted the term "open shop." The menace of Red Russia was taken very seriously, property rights were exalted as the citadel of patriotism, and organizations such as the Better America Federation made antiliberalism and antiunionism the prime virtues. The decade ended with unionism and liberalism at low ebb.

CHAPTER 23

Traffic Congestion, Downtown Los Angeles, 1925

Title Insurance and Trust Company

You know, I think we put too much emphasis and importance and advertising on our so-called High standard of living. I think that "High" is the only word in that phrase that is really correct. We sure are a-living High.

Will Rogers

The Boom of the Twenties

Since the discovery of gold, California has enjoyed practically uninterrupted growth. The steady climb has been punctuated dramatically by accelerated spurts of very rapid growth. One came with the boom of the eighties; still another in the twenties.

In 1914 the state's population was less than 3 million. By 1930 it was 5⅔ million, by 1940 just short of 7 million. The statistics on bank clearings, postal receipts, freight shipments, property assessments and tax receipts, building permits, crop harvests, and industrial production advanced even more.

This rapid growth involved a wholesale transformation. By 1940 the majority of Californians lived in dwellings constructed within the quarter century, did business in buildings equally recent, and moved about on a network of paved streets and highways that had not existed in 1914. For a few commodities like gold, wheat, and beef, the aggregate totals for pre-1914 production were not matched in the span between 1914 and 1940. For other old standbys, including oranges, walnuts, wines, and deciduous fruits, the output of this period surpassed that of all the preceding years. For another long list, including cotton, moving pictures, head lettuce, airplanes, and raisins, the years this side of 1914 were the only ones of importance. These new products suggest that the economic development of this more recent time was not a mere automatic outgrowth of the processes initiated by the historic leaders from Serra and Anza to Stanford and Huntington. The new era gave promise of earning recognition as the most significant thus far in the pageant of local history.

Enthusiasm for the Automobile

That new day is perhaps best characterized by the automobile. The preceding years had belonged to the railroad; now the motorcar

was dominant. In car manufacture California lagged far behind Michigan and its neighbors and did not generate any great corporation comparable to the Central Pacific–Southern Pacific Railroad. Through local emphasis on designing and building racing cars it did contribute to the evolution of the automobile. In the matter of using the new machines, Californians yielded to none. Here the contributions are even more notable, including the center line that bisects highways the world over and the automatic traffic signal that also became universal.

Californians geared their culture to the automobile to an unsurpassed degree. Los Angeles citizens became more dependent on their private automobiles to get to work and play than did the inhabitants of any other city, and the University of California at Los Angeles earned the doubtful distinction that a larger fraction of its faculty and students drove daily to and from its campus than was the case with any other reputable university. In 1936 California exceeded even New York in the number of fatalities charged to the automobile.

Pleasanter evidences may be mentioned. Radio came to the state virtually as an automobile accessory, with the first large stations controlled by the Packard and Cadillac distributors, and an automobile club organ, *Westways*, ranked as the best California monthly.

This enthusiastic reception came in spite of the fact that acquisition and operation of automobiles were not easy. California car registrations were surprisingly high in view of the price differential of $150 to $300 maintained against western purchasers under the guise of rail freight charges from Detroit. Even after assembly plants opened at Oakland, Long Beach, and Los Angeles, this charge continued. California's urban parking facilities were by no means ideal; its streets were originally laid out for horse and buggy traffic. The

San Francisco Bay barrier to vehicular circulation was conquered only in part by ferries and bridges, and after a quarter century of construction the state's network of paved highways was still less extensive than those of several more compact states such as New York, Illinois, Pennsylvania, and Ohio.

Offsetting these disadvantages there were numerous favorable conditions, in particular the benign climate, which imposes no closed season for automobile use. Large-scale production of petroleum made for a reasonable gasoline price. A most conservative height limit for office buildings and the preference for individual houses rather than apartments promoted in Los Angeles a tendency to spread out. In this city and elsewhere throughout the state, population grew more rapidly than existing systems of public transportation could be expanded to meet the demand, and dependence on private automobiles seemed a simpler solution. The automobile, at any rate, became an essential in the California scene.

Many of the consequences seem to have been inevitable or were a part of the national experience. Every American soon took it for granted that a large fraction of any city's police force would be assigned to traffic duty, that state troopers, officers, or rangers would patrol the highways by motorcycle, that state and local governments would spend more for highway construction and maintenance than for any other function except public education and perhaps relief, and that there would be a garage for every house and a filling station at practically every other corner. California lived up to this standard if not beyond it. When a sociologist arises to assess the role of the automobile in American civilization, this state can provide the more striking illustrations.

Passing notice should be accorded several industries subsidiary to the automobile, such as the manufacture of Portland cement. This product, of course, has a variety of uses. It goes into sidewalks and foundations, by the carload into steel-skeletoned business blocks and factories, and by the trainload into such structures as Boulder Dam. Nevertheless, it was the demand for paving material that maintained California cement manufacturers a comfortable second to Pennsylvania's through the thirties with annual production at times mounting as high as 13 million barrels.

Advertising California

Advertising of the booster sort was characteristic of the period. Earlier enthusiasts, newspaper editors, railroad land agents, and chambers of commerce had established a tradition of proclaiming California's advantages. Such organizations as Californians, Inc. and the All-Year Club expanded this art and obtained city, county, and state funds allotted to finance promotion efforts. Whereas the stress was once on getting farmers to move to California, it now shifted to persuading industries to locate new plants on the West Coast, opening new markets for California products in the East or abroad, bringing conventions to California cities, and promoting tourist travel. Illustrated brochures and special editions of newspapers were distributed and a more glamorous assist came from the movies.

Two other advertising media proved effective. One was annual celebrations such as Santa Barbara's summer fiesta, the Salinas rodeo, and the San Bernardino Orange Show; most famous and successful were Pasadena's Tournament of Roses and the Rose Bowl game. Special celebrations were more pretentious. In beautiful Balboa Park, San Diego staged the Panama-California Exposition in 1915, and San Francisco celebrated the completion of the canal with an even larger display, the Panama-Pacific Exposition. In 1932 Los Angeles hosted the Olympic Games, and in 1939 and 1940, on an island created for the purpose north of Yerba Buena, San Francisco

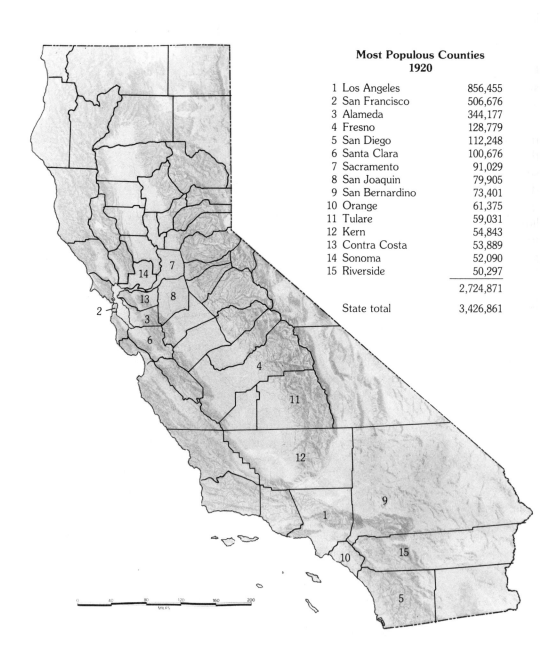

Most Populous Counties
1920

	County	Population
1	Los Angeles	856,455
2	San Francisco	506,676
3	Alameda	344,177
4	Fresno	128,779
5	San Diego	112,248
6	Santa Clara	100,676
7	Sacramento	91,029
8	San Joaquin	79,905
9	San Bernardino	73,401
10	Orange	61,375
11	Tulare	59,031
12	Kern	54,843
13	Contra Costa	53,889
14	Sonoma	52,090
15	Riverside	50,297
		2,724,871
	State total	3,426,861

Census of 1920; Most Populous Counties

signaled the completion of her great bridges with the Golden Gate International Exposition. How many visitors were brought by these special attractions was difficult to measure, for the standard inducements such as Yosemite and the big trees, Death Valley, Catalina, San Francisco, and Hollywood drew large numbers even in exposition years.

In the longer view the fairs, parades, and conventions were only surface waves on a much deeper current, part of which was merely coming to visit friends and relatives. All told, tourists had become a most profitable California crop.

Offhand the tourist element in the economy may seem unsubstantial but it engaged many in service occupations such as grocers, haberdashers, druggists, bankers, salespersons, clerks, lawyers, teachers, physicians, dentists, and barbers. Besides firmly contributing to the roster of permanent residents, these visitors boosted the budget for "nonproductive" employments.

First Place in Agriculture

In 1909, a representative year toward the close of the second American generation, the total value of California field crops was calculated at $95,757,000, and of fruit crops at $48,718,000. By 1937 the total had advanced to $648,200,000, which put California first among the 48 states. This phenomenal advance was achieved through far-reaching alteration of the crop list and by innovations of method in several of the older branches of agriculture. Certain crops, such as the grains, shared only minutely in this advance. Others, like potatoes, sugar beets, and alfalfa, advanced as much as 150 percent in the three decades, but without keeping pace with the industry as a whole. Most of the increase was accounted for by expansion of

orange raising and wine production and by several crops insignificant prior to 1914.

The California orange since the seventies had been the winter ripening navel, but early in the new century growers began to set out Valencias. The new variety possessed several points of superiority, not least of which was that it ripened in the summer when the nation's appetite for cool drinks was at its highest. The two varieties made available a year-round supply, which fell in line admirably with the marketing program of the Fruit Growers' Exchange.

By the early twenties the Valencia caught up with the navel and thereafter continued to gain steadily until in 1936 the acreages were 143,000 and 88,000 respectively. In 1909 the value of the orange crop was put at $12 million. In the thirties, despite adverse prices, there were several $100 million years, and acreage and total production still increased.

Most of the expansion of orange plantings was predicated on uninterrupted prosperity. When the depression of the thirties slashed prices 60 percent or more, the growers faced serious difficulty. A satisfactory remedy was not easy to find. Production costs, including irrigation, fertilizing, spraying, and orchard heating, were more or less fixed, and production itself was not subject to annual regulatory control. The Exchange continued its efforts to expand the market but the main reliance was upon the prorate, a device to regulate the quantity of fruit offered for sale. By this method, which entailed destroying quantities of good fruit, the industry bolstered its price structure though, according to the growers' definition, prices were still too low. It is a narrow and artificial view, however, to judge an industry solely in terms of the monetary value of its product. The more significant criterion for the orange business was its remarkable increase in acreage, production, and consumption, not only in the prosperous

Lettuce and Dates, Imperial Valley   *William Graham*

twenties but also in the hard times of the thirties.

On a smaller scale the walnut growers enacted the same drama. From very modest beginnings in the prewar era, they expanded their plantings so that the annual crop approached 100 million pounds. Since that was more than could be marketed, through their Exchange they too attempted to set up a prorate to peg the price above the cost of production. In size the walnut industry compared with the orange industry approximately as does a walnut with an orange. The walnut crop, however, was not trivial; 100 million pounds represented a considerable quantity in the twenties and thirties, surpassing in value the total crop production of New Hampshire, Vermont, Rhode Island, Delaware, Nevada, or Wyoming.

Viticulture ranked as the second branch of California agriculture. Building on the Spanish stock and benefiting from the new varieties imported by Agostón Haraszthy in the sixties and from the experience gained by the pioneer vineyardists in succeeding decades,

the industry became one of California's most distinctive and successful. In 1918 the Eighteenth Amendment threatened the vineyardists with ruin, for up to that time by far the largest fraction of California grapes had gone into wine. Long before repeal the wine market was reentered through the sale of "grape concentrate" and "wine bricks" from which wine of a sort could be concocted in the home.

Meanwhile, the vineyardists set out to sell their produce as table grapes and raisins. The former had been popular in the local markets; now refrigeration and rapid transit made it possible to whisk them across the continent to eastern markets. Raisins, on the other hand, had been so indifferent in quality that they were practically unmarketable. Dried grapes was their unappetizing name. A modern triumph of the industry was the introduction of better processing methods and stimulation of sales under the Sun Maid label and organization. By the late thirties wine grapes, table grapes, and raisins brought California vineyardists an annual income of approximately $50 million. In 1937 the state produced almost 2½ million tons, or 90 percent of the nation's total.

The list of crops in which California by that time led the nation goes on. In fruits for canning and drying she was easily first. The peach crop exceeded the total for the next ten states on the list, and domination in apricot production was still more pronounced. The pear crop was a trifle larger than the Oregon-Washington total and almost as large as the total for the other 45 states. The prune, once rated as plebeian as the dried apple, was another California specialty. Production mounted steadily throughout the twenties and thirties, until the annual output reached half a billion pounds. At the same time, improved techniques in drying made the prune a much more delectable morsel.

California apples reached the $10 million class. The potentialities appeared greater for certain subtropical fruits. Figs had been raised for many years. The date palm was introduced by the Spanish missionaries as a decorative tree, and commercial plantings were of little significance until this century. The avocado, a still more recent importation from Mexico, quickly became popular. Miscellaneous groves of olives, almonds, cherries, and the like aggregated still another $10 million annually. The grand total was a diversified yet specialized fruit industry comprising almost half of the state's crop production.

In field crops, likewise, phenomenal expansion characterized the period. Truck gardening, which had flourished earlier for the supply of the local market, led in the expansion. The state's increased population and the trend toward a larger per capita consumption of vegetables would have permitted a trebling of production. That the increase was much greater was because a nationwide market was opened by the devices of canning and refrigeration. Canneries operated before 1914 but

with disturbing uncertainty as to quality of output. Only more recently were processes perfected to insure standardized and palatable products. Refrigerated cars to make possible Atlantic seaboard delivery of Salinas Valley lettuce, Imperial Valley cantaloupes, or Tagus Ranch pears were a new facility.

On this multiple basis California advanced to first place in production of tomatoes, lettuce, asparagus, artichokes, cantaloupes, carrots, cauliflower, celery, peas, and garlic. Truck farmers were capitalizing on California's long season which makes possible several harvests, the early season which gives her first call on the eastern markets, and the boon of irrigation which accounts for much of the uniformity in size and attractive appearance of California vegetables.

In the Sacramento Valley, Japanese introduced rice cultivation. The acreage was smaller than in Louisiana, Texas, or Arkansas, but the yield per acre was the highest in the United States and placed California third in production. In 1937 the harvest exceeded 10 million bushels. The reclaimed swamp land on which the rice plantations were located soon ranked with the most valuable farm land in the state.

Another lusty upstart was cotton. Early experiments had been made in the sixties and seventies but with disappointing result. In 1910 a fresh attempt was made with a new variety, the Acala. Results were more encouraging and, when World War I boomed the market, plantings were greatly increased in Imperial Valley, Riverside County, and the southern part of the San Joaquin Valley. Largely because the plantings throughout were restricted to a single variety, thereby avoiding mongrelization through cross-pollenizing, the yield per acre was more than twice the national average, and because of longer staple the price was better too. Cotton became a $40 million crop, which put California ahead of Oklahoma, Missouri, Tennessee, Virginia, and Florida and within challenging distance of such cotton kingdom strongholds as the Carolinas, Georgia, Alabama, and Louisiana.

The remaining third of California agriculture centered on livestock and poultry. Dairying headed this division, consuming the larger share of the state's $50 million alfalfa crop and producing enough milk, cream, butter, cheese, ice cream, and condensed milk to meet the major requirements of the state's population. As a dairy producer California by 1940 was surpassed only by eight states clustered around Wisconsin.

Meat production was second to dairying on California stock farms. Although the state lagged far behind Texas in cattle and Iowa in hogs, and, although East Los Angeles and South San Francisco did not rank with South Chicago or Kansas City in meat packing, California had more cattle than any state in the old South or west of Kansas. In wool production its rank was third.

Poultry raising was much emphasized with many turkey ranches in the semiarid south and with myriad chicken ranches all over the state. Petaluma and San Fernando were the chief centers, but the standardized and streamlined versions of the old-fashioned hen roost were encountered almost everywhere. In 1929 the egg count was 159 million dozen.

In butter, eggs, meat, potatoes, cabbage, onions, and numerous incidental crops, California had, so to speak, lifted herself by her own bootstraps. Increased local demand required a threefold increase in production. The distinctive note was provided rather by production for the national and to some extent the world market. This production spread over a long list of commodities from exotic dates and avocados to things as common as carrots, yet in each instance California climatic and soil conditions afforded either a monopoly of opportunity or at least a very great advantage over the less fortunately situated portions of the United States. Availing themselves of these opportunities and contributing considerable ingenuity, California agriculturists forged into first place.

A prevailing characteristic of this agricultural development was its industrial technique and method. Profiting by the findings of agricultural research, tooling for assembly line operations, and incorporating on the scale of big business, the typical farms became, in Carey McWilliams's phrase, "factories in the fields." A correlative fact was the presence of an exploitative attitude toward farm labor. From Indians to tramps, to Chinese, to Japanese, to Filipinos, to Hindus, to Mexicans, the farm labor force had been in a position of inferiority. This inherited pattern and the nationwide practice in the twenties go far to explain the attitude.

Black Gold and Other Minerals

In mineral production California rose to third with Texas and Pennsylvania in the lead. Annual value of output ran beyond $440 million, most of it accounted for by the yearly outflow of more than 200 million barrels of oil.

Even without petroleum California would have been an important mining state. The annual gold output exceeded a million ounces, and the price had been boosted to $35.02 an ounce. Other metals were of less significance, but the list of nonmetallic minerals was long and imposing, some 50 different minerals being produced in San Bernardino County alone. The cement industry, with a yearly production in excess of 10 million barrels, has already been mentioned. Sand and crushed rock were used in proportion, and clay products, from rough tile and brick to glazed tile and tableware, were an embellishment and a continuation of one of the old mission industries.

The petroleum industry after 1914 was furnishing fuel for locomotives, heating furnaces, and orchard heaters. It was finding favor in paving operations and gaining an even larger market in gasoline for automobile consumption. There also was technological progress, especially in the latter portion of the period, including improved methods of drilling and refining, the construction of pipelines, tank cars, and tankers, and the solidification of financial control in the hands of a few large companies.

From 1914 to 1920 production ranged between 89 million and 105 million barrels with no important new fields being opened. Whatever excitement was missing in these years was more than made up for in the ensuing decade when one fabulous strike followed another. First came the Huntington Beach field in 1920 and the next year Santa Fe Springs and Signal Hill. By 1923 these three fields, all in the Los Angeles area, were producing, respectively, 113,000, 332,000, and 244,000 barrels a day, carrying the state's total for the year to 264 million barrels. In such an outpouring the existing facilities for storage and refining were completely engulfed. The oil companies escaped inundation by putting their tankers on a rapid shuttle service through the Panama Canal to refineries on the Atlantic seaboard. In 1924 there were 1,704 transits by tankers, the best business the canal had enjoyed up to that time, and good business for the oil companies too, since this was a cheaper method of delivering oil than to ship it from the midcontinent fields.

Canal shipments of oil soon fell off about a third, partly because of the availability of Mexican and South American oil and the opening of the tremendously productive mid-continent field in Texas and Oklahoma. California production, however, declined only slightly. In the late twenties it maintained an average of 241 million barrels, in the early thirties was off to 184 million, but then mounted again to more than 200 million barrels. The same major fields were still heavy producers, in some instances from deeper sands, and in 1928 Kettleman Hills near Coalinga came in as another bonanza.

New wells, however, were a less striking feature than were some of the other changes in the industry. One development was the expansion of storage facilities with huge tank farms at Richmond, Bakersfield, Coalinga, El Segundo, and Long Beach so that almost two years' production could be held in storage. Refineries also expanded, turning out $3\frac{1}{3}$ billion gallons of gasoline annually and other products in proportion. Significant also was the expansion of the local market. The state's automobiles, airplanes, trucks, buses, and tractors consumed annually a quantity of gasoline exceeded only in New York, and the demand for fuel oil grew correspondingly, thanks to diesel motors and engines, the augmented number of orchard heaters, and the expansion of California industry. Only an eighth of the electricity consumed was generated in steam plants such as the huge installation of the Southern California Edison Company at Long Beach, but the cost of this oil-generated current was the yardstick for determining the price of hydroelectric power from Boulder Dam.

After 1920 production and consumption of natural gas also increased tremendously. For domestic uses, including home heating, it became the favored fuel and had industrial significance as well. Over a 16-year period the increase in billions of cubic feet consumed was from 66 to 320, while other large quantities were converted into natural gas or reintroduced into the oil sands to rejuvenate faltering wells.

Another important extractive industry was the making of cement for paving and building purposes and also for the demands of irrigation, flood control, and aqueduct construction. Lumbering, centered in the northwestern quarter of the state, also expanded.

In lines necessarily conducted near the point of consumption, manufacturing increased, among them baking, printing, foundry operation, machine shops, and planing mills. More ambitious branches looked far beyond the state. Among these were canning of fruits, vegetables, and fish, wine making, clothing, especially for women, and, by no means last, motion picture production.

Movie Making
Comes to Hollywood

Pictures that moved were being made as early as the nineties at the Edison laboratory in New Jersey and in Brooklyn, but the art was still in its infancy when Hollywood was discovered by a refugee from Brooklyn's gloomy skies.

Once Hollywood was tried, tangible assets were evident. The air in those days was clear. At a time when indoor sets often were roofless,

Beverly Hills, Speedway, and Oil Wells, 1921   *C. C. Pierce Collection*

the year-round availability of outdoor shooting was a great advantage. In and around Hollywood a rich variety of backdrops was available as well as locations near at hand that could pass for South Sea beaches, the Sahara, Sherwood Forest, and the open range. Los Angeles was enough of a city to provide supplies and services, and because the product was compact it did not matter that the major market was 3,000 miles away.

The beginning was small and casual. A camera and cameraman, a director, a skeletal cast, and a story line seemed all that was needed. Behind the scenes support including a film developer, editor, and a week's wages also was necessary. That is where the producer came in.

For some time all the movies were one-reelers, and they could be ground out in a matter of days. Essanay at its ranch near Niles produced 375 Bronco Billy westerns over a six-year stretch, and Biograph with David Wark Griffith ran on a similar treadmill. Everything was to be learned: how to employ close-ups and long shots, shoot from different angles, capitalize on a moving camera, modify the lighting, and assemble the bits and pieces.

Griffith broke through the time barrier with a two reeler. Exploiting a California theme, he filmed *Ramona* and paid the publisher $100 for the right to adapt. A $50,000 award to the author and publisher of *Ben Hur* taught respect for copyrights. The movie makers hired well-known authors such as Richard Harding Davis and Elbert Hubbard. Meanwhile, script writing keyed precisely to the methodology of film making developed a format of its own.

Early arrivals included Mack Sennett, Mary Pickford, Jesse L. Lasky, Cecil B. DeMille, and Charlie Chaplin. As soon as the distributors became aware that fans identified primarily with leading actors, the star system was born,

with salaries inflated as a publicity device. As early as 1915 Mary Pickford was on salary at $1,000 a week and a few years later at $20,000. Though more crucial to a picture, directors gained recognition more slowly, a landmark being Griffith's *Birth of a Nation* in 1915 which grossed $15 million. The producers, meanwhile, became the real magnates.

By the twenties production was geared to feature pictures several reels long. Admissions rose above a nickel, but still it was inexpensive entertainment with mass appeal surpassing any competitor. Californians and the entire nation took up the habit of movie-going, bought film magazines, joined fan clubs, and in many subtle ways were influenced by what they saw.

For Hollywood and at least southern California, the industry soon became a significant element in the economy. By the twenties it grossed more than the orange crop and much more than the gold miners did at their peak. The California economy had had and would have other incomes out of proportion to the labor and energy and tangibles involved, such as the honey harvest, revenue from tourists or conventions, and appreciating real estate, but this suddenly emerging industry on celluloid, in which the movement on the screen was itself an illusion, quickly took an important place in the state's economy.

The movie industry released in southern California a very considerable purchasing power, esteemed by builders, tradesmen, salesmen, domestics, and members of the professions. Quantitiative measure is difficult because not even the stars spent all their income locally, and, since the industry put its financial center in New York, some of the profits were diverted from the state. Nevertheless, what was left was large. In 1935 salaries and wages totaled $98 million out of cost of production of $165 million. How far income exceeded cost was not revealed, but there are indirect benefits that must be added such as the swelling of the tourist dollar. Movie making stimulated the local apparel industry and led the radio broadcasters to establish studios in Hollywood second only to New York's.

Public Improvements

In this era of prosperity the engineers were working on a variety of projects and planning others still more ambitious. In the 1850s stage lines had spread to the far corners of the state over unimproved roads. With the coming of the railroads, wagon roads fell back into strictly local use from which the automobile elevated them only gradually. However, new ideas took hold. Roads should not merely be graded and graveled but paved and should extend from one end of the state to the other.

In 1909 the legislature ordered a survey for a state highway system, and in 1911 it set up a highway commission to supervise such a program. In 1910 bonds were voted in the amount of $18 million followed by $15 million in 1915 and $40 million in 1918 to finance paved roads approximating the course of present highways 99 and 101 and with connections with every county seat.

In 1923 the legislature followed the Oregon inspiration and voted a two cent per gallon gasoline tax together with higher fees for trucks, the income to be allocated to highway improvements. This device had the virtues of pay-as-you-go financing and also was a neat approximation of payment in proportion to use. From that time on the gas tax has been the main reliance for highway and later freeway construction, assisted at intervals by federal aid, much of it derived from a superimposed federal gas tax. One testimony to the inherent logic of the gas tax was that the repre-

sentatives of the people saw fit to advance the tax step by step to bring the state and federal levy up to as much as 11 or 12 cents per gallon. There have been pressures to divert part of this tax to other worthy purposes such as school support, but for the most part that temptation has been resisted.

The first so-called highways were not much more than surfaced wagon roads, not engineered specifically as a runway for motor driven vehicles. By the twenties, however, rapid progress had been made. One main artery followed the approximate route of El Camino Real, through the Santa Clara, Salinas, and Santa Maria valleys from San Francisco to Santa Barbara, and then by the inland route to San Fernando and Los Angeles, and on by the coast to San Diego. The other main artery reached south from Oregon, took advantage of the open expanse of the great Central Valley, and crossed Tejon Pass to Los Angeles.

Laterals attached most of the centers of population with these main arteries, and highways reached eastward to the Colorado crossings at Yuma and Needles and to the trans-Sierra gateway at Reno. Extension of the Redwood Highway northward along the coast came more slowly, but by mid-decade it was surfaced and open all the way to Oregon.

Since many of the property lines in California antedated the quadrangular surveys typical of the United States as a whole, roads and highways were less rigidly held to the straight lines and square corners of the section lines. The terrain set up many difficult problems. One, on the coast route, was to negotiate the transfers from valley to valley, as at Cuesta grade near San Luis Obispo. Another was to cope with the constantly shifting sands near Yuma. Several miles of movable plank road were the initial solution to this problem.

Still another difficulty was how to surmount

Remnant of Plank Road, Colorado Desert

*California Department of Public Works,
Division of Highways*

the mountain barrier between Bakersfield and Los Angeles. The twisting, switchbacking old ridge route was a devious answer to that problem, achieved in the pattern of the period with as little earth moving as possible and with no compunction about the number or sharpness of the turns. It was an adventurous ride, blamed for much carsickness and calling for prodigious exercise of the steering wheel.

The arms of San Francisco Bay, such a boon to water transportation, were an equivalent obstacle to automobile traffic. An obvious response was to add automobile ferries to those already serving railroad passengers and commuters. In the twenties this service was available from San Francisco to Sausalito, Oakland, and Berkeley, from Richmond to San Rafael, and across Carquinez Straits at Vallejo and Benicia. Bridges, it was suggested, would speed up this traffic. Several were built—at Antioch, Crockett, Dumbarton, and San Mateo. They helped but in each instance they merely cut off the end of an arm of the bay. A bolder remedy in the form of bridges

319

direct from San Francisco to Oakland and to Marin County advanced to the planning stage, but in the twenties neither got beyond paper.

The problems of water and power were recognized as even more vital. In earlier days the water resources most conveniently available for irrigation and for municipal supply had been developed. In the time of George Chaffey several more dramatic steps had been taken, most rewardingly in the diversion of Colorado River water into Imperial Valley and most flamboyantly in the siphoning of the Owens River to Los Angeles. In many instances hydroelectric energy had been generated as a sort of by-product of the water supplying. In the teens and twenties still other power plants were installed along Sierra streams. Just prior to the completion of the big dams at Boulder, Shasta, and Friant the aggregate of this hydroelectric output was almost a fifth of the national total.

Through the twenties the Owens Valley Aqueduct was much in the news. In 1923, following a succession of dry years, Los Angeles began to buy up additional farms in the valley and to transfer their water to the aqueduct. The remaining residents of the valley, especially the townspeople, were incensed at this blighting of their homeland. The Owens Valley champions first protested vocally and editorially, then by a token charge of dynamite alongside the aqueduct, then by seizing a spillway in the Alabama Hills and turning the flow of water out upon the desert, and finally by more damaging sabotage of wells, pumps, and aqueduct sections. The city put detectives to work but never brought any of the dynamiters to trial.

The protesters took it the more amiss because much of their water was not piped to Angeleños' homes but was used instead to irrigate the San Fernando Valley. A syndicate dominated by the Otis-Chandler interests had

bought 47,000 acres in this valley in 1910. The aqueduct water increased its value as much as a hundredfold.

On March 12, 1928, a 180-foot dam that Mulholland had built in San Francisquito Canyon near the southern end of his aqueduct suddenly gave way, sending a monstrous wall of water cascading down the narrow valley of the Santa Clara. When it struck Santa Paula, 50 miles away, the crest was still 25 feet high. The toll of lives was between 400 and 450, almost as many as in San Francisco's great fire. The property damage was millions of dollars.

An appraisal committee assessed the property losses and the city promptly met these claims. With the dynamite blasts along the aqueduct still in mind, there was an impulse to blame the disaster on sabotage, but inspection revealed that the dam was built on and anchored to a weak and faulted rock formation. Capable geological advice would have prevented this catastrophe.

San Francisco also was at work on its water problem. Initially it had depended on local wells. By 1901, however, when it was apparent that a supplement was needed, Major James D. Phelan filed an application for water from the Tuolumne River in Yosemite National Park. The Sierra Club and other nature lovers protested and nothing was accomplished until 1913 when Congress authorized the diversion and confirmed San Francisco's title to water rights in the amount of 420,000 acre-feet a year. Legal, financial, and physical difficulties, together with the opposition of Pacific Gas and Electric and the Spring Valley Water Company, delayed the work. Finally, in 1931, after an expenditure of $121 million, the Hetch Hetchy Dam, the transmission lines, and the 186-mile aqueduct were realities, and San Francisco had all the water it would need in the foreseeable future.

The Speculative Urge

For the United States as a whole the twenties were a sort of binge, with prohibition, bootleggers, and speakeasies, a runaway stock market, an increasing degree of corporate concentration as exemplified in chain stores, and a resurgence of hyperpatriotism and nativism as expressed in isolationism, the Ku Klux Klan, and the Scopes and Sacco-Vanzetti trials. California shared in these aberrations.

Through mergers and consolidations, locally owned banks gave place to the branches of a few mammoth organizations, chief of which was Gianinni's Bank of Italy. By removing much of the personal equation from their lending and collecting, these banks improved soundness and security, at the same time concentrating power to an alarming degree. They also had a hand in broadening interest in investment, some of it highly speculative. A host of persons who had never previously paid attention to stock quotations bought shares in Transamerica and other such issues and hung on the rise and fall of the market.

The speculative urge was more purely evident in the uncritical support given to real estate schemes, such as at Atascadero, and in the rage especially in Los Angeles for oil stocks. The particular darling of the Los Angeles public was C. C. Julian, an ornate showman and a master of breezy, folksy, spellbinding appeal. In the chatty monologue of his newspaper ads he invited the folks to take shares in the bonanza of Santa Fe Springs' gushing wells. Julian Petroleum stock sold rapidly and paid handsome dividends. From 1922 to 1925 his ventures spiraled upward, but at that point the major interests protested his stock issues, pressured the newspapers to refuse his advertising, and persuaded the refineries to stop handling his oil. In the crisis that followed Julian lost control of his company.

His successors, S. C. Lewis and Jacob Berman, had to borrow money extravagantly to keep the company afloat. A favorite speculation was in lending money at exorbitant interest and bonuses to Julian Petroleum. It was participated in by a bankers' pool from the most respected element in the community, a group known as the Jewish pool made up of affluent merchants and bankers, and the Tia Juana pool, composed of gamblers and racetrack habitués. As security for these loans, Lewis and Berman resorted to counterfeiting stock, eventually in the amount of 3,000,015 shares. On May 7, 1927, this bubble burst and $150 million in supposed worth vanished from the grasp of 40,000 eager investors. Julian had set the stage for such a disaster but there is no evidence that he was culpable for what others did to Julian "Pete."

This spectacular failure was followed by the receivership of the Richfield Oil Company in 1931, with revelations of unconscionable extravagances by its officials and an operating loss of $56 million. Embezzlement, fraud, and poor judgment brought many other companies to bankruptcy, including the Guarantee Building and Loan Association and the American Mortgage Company. Indeed, in bankruptcies for fraud Los Angeles led the nation at the end of the twenties.

Slightly translated, the speculative urge of southern Californians in the twenties was expressed also in attention to new cults of philosophy and religion. The region abounded in health faddists, exponents of medical unorthodoxy, apostles of new thought variously defined, and indigenous sects. The latter may be illustrated by a funerary establishment, Forest Lawn, designed to banish all that is somber and depressing.

The dramatic evangelism of Aimee Semple McPherson suited the twenties. Sister Aimee began to preach the Four Square Gospel in Los Angeles in 1922. Within a very short time she had a devoted following of thousands, who built the huge Angelus Temple with an auditorium to seat 5,000. In 1926 Sister Aimee disappeared. Last seen on the beach near Ocean Park, she was presumed to have drowned. Eight days later she reappeared at Agua Prieta, Sonora, returned to a triumphal reception at Los Angeles, and gave out a story that she had been kidnapped. When reporters exposed this story as a hoax, she was arrested on the charge of falsifying and thereby interfering with the orderly processes of the law. The charge was later dropped. Her followers continued loyal to the time of her death in 1945, never, however, exceeding in numbers or vigor the peak attained in the twenties. Because of her penchant for showmanship the Los Angeles press and the more sophisticated element in the community lampooned Sister Aimee. Thereby they obscured the substantial amount of real good that she did in helping the sick and needy, cheering the unhappy, providing social opportunity for the lonely, and uplifting her followers.

Reapportionment and Reassessment

The prosperity of the twenties seemed to promote complacency about politics. Legislatures met with calendrical regularity but enacted few measures of much moment and sedulously avoided one important duty, reapportionment. The unequal growth of the state, with the center of gravity shifting southward, made for an unrepresentative legislature and congressional delegation.

After the census of 1910 Congress assigned 11 seats to California. That of 1920, recording a 44.1 percent increase in the state's population, entitled California to three or four additional congressmen. Similar change in the state legislature would also be in order.

In the state several alignments were discernible: Republicans against Democrats, north against south, San Francisco against Los Angeles, and rural against urban. The first was muted because Republican proponderance was so great that no conceivable redistricting could do the party much harm or good. North-south tension was not acute; out of habit there was occasional mention of state division but without expectation. The rivalry of the two cities had some reality and the city-county standoff even more.

Two initiatives were put on the ballot in 1926. One, ineptly called the Los Angeles plan, would have reapportioned Senate and Assembly according to population. The other, the Federal plan, proposed one to three counties for each Senate seat, which inevitably would create rotten boroughs and grossly overrepresent the countryside. The voters, however, rejected the Los Angeles plan.

Almost immediately Congress voted reapportionment of the House as soon as the 1930 census figures were available. That made reapportionment necessary business for the state legislature in 1931. The choice was between allotments of congressmen ten to the north and ten to the south, and assemblymen at or about 40 to 40, or a recognition of the more populous south by allotments of 9 to 11 and 38 to 42. The San Joaquin Valley delegation cast the balance in favor of the second of these alternatives, leaving the state senate heavily northern.

Statewide reassessment for tax purposes soon followed. To meet pressing needs the state agreed to assist public schools up to and including junior colleges on the basis of daily attendance. To fund that program, utilities would be shifted from local to state taxrolls and a state income tax and a one penny sales tax would be instituted. To save the schools that package was voted in 1933.

Two important details did not work out as specified. Other costs kept local taxes from going down and, although the income tax was supposed to balance the sales tax's heavier impact on the poor, Governor James M. Rolph found excuse to veto it. Thus those who paid the sales tax had the privilege of saving the schools while taxable incomes went unscathed and the corporations had their tax burdens lightened.

CHAPTER 24

Migrant Family from the Dust Bowl　　　　　　　*Dorothea Lange, Farm Security Administration*

The cars of the migrant people crawled out of the side roads onto the great cross-country highway, and they took the migrant way to the West. In the daylight they scuttled like bugs to the westward; and as the dark caught them, they clustered like bugs near to shelter and to water. And because they were lonely and perplexed, because they had all come from a place of sadness and worry and defeat, they huddled together; they talked together; they shared their lives, their food, and the things they hoped for in the new country. Thus it might be that one family camped near a spring, and another camped for the spring and for company, and a third because two families had pioneered the place and found it good. And when the sun went down, perhaps twenty families and twenty cars were there.

In the evening a strange thing happened: the twenty families became one family, the children were the children of all. The loss of home became one loss, and the golden time in the West was one dream.

John Steinbeck
The Grapes of Wrath

The Great Depression

Viewed with hindsight, imperfections show up in the American prosperity of the twenties, some of which were suspected at the time. The boom in business was highly selective; automobiles and radios sold as never before, but such key industries as soft coal mining, textiles, and agriculture were not prospering. Labor-saving machinery gave production a tremendous boost, but nothing gave a similar lift to consumer purchasing power. Installment buying was the closest approach, but at most it was a palliative. The unevenness of prosperity showed in the 312 percent increase in speculative gains from 1923 to 1928, while wages crept up only 12 percent. In the midst of the prosperity, too, there was an alarming amount of poverty. Unemployment, to cite one example, went up from 1.5 million in 1926 to 1.8 million in 1929.

The speculative superstructure toppled first. To many Americans it seemed a matter of comparative indifference that the paper profits of the market players were swept away. Soon, however, the paralysis spread through the whole economy. Wages, salaries, and dividends were slashed; national income dropped from some $81 billion in 1929 to $41 billion in 1932; stores and factories closed, "Hoovervilles" and apple-selling sprang up; and the roster of unemployed mounted to 10 million in 1931 and to 14 or 15 million the next year.

Earlier drops in the business cycle, such as the panics of 1857, 1873, and 1893, had had only a delayed reaction in California. By 1929 the state was closely enmeshed with the nation. Furthermore, much that it had to offer in the national market was particularly sensitive to recession. Its fruits were only partially regarded as staples. Its moving pictures were less than necessities. Its vacation opportunities would go begging in a period of austerity.

This time California felt the impact as abruptly as any part of the country except perhaps Wall Street itself. Before the depression was over some of its consequences would be brought home in aggravated form. California became a special asylum for the unemployed. They were attracted by the mildness of the climate, which made it seem a better place in which to endure privation, and they were lured by the state's traditional aura as a land of promise and opportunity.

In the state as in the nation the very volume of distress among the impoverished and the unemployed cried for action. The Hoover administration sought to cope with the depression by pronouncements of confidence in America. Through the Reconstruction Finance Corporation, it gave aid to major industries. Its philosophy, however, was that relief to individuals should come from private sources or local governments. The California state government was equally hesitant. The first major decision toward dealing with the depression was the election of James (Sunny Jim) Rolph as governor in November, 1930.

In his long tenure as mayor of San Francisco, Rolph's major qualifications were as official greeter, hand shaker, and parade reviewer. Unfortunately, in his term at Sacramento there was not much to be sunny about. It was not in the cards that he would mobilize the state government to meet the emergency. With the accession of Franklin Delano Roosevelt as President in 1933 the national government launched the New Deal as an effort to achieve relief, recovery, and reform. Many phases of the New Deal had impact on California. The state government, however, declined to get in step and continued, insofar as possible, to practice the philosophy of Coolidge and Hoover Republicanism.

The Coming of the Okies

In at least one part of the nation the depression struck harder than in California. On the southern plains falling prices, foreclosures, and unemployment coincided with a shift to larger farms and more mechanization. Some people had to leave because of foreclosures; others spoke of themselves as tractored off. In addition, a series of dry years turned the whole region into a Dust Bowl.

Such was California's reputation that when refugees had to leave their homes they almost automatically went West. This flight was by families in rundown jalopies, a migration vividly depicted in Dorothea Lange's *American Exodus* and in the first part of Steinbeck's *Grapes of Wrath.*

Displaced farmers and their families came pouring in from many states, particularly those in the tier from Texas to the Dakotas. Oklahomans had the catchiest nickname and lent it to the whole migration. Being farmers, these newcomers looked for work in the fields of California. They came in sufficient numbers to glut the market for migratory farm labor and at a time when the growers were least able to pay a living wage. The Okies brought more women and children than had characterized earlier harvests. Consequently, even at a time

The Road West *Dorothea Lange, Farm Security Administration*

when people were suffering almost every-where, the distress of these new arrivals was extraordinarily heartrending. The Okies, with the Dust Bowl and the rigors of Highway 66 behind them, and with the organized, implac-able, and police-supported growers confront-ing them, stand as the most touching symbol of the Depression.

The Restiveness of Labor

Predictably labor was restive. With prices tumbling, employers sought to protect their interests by slashing wages, and workers often felt this was carried too far. The feature of greatest novelty was the attempt to organize farm labor and to stage a series of great agri-cultural strikes.

Prior to 1929 there had been some ges-tures toward organizing agricultural workers in the state—by the American Federation of Labor among the cannery workers, by racial associations among the Japanese and the Mexicans, and by the IWW in its peculiar and impractical program among the casual labor-ers. None had appreciable effect on the status of farm labor.

Early in 1930 two spontaneous strikes took place in Imperial Valley protesting lowered wages in the fields and the packing sheds. After the strikes failed, the heads of the Trade Union Unity League called a conference of worker delegates from the entire valley. This move provoked arrest of 100 workers, trial of a number of the leaders for violation of the criminal syndicalism statute, and conviction of eight of them.

Capitalizing on the resentment that this repression produced, the Communist party began a drive to organize the farm workers. The strategy was to take advantage of every labor dispute and every strike that developed spontaneously and to try to build these pieces

into a cohesive statewide movement. Added to the rise of unionism where it had never existed before, the label Communist roused bitter resistance.

At Vacaville late in 1932 a masked mob answered a fruit workers strike by seizing six of the leaders, flogging them, shearing their heads, and smearing them with red enamel. Strikes followed among the pea pickers at Decoto, the cherry pickers at Mountain View and Sunnyvale, the peach gatherers at Mer-ced and elsewhere, the grape workers at Lodi and Fresno, the pear harvesters in the Santa Clara Valley, and the general fruit gatherers on the Tagus Ranch.

Although not always initiated by Commu-nist organizers, these strikes were incor-porated into the program of the Cannery and Agricultural Workers' Industrial Union. CAWIU went on in the fall of 1933 to organize a cotton pickers strike that boycotted the fields throughout the San Joaquin Valley, main-tained a headquarters camp of 5,000 persons near Corcoran, and withheld 18,000 workers from the fields. This was followed by an Im-perial Valley strike in the winter of 1933–34 and another wave of walkouts in the northern fruit districts in 1934.

Opposition to these strikes took the form of bitter denunciation in the press, vigilante vio-lence aimed primarily at the leadership, and use of local and state police to break up strike meetings and disperse their camps. As in the routing of the TUUL, the criminal syndicalism law was invoked against the CAWIU. After its second state convention in 1934, all its remaining leaders were brought to trial and convicted under this act. The union was bro-ken, despite its record of winning 21 strikes out of 24 and advancing the prevailing wage from 15 to 25 cents an hour.

A parallel effort sought to rebuild unionism in San Francisco. From 1921 to 1933 the city's unions were at minimum strength and

Cotton Picker Headed for the Field   *Dorothea Lange, Farm Security Administration*

the port was on what amounted to an open shop basis. During these years San Francisco by no means kept pace with other Pacific Coast ports. Its share of tonnage decreased from 36 to 21 percent and other indexes went down in proportion. Company-controlled hiring did not prevent this decline.

When Section 7A of the National Recovery Act outlined a procedure whereby labor could choose its bargaining agency, the waterfront workers with little delay chose the International Longshoremen's Association. In May, 1934, the ILA demanded a minimum wage of a dollar an hour, a six hour day and a 30 hour week to spread the work, union control of hiring halls, and various lesser concessions.

The operators rejected all these demands and charged that the ILA was Communist and radical. President Roosevelt, Senator Robert

Wagner, and members of the national and regional boards tried to bring about a settlement but failed, and on May 9 the strike began, tying up all the ports on the coast. On July 5 when strikebreakers under police escort tried to move cargo at San Francisco, the strikers overturned trucks and burned them, dumped goods into the streets, and answered tear gas and pistol fire with cobblestones and brickbats. Two strikers were killed and more than a hundred seriously injured. A funeral procession, 10,000 strong marching up Market Street, created a profound impression on the entire community. When Governor Frank Merriam deployed the National Guard, the labor leaders invoked a general strike, that is, a strike designed to paralyze the community and force surrender.

This strike took place from July 16 to 19.

Except for a few authorized necessities nothing was sold or delivered. Conservative union leaders sabotaged the strike. The "sympathetic strikers," including even the teamsters, went back to work and by the end of July the longshoremen also were back on the job. An arbitration award in October assigned control of the hiring hall to the union. With Harry Bridges heading the ILA and with the organization of the Maritime Federation of the Pacific, the strike marked a long step in the direction of industrial unionism, a trend represented on the national scene by John L. Lewis and the Congress of Industrial Organization (CIO) defecting from the AF of L.

There was, however, a division of opinion. Bridges and the longshoremen went with the CIO; Harry Lundeberg and the sailors' union stayed with the AF of L. Out of this schizophrenia arose a bewildering array of petty strikes and work stoppages, some 561 in 25 months, crippling to operators and shippers, a nuisance to the public, and extremely damaging to the goodwill that union labor might otherwise have had. These jurisdictional disputes were more damaging to labor's reputation than the recurrent charge that the unions were Communist dominated.

Despite the drawbacks the maritime unions continued in strength throughout the thirties. Unionism in general also made great strides, first under the temporary benediction of the Blue Eagle of the National Industrial Relations Administration (NIRA), and later under the National Labor Relations Board. By 1940 San Francisco and the Bay region had more union members than ever before, even including newsboys and bootblacks.

Although Los Angeles still purported to be open shop, it had a nucleus of solid unionization in the harbor district. The more concentrated industries, such as airplane building,

Pea Pickers Waiting for the Weigh-in   *Dorothea Lange, Farm Security Administration*

automobile assembly, tire manufacture, and oil production and refining, were thoroughly organized; the motion-picture industry was practically solid; and organizers had made some progress in other lines such as the building trades and truck driving. Between 1933 and 1940 union membership advanced from 33,000 to 200,000.

As to rural labor, however, there was no revival of effective unionism. On the contrary, the larger agriculturists formed a union of employers, the Associated Farmers, and, whenever labor troubles occurred, they supplanted the regular peace officers, armed enough men with guns, pick handles, and tear gas, and resorted to enough violence to crush the strike. Farm fascism or vigilantism seemed an effective check on the movement to unionize farm labor. The most hopeful sign was at the close of the decade when McWilliams' *Factories in the Fields* and Steinbeck's *The Grapes of Wrath* called attention to the plight of the migratory workers and stirred the public conscience.

Technocracy and Utopia

In the prosperous twenties Californians had shown a remarkable waywardness in philosophy and religion. In the depression decade the state spawned equally fantastic schemes for economic sleight of hand. Since the state had contributed Henry George and the Single Tax and had harbored communitarian ventures at Kaweah, Delhi, Llano, and elsewhere, perhaps this susceptibility should not surprise. The degree with which visionary and unscientific programs took hold was, nevertheless, amazing.

The first of any consequence was Technocracy. It had honorable origin at Columbia University as a study of energy as the foundation of civilization. Howard Scott brought it to California as a crusade encrusted with an impressive pseudoscientific vocabulary. He quickly recruited many adherents, who made up in enthusiasm for whatever they lacked in understanding. The most notable of the new disciples was Manchester Boddy, owner and editor of the Los Angeles *Daily News*. He used its columns to spread the new gospel and did so with such effectiveness that Technocracy swept the state. Twenty years later a few clubs devoted to economic salvation through the proper use of modern science were still meeting.

In July, 1933, a competitor arose in the Utopian Society. An "educational" organization with initiation ceremonies, secret rituals, and pageantry borrowed from the old morality plays, it claimed to be the answer to the ills of society. From modest beginnings with initiations performed in private homes, it grew so rapidly that the largest auditoriums in Los Angeles were filled. At the peak a half million Utopians was the estimate, practically all of them in southern California. The doctrine of Utopia was, in essence, that private ownership and the profit system were to blame for all evil. With modern machines and proper management, three hours' work a day by those between 25 and 45 years of age could produce all that was needed by the entire population. Education until 25 and pensions after 45 was the motto. Inspirational qualities of the meetings probably outweighed the teachings. After about two years the movement faded away almost as rapidly as it had risen. It was part of the ferment out of which arose Epic.

The Epic Crusade

The Epic movement obviously was nurtured on the distress of the depression. It also was encouraged by the New Deal, by Roosevelt's remarks about the forgotten man, and by the nationwide fervor that was engendered when the NIRA was introduced to the country.

Upton Sinclair in 1934

Some months before the 1934 primary, a group of liberal Democrats and Socialists persuaded Upton Sinclair to register as a Democrat and seek that party's nomination for governor. Lifelong Socialist, writer rather than speaker, idealist rather than practical politician, Sinclair was in some respects as unpromising a candidate as could have been found, but he had boldness of imagination, determination, incorruptible character, and unexpected powers of dynamic leadership.

The author of some 48 books, plays, and pamphlets, Sinclair adopted the novel expedient of building his campaign around a book. Formulating the program he wanted to carry into effect, Sinclair envisioned the obstacles that would confront him, the way they would be overcome, and the eventual triumph of his plan. All this he wrote up in a booklet entitled *I, Governor of California, and How I Ended Poverty: A True Story of the Future.* The campaign was then simply an endeavor to make this book come true.

Sinclair's plan had 12 points, chief of which were the proposals for state land colonies where the unemployed might farm under the guidance of experts, similar operation of idle factories, and a state distribution system for the exchange of these various products—all to be financed by state-issued scrip. His plan proposed repeal of the sales tax, enactment of a steeply graduated income tax, and increases in inheritance and public utility corporation taxes.

It contained a proposal for tax exemption on homes occupied by the owners and on ranches cultivated by the owners, provided the assessed value did not exceed $3,000. There was a Georgean proposal for a 10 percent tax on unimproved building lots and on agricultural land not under cultivation. Finally, there was provision for $50-a-month pensions to the aged needy, the physically incapacitated, and widows with dependent children.

How the plan would have worked can be answered only on the basis of theory. It had elements that were most attractive to the unemployed, the poor, and the left wing. Those same elements antagonized and alarmed the propertied classes. The campaign was waged, therefore, with reforming fervor and hope arrayed against distrust and resistance to change. The Epics had only a minimal financial support, not enough to buy much radio time or to make available the other channels of campaigning usually employed. Sinclair's supporters had to depend instead upon volunteer workers, rallies, and clubs, upon their candidate's pamphlets, which, after all, were better than his radio performances, and upon the mistakes of the opposition.

Although handicapped with the colorless Frank Merriam as a candidate, the opposition had a wealth of political experience and an unlimited war chest. Practically all the newspapers were against Sinclair. The radio beat out heated warnings against giving him office, billboards carried the same message, and the voters were deluged with handbills, pamphlets, and letters urging them to "save the state" with Merriam. Sinclair was maligned as "an Anarchist, a free-lover, an agent of Moscow, a Communist, an anti-Christ."

Just before the election the motion-picture industry released what purported to be newsreels introducing the tramps who allegedly would descend upon California if Epic were adopted. In actuality they were bit players from Central Casting. A *Literary Digest* poll, perhaps in honest error, found 62 percent of the voters for Merriam, though in the election he got only 49 percent.

On top of all this Sinclair was opposed by many Socialists and Democrats. Norman Thomas and other Socialists complained that he had deserted true socialism. Conservative Democrats announced for Merriam, and many liberal Democrats threw their votes to Raymond Haight, the Progressive candidate. George Creel, a leading Democrat, denounced Sinclair, and President Roosevelt, though hinting that he would endorse Sinclair, never did. In the end it was virtually Sinclair and the Epics against the world.

In retrospect it is difficult to recapture the feeling of bitter partisanship that suffused the state. Part of it was due, no doubt, to the threat to entrenched privilege which Sinclair's plan obviously contained. Others were sure that his real intentions were to go far beyond the announced plan and use it as an entering wedge for a program of socialization which would exceed anything Russia had seen. Many conservatives were also habituated to the thought that the Soviets were behind every movement in America bearing the reform label.

The combination of fear and hate, concern for the preservation of property rights and national institutions, and political experience and financial resources was more than the Epics could overcome. The Epics won Sinclair the nomination and elected a number of assemblymen, state senators, and congressmen, but they fell short in the final vote for governor. It was 1,138,620 for Merriam, 879,557 for Sinclair, and 302,519 for Haight, an illustration of the efficacy of a third party. The state was saved from however much of his platform Sinclair might have tried to carry into effect and had instead a continuation of the cautiousness and laissez faire with which Merriam had been facing the depression crisis.

The Townsend Plan

The inspiration for the Townsend Plan came to a retired physician of Long Beach, Dr. Francis E. Townsend, about the time Epic was taking shape. He proposed to cure the depression by the simple device of giving $200 a month to every person over 60, with the proviso that each installment be spent within the month. The funds would be raised by a 2 percent transactions tax. Notwithstanding the obvious fallacies involved, the package of old age pensions and limited inflation had instantaneous appeal. Townsend clubs sprang up as if by chain reaction; contributions from hopeful oldsters poured in to the "national headquarters." The publications that Townsend set up sold in great quantity.

Although not launched until a few months before the 1934 election, the Townsend Plan was a factor in its outcome. Sinclair denounced the plan as economic heresy. Merriam endorsed it and there can be no doubt that it helped elect him. At the 1935 legislature, too, an early order of business was to consider a memorial to Congress in favor of enactment of the plan. Republican votes put it over, and the Townsendites in appreciation began to boom Merriam for President. That the Republicans, who had been so righteous about saving the state from Sinclair's experiments, should plump for the folly of Townsendism is only explainable as politics or as confidence that the federal government would not be stampeded.

The Townsend idea had a lively persistence. It moved out into the national arena and got support from candidates in many states. As a matter of fact, its original intention was that the federal government should be the agency to give it effect. At the state level it also continued to exert pressure. Exactly how much influence can be attributed to it is hard to measure, but certainly it accelerated the increase in California old age pensions and the adoption of the national social security program.

In 1938 Robert Noble conjured up a plan for rewarding every Californian over 50 with $25 every Monday in state warrants redeemable at the end of the year, provided that a weekly stamp tax of 2 percent was affixed. Since its moneymaking apparatus was self-contained, the economic fallacy should have been apparent even to the most unwary, but, taken in hand by an astute promoter, Willis Allen, the scheme came close to adoption. By advancing the amount and the day, Allen achieved the alliterative title, Thirty Dollars Every Thursday. In the course of the campaign the nonsensical nickname "Ham and Eggs" was added, and for a while this seemed to help in the promotion.

With relative ease Allen got 700,000 signatures, far more than were needed to qualify his proposed constitutional amendment for the November ballot. He took a leaf out of Townsend's method in appealing to the old folks for contributions for the drive to get them something for nothing and at the same time stimulate recovery from the depression.

Backed by these contributions and by the advertising revenue of the pension paper that he published, Allen staged a vigorous campaign. He used radio but depended largely on mass meetings and volunteer solicitation of votes. Candidates including Culbert Olson and Sheridan Downey, Democratic aspirants for governor and United States Senate, endorsed Ham and Eggs, but the sober element in the state was solid against it. There was a counter-campaign, but the general attitude was that a proposal so fantastic had no chance of adoption. It was a shock, therefore, when the count showed more than a million votes cast in its favor. A shift of a few hundred thousand more would have enacted it.

A greater jolt came in Allen's announcement that the Retirement Life Payments proposal would immediately be requalified for the ballot, this time with a million signatures. The petition went into circulation, the radio and the newssheet continued, and the campaign of soliciting dollars from the aged was intensified. The State Chamber of Commerce and its business cohorts had no choice but to continue and step up their opposition. The million signatures were achieved and publicly delivered to Governor Olson on May 18, 1939, putting him on the spot to call an election. The Ham and Eggers hoped for an August date, but Olson set November 7, and by that time the fervor had waned to the extent that the proposition got only 993,000 out of 2,975,000 votes.

Except for the scene-stealing Epic campaign, Californians throughout the thirties were more absorbed in national issues than in those of the state and were more attentive to national politics. The recovery and reform efforts of the New Deal, the reciprocal trade agreements, labor relations as provided for in Section 7A, agricultural benefits, devaluation of the dollar, the threat to pack the Supreme Court, and the third term issue—questions like these got attention almost to the exclusion of matters concerned merely with the state.

California voting behavior was equivocal and contained a paradox. At each opportunity the state went for Roosevelt, and as regularly it returned its old hero, Hiram Johnson, to the Senate. It elected a fair number of New Dealers to Congress but not until 1938 did it choose a Democratic governor or legislature. Throughout most of the decade, in fact, the state government was so out of sympathy with the New Deal program that it held cooperation to a minimum. For example, not until the very end of the Public Works program were the regents of the University of California willing to accept federal money for much needed university buildings.

In national politics bitterness intensified. In California, however, the reactionary and radical factions of 1934 moved toward each other and by 1938 were merely conservative and liberal. Another four years of depression made almost everyone accept government relief as a matter of course.

In 1938 the Democrats offered a more conventional candidate for governor, politically experienced Culbert L. Olson, and elected him without much difficulty. A former Epic, Olson was committed to modest reforms, which incorporated a few of the Sinclair planks, for example, relief through production for use. He entered office handicapped by ill health. His friends in the assembly were a majority, but proved disunited and inept, and the unrepresentative senate was still dominated by the conservatives. Olson pardoned Mooney and took a few other liberal steps. At the time Hitler and Mussolini were plunging toward war. The war came in the ninth month of his governorship, and thereafter the thoughts of Californians ran far more to national and world problems than to what might be done at Sacramento.

The most notable fact about the Olson administration was a facing up at last to the problems of the migrant laborers in California agriculture. In cooperation with federal agencies, the state moved to enforce minimum sanitary requirements at the labor camps and to set up government camps where at least a part of this working force could be accommodated. It tried to regulate the calls for labor in particular harvests so that they would not exceed the actual needs. It also tried to restrict the police to police activity rather than strikebreaking.

At the same time many of these problems were under federal investigation by the LaFollette Committee. Before major corrective legislation could be achieved at the state or national level, however, the labor requirements of defense preparations and then of the war effort siphoned off the labor surplus and decidedly altered the problems. The working out of durable and mutually satisfactory farm labor relations consequently was deferred to a later day. Meanwhile, the Okies and the Arkies, who for a time were regarded as such a problem group, were quickly assimilated into the state's already heterogeneous population.

The Boulder Canyon Project

In a planned economy, which California has never had, a depression would be the time for public works. One such enterprise of major proportions was ready for action early in the thirties, damming the Colorado.

In 1921 Phil Swing went to Congress as representative of the seven southern and southeastern counties of the state. His foremost purpose was to win federal support for a canal, an All-American Canal that would eliminate the valley's reliance on Mexico, and for a flood control program that would make impossible a repetition of the 1905–07 disaster to Imperial Valley. Prior to that time the Southern California Edison Company had under consideration a hydroelectric power installation on the Colorado in Boulder Canyon and the Reclamation Service had proposed dams far upstream to impound floodwaters. In 1920 Arthur Powell Davis of the Reclamation Service had proposed coalescing these two functions in a great dam in Boulder Canyon, which would control the flow of the river and yield a tremendous amount of electric power. Swing knew of this proposal and, en route to Washington, made a detour to Boulder Canyon and inspected the site.

As a lawyer who had represented an irrigation district, Swing saw the need for federal involvement in control of the Colorado and resolution of the claims of the seven basin states and of Mexico. The upper states pushed

Parker Dam on the Colorado   *Los Angeles Chamber of Commerce*

ahead with a compact in 1922 limiting the volume that California and the other lower states could take from the river. In collaboration with Senator Hiram Johnson, Swing introduced a bill to authorize construction of an All-American Canal and a multipurpose dam in Boulder Canyon. By regulating the flow of the river, this dam would safeguard against flooding, and as a high dam it would produce electric power. Over a 50-year period the sale of power could return to the federal government all its investment plus interest.

In the 67th Congress this bill died in committee. In the 68th Congress, Democrats bottled it up as a favor to Senator Carl Hayden of Arizona. In the 69th Congress, Republicans defeated it as requested by private power interests. In 1928, following the Teapot Dome scandal, the private power lobbyists were at a low ebb of influence and passage was possible. It took a few more years before an appropriation was made—$10 million on July 3, 1930. On March 11, 1931, a contract in the amount of $48,890,990 was signed for the construction of the dam and powerhouse.

In September, on the occasion of the driving of the first spike of the access railroad, Secretary of the Interior Ray Lyman Wilbur seized the opportunity to christen the dam-to-be in honor of the current President, Herbert Hoover. He had presided over the drafting of the compact in 1922 but from start to finish he had preferred a low dam merely for flood control. Those alert to the steps by which enabling action had been achieved were outraged at this "stealing" of the dam. Johnson was not the sort to take such an affront philosophically but, as Beverley Moeller reports, Swing did, merely remarking that "many a child has been named for a man who admittedly was not its father."

Swing had one more task to perform in Washington, the funding of the All-American Canal, which would disentangle the delivery system from international complexity, bring the water in at a higher level, and make lands on the east side of Imperial Valley irrigable. In 1933, when he set out on this mission, there was no need to ask Congress for the money. As one means of combating the depression, Congress had authorized $3.3 billion for public works projects. Secretary of the Interior Harold L. Ickes and the Public Works Administration held these purse strings, but the President was the man to see. After carefully laying the groundwork and gathering a delegation representing most of the basin states, Swing successfully took his appeal to Franklin D. Roosevelt. The irrigation customers in prospect were a good risk to repay the $78 million involved.

In addition to their obligations to the federal government for electric power to be picked up at the dam, the southern California contractors planned the financing of $56 million worth of transmission lines. Los Angeles and 44 neighboring communities joined in the Colorado River Water District and prepared to invest $200 million building Parker Dam, the Metropolitan Aqueduct, its branches, pumping plants, storage reservoirs, and treating plants, through which Colorado water would be delivered at the rate of a billion gallons a day.

Because the great dam, 1,282 feet in length, 727 feet high, 661 feet thick at the base and 45 feet at the top, was a bigger job and risk than any one company was prepared to handle, the contract was taken by a combine known as the Six Companies. Under the driving direction of Frank Crowe, the task, including preliminary diversion of the river, building a railway spur to the site, and creation of Boulder City to house the workmen, was completed by March, 1936. The dam freed Imperial Valley of flood danger. It created a lake that would store 32 million acre-feet of water, and its generators would produce power at the rate of more than one million kilowatts.

While the dam was rising, work began on the delivery adjuncts, the transmission lines, the All-American Canal, and the Colorado River Aqueduct, which in sum cost several times as much as the dam itself. By 1941 all three of these depression decade products were in operation.

The Central Valley Project

In this decade California finally decided to come to grips with the water problem of the Sacramento–San Joaquin Valley. The basic idea was to divert surplus water from the northern half of the valley to the southern, thereby minimizing flood danger in the north and alleviating aridity in the south. Supplementary aims were to develop hydroelectric power, improve navigability of the Sacramento, prevent saline intrusion in the Delta area, and furnish water to several towns and cities along the straits.

As early as 1874 B. S. Alexander had proposed such a project. In 1919 Robert Bradford Marshall adopted it and began to popularize it as the Marshall Plan. Some of his details were unduly simplified; he made drawings of canals, wide enough for sailing ships, along each side of the great valley. In 1921 the legislature appropriated $200,000 for a scientific study of the plan, but voted down a Water and Power Bill which would have supported the project. In 1922, 1924, and 1926 William Kent, John R. Haynes, James D. Phelan, and Rudolph Spreckels saw to it that the proposal was on the ballot as an initiative measure. Each time the Pacific Gas and Electric Company vigorously opposed it and the measure did not pass.

In 1933, however, the legislature, conservative though it was, passed the Central Valley

Project Act, authorizing a bond issue of $170 million to cover construction costs. The private utility companies forced a referendum, but the measure was upheld by 459,712 to 426,109. Instead of trying to find takers for the bond issue, the state government pinned its hopes on getting the federal government to adopt the project and succeeded in 1935 to the extent of a $12 million initial appropriation. Two years later Congress officially declared it a federal reclamation project.

The engineering plans, meanwhile, were carried forward, and by the end of the decade work was launched on the two major dams, Shasta and Friant. Shasta Dam impounds 4.5 million acre-feet of water on the upper Sacramento, regulates the flow, and generates electric power, some of which is used for pumping to the canal that carries water a hundred miles up the San Joaquin Valley. Friant Dam, near Fresno, impounds the San Joaquin River, and the 160-mile Friant-Kern Canal diverts this water southward to the driest part of the Central Valley.

Most of the work on these key units came in the following decade, and other amplifications of the project were reserved for the more distant future. Decision was deferred also on many knotty problems of administration and control. Should the Reclamation Bureau, the Army Corps of Engineers, or the state exercise control? Should publicly owned distributors have preference in sales of power? Should the Reclamation Bureau's customary 160-acre limitation on water sales be enforced? These and other fundamental questions were left to be answered later.

Because the project lay entirely within the state, some of the patterns in other river developments were not entirely applicable. Since if fully developed its potentialities so far exceeded others, even the Tennessee Valley Authority, the ultimate arrangement would be a matter of great moment. With the advocates of effective public control on the one hand and private interests, as represented by the Pacific Gas and Electric and the great landowners on the other, an epic tug of war was in the making. The depression-ridden thirties left these matters unresolved but did crystallize the plans and the launching of this most ambitious project.

In the never ending task of modernizing the state highway system and in a public building program involving schools, libraries, courthouses, and government office buildings, much of it federally financed, California advanced during the thirties. It was a period during which private enterprise was less venturesome. With the Federal Housing Authority as angel, however, a fair amount of residential construction took place. The railroads also began to re-equip with diesels and streamliners. In agriculture cotton raising and dairying expanded rapidly as did the commercial fishing based at California ports. Several branches of industry gained, notably cement making, but the most striking innovation was the rise of airplane building.

Until the midthirties California's best-known contribution to aviation was that Charles Lindbergh's *Spirit of St. Louis* had been assembled and conditioned at San Diego. Shortly thereafter the plants of Douglas, Lockheed, and North American at Santa Monica, El Segundo, Inglewood, and Burbank gave the state high rank in airplane manufacture. The availability of electric power was a factor as was the reservoir of skilled labor. The climate of southern California was congenial to the sprawling plants and afforded fair weather for test flights the year round. By the end of the decade this industry accounted for more than 10 percent of industrial employment in the state.

The inescapably dominant note of the thirties was the reality of the depression, its body blows to the economy and its disjointing of society. A feature of almost comparable significance was the tendency to look to the federal government to provide a remedy. The graphs and the indexes were down. Nevertheless, in addition to construction on the Colorado and planning in the Central Valley, California made substantial progress. The annual totals in many lines of production advanced, including cotton, fruits, milk, canned goods, oil refining, moving pictures, airplanes, and paved highways. Though not so spectacularly as in better times, the state continued its population climb, moving from 5,677,251 in 1930 to 6,907,387 in 1940, a larger increase than any other state. All told, there was solid achievement despite adversity.

CHAPTER 25

Robinson Jeffers

Sonya Noskourak, The Huntington Library

Physically attached to the West rather than belonging to the West, culturally isolated from the rest of America during decades when it grew "like a gourd in the night," California has always struggled, however, uncomprehendingly, for independent expression.

Carey McWilliams
Southern California Country

A California
Way of Life

The Environment Rediscovered

The men of the gold rush era, though engaged in work that was often peculiar, did their utmost to reproduce the pattern of living they had known back home. Likewise, the people of the next generation, though operating an economy that was different, felt a compunction to conform to the national standard in things cultural. California women, to the best of their ability, dressed exactly like their sisters in the East, and male attire ran to the conventional somber colors, hard collars and cuffs, high shoes, and no laying aside of vests or hats. In architecture the fearsome ornateness and eclecticism of the period had full force locally as well as in the East.

Upon the next generation, bounded roughly by the two world wars, national urges in things social continued to have weight. The people of the state were Americans first and Californians second. They went hand in hand with the rest of the country in discarding chewing tobacco and taking up the cigarette, in filling the home with gadgets and machines, in stepping up mobility, chain stores, and packaged goods, and in recognizing that many problems were beyond solution by local authority or by private initiative. Women had won acceptance at the polls and in employment. In some respects the Californians of these years went beyond the national average, as in gearing themselves to the automobile, shifting to suburban residence, and adapting their dress and dwellings to the climate. In significant particulars they moved toward a cultural pattern distinctively Californian.

Not least among the factors promoting this movement was rediscovery of the environment. The wonders of the Yosemite had been extolled for a generation, and the High Sierra had its devotees. The health rush had

involved appraisal of the state's many subclimates, and the state's agriculture, by trial and science, had achieved an adjustment to the environmental facts. Yet overall appreciation of what nature offered waited until the twentieth century when highways and the automobile made the remote parts of the state accessible.

With literally thousands and tens of thousands turning out where only dozens had gone before, problems arose of how to accommodate such crowds and at the same time preserve the beauties and wonders of nature. One answer, now commonplace, was through the National Parks Service or the state taking charge of parks, monuments, forests, beaches, and historic sites.

As long ago as 1864 Yosemite Valley was designated a state park. In 1890, alerted by the intrusions of cattlemen and sheepherders, the federal government set aside about a thousand square miles adjoining this valley as Yosemite National Park. Stirred by the Kaweah communitarians and their project for lumbering in the vicinity of the big trees, Congress also created Sequoia and General Grant National Parks, embracing about 250 square miles. In most cases the military was put in charge, which usually meant control without specialized personnel. This was one reason for the friction with the civilians whom the state had placed in charge at Yosemite Valley. In 1906 Yosemite was unified through reconveyance of title to the federal government, but not until 1916 with the creation of the National Parks Service was the care put on a satisfactory basis. At Sequoia civilian control began in 1914.

Additions were made to the areas protected by park control. In 1926 about 350 square miles in the Mt. Whitney–Kern River district were added to Sequoia. In 1933 Death Valley and its environs, almost 3,000 square miles of exposed geology and unbelievable color effects, became a national monument. In 1940 the Kings Canyon area immediately to the north of Sequoia, some 700 square miles, was made a national park. Mt. Lassen, the Lava Beds, the Pinnacles, the Devil's Postpile, and Muir Woods also became national parks or monuments.

The state took jurisdiction over a number of sites, some of them historic, such as the Mother Lode town of Columbia and the Marshall monument at Coloma. Most were at threatened beach frontages or at the most spectacular of the redwood groves from Del Norte County south as far as the Big Sur. A few of these sites, such as Santa Cruz Big Trees, were subject to earlier pilgrimage by rail, but most came to be of major interest only in the automobile era. Thus the state park system, like the national, assumed its real proportions and importance in the period after World War I.

Attuning to the Land

In 1915 San Francisco celebrated the completion of the Panama Canal with the Panama-Pacific Exposition, of less enduring influence than the concurrent Panama-California Exposition at San Diego. The directors of the San Diego fair dramatized the regional culture of the Southwest, presenting a review of the patterns of living from prehistoric times to the twentieth century, with stress on the blossoming of the desert and the semiarid land whenever irrigation was applied, and displays of architecture skillfully attuned to the land and climate.

Some of the buildings were permanent structures for Balboa Park, but the architectural influence was even more pervasive. Asked to accent Pan American relationships, Bertram Goodhue drew on elements of the Spanish Renaissance and the Spanish colonial. Working primarily in bright tones of tile

and stucco, with towers, domes, and arcades, he achieved variety, sparkle, and brilliance. Enthusiastically received by visitors to the fair, this theme infected the architectural trends of the time, especially in southern California.

In residential design Richard Neutra, Frank Lloyd Wright, and others introduced a functional approach that took into account the opportunities of the locale. Once it was conceded that a California house did not have to look like a Spanish castle, a Cape Cod cottage, or a midwestern farmhouse, it was possible to open it so that the patio or garden became an integral part of the living area. Much construction was as conservative as ever, but the leaven of indoor-outdoor architecture was increasingly present. The Los Angeles Union Station, Cliff May's Sunset Building in Menlo Park, and Carmel as it was in the 1930s are examples of this adaption of architecture to its environment.

In dress this generation of Californians became less formal and less confined. The escape from corsets, collars, and excess layers of cloth was not confined to California, but the benign climate, the spirit of vacationing, and the boldness of the state's own clothing designers made unconventional attire more tempting.

Californians devised ways to capitalize on the outdoors. One was through staging special events such as the Los Angeles Olympic Games in 1932, another fair at San Diego in 1935, and the Golden Gate International Exposition at Treasure Island in 1938. Other activities were annual performances such as the Salinas Rodeo, the Santa Barbara Fiesta, and the Pasadena Tournament of Roses and Rose Bowl game. Another salute to the climate was in carrying the theater and the concert outdoors. The beginning may have been the High Jinks of the Bohemian Club in Marin County. Then came outdoor theater and pageantry in the Greek Theater in Berkeley. John McGroarty's *Mission Play* ran for

A California Ranch House by Cliff May

Maynard L. Parker

many years at San Gabriel, and *Ramona* had even longer popularity at Hemet. Hollywood's *Pilgrimage Play* was another hardy perennial.

At the turn of the century the Point Loma Colony had an amphitheater in which Greek plays and classical music were performed. Open-air concerts at the Ford Bowl in Balboa Park were a feature of the 1915 exposition. At Ojai some years later an annual festival was initiated. Most ambitious of all were the Symphonies Under the Stars in Hollywood Bowl, begun in 1921 and continued in spite of the competition of radio and television and the handicaps of traffic congestion and airplane interference.

Besides these al fresco concerts, Los Angeles had opportunity to hear its Philharmonic Orchestra, established in 1919 through

the philanthropy of W. A. Clark, Jr. The San Francisco Symphony Orchestra was much older and since 1911 had been in part municipally supported. San Francisco also supported its own opera company and in 1932 outfitted it with a home in the Civic Center, the first municipal opera house in the United States. No less significant as an institution in this epoch, and reaching a much larger audience, was the Standard Hour, a weekly radio program in which the San Francisco and Los Angeles orchestras were the most frequent performers.

Art

Since the time of the first railroad and Comstock fortunes, the number of privately owned art masterpieces in California constantly mounted. Hung side by side these would make something less than a Louvre but a very creditable, instructive, and inspiring display. Although many of these canvases remained in sterile seclusion, there was encouraging progress in making them available to the public. Old museums such as the M. H. de Young in Golden Gate Park were enlarged and enriched and new galleries of even greater size and distinction opened. These include the Palace of the Legion of Honor in San Francisco, the Los Angeles Museum of History, Science and Art, the Fine Arts Gallery in San Diego's Balboa Park, the Louis Terah Haggin Memorial Galleries in Stockton, and the Henry E. Huntington Art Gallery in San Marino. Several of these galleries became focal points for contemporary work. The Carmel and Laguna Beach art colonies attracted large contingents of poets, painters, composers, and kindred spirits.

In a drab neighborhood in Los Angeles, Simon Rodia, a poor immigrant from Italy, built a gigantic fantasy of folk art known as the Watts Towers. For many years he collected seashells, discarded pipe, bedsprings, scrap iron, colored bottles, and broken tile to make a unique present for the people of his adopted country. He worked without blueprint or scaffolding or help. The tallest of the towers is almost ten stories high.

Ansel Adams personified an art form that has had special flowering in California. He achieved fame as photographer of Yosemite and the Sierra Nevada. That is only a fraction of his contribution in this art, but it is central and seminal to the appreciation of wilderness and dedication to conservation by the Sierra Club and the Wilderness Society. Associates and disciples, including Philip Hyde and Wynn Bullock, carry on. His neighbor Edward Weston found beauty lurking not only at California's showplaces but in the most casual scenes.

Film making and climatic advantages were among the lodestones drawing some of the world's most famous musicians to California. Among them were Lawrence Tibbett, Amelita Galli-Curci, Arnold Schoenberg, and Otto Klemperer.

Writers

Among the eminent writers imported in the twenties and thirties by the moving picture studios, Theodore Dreiser stayed briefly and F. Scott Fitzgerald and Eugene Manlove Rhodes only a little longer. Others remaining from a few weeks to the rest of their lives included Irvin S. Cobb, Will Rogers, James M. Cain, John O'Hara, Nathanael West, and Aldous Huxley.

Each made some contribution to films. As California writers, however, they are judged not by their scenarios but by their "moonlighting," Huxley for his *After Many a Summer*, West for *The Day of the Locust*, and Fitzgerald for *The Last Tycoon*. *After Many a Summer* is memorable for its deflating of Los Angeles, William Randolph Hearst, and Forest Lawn, a formidable trinity. *The Last Tycoon*, unfinished, gave promise of being the most revealing vignette of Hollywood, which was more devastatingly achieved in Budd Schulberg's *What Makes Sammy Run?*

The attitude of the eastern establishment toward writers in the plush exile of Hollywood is well illustrated in Edmund Wilson's greeting to *The Day of the Locust*: "Nathanael West, the brilliant author of Miss Lonelyhearts, went to Hollywood several years ago, and his silence had been causing his readers alarm lest he might have faded out on the Coast as so many of his fellows have done. But Mr. West, as this new book happily proves, is still alive beyond the mountains, and can still tell what he feels and sees—has still, in short, remained an artist. His new novel, *The Day of the Locust*, deals with the nondescript characters

Simon Rodia's Towers

Nick King

on the edges of Hollywood studios.

"Mr. West has caught the emptiness of Hollywood; and he is, as far as I know, the first writer to make this emptiness horrible."

The state had more than its share of writers of westerns, including the inordinately productive Frederick Faust. It also abounded in mystery writers. Raymond Chandler, as Philip Durham pointed out in *Down These Mean Streets*, used the detective story to support a vivid documentary on the southern California scene.

Edwin Corle in *Mojave* (1934), *Fig Tree John* (1938), and several other books proved an adept storyteller, primarily interested in the southern California interior, with which he dealt in a few works of nonfiction, notably *Desert Country* (1941).

John Steinbeck

The Bancroft Library

John Steinbeck

It is rare good fortune when a sympathetic and prepared writer and an epic story of human tragedy coincide in time and place. John Steinbeck seemed to be waiting for them when the Dust Bowl refugees dragged in to bitter disappointment and disillusionment in the fields of California.

The story line for the powerful novel that resulted was not difficult to find. Here was a whole migration of people foreclosed from their farms by ravaging dust storms, hopelessly in debt, exhausted and ill from maneuvering broken-down cars loaded with their possessions across Highway 66 to get to the promised land. After that they then faced ominous reality that California for them was not going to be much of an improvement over what was left in the Dust Bowl. They found land abundant but not for the penniless, work at certain seasons but at starvation wages, beautiful landscapes but unsightly and unsanitary camps for migrants, and at the

slightest provocation brutal suppression by police and self-appointed vigilantes.

Steinbeck had become identified as champion of the downtrodden, the underprivileged, and the insecure in *Pastures of Heaven* (1932), *Tortilla Flat* (1935), *In Dubious Battle* (1936), and *Of Mice and Men* (1937). His writing was vigorous; his arguments and vocabulary were earthy and blunt. The vintage tramped out in *The Grapes of Wrath* (1939) is bitter. The book calls to mind Dickens' exposés. It dwarfs the earlier California novels of protest such as Jackson's *Ramona* and Norris' *The Octopus*. The Nobel Prize was awarded to Steinbeck for the sequence of novels concerned with social ills but principally for *The Grapes of Wrath*.

Robinson Jeffers

Robinson Jeffers stands as California's epic poet. Much of his youth was spent in Los Angeles where he was an undergraduate at Occidental College and graduate student at the University of Southern California. But after he and his wife Una chose Carmel for their home in 1914, the man and his poetry became inseparable from the rugged Big Sur country.

In 1925, after two largely unnoticed volumes of poems, Jeffers attracted immediate attention with the publication of *Roan Stallion*. More than a dozen volumes followed, among them *Dear Judas*, *Thurso's Landing*, and *Give Your Heart to the Hawks*. All were set against the magnificent scenery of the Monterey peninsula. This coastline with its bold headlands jutting into sea and fog, its "savage beauty of canyon and cliff," its redwoods and tortured cypress, its gulls and hawks, came to be known as "Jeffers Country."

Universals are Jeffers' chosen subjects and

Bixby Creek Bridge on the Big Sur Coast   *Department of Public Works, Division of Highways*

a steady seriousness dominates his writing. To him only nature is significant and worthy of being eternal. He relentlessly rages against man's inhumanity, shortsightedness, and lack of respect for truth. In poem after poem he warns of the inevitable destruction of the human race if it continues the senselessness and horror of war, the onslaughts on the planet, and the population explosion—"the torrents of newborn babies, the bursting schools."

Jeffers was not the people's poet. His obsession with violence and tragedy brought harsh criticism. When *The Double Axe* was published in 1948, his publisher for 15 years did the unheard of by prefacing the book with a statement of disassociation from the politics expressed.

Tor House, which Jeffers built of stones rolled up from the ocean, is now a protected monument, and the poet is increasingly acclaimed not only for the splendor of his writing but for his passionate concern for the plight of the world.

Schools

Along with the substantial population increase from World War I to World War II, public school enrollments kept pace and in higher education considerably exceeded it. The state met the challenge and at the same time upgraded the programs.

In the certification of teachers the state now required a college degree for elementary teachers and a year of graduate work for high school teachers along with special studies in education and supervised practice teaching. The state specified minimum salaries and, to eliminate extreme differences in school district tax rates, it made substantial contributions to school district costs on the basis of average daily attendance. As of 1950 the per capita

expenditure was exceeded only in New York.

The state also moved to consolidate districts that were too small for effectiveness. In most instances busing was the enabling factor and was warmly welcomed. Schools also were being better equipped, as for example with science laboratories in the high schools.

At the college level a much larger increase in enrollments occurred. President Robert Gordon Sproul and the regents of the University of California were determined not to allow it to be fragmented into many separate institutions competing for public funding. They could point to states where that kind of fracturing had been disastrous. A generation later New York would follow the California example and at great expense create a statewide university operating on ten or a dozen campuses.

Early in the twenties the state normal school in Los Angeles became the southern branch of the University of California, later moved to a new campus and rechristened the University of California at Los Angeles. That experiment was followed by annexation of the state teachers college at Santa Barbara and its incorporation into the university system. For decades these outposts were essentially undergraduate colleges. UCLA awarded its first Ph.D. in 1936. But the pattern was set that would permit additional general instruction campuses at Riverside, Davis, Santa Cruz, San Diego, and Irvine. By 1940 the University of California was the largest of all universities and its Berkeley faculty, according to a Carnegie Institution survey, was surpassed in "distinction" only by Harvard's.

The state college system under its own board of trustees also began to expand and there was a comparable flourishing of private universities and colleges.

More spectacular was the sudden emergence of a battery of junior colleges, a phenomenon in which California led the way. By

Berkeley Campus, University of California   *Ansel Adams,* Fiat Lux, *University of California Press*

1939 there were 49, of which 42 were public, each with its own board of trustees, district, and tax base, plus state appropriations. By 1951 there were 75 with a total enrollment of 302,130, much larger than the statewide university or the state college system. These were two-year colleges, rationalized as reducing the enrollment pressure on the four-year schools but also serving many students not intending to go further and offering programs not available elsewhere.

Libraries and Laboratories

By resorting to branch libraries and interlibrary loans the state, county, and city libraries conspired to make books readily available at a multitude of stations. Without such machinery the Los Angeles Public Library could not have achieved the largest circulation among American libraries. This expansion paralleled the proliferation of schools.

In development of research libraries, which in large degree is dependent on time, California in this between-the-wars generation did well. As a general research collection the University library at Berkeley was preeminent, followed at some distance by Stanford University, the State Library, and half a dozen university, college, and city libraries.

Henry E. Huntington's endowed holdings on English history and literature and secondarily on California had become an active research center. So had the Hoover Library at Stanford in its World War I and Russian Revolution specialization.

Not surprisingly investment in research went far more heavily into the sciences, some of it directly by industry at company laboratories but much of it at the universities in part state financed but with important injections from industry and the federal government. University of California researchers made

advances tremendously valuable to California agriculture. Another example is available in the record as to astronomy.

In 1874 an eccentric millionaire, James Lick, donated $700,000 to the University of California for the building of an observatory. His first thought was to put it at Fourth and Market in San Francisco, then he veered to the inspiration of a mountaintop and settled on Mt. Hamilton, south of San Jose, partly because it overlooked the site of a flour mill of his. Thus was initiated the scientifically advantageous device of perching a telescope in the clear atmosphere of the mountains. With a 35-inch refracting telescope, for many years the second most powerful in existence, the Lick Observatory was a focal point for astronomical research.

Thaddeus S. C. Lowe, Lewis Spence, and other promoters and popular scientists were inspired by the Lick Observatory and longed for something like it, only larger, in southern California. Their notion was taken up at the turn of the century by astronomer George Ellery Hale, who raised support for a scientific search for an ideal observatory site. The specifications included such factors as latitude 30 to 35 north, moderate but not excessive altitude, equable temperature, stability of weather, a minimum of clouds and overcast, no undue turbulence of air currents, and accessibility to an inhabited center where machine shops, supplies, and accommodations for visitors could be had. Mt. Wilson met the specifications. Hale then went to work on acquaintances of means, many of whom had retired to Pasadena's millionaires' row. By 1917 he had a 100-inch telescope ready to operate, for the next 20 years the world's largest.

As the work at Mt. Wilson progressed, Hale raised his sights to a still more ambitious project. In 1928 he persuaded the Rockefeller Foundation to commission a still larger telescope and to budget $6 million for the purpose. The sea of lights that had developed on the plains below Mt. Wilson ruled it out as the location. While the 200-inch refractor was being ground, southern California was combed for the most eligible site, the choice falling on Mt. Palomar in San Diego County. The partly ground glass arrived in Pasadena in 1936; another 12 years of painstaking work was necessary before the telescope was completed and installed, ready to reach out to the very boundaries of the universe.

Meanwhile, other arsenals for scientific research were being prepared. At Pasadena as a sort of adjunct to his observatory, Hale envisioned a scientific institute, which he convinced a number of wealthy Pasadenans to finance. In 1917 Robert A. Millikan joined forces with Hale. He was as adept as Hale in enlisting benefactors of great wealth and he had a remarkable gift for selecting areas of research in which the prospect for significant findings was at a maximum. Within a very few years the California Institute of Technology won recognition as one of the most effective agencies of its kind.

At the university at Berkeley a noteworthy scientific improvement took place in the period before 1940. It was interdisciplinary, embracing practically all the branches of science, but its most arresting feature was the Radiation Laboratory at work on the then mystical experiment in splitting the atom. Perhaps most surprising was that a state as new as California, only recently graduated from frontier status, should be almost without peer in its marshalling of forces for exploration of the frontiers of scientific knowledge.

Historical Scholarship

California history, meanwhile, was brought under scrutiny by a number of very competent amateurs, that is, historians in the business for the fun of it rather than because of economic urge. Many of the best results in this quarter century were achieved by historians of this group. Their works are cited by the score in this book's bibliography, but too much emphasis cannot be laid on the great service to local historiography rendered by them. At the head of the lists in their respective divisions stand the bibliographies of Wagner and Cowan, Hanna's chronological commentary, Wagner's analyses of cartography and explorations, the biographies by Harding, Lyman, Watson, and Dakin, and the miscellaneous writings of a host of others, among them Camp, Wheat, Chalfant, Robinson, Paden, and McWilliams. In this connection it is significant that the California Historical Society, the Historical Society of Southern California, and numerous local societies actively meeting, collecting, and publishing were maintained by energetic groups of dedicated nonprofessional enthusiasts.

The normal expectation in this era of specialization was that historical research should be primarily the work of professionals. In Bancroft's day California history was not written thus and, as recently as 1907, when the Native Sons of the Golden West proposed to endow a chair of California history, the president of the University of California demurred, in chagrin it is to be hoped, because there was no scholar at the university or elsewhere competent to fill such a chair. To the credit of the university it must be admitted that, assisted by the Native Sons, it set out at once to remedy that defect. Nevertheless, at this writing, more than 70 years later, no such chair has been set up.

In 1906 the university acquired the Bancroft Library, consisting of some 60,000 volumes of books, manuscripts, and newspapers. In 1910 H. Morse Stephens, head of the history department, persuaded the Native Sons to advance funds sufficient for two annual traveling fellowships. The following year Herbert E. Bolton was brought to the department expressly for the purpose of directing and leading the utilization of the resources of the Bancroft Library in graduate work and research. These elements, the Bancroft materials, the fellowships, Stephens and Bolton, explain much of the renown earned then by the Berkeley history department.

Two particular concepts were fundamental to the Berkeley graduate work in American history. One was the realization that the archives of Spain and Mexico contained a marvelous wealth of materials for the history of California and of every other part of the New World in which Spain had once been interested. Bancroft had had only a slight awareness of the existence of these materials; Stephens gained a notion of the extent of the Spanish archives when he made a preliminary survey in 1910. Bolton was already conversant with Mexico's archival riches, for he had examined them with care and had prepared a guide to their resources for United States history.

For the other fundamental, Bolton was primarily responsible. It was a simple idea, yet revolutionary, namely, that American history is best studied not within state or national confines but on a continental or, better still, on a hemispheric basis. Thoughtful analysis of California's history would seem to point inevitably to this deduction, but, if Bancroft grasped it, the only evidence is that he decided to broaden his project to take in the entire Pacific slope. Other historians had been content to stay within the United States, or even within a portion of it.

Catalyzed by this vision of broader horizons, nurtured on the riches that Bancroft had stored up, vitalized by the magnificent documentation preserved in the Spanish and Mexican archives, stimulated and assisted by the Native Sons fellowships, and inspired by the leadership of Stephens and Bolton, the Berkeley graduate group in American history made itself one of the most dynamic, prolific, and significant in the country. Its doctors of philosophy predominated in the field of Hispanic American history. They became major workers in the field of the Spanish borderlands, prominent in the field of the American westward movement and the American West, including Hawaii, and the leading exponents of the study of the history of the Americas, the Western Hemisphere in its entirety. Concerning this group the term "California school" gained currency.

Many of these historians engaged in studies that relate distantly or not at all to California. Others turned their attention to local problems with such commendable result that of the references, other than first-hand accounts, tabulated in the accompanying bibliography at least a quarter are credited to this California school. Outstanding among these are Bolton's works on Kino, Anza, Crespi, and Palóu, Charles E. Chapman's *Catalogue*, his volume on the founding, the Chapman-Cleland *History*, Owen Coy's work on the gold rush era, Cardinal Goodwin's studies of the establishment of state government and of Frémont, and Joseph Ellison's account of early federal relations. Thus the list begins; it goes on to include published items running the whole gamut of the state's history, not to mention scores of manuscript theses deposited in the university library.

CHAPTER 26

Building a Bomber, Long Beach   *Palmer, Office of War Information*

1939 to 1945

The Second World War removed the last traces of California's isolation; it increased her manufacturing output, measured in dollars, more than three times over; it established her as the center of American aviation, military and civilian; and, because a Japanese submarine popped out of the ocean one day and took a random shot at a pier near Santa Barbara, it made her the only State in the Union to lose even a few slivers of wood by enemy action. . . .

The hold of venerable traditions loosened. Even in San Francisco people didn't look back to the Gold Rush or to the "Earthquake and Fire" as earnestly as they used to; they looked forward; after all, they did have those bridges. In Los Angeles the annual Iowa picnic would never again be the event of the year.

R. L. Duffus
Queen Calafia's Island (1965)

Wartime Upsurge

In 1939, though the decade just closing had been difficult, California could look back on an epoch of lusty growth. In the comparatively short span of 90 years as an American state it had come from nowhere to be fifth among the states in population, fifth in taxable income, at the top in agricultural production, and perhaps over the top in attention claimed. No other state had matched this increase; sober opinion doubted that even California could maintain the pace.

In September, 1939, however, Hitler sent his Panzers into Poland, and overnight Europe was caught up in a war that soon had world dimensions. For a time the United States remained neutral, though this was a war about which it was impossible to remain dispassionate and from which it was most difficult to remain detached.

Existence of a world war, even though the United States was not a belligerent, radically changed the outlook for California. Then, on December 7, 1941, the attack on Pearl Harbor snatched away neutrality and plunged the nation into the vortex of the European as well as the Pacific war. This development was a stimulant to the economy such as the state had never experienced. It demanded planned and coordinated effort and provided a patriotic incentive that mobilized California for an unprecedented effort.

Plant and Potential

When the war started, California's annual income was approximately $5 billion. Primary production in fisheries, forests, mines, farms, and factories accounted for about half of the total. Fisheries yielded $20 million; forests $87 million; mines about $400 million, the greater part in petroleum; agriculture $625 million; construction $417 million; and manufactur-

356

ing, on goods with a market value of $2,798 million, was credited with addition of $1,135 million through processing. The other half of the annual income came from values added through distribution and services, a broad category including everything from wholesale and retail trade to utilities, transportation, hotels, laundries, theaters, personal service, and the professions. Part of this income was derived from investments outside the state and from expenditures by tourists and other visitors within the state.

A peculiarity of the economy was that, whereas the nation as a whole had an almost equal number engaged in primary production industries and in the distribution and service trades, in California the division was more nearly on a one-third, two-thirds basis. Clerks, salesmen, businessmen, service station operators, teachers, money lenders, lawyers, and the like outnumbered mill hands, farmers, construction workers, and miners two to one. For the waging of old-fashioned war this personnel factor would not have been a good omen.

Several lines of production also seemed unwarlike. An early move was to shut down the $50 million a year gold mining industry in an effort to shift its skilled labor to producing more critical minerals. In the nineteenth century the fruits and nuts that constituted about 30 percent of the agricultural output and the vegetables that ran to another 18 percent would not have been counted sinews of war. Of the 381,000 persons engaged in manufacturing it appeared that the 71,700 engaged in food and beverage production, the 31,000 motion picture makers, the 22,400 apparel workers, and the 13,200 furniture makers, to cite just a few examples, were hardly in position directly to win the war. Iron and steel workers in 1939 numbered only 26,900 and aircraft and ship builders, only 22,600. The war, of course, was waged in a more modern fashion, utilizing new skills and materiel. Even so, to meet the war's requirements many Californians would have to shift to entirely different work.

The other side of the picture was that by 1939 California had in production several requisites for up-to-date warfare. Since this war would not be fought on hardtack and embalmed beef, the state's agriculture did not have to be completely revamped. In gasoline and fuel oil the petroleum industry was producing two prime essentials. In machine shops, automobile assembly plants, tire factories, electrical equipment plants, and precision instrument shops the state had nuclei for military production. Furthermore, it was off to a good start in airplane building and possessed certain natural advantages for shipbuilding.

In the face of Japanese aggression against China and the rise of militarism in Europe, the United States began to step up its preparedness for war. The most spectacular dividends for California were the contracts for training and combat planes and for ships, mostly Liberty and Victory type freighters and transports. Federal funds covered part of the cost of airplane factory expansion and almost the entire outlay for shipbuilding facilities. A rapid buildup of plants occurred. Employment rolls in these industries mushroomed by 1941 to five and a half times what they had been in 1939, and production advanced from $106 million to $708 million—all before the United States entered the war.

The federal authorities also turned to California for troop training. Held over from earlier wars and alarms were a number of installations, including naval facilities at Mare Island, San Francisco, and San Diego and army posts at the Presidio in San Francisco, Fort Ord, Fort MacArthur, and air bases at March Field and Hamilton Field. The Navy was at work on an airfield at Alameda and had plans for Treasure Island when the exposition closed. As the prewar draft put more and more men into uniform, California began to bristle with an array of mammoth training stations.

War Industries

In aircraft production California had made a good beginning. This program was now stepped up to an all-out effort. The national government put up $150 million for plant expansion, to which was added $79 million in private capital. Vast, sprawling plants took shape at Burbank, Santa Monica, El Segundo, Inglewood, Long Beach, and San Diego, camouflaged in imitation of residential subdivisions. A rumor circulated that the Ocean Park pier, which drew a bead on the Douglas plant, was to be realigned to set up the UCLA campus as a decoy. The contracts poured in to Douglas, Lockheed, North American, Vultee, Hughes, and a host of subsidiary parts suppliers. By June, 1945, they totalled $2,136,119,000 in San Diego County and $7,093,837,000 in Los Angeles County.

From considerably fewer than 20,000 employees in 1939 the work force rose to a peak of 243,000 in August, 1943. Some workers came to the job sufficiently skilled. A larger number had to be trained as riveters, welders, machinists, and the like. The saving factor was that a division of labor approximating the assembly line was possible and narrowly specialized skills sufficed.

The shipbuilding story is strikingly similar. From a mere 4,000 on the job in 1939 there was an upsurge to a peak of 282,000 in August, 1943. Contracts amounted to $5,155,516,000. Some $3,053,119,000 went to the yards at Richmond, Sausalito, South San Francisco, and elsewhere in the Bay region. Los Angeles was far behind with $1,709,974,000 in contracts. The plants were financed almost entirely by the federal government, which posted $409 million to go

Los Angeles Harbor after the War   *Los Angeles Chamber of Commerce*

with $29 million in private capital. Several companies engaged in the work, but the one enterpriser who emerged as a public figure was Henry J. Kaiser.

His fame derived in part from his other interests, which included cement, aluminum, steel, a tank factory at Willow Run, and plans for automobile manufacture, but for a time he was thought of primarily as Kaiser the ship-builder. His approach to the problem resembled that in the great construction projects at Boulder, Friant, or Shasta. For transforming plans and blueprints into reality he relied on the methods of organization and procedure and some of the key personnel that had been used in such projects.

Although by the year 1939 California had 675 plants producing and fabricating iron and steel, the majority were relatively small, supplied only a small fraction of the western market, and were at the fabricating level. A regional deficiency long recognized was the slight development of basic production of iron and steel. As of 1939 the available capacity was no more than a million tons of ingots a year. Wartime concern about decentralizing industry, lessening the load on the railroads, and insuring a supply of material to the western warplants led to a sudden expansion of plants. At Geneva, Utah, the federal government built a $200 million steel mill rated at 1,280,000 tons capacity. Through government loans it assisted in the enlargement of the United States Steel, Bethlehem Steel, and independent mills at San Francisco and Los Angeles.

Also, with a loan from the Reconstruction Finance Corporation, Kaiser built at Fontana an integrated blast furnace and rolling mill of 700,000 tons capacity. Some 50 miles east of Los Angeles, dependent on coal from Utah 500 miles away, iron ore from Eagle Mountain 150 miles away, and rail freight for the delivery of its products, it was expected to be at a disadvantage in competition with tidewater-located mills. Nevertheless, the mill prospered sufficiently to justify a postwar enlargement. Percentagewise the California steel industry was an infinitesimal part of the national total. By 1945, after all this expansion, the state accounted for only 1.5 percent of the nation's pig iron. The wartime increase, however, was a tonic to the West and a harbinger of a better rounded and possibly unmonopolized basic industry.

With the particular assignment of fueling the war in the Pacific, the California oil companies stepped up production of crude oil, added to their refineries, and increased the output of gasoline and fuel oil by more than 50 percent between 1939 and 1945. New cracking equipment distilled a considerably higher proportion of high test aviation gasoline. Another series of plants transmuted crude oil into rubber. The process was fantastically expensive and noisome, but, as Japanese conquests in Malaya and the Dutch East Indies cut off access to natural rubber, it was a war necessity. The product was a synthetic with certain marked superiorities over natural rubber and therefore of continuing importance beyond the war years.

Many other industries were boosted by the war effort. Older factories were converted, for example, from the making of furniture to plywood boats or from radios to sonar equipment. New factories were improvised to produce airplane parts, shell casings, landing field lights, electronic equipment, and other war supplies. The largest expansion was in machinery, electrical equipment, rubber goods, sheet metal, and light metal products. Even with certain industries such as automobile manufacture officially restrained, the overall picture was one of tremendous growth. Factory output rose from $2,798,180,000 in 1939 to $10,141,496,000 in 1944.

For reasons of convenience this manufacturing was clustered in the localities where industrial beginnings had already been made—the Los Angeles area, the San Francisco Bay region, and the San Diego area. Los Angeles had the largest population increase during the war years, better than 300,000, but more startling gains included San Diego's spurt from 203,000 to 362,000; Richmond's from 23,000 to 93,000; and Alameda's from 36,000 to 90,000.

Agriculture at War

At the outset of the war certain specialties in California agriculture such as flower growing were candidates for curtailment. By plan or otherwise there was a reduction in the acreage planted to strawberries and sugarbeets. All the other 48 crops on the Department of Agriculture's list held their own or showed an increase. The handicaps of competition for labor and transport to market were offset by the nationwide prosperity, the enlarged number of consumers in California, and government purchases for servicemen in training in the state and for provisioning the armed forces in the Pacific theater.

The increase was felt by all branches of agriculture. From 1940 to 1944, for example, income from dairying advanced from $91 to $192 million, that from beef cattle, hogs, and lambs from $88 to $175 million, that from poultry went from $45 to $119 million, with the total for livestock and livestock products going from $232 to $500 million.

Cotton advanced from $25 to $51 million, other field crops from $74 to $161 million, and vegetables from $123 to $284 million. In this general category, as in livestock raising, farm income more than doubled.

Fruits and nuts showed an even more striking growth. Citrus went from $91 to $262 million, grapes from $35 to $184 million, the deciduous fruit crop from $57 to $217 million, and nuts from $14 to $39 million. Overall, this meant three and a half times as much income.

These figures remind that California agriculture is responsive to the market and that even the tree-borne part of its output can be stepped up by more intensive cultivation, application of more water and plant food, and more thorough harvesting. The total realized, $1.744 billion in 1944 as against $625 million in 1939, was almost a threefold increase and only less startling than the strides being made in industry. Furthermore, while climbing only to eighth or ninth among the states in manufacturing, in agriculture California was in first place.

The Manhattan Project

Meanwhile, California scientists applied their talents to the problems of the war. At Stanford, Berkeley, and Los Angeles training programs were started for those who might be assigned responsibilities of military government in occupied countries. The California Institute of Technology and UCLA had elaborate training programs in meteorology. A variety of other specialized training programs were conducted at the colleges and universities. Conventional civilian instruction continued alongside these programs, except at the Davis campus of the university, which was turned over to the Air Force for the duration.

Capitalizing on the reservoir of researchers in the state, the national authorities turned to them for a variety of services. Some went into the field with the armed forces, as for example a geologist, who advised on problems of terrain that would be encountered in the island-to-island progression in the Pacific. Others pursued research studies at laboratories set up by the armed forces, such as the sonar laboratory on Point Loma or the Naval Research Center at Inyokern. Still others, with contracted support, stayed on in their laboratories to work on specified problems critical in the war effort. Some scientists feared there would be an exhaustion of the pure or theoretical science waiting application. The range of assignments was broad and basic research was involved. The dimensions are suggested by the total of $57 million in research contracts entered into by the University of California. Other institutions in the state had proportionate shares.

The most spectacular project was in atomic research. At the Radiation Laboratory in Berkeley, E. O. Lawrence had built the first cyclotron, thus paving the way for production of U-235 and the atomic bomb. Discovery of two other elements, neptunium and plutonium, also took place at the Radiation Laboratory. Under the Manhattan Project, the University of California accepted responsibility for setting up and exercising managerial supervision over the facility at Los Alamos in New Mexico where further atomic research was conducted and the first atomic bombs were actually produced.

The project at Los Alamos was shrouded in secrecy, and many facts about it were kept confidential after the war. Only a limited number of persons knew that the university's involvement was not just in research but in the production of the atomic bombs that would be dropped on Hiroshima and Nagasaki. They did not challenge this participation, and the university went on after the war at another installation to make the key contribution to development of the hydrogen bomb and to supervise production of these bombs.

After the atomic bombs were dropped many Americans were appalled. Feverishly the government called on other nations to covenant not to use this fearsome weapon and at the same time raced to stockpile as many bigger nuclear bombs as possible.

Years went by before the question was faced whether war-serving research was a legitimate or condonable university function. Clearly there were basic researches that might be applicable in the service of mankind or for the destruction of mankind. As a legacy from World War II the University of California continued to run the laboratories at Los Alamos and Livermore where America's nuclear bombs are produced. Controversy on the legitimacy of a university performing such a role extended into the 1980s.

Many Americans felt remorse that, besides being the first to make the bomb, the United States has been the one nation that used it.

Troop Training and Staging Area

Notoriously wars are fought without sparing cost. Except for a strong effort to curb inflation, the United States made no pretense of economizing on World War II. There were times, however, when factors quite extraneous led to provident decisions. One was the selection of California as a major area for troop training. Continuing the process begun before American involvement as a belligerent, the Army developed huge training camps near Monterey, Paso Robles, San Luis Obispo, and Santa Maria. The Marines opened a west coast Quantico near Oceanside; the Navy built up its facilities at San Diego; and the Air Force added major training fields near Victorville, Merced, and Santa Ana. These training

centers amounted to more than 10 percent of the national total.

Much of the construction was routine. Barracks, for example, were built according to blueprints left over from World War I, yet there was some accommodation to the environment and some use of its particular features. At Oceanside the Marines had an ideal setting for practice landings, and on the desert beyond Palm Springs, General George S. Patton's Third Army found plenty of heat and sand in which to prepare for the African campaign.

California also was the principal staging area for the Pacific War. The Navy enlarged and improved its facilities at Mare Island, San Francisco, and San Diego. It converted Treasure Island into a naval station and Terminal Island in Los Angeles Harbor into a base. By comparable effort it developed Port Hueneme as an efficient working port. Most of the troops sent out into the Pacific embarked at San Francisco or Los Angeles. In cargo loading for the Pacific convoys Port Hueneme had a substantial share.

Relocation of the Japanese

Californians in 1941 had not entirely escaped from the heritage of anti-Japanese sentiment built up earlier in the century. The Japanese seemed inscrutable. Many had not become Americanized in language and looks. In several lines of business they were formidable competitors. Their imperial homeland, too, roused fears by its aggressions in China.

In this setting horror fiction anecdotes circulated about what the Japanese Americans would do if war came. This fisherman, it was said, would put on his uniform as an officer of the Imperial Navy and lead the Japanese fleet into Los Angeles Harbor. That gardener would signal in a landing party. Another would dynamite the Los Angeles Aqueduct,

Assembly for Relocation   *War Relocation Authority*

others would demolish the San Francisco bridges, while the maid in the Beverly Hills mansion would assassinate her mistress. Those who retold these scare stories did not always believe them; nevertheless, there was at least a suspicion that some might come true.

Against this background the news on December 7 from Pearl Harbor had particular impact. The losses officially admitted were heavy. Rumor multiplied them, and the popular supposition was that, with the Pacific fleet and the Hawaiian bastion knocked out, the West Coast was wide open to attack. Except through limited submarine action, the sinking of a tanker off Crescent City, and the lobbing of a few shells into the Goleta oil fields, the attack did not come. The general belief, however, was that it could have happened.

On December 7 the Department of Justice took prompt action to restrain enemy aliens. It imposed contraband rules, travel restrictions and inspections, and moved in quickly to arrest aliens suspected to be dangerous. That day 736 Japanese aliens were arrested; by February, 1942, more than 2,000 were being detained. A difference of opinion developed, however, between the Department of Justice and General John L. DeWitt, head of the Western Defense Command, on what further steps should be taken. At his urging the department stepped up its raids but, without more specific evidence than he presented, it was unwilling to go further. By mid-February an impasse had developed.

In large part DeWitt's demands for more drastic measures were the outgrowth of heavy pressures exerted by West Coast civilians. The first loud voice in this campaign was that of radio commentator John B. Hughes. On January 5 he insisted that all the Japanese must be removed. His cry drew immediate support from groups habitually anti-Japanese, including the California Joint Immigration Committee, the Native Sons, and the American Legion. Agricultural and marketing organizations and certain labor unions joined the chorus, and practically all the newpapers agreed that "the Japs must go."

Public officials and politicians were equally clamorous. The West Coast delegations in Congress were unanimous on the issue, while on the scene the most active official spokesmen were State Attorney General Earl Warren and Mayor Fletcher Bowron of Los Angeles. Speaking to the district attorneys and sheriffs of the state, Warren interpreted the total absence of fifth column and sabotage activity as "a studied effort" on the part of the Japanese to hold any such action until the zero hour. Bowron saw to it that all Japanese were removed from city jobs, pressed the issue of exclusion in Washington, and declaimed over the radio that the Japanese in California were "a hotbed and a nerve center for spying and sabotage." Both Warren and Bowron carried their urgings directly to DeWitt. Later both publicly expressed profound regret for their part in this agitation.

At first DeWitt asked merely for more controls on enemy aliens. On February 5 his office gave out a statement that "military judgment" called for the removal of all Japanese. Subsequently this demand was laid more categorically before the Department of Justice. It pled lack of authority and facilities for any such undertaking and lack of demonstration that removal was called for. The department declared, however, that it was not in a position to deny the military necessity alleged by DeWitt. Higher authority would have to decide.

The most simplistic explanation of the indiscriminate removal of all persons of Japanese ancestry is to blame DeWitt. Research in military records pinpoints Colonel Karl R. Bendetson as the man who drew up and defended the detailed plan. Further research suggests that he was not much more than an active and willing emissary, with the decision making centered more in Assistant Secretary of War John J. McCloy and Secretary Henry L. Stimson, with minimal resistance by Francis Biddle, the head of the Department of Justice. They could recommend, but the ultimate decision to issue Presidential Order 9066 was Franklin D. Roosevelt's. The impetus, however, for all these actions is traceable to the West Coast agitators and the groundswell of public clamor, especially in California.

On February 19, 1942, President Roosevelt took the fateful step of transferring control of enemy aliens to the War Department. Through a series of public proclamations DeWitt then ordered "voluntary" departure of Japanese from designated coastal areas, an 8:00 P.M. to 6:00 A.M. curfew and, on March 27, evacuation of all Japanese, citizens and aliens alike. Some 110,000 persons were subject to this order, two-thirds of them American citizens. The Japanese Americans of western Washington and Oregon and southern Arizona were included, but the main body to be evacuated was from California.

In an age when almost that many persons turned out for a football game and several times as many flocked to the beaches on a holiday or to the Tournament of Roses parade, it might seem that the removal could have been accomplished overnight. Actually it took from April to August. Assembly centers were improvised at racetracks and fairgrounds. Summoned to register and then to report on specified dates, the Japanese assembled at these centers. At best there was little time to wind up business affairs, dispose of property, and get ready to leave. From these makeshift quarters the evacuees were transferred to more distant sites, two on the eastern margin of California, the other eight scattered as far east as Arkansas. These were called relocation centers, but the barbed wire fences and armed guards stamped them as concentration camps. Decades later, the historical markers officially erected at the desolate Tule Lake and Manzanar sites use those inevitable words.

Without the goodwill of the administrators headed by Dillon Myer, the lot of the evacuees would have been much worse. Even so, the uprooting and the detention imposed severe psychological strain. The inescapable imputation of disloyalty and inferiority before the law was hard to bear. All felt the stigma of being sentenced to sit out the war idle and unproductive. In time some were released from the centers. Through enlistment or the draft many of the young men went off to the battlefields in Europe and later in the Pacific where they performed with extraordinary valor. Others were released to go to guaranteed jobs outside General DeWitt's proscribed area. Late in the war a few were permitted to come back to California. Most were kept in camp until after V-J Day, and the centers were not closed until January 1, 1946.

Since there was no Japanese assault on the mainland, the question of military necessity was not tested. Several of the arguments for relocation, such as the citing of sabotage in Hawaii, have been proven false. Some of the pressure groups were frank about their ulterior motives. The fundamental cause clearly lay in California's long and accumulated opposition to Orientals, quickened by considerations of economic or political advantage. The clamor and hysteria were nonetheless genuine. There was a measure of accuracy in the claim that relocation was to protect the evacuees from mob violence—certainly no compliment to the law-abiding character of the Caucasian Californians.

Most of the sympathy for the removed

Japanese came long after the fact. A few Californians at the time questioned the propriety of the removal and did what they could to ensure good treatment and provisions for their ultimate return. Their principal agency was the Fair Play Committee, headed by Galen M. Fisher. President Sproul of the University of California persuaded other colleges and universities to welcome students from the detention camps. Mere civilians, no matter how distinguished, were not in position in 1942 to challenge the asserted military necessity for removal.

That justification, on the other hand, was suspect because of the contrast of Hawaii. There, a larger number of Japanese, less Americanized than those on the mainland, were not removed. The area was at least as critical as the West Coast, but the general in charge was not a DeWitt and the community far less prone to racist extremism.

In California the Japanese were missed. At a time when production for the war effort was at a premium the retirement of these thousands of competent enterprisers and workers was unsound. To the Japanese it meant a more direct loss, which by one calculation amounted to $365 million. What scars it would leave on their regard for America could not be forecast.

There was an inescapable consequence for the constitutional system of the United States. Except for the weaker parallel of Indian removal in Andrew Jackson's day, there was no American precedent for a mass internment of aliens and citizens alike, without evidence of disloyalty and with race as the sole basis of determining who should be interned. Prior to 1942 most Americans assumed that the Constitution was a safeguard against such arbitrary treatment. Belatedly, the issue was taken to court and, about the time the war ended, there were rulings that the color of military necessity had been sufficient, but that the federal government had a limited liability for damages.

Thereby, a most unfortunate precedent of group proscription was set, a legacy of the hysteria which led to the expulsion of the Japanese Americans.

The Population Spiral

The war transferred more than 700,000 Californians into the armed services. It also brought about major changes in employment and a flood tide of migration to the state that exceeded any rate previously attained. The population movements in the gold rush and the boom of the eighties were small by comparison. That in the booming twenties was more grandiose, but the war years' increase, 1,916,000 between 1940 and 1945, was almost as large as that for the entire decade of the twenties, 2,251,000.

The tremendous increase in industrial activity required expansion of the industrial labor force. In 1939 there had been 381,000 thus employed. In 1943 almost three times as many, 1,121,200, were at work. Over the same four years the personnel employed in agriculture increased by 31,000, in utilities and transportation by 58,000, in trade by 54,000, and in government by 188,000. Thus, the aircraft and shipbuilding plants, which boosted their labor force by 462,000, were not the only elements active in increasing employment.

In many instances the workers moving into these expanding fields of employment came by a shift over from other elements in the state's economy. Bakers became riveters; gas station attendants turned welders; clerks took hold of factory tools; and so on down the line. In the overall picture the statistics show clearly where the extra workers came from. The service trades released a net total of 55,000; mining, 15,000; construction, 8,000; printing, 1,400; and automobile making, 1,300. Those were the only lines of employment reporting a net decrease, and, with a million new jobs to fill and half that many servicemen and Japanese to replace, these transfers left about 95 percent of the new jobs unfilled.

The new recruits included some young people going to work a year or two earlier than they normally would have. They included thousands of women who in peacetime would have stayed at home. Among them were a few persons who had other work but took on a war job in addition. A much larger number were new arrivals pulled in from all the outlying states by the war's requirements and the prevailing good wages. Some Mexican nationals joined the trek. The vast majority, however, were from other parts of the Union. They were a reasonably accurate cross section of America, drawn, however, more from the South and West than from the industrialized Northeast. They also were much more concentrated in the working-age bracket than had been true in the eighties or the twenties. More blacks came in this migration than had been present in California.

Even without the complications of war such an influx of new inhabitants would have created a serious housing problem. Curtailment of nonessential construction released certain materials. Highway building, for example, was practically called off for the duration. On the other hand, military priorities hampered the building program. The most effective solution was the company construction of temporary housing units as an adjunct to the war plants. On hills above Vallejo and Marin City, on the flats at Richmond, and at various locations in southern California, seried ranks of these structures took shape. Built without much benefit of architecture, intended to provide only minimum shelter, and that only for the duration, these buildings did not adorn the landscape or provide for California living at its best.

A limited amount of private dwelling construction went on, most of it held to

High-Octane Refinery of the Vintage Coinciding with
the First Appearance of Smog in Los Angeles

Los Angeles Chamber of Commerce

unpretentious small homes and to even starker prefabricated houses. Many newcomers substituted a trailer. Trailer camps blossomed as a new variety of real estate subdivision.

The added throng strained utilities—water, electricity, gas, telephone, and sewer—hard put to achieve the sudden expansion that was necessary. The same was true of public transportation. School districts in the vicinity of the war plants were confronted with a sudden enrollment jump, and the problem was complicated because at war's end the workers might all depart and the school population revert to what had been normal. The state program of equalizing school costs helped greatly, though the system of allotment on the basis of average daily attendance in the preceding year did not fit the emergency. The

answer in some instances was to erect and staff a new school. More often it was to crowd more pupils into the existing buildings and to make these schools and teachers do double duty through half-day sessions.

The problem of accommodating the newcomers involved governmental service, such as police and fire protection, garbage collection, and public health; shopping centers and the supply of groceries, drugs, clothing, and furniture; social provision, churches, theaters, public parks, and the like. In earlier growth such elements had tagged along or had seemed to come automatically as population grew. The war did not repeal the natural impulses to try to fill these needs, but shortages and priorities made it difficult, if not impossible, to do so.

A fixed impression of the period is one of

standing in line to board a crowded bus, standing in line to buy vegetables, taking a number and waiting one's turn at the meat counter, or queueing up at Christmas time to buy a box of candy. A penalty for California's very rapid growth was that shortages were more acute, the ration point system therefore subjected to more strain, and its abuses more of a temptation than in more normal parts of the country.

One element of shortage and rationing came home to California with special force. In the more compact eastern communities, where public transportation was convenient and cheap and the private automobile something of a luxury, gasoline rationing was just an incident. The average Californian, however, was as dependent on his car as an Eskimo on his snowshoes. The full gasoline tank was a more compelling symbol than the full dinner pail had ever been, and to qualify for a B ration book was an achievement supreme.

Streets and parking lots had good business hour patronage, but the open highways were strangely deserted. The fact was that pleasure driving all but disappeared. To avoid being grounded most people had to confine their driving to business and essential shopping.

Another respect in which California was unusual was in its presumed exposure to attack. At continent's end and with its population massed near the coast, it seemed in position to catch the first blows of a Japanese assault on the mainland. Furthermore, its war plants and military installations seemed to set it up as a target worth striking. Accordingly, there was concern.

California was a flourishing area for civilian defense. Householders laid in primitive fire fighting equipment—ladders, axes, and sand. Enrolled as air raid wardens, they were issued stirrup pumps, helmets, armbands, and stickers for their cars. They organized telephone chains to spread warnings, and wardens stood watches at the communications centers. Perhaps more usefully, many citizens worked as airplane spotters. The defense authorities designated bomb shelters, decreed blackouts, and sounded several alerts.

Barrage balloons, radar emplacements, searchlights, and antiaircraft batteries provided the similitude of war. On one occasion, which went down in history as the "Battle of Los Angeles," the guns were actually unlimbered. Whether the target was a cloud, an escaped balloon, successive shell bursts, a strayed plane, or enemy aircraft was never announced. Rumors quickly encompassed all conceivable explanations, and the authorities did not bother to clear up the mystery. Seemingly the "battle" involved warlike exercise and no casualties. In retrospect civilian defense seems to have been waste motion, though perhaps worthwhile as a morale builder.

The more solid achievement of California's war effort was the production of the sinews of war. In these accomplishments California could take real pride. In them, too, very substantial profits were reaped. During the war years their annual income advanced from a gross of just over $5 billion to almost $13 billion, while the holdings in liquid assets increased from $4.5 billion to $15.25 billion. Even with allowance for inflation, estimated at 30 percent, this was a remarkable prospering. Although proprietors and labor each had a threefold increase in cash income, it was not shared evenly. White-collar workers lagged behind, farmers ran ahead of everyone else in the gains in cash income, and many industrialists had capital gains not yet converted into cash. The most striking feature was that California had built a complex and high-powered economic machine which in time of war, at least, could produce at a prodigious rate.

CHAPTER 27

Construction Detail, University of California,
Riverside

Ansel Adams, Fiat Lux

What will happen when California is filled by fifty millions of people, and its valuation is five times what it is now, and the wealth will be so great that you will find it difficult to know what to do with it? The day will, after all, have only twenty-four hours. Each man will have only one mouth, one pair of ears, and one pair of eyes. There will be more people—as many perhaps as the country can support—and the real question will be not about making more wealth or having more people, but whether the people will then be happier or better.

Lord James Bryce
in a speech at Berkeley in 1909

A Touch
of Midas

Elements of Growth

In the immediate postwar years the California economy stumbled slightly because of shortages in various lines of merchandise, building materials, and film for the moviemakers. Nationwide there was a similar hesitation before the readjustment to peacetime pursuits was achieved. Then followed a long stretch of prosperity, occasionally slacking off slightly but generally continuing strong for two decades and more. In this greatest of American prosperities California surpassed the national average.

Throughout that long period the state's population increased at a formidable rate. Newcomers poured in from every state in the union but particularly from Texas, Illinois, and New York. They came from the Deep South and from foreign lands, notably Mexico and Canada. Part of the migration consisted of elderly people, some of whom would be active. Most of the newcomers were young, capable, and immediate additions to the work force. They brought children and also contributed to an explosion of babies, ultimately a second wave of workers and immediately an addition to the roster of consumers. With migration as the main source, population growth averaged more than 500,000 a year for 25 years.

The tourist business grew correspondingly with added attractions, such as Disneyland and Hearst's Castle. By the sixties the State Chamber of Commerce listed it third in dollar volume.

Both public and private construction boomed. Industry also faced the challenge to retool and refit. Kaiser Steel enlarged its mill. As wartime models became obsolete, aircraft companies changed to more advanced designs for the civilian market.

The railroads reequipped. In the 1930s the Southern Pacific had used articulated streamliners—the Daylights and the Lark—between San Francisco and Los Angeles. The Santa Fe had a streamliner on the San Joaquin Valley run and the Chief and El Capitan to Chicago, to which it added the diesel-powered Super Chief in 1937. The Union Pacific was pioneering even more venturesomely with the diesel-powered City of San Francisco and City of Los Angeles from Chicago. By the time of the war all the railroads were turning to diesels for freight hauling and for switching.

In the postwar era the trend continued. The Santa Fe converted practically all its operations to streamliners and diesels; the Union Pacific moved in the same direction. The Southern Pacific put new Daylights on the San Joaquin and Cascade runs and shiny new trains on the Golden State and Sunset routes to Chicago and New Orleans. The Western Pacific, in cooperation with eastern affiliates, launched the California Zephyr on the Feather River—Moffat Tunnel route to Chicago. Even the most casual observer could see that California railroading had entered a new day.

With diesels the railroads could lay off the servicing crews at every second or third division point. On the mountain runs, whereas every helper steam locomotive had to have its own engineer and fireman, a set of diesels operated from one control and required only one crew. The unions insisted that a fireman or substitute engineer accompany every engineer. The unions sought to prevent train lengthening and other economizing in labor costs, yet step by step a number of such changes were made.

For a brief time railroading was at its pinnacle of convenience and comfort, thanks to smooth diesel power and air-conditioned cars. The companies sought business, using their boxcars as rolling billboards to advertise their crack passenger trains. In the sixties this part of

Southern Pacific Freight, Tehachapi Loop

Southern Pacific Railroad

railroading ran into its private depression. Patronage shifted to the airlines. The railroads began to cut back on service and to withdraw these trains as rapidly as possible. The Southern Pacific in particular used every device to discourage anyone from boading a train. The Post Office cancelled the mail contracts and, by the centennial of the Pacific Railroad, passengers were almost as ghostly as the Irish paddies and the Chinese who long ago had laid and joined the rails.

Meanwhile the railroads boosted their freight business. They put better springs and shock absorbers on boxcars and could promise dead freight a gentler ride. They replaced the old iced cars with mechanically cooled cars. They offered special cars for special cargoes such as the many tiered automobile carriers and the flatcars for piggyback or containerized freight. With vast sorting yards they speeded up the assembling of trains. They advertised faster freight schedules and kept

track of every boxcar by computer. The pride of the Santa Fe was a big-hopper ore train carrying coal by the trainload from Raton to the steel mill at Fontana.

By the late sixties Californians owned and relied on 10 million autos but had very little part in their manufacture. Similarly Californians were avid airplane passengers. The San Francisco–Los Angeles route was said to be the world's most traveled. But no major airline was based in California.

Military Procurement Continues

California's peacetime growth turned out not to be so peaceful after all. Some Americans distrusted Russia even in the midst of the defense of Stalingrad. After 1945, challenged by the Soviets on many fronts, the United States moved to stiffen its defenses, at first with the idea of containing the Soviet Union and then of intimidating her through capacity to retaliate in greater force.

The rivalry escalated after 1949 when the Russians exploded an atomic bomb. In 1950, when Chinese Communists poured into Korea, the United States on behalf of the United Nations took up the fighting. In 1957 Russia scored with Sputnik, whereupon the United States redoubled its commitment to rocket launching and missile development.

The emergency suggested a new dedication to mathematics and science. Four years later President John F. Kennedy promised that the United States would put a man on the moon by 1970, a feat duly accomplished on July 20, 1969, at a quoted cost of $24 billion. Meanwhile, the United States embarked on undeclared war in Vietnam in 1964. This war grew and intensified, rose in costs to about $80 billion a year, became the United States' most unpopular war, but seemingly defied all efforts at resolution.

American involvement in the Cold War, the hot wars in Korea and Vietnam, and the intensely competitive space race had momentous repercussions on the California economy. Adversely it resulted in a larger siphoning of income, excise, and special tax payments to the federal government and in required expenditures by California agencies in support of war-related activities. Some of the outlay for the buildup of the colleges and universities, for example, was to equip them to support the kinds of teaching and research that would contribute to the military and space efforts. Nevertheless, the reverse flow of money and credits to California was much greater. For military and space procurement and for development and delivery of what would be needed in these interrelated endeavors, the federal government looked particularly to this state. California led in the dollar value of military and space contracts.

Through its schools, particularly the University of California and California Institute of Technology, the state participated in contracted research on nuclear energy, rocket fuel, guidance systems, remote controls, navigation in space, problems of weightlessness, biological hazards and protections, improved missile launchers and warheads, methods of detection and interception, and many other problems in basic or applied science. Through these schools or the Rand Corporation came contracts to measure the effectiveness of a propaganda device, the cost of achieving a political result, or the methods best calculated to ensure the fall of a particular ruling faction.

California firms received contracts to produce planes and helicopters for use in Korea and Vietnam, napalm for the fire bombings in Vietnam, first- and second-stage boosters for spaceflights, landing gear for the moonflight, control systems for satellites, camera controls for the fly-by of Mars, and a good fraction of the communications equipment for the first landing on the moon.

Vandenberg Air Force Base was the launching pad for many unmanned satellites and space probes. More prosaically Port Chicago was the principal loading point for munitions for the Korean and Vietnamese wars. For these later wars in the Pacific, California was a staging area, through San Francisco Bay, Port Hueneme, Los Angeles, San Diego, and the California airfields.

That California, the great vacationland, the home of orange groves and make-believe, of Sinclair's Epic and the Townsend Plan, should lead in the most sophisticated military hardware and the greatest extrapolation of scientific technology was incongruous. The industrial might of the Northeast dwarfed the West Coast. But the state's new industries, with the cooperation of the universities, moved readily to supersonic craft and the problems of outer space.

Still First in Agriculture

Urban and industrial expansion relentlessly challenged agriculture's hold on much of the best land in the state. Sometimes it was by condemnation of a wide swath for a freeway or by polluting the air and thus foreclosing successful crop production. More often it was by urban sprawl, the proliferation of housing tracts, airport runways, industrial sites, and new school campuses.

In 1969 almost a square mile of prime cropland west of Bakersfield was dedicated to the new state college. The Santa Clara Valley, once 200 square miles of prune, peach, and pear orchards, soon was so decimated by the subdividers that not a single square mile remained intact. In San Diego County avocado groves proved a lodestone for housing developers well aware of the avocado's need for good soil, level or slightly rolling land, and benign climate. In Orange County the assaults on farmland were so relentless that the name ceased to fit. And Los Angeles, for many years the nation's number one farm county, was violated to such an extent that it barely held on in the first ten.

Year by year land became too valuable to farm. Each year the number of active farmers dropped, as did the number of farms and farmworkers. The cost of implements and supplies rose more rapidly than farm prices. Nevertheless, over these years the state's farmers so adjusted their methods that they substantially increased production. They kept California first in agriculture with annual output approaching $5 billion.

Redeployment was one necessary tactic. Poinsettia growing had to retreat from Los Angeles to new and larger fields near San Diego. Major milk producers in the San Fernando Valley and Norwalk had to move out. Orange growers could not relocate so readily. In most instances they had to go to poorer soils and greater exposure to frost, yet some were able to compensate with larger acreage which promised greater efficiency. The wise farmer protected himself with a soil test, a report on the microclimate, and expert advice on the most suitable planting.

Scientists also cooperated with mechanization. To meet the requirements of the tomato picking machine they developed a tomato with slightly tougher skin and all ripening at once. Giant lettuce pickers moved through the field with rubber hands that determined by feel whether a head should be picked. The long dry summer season that favored the California wheat harvests a century ago similarly favored cotton picking by machine, the California way, and a major reason why cotton rose to be the most valuable field crop. Mechanization extended to many operations once done by hoe or pruning shears. Packing sheds were now equipped with electronic fruit sorters and automatic box movers. Because of such advances the number of year-round workers on the farms dropped from 100,000 in 1955 to 92,000 in 1965, though over that same period production doubled.

By the sixties the Central Valley water project provided for considerably more irrigation in the upper San Joaquin Valley. Funded originally with a bond authorization of $170 million, the project moved slowly until the federal government became a participant. By the end of the sixties $1 billion had been invested, resulting in additional irrigated farming in Tulare, Fresno, and Kern counties. Elsewhere irrigation was extended, as in the upper Salinas Valley by Nacimiento Dam and in Santa Barbara County by the Cachuma project.

Vineyardists lost to industry some of their proven acreage in Napa, Sonoma, Livermore, Santa Clara, and Los Angeles counties. Agricultural zoning gave a tax saving that protected some vineyards. Scientists, principally

Friant-Kern Canal

B. G. Glaha, Bureau of Reclamation

at the University of California at Davis, scouted for new sites with soil and climate needed for fine wine grapes, developed promising new varieties, and devised more efficient ways of making wine.

The long growing season and the long dry season plus irrigation made much of the state one great hothouse or assembly line over which moved almost the entire commercial supply of pears, plums, prunes, garlic, grapes, apricots, lemons, lettuce, carrots, asparagus, dates, walnuts, and a substantial fraction of many other foods. California held the lead in beef, tomatoes, sugarbeets, strawberries and turkeys, second place only to Texas in cotton, and third to Wisconsin and New York in milk. The state's agriculture looked to more than 24 million California customers and selectively to another 200 million across the nation. The production process was a marvel, the more so because it had emerged in a state with relatively few farmers and very few farm-minded people.

Diversified Industry

From midway in World War II, Californians were told that their economy was so heavily weighted to military purchasing that if peace were to break out the state would be a shambles. The involvement was real. At its peak in the early sixties, with NASA contracts piled on the Pentagon's, southern California had 40 percent of its manufacturing workers so employed and traced about that same fraction of its personal income to military and space work.

With the passage of time panic over the pending cutback proved difficult to sustain. There was skepticism that peace would terminate the federal programs and, besides, much of the state's economy was not visibly aimed at Vietnam or the moon. Agriculture, the tourist trade, the oil companies, and the construction industry had independent justification. Even in transportation equipment and electrical machinery, which bracketed most of the military and space projects, the companies engaged had a substantial civilian business or the potential to acquire it.

The postwar decades saw several declines. Monterey's Cannery Row and the sardine fishery were virtually wiped out by disappearance of the sardines. The Hollywood movie industry dropped from its immediate postwar peak at the box office. Film making spread to France, Italy, Mexico and elsewhere. But Hollywood rallied and continued as the leader in the industry, and it shared with New York the leadership in television production.

Other industries flourished. Food processing, for instance, rose proportionately to the increase in farm output. Principal elements included large-scale canning and quick freezing of fruits and vegetables, wine making, and dehydrating and packing raisins, prunes, figs, dates, and apricots. In all these industries California led the nation. Its meat companies converted animals shipped in and the endproduct of its massive feedlots into cuts for the state market. Most of the milk produced in the state was consumed fresh, but a substantial part was condensed or powdered or used in ice cream and cheese making. Of the cotton raised a much smaller fraction was processed in the state; a third or more was compressed and shipped to Japan.

A miscellany of other manufacturing flourished with products as diverse as tires, buses, trailers, small boats, plastics, toys, drugs, furniture, and leisure wear. To these may be added the roll-out of planes, radios, television sets, tapedecks, record players, computing and copying machines, and many other such commodities. California acquired branch offices of many national or international firms in banking, investment, insurance, publishing, and merchandising.

The overall trend was to larger and fewer companies. Giants such as Standard Oil of California simply grew bigger. Or growth was by merger, North American acquiring Rockwell, Security First National Bank taking in Pacific, and Times Mirror annexing a map company, a book bindery, a timber company, and a land company. Signal and Litton pursued the popular route of the conglomerates.

Amalgamations could have the effect of making a major California company subordinate to out-of-state management and control, as happened to Douglas in the merger with McDonnell. Many other big businesses moved into the state, among them Standard Oil of New Jersey as Humble Oil, Standard of Ohio as American Oil, and Phillips 66, Xerox, and IBM. With the federal government relaxing its objections to mergers and acquisitions, the trend nationally and in California was increasingly toward bigger business. This trend ran strong both in urban and rural California.

Mass Production of Housing

The construction industry, dormant during the war, set new records. In addition to replacements, over the next 25 years housing would be needed for an additional 13 million Californians. The answer was single-family residences, alone or in tracts; apartments, small, medium, and high rise; rentals, condominiums, and separate ownership. Occasionally it was with cash on the escrow line, but primarily with mortgages and time payments.

The first starts were small apartments and

Tract Housing, Daly City

single-family dwellings on city lots left over from earlier promotions. Pent up and spiraling demand suggested mass production. That is the way most of the postwar housing construction arose, most flamboyantly in tract housing. Examples had been set in Los Angeles' Westchester district and in the Levittowns of New Jersey and Long Island.

In the boom of the eighties the promoters did little more than flag the corners of the lots. By the twenties the practice was to survey, lay out streets, and even pave and bring in utilities. The postwar tract developers did much more. Acquiring a sizable piece of raw or agricultural land, they marked it off, put in improvements, and erected a house on every lot. To the prospective purchaser they offered immediate occupancy, the house complete even to the financing.

Builders discovered that tract housing saves substantially on costs, particularly of labor. In its ultimate form the assembly line is brought to the site. Advance crews pave the streets and put in utility lines, a machine quickly digs the foundation trenches, other crews pour the concrete, raise the precut and perhaps prefabricated frame, shingle the roof, plaster, hang doors and windows, paint, and clean up. Selling of the first houses can be in full swing while the construction crews are approaching other parts of the tract.

Some tracts were laid out on a conventional grid of streets. Others used the curved line and a maze of streets out of reach of through traffic. Some tracts endlessly repeated one house plan; others used two or more plans and broke the monotony by varying placement and ornamentation. The habit of the tract house is to sidle close to its neighbors. When tract adjoins tract, as they characteristically do, this compactness seems appropriate. But where a tract stands apart from any other habitations, as occurs south of Laguna, on the road to Castaic, and on the road to Palmdale, the crowding seems incongruous.

Tract housing has its critics, as in Malvina Reynolds' song, "Ticky-Tacky Houses," inspired by the view from the Bayshore Freeway south of San Francisco. Examined more closely, the tract house is seen to be true to the central precept of individual ownership, most especially in the fenced-in back yards giving at least the illusion of privacy.

Initially tract housing was the major element in the urban sprawl predicted to blanket from San Diego to San Bernardino and Santa Barbara and from San Jose to Santa Rosa and Sacramento. It was particularly in evidence in San Diego, Orange County, Lakewood, Downey, Torrance, Hawthorne, south of Los Angeles, and all across San Fernando Valley. It proliferated in Santa Clara County, the East Bay and North Bay, and Sacramento. In fact, it became commonplace roundabout every California city.

The trailer park initially was a port of call for those who wanted to be footloose to follow the seasons or to move on whim. Mobile homes are used, as can be seen at the beaches and at mountain and desert resorts, but the new feature was the trailer home that took root and sprouted ramada, patio, and even a small garden. It amounts to an individually owned residence but on leased ground.

Apartment building advanced at a more rapid rate and by the sixties accounted for more than half of the new units. The start was with two- or three-story structures occupying a single or double lot, some on virgin ground but many owing their existence to bungalow or mansion clearance. In West Hollywood, apartment projects repeatedly threatened an architectural treasure, the Dodge House by Irving Gill. Aroused admirers stayed the wrecking crew but only temporarily. In 1970 Dodge House was demolished to be replaced by the Dodge House Apartments. In many a residential area the apartment invasion was enough to change the character of an entire neighborhood.

More impressive were the complexes that occupy the equivalent of several city blocks, the units generously spaced and with a park-like environment made part of the development. Often the builder was content with two-story design and the trees could outreach the roofs. Other variations include the ten-story Park La Brea Towers in Los Angeles, convenient to the Farmers' Market, the Miracle Mile stores, the Tar Pits, and the Los Angeles Museum of Art. Considerably higher apartment complexes have risen in San Francisco, in Inner City Los Angeles where Bunker Hill once stood, and lining Wilshire Boulevard to the west.

To many of these multiple-unit residences participatory co-ownership was applied. Condominiums, which are bought rather than leased, make possible a more predictable set of residents. Maintenance and services are centralized, and tax savings may result. The condominium principle was also applied in many of the more elaborate tract developments with varying restrictions to pets, children, age, and marital status. They feature communal facilities such as lawns, swimming pool, hobby rooms, a restaurant, shops, and access to a golf course. They range up to self-contained communities, some of them actually unincorporated towns as a further tax shelter.

Notwithstanding these economies many Californians of the postwar epoch made substantial investments in individually constructed residences. None is as grandiose as Hearst's Castle or the mansions of Nob Hill, the Peninsula, Oak Knoll, or early Bel Air. Many are distinguishable from the better tract houses mainly in the higher cost per foot. A great many lend themselves to comfortable living, and a sprinkling are triumphs in design to fit a particular site and to suit a given family.

Commercial and Industrial Building

Queues of customers at stores and theaters in the summer of 1945 demonstrated the state's need for commercial construction. New suburban shopping centers sprang up facing existing streets in Beverly Hills, Westchester, and Crenshaw in the Los Angeles area, and elsewhere. The preferred pattern made the center an island to itself, near an artery but not right on it, with inviting turnoff and accommodation for the car as well as the customer. The typical center offered food, drink, clothing, barbering and beauty applications, cleaning and laundry, appliances, furniture, and all other vital needs. The more ambitious boasted major department stores. In Los Angeles the bulk of the trade shifted from downtown to the satellites. Smaller cities felt similar pull; Santa Barbara shared its business with Montecito on the east and two new centers to the west. Small towns also were affected, as by the so-called Five Cities center south of Pismo Beach.

The satellite shopping centers accelerated urban sprawl. So popular did they become that tract developers increasingly included them in their plans. They competed so heavily with the older shopping districts that renovation at the city cores appeared the only way to survive. Not every city attempted it; not every effort succeeded. The Fresno Mall is a showplace; that of Hillsdale draws visitors. Santa Monica's two efforts have been criticized as uninspired.

The new building in San Francisco was primarily for financial institutions, law and corporate offices, and hotels. In Los Angeles, banks, oil companies, and office buildings dominated the scene together with the cluster of new city, county, state, and federal buildings. The urban renewal constructions included a few display performances in architectural design and occasionally a notable restoration, as of the unique Bradbury Building in Los Angeles. Downtown survived but without slowing the satellite cash registers.

Postwar California added new hotels but accommodations many times more numerous in the motels that festooned every highway. Most of this growth was in chains with repetitive plans and services at scores of locations throughout the state. The larger looked more and more like hotels and did not hesitate to invade the inner city, as for instance the Jack Tar and Del Webb's in San Francisco. The motels en masse represent a tremendous investment and a major layout in construction.

Industrial construction also was noteworthy. Some of it was massive, as in the nuclear power plants at San Onofre, Elk Grove, and Diablo Canyon. Most were smaller buildings, laboratories, workshops, and computer housings for the production of electronic, missile, or space-age devices. Los Angeles International Airport is ringed with hundreds of such plants. Other locations are San Diego, Orange County, Pasadena, San Fernando Valley, Livermore, and Sacramento, and along "Silicon Valley" near Palo Alto, an unforeseen distribution of industry.

Public Building

The public construction needs of the postwar period were symbolized by the Governor's Mansion, combustible, obsolete, and at a noisy intersection, and the State Capitol, much in need of repair. By 1975 a new mansion was ready on the American River north of Sacramento and by 1980 $80 million had been authorized and spent for strengthening the Capitol to withstand earthquakes and refurbishing it all the way to its gold dome.

More pressing were some of the other

needs, represented by new office buildings along Capitol Mall and in San Francisco, Los Angeles, and elsewhere; new courthouses and branch courthouses, as in Long Beach, Santa Monica, Van Nuys, and Pomona; and new correctional institutions in Vacaville, Soledad, and San Luis Obispo. The federal and local government also had extensive building programs.

Much more money went into school construction. The University of California entered the postwar period with projects totalling $170 million. Existing campuses expected larger enrollments and new campuses were to be opened at Santa Cruz, Irvine, and San Diego. The university built dormitories and parking structures to be paid for by the fees charged. Pushed to charge tuition, the regents raised the "incidental fee," which financed the building of student unions and recreational facilities. Some new building was endowed or federally financed. The state paid for education-oriented buildings. Statewide the university plant is mostly postwar construction with much of it now in disrepair.

The state university system, meanwhile, grew from six colleges to 21 much larger institutions, necessitating another impressive building program. Community colleges new and old participated, and so did the hundreds of school districts, trebling their classroom capacity. This new construction could have accommodated the entire school enrollment of any state in the union except New York.

Water Projects

After the war work resumed on the Central Valley project. Shasta Dam and Friant Dam were completed as well as the Friant Canal to Bakersfield and a dam on the Kern. With Shasta power at Tracy, water could be pumped to flow "uphill" to Mendota.

A severe drought in 1947–48 catalyzed Santa Barbara to dam the Santa Ynez at Cachuma and tunnel through the unstable mountain range to fill its reservoirs. Other communities, such as La Canada and Flintridge, were almost out of water. The towns and cities organized earlier continued construction of the Metropolitan Aqueduct from the Colorado.

As successor to the Spanish pueblo Los Angeles shored up its claim to paramount right as needed to the water of the Los Angeles River and its drainage and storage basins. A suit enjoining upstream towns, persons, and corporations, after many years of litigation, was decided by the California Supreme Court in 1975 supportively of this water right.

Though eligible for Colorado River water through the Metropolitan Aqueduct, Los Angeles looked again to Owens Valley and the Mono Basin to the north. Without fanfare it proceeded with a second aqueduct paralleling Mulholland's 1913 tube which came into operation in 1970. Conservationists protested the damage to Mono Lake, and Inyo County brought suit which succeeded to the extent of a court ruling that the valley water users had prior right to ground water, which could reduce the city's water appropriation by about an eighth.

Meanwhile, state water engineers foresaw a time when the needs of the arid south would exceed the yield from local rainfall and streams. A science writer proposed towing icebergs from the Antarctic to the lee of Catalina Island and ladling out the melt. Diversions from the Snake or the Columbia were suggested. More conservatively the engineers centered on the surplus water in the Feather and the Eel. They drafted the $12 billion California Water Project, the gist of which was to impound the waters of these two rivers and move the surplus to the parched upper San Joaquin Valley and part of it through the

Shasta Dam

Bureau of Reclamation

mountains to thirsty southern California.

On becoming governor in 1959, Edmund G. (Pat) Brown put this project at the head of his agenda, persuaded the legislature to endorse it, and urged the people to authorize the first installment, a $1.75 billion program calculated to meet the needs through the 1980s. On his urging, the voters approved in 1960.

Construction went forward on a record high earthfill dam (735 feet) at Oroville on the Feather, a mammoth pumping plant at the Delta, an aqueduct skirting the western San Joaquin where most of this water was put to use, another huge pumping plant to a tunnel and more aqueducts through the mountains and on south of the Tehachapi.

The Freeway Explosion

On December 30, 1940, Mayor Fletcher Bowron of Los Angeles officially opened the Arroyo Seco Parkway, more commonly known as the Pasadena Freeway, California's first. This 8.9 mile, six-lane divided roadway had evolved from suggestions of an access road to picnic grounds in Arroyo Seco Park. As an artery the road needed approval by the cities of Pasadena, South Pasadena, and Los Angeles, not to mention the businessmen of Highland Park. It needed designation as part of the state highway system and state participation. With the right of way transferred from the park and free fill obtained from the flood control work in progress in the Arroyo, the construction still cost $560,000 a mile, and that in depression dollars.

As Marshall Goodwin, the chief authority on this and all California freeways has pointed out, by modern standards the Pasadena Freeway was too narrow, too sharply curved, insufficiently banked, deficient in turnouts, too abrupt in its entrances and exits, and too

stingy in its center divider. But thanks to studies made by the Automobile Club of Southern California, the Los Angeles city engineer, and the state highway engineer, there was awareness of the central concept in Germany's autobahns and the parkways being developed in New York, Connecticut, and Pennsylvania. All cross traffic was eliminated, which is the essence of a freeway. Traffic began to flow at the speed for which this freeway was designed—45 miles an hour, at the time the posted state speed limit.

The war came and so did a moratorium on nonmilitary projects. The Pasadena Freeway was a thrill and a boon to motorists. It whetted the appetite for more roadways free of cross traffic and left-hand turns. It also served as a laboratory for improving design. Accidents so trivial as a flat tire or running out of gas brought home the need for turnouts. Bottlenecks at stop-signed exits underlined the advisability of merging in motion. Speeders who jumped the divider into oncoming traffic illustrated the wisdom of more width or deterrence in the divider.

In 1911 the legislature had entrusted supervision of the highway program to the Highway Commission. Through the fifties and sixties Senator Randolph Collier of Siskiyou, long-time chairman of the Senate Committee on Transportation, sedulously protected the gas tax against raids and the Highway Commission against challenges to its authority to determine where and how and what freeways should be built. In administering the program the commission has been more autonomous than the regents of the university. In 1923 the legislature had endowed the highway program by initiating the gas tax, thus providing an allocated income which by the late sixties amounted to $800 million a year, "bubbling up," as one critic put it, from the "sacrosanct fountain" of the gas tax.

In 1946, when the number of licensed cars

had risen to 3 million, the Highway Commission could point to 14,000 miles of highways in use, some of them prodigiously difficult in construction, for instance the Feather River Canyon route and the coast road from Carmel to San Simeon. Because both maintenance and construction were in arrears, the commission asked for more money. The legislature in 1947 voted the Collier-Burns Act, raising the gas tax, revising the formula for sharing with counties, accepting state responsibility for highway construction through cities, and authorizing a statewide freeway and expressway system. This measure was the enabling act for freeway construction.

Other modifications followed, including partial correction of a sectional inequity under which for many years southern California motorists paid well over half the tax but well over half the construction was in northern California. But the same guiding principles continued—financing through the gas tax rather than by bonding, decision-making by the Highway Commission rather than by the more political legislature, emphasis on freeways, and freeways that would be free rather than toll roads. Senator Collier is chiefly credited with holding California to this line.

In the fifties and sixties the freeway builders addressed themselves first of all to long distance driving and the problem of easing, speeding, and making it safer. Where traffic snarled or slowed on the great arteries, such as Highways 99 and 101, a section of multilane divided freeway was built. The tortuous Ridge Route was one such candidate. The Grapevine ascent was widened and straightened and an entirely new route was opened replacing the twisting ridge. In the late sixties what seemed to be an almost perfect divided highway from Lebec to Gorman was replaced by a wider and slightly faster freeway. As an added dividend the grading at the summit finally got rid of the "Impeach Earl Warren" billboard

placed there by his detractors shortly after he wrote the Supreme Court ruling in *Brown vs. Board of Education.*

Bypassing of cities was another standard device. On 101, Ventura, which had been an aggravating bottleneck, was avoided by swerving the freeway a little farther to the south. San Luis Obispo was negotiated by a depressed freeway with several overpasses. The freeway circled San Jose, and the Bay Shore section on toward San Francisco was one long bypass of the Peninsula cities. Bypasses were thrown around Santa Maria, Salinas, Carpinteria, and King City, in approximately that order, and even around so small a community as Buelton. Some of these communities must miss the revenue that once came from gas, lunch, and coffee breaks. The dire prediction of doom for Buelton, fictionalized in Eugene Burdick's *The Ninth Wave,* did not come to pass, perhaps because the novelist underestimated the loyalty to split pea soup.

In certain localities the freeway planners have been rebuffed. The Monterey-Carmel community vigorously protested a plan to cut through the scene they treasure and push on to Hearst's Castle. To date this opposition prevails. For decades Santa Barbara and the Highway Commission remained at loggerheads over whether streets or freeway should go underground where State Street and 101 intersect. Whichever did would plunge slightly below sea level, and neither side had perfect confidence in pumps and drains. Therefore, the motorist on 101 encounters in rapid succession four grade crossings with traffic lights, cross traffic, and left turns. Once these are negotiated, the southbound driver can proceed without another such interference all the way to the state line at Blythe.

Conservationists have objected strenuously to proposals for a freeway through the redwoods, additional routes across the Sierra, and any freeway that would disfigure the beach or waterfront or the mountains from Santa Monica to Point Magu. Another school of conservationists regrets the retirement of a wide swath of agricultural land for the full length of 99 through the Central Valley. The freeway program encounters more spirited resistance and astronomical expense when it penetrates urban areas. The citizens of Beverly Hills want no freeway invasion. If it must come, they want it underground and with no exits or entrances.

Entering urban areas, the freeway builders understandably found their problems compounded. Acquiring right of way can be extremely expensive, and all the country problems were complicated by the mass of urbanites crowding onto the freeway just to go to work or to shop or to a ball game. The urban sections of the freeway system are by all odds the most heavily traveled. They are the samples by which the freeways are most often judged, which is not quite fair. To be sure of being able to cruise along at the speed limit (70 miles an hour until 1975) on any of the freeways in metropolitan Los Angeles, a motorist had to choose carefully the day and the hour. For any stretch of 5, or 101 between Santa Barbara and San Jose, or 99 between San Fernando and Stockton, that condition did not apply.

The federal government belatedly plunged into the interstate phase of freeway construction. To its largess must be credited, for example, the magnificent divided freeway east from Barstow, bypassing Amboy, Bagdad, Cadiz, and Needles, all the way to the Colorado River. In the main, the state gas tax produced California's network of freeways which are the most visible, pervasive, and massive monument raised in the great postwar building boom.

Growth and the GSP

Toward the end of the sixties California reached a plateau where its Gross State Product approximated $100 billion a year. On a per capita basis that surpassed the average in the most prosperous nation in the world. The magnitude may be better grasped by thinking of this state, in its economy, as a nation. Its Gross "National" Product in 1970 would have weighed in at sixth in the Free World, exceeded only by Russia, Great Britain, West Germany, France, Japan, and the rest of the United States. California had grown to the dimensions of a nation more populous than Canada, an area equal to that of eight or ten of the original 13 states, and an economy more productive than that of any nation on the Asian, African, or American continents and of most of the nations of Europe.

CHAPTER 28

California Supreme Court, 1972. Standing: Justices Burke, Tobriner, Mosk, Sullivan.
Seated: Justices McComb, Chief Justice Wright, Peters.

1942 to 1966

"What," James Reston asked me, "does California have to give to the nation?"

Well, I said, for one thing it offers the example of a large number of people who have scrapped the party system in its orthodox American form, and have got along fairly well nevertheless.

Gladwin Hill
Dancing Bear (1968)

Issues
and Politics

At the earlier peaks of attention to politics and government, at the time of the first and second constitutional conventions and the Lincoln-Roosevelt reform drive, the problems calling for solution were state or local. With the Great Depression, Sinclair suggested a state-level response but the real effort was by the national government. During World War II state politics to great extent were subdued and it was the national government that exercised extraordinary powers. In the postwar years, as was made evident in taxation and in decisions to go to war in Korea, to send men to the moon, and to go to war in Vietnam, the national government was again in the ascendant.

Beginning a bit earlier, California voters showed a split personality. In presidential years they voted Democratic but in gubernatorial years Republican. That swaying back and forth led pundit Gladwin Hill to call the state the "Dancing Bear." The reformers of 1911 had downgraded party labels and loyalty. Issues changed rapidly and so did the roster of registered voters. Cross-filing and candidate shifts from one party to another weakened party discipline. Rolph, Sinclair, Merriam, Olson, and FDR for that matter, had trouble sailing these seas. Earl Warren was the first to combine a technique and a personality that resulted in their mastery.

Earl Warren

A native of Los Angeles and a graduate of the University of California School of Law, Warren drew attention as a vigorous law-enforcing district attorney of Alameda County. When the engineer of the ship *Port Lobos* died after a beating by thugs, Warren prosecuted the labor officers responsible and won convictions for second-degree murder.

Earl Warren
UCLA Library

He also was active in the Republican party and was state chairman in 1934.

On that basis Warren ran for state attorney general in 1938, cross-filed, and won the Democratic as well as the Republican nomination. Coming into office with the aura of rising above party, and applying the merit system, he chose as his chief assistant a Democrat. One of his first actions was to prosecute a county judge recently appointed by Merriam and found guilty of bribe taking. In person Warren headed the process servers on Tony Carnero at his gambling ship outside the three-mile limit in Santa Monica Bay. Early in 1942, along with Mayor Fletcher Bowron of Los Angeles, he argued vehemently that all Japanese Americans be removed.

Efficient and popular for his stands against corruption, crime, and the Japanese, and blessed with a nonpartisan image, Warren loomed as a formidable challenger against Olson in 1947. Again Warren cross-filed while on principle Olson did not. That gave Warren a headstart in cultivating Democratic votes. Leaving nothing to chance, he retained public relations expert Clem Whitaker to manage his campaign. Whitaker claimed that he taught Warren to smile. More important, he insisted on a Warren-for-Governor campaign separate and distinct from the Republican party ticket and stress on the good citizenship of voting for the best qualified candidate irrespective of party. Whitaker found a number of prominent citizens willing to announce as "Democrats for Warren." The end result was that Warren came into office with what appeared to be a bipartisan mandate.

The California that Warren began governing in 1943 was bustling with war industries and employment close to its peak. Because the war imposed a shutdown on several activities that stood high in state budgets, the state could economize. Warren proposed and achieved lower taxes and at the same time built a reserve for postwar catch-up on building needs.

All Californians applauded that good housekeeping. Democrats took it in stride that his keynote address at the Republican national convention in 1944 was stridently partisan and that in 1945 he named a comparative unknown, William Knowland, son of his champion, publisher Joseph Knowland, to a vacancy in the United States Senate.

Warren's proposal for employee-employer financed medical insurance—in modern parlance Medicare—stirred up bipartisan opposition. The legislature blocked the program, and in 1945 Whitaker and Baxter turned against him to manage the California Medical Association's campaign to defeat an initiative for, as they called it, socialized medicine. The voters, however, recognized rectitude, efficiency, and commitment to the best interests of Califor-

nians. In 1946 they reelected Warren in the primaries, which no governor ever achieved before or since.

In 1948 Warren headed the delegation to the Republican national convention and emerged as the vice-presidential candidate. Harry Truman's "give-'em-hell" campaigning, which confounded the experts and won a narrow victory, was mostly directed at the Republican presidential nominee, Thomas E. Dewey. Truman had a witticism for Warren. "He's a Democrat—and doesn't know it."

In 1950 the Democrats fielded an active campaigner, Franklin D. Roosevelt's son James. Warren won reelection by a million votes, approximately the edge of Democratic voters over Republican, which was carrying nonpartisanship about as far as possible.

In September, 1953, President Dwight Eisenhower fulfilled a campaign promise and appointed Warren Chief Justice of the Supreme Court. Irked by some of the decisions of the Warren Court, Eisenhower later spoke of this appointment as his worst mistake. The John Birch Society and some others agreed. The consensus is that he was one of the most effective of all the heads of this Court. Popular as he had been as governor, his greatest contributions were as Chief Justice.

Lobbying the Legislature

In the twenties and thirties special interests saw advantage through influencing the legislature, the more so because of its unrepresentative character. In the thirties, with the return of legalized liquor, racing, and gambling, additional special interests entered the field. Detective H. R. Philbrick gave the Sacramento grand jury in 1939 itemized accounts of retainers, donations, and campaign contributions to certain legislators and how this money was funneled to them by professional lobbyists. The accounts of one lobbyist, Arthur H. Samish, traced $496,138.26 delivered in 1935–38.

A legislator or two failed to be reelected, but concern about "government by lobbyists" was postponed until 1949 when Carey McWilliams in the *Nation* and Lester Velie in *Collier's* candidly exposed Samish and his methods. Velie quoted Governor Warren, "On matters that affect his clients, Artie unquestionably has more power than the governor." Samish freely admitted that he had influence; he posed for a photograph with a "Mr. Legislature" puppet on his knee.

Samish's system was within the law and partly by using the law. As public relations counselor for brewers, liquor wholesalers, truck companies, and others, he worked through front organizations that put on public relations drives, donated to campaigns, and retained lawyers, especially lawyer-legislators. The reciprocal favors asked were mere details in the grand total of bills and in many instances remote from the interest of a particular legislator's constituents.

The weight of lobbyist control was felt most in the "fair trade and practices" laws, principally those against price cutting, and the Alcoholic Beverage Control Act of 1934.

Even after a law to the advantage of such a client was passed and in force, it was comparatively simple to point to agitation against it or a proposed amendment and thus get a continuing retainer for "the man who gets things done."

For his bragging Samish was barred from the floor of the 1949 legislature. In 1953 he was convicted of income tax evasion. A speaker of the assembly was convicted for accepting bribes and another was indicted. An investigator in the fifties found that contributors "carefully refrain from asking a quid pro quo." "The Third House," outnumbering the legislators, still operated but circumspectly.

Propositions Unlimited

If Warren's high repute as governor seems to rest on capable administration rather than on leading the state into bold new programs, it may be because of the emphasis the California system puts on the direct democracy of initiatives, referendums, and constitutional amendments.

Legislators, executives, and even judges learned to sidestep thorny issues by referral to the electorate. Special interests recognized such propositions as better vehicles for their purposes. All this was foreshadowed in the twenties and thirties. Joseph Robinson had gone into the business of qualifying propositions by collecting the necessary signatures. Unions, state employees, a movement such as Ham and Eggs, or the opponents of "forced busing" might prefer to rally support by circulating petitions, but for a few hundred thousand dollars that work could be bypassed. As propositions claimed more and more space on the ballot, a special breed of lobbyists sprang up, their specialty lobbying the electorate.

Clem Whitaker blazed a trail in 1930. An association of barbers wanted a state regulatory board set up. They could not stir the legislature, but Whitaker offered to do the job for $4,000. Instead of going to legislators, he carried the message to the people, stirred attention and interest, and the measure soon became law.

In 1933 Whitaker and Baxter masterminded defeat of the PG&E referendum against the Central Valley Project. In 1936 Don Francisco orchestrated the campaign against a graduated chain store tax. In 1948 Whitaker and Baxter handled the antifeatherbedding initiative for the railroads which wanted to economize with longer trains but no more brakemen. They also persuaded the voters partly to disenfranchise themselves by continuing malapportionment. On the basis of these performances Whitaker and Baxter were retained by the American Medical Association to stage a nationwide fight against medicare.

Other defects in this direct democracy became evident. These propositions were not subject to hearings, amendments, and argument to eliminate faults as can happen in consideration by the legislature. All too often a proposition on its face violates the state or federal constitution but operates for months or years until judicial review can overtake it. It often centers on a catch phrase that covers a broader or more fundamental issue. The millions upon millions of California voters are a far cry from the town meeting which was the early form of direct democracy.

As a recourse of last resort, however, some form of action by the electorate is needed. Without Proposition 13 and its ceiling on taxation of real estate, local governments were obstinate against any relief, and until a 1980 proposition the state government did nothing toward indexing state income taxes.

Anticommunism and Its Repercussions

Anticommunism was institutionalized in California a year before Warren became governor when the state senate set up its own Un-American Activities Committee, the Tenney Committee. As a legislative investigating committee it was beyond the governor's reach. As an instrument of federal government, the House Un-American Activities Committee was still further removed.

In 1947 HUAC made its famous safari into Hollywood, alleging procommunist propaganda in Ambassador Davies' *Mission to Moscow*, Louis B. Mayer's *Song of Russia*, and *None but the Lonely Heart*, in which actress Ginger Rogers' mother saw Communist infection. Armed with a list of suspects, the committee returned to put the question, "Are you now or have you ever been a member of the Communist Party?"

Writer John Howard Lawson attempted to explain to the committee why he could not answer that question. A staff member read into the record a representation of Communist-related activities. Writer Dalton Trumbo and eight others followed suit. The chairperson adjourned the hearing, announcing that there were 68 other witnesses to be called.

Each of the Hollywood Ten was cited and tried. Each pled a First Amendment protection against having to answer such a question. At that time this defense did not hold and all were fined and imprisoned. Out of this episode rose the infamous Hollywood blacklist barring hundreds of actors, writers, directors, and producers from employment in the industry. A pleading of the Fifth Amendment might ward off imprisonment but not blacklisting.

In 1949 the Tenney Committee injudiciously named several members of the legislature as Communist tainted. The legislature promptly discontinued his committee, thereby depriving Tenney of his role. The vacuum was filled, however, by a new committee headed by Senator Hugh Burns, who used the role more discreetly and made it his power base for 20 years.

Meanwhile anticommunist fervor produced an epidemic of loyalty oaths and checks. Los Angeles County instituted such an oath from every employee. The City of Los Angeles required an oath of denial, and radio station KNX put its 200 employees to the same test. The Los Angeles County supervisors ordered every Communist book removed from the county library, and Burbank moved to have every such book in its city library branded. In 1949, shortly before losing his committee, Tenney conferred with the University of California lobbyist about the need for a faculty loyalty check, and in March President Sproul recommended such an oath to the regents. In June it was revealed to the faculty.

Thus began the "year of the oath," in which all employees of the university, clerical and custodial as well as faculty, were in prospect of losing their jobs unless they complied. Most members of the faculty saw the requirement as a violation of academic freedom, though many thought that fighting it would do more harm than good. The regents also were divided. John Francis Neylan, in an earlier loyalty crisis the staunch defender of Anita Whitney, was determined that the regents not forfeit control of the university. Governor Warren, ex officio president of the regents, favored withdrawal of the oath requirement but at most could muster half the votes and that was not enough to prevent the firing of the last of the nonsigners. The record showed that the firings were not for Communist party affiliations but for insubordination. At the July, 1950, meeting there were 46 nonsigners; a month later the number was reduced to 31, of whom 5 subsequently signed.

The nonsigners brought suit in *Tolman* v. *Underhill* and in April, 1951, the district court held that the oath requirement was a violation of tenure and unconstitutional. The regents appealed. A year and a half later the state supreme court upheld the trial court, though on the narrower ground that years earlier the state had "occupied the field" of spelling out oaths and who should be required to swear to them. As it turned out another suit was needed for restoration of tenure, accrued rights, and the like. By the time that suit was settled another six years had been added to the year of the oath and the American Association of University Professors had censured the board of regents.

The legislature, meanwhile, added a series of loyalty checks and oaths, one for all state employees known as the Levering Oath, a special one for school teachers, and one for churches and veterans claiming tax exemptions. One by one these requirements were held unconstitutional. Not until 1967 did the state supreme court reverse itself and strike down the oath for all public employees.

Two years later the regents felt free to fire Angela Davis, an assistant professor of philosophy at UCLA, because she was a member of Che Lumumba, a black cell of the Communist party. At the next meeting they backed off slightly. Davis was allowed to continue on the payroll and teach but not for credit. That concession did not deter the AAUP from again putting the University of California on the censure list, where it remained until 1980 when proof was offered that the chancellor on each campus would make final decision on appointments and the faculty on courses of instruction.

The Hollywood blacklist was not absolute. Under an alias Dalton Trumbo wrote a script that won an Oscar. Later some blacklisted artists were allowed to return openly to work. As with McCarthyism nationally, the winddown of blacklisting was slow and uncertain. Many of those ejected from work in the entertainment industry, the schools, or other employment were never taken back.

Knight and the Musical Chairs

On Warren's departure Goodwin J. Knight became governor. In the undemanding role of lieutenant governor he had traveled up and down the state making countless appearances. On a few issues, such as the university loyalty oath, he had disagreed with Warren. The expectation was that he would be more Republican and more conservative.

Knight proved more astute. He had no intention of narrowing his support to Republican registrants and he was much more cooperative with labor. He backed an increase in workmen's compensation and boosted the unemployment insurance from $25 to $40 a week. He signed a bill protecting pension and union welfare funds. He was easily elected in 1954, and his prospects seemed good for winning in 1958 despite the large bulge in Democratic registrations.

There was one cloud on the horizon, the newly organized California Democratic Council, modelled on the Republican Assembly. Backed by 100 clubs, eventually 500, the CDC raised money, did precinct work, developed candidates, and would help some of them into office. Adlai Stevenson was the patron saint, and preprimary endorsements the answer to crossfiling.

Lightning struck from another quarter. Senator Knowland announced that he would not seek reelection. His plan was to run for governor and then be based for mounting to the presidency. Had he been California's only prominent Republican, this maneuver might have been as graceful as it was calculated. But Knight was not one to be cavalierly set aside, and Richard Nixon, as Eisenhower's choice for vice-president, saw himself closer to the presidency than either Knowland or Knight. Only the year before, the three had to be taken into account in the delegation to the Republican national convention. Supporters of each were made equal in number, plus one spot for Senator Thomas Kuchel, a neutral.

Nixon is credited with suggesting how to avoid a knockdown primary between Knowland and Knight. Knight should be persuaded to step aside and run for Knowland's vacated Senate seat. Knight refused, and advisedly when it became clear that Knowland planned to run on a "right-to-work," that is, on an antiunion, antilabor plank. With support from labor, Knight thought his chances were good and so stated. But a month later he dolefully announced that his "most constructive course" would be to run for the Senate; a Knight-Knowland battle was too likely to split

the party and turn California over to the Democrats. Later he was more explicit. He had been notified that if he fought on for the governorship the big campaign contributors would find their conservative way to Knowland. "Standing on the burning deck in midocean," he soliloquized, "I had no choice."

Knowland was a bumbling campaigner. Labor baiting, even brightly packaged as the "right to work" or the "American way," had the feel of a return to the nineteenth century or at least to Herbert Hoover. Native son though he was, Knowland came back for this race as an outlander, and the shunting of "Goody" Knight into an inferior position was held against him. To the voters it all appeared too manipulated.

On the countdown Knowland lost by 3,140,000 to 2,111,000, and Knight by 2,927,000 to 2,204,000. In the races for Congress and the legislature the landslide was more moderate, but the end result was an across-the-board Republican defeat. For the first time in many a year Republicans would be a minority (14 to 16) in the House delegation, for the first time since 1942 a minority (33 to 47) in the assembly, and for the first time since 1890 a minority (13 to 27) in the state senate.

The general opinion was that Knowland got the comeuppance he deserved. Almost as widespread was the sentiment that Knight deserved a better fate, though not necessarily the Senate seat. The consensus was that Knowland and Nixon and Knight had played musical chairs; when the music stopped, as Robert Kenny remarked, Nixon was sitting in both chairs. That oversimplifies. Knowland's influence was cut down to one newspaper and one vote. Knight was retired. Nixon's ploy had not really saved the Republicans from splitting. And there was another way to read the election returns. With Edmund G. (Pat) Brown moving into the governor's seat and Clair Engle into the Senate, the election was a Democratic victory, not just a Republican defeat.

Edmund G. (Pat) Brown

A native of San Francisco, Brown grew up in its Mission district and worked his way through law school. He also worked his way up to the post of district attorney, attained in 1944. Initially he was a Republican, natural enough for an admirer of Hiram Johnson, but in 1934, prompted by FDR and the New Deal rather than by Sinclair and Epic, he changed his registration to Democratic. Open and warm-hearted, he also demonstrated unmistakable integrity. In a much publicized case, on the verge of getting a conviction, he learned that a key witness had lied. Unhesitatingly he asked for dismissal. In 1950 he won election as attorney general.

Against Knowland, Brown could capitalize on the selfish conniving of the opposition, imply less radical departure from the good features of the Warren and Knight regimes, and count on union support. He came out flatly against Knowland's pet antiunion initiative. Invoking the tradition of Hiram Johnson

Edmund G. (Pat) Brown

The Bancroft Library

and Warren, he announced that as governor he would call on the most able Californians regardless of party. His road to the governor's mansion thus closely paralleled Warren's.

In his first message to the legislature Brown emphasized the need to combat racial discrimination. The legislature responded with a Fair Employment Practices Act and a Civil Rights Act authored by the new speaker of the assembly, Jess Unruh. Attorney General Stanley Mosk was committed to these same purposes; his staff was soon exerting itself to persuade business people in many lines to avoid discriminatory practices.

Well aware of the way in which cross-filing had benefited the Republicans, the new legislature joyfully abolished this practice. Brown asked and got an increase in unemployment benefits, improved compensation to injured workmen, and an increase in state aid to local school districts. He did not succeed in having the minimum wage law extended to agricultural workers. He appointed a dedicated humanitarian as consumers' counsel, essentially to help buyers beware, but for lack of anything more than a very short hatpin her work was not highly effective.

In 1959 Brown appointed a new state economic planning board and he called for a master plan for higher education. The appointed committee confirmed that the junior colleges should prepare some students for further studies and some for vocations; that the state colleges have rounded rather than merely teacher-training programs and, where resources permitted, include some graduate work; and that the university continue with a four-year undergraduate program along with graduate and professional programs.

The Donohue Act of 1960 incorporated the gist of the master plan and set up a board of trustees for the state colleges. Subsequently a similar statewide board was set up for the junior colleges. The 79 junior colleges soon were rechristened community colleges and the state colleges as the State Universities and Colleges. By the late sixties the 79 community colleges enrolled 500,000 students, the 21 state universities and colleges 200,000, the 8 general campuses of the University of California 100,000, and private universities and colleges 100,000.

From his predecessors Brown inherited a deficit and a need for state services that was growing in step with the rapid rise in population. He recommended a budget approaching $2.5 billion and increases in income, inheritance, corporation, and excise taxes to bring it into balance. The legislature voted approximately what he requested; indeed, of the 40 measures which he urged 35 were made law. All told, the 1959 legislative achievement was perhaps as lustrous as that of the famous legislature of Hiram Johnson and the Lincoln-Roosevelt reformers.

A great assist came from Speaker Unruh, who was in the process of upgrading the legislature by providing consultants and technical assistants, and raising salaries and expectancy of year-round attention. By such means and by running a tight ship, Unruh brought the legislature to recognition as one of the most effective in the land, in the process incurring a few enmities. On the whole the governor and the speaker cooperated effectively.

Alongside the legislation of this session Brown was laying foundation for a larger achievement. Eight years earlier the legislature had approved a Warren-recommended plan for capturing the water of the Feather River and conducting it to the Bay cities, the parched west side of San Joaquin Valley, and southern California. Funding the project hung fire. Northern Californians were reluctant to see a natural resource of their section siphoned off to Los Angeles, and the Senate had the votes to prevent a commitment. On January 22, 1959, midway in his first month in office, Brown urged the legislature to take action to bring into use 3 billion acre-feet

of water that was going to waste each year.

Brown made several very practical suggestions. One was to give prospective water purchasers commitments by contracts with the state rather than by more cumbersome constitutional amendment. Another was to allocate the state's Investment Fund (tideland oil royalties) to this resource project, with water bonds accepted in exchange. This feature would later come in for criticism as robbing the schools to pay for water. To make the project manageable Brown proposed leaving until later the $11.8 billion package for the projected needs of the year 2050 and an immediate commitment to $1.75 billion which should suffice for the seventies and early eighties.

Choosing to crack the harder nut first, Brown began with the senate. He concentrated on trying to persuade reluctant senators. During the luncheon recess on May 29 he was in touch with several of them and that afternoon the senate voted to put the bond issue on the ballot. The assembly was sufficiently committed; it approved the Burns-Porter bill without amendment, thereby avoiding the necessity for a conference where the bill might have died.

Throughout the next year and a half Brown continued to plead for his water bonds at every opportunity. He met opposition from conservatives who questioned the investment and from liberals who criticized the shelving of the 160-acre requirement. But in November, 1960, the voters validated this largest of all state bond issues.

A Cause Celébre, Capital Punishment

As governor Brown inherited the case of Caryl Chessman. In 1948, with a record of earlier felonies, Chessman was arrested in a stolen car. He had not killed, but he was brought to

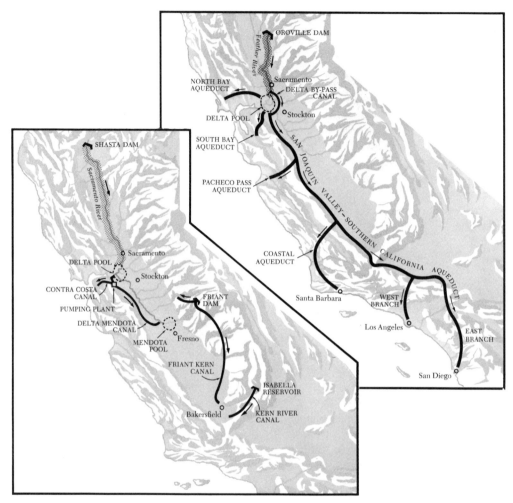

Central Valley and California Water Projects

trial and charged with forcing a woman to move to another car with intent of sexual assault. The state's definition of kidnapping in its Little Lindberg Act led to a death sentence. Irregularities in the trial and glaring deficiencies in the record available on appeal cast grave doubt that Chessman had received full protection of the law.

In prison Chessman read law, acted as his own counsel, and was articulate in letters, interviews, and his book, *Cell 2455, Death Row*. He became San Quentin's best known resident and his case a cause celébre. As with Tom Mooney, his arrogance provoked hostility and sensationalism in the press. He substantially rehabilitated himself though some said not enough. He endured the torture of 11 years on Death Row before being put to death.

The case roused serious question of the death penalty. Most European nations and several American states had abolished it.

Wardens testified that it was a handicap to prison operation. Experts denied that it deterred crime and insisted that by it the state set the ultimate example in violence. Clearly it was inflicted disproportionately on black and other minorities and the poor. Yet public opinion seemed to be that certain crimes called for capital punishment and that lawmen needed this backup.

Brown's lifelong experience with law enforcement convinced him that capital punishment was a mistake. He issued several stays and proposed a moratorium. He tried to get the legislature to abolish the death penalty. Because of Chessman's earlier conviction, Brown could not commute the sentence without the consent of the Supreme Court. Through an intermediary he sounded out the court and found it opposed, certainly not the same as confronting the court with a commutation and requiring the justices to register yes or no. He had sworn to uphold the law, and on the basis of the intermediary's report he allowed the execution to proceed.

The American Civil Liberties Union of Southern California had intervened in many death sentences on the basis of procedural defects in the original trial or review. In 1959 it advanced to the position that capital punishment itself, commonplace at the time of the adoption of the Bill of Rights, had now become a relic of barbarism and was a violation of the Eighth Amendment ban on cruel and unusual punishment.

This position proved to be revolutionary. Several years passed before the national ACLU was persuaded of its constitutionality. In 1972 the California Supreme Court reversed a death sentence on the basis of the state constitution's ban on cruel or unusual punishment. Soon after the Supreme Court of the United States held similarly on the basis of cruel and unusual punishment. In the changing scene both courts gave ground, but more

than two decades after the California ACLU entered its constitutional objection, only one person in California had been sent to the gas chamber.

Brown's Second Term

In 1960 Brown headed the California delegation to the Democratic convention in Los Angeles and swung most of its votes to John Kennedy, even though the gallery was vociferously for Stevenson and a third of the delegation so voted. At the polls Kennedy edged Nixon but, when the absentee ballots were counted, the state ended up in the other column. That meant that California might not be so influential in Washington as hoped. Brown, however, had maintained good liaison with the state's representatives and with the Eisenhower administration, a relationship that improved when Kennedy came into office.

In 1961 the Birch Society was exposed by Thomas M. Storke in his Santa Barbara News – Press and then by the Los Angeles Times. What set Storke off was a covertly backed student essay contest on impeaching Earl Warren. Storke's paper let wealthy reactionaries know where to put their money to work against the income tax, the United Nations, school integration, social security, medicare, and fluoridation. "Bircher" entered the lexicon signifying an extremist of the right, all out for private enterprise as opposed to reliance on government programs or regulations. In southern California in particular the Birch Society visibly flourished.

In 1962 Nixon attempted a comeback by running for governor. Illness forced Knight's withdrawal and Nixon was nominated. Conscious that he must woo middle-of-the-road Democrats, Nixon pointedly rejected Bircher support, thereby forfeiting some campaign

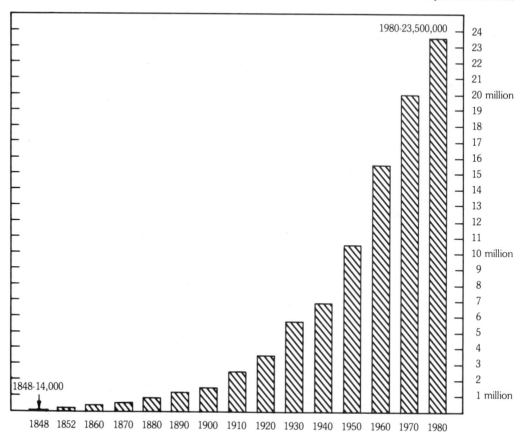

1980-23,500,000

1848-14,000

1848 1852 1860 1870 1880 1890 1900 1910 1920 1930 1940 1950 1960 1970 1980

Population Growth to 1980

contributions. Brown ran on his record as governor, made much of Nixon's long absence from the state, and accused his opponent of intending to use the governorship as a stepping-stone for another try for the presidency in 1964. To the surprise of many Brown won by over 500,000 votes. The next morning Nixon called in the press, berated them for the way his campaign had been reported, and told them they would not have him "to kick around any more." He left California to join a New York law firm.

Brown's second term began auspiciously with the Rumford Act, which banned discrimination in sales or rentals except in owner-

occupied housing of two to four units. The realtors immediately reacted with Proposition 14, an elaborate ban on any such legislation past, present, or future. That proposition shared the limelight with the 1964 presidential campaign, helped mightily by California and the Birchers, in which Barry Goldwater won the Republican nomination for President. Lyndon Johnson carried California handily, but the state Democratic clubs had hard going, partly because of the reactionary resurgence and partly because the stand of the clubs on such issues as recognition of Red China were an embarrassment to incumbents and to candidates. Reactionary posture did not prevent song and dance man George Murphy from making his way to the Senate.

In 1964 the state board of education called for textbooks for the basic eighth-grade course in United States history which would, among other things, give balanced coverage of the contributions by Americans of all backgrounds. Of the books submitted, the board was advised that a new book, *Land of the Free*, best met the requirements. In May, 1966, the board voted the adoption.

What had been a small rumbling of criticism now became an angry attack manifested in representations to the board, letters to the editor, fliers, phone calls, radio and television talk shows, sermons, political speeches, pamphlets, and a film strip. The book, so the critics said, was too attentive to blacks, too frank in reporting American mistakes, insufficient in its praise of captains of industry and Republican Presidents, critical of atomic warfare, and calculated to break down pride in America. The Birch Society actively circulated these materials, and a small group of Republican legislators held up the general appropriation bill for 1966–67 because it included purchase of *Land of the Free*. The state Junior Chamber of Commerce, the vast majority of whose members had never opened the book, by statewide referendum condemned it. Not since *The Grapes of Wrath* had any book stirred up so much hatred.

The hue and cry over this textbook contributed in 1966 to the election of Ronald Reagan as governor. By appointments he remade the state board of education and, promptly after the adoption period ended, it shifted to a more conventional text. Responding to another group of critics, that board also directed that in the teaching of science, along with "the theory of evolution," texts and teachers must present the Biblical "view of special creation." That official position of "giving God equal time" was only one step

removed from Tennessee's in the 1920s.

In his eight years as governor Brown proved himself not only an adept promoter of legislation but a highly efficient administrator. He took particular pride in making government work. The parts that were within his reach were operating well and, as indicated, excellent relationship was maintained with the federal government.

The legislature, as restructured by Unruh with support from Brown, had won recognition as one of the most efficient in the land. In 1966 it was further improved by reapportionment. Impetus came in 1964 from the Warren Court, in the now archaic language of "one man, one vote" required by the equal protection clause of the Fourteenth Amendment. The test case came from Tennessee, but California could readily have set the scene with its state senate and its rotten boroughs in the most sparsely populated counties. For example, one lone senator represented 40 percent of the state's voters in the most populous county. The legislature put off to the last minute but then voted the reapportionment that would put the 1966 election on the new and constitutional basis.

By the luck of the draw, Warren in his long governorship had named no one to the state supreme court and Knight but one. Brown had opportunity to appoint six. By his choices he endowed the state with an outstanding court which in the course of the sixties and seventies impressed experts on the American judiciary as unexcelled.

Thus at midsixties California state government was at a high water mark. By happy coincidence this peak had been reached in the smooth sailing of the Warren, Knight, and Pat Brown administrations which also saw California double in population and become the most populous state. Nevertheless, under Brown tensions that had been muted became more evident and demanding.

CHAPTER 29

The View from Watts

Paul Conrad, Los Angeles Times

1959 and after

We believe that in California we have the greatest scientific and engineering community in the world. Its members have created and built machines to land on the moon, photograph Mars, circle the sun, explore the bottom of the oceans, and very soon, perhaps, decipher the genetic code of life.

Yet, at the same time, the rest of us in California are still struggling to solve economic and social problems as old, in many cases, as civilization itself.

Edmund G. (Pat) Brown

A Time of Confrontations

Toward Equal Opportunity

In the summer of 1954 repressive hysteria reached its peak when the maker of the atomic bomb, J. Robert Oppenheimer, was found dangerous to national security and was ordered "walled off" from all atomic secrets. Soon thereafter the Army-McCarthy hearings undermined confidence in Senator Joseph McCarthy. McCarthyism carried on but dwindled perceptibly.

That same summer Chief Justice Warren, speaking for a unanimous Supreme Court, announced the landmark decision in *Brown* v. *Board of Education, Topeka*. Addressed specifically to a set of schools in the South, *Brown* spoke to all governmental agencies. The decision rejected the long standing fallacy of "separate but equal" and resuscitated the Fourteenth Amendment guaranty of "equal protection of the law" without distinction by race or color. This decision became the American Magna Carta of civil rights.

Californians hailed this decision, but the immediate impression was that it was strictly an order to the Old South. The temptation was to see segregation as a distant problem. After all, it was California's Jackie Robinson who had integrated baseball. A California case, *Barrows*, had closed a loophole that could have revived restrictive covenants. On the university campuses and in the professions blacks were visible, and with the Korean War the armed services were integrating. At that time, however, a black student could make reservation by mail to stay at the UCLA dormitory and be told when seen that there was no room. Hotels, restaurants, employers, and property owners as a matter of practice segregated extensively.

Californians took a strong spectator interest in the heroism of the black children who had to be escorted past the white demonstrators in order to integrate Central High in Little Rock. They felt empathy with the blacks of the Montgomery boycott who walked to work rather than sit in the back of the bus. They were moved by the eloquence of Martin Luther King and his formula of passive resistance.

Governor Knight and the Republican legislature felt no need to enforce the mandate in *Brown*. Thus it was a startling stroke of leadership in 1959 when Governor Brown requested and the legislature voted the Unruh Civil Rights Act and a Fair Employment Act. Attorney General Stanley Mosk promptly set up a division on constitutional rights, appointed a committee of consultants, and systematically notified businesses, motels, restaurants, bars, and stores to cease denying equal access.

In 1961, when President John Kennedy initiated the Peace Corps, California students were among the most numerous volunteers. Others went as Freedom Riders to Mississippi and neighboring states to break the hold of Jim Crow or to help in voter registration drives. By easy extension came participation back home in marches, picketing, and sit-ins against discriminations in employment, housing, and commerce.

Not until the sixties, however, did Californians generally recognize segregation in the very field that had provided the base for the decision in *Brown*. At loggerheads on much else, the Democratic-led state board of education and Max Rafferty, the Republican superintendent of instruction, were agreed on this point. Besides ordering integrated texts, in order to identify the segregated schools, they ordered annual school-by-school racial and ethnic censuses. They put every school district on notice that it was under obligation to deseg-

"A White Man's Home Is His Castle."   *Dennis Renault*

regate, and on that point in 1963 the state supreme court was equally explicit in *Jackson v. Pasadena*.

Anti–Fair Housing

In 1963 the legislature had enacted the Rumford Fair Housing statute. Thereupon, the California Real Estate Association reacted in the classic California tradition; it appealed to the voters to amend the constitution. CREA hired the drafting of an amendment, hired the gathering of the necessary signatures, and entrusted the campaign to the best public relations firm available. Along with protection of the "God-given" property rights of absentee as well as live-in owners, the campaign was keyed to the heartthrob pitch, the sanctity of the home.

Recognizing that this Proposition 14 threatened to paralyze the entire civil rights movement, ACLU and NAACP dropped most of their other work to do battle against it. The fight was uphill all the way. Proposition 14 was overwhelmingly adopted in 1964.

Immediately after the vote owners began refusing to rent, lease, or sell, particularly to blacks. Dozens of suits were brought. In the spring of 1966, with Herman Selvin as volunteer counsel for ACLU, several of the cases were consolidated and appealed to the California supreme court which in June found the amendment unconstitutional.

CREA spokesmen expostulated that they had hired the best legal minds in the state to write their Anti–Fair Housing Amendment. CREA appealed to the Supreme Court of the United States. A year later that Court struck down this baleful proposition.

The Anti–Fair Housing Amendment thus had a lifespan of only two and half years, or so it might seem. Actually it had dominated the scene through much of the preceding year, and many of its effects lingered on, as did those of restrictive covenants, long after the courts had outlawed them and many of their substitutes.

On California blacks in particular the psychological impact of Proposition 14 was indelible. Given the overwhelming endorsement at the polls, 4.5 million to 2.4 million, it could only be read as a clear exposure of the prevailing white attitude. This disillusionment undoubtedly set the scene for the race riot that exploded in late August, 1965.

The Watts Riot

The time was a warm August evening after a hot and sultry day. In Los Angeles' ghetto many sought relief by coming out on their porches or into the streets. A police incident with appearance of unnecessary harshness touched off the riot. Once started, the striking back at the police spread to a general attack on ''whitey.'' Windows were smashed, especially of those businesses blamed for exploiting ghetto customers. Fires were set, again selectively, and the firemen answering the calls were turned back. Many who committed no other violence joined in looting supermarkets, clothing stores, liquor shops, and appliance

Interlude in the Watts Riot

The Los Angeles Times

shops. The rationale was that they were collecting something white society had been denying them for a long time.

At first Police Chief William Parker was confident that his men could restore order. By the second day he was ready to ask for the National Guard. In Governor Brown's absence Lieutenant Governor Glenn Anderson had been legally powerless to act until asked. He now responded promptly and within hours guardsmen reached the riot area. The outbreak turned into a six-day shoot-out, snipers on one side and police and guardsmen on the other. Meanwhile, the riot spread over an area of 50 square miles, most of the ghetto, with added flare-ups in Venice and at the harbor. The toll mounted to 34 killed, 31 of them blacks; 1,032 injured; 3,952 arrested; and 3,411 charged with felony or misdemeanor. Property damage reached $40 million. By several measures it was the largest race riot ever.

It was clear that neither agitators nor the black leadership precipitated this riot. Frustrations over unemployment and poor schools, anger over police practices, and resentment of the white segregationist attitude manifested so clearly in the vote for Proposition 14, fueled the outburst.

The post-mortem by the state-appointed McCone Commission exculpated the police, made Anderson the scapegoat for alleged delay in bringing in the National Guard, and called for improvements in ghetto employment, housing, and education. Sixteen years later the Urban League and the American Jewish Committee were influential in getting former Governor Brown appointed to advise another task force looking into the problems of this ghetto. The troubles to be focused on had a familiar ring—high unemployment, poor education, inadequate housing, and bad police-community relations. It was not to have been expected that the riot itself would solve

the problems, but as the 1981 committee spokesman noted, "conditions have changed very little since the 1965 riot."

Alienation and Student Unrest

In the fifties McCarthyism with its pressures for conformity led to the silent generation when college students and many of their elders chose pragmatic goals and were circumspect to a fault about memberships in organizations and political activity. Alongside that pattern of noninvolvement and out of dedication to the capitalist system, another form of disengagement arose in the spirit of Sam Goldwyn's famous phrase, "Include me out."

Beatniks and the hippies chose to be unkempt and declined to participate. They clustered in select parts of the state, such as the Big Sur, Venice, Berkeley, San Francisco's Columbus Avenue, and later its Haight-Ashbury neighborhood. Some of these young people held jobs. Allegedly some were bank clerks during the week and hippies over the weekend. Some accepted remittances from parents left behind in the world of the squares. Beards and unkempt attire spread across the generation gap. By the sixties many of the disaffected had taken to escapism in marijuana, LSD, or heroin.

The sixties saw renewed willingness to be involved. In May, 1960, students from many campuses came to City Hall in San Francisco to show disapproval of the House Un-American Activities Committee. Finding that passes to the auditorium were given only to "friendly" spectators, they filled the corridor to chant and sing until the police drove them out with clubs and firehosed them down the steps.

In the spirit of the activism of the Freedom Rides, the Peace Corps, and particularly against Proposition 14, students assembled at

**Hosing Protesting Students down the Steps
of City Hall, San Francisco, 1960**

San Francisco Chronicle

Berkeley for the 1964 fall semester. A show-down on the right of students to participate in politics triggered the Free Speech Movement. The proposition was that, although the university must stay clear of partisan politics, its students need not be political neuters. The protesters, aided tremendously by the charismatic appeal of quick-witted Mario Savio, gained many supporters even among the faculty. Savio and his collaborators broadened the issue. They wanted the university made more relevant to the times and to student needs as they identified them. They called for a different deployment of professors' attention, less to contract research and off-campus employment and more to teaching. They proposed an overhaul of courses and degree programs and more student voice in decision making. Nothing in the past experience of many of the professors and most of the administrators conditioned them favorably to these proposals. Concessions came haltingly.

The Free Speech Movement soon degenerated to the Filthy Speech Movement and to tactics learned in off-campus protest. "Street people," often indistinguishable, infiltrated the student ranks. Climax came in a sit-in in Sproul Hall, the administrative nerve center of the university but paradoxically the building least essential to the day-to-day learning processes and research.

President Clark Kerr proposed that he and Governor Brown go in and talk it over with the demonstrators but the chancellor took the hard line that the state police be sent in to clear the building. Some 700 persons, not all of them students, were forcibly evicted and eventually 578 were found guilty of trespassing or resisting arrest.

Although many classes went on as usual and credits were earned, degrees awarded, and researches continued, the sound and fury of the Free Speech Movement dominated the scene through the whole academic year. The university emerged intact from the year's buffeting, but there was a question how much more it could stand.

Alongside the escapism of the hippies, the student unrest, and the insistent minorities in the late sixties, there rose a groundswell of dissatisfaction with the war in Vietnam, which had taken on the aspect of a ghastly mistake.

Harold Willens' Business Executives for Peace hoped for a "man-to-man" talk with the President. The volunteers of Another Mother for Peace circulated widely its appealing logo. Others pinned their hopes on marches and picketing. In 1967 when President Johnson came to speak at a $100-a-plate dinner in Los Angeles, thousands of nonviolent demonstrators marched to the Century City Hotel. The President was whisked in and out the back door. Ordered to break up the demonstration, the police moved in, whacking away at skulls and followed up with wholesale arrests and prosecutions.

Logo of Another Mother for Peace

As the war in Vietnam dragged on and escalated, and with assassinations of Martin Luther King in Memphis and Robert Kennedy in Los Angeles, opposition grew. In particular there was objection to the draft. In the late sixties on many campuses across the country the pattern became nonnegotiable demands, takeover by force, arson, and bombs.

The most violent confrontations were at Wisconsin, Columbia, and Kent State, but California schools had their share. At Stanford a fire was set at a war-related laboratory and student records were seized and trashed. At the University of California at Santa Barbara a bomb killed a custodian, and a student riot at nearby Isla Vista featured the burning of the Bank of America branch. For the better part of two years student demands paralyzed San Francisco State University. Only by herculean effort could the police clear the campus.

At Berkeley the aroused students renewed some of the demands of the Free Speech Movement, threatened to burn the University

405

Library, perhaps the state's greatest cultural asset, and seized People's Park. The National Guard was summoned, shots were fired, one rooftop spectator was blinded and another was killed. A national guard helicopter sprayed demonstrators with tear gas which was wafted into the university infirmary.

This madness melted away. As Walton Bean phrased it, "by the fall of 1970 the volcano of student rebellion had become dormant, if not extinct. Soon even radical students were referring to " 'the old New Left' of the 1960s."

Off campus and apart from what the black community stood for, a strain of nihilistic violence carried on, as extreme as that of the Weathermen bombmakers. Three heinous outbursts stand out. In 1970, with guns purchased by Angela Davis, a rescue attempt of black prisoners was made at the Marin County courthouse. A judge and two others were killed and the convicts who had fled the scene were quickly recaptured. In 1973 Oakland's black superintendent of schools, Marcus Foster, was the victim of an execution-style assassination by the Symbionese Liberation Army, which also kidnapped Patricia Hearst and for a year exploited her as a hostage.

The Blacks as a Force

During the sixties blacks became a force in California. Martin Luther King had given them inspiration at an overflow rally in 1963 at Wrigley Field set up by the NAACP and other civil rights leaders. Chilled by local inattention to redressing old wrongs, they had invited King to come and speak. Reviewing the struggle for equal opportunity in the South, he pleaded eloquently for a like commitment in the West. Asked what could be done to help the blacks in Birmingham, he answered, "The best thing you can do is to make Los Angeles free."

That cry, "Make Los Angeles free!" galvanized the community to action. The blacks took the lead by organizing the United Civil Rights Council. Reflecting the rally, UCRC became an umbrella coalition for all concerned groups and all races, religions, and shades of politics. The historic areas of flagrant violations of black rights were singled out—employment, housing, police practices, and education—and interracial committees were set up to press for action. They went directly to local and regional employers, employee organizations, and labor unions; to realtors and regulatory agencies; to the police commission, the chief of police, and the sheriff; and to the board of education. This beginning of black solidarity intensified and spread statewide.

Blacks had been a presence throughout California history. The small band of settlers of the pueblo of Los Angeles included blacks and mulattoes. A thousand blacks, it is estimated, came in the gold rush. Early in the American period an impressive black delegation from San Francisco, Stockton, and Marysville had urged the legislature to give protection to black rights, particularly in court.

By the 1920s and 1930s the black population was noticeably larger. The huge influx of war workers in the airplane plants and shipyards brought a sudden and great increase both in the Bay region and in southern California. The migration continued, and by the midsixties Los Angeles had eight times as many blacks as in 1940 and almost enough to match the total population of San Francisco.

Along the way many gained distinction, among them Ralph Bunche as undersecretary of the United Nations, Carlotta Bass as editor of the Los Angeles *Eagle*, Loren Miller as editor and lawyer, and Jackie Robinson by integrating baseball. What was lacking was a united black effort. In the sixties several factors contributed—the heroism of King and his followers in the face of extreme abuse in the

Tom Bradley, Mayor of Los Angeles

South, the encouraging gains in equal access here in California, and the upswing of black pride.

This was the time when the historic appellation "Negro" was retired in favor of flat identification by race and color. There was defiance in the proud declaration that "black is beautiful." "Brother" and "sister" rose above church usage, and "skin" replaced the handshake.

Opinion differed on how to proceed: by the Black Panther route, through a rival brotherhood called US, through the traditional approach of the NAACP, through the more militant program of the Congress of Racial Equality, through the nonviolent teachings of King or of Malcolm X, through separatism, or by challenging the establishment. In fact all these methods were tried.

At times rivalries between factions spilled over into violence. With federal agents as provocateurs in a struggle for control of the UCLA black studies program, two Black Pan-

ther leaders were killed by members of US.

The Panthers, first in Oakland and then in many cities, had a stormy time. Dedicated to helping the unfortunate, as with breakfast programs for young children, they also took a tough stance and openly carried arms. A confrontation occurred in Oakland in 1967 in which a policeman was killed and Huey Newton, the founder of the Panthers, was wounded. After two hung juries, he left the country.

Then in December, 1969, federal agents made simultaneous raids on Panther headquarters in Los Angeles, Vallejo, Chicago, Philadelphia, and several other cities. The mayor of Vallejo was horrified at the damage to the commissary as well as the headquarters. In Los Angeles the exchange of fire lasted long enough for television cameramen to cover the finale when men, women, and infants were brought out and hustled off to jail. Senator Mervyn Dymally reached the scene to protest and was beaten by the police.

For a time blacks reached for things African—natural hairdos, African dress, Swahili phrases, and soul food. With the further inspiration of *Roots*, Alex Haley's book and television special, many sought to establish African roots, but that passed. In contrast to white Americans, the majority of whom are descended from nineteenth and twentieth century immigrants, black Americans trace back mainly to seventeenth and eighteenth century immigration, which makes them much longer and farther removed than many whites from the Old World.

Blacks have unquestionably made giant strides in politics. By the seventies Tom Bradley became mayor of Los Angeles and Wilson Riles became state superintendent of instruction, the first black elected to statewide office. Yvonne Brathwaite Burke was elected to the assembly and the House of Representatives and appointed to the Los Angeles board of supervisors. Dymally became state senator, lieutenant governor, and congressman. Ronald Dellums was elected to Congress and Diane Watson to the state senate. Wiley W. Manuel and Allen E. Broussard were appointed to the state supreme court and Willie Brown to the powerful role of speaker of the assembly. Many blacks have served on school boards. In the heated struggle over integration in Los Angeles, Rita Walters, the only black member, was projected into crucial leadership on behalf of the victimized children.

The Grape Boycott and La Raza

After boyhood in a family of migratory farm workers and several more years in such work, in 1952 César Chávez found a job in the community service program of the AFL-CIO

César Chávez
Los Angeles Times

among Mexican laborers. Failing to persuade this organization to start a farm workers union, he decided in 1962 to organize one himself. With Delano as his base he launched the National Farm Workers Association and in two years membership was a phenomenal 50,000, most of them Mexicans.

In 1965 Filipino grape pickers came up from the Coachella Valley organized as an AFL-CIO union. When they struck for the wage paid imported workers, Chávez and his union had to decide whether to join the strike. The fervor of Mexico's Independence Day readily transferred to the cause. *Viva México!* became *Viva la Huelga* (the strike)! *Viva la Unión!* Chávez was the binding force in the collaboration and soon the two unions merged.

Because table grapes had to be picked with special care, Chávez focused on this most vulnerable part of the business. That this boycott could succeed against so mouthwatering a morsel as the grape ran contrary to nature. Yet the state's monopoly was such that any table grape other than Concord in any market in the nation was in high probability from California.

La Huelga gained from public remorse about exploitation of migratory stoop-labor, remembrance of Steinbeck's *Grapes of Wrath*, and the inspiration of the Montgomery bus boycott. Chávez tied the strike to Catholic endorsements of social reform and the resurgent pride of being Mexican. Dedication to nonviolence and his self-sacrificing example, as well as that of Dolores Huerta and other NFWA leaders, were fundamental to the initial success in this move to upgrade the agricultural branch of California labor.

The boycott also drew support from Robert Kennedy, Jess Unruh, Eugene McCarthy, Chicago's Mayor Richard Daley, and from Democratic clubs and student groups. The Pentagon, it is said, boosted its purchases of grapes, but the boycott reached the eastern states and the Scandinavian countries. A surprising number of persons, including children who had never tasted the forbidden fruit, took the pledge and kept it.

The boycott's most tangible achievement was a permanent reduction in the per capita consumption of table grapes. The growers fought back by angling for more laborers from Mexico, including many illegals, by mechanizing more farm tasks, and by allying with the Teamsters Union. Through the seventies and into the eighties Chávez continued to be a potent factor in upholding the interests of farmworkers and a force to be considered in politics.

Urban Hispanics

Through the decades of the great prosperity Hispanics came to California in ever increasing numbers, some from Spain, Cuba, Central America, Peru, Chile, New Mexico, and Texas, but most of them from Mexico. By 1980 Hispanics were put at 2 million, far and away more than any other ethnic minority. The number may have been somewhat exaggerated due to stress on identification by Spanish surname. The school censuses failed to recognize that many such persons are indistinguishable in the white majority and that Spanish-named blacks and Asians are inaccurately included.

By the eighties the great majority of Hispanics were city dwellers, in Los Angeles' eastside barrio in particular but also in many other southern California and Central Valley cities. They were found in many employments—as day laborers, domestics, clerks, office workers, garment makers, bus boys, car washers, gardeners, maintenance workers, as storekeepers, teachers, artists, executives, and members of the professions.

Both in farm labor ranks and in the cities many of the newcomers were legal entrants but, by American law, some were illegal. Policy on law enforcement vacillated. Furthermore, among both the legal and illegal, a sizeable number were nonimmigrants. As the Chinese had done a century earlier, many from Mexico came to stay only as long as necessary to earn enough to return home to live comfortably. Traditional attitudes made it difficult to welcome such entrants.

When the courts ruled that Hispanic children assigned to segregated schools were victimized and equally entitled to redress, these findings were taken to cover the entire ethnic group even though many Hispanics were unmistakably in the mainstream.

Following the lead of the blacks and Indians trying to preserve their roots, Hispanics insisted on bilingual/bicultural education, and the courts certified their right to vote in Spanish and to be taught in Spanish. Raising the banner of La Raza (The Race), Chicanos complained about the poor quality of their schools, lack of attention to Mexican culture and achievements, lack of voice in setting school policies, and the small number of Hispanic teachers and administrators. In the early seventies, as part of this effort, there were demonstrations and confrontations with the police. In the course of one of these, their most effective spokesman, reporter Reuben Salazar, was killed by a tear gas cannister fired into an eastside bar. Some concessions were made; in the colleges Chicano study programs became commonplace, along with Chicano professors. Per capita the Hispanics had less political clout than the blacks, but Governor Jerry Brown made more Hispanic appointments as judges and to various commissions than any of his predecessors and particularly to the state board of education.

California's Rich Multiethnic Mix

It was appropriate in 1945 that the Charter of the United Nations was signed in cosmopolitan San Francisco. Los Angeles was then the all-American city with the closest match to the nation's racial and ethnic makeup.

Migration to California mounted, including a special surge of immigrants in the late seventies. The 1980 census found a rise in the Indian and black contingents and more striking increase in Asians and Hispanics. Los Angeles had more of every minority, but San Francisco was still the most cosmopolitan center. Prophets saw Los Angeles as a Mexican city within a few years and California as a mostly minority Third World state.

What the 1980 count really showed was that the white/black ratio in the state was 8 to 1, the white/Asian 13 to 1, and the white/Hispanic 3½ to 1. Inquiry put to the Hispanics revealed that more than half identified themselves as white rather than as minority, which should alter that ratio significantly. Squarely in the tradition of America as a nation of descendants of immigrants, California has a richly multiethnic population.

In the early and biggest migrations, although there was temporary cohesion of Germans or Scandinavians or Poles, the pragmatic goal had been to pick up the national language as soon as possible and qualify for earning a living, the prerequisites for entering the mainstream. These immigrants intended to remain in America and their children, if not

The Ethnic Mix

INDIAN
1%

HISPANIC
19%

BLACK
8%

ASIAN
5%

ANGLO
67%

Largest Cities
1980

Los Angeles	2,952,198
San Diego	874,348
San Francisco	674,150
San Jose	627,955
Long Beach	356,734
Oakland	338,721
Sacramento	274,547
Anaheim	218,468
Fresno	215,396
Santa Ana	205,730

they themselves, would be Americans. These immigrants soon became hyphenated Americans and then simply Americans.

In its pastoral and gold rush periods California attracted immigrants in abundance and great variety. By World War II it was higher than any other state in Japanese and Chinese Americans and high in several other classifications. Thereafter it became the state most favored by refugees from Vietnam and immigrants from Korea.

After the shattering experience of exile during the war, some Japanese chose repatriation with their families to Japan. Others relocated elsewhere in the United States, but most came back to pick up the pieces of their life in California.

Japanese tourists come in such numbers that a publisher plans to publish this history of California in Japanese translation. In 1980 a Tokyo corporation with great fanfare scheduled a Pacific Coast Conference football game in the Tokyo stadium. Along with the tourists immigration has resumed and, because of Japan's rapid Westernization, acculturation is swift. A few California cities may have a Little Tokyo and here and there a block or two of houses where bonzaied landscaping recalls a neighborhood once Japanese, but geographically the California Japanese are substantially dispersed.

With mainland China as an ally in the War in the Pacific, the United States terminated its racist ban on immigration from China and placed Chinese on the quota system. In business and housing most barriers came down. Immigration picked up, bringing a substantial amount of Chinese capital. Meanwhile, San Francisco Chinatown has a durability of its own, with well maintained contacts and a zeal to retain its publicly supported Chinese school. In 1971 the president of the Chinese Six Companies mustered 600 angry parents who objected so vigorously to the school

board intention to "use their children as guinea pigs" for integration that they broke up the board meeting. When the superintendent came to speak at a public meeting, he had to run for his life.

California attracted so many immigrants from so many nations that it was suggested that Ellis Island be relocated on the Los Angeles River and perhaps the Statue of Liberty at the airport. The Los Angeles school district enrolled pupils with 82 mother tongues. The flight of the Shah of Iran and the siezure of the American hostages called attention to the presence in Los Angeles, or more especially in Beverly Hills, of hundreds of Iranian students and vast sums of Iranian and OPEC money invested in residential and business property.

Centering around the Los Angeles Harbor and especially Carson, California has the principal overseas cluster of Samoans. Family and religious ties are strong and much of Samoan culture, as modified by missionary and trader contacts, is kept intact. Americanization has grown apace.

Although the native Gabrielino have disappeared, Navajo, Sioux, and members of other Indian tribes have come in sufficient numbers to give Los Angeles more Indians than any other city. Pride in Indianness is strong and on a Pan-Indian basis. Thus *The Indian Historian*, published in San Francisco by Rupert Costo, a Cahuilla man, and Jeannette Costo, a Cherokee, is a strong voice for all things Indian. Near Point Conception the proposed liquid natural gas facility for landing gas from Alaska and the Orient was held up because it would desecrate a sacred Chumash site. In higher dramatics, late in 1969, a war party made headlines by occupying Alcatraz Island, just abandoned as a federal prison, and offering to buy it for $24 in baubles and beads. On intercession by Jane Fonda, the state assembly adopted a resolution urging the Great White Father to assign the island to this group. Negotiations dragged on, but after a time the Indians struck their tipis.

Belated Focus on Women's Rights

In 1980 California women numbered 12 million. They may well be the last group to receive equal protection of the law because of the very pervasiveness of their victimization.

By the Nineteenth Amendment in 1920 women were effectively guaranteed the right to vote, long before that right was enjoyed nationwide by blacks and Indians. But women are not spoken to directly by the Fourteenth Amendment, though that document was long ago interpreted to include corporations as "persons" protected against discriminatory state enactments or enforcements.

As a group women are endowed with less physical strength than men. They have the sole responsibility for childbearing and, as a not inevitable but traditional corollary, frequently that of childrearing and housekeeping, as "women's work" not paid for in cash. Women are far more exposed to rape and other forms of sexual molestation and to assault and battery and other social hazards. Logic would seem to call for certain more-than-equal protections.

Women bear the yoke of discriminations encased in our culture and entrenched in the language. Because English lacks a generic term that links men and women, women are lost in elipses such as "mankind," "God of our Fathers," and the State Capitol's prayer, "Give Me Men To Match My Mountains."

Using the "King's English," even a writer with the fairest of intentions may inadvertantly use a phrase that denigrates women. It was a well-intentioned senator who held up Califor-

nia's ratification of the Equal Rights Amendment on the ground that it was unnecessary. In time, he withdrew his objection and California ratified. In accord with a city ordinance, Mayor Dianne Feinstein of San Francisco in 1981 cancelled participation in a convention in Nevada, one of the nonratifying states.

The Shame of Los Angeles

Without waiting for court action some districts such as Berkeley, Riverside, and Sacramento integrated their schools in compliance with the ruling in *Brown*. Others, among them Pasadena, San Francisco, Oxnard, and Inglewood, waited for court action and then followed the law. After nearly a decade, the ACLU found it necessary to go to court to compel the Los Angeles school authorities to integrate.

The Los Angeles district, the largest in the state, had by far the most segregation. ACLU's prolonged attempts to persuade the board of education were joined by NAACP, CORE, and many other organizations. The intensity of the pleadings, the marches, the sit-ins, and other demonstrations were a replay of the bitter struggle in the South, but the school authorities would not even acknowledge the existence of segregation.

Suit was brought in 1963 in *Crawford* v. *Board of Education, Los Angeles* and reached trial in 1968–69. In 1970 Judge Alfred Gitelson found the board guilty of many and prolonged acts of bad faith that made it responsible for the segregated schooling. He ordered an immediate end to segregation. Elimination of minority segregated schools, he ruled, must begin at once and be completed by the end of the second school year.

Although in 1969 the board had laid out a program of pupil exchanges that would have eliminated all segregation at a cost of a mere $22.5 million a year, less than 3 percent of the

1969 school budget, the president of the board and the superintendent immediately went on television and denounced the court order as unfounded and so expensive that it must be appealed.

State and nationwide shock waves followed. Integrationists could see victory at last, but to others and to most public officials this "busing decision," as they termed it, was an alarum. Ironically, the word "busing" did not appear in the order.

Mayor Sam Yorty predicted "real trouble." Governor Reagan called the decision "utterly ridiculous." He proclaimed that California had no segregation—imbalance, perhaps, in some metropolitan areas, but that "is going to disappear." Senator Murphy fumed that desegregation would cost $50 million, and "that we don't have." The city council, the board of supervisors, the county superintendent, the state superintedent of instruction, the California congressional delegation, HEW Secretary Robert Finch, and President Nixon all belabored the decision. The state board of education went so far as to repeal every provision in the education code that pertained to integration.

On appeal, counsel for petitioners argued strongly for the order. Counsel for the board challenged the applicability of *Brown*, claimed that the separation of races in the Los Angeles schools was different, and insisted that all decision-making about education should be left to the expertness of the board. It also argued that, since it had not been proved that blacks were not genetically inferior, integration might be futile. Meanwhile, the board turned its back on any desegregation.

Time dragged on. The court of appeals in 1975 found for the board, but in June, 1976, the California Supreme Court upheld Judge Gitelson's order, and the case was remanded to the trial court to supervise compliance.

The trial court, with a newly assigned judge, allowed the board to concentrate not on desegregating the minority schools but on "desegregating" white schools which in the meaning of *Brown* and *Crawford* were not segregated to begin with. The board's game plan was to bring to these schools just enough minority pupils to meet an arbitrary definition of integrated and then exempt them from any further participation in the desegregation process. These schools thus were preserved predominantly white, in sharp contrast to the much larger number of ghetto and barrio segregated schools which the board announced would be permanently segregated.

After court hearings spread out over five school years with prolonged debate over plans submitted by the board, and implementation of several programs costing hundreds of millions of dollars, not one of the minority schools had been desegregated. In 1981 a third judge, asserting that "all facts material to the case had changed, retracted all prior orders and dismissed the case.

In the main Los Angeles has been blessed with a happy history, though with some shameful entries. In the 1850s a slave market was held every Monday where Indians were auctioned off to work out fines for weekend drunkenness. In 1871 a large mob of whites invaded the Chinese quarter and perpetrated a wanton massacre. Later the Times Building was bombed, and subsequently police and vigilantes beat and arbitrarily imprisoned striking dock workers. In 1942 in the wartime hysteria all Japanese Americans were sent into exile.

No count was kept of the Indians auctioned but they were relatively few. In the Chinese massacre and the Times Building bombing the direct casualties ran to about 20 each. The mistreated strikers numbered 1,000 men and one girl. Of the 110,000 West Coast Japanese sent to concentration camps, Los Angeles provided the largest contingent, but that was less than a tenth of the number of more than 300,000 black and other minority boys and girls assigned to second class citizenship on the segregated campuses. A case can be made that the school segregation is the worst infamy of all. This gargantuan injustice dwarfs the historic atrocities.

Several of this city's earlier dark episodes were spur-of-the-moment incidents. Some operated only briefly and in some instances restitution was made. But Los Angeles' segregated schools, far from being temporary, remained intact, grew in number, and in 1981 hundreds of them were classified as permanently segregated not only by the board but also by the court. Thus 27 years after *Brown*, 11 years after Judge Gitelson's explicit order to desegregate, 5 years after the California Supreme Court upheld that order, most of the petitioners in *Crawford* remained sealed off from the mainstream.

ACLU, Watchguard for Justice

In 1981 President Jimmy Carter awarded the Medal of Freedom to Roger Baldwin, the founder in 1920 of the American Civil Liberties Union. The California branch dates back almost that far. In 1923 at a meeting in San Pedro when the longshoremen were trying to organize and Upton Sinclair began to read the Constitution, the police interfered and arrested him and many others. That violation of the First Amendment guaranty of freedom of speech led to the founding of the California ACLU. In time it divided into two affiliates, centered in Los Angeles and San Francisco.

A single issue organization, ACLU is dedicated to upholding the freedoms guaranteed in the Bill of Rights and related parts of the Constitution. When its chief counsel, A. L. Wirin, named for the Great Emancipator, was

asked if it was true that he had taken more cases to the Supreme Court than any other attorney, his answer was, "That may be so, and I have lost more."

In the thirties Wirin was kidnapped and threatened with death when he supported Mexican field hands in Imperial Valley who were trying to organize. In the forties, in the hysteria following Pearl Harbor, it was the ACLU that voiced strong opposition to the removal and lockup of the Japanese Americans.

In the fifties during the panic about security, and the widespread denial of constitutional protections, the ACLU challenged the loyalty oaths required of churches and veterans and, on a longer term basis, the investigative committee exposures and the firings and blacklistings. Eason Monroe, a professor at San Francisco State University, who was dismissed for refusing to sign the Levering oath, became the director of ACLU of Southern California. Two decades later an ACLU suit extinguished that oath which had blanketed all public employees.

As has been described, the ACLU found constitutional basis for attacking the death penalty. It carried the appeal against the Anti–Fair Housing Amendment, saw to it that everyone arrested in the Watts riot—and there were thousands—had counsel, provided that same protection for black students arrested for takeover of a building of the State University at Northridge and for the clubbed and arrested antiwar demonstrators in the Century City peace march. ACLU's persistence in the unpopular school desegregation case took it almost to bankruptcy.

In the seventies violations of women's rights were increasingly challenged. In 1972, when a new director for the ACLU of Southern California was being chosen, the subtle hold of sexism showed even in that organization. The leading candidate for the first time was a woman, Ramona Ripston. She was asked, "You are married and the mother of three; will you be able to care for your children and home and also run this large active organization?" Her answer was direct and resounding: "That is an improper question that never would have been put to a man."

Subsequent ACLU efforts included support of the Equal Rights Amendment, legalizing of abortion, and elimination of abuses in rape prosecutions. In 1980 it successfully challenged stark inadequacies in military justice as meted out to young women of the crew of the *Norton Sound* in which homosexuality was loosely charged by the Navy.

Civil liberties issues often are complex. Affirmative action, for example, which ACLU strongly supports, calls for preference to blacks, other minorities, and women to compensate in part for historic denials of equal rights. Such action involves a double standard. In *Bakke*, a male Caucasian sought admission to the medical school of the University of California at Davis but was passed over in favor of several minority and women applicants with lower academic qualifications. The state supreme court upheld this white male's claim to equal opportunity. After strong protest by the NAACP, Harvard and other prominent schools, and the ACLU, the Supreme Court found that race could be one but not the only criterion.

Upholding the freedoms of speech, the press, religion, and the right to fair and equal treatment, the ACLU often found itself standing alone defending unpopular and disreputable persons—conscientious objectors, draft dodgers, and demonstrators against the war in Vietnam; professors, writers, actors, and others who refused to swear they were not Communists; and Nazis and Klansmen denied right of free speech. Without the work of this organization the history of California would have been far different.

Resurgence of the Right

Not least of the turnabouts in the sixties was that of extreme conservatism. California Democrats may have been reassured by Brown's victory over Nixon in 1962 and by Johnson over Goldwater in 1964, but the Republican right at that latter election sent Murphy to the Senate and succeeded overwhelmingly with Proposition 14. Henry Salvatori and other major campaign contributors saw another good omen in the speechmaking of Ronald Reagan, a well-known actor, first for General Electric and then in support of the Goldwater campaign. They began to promote him for governor.

Undaunted by the anti-third-term tradition, which only Warren had been able to overcome, Brown was again a candidate in 1966. The Democrats were deeply divided; remembering promises that this would be his turn,

Ronald Reagan

UCLA Library

Unruh gave no support. Brown was unfairly criticized for the Watts Riot and the student uprising at Berkeley, neither of which was directly traceable to him. By 1966, although President Johnson had shouldered responsibility for carrying on the war in Vietnam, some of the blame for the war rubbed off on Brown. Reagan won by more than a million votes. On analysis by precincts, the vote distribution closely resembled that two years earlier for Proposition 14, a strong hint on what the voters wanted from the new governor.

Instead of being sworn in at the traditional hour, Reagan dramatized the urgency of his promised tax reductions by scheduling the ceremony for the first minutes of his term, just after midnight. Lest anyone be misled, he chose the most conservative of the justices of the supreme court to administer the oath of office. In his address he emphasized his determination "to squeeze, cut, and trim."

Unruh with relish promised that the legislature would give the new governor "on-the-job training," and that is about what happened. Reagan put a freeze on state hiring, asked state employees to work on Washington's Birthday, instructed department heads to list in preferential order budget items that could be reduced or deleted, and went to work on the budget that had been submitted by his predecessor and tried to carry out his promise to economize.

Under the California system, however, most of the state expenditures were tied up by ongoing commitments and could not be struck by the governor. Gas tax revenue went into a fund for building, repairing, and policing freeways, highways, and lesser roads. Cities and counties received fractions for street paving and repair. On the basis of average daily attendance the state was committed to disbursing large sums to the school districts. There were other fixed charges. The reachable items in the budget almost came down to the annual outlay for the University of Califor-

nia, the State Universities and Colleges, the correctional and custodial institutions, and the state contributions to welfare programs.

Even in these restricted branches Reagan needed cooperation by the legislature, which the Democrats controlled during all but two of his eight years in office. He inherited a budget of approximately $5 billion a year and passed on to his successor a budget of $10.2 billion, only part of which is attributable to inflation, or to population increase, which was moderate during his years in office.

Brown had been criticized for not being able to control the university students, a responsibility which the constitution assigns to the board of regents. Reagan set out to control them. As the ex officio president of the board he attended meetings regularly. Except at the height of the loyalty oath controversy, earlier governors had held themselves more at arms' length in keeping with the constitutional mandate that the university be kept free from partisan politics. Reagan had called for the dismissal of Clark Kerr as president and at his first meeting with the regents, when Kerr asked for a vote of confidence, he was instead asked to resign.

Reagan's presence at meetings of the regents and of the trustees of the state colleges seemed to catalyze student outbursts. Both boards were rotating meetings to the various campuses, several of which seemed to vie in demonstrating against the governor. The causes were a mixture of demand for educational reform, insistence on student participation in educational planning, support for the demands of blacks and other minorities for special attention and special programs, and cooperation in the nationwide protest against the war in Vietnam.

The Reagan family moved into the historic but decrepit governor's mansion, now exposed to distracting traffic noise, and as quickly moved out. Admirers found and furnished a more suitable home in Sacramento.

Reagan had his idiosyncracies. He was adamant against withholding for state income taxes, though, in addition to the forfeited interest, the state lost substantially because of unreported incomes. In the end, he allowed this reform to become law.

In the face of his popularity there was no rush of Democrats eager to file against him in 1970. Out of a feeling of obligation to the party, Unruh became the nominee and, as expected, found himself badly handicapped by lack of campaign funds. Unable to get Reagan to face the issues, Unruh, in a bid for attention, contrived a confrontation with Salvatori. The outcome of the election was a foregone conclusion; Unruh did well to narrow the margin to about 500,000 votes, but, once defeated, as is almost inexorable in California politics, his star fell. He managed a comeback years later as state treasurer, an obscure office in which he saved the state millions of dollars, but his viability for a leading role became minimal.

Continuing his drive to reduce state expenditures, Reagan pushed for lowering outlay for relief of the unemployed and for medical expenses of the poor. Unable to get cooperation from the legislature, in 1973 he took the unprecedented step of calling for a special election and personally submitted a constitutional amendment to lower the level of state spending from 8.3 to 7 percent of personal income. That proposal was roundly defeated.

As it worked out, Reagan's California let him down. He often must have felt thwarted. His campaigning had revealed little enthusiasm for conservation of natural resources or the beauties of nature; his interest was more in promoting prosperity and helping businessmen produce more wealth. He had stressed that it would be good to have the oil that would flow from the offshore wells, but in 1967 a Union Oil rig sprang a leak that polluted water and beaches all along the Santa Barbara Channel. When enlargement of Redwood National Park was proposed, he had quipped, "If you have seen one tree you have seen them all." Soon a flood felled several giant trees and threatened to destroy one entire stand and Reagan's remark returned to haunt him.

To him and to the state chamber of commerce continued population growth was vital to prosperity, but in his first term population leveled off, and after the Sylmar earthquake San Fernando Valley suffered more departures than arrivals. An astute investment allowed him to show no taxable income one year, and critics pointed to that as an evidence of bad citizenship.

In 1968 and 1972, Reagan headed the California delegations to his party's national conventions as a favorite son, but Nixon had the nominations sewn up both years. In 1976 and 1980 as a candidate Reagan would not have an in-office base.

No matter how he pressed for economies, the times and the California system were refractory and Reagan could not lower state expenditures or taxation. His main achievement in economizing was to hold the number of state employees at about 100,000.

CHAPTER 30

**The Santa Monicas Temporarily Block
Urban Sprawl**

*Graphics Section, Los Angeles
City Planning Department*

Paradoxically Californians cringe at the specter of no growth, but growth itself can be a specter. We are entering the age of the ecological imperative. To preserve our way of life, can we bring ourselves to roll back consumption, restrain the machines, housebreak science, and, rather than as parasites, live as symbionts at peace with our environment?

J. C.

New
Challenges

Farewell to Exuberant Growth

Spain had been content to send only a very few persons to California. In the Mexican period growth picked up and by its end the colonizers, including acculturated Indians and "blue-eyed Anglos," amounted to perhaps fifteen thousand. American takeover and the gold rush touched off a rapid increase to half a million by 1868. That number increased to a million by 1888, 2 million by 1908, 5 million by 1928, 10 million by 1948, and 20 million by 1968, a doubling or more every 20 years. In every round the task of fitting in that many more was gargantuan, but the momentum was impressive. One expert predicted that California would catch up with Japan.

How the state had achieved growth is clearly on record. One way was to seize on a natural resource such as cowhides or beaver pelts and exploit it to the point of leveling off or all the way to exhaustion. Gold was the next such resource, then the great wheat harvests, a rush of healthseekers, and a real estate boom, followed by irrigation, many different crops, the railroads, and a flow of visitors and new residents. Bungalows, oil wells, an expanded crop list, the automobile, and the unsolicited arrival of the movie makers produced the boom of the twenties. Wartime incentives accounted for the spurt in the forties, and a great construction splurge, along with remarkable applications of science, was central to the postwar population explosion. In retrospect it is clear that repeatedly Californians found a windfall to exploit—gold, the health rush, the navel orange and cooperative marketing, the cinema, those ships to build, and the race to the moon.

Although population might edge up in hard times such as the 1870s or the 1930s, the totals swung upward most giddily when the state, the nation, and the world were prospering. California, it was said, was populated by those who wanted to come and could afford to. Many were ready to join the workforce immediately and many brought capital with them. Most Californians were convinced that prosperity depended on continued increase in population. Consequently, there was rejoicing in 1962 when California overtook New York and became the most populous state, and there was dismay a few years later when it appeared that population growth was at or near zero.

An official reading became available in the census of 1980 with its count at only 23.5 million. Clearly the curve that had been mounting so sharply had flattened drastically and was not headed for that seventh doubling by 1988. The omens seemed to say that the age of exuberant population growth had ended. To the chambers of commerce and promoters and developers, that was bad news. To environmentalists and to others nostalgic for a less cluttered scene, the news was heartening, but even among them there was concern that no growth might mean no prosperity.

Lowered Support Elements

By the seventies and eighties it was evident that several of the economic mainstays had shrunk or disappeared. The most noteworthy decline was in the construction industries. The federal subsidy for interstate freeways came to an end. A similar fate befell the state freeway funding. When inflation came, the tax pennies per gallon were much less valuable, while the costs billed ran to many more dollars. The Department of Transportation needed all that income for upkeep and repairs. It would try to

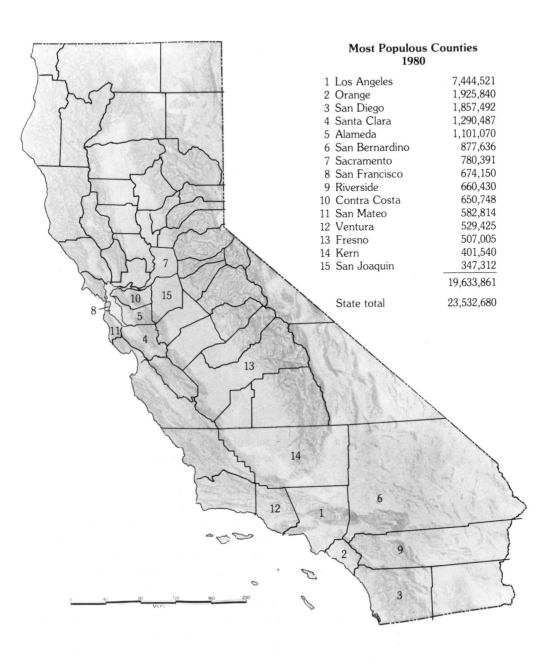

**Most Populous Counties
1980**

1	Los Angeles	7,444,521
2	Orange	1,925,840
3	San Diego	1,857,492
4	Santa Clara	1,290,487
5	Alameda	1,101,070
6	San Bernardino	877,636
7	Sacramento	780,391
8	San Francisco	674,150
9	Riverside	660,430
10	Contra Costa	650,748
11	San Mateo	582,814
12	Ventura	529,425
13	Fresno	507,005
14	Kern	401,540
15	San Joaquin	347,312
		19,633,861
	State total	23,532,680

Most Populous Counties, 1980

complete work on a few freeways already begun but held out little hope for new starts.

With the California Project delivering water to the west San Joaquin Valley and to cities and farms south of the Tehachapi, that kind of construction virtually halted. With lowered enrollments, school construction was slowed almost to a standstill. The building of houses was also at a low ebb. New apartment building did not keep up with those torn down or converted. There was some construction of new office buildings and hotels but few new industrial plants.

On environmental grounds certain proposed industrial developments were discouraged—a chemical plant on Suisun Bay and a Standard Oil of Ohio unloading facility at Long Beach. Utilities backed off from nuclear power plants and coal-fired desert projects, partly because of environmentalist opposition but also because, with fewer people than once expected, the need was smaller.

The sleek streamliners which had reached their climax in the fifties—some two dozen departures per day—were gleefully withdrawn by their sponsors and only the token operations of Amtrak remained. Admittedly there was a concomitant rise of traffic at the major airports, but to railroad buffs it is a sobering thought that each widebodied plane can carry more passengers than did the Lark, the California Zephyr, the Chief, or the Super Chief.

Automobile companies closed their California assembly lines as did the tire manufacturers. The garment industry increasingly had its work done across the border or across the Pacific. The same changes occurred in various forms of light industry and in printing. In the fifties half of the world's scheduled passenger flights were in Douglas planes. By 1980, although California plants supplied parts and components, they seldom figured as prime

contractors for commercial or military planes.

Mergers changed the corporate landscape. In a few instances a California company aggrandized at the expense of other states; Times-Mirror, for instance, picked up a Long Island newspaper and an out-of-state cable television company. More often the tide of corporate control flowed out: Douglas Aircraft was merged into McDonnell, Hughes Aircraft into Republic, Dart into Kraft.

Buffeted by urban and industrial sprawl, some leading agricultural counties dropped several notches in the state and national rankings in value of production, Los Angeles and Santa Clara among others.

Science and the application of science were of continued importance, but without the extraordinary contracts for the wars in Korea and Vietnam and the race to the moon.

Jerry Brown as Governor

In 1974 the Republicans nominated Houston Flournoy for governor. He was state controller and had been an assemblyman. The Democrats turned to Jerry Brown (Edmund G., Jr.), son of a well-remembered governor. After two years as a Jesuit novitiate he had switched to classical studies and then to law. In 1969 he was politically active as a member of the community, colleges board in Los Angeles, then was elected as the state's secretary of state. In that normally inconspicuous office he won notice by more vigorous exercise of its powers and by advocating tightened restrictions on campaign contributions. Unruh, the best-known Democratic prospect, had been sidelined by defeat. Because of his father, Brown had instant name recognition and support, and he proved an energetic and cagey campaigner. Elected at 36, he was the state's youngest governor and, with one exception, the least experienced.

Edmund G. (Jerry) Brown
Los Angeles Times

Taking over, Brown dramatized the contrast to Reagan. Instead of the official Cadillac he chose a blue Plymouth. Instead of moving into the palatial new governor's mansion, he chose a spartan bachelor apartment. In his brief inaugural remarks he startled his supporters by calling for austerity and lowered expectations for the state. Specifically he promised that for the first two years there would be no new taxes and no tax rate increase. When the legislature exceeded his recommendations, he vetoed items totaling $100 million.

Early in his third year in office Brown charged at a regents meeting that the university was overbudgeted and less distinguished than it claimed. The second charge was somewhat nebulous; the measure usually relied on had been a composite of opinion polls on preeminence in 20 or 30 subject fields, and the dilemma of campus by campus or systemwide ratings had been left up in the air. Nevertheless, Brown pressed some Reagan-like austerity on the university.

Bitten by the presidential bug, Brown spent much time and energy trying to win Democratic convention votes in 1976 and 1980. In the latter year that was tricky because a Republican, Mike Curb, had been elected lieutenant governor and threatened to make appointments whenever the governor was out of the state. Even apart from these forays into national politics there were criticisms that Brown was mercurial.

On environmental issues he was consistent, supportive of the regulatory work of the Coastal Commission, opposing the commercial development of Mineral King in the Sequoia back country, favoring postponement of nuclear power plants at least until safe disposal of nuclear wastes was worked out, and willing to forego industrial developments on the basis of probable damage to the environment.

Of particular importance were his appointments. Politically the key one was that of Gray Davis as his chief assistant—with time off intermittently to manage Brown's political campaigns. Davis doubled as chief spokesman, projecting a firm grasp of the problems and programs that counterbalanced Brown's style.

Brown went far beyond earlier governors in putting affirmative action into practice and appointing blacks, Hispanics, and women. His most elegant appointment was of Theodora Kroeber to an unexpired term on the board of regents. Her sensitive and eloquent farewell message to her colleagues went to the heart of the problems of governance of an institution of learning. His most controversial appointments were of Adriana Gianturco as head of the department of transportation and Rose Elizabeth Bird as chief justice of the supreme court.

The legislature found so much fault with Gianturco that it repeatedly deleted her name from the payroll. Repeatedly Brown found other funds from which she could be paid. A boiling point in complaint came over her experiment with "diamond lanes" on the Santa Monica Freeway, inner (fast) lanes so marked and reserved for buses and carpools. Traffic snarls of mammoth proportions were created.

The trouble was that the crucial stretch of that freeway between the San Diego and Harbor Freeways begins in each direction with left hand as well as right hand entrances and ends with left hand and right hand exits. En route there are ten or a dozen right hand entrances and exits. In consequence a great many drivers had to work their way all across

the freeway in the course of all these mergings. There was no hint that the planners understood what the problem was, but tie-ups and complaints were so voluminous that the diamonds at length were erased.

Not all was lost. Another part of this trial and error approach, which is how most lessons about freeway design and operation have been learned, was brilliantly successful. Metering access, particularly for cars carrying only one or two persons, worked like a charm and improved the carrying capacity of the freeway.

Gianturco was also much in the news in 1980 after the slide at Big Rock Canyon closed the Pacific Coast Highway near Malibu. For a time commuters were ferried around it. An effort was made to pin responsibility for

Freeway Geometry, the Four-Stack Interchange at the Civic Center, Los Angeles

California Department of Transportation

repair on the uphill landowner, but in the end responsibility came to rest on the Department of Transportation. A giant boulder was hauled away by a sculptor and converted into a glyph of John Wayne. Dirtmovers transported the fallout to distant sites, the most visible being an old slide area in Pacific Palisades where it was compacted buttresslike. The laborious task of stabilizing the uneasy hillside was eventually certified to by geologists. More than a year was required for the work and the cost at this 700-foot strip was more than the cost of the original construction of the road from Santa Monica to Port Hueneme.

In the supreme court appointment Brown's intent clearly was to make an unmistakable affirmation of women's rights. As was characteristic in American supreme courts, California's had been an exclusive male club where decisions were by "the Brethren." Playwright Arthur Miller has explored the trauma in being the first woman on an American court. The double burden of being chief justice made Bird's role exceedingly arduous. There were other new appointments, and the court was in transition. Rumors circulated that animosities were disrupting its work.

In 1978 Chief Justice Bird had to stand for election to a regular term. Just before election day the Los Angeles *Times* published a charge that decision on a rape case was being held up because of the damage it might do her chances at the polls. That accusation was without merit. It did not lose her the election, but it led to what amounted to a trial of the supreme court by a televised kangaroo court on the alleged delay and a miscellany of other charges.

A couple of justices testified disparagingly. The senior justice insisted that the work on the opinions had not been completed and that they were not ready for release. After several weeks Justice Mosk's counsel brought suit challenging the legitimacy of the hearings and

Chief Justice Rose Elizabeth Bird

Wide World Photos

won a ruling which led to halting the action.

It was a Pyrrhic victory. The prestige of the supreme court had been tarnished and Chief Justice Bird had been put through an initiation with strong overtones of sexist discrimination. New appointments brought the court to full strength and gave it opportunity to concentrate on its central function.

Toward a Taxpayers Revolt

Even the politicians complained in the sixties and seventies of too much government and too much taxation. Much of both was federal and military and thus only by impact a part of California history. A great part, nonetheless, was state, local, and school and clearly Californian. The classic statement of the complaint would be by a Californian in the presidential campaign of 1980.

Certain citizens and enterprisers were restless under the multiple-level regulations imposed by the many elements of government. Others were more concerned about taxes, and it was seen that tax reduction might also shrink government. Within living memory taxes had been much fewer and much lower. Early in the twentieth century the federal government subsisted on excise and import levies, and schools and local governments relied mainly on the property tax. In Wilson's presidency the federal government instituted an income tax, which the state copied about 20 years later. In 1933 California began to use a sales tax which expanded in 40 years from 1 to 7 percent. Oregon invented the gas tax which California copied and raised. Other added taxes included those on estates and inheritances.

In 1915 a couple of weeks work would pay the average Californian's taxes. Sixty years later the typical taxpayer had to work for the tax collector up to about the 15th of April.

At all levels of government taxes had mushroomed. The federal government claimed the most, and that is where the objection might have centered. The sales tax which disproportionately burdens the poor would also have been a logical target. The gas tax may have escaped because its collection is piecemeal and not shown in the actual billing. The income tax was somewhat shielded by withholding. The property tax, on the other hand, was based on valuation put by the assessor and billed by the collector as a large lump sum. The assessments, furthermore, were boosted for an entire neighborhood whenever similar properties there had sold at an appreciably higher figure. That is where the realtors association decided to strike.

Howard Jarvis, acting for that group, drew up a constitutional amendment in 1978 to roll back assessments to where they stood in 1975 and to limit taxes on such property to 1 percent of the assessed value. It was also pro-

vided that taxes could be added for specified purposes if approved by not less than a two-thirds vote. Jarvis made clear that the amendment was intended as an object lesson to other branches of government to reduce taxes—to the state, for instance, because of its unindexed income tax. Because of inflation that tax was pushing more and more people into higher brackets, and by election day would show a state surplus of about $5 billion, a potent argument for the Jarvis Amendment, Proposition 13.

Homeowners and other property owners would benefit. Benefits might be passed on to renters, leasers, and in prices of many goods sold, though that was something the amendment could not guarantee. There were warnings that local and state bonds would decline in their ratings, and that police, fire, and other public services and the schools would be ruined. Most politicians opposed the amendment, especially those involved in local governments and schools. But this tax relief was popular enough to carry in every county.

Brown had campaigned against Proposition 13 but he was far too good a politician not to jump on the bandwagon. When the legislature assembled in January, 1979, he proposed several economies in state government and suggested how to use the state surplus to bail out schools and local governments. Jarvis had said that the surplus ought to be returned to the income taxpayers who had been overtaxed; he was convinced that all branches of government were overspending and could cut back.

As it worked out, through the next two fiscal years state bailout at $5 billion per year relieved the pressure on school boards and local governments. Local governments in particular showed great ingenuity in adopting utility taxes, new sets of fees and licensing charges, and other sources of income. Jarvis was piqued that the lesson on economizing

The Ferry Building's New Neighbors, the Financial District and a Freeway

San Francisco Convention Bureau

had been blurred. Petitions circulated for "Jarvis II," an amendment to roll back the indexing of state income tax. The legislature had voted the indexing as of 1980, but that could be repealed by the legislature at any time. Jarvis II, however, did not pass.

The long-range effects of Proposition 13 would not be visible until some years down the road. In the first couple of years the amendment saved many homeowners from being taxed out of their homes.

An Improbable Prosperity

In spite of all the discouragements in the economy, the supports that crumbled, and the

lowered expectations, California in the seventies and into the eighties perversely enjoyed an unmistakeable prosperity. It did not benefit all uniformly. At the bottom of the ladder there was serious unemployment, and the retired and others found living on fixed incomes distressingly difficult. But as in the past some unexpected new supports for the economy appeared.

The completed freeway system was one such asset, all the more remarkable because what had begun as a carrier of long-distance intercity traffic came into its own as the indispensable carrier within cities and within entire metropolitan areas. Though pushed aside by suburban and industrial sprawl, California agriculture readjusted and continued as a

427

major contributor as did science and mechanics and their applications.

Communal living had not been forecast as a pillar in the economy. In fact, the city fathers of Santa Monica, for instance, used all their ingenuity to try to forbid the practice. In the seventies the condominium became the rage. The governing attraction was having a share in appreciating values should they come. That was a strange answer to the question, who would want to buy an apartment?

In many instances the condominium was merely an apartment slightly refurbished. In other instances older buildings were razed or a new site was found and an entirely new building was constructed. The going price was substantially higher and the cost of occupancy, with interest, taxes, and management fee included, averaged well above what comparable rentals brought. Consequently here was a business in which quick fortunes were made. A well publicized example is Dr. Jerry Buss, whose activities as a condominium developer, promoter, and owner soon put him in position to buy the Los Angeles Lakers, the Forum, the Kings, and Pickfair, the legendary palace of Mary Pickford and Douglas Fairbanks, and to be in position at the drop of a hat to add the Rams to his constellation.

The entertainment industry also created large purchasing power. A country singer accumulated enough gold discs to pay approximately $15 million for The Knoll, a single-family residence with garage space for thirteen cars and other refinements to match.

Since the time of Henry George, Californians frequently have capitalized on appreciating values. Buying in early, sometimes with the immediate purpose of having a tax write-off, they gained when properties appreciated. The OPEC manipulation of oil prices, combined with double-digit inflation, appearance of foreign investors, and a minimal amount of building activity combined to produce drastic

appreciation for much California real estate.

Soon after Ronald Reagan was elected President, a story broke that the Reagan residence in Palisades Riviera would be on the market at $1.9 million. In 1956 this home cost $26,500. More revealing was the phrase that it was "in a neighborhood of million dollar homes," many of which 30 or 20 or 10 years earlier had cost only a small fraction of the appreciated value. Here was a neighborhood of "home-made" millionaires in the most literal reading of that phrase. And it was one of many such neighborhoods up and down the state.

Similar unearned increments in business, industrial, and agricultural property added greatly to net worth and to the yearly gross state product.

Inflation, higher prices, and the gas shortage led many Californians to vacation in California rather than farther away as had been customary. The depreciation of the dollar also contributed to substantial increase in the number of foreign tourists and the amount of money spent in the state.

By 1978 California led the nation with receipts of $16.2 million in expenditures received from foreign tourists for transportation, meals, accommodations, entertainment, and purchases. In addition, foreigners were investing heavily in California properties, farm and city real estate, banks, and businesses.

Usuriously high interest rates, present under the Carter administration and for a time under Reagan, were seized upon by a select strata in California. The poor could not participate and many of the richest preferred longer term investments, but in 1981, the news broke that Beverly Hills and Palm Springs had been eclipsed and that Hemet in Ramona country was "the richest town in the West." Rather than Beverly Hills' Rodeo Drive, its Florida Avenue with its modest-appearing banks and savings companies was the street that had by far the largest deposits per capita. Hemet's pensioners and retired, though content to live in cottages and mobile homes, were heavily into money market accounts. Here was another unprophesied support for the California economy.

The State of the Arts

Patronage of the arts advanced in the postwar generation. Dorothy Chandler spearheaded a drive to give the Los Angeles Philharmonic a new home in the Music Center at the Acropolis of the Civic Center. In 1980 San Francisco opened a new Opera House at its Civic Center.

Oakland combined museums of history, art, and science most effectively in a new integrated museum. In Los Angeles the art section of the County Museum moved into spacious quarters at the Wilshire Boulevard site of the tar pits, which had provided the articulated skeletons from the age of the dinosaurs featured at the old site in Exposition Park. San Francisco voted a bond issue to build a wing on the De Young Museum to house the Avery Brundage collection of Oriental Art. Norton Simon took over the Pasadena Art Museum and substantially shifted its emphasis. By 1981 a new Museum of Contemporary Art to be built in the Bunker Hill renewal area had commissioned a Japanese architect to design the building. The enormously endowed Getty Museum a few years earlier opened in Pacific Palisades.

Through its exhibit-format books the Sierra Club paid tribute to California's master photographers: Edward Weston, Ansel Adams, Philip Hyde, and many others. The California Historical Society also used pictorial exhibits along with its books and its quarterly to stir interest in the history of the state, and the Historical Society of Southern California

worked toward this same end. *Ramparts* and *Frontier* as journals of opinion and the *Pacific Spectator* as a literary journal came and went. They were succeeded by *Los Angeles* and *New West*, ultimately renamed the *California Magazine*, glossy and rich in advertising, and on occasion achieving incisive investigative reporting and commentary.

Over the same decades, encouraged by the Roxburghe and Zamarano clubs, California has been well served by master book designers such as the Grabhorns and Kennedys, Ward Ritchie, Saul and Lillian Marks, Grant Dahlstrom, and by publishers such as the University of California Press, Howell, Clark, Westernlore, and Talisman, all interested in Californiana. Booksellers Dawson, Elder, and Howell stress that field. California became a major market for books. In 1980 the largest reviewing outlet in the West established the Los Angeles *Times* Book Awards. One of them, the Robert Kirsch Award, honoring the paper's longtime chief reviewer, went to Wallace Stegner for his body of writings, heavily western and including California titles such as *The Preacher and the Slave* and *Angle of Repose*.

The architectural achievements most praised include such gems as the Golden Gate Bridge, Frank Lloyd Wright's Marin County Courthouse, Lloyd Wright's Wayfarers Chapel in Palos Verdes, and the Bradbury Building, all of a generation or more ago. The jewel-like Glass Chapel in Palos Verdes contrasts sharply with the grandiose Glass Cathedral completed in 1980 in Garden Grove which, despite some acoustical problems, well serves the intended purposes of Rev. Robert Schuller and his congregation.

In the grand design of the freeways and of the huge aqueducts, function dictates form as it does in the building-block starkness of the high rises. These magnitudes impress, but they are triumphs of engineering rather than of architecture. There are vantage points from which the geometry of these structures or the carpet of urban development is breathtaking.

Where Have All the Heroes Gone?

Historic California is rich in heroes: Serra, Portolá, Anza, Lasuén, Smith, Bidwell, Coleman, Judah, Huntington, Swett, Bancroft, Muir, Chaffey. One could say that the motto "Give Me Men To Match My Mountains" has been realized.

Suddenly on the modern scene where have all the heroes gone? There are churchmen better versed in theology than was Serra, test pilots carrying on in the Anza tradition, engineers ushering in new developments in transportation, school people with more power than was granted to Swett, and historians better trained than Bancroft.

Some individuals stand out. Among them two undaunted environmentalists for decades have spearheaded the never-ending fight to preserve the natural endowment—Ansel Adams as the state's premier photographer and David Brower as the executive secretary and director of publications of the Sierra Club and then of the Friends of the Earth.

Otis Chandler elevated the Los Angeles *Times* to just about the best American newspaper.

Cartoonist Charles Schultz, in a daily strip, *Peanuts*, through Charlie Brown and his friends poignantly mirrors universal realities and our dreams and frustrations.

Fulfilling the awesome responsibilities of a Chief Justice, Rose Elizabeth Bird symbolizes the long-overdue breakthrough toward equal opportunity for women.

In a race-conscious time Tom Bradley, elected for three terms as mayor of the largest city in the West, sets an inspiring example of how to win and hold across-the-board public support.

In their day Huntington and his partners were the Southern Pacific Railroad, and A. P. Giannini was the Bank of America. But who can name the heads of Standard Oil of California or PG & E? Who is chairman at Wells Fargo? Who is on first at Union Oil or Foremost-McKesson?

As long ago as the thirties when the first gigantic dam was to be erected on the Colorado, no individual builder or corporation was big enough for the task, and the bid had to be made by the Six Companies. The Central Valley project had to be a coalition effort. In 1970 the second tube paralleling Mulholland's Aqueduct was known merely as a construction by the Department of Water and Power, and the nuclear plants on the drawing boards belonged to PG & E and Southern California Edison. The motto should now read, "Give me corporations to match my problems."

This shift from emphasis on the individual to the group flows naturally from the tremendous increase in all California magnitudes. Certain tasks are so large, the California Water Project, for instance, that only the federal government or the state can handle them. Many undertakings can be carried in the private sector only by a pooling of resources. Most require more ongoing attention than any one individual could give.

Reagan as President

In 1980 by a landslide Ronald Reagan was elected president. As he departed for Washington it could be assumed that he was leaving the stage of state history for another that was national and global.

There were hints that it might not be so. His inaugural ball was staged by Frank Sinatra and early on he made clear that his Rancho de Cielo above Santa Barbara would be his second White House and his vacation retreat. More to the point, he took along a double quartet of close advisers and installed them in key roles. He also took along the main planks in the platform on which he had twice run for governor.

Circumstances also had changed. Many early presidents affected California only slightly, but now the federal government, besides having title to half the land, exercises controls that are numerous and penetrating.

Reagan began by intercepting appropriations and programs that he thought extravagant or unnecessary, among them purchase of additional land for parks. Attacking the budget, he called on Congress to cut welfare, revenue sharing, support of regulatory agencies, and building programs. These economies were more than matched by tax cuts, particularly for corporations and the wealthy.

Supply-side economic theory promised that business thereby would be greatly stimulated, the more so because many governmental controls would be eliminated and the benefits would soon be felt by all. The immediate result was disappointing, perhaps because enormous increases for armaments and the military were called for outside the budget.

When the air controllers struck, Reagan declared their union defunct, assigned military controllers to assist the volunteers, and sharply reduced the number of flights. That meant that many pilots were laid off as were flight attendants, ground crews, and suppliers. One California air line closed down. More air-minded than the average state, California suffered disproportionate loss and inconvenience.

As an announced supporter of the "Sagebrush Rebellion" Reagan moved to curtail the parks service and to open more federal land in and out of the parks for lumbering, mining, oil drilling, and recreational development. With some of the best and most valuable of the nation's natural resources, California was seriously threatened by this reversal of federal policy.

Similarly Reagan determined to downgrade regulatory agencies. He asked for the resignation of Chairman Arthur Flemming of the United States Commission on Civil Rights in order to replace him with a much less zealous investigator. Attorney General William French Smith forecast fewer prosecutions and that the Justice Department would enter argument against the petitioners in Seattle and Los Angeles school integration cases that were to be heard by the Supreme Court.

Reagan relished the role of the most active president since Franklin Delano Roosevelt. In his first year as president he made more of a mark on California than he was able to do in eight years as governor.

Eden in Jeopardy

Within a dozen years after the United States dropped the first atomic bombs, the United States and the USSR had far more powerful nuclear weapons, and the ultimate fear had become that a nuclear war could destroy the human race. Short of that, accidental explosion of a warhead or meltdown of a nuclear reactor could wipe out much more than a city.

California had three nuclear power plants, a small number compared to those in eastern and midwestern states. Several more had been proposed. A Bodega Bay project was faulted because it would have spoiled a marine study area. Another at Diablo Canyon was delayed because it was sited near an earthquake fault and then because of confused blueprints. No-Nuke demonstrators vigorously opposed, and Governor Jerry Brown was adamant against expansion until a safe and sure method of disposing of nuclear wastes became available. Rising costs and lowered estimates of energy needs led to abandonment of nuclear projects for Los Angeles Harbor, the Colorado Desert, Lucern Valley, and a site northeast of Bakersfield.

As long ago as the 1890s voices were raised, John Muir's in particular, for the protection of wilderness. The Sierra Club dedicated itself to that cause. On a narrower front the Save-the-Redwoods League bought up one grove after another. Later it was realized that saving whole habitats was necessary. In 1963 the Point Reyes seashore was made a national park. Congress so voted in the seventies for the Santa Monica Mountains and four of the off-shore islands but enabling appropriations were intercepted. The Disney interests were dissuaded from developing a mammoth resort that would have devastated the Mineral King backcountry of Sequoia. The Nature Conservancy carried out a program whereby individuals could "buy an acre" or ten or a thousand so that the preservation of Santa Cruz Island could be achieved, with ARCO and Irvine Foundations as prime contributors. Residents on and near the Big Sur checked a plan for a four-lane divided highway on that spectacular but precipitous mountainside.

The Sierra Club, meanwhile, had extended its concerns far beyond California. It took the lead for preservation in Alaska. Then in Utah when a large dam was proposed that would have flooded the prehistoric remains in Dinosaur National Monument, the club led the protest. In 1966 the Reclamation Bureau sought approval for two much larger dams on the Colorado in the Grand Canyon National Park. A full-page Sierra Club ad in the Washington *Post* and the New York *Times* brought immediate challenge by the Internal Revenue Service and the organization's tax exemption was struck down. That crimped the club's style but not its effectiveness. It continued as the principal guardian of the nation's natural inheritance.

In 1981 in a nationwide effort conserva-

Interlandi, Los Angeles Times

tionists gathered signatures for a petition to Congress to dismiss Secretary of the Interior James Watt. They charged in full-page ads that Reagan's appointee was representing private interests rather than following the laws that defined his responsibilities. He was sabotaging conservation goals supported by a majority of the American people. He was defying decades of legislation designed to protect the natural resources. His destructive policies were aimed across the board at national parks, wilderness areas, rivers, wildlife, and desert land and would damage the oceans and the very air.

As Wallace Stegner summed it up, "Mr. Watt feels that the continent is a vast warehouse to be plundered and emptied, and the devil take the hindmost."

Because of the presence of more than 24 million Californians, with almost that many automobiles to take them to the most remote parts of the state, and with off-road motorcycles, autos, and trucks capable of churning up a trail almost anywhere, the desert, hill country, and forest lands have taken a severe beating. A vast acreage is under the federal Bureau of Land Management, which has much to do besides policing these great open spaces. The best efforts have been in the state and national parks and monuments.

For one key part of the California inheritance an initiative in 1972 and a statute in 1976 set up a special protection in the Coastal Commission. It became guardian of the few wetlands along this almost thousand-mile coast and has insisted that the public must have access to the beaches. Its principal task has been to monitor building permits in the coastal strip and to insist on environmental impact reports and protections before developments are authorized.

Until the fifties disposal of wastes was not an insurmountable problem. Every householder in Los Angeles, for example, had a backyard incinerator. Only when smog became a nuisance were these burners eliminated and replaced by cut and fill. Hungry sea gulls learned a new flight pattern and the Santa Monicas were renamed the Santa Garbage Mountains. That great fill was temporarily closed with the possibility of reopening for another few years, but thereafter much more distant locations would have to be found.

When the San Francisco fill near Candlestick Park was about to top out, the city considered running a daily garbage train across the Sierra to Lassen County, which aspired to become the garbage capital of the world.

The miracles of chemistry compounded the waste problem. Its creations include inert materials that simply persist. Worse are the pesticides and fertilizers that enter the food chain or otherwise continue. When DDT was at its height of popularity, it passed to lakes and the ocean and, through plankton and fish, rendered the brown pelicans incapable of laying hatchable eggs and poisoned mothers'

milk. In the eighties several water districts had to close wells because of tainted ground water.

Industrial wastes too noxious to dispose of at any dump in Los Angeles County were held in storage or shipped out by rail, truck, or ship. In 1980 a tanker truck with such a load spilled its contents on an eastbound freeway. Wastes that are nonbiodegradable were the most perplexing.

Smog became the most widespread and frequent pollutant, but the quality control agencies made it somewhat less visible by reducing particulates and in emergencies shutting down certain plants or requiring shift to cleaner fuel. But the areas affected spread far beyond the Los Angeles air basin and the San Francisco Bay Area, and the standard was far short of clean air. Pollution was allowed up to the maximum that "a normal insensitive person could endure." In 1969 the Los Angeles County coroner's chilling report after an autopsy was that a girl murdered on Mulholland had not been identified but must have come very recently "because her lungs were clean." Few deaths were certified as smog caused, but the smog drove out several commercial plantings and is confirmed as having killed more than a million pine trees in the San Bernardino Mountains.

Since the midsixties Californians have been on notice from earth scientists that the impact put on the California environment comes very close to matching its recuperative capacity. The ecology hovers near breakdown. Raymond Dasmann hit hard on this theme in *The Destruction of California* (1965), the quarterly *Cry California* kept up that refrain, William Bronson pinpointed it in *How To Kill a Golden State* (1968), as did Richard Lillard in *Eden in Jeopardy* (1966). OPEC and the hikes in gas prices, the 55 mile an hour speed limit, and the switch to diesel gave the ecology a little relief, but the margin for survival of the environment remains razor thin.

Selected References

General Works

First in dimensions and in significance are the 39 volumes of the *Works* (1884–90) of Hubert Howe Bancroft. Bancroft and his staff amassed and presented a tremendous amount of data on the history of the western half of North America. Seven of the volumes are labeled *History of California*, another four are purely Californian, and most of the rest tie in closely. They are the foundation for much subsequent work in the field. Theodore H. Hittell, *History of California* (4 vols., 1885–97), is especially rich on the early American period. Zoeth S. Eldredge, ed., *History of California* (5 vols., 1915), is a fluent narrative. In 1929–31 the Powell Publishing Company issued a nine-volume set entitled *California*, individual volumes of which will be cited. In 1960 Richard F. Pourade began issuance of a spritely and richly illustrated *History of San Diego*, which by 1977 had reached the seventh volume and the 1960s; in the process this set recites a substantial part of the history of the state. The Golden State Series, launched in 1979 under the editorship of Norris Hundley, jr., and John A. Schutz, included by 1982 eleven short books on major aspects of California's past. Additional titles are forthcoming and those already published will be cited.

The first authoritative survey was in the companion volumes, Charles E. Chapman, *A History of California: The Spanish Period* (1921), the first general work using the results of research in the archives of Spain and Mexico, and Robert G. Cleland, *A History of California: The American Period* (1922), which emphasizes the processes leading to acquisition by the United States. Single-volume analyses preceded and followed, e.g., those by McGroarty (1911), Norton (1913), Atherton (1914), Tinkham (1915), Hunt and Sán-chez (1929), Caughey (1940), Rolle (1963), Bean (1968), Roske (1968), Hutchinson (1969), Lavender (1976), and DeWitt (1979). A valuable encyclopedia is James D. Hart, *A Companion to California* (1978).

Robert E. and Robert G. Cowan's *A Bibliography of the History of California, 1510–1930* (4 vols., 1933–64) is the most useful research aid, even though its annotations are addressed to the collector. Helpful specialized bibliographies include: Margaret Miller Rocq, *California Local History* (1970); Doyce B. Nunis, Jr., *Los Angeles and Its Environs in the Twentieth Century: A Bibliography* (1973); Henry R. Wagner, *The Spanish Southwest* (1924; revised 1937) and *The Plains and the Rockies* (1920; revised 1937); and Oscar O. Winther and Richard A. Van Orman, *The Trans-Mississippi West: A Guide to Its Periodical Literature, 1811–1967* (1972). *Libros Californianos* (1931; 1958) and *The Zamorano Eighty* (1945) are book lovers' choices of outstanding books. In addition to catalogues, information on new publications is available in the book review sections of *California History (CH)*, *Southern California Quarterly (SCQ)*, and *Pacific Historical Review (PHR)*.

The best work on its subject is Warren A. Beck and Ynez D. Haase's *Historical Atlas of California* (1973). Robert W. Durrenberger, *Patterns on the Land* (1965); Hammond's *California Atlas* (1969); and Michael W. Donley et al., *Atlas of California* (1979), offer descriptive maps, many of them historical. William J. Miller's *California through the Ages* (1957) is a summary of geological history. Clifford M. Zierer, ed., *California and the Southwest* (1956), and David W. Lantix, Rodney Steiner, and Arthur E. Karinen, *California, Land of Contrast* (1963), give geographical analyses. William Kahrl's (ed.) *The California*

Water Atlas (1979) is both good history and geography. Peveril Meigs III, *Climates of California* (1938), and Ernest L. Felton, *California's Many Climates* (1965), deal with a fundamental of the environment.

Piecemeal descriptions abound in topical studies such as William L. Dawson, *The Birds of California* (4 vols., 1921); Willis L. Jepson, *The Trees of California* (1909) and *A Manual of the Flowering Plants of California* (1925); Howard E. McMinn, *An Illustrated Manual of California Shrubs* (1939); Edith S. Clements, *Flowers of Coast and Sierra* (1928); Francis M. Fultz, *The Elfin-Forest of California* (1923); and Tracy I. Storer and Lloyd P. Tevis, Jr., *California Grizzly* (1955); and in regional studies by François E. Matthes, *The Incomparable Valley: A Geologic Interpretation of the Yosemite* (1950) and *Sequoia National Park: A Geological Album* (1950); John Muir, *The Mountains of California* (1894) and *The Yosemite* (1912); Roderick Peattie, *The Sierra Nevada* (1947) and *The Pacific Coast Ranges* (1946); Godfrey Sykes, *The Colorado Delta* (1937); E. C. Jaeger, *The California Desert* (1906); Edwin Corle, *Desert Country* (1941); Mary Austin, *The Land of Little Rain* (1903); Anne B. Fisher, *The Salinas, Upside-down River* (1945); and J. Smeaton Chase, *California Coast Trails* (1913).

Rhapsodic description had early representation in titles by Charles Nordhoff, *California for Health, Pleasure, and Residence* (1872); Sutton Palmer and Mary Austin, *California: The Land of the Sun* (1914); and George Wharton James, *California, Romantic and Beautiful* (1914). This message is better documented in photographically enriched books by Edward Weston, *California and the West* (1940); Ansel Adams, *The Eloquent Light* (1963); Richard Kaufmann, *Gentle Wilderness: The Sierra Nevada* (1964); Philip Hyde and François Leydet, *The Last Redwoods* (1963); and David Brower, *Not Man Apart* (1965). Elna Bakker, *An Island Called California* (1971), is an ecological pilgrimage from the Golden Gate to Mono Lake and south to the Joshua Trees. In addition, the University of California Press and the Sierra Club have each issued a series of nature guides.

1. The First Californians

Recording data on the California Indians began with the early Spaniards, the most illuminating record being Gerónimo Boscana's "Chinigchinich" on the Juaneño and Gabrielino. Alfred Robinson included an English translation in his *Life in California* (1846). Hugo Reid's notes on the Gabrielino, written for the Los Angeles *Star* in 1852, were reprinted as *The Indians of Los Angeles County* (1926). Similarly, John Caughey, ed., *The Indians of Southern California in 1852* (1952), makes available the B. D. Wilson report, serialized in the Los Angeles *Star* in 1868. Alexander S. Taylor contributed "Indianology of California," a vast miscellany on all aspects of Indian history, some of it otherwise lost to memory, to the *California Farmer* in many installments, from 1860 to 1863. Stephen Powers's *Tribes of California* (1877) is based on observation and empathy for the Indians. In that same decade Bancroft and his staff were combing the written and published records and compiling *The Native Races* (5 vols., 1874–75), which took stock of pre-Columbian culture in the whole of western America.

Scientific study of the Indians came later. The results to the 1920s are set forth in A. L. Kroeber, *Handbook of the Indians of California* (1925), and modernized in William C. Sturtevant and Robert F. Heizer, eds., *Handbook of North American Indians: California* (1978). Monographs abound, particularly in the University of California *Publications in American Archaeology and Ethnology* and the series *Ibero-Americana*. Robert F. Heizer and M. A. Whipple's (eds.) *The California Indians: A Source Book* (1951) is made up of selections from this scholarship. Especially valuable is Robert F. Heizer and Albert B. Elsasser, *The Natural World of the California Indians* (1980). George Phillips, *The Enduring Struggle: Indians in California History* (1981); Robert F. Heizer, *Languages, Territories, and Names of California Indian Tribes* (1966); and C. Hart Merriam, *Studies of California Indians* (1955), have broad range. Lorraine M. Sherer, *The Clan System of the Fort Mojave Indians* (1965); Lowell J. Bean, *Mukat's People: The Cahuilla Indians of Southern California* (1972); Harry C. James, *The Cahuilla Indians* (1960); Bernice Eastman Johnston, *California's Gabrielino Indians* (1962); Campbell Grant, *The Rock Paintings of the Chumash* (1965); Annie R. Mitchell, *Jim Savage and the Tulareño Indians* (1957); and Robert F. Heizer and John E. Mills, *The Four Ages of Tsurai* [Trinidad Bay] (1952), present scholarly analyses of various Indian groups. The latest word on population is S. F. Cook's *The Population of the California Indians, 1769–1970* (1976).

George Wharton James, *Indian Basketry* (1904), deals with one culture trait. The Indians' traditional literature is sampled in Edward W. Gifford and Gwendoline H. Block, *Californian Indian Nights Entertainments* (1930); Jaime d'Angulo, *Indian Tales* (1953), stories collected from the Pit River Indians; Thomas C. Blackburn, ed., *December's Child* (1976), a collection of Chumash oral narratives; and Theodora Kroeber, *The Inland Whale* (1959).

Theodora Kroeber's *Ishi in Two Worlds* (1961) is a biography of the last wild Indian in North America, as is *Ishi, Last of His Tribe* (1964); and W. W. Waterman, "Ishi, the Last Wild Indian," *Southern Workman*, 46 (1917), 528–37. Florence C. Shipek's (ed.) *The Autobiography of Delfina Cuero* (1968) concerns a twentieth-century Diegueño. *The Indian Historian* (1968 on), a San Francisco publication, is alert to current issues as well as past experiences.

2. Explorers and Empire Builders

Excellent brief narratives of the first Spanish activities in America are I. B. Richman, *The Spanish Conquerors* (1919); E. G. Bourne, *Spain in America* (1904); and Charles Gibson, *Spain in America* (1966). S. E. Morison's *Admiral of the Ocean Sea* (1942) is a masterpiece on Columbus and the early exploration.

The whole sweep of northward searching is sketched by H. E. Bolton, *The Spanish Borderlands* (1921), and John Francis Bannon, *The Spanish Borderlands Frontier, 1513–1821* (1970). Much is available on individual expeditions and explorers from Ponce de León across country to Coronado. Examples are: Morris Bishop, *The Odyssey of Cabeza de Vaca* (1933); Haniel Long, *The Power within Us* (1944); Cleve Hallenbeck, *Alvar Nuñez Cabeza de Vaca* (1933) and *The Journey of Fray Marcos de Niza* (1949); Carl Sauer, *The Road to Cíbola* (1932); A. Grove Day, *Coronado's Quest* (1940); H. E. Bolton, *Coronado* (1949); G. P. Hammond and Agapito Rey, eds., *Narratives of the Coronado Expedition* (1940).

The most prolific scholar on West Coast exploration was Henry Raup Wagner. See his *Spanish Voyages to the Northwest Coast* (1929), consisting of Spanish texts, translations, and annotations; *Cartography of the Northwest Coast of America to the Year 1800* (2 vols., 1937); *Juan Rodríguez Cabrillo, Discoverer of the Coast of California* (1941); and *Sir Francis Drake's Voyage around the World* (1926). See also Donald C. Cutter, ed., *The California Coast* (1969), and Michael Mathes, ed., *California: Documentos para la historia de la demarcación comercial de California, 1583–1632* (1965). On Drake's visit, consult Warren L. Hanna, *Lost Harbor: The Controversy over Drake's California Anchorage* (1979); and James Hart, *The Plate of Brass Reexamined* (1977) and *The Plate of Brass Reexamined—Supplement* (1979). W. L. Schurz's *The Manila Galleon* (1939) is the first book on the Philippine-Mexican trade. On Vizcaíno, see W. Michael Mathes, *Vizcaíno and Spanish Expansion in the Pacific Ocean, 1580–1630* (1968).

For the Jesuit advance into Sinaloa and beyond, Peter M. Dunne is the principal historian, represented by his *Pioneer Black Robes on the West Coast* (1940), *Pioneer Jesuits in Northern Mexico* (1944), and *Early Jesuit Missions in Tarahumara* (1948). On Kino the basic work is his own "Celestial Favors," translated by Herbert E. Bolton as *Kino's Historical Memoir of Pimería Alta* (2 vols., 1919). Bolton's *The Padre on Horseback* (1932) is an admiring sketch of Kino's career. R. K. Wyllys, *Pioneer Padre* (1935), gives more detail, but in turn is surpassed by Bolton's *The Rim of Christendom* (1936), a full-length, lifelike portrait of this most remarkable man. Miguel Venegas's laudatory biography of the founder of the first peninsular missions, *Juan María de Salvatierra* (1754) has been translated by Marguerite Eyer Wilbur (1929). Francisco María Pícolo's *Informe del estado de la nueva christianidad de California* (1702) is a report on the first five years of the missions. Juan José Villavicencio, *Vida y virtudes de el venerable y apostólico padre Juan de Ugarte* (1852) eulogizes Salvatierra's successor. The melancholy facts of declining Indian population are set forth by S. F. Cook, *The Extent and Significance of Disease among the Indians of Baja California, 1687–1733* (1937). For an overall view of the Jesuit period, see Peter M. Dunne, *Black Robes in Lower California* (1952).

3. A Spanish Outpost

The immediate background for the occupation of Alta California is delineated in Herbert I. Priestley, *José de Gálvez, Visitador-General of New Spain* (1916). Charles E. Chapman, *The Founding of Spanish California* (1916), analyzes the problems of frontier advance from the 1680s to the 1770s. See also I. B. Richman, *California under Spain and Mexico* (1911). These volumes were pioneers in drawing on the resources of the Spanish and Mexican archives. Original narratives of 1769–70 written by Portolá, Costansó, Vilá, and Fages appear in the *Publications* of the Academy of Pacific Coast History, 1–2 (1910–11). Herbert E. Bolton's *Fray Juan Crespi, Missionary Explorer* (1927) and Douglas E. Watson's *The Spanish Occupation of California* (1934) are mainly documentary. Theodore E. Treutlein reassesses the evidence in *San Francisco Bay, Discovery and Colonization, 1769–1776* (1968). Also useful is Frank M. Stanger and Alan K. Brown's *Who Discovered the Golden Gate?* (1969).

Francisco Palóu's *Noticias de la Nueva California* is the major compendium of primary material on the first dozen years of Spanish California. Completed in 1783, it was published in Spanish in 1857 and 1874 and in English translation by Herbert E. Bolton as *Historical Memoirs of New California* (4 vols., 1926). Palóu's *Junípero Serra* (1787), translated by C. S. Williams (1913) and by Maynard J. Geiger (1955), is the earliest California biography. The story of Serra's life has been capably sketched by Abigail H. Fitch, *Junípero Serra* (1914); Agnes Repplier, *Junípero Serra, Pioneer Colonist of California* (1933); Theodore Maynard, *The Long Road of Father Serra* (1954); and Omer Engelbert, *The Last of the Conquistadors* (1956). The most satisfactory, though doubtless not the ultimate biography of Serra, is Maynard J. Geiger's *The Life and Times of Fray Junípero Serra* (2 vols., 1959). On individual Franciscan missionaries, see Geiger's *Franciscan Missionaries in Hispanic California, 1769–1848: A Biographical Dictionary* (1969). For the mission beginnings and on every phase of their history, see Zephyrin Engelhardt, *The Missions and Missionaries of California* (4 vols., 1908–15). Engelhardt also wrote separate volumes on most of the individual missions. Bernard E. Bobb, *The Viceregency of Antonio María Bucareli in New*

Spain (1962), takes issue with Chapman's high praise of Bucareli as a positive force. John Galvin, *The Coming of Justice to California* (1963), and Sidney B. Brinckerhoff and Odie B. Faulk, *Lancers for the King* (1965), reproduce the rules and regulations issued in 1772 for frontier presidios.

Herbert E. Bolton, *Anza's California Expeditions* (5 vols., 1930), is the complete record of the opening and use of the trail from Sonora. The first volume, reprinted as *Outpost of Empire* (1931), narrates the two expeditions and the founding of San Francisco. John Galvin's *A Record of Travels in Arizona and California, 1775–1776* (1967) centers on Francisco Garcés.

4. Spain's Hold Established

Many of the same sources cited in the previous section apply here as well. On the province in 1775, see Herbert I. Priestley, *A Historical, Political and Natural Description of California by Pedro Fages* (1937) and Francisco Antonio Maurelle, *Journal of a Voyage in 1775 to Explore the Coast of America Northward of California* (1781). Alfred B. Thomas, *Teodoro de Croix* (1941), supplies background on the Yuma Massacre. Herbert I. Priestley, "The Colorado River Campaign, 1781–1782," *Publications* of the Academy of Pacific Coast History, 3 (1913), translates a Fages diary on the aftermath. On Felipe de Neve, see Edwin A. Beilharz, *Felipe de Neve, First Governor of California* (1971). The 1931 *Publication* of the Historical Society of Southern California contains the basic materials on the founding of the pueblo of Los Angeles. For the next 40 years of the pueblo's history the principal reference is John Caughey's "The Country Town of the Angels," in John and LaRee Caughey, *Los Angeles: Biography of a City* (1976), pp. 73–78. A special issue of *California History*, 60 (Spring 1981), edited by Larry L. Meyer, "Los Angeles, 1781–1981," marked the bicentennial.

5. Local Annals

Bancroft deals generously with these latter years of Spanish control, devoting to them half of the first volume and the entire second volume of his

History of California, a full thousand pages. Engelhardt's account is almost as voluminous. Chapman's *History of California* and Richman's *California under Spain and Mexico* are detailed. Bancroft, *California Pastoral* (1888), plays up the romance of the period, as do Nellie V. Sánchez, *Spanish Arcadia* (1929), and Alberta Johnson Denis, *Spanish Alta California* (1927). Of dozens of rhapsodic tributes to the missions, George Wharton James, *In and Out of the Old Missions of California* (1916); Charles Francis Saunders and J. Smeaton Chase, *The California Padres and Their Missions* (1915); John A. Berger, *The Franciscan Missions of California* (1948); Will Connell, *The Missions of California* (1941); and Paul C. Johnson, *The California Missions: A Pictorial History* (1964), furnish representative accounts. Kurt Baer, *Architecture of the California Missions* (1958) and *Paintings and Sculpture at Mission Santa Barbara* (1955); and Ruth Mahood, *A Gallery of California Mission Paintings* [by Edwin Deakin] (1966), concentrate on the structures. On Lasuén, see Francis F. Guest, *Fermín Francisco de Lasuén (1736–1803): A Biography* (1973).

Descriptions by visitors to the province are found in *Voyage de la Pérouse autour du monde* (4 vols., 1797); Donald Cutter, *Malaspina in California* (1960); George Vancouver, *A Voyage of Discovery to the North Pacific Ocean* (3 vols., 1798); Marguerite Eyer Wilbur, *Vancouver in California* (1954); William Shaler, *Journal of a Voyage* (ed. Lindley Bynum, 1935); and Louis Choris, *Voyage pittoresque autour du monde* (1822), translated with some additions in August C. Mahr, *The Visit of the Rurik to San Francisco in 1816* (1932). On the sea otter, see Adele Ogden, *The California Sea Otter Trade* (1941).

The new stirrings of activities to the north are related in Henry R. Wagner, *Spanish Explorations in Juan de Fuca Strait* (1933) and W. R. Manning, *The Nootka Sound Controversy* (1905). T. C. Russell, *The Rezanov Voyage to Nueva California in 1806* (1926); Georg Heinrich von Langsdorff, *Narrative of the Rezanov Voyage to Nueva California in 1806* (1927); Gertrude Atherton, *Rezanov* (1906); Hector Chevigny, *Lost Empire: The Life and Adventures of Nikiolai Petrovich Rezanov* (1937); James R. Gibson, *Imperial Russia in Frontier America* (1976); and C. Bickford O'Brien, Dianne Spencer-Hancock, and Michael Tucker, *Fort Ross: Indians-Russians-*

Americans (1978), cover the first Russian visits to California.

Jeanne Van Nostrand, *Monterey, Adobe Capital of California* (1968), is a pictorial, complemented in the south by Richard F. Pourade, *Time of the Bells* (1961). On rancho beginnings, see W. W. Robinson, *Land in California* (1948) and Robert H. Becker, *Diseños of California Ranchos* (1964).

6. A Mexican Province

The works of Bancroft, Sánchez, Denis, Richman, and Chapman, cited earlier, apply also to the Mexican regime. Gertrude Atherton's *The Splendid Idle Forties* (1902) is another glowing description. Alexander Forbes, *California: A History of Upper and Lower California* (1839), the first book on California written in English, reported on the province from the author's vantage point in Mexico. Foreigners who came to trade or to settle contributed important accounts. Richard Henry Dana, *Two Years Before the Mast* (1840) and Alfred Robinson, *Life in California* (1846), head this class; many others are mentioned in the next section of this bibliography.

The most thorough exposition is an unpublished dissertation by George Tays, "Revolutionary California: The Political History of California during the Mexican Period" (Berkeley, 1932). See also his "Mariano Guadalupe Vallejo and Sonoma—A Biography and a History," six installments in *CH*, 16–17 (1937–38); Marion L. Lothrop, "The Indian Campaigns of General M. G. Vallejo," *Quarterly of the Society of California Pioneers*, 9 (1932), 161–205; Myrtle M. McKittrick, *Vallejo, Son of California* (1944); Madie Brown Emparan, *The Vallejos of California* (1968); Terry E. Stephenson, *Don Bernardo de Yorba* (1941); George L. Harding, *Agustín V. Zamorano, Statesman, Soldier, Craftsman, and California's First Printer* (1934); Jeanne Van Nostrand, *Monterey, Adobe Capital of California, 1770–1847* (1969); Charles F. Lummis, *Flowers of Our Lost Romance* (1929); Robert G. Cleland, *The Place Called Sespe* (1940) and *The Cattle on a Thousand Hills* (1941). The years 1820 to 1849 receive close attention in Woodrow James Hansen's *The Search for Authority in California* (1960).

J. N. Bowman's "The Resident Neophytes of the California Missions, 1769–1834," *SCQ*, 40 (1958), 138–48, and "The Number of California Indians Baptized during the Mission Period," *SCQ*, 42 (1960), 273–77, present statistical tables. S. F. Cook's *The Conflict between the California Indian and White Civilization* (1943) is an analysis of population decline. Gerald J. Geary, *The Secularization of the California Missions* (1934), is a fair statement from the viewpoint of the churchmen. Manuel P. Servín, "The Secularization of the California Missions: A Reappraisal," *SCQ*, 47 (1965), 133–49, is considerably more critical of the missionary program; and Martha Voght, "Shamans and Padres: The Religion of the Southern California Mission Indians," *PHR*, 36 (1967), 363–73, finds that the religious impact of the missions was ephemeral. C. Alan Hutchinson, *Frontier Settlement in Mexican California* (1969) centers on the Padrés-Híjar colonization project but is informative on much else.

The classics on the hide trade are Richard Henry Dana, *Two Years Before the Mast* (1840), edited, with passages restored and other additions, by John H. Kemble (2 vols., 1964), and Alfred Robinson, *Life in California* (1846). William D. Phelps, *Fore and Aft* (1871), is by another sailor; Doyce B. Nunis, Jr., ed., *The California Diary of Faxon Dean Atherton, 1836–1839* (1964), is by another of the agents ashore. George P. Hammond, ed., *The Larkin Papers* (10 vols., 1951–66), is a great collection of documents on trade and other topics.

7. Trappers and Settlers

Of the general works on the fur trade, the one most relevant to California is Robert G. Cleland's *This Reckless Breed of Men* (1950). Firsthand material on the earliest entrances to the state are H. C. Dale, *The Ashley-Smith Explorations* (1918); Maurice S. Sullivan, *The Travels of Jedediah Smith* (1934); and *The Personal Narrative of James O. Pattie* (1831), a vivid adventure tale with frequently embellished facts. Charles L. Camp, *George C. Yount and His Chronicles of the West* (1966) describes a later entry from New Mexico. Two members of the Walker party left accounts: *Narratives of the Adventures of Zenas Leonard* (1839; John C. Ewers, ed., 1959) and William H.

Ellison, ed., *The Life and Adventures of George Nidever* (1937).

Dale L. Morgan's *Jedediah Smith and the Opening of the West* (1953) heads a long list of biographies: Maurice S. Sullivan, *The Life of Jedediah Smith* (1936); Stanley Vestal, *Kit Carson: The Happy Warrior of the Old West* (1928); John E. Sunder, *Bill Sublette, Mountain Man* (1959); LeRoy R. Hafen and W. J. Ghent, *Broken Hand: The Life Story of Thomas Fitzpatrick* (1931); Douglas S. Watson, *West Wind: The Life Story of Joseph Reddeford Walker* (1934); T. D. Bonner, *The Life and Adventures of James P. Beckwourth* (1856); and Charles Kelly, *Old Greenwood* (1936; 1965). Alice B. Maloney, ed., *Fur Brigade to the Bonaventura* (1945), and John S. Galbraith, *The Hudson's Bay Company as an Imperial Factor, 1821–1869* (1957) bear on British activities.

As an appendix to volumes 2 to 5 of his *History of California*, Hubert Howe Bancroft inserted a "Pioneer Register," a Who's Who of Californians to 1848, with an almost complete roll call and thumbnail sketches of many inhabitants. In 1964 Glen and Muir Dawson reissued this *Register of Pioneer Inhabitants of California* as a book.

Reuben L. Underhill's *From Cowhides to Golden Fleece* (1939) is a biography of Larkin intended for the general reader. Susanna B. Dakin writes on *The Lives of William Hartnell* (1949) and *Scotch Paisano: Hugo Reid's Life in California* (1939); Doris Wright on *A Yankee in Mexican California: Abel Stearns, 1798–1848* (1977); and Sheldon G. Jackson on *A British Ranchero in Old California* [Henry Dalton] (1977). Andrew F. Rolle, *An American in California* (1956), covers the life of William Heath Davis. William H. Ellison and Francis Price's *The Life and Adventures in California of Don Agustin Janssens, 1834–1856* (1953) is the narrative of a Belgian who came with the Híjar-Padrés expedition. J. J. Hill's *History of Warner's Ranch and Its Environs* (1927) is, in passing, a life of a former fur man, J. J. Warner.

There are several books on Sutter: Douglas S. Watson's edition of Sutter's *Diary* (1932); Edwin G. Gudde's editing of Sutter's dictation to Bancroft (1936); Julian Dana's journalistic *Sutter of California* (1936); James P. Zollinger's *Sutter: The Man and His Empire* (1939); and Richard Dillon's *Fool's Gold: The Decline and Fall of*

Captain John Sutter of California (1967). George D. Lyman's *John Marsh, Pioneer* (1930) is a well-rounded biography.

There is general coverage on the overland pioneers by W. J. Ghent, *The Road to Oregon* (1929); Owen C. Coy, *The Great Trek* (1931); George R. Stewart, *The California Trail* (1962); and much detail in tracing the routes in Irene D. Paden's *In the Wake of the Prairie Schooner* (1943) and *Prairie Schooner Detours* (1949). John Bidwell's *A Journey to California in 1841* (1842; Francis P. Farquhar, ed., 1964) is supplemented by Nicholas "Cheyenne" Dawson's *California in '41, Texas in '51* (1894) and Rockwell D. Hunt's scholarly and laudatory *John Bidwell, Prince of California Pioneers* (1942). Other pioneer settlers are presented by Charles L. Camp, ed., *James Clyman, American Frontiersman* (1928; enlarged edition, 1960); Ruby Swartzlow, "Peter Lassen, Northern California's Trailblazer," *CH*, 18 (1939), 291–314; and John Caughey, "Don Benito Wilson," *Huntington Library Quarterly*, 2 (1939), 285–300.

Edwin Bryant, *What I Saw in California* (1848); J. Q. Thornton, *Oregon and California* (2 vols., 1849); and Heinrich Lienhard, *From St. Louis to Sutter's Fort, 1846*, translated by Erwin G. and Elisabeth K. Gudde (1961), report on successful overland expeditions in 1846, a year covered in detail by Dale L. Morgan, *Overland in 1846* (2 vols., 1963), and Bernard De Voto, *The Year of Decision, 1846* (1943). For the migration of 1847, see Douglas M. McMurtie, ed., *Overland to California in 1847, Letters . . . by Chester Ingersoll* (1937).

The stark tragedy of the Donner party dominates. Charles F. McGlashan, *History of the Donner Party* (1879) is the product of a patient assembling of information; Eliza P. Houghton, *The Expedition of the Donner Party and Its Tragic Fate* (1911), is by one of the Donner children who, as a four-year-old, survived the ordeal. The authoritative treatment is George R. Stewart, *Ordeal by Hunger* (1936; 1960).

8. American Takeover

Robert G. Cleland's "The Early Sentiment for Annexation of California," *SHQ*, 8 (1915) may be read in association with John A. Hawgood, "The Pattern of Yankee Infiltration in Mexican Alta California," *PHR*, 27 (1958), 27–38, and *First and Last Consul: Thomas Oliver Larkin and the Americanization of California* (1962); Norman A. Graebner, *Empire on the Pacific* (1955); Glen W. Price, *Origins of the War with Mexico: The Polk-Stockton Intrigue* (1967); E. I. McCormac, *James K. Polk* (1922); Charles G. Sellers, *James K. Polk, Continentalist* (1966); Neal Harlow, *California Conquered* (1981); and Mary Lee Spence and Donald Jackson, eds., *The Expeditions of John Charles Frémont* (2 vols., 1970, 1973).

Frémont's role in the conquest of California has been the subject of a manysided debate. With the exception of Cardinal L. Goodwin in his *John Charles Frémont, An Explanation of His Career* (1930), biographers have been lavish in praise. Herbert Bashford and Harr Wagner used the title *A Man Unafraid* (1927); and Allan Nevins's titles were *Frémont, The West's Greatest Adventurer* (2 vols., 1928) and *Frémont, Pathmarker of the West* (1939). Better balanced is Ferol Egan's *Frémont, Explorer for a Restless Nation* (1977). Beginning with John S. Hittell, *A History of the City of San Francisco and Incidentally of the State of California* (1878), Bancroft, Theodore H. Hittell, and Josiah Royce, *California* (1886), historians have been less entranced with his performance in California. See also Kenneth M. Johnson, *The Frémont Court Martial* (1968).

On the Bear Flag revolt, see Werner H. Marti, *Messenger of Destiny: The California Adventures, 1846–1847, of Archibald H. Gillespie* (1960); William B. Ide, *Who Conquered California?* (1880); Fred B. Rogers, *Bear Flag Lieutenant: The Life Story of Henry L. Ford* (1951) and *William Brown Ide, Bear Flagger* (1962); John A. Hussey, "New Light on the Original Bear Flag," *CH*, 31 (1952), 205–17; and John A. Hawgood, "John C. Frémont and the Bear Flag Revolution," *University of Birmingham Journal*, 7 (1959), 80–100, and *SCQ*, 44 (1963), 67–96.

The general histories of the war with Mexico say little about the California campaigns. The U.S. Navy's operations are represented in Fred B. Rogers's (ed.) *A Navy Surgeon in California* [Marius Duvall] (1956), *Filings from an Old Saw* [Joseph T. Downey] (1956), and *Montgomery and the Portsmouth* (1958); and Howard Lamar's (ed.) *The Cruise of the Portsmouth* [Joseph T. Downey] (1958).

On the progress of Kearny's Army of the West, see Dwight L. Clarke, *Stephen Watts Kearny,*

Soldier of the West (1961); Ross Calvin, *Lieutenant Emory Reports* (1951), reproduced from William H. Emory, *Notes of a Military Reconnaissance* (1848); George W. Ames, Jr., ed., *A Doctor Comes to California: The Diary of John S. Griffin* (1943); and Arthur Woodward, *Lances at San Pascual* (1948).

9. Gold

Materials on the gold rush are abundant, and almost all of them are specialized. The most comprehensive account is John Caughey's *Gold Is the Cornerstone* (1948). Joseph Henry Jackson's *Gold Rush Album* (1949) is a picture book viewing the subject in the round. Hubert Howe Bancroft, *California Inter Pocula* (1888), inspired in title (California in her cups), deals with most phases, as do Stewart Edward White, *The Forty-niners* (1918); Valeska Bari, ed., *The Course of Empire* (1931); and John Caughey, ed., *Rushing for Gold* (1949). A fascinating account of one gold seeker and his family is J. S. Holliday, *The World Rushed In: The California Gold Rush Experience* (1981).

California Gold Discovery, Centennial Papers on the Time, the Site, and Artifacts (1947), a special publication of the California Historical Society, assembles reports ranging from contemporary to archaeological; Rodman W. Paul's *The California Gold Discovery* (1966) is a meticulous analysis of the evidence. Theressa Gay's *James W. Marshall* (1967) is an indepth study of the discoverer. Records of 1848 include E. Gould Buffum, *Six Months in the Gold Mines* (1850; 1959); James H. Carson, *Early Recollections of the Mines* (1852); William McCollum, *California as I Saw It* (1850; 1960); William R. Ryan, *Personal Adventures in Upper and Lower California* (2 vols., 1851); and Erwin G. Gudde, *Bigler's Chronicle of the West* (1962). Elizabeth L. Egenhoff, *The Elephant as They Saw It* (1949), features contemporary statements and pictures on gold mining.

Joseph Ware's *The Emigrant's Guide to California* (1849; ed. John Caughey, 1932) is the best of the two dozen guides prepared for the forty-niners.

Octavius T. Howe's *Argonauts of '49* (1923), though limited to companies from Massachusetts, is the nearest approach to a monograph on the Cape Horn argonauts. For briefer treatments, see Oscar Lewis, *Sea Routes to the Gold Fields* (1949), and the appropriate chapter in Raymond Rydell, *Cape Horn to the Pacific* (1952). Carolyn Hale Ross's (ed.) *The Log of a Forty-niner* (1923); Franklin A. Buck's *A Yankee Trader in the Gold Rush* (1930); Enos Christman's *One Man's Gold* (1930); and Robert S. Fletcher's *Eureka: From Cleveland by Ship to California* (1959) are representative accounts. On argonauts from even more distant places, see Charles Bateson, *Gold Fleet to California: Forty-Niners from Australia and New Zealand* (1964).

On the Panama route, see Bayard Taylor, *Eldorado, or Adventures in the Path of Empire* (2 vols., 1850); Carl Meyer, *Nach dem Sacramento* (1855; translated by Ruth Frey Axe, 1938); Charles A. Barker, ed., *Memoirs of Elisha Oscar Crosby* (1945); and John W. Caughey, ed., *Seeing the Elephant: Letters of R. R. Taylor, Forty-niner* (1951). John H. Kemble's *The Panama Route* (1943) is authoritative on the steamers. Standard on its subject is David I. Folkman, Jr., *The Nicaragua Route* (1972).

The saga of the overland march of the gold seekers is best read in some of their journals, notably, Alonzo Delano, *Life on the Plains and among the Diggings* (1854); Georgia Willis Read and Ruth Gaines, eds., *Gold Rush: The Journals, Drawings, and Other Papers of J. Goldsborough Bruff* (2 vols., 1944); David M. Potter, ed., *Trail to California: The Overland Journal of Vincent Geiger and Wakeman Bryarly* (1945); *Autobiography of Isaac J. Wistar* (2 vols., 1914); Sarah Royce, *A Frontier Lady* (1932); Walker D. Wyman, *California Emigrant Letters* (1952); Howard L. Scamehorn, *The Buckeye Rovers in the Gold Rush* (1965); Elisha D. Perkins, *Gold Rush Diary* (ed. Thomas D. Clark, 1967); and Dale L. Morgan, ed., *The Overland Diary of James Avery Pritchard* (1959). With the Pritchard diary Morgan supplies a table of 100 forty-niner diarists passing waypoints along the trail. Excellent later studies are Irene D. Paden's *The Wake of the Prairie Schooner* (1943) and *Prairie Schooner Detours* (1947); Owen C. Coy's *The Great Trek* (1931); and, with exaggerated drama, Archer B. Hulbert's *Forty-niners* (1931). The most perceptive study may be John D. Unruh's *The Plains Across: The Overland Emigrants, 1840–1860* (1979). A valuable specialized work is John P. Reid's *Law for the Elephant: Property and Social Behavior on the Overland Trail* (1980).

Southwestern offshoots from the main trail are described by W. L. Manly, *Death Valley in '49* (1894); John W. Caughey, "Southwest from Salt Lake in 1849," *PHR*, 6 (1937), 143–81; John G. Ellenbecker, *The Jayhawkers of Death Valley* (1938); and Carl I. Wheat, "Trailing the Forty-niners through Death Valley," *SCQ*, 24 (1939), 74–108. Still more southerly routes are described by Ralph P. Bieber, *Southern Trails to California in 1849* (1937); Grant Foreman, *Marcy and the Gold Seekers* (1939); H. M. T. Powell, *The Santa Fe Trail to California* (1931); Charles Pancoast, *A Quaker Forty-niner* (1930); John W. Audubon, *Audubon's Western Journal* (1906); and George W. B. Evans, *Mexican Gold Trail* (1945).

Rodman W. Paul's *California Gold* (1947) is a masterly analysis of the miner at work. On mining methods, see Otis E. Young, Jr., *How They Dug the Gold* (1967). See also Buffum, Delano, Buck, Chistman, and a few other travel accounts that carry on into the diggings, and J. D. Borthwick, *Three Years in California* (1857); Vicente Pérez de Rosales, *Recuerdos del pasado* (1890), translated by Edwin S. Morby as *California Adventure* (1947); John Steele, *In Camp and Cabin* (1928); Frank Marryat, *Mountains and Molehills* (1855); John W. Caughey, ed., "Life in California in 1849, as Described in the Journal of George F. Kent," *CH*, 20 (1941), 26–46; Dale L. Morgan and James R. Scobie, eds., *William Perkins' Journal of Life at Sonora, 1849–1852* (1964); Friedrich Gerstäcker, *Scenes of Life in California*, translated by George Cosgrave (1942); and Carvel Collins, *Sam Ward in the Gold Rush* (1949). The classic description is in the "Shirley Letters," contributed to the *Pioneer* in 1854 by Louisa Amelia Knapp Smith Clapp and several times reissued in book form. Rodman W. Paul, "In Search of 'Dame Shirley,' " *PHR*, 33 (1964), 127–46, draws together the fugitive details about the author. G. Ezra Dane's *Ghost Town* (1941) is a capital recounting of the foibles of the gold miners.

For a guide to the diggings, see Erwin G. Gudde, *California Gold Camps* (1975). Charles H. Shinn, *Mining Camps* (1885), emphasizes the development of law and government. Rudolph M. Lapp, *Blacks in Gold Rush California* (1977); Richard Henry Morefield, "Mexicans in the California Mines, 1848–53," *CH*, 35 (1956), 37–46; Robert E. Levinson, *Jews in the California Gold Rush* (1978); and David V. DuFault, "The Chi-nese in the Mining Camps of California, 1848–1870," *SCQ*, 41 (1959), 155–70, concern minorities.

10. *Mushrooming Economy*

The first six chapters of the final volume of Bancroft's *History of California* pertain to this economic transformation. See also Robert G. Cleland and Osgood Hardy, *March of Industry* (1929). There are excellent local histories, among them Owen C. Coy's *The Humboldt Bay Region, 1850–1875* (1929) and George W. and Helen P. Beattie's *Heritage of the Valley* [San Bernardino] (1939). See also the county histories, such as those published by Thompson and West about 1880.

Of the volumes compiled expressly to describe California's economy, the most successful was John S. Hittell's *The Resources of California* (1863), which ran through seven editions. Hittell also assembled a handbook on *Mining in the Pacific States of North America* (1868). Titus Fey Cronise's *The Natural Wealth of California* (1868), even bulkier than Hittell's *Resources*, rivaled it in popularity, while on the West in general, J. Ross Browne's *Resources of the Pacific Slope* (1869) was an alternative choice.

The state's banking history is detailed in Ira B. Cross's *Financing an Empire* (4 vols., 1927), while biographies of William Ralston by Cecil J. Tilton (1935), Julian Dana (1936), George D. Lyman (1937), and David Lavender (1975) summarize the problems and progress of San Francisco. See also Frank Soulé, John H. Gihon, and James Nisbet, *The Annals of San Francisco* (1855) and Robert W. Cherny and William Issel, *San Francisco: Presidio, Port and Pacific Metropolis* (1981).

There is information on Los Angeles in books by Harris Newmark, *Sixty Years in Southern California* (1916); Benjamin Hayes, *Pioneer Notes* (1922); Horace Bell, *Reminiscences of a Ranger* (1881) and *On the Old West Coast* (1930); J. J. Warner, Benjamin Hayes, and J. P. Widney, *An Historical Sketch of Los Angeles County* (1876); Robert G. Cleland and Frank B. Putnam, *Isaias W. Hellman and Farmers and Merchants Bank* (1965); and particularly in William B. Rice, *The Los Angeles Star, 1851–1864* (1947).

Kenneth M. Johnson, *The New Almadén*

Quicksilver Mine (1963); Robert L. Kelley, "Forgotten Giant: The Hydraulic Gold Mining Industry in California," *PHR*, 32 (1954), 343–56, and *Gold vs. Grain: The Hydraulic Mining Controversy in California's Sacramento Valley* (1960); H. Brett Melendy, "Two Men and a Mill: John Dolbeer, William Carson, and the Redwood Lumber Industry of California," *CH*, 38 (1959), 59–71; John E. Baur, "Early Days and California Years of John Percival Jones," *SCQ*, 44 (1962), 97–131; Patricia M. Bauer, "The Beginnings of Tanning in California," *CH*, 33 (1954), 59–72; and Lloyd C. Miltare, *Salted Tories: The Story of the Whaling Fleets of San Francisco* (1960), follow the rise of selected industries.

On the agricultural development in the first American decades, see the appropriate chapters in Lawrence J. Jelinek, *Harvest Empire: A History of California Agriculture* (1979) and in C. B. Hutchison, ed., *California Agriculture* (1946); see also Paul W. Gates, *California Ranchos and Farms, 1846–1862* (1967); Edward F. Treadwell's rather superficial biography of Henry Miller, *The Cattle King* (1931); Vincent P. Carosso, *The California Wine Industry, 1830–1895* (1951); Walton Bean, "James Warren and the Beginnings of Agricultural Institutions in California," *PHR*, 13 (1944), 361–75; John W. Caughey, "Don Benito Wilson, *Huntington Library Quarterly*, 2 (1939), 285–300; and Robert G. Cleland, *The Cattle on a Thousand Hills* (1941). Rodman W. Paul deals with a substantial subject in "The Great California Grain War: The Grangers Challenge the Wheat King," *PHR*, 27 (1958), 331–49, and "The Wheat Trade between California and the United Kingdom," *Mississippi Valley Historical Review*, 45 (1958), 391–412.

The glories of the Comstock are recorded by Mark Twain, *Roughing It* (1872); by his crony William Wright, who wrote under the pen name Dan DeQuille, in *The Big Bonanza* (1876) and *A History of the Comstock Mines* (1889); and by Charles H. Shinn, *The Story of the Mine* (1896). A later flood of writing includes Swift Paine, *The Big Bonanza* (1931); George D. Lyman, *The Saga of the Comstock Lode* (1934); Wells Drury, *An Editor on the Comstock Lode* (1939); Grant H. Smith, *The History of the Comstock Lode* (1943); Oscar Lewis, *Silver Kings* (1947); Duncan Emrich, ed., *Comstock Bonanza* (1950); Lucius Beebe and Charles Clegg, *Legends of the Com-*

stock Lode (1950); and Zeke Daniels and Ben Christy, *The Life and Death of Julia C. Bulette* (1958).

11. Politics and Land Titles

For broad views of politics in this formative period, see Josiah Royce, *California, from the Conquest in 1846 to the Second Vigilance Committee* (1886); and Spencer Olin, Jr., *California Politics: 1846–1920: The Emerging Corporate State* (1981). Theodore Grivas, *Military Governments in California* (1962), is the principal reference on its topic. Contemporary comment is available in Walter Colton's *Three Years in California* (1850). The road to statehood is followed by Cardinal L. Goodwin, *The Establishment of State Government in California* (1914); Joseph Ellison, "The Struggle for Civil Government in California," *CH*, 10 (1931), three installments; and James A. B. Scherer, *Thirty-first Star* (1942). See also Rockwell D. Hunt, *The Genesis of California's First Constitution* (1895); and J. Ross Browne's official *Record of the Debates in the Convention of California on the Formation of the State Constitution* (1850).

William H. Ellison, *A Self-governing Dominion* (1950), follows politics through the fifties; Joseph Ellison, *California and the Nation* (1927), deals with federal relations through another decade. Bancroft, Hittell, and Royce have much to say about politics in this period. William H. Ellison, ed., "Memoirs of Hon. William M. Gwin," *CH*, 19 (1940), four installments, is an important source. See also James O'Meara, *Broderick and Gwin* (1881); Lately Thomes, *William McKendree Gwin* (1969); David A. Williams, *David C. Broderick: A Political Portrait* (1970); A. Russell Buchanan, *David S. Terry of California, Dueling Judge* (1956); and Peyton Hurt, *The Know Nothing Party in California* (1930).

For information on California and the Civil War, see the December, 1961, issue of *CH*; Milton H. Shutes, *Lincoln and California* (1943); Aurora Hunt, *The Army of the Pacific* (1951) and *Major General James Henry Carleton* (1958); Fred B. Rogers, *Soldiers of the Overland* (1938); Oscar Lewis, *The War in the Far West* (1961); and John W. Robinson, *Los Angeles in Civil War Days, 1860–65* (1977).

The resolution of holdover land titles in newly

acquired California is a principal subject in W. W. Robinson's *Land in California* (1948), useful because it describes the setting as well as the processes. Henry W. Halleck, *Report on Land Titles in California* (1850), and William Carey Jones, *Land Titles in California* (1850), present the findings of two assigned investigators. These works are included in the Executive Documents series of Congress. Ogden Hoffman, *Report of Land Cases Determined in the United States District Court of the Northern District of California* (1862) and California Surveyor-General, *Reports, 1879–80* are useful government records. Robert H. Becker, *Diseños of California Ranchos* (1964), illuminates a specific involvement. There is a four-volume printing of the proceedings in the litigation that exposed Limantour's fradulent claim to half San Francisco, *United States* vs. *José Yves Limantour* (1858), well summarized in Kenneth M. Johnson's *José Yves Limantour* vs. *the United States* (1961). Useful on the makers of southern California is Robert G. Cleland's *The Cattle on a Thousand Hills* (1941).

Bancroft, Hittell, and several others sharply criticize the legal process. In contrast, Alston G. Field, "Attorney General Black and the California Land Claims," *PHR*, 4 (1935), 235–45, supports the thesis that Black rendered a great service by fighting fraudulent claims. And in a series of articles, "The Adjudication of Spanish-Mexican Land Claims in California," *Huntington Library Quarterly*, 21 (1958), 213–26; "California's Embattled Settlers," *CH*, 41 (1962), 99–130; and "Pre–Henry George Land Warfare in California," *CH*, 46 (1967), 121–48, Paul W. Gates insists that the United States was only doing what it had done in earlier acquired territories.

12. The Vigilante Habit

Hubert Howe Bancroft's *Popular Tribunals* (2 vols., 1887) has a wealth of detail on the California vigilantes, both urban and rural. In his *California*, Josiah Royce seriously addressed himself to this phenomenon. Charles H. Shinn, *Mining Camps* (1885), has much to say about people's courts in the diggings, as do many of the forty-niner narratives. Mary Floyd Williams edited the *Papers of the San Francisco Committee of Vigilance of 1851* (1929) and wrote *History of the San Francisco Committee of Vigilance of 1851*

(1921), to which can be added George R. Stewart, Jr., *Committee of Vigilance: Revolution in San Francisco, 1851* (1964). James A. B. Scherer's *The Lion of the Vigilantes* (1939) is about William T. Coleman and his work in 1851, 1856, and 1877.

The case for the second committee is stated in moderation in Frank M. Smith's *The San Francisco Vigilance Committee of 1856* (1883), and with less restraint in Stanton A. Coblentz's *Villains and Vigilantes* (1936); and Alan Valentine's *Vigilante Justice* (1955). See also Doyce B. Nunis, Jr., ed., *The San Francisco Vigilance Committee of 1856: Three Views* (1971). The law and order viewpoint is reflected in James O'Meara's *The Vigilance Committee of 1856* (1887); William Tecumseh Sherman's *Memoirs* (2 vols., 1875) and in his article in *Century*, 43 (1891), 296–309; and bluntly in Issac J. Wistar's *Autobiography* (2 vols., 1914). A. Russell Buchanan, *David S. Terry of California* (1956); William H. Ellison, *A Self-governing Dominion* (1950); Roger W. Lotchin, *San Francisco, 1846–1856: From Hamlet to Modern City* (1974); and John W. Caughey, *Their Majesties the Mob* (1960), are more critical, as is Walter Tilburg Clark in his novel, *The Ox Bow Incident* (1942).

Rufus K. Wyllys's *The French in Sonora, 1850–1854* (1932) is the prime authority on California-based filibustering. See also his "The Republic of Lower California, 1853–54," *PHR*, 2 (1933), 194–214; "An Expansionist in Baja California, 1855," *PHR*, 1 (1932), 477–82; and "Henry A. Crabb: A Tragedy of the Sonora Frontier," *PHR*, 9 (1940), 183–94. On a Sam Brannan venture, see Andrew F. Rolle, "California Filibustering and the Hawaiian Kingdom," *PHR*, 19 (1950), 251–63.

13. A White Man's Country

Bancroft castigates the treatment of the Indians in his *History of California* and *California Inter Pocula*. William H. Ellison's "The Federal Indian Policy in California, 1846–1860," *Mississippi Valley Historical Review*, 9 (1922), 37–67, is to the point, as are his "The California Indian Frontier," *Grizzly Bear* (March, 1922) and "Rejection of California Indian Treaties: A Study of Local Influence on National Policy," *Grizzly Bear* (May–July, 1925). Alban W. Hoopes, *Indian*

Affairs and Their Administration, with Special Reference to the Far West, 1849–1860 (1932), notes the spread of the reservation system. Edward E. Dale's *The Indians of the Southwest* (1949) has greater breadth. See also Charles C. Royce, *Indian Land Cessions in the United States* (1899); and Stephen Bonsal, *Edward Fitzgerald Beale: A Pioneer in the Path of Empire, 1822–1903* (1912), a biography of the originator of the reservation system.

Indian experiences in this period are described by John W. Caughey, ed., *The Indians of Southern California in 1852* (1952); George H. Phillips, *Chiefs and Challengers: Indian Resistance and Cooperation in Southern California* (1975) and his "Indians in Los Angeles, 1781–1875: Economic Integration, Social Disintegration," *PHR*, 49 (1980), 427–51; and William R. Benson, "The Stone and Kelsey 'Massacre' on the Shores of Clear Lake in 1849—The Indian Viewpoint," *CH*, 11 (1932), 266–73; Lafayette Bunnell, *The Discovery of the Yosemite and the Indian War of 1851* (1881); Annie Mitchell, *Jim Savage and the Tulareño Indians* (1957); C. Gregory Crampton, ed., *The Mariposa Indian War* (1958); Helen S. Giffen and Arthur Woodward, *The Story of El Tejón* (1942); and Theodora Kroeber, *Ishi in Two Worlds* (1961).

Keith A. Murray's *The Modocs and Their War* (1959) is an account of resistance against formidable odds. In *The Indian History of the Modoc War*, by Jeff C. Riddle (1914), the adjective in the title is at least partly justified. A. B. Meacham's *Wigwam and War-path, or, The Royal Chief in Chains* (1875) is the melodramatic account of an Indian agent. The military are represented in LaFayette Grover's *Modoc War* (1874); Alvan Gillem's *Final Report of the Operation of Troops in the Modoc Country* (1877); and Max Heyman's *Prudent Soldier* (1960), a biography of E. R. S. Canby.

Reports on the mission Indians of southern California by John G. Ames and C. A. Wetmore were printed as government documents in 1873 and 1875. The pleas for a just and more generous treatment voiced by Helen Hunt Jackson in *A Century of Dishonor* (1881) and *Ramona* (1884) and, with the collaboration of Abbot Kinney, in *Report on the Conditions and Needs of the Mission Indians* (1883) were continued and reinvigorated by Charles F. Lummis in the columns of *Land of Sunshine* and *Out West*. Ruth Odell did a thorough study of Helen Hunt Jackson's life in 1939. Twentieth-century review of the dispossession of the California Indians and their claims for compensation are described by George Phillips, *The Enduring Struggle: Indians in California History* (1981); Robert W. Kenny, *History and Proposed Settlement of Claims of California Indians* (1944); and Kenneth M. Johnson, *K–344, or the Indians of California vs. the United States* (1966).

The problems of minorities in the early American decades are touched on by Ferdinand F. Fernández, "Except a California Indian: A Study in Legal Discrimination," *SCQ*, 50 (1968), 161–75; Rudolph M. Lapp, "Negro Rights Activities in Gold Rush California," *CH*, 45 (1966), 3–20; William E. Franklin, "The Archy Case," *PHR*, 33 (1963), 137–54; Robert Seager II, "Some Denominational Reactions to Chinese Immigration to California, 1856–1892," *PHR*, 28 (1959), 49–66; Elmer Sandmeyer, *The Anti-Chinese Movement in California* (1939); Ping Chiu, *Chinese Labor in California, 1850–1880* (1963); Gunther Barth, *Bitter Strength: A History of the Chinese in the United States, 1850–1870* (1964); Leonard M. Pitt, *The Decline of the Californios* (1966); and Pedro Castillo and Albert Camarillo, *Furia y Muerte: Chicano Social Banditry* (1973).

14. Cultural Awakening

City of the Golden 'Fifties (1941), by Pauline Jacobsen, pictures the life of San Francisco and, to a degree, that of the state. Other works, by T. A. Barry and B. A. Patten, *Men and Memories of San Francisco* (1873); Idwal Jones, *Ark of Empire: San Francisco's Montgomery Block* (1951); and Robert E. Cowan, *Forgotten Characters of Old San Francisco* (1938), support her description. William H. Brewer's *Up and Down California in 1860–1864* (1930) is an important source on the interior.

Irving G. Hendrick's *California Education: A Brief History* (1980) is a succinct overview. William W. Ferrier's *Ninety Years of Education in California* (1937) is the basic reference on educational beginnings. David F. Ferris, *Judge Marvin and the Founding of the California Public School System* (1962); John Swett, *History of the Public School System of California* (1876) and *Public Education in California* (1911); William G. Carr,

John Swett: The Biography of an Educational Pioneer (1933); and Nicholas C. Polos, *John Swett: California's Frontier Schoolmaster* (1978) chart the growth of public schooling. On higher education, see Gerald McKevitt, *The University of Santa Clara* (1979); Verne A. Stadtman, *The University of California, 1868–1968* (1970); William W. Ferrier, *Origin and Development of the University of California* (1930) and *Henry Durant: First President of the University of California* (1942); and Abraham Flexner, *Daniel Coit Gilman* (1946).

William Hanchett's "The Question of Religion and the Taming of California, 1849–1854," *CH*, 32 (1953), 49–56, 119–44, and his "The Blue Law Gospel in Gold Rush California," *PHR*, 24 (1955), 361–68, introduce some of the Protestant churchmen. John B. McGloin's *California's First Archbishop: The Life of Joseph Sadoc Alemany, O.P.* (1966) and Francis J. Weber's *California's Reluctant Prelate: The Life and Times of Right Reverend Thaddeus Amat, C.M.* (1964) are biographies of San Francisco's first Catholic archbishop and Los Angeles's first bishop, respectively. See also John B. McGloin, *Jesuits by the Golden Gate* (1972).

Constance Rourke's *Troupers of the Gold Coast* (1928) is a lighthearted volume with long applause for Lotta Crabtree. G. R. MacMinn's *The Theater of the Golden Era* (1941) and Edmond M. Gagey's *The San Francisco Stage* (1950) are supplemented by a series of articles by Lois Foster Rodecape in *CH* in the 1940s. A pioneering study is John Baur's *Growing Up With California: A History of California's Children* (1978).

Early journalism is described by E. C. Kemble, *A History of California Newspapers, 1846–1858* (1858; 1927; and, with annotations by Helen Harding Bretnor, 1962); John P. Young, *Journalism in California* (1915); and John Bruce, *Gaudy Century: The Story of San Francisco's Hundred Years of Robust Journalism* (1948). William B. Rice, *The Los Angeles Star, 1851–1864* (1947) covers the beginnings of journalism in southern California. Francis P. Weisenburger, *Idol of the West* (1965), follows the western career of journalist Rollin M. Daggett. Benjamin S. Harrison, *Fortune Favors the Brave* (1953), traces, among many other adventures, Horace Bell's editorship of the *Porcupine*.

Franklin Walker's *San Francisco's Literary Frontier* (1939) is a sheaf of sketches of early

California writers colored by sage comment on their works and on the society in which they moved. His *A Literary History of Southern California* (1950) has a longer time span and likewise is social as well as literary history. Also valuable are Kevin Starr's *Americans and the California Dream* (1973); Roger Lotchin's *San Francisco, 1846–1856* (1974); and Gunther Barth's *Instant Cities: Urbanization and the Rise of San Francisco and Denver* (1975). Ella Sterling Cummins [Mighels], *The Story of the Files* (1893), is a useful general survey. Hubert Howe Bancroft has a long chapter on the subject in *Essays and Miscellany* (1890).

Notable biographies include George R. Stewart, *Bret Harte: Argonaut and Exile* (1931); Bernard De Voto, *Mark Twain's America* (1932); Ivan Benson, *Mark Twain's Western Years* (1938); Edgar M. Branch, *The Literary Apprenticeship of Mark Twain* (1950); Henry Nash Smith, ed., *Mark Twain of the Enterprise* (1957); Bernard Taper, ed., *Mark Twain's San Francisco* (1963); George Stewart, *John Phoenix, Esq., the Veritable Squibob* (1937); Rodman W. Paul, "In Search of 'Dame Shirley,'" *PHR*, 33 (1964), 127–46; Thurman Wilkins, *Clarence King* (1958); Martin S. Peterson, *Joaquin Miller, Literary Frontiersman* (1937); M. N. Marberry, *Splendid Poseur: Joaquin Miller* (1953); and David Michael Goodman, *A Western Panorama, 1849–1875: The Travels, Writings, and Influence of J. Ross Browne* (1966).

15. Steamboats and Stages

Oscar O. Winther, *Express and Stagecoach Days in California* (1936), and William and George Banning, *Six Horses* (1930), describe western staging with special reference to James Birch. Charles Outland, *Stagecoaching on El Camino Real* (1973), covers the route between Los Angeles and San Francisco. Maymie Krythe's *Port Admiral, Phineas Banning* (1957) is a biography of southern California's most enterprising stage operator. The rise of riverboats and ferries on San Francisco Bay is the subject of Jerry MacMullen's *Paddlewheel Days in California* (1944). Jack McNairn and Jerry MacMullen wrote a companion book on the coast trade north of San Francisco: *Ships of the Redwood Coast* (1945).

John H. Kemble's *The Panama Route, 1848–*

1869 (1943) is a masterly account of the mail steamers and their runs. A. H. Clark's *The Clipper Ship Era, 1843–1869* (1910) relates largely to California voyages. There are pertinent chapters in books by Samuel Eliot Morison, *The Maritime History of Massachusetts* (1921); Raymond Rydell, *Cape Horn to the Pacific* (1952); and Robert G. Albion, *The Rise of the Port of New York, 1815–1860* (1939). Victor M. Berthold, *The Pioneer Steamer "California," 1848–1849* (1932), centers on the first steamer on the Panama run. John H. Kemble's *San Francisco Bay, a Pictorial Maritime History* (1957) is a rich compilation on ships and shipping in and out of the great bay. Much of the maritime history of the period is covered by Felix Rosenberg, Jr., *Golden Gate: The Story of San Francisco Harbor* (1940), and William M. Camp, *San Francisco, Port of Gold* (1947).

Lewis B. Lesley's *Uncle Sam's Camels* (1929) and Harlan D. Fowler's *Camels to California* (1950) are book-length studies of one of the more fanciful transportation experiments. W. Turrentine Jackson, *Wagon Roads West* (1952), reports of western demands for federal aid and subsidy for road improvements to California. On the women who came overland, consult Sandra Myres, ed., *Ho for California* (1980).

The account by LeRoy R. Hafen in *The Overland Mail, 1849–1869* (1926) is much elaborated in Roscoe P. and Margaret B. Conkling's *The Butterfield Overland Mail, 1857–1869* (3 vols., 1948). There are popular histories of Wells Fargo by Neill C. Wilson (1936), Edward Hungerland (1949), and Lucius Beebe and Charles Clegg (1949), the latter largely in pictures. *Seventy Years on the Frontier* (1893) by Alexander Majors contains one of the few accounts of wagon freighting, also prominent in Raymond W. and Mary Lund Settle's *War Drums and Wagon Wheels* (1966), a history of the firm of Russell, Majors, and Waddell.

The dashing but brief episode of the Pony Express has half a dozen histories: William L. Visscher, *A Thrilling and Truthful History of the Pony Express* (1908); Glenn D. Bradley, *The Story of the Pony Express* (1913); Arthur Chapman, *The Pony Express* (1932); Raymond W. and Mary Lund Settle, *Saddles and Spurs* (1955); Roy S. Bloss, *Pony Express—The Great Gamble* (1959); Noel Loomis, *Wells Fargo* (1969); Waddell Smith, *The Story of the Pony Express* (1960),

and his *Pony Express versus Wells Fargo Express* (1966), a rebuttal of W. Turrentine Jackson's "A New Look at Wells Fargo Stagecoaches and the Pony Express," *CH*, 45 (1966), 291–324. Smith's contention is that Wells Fargo was one of the travel agents or ticket agents for the Pony Express but not its operator. The conqueror of the Pony Express is the subject of Robert Luther Thompson's *Wiring a Continent* (1947).

Walter B. Lang, ed., *The First Overland Mail* (2 vols., 1940, 1945), and Lyle H. Wright and Josephine M. Bynum, eds., *The Butterfield Overland Mail* (1942), make available the one through passenger's account of the first westbound stage run. An eastbound report with an expressive subtitle is William B. Tallack's *The California Overland Express: The Longest Stage Ride in the World* (1935). Horace Greeley, Samuel Bowles, and many others wrote with feeling about riding the stage, none more vividly than Mark Twain in *Roughing It* (1872).

16. Rails over the Sierra

The *Pacific Railroad Reports*, 13 quarto volumes with numerous maps, plates, and colored plates (1855), were of little practical assistance to the builders but are concrete evidence of governmental interest. George L. Albright attempted, without total success, to reduce the meat of these reports to one slender narrative, *Official Explorations for Pacific Railroads, 1853–1855* (1921). Grant Foreman's *A Pathfinder in the Southwest* (1941) reproduces Whipple's report of the survey along the 35th parallel.

E. L. Sabin, *Building the Pacific Railway* (1919); Robert L. Fulton, *Epic of the Overland* (1924); John D. Galloway, *The First Transcontinental Railroad* (1950); Robert West Howard, *The Giant Iron Trail: The Story of the First Transcontinental Railroad* (1963); and Wesley S. Griswold, *A Work of Giants: Building the First Transcontinental Railway* (1963) range from sketchy to detailed and from matter of fact to vibrant in telling the story of this epoch-making construction project.

Chief engineer Grenville M. Dodge committed his memoirs to print on *How We Built the Union Pacific Railway* (1903). This narrative is expanded and made more effective in J. R. Perkins, *Trails, Rails and War* (1929). Belatedly, in 1960, economist Robert William Fogel ran an economic analysis which led him to the conclusion that, with a few years' patience, the road could have been built without the need for a great federal subsidy: *The Union Pacific Railroad, A Case in Premature Enterprise.*

Carl I. Wheat's "A Sketch of the Life of Theodore D. Judah," *CH*, 4 (1925), 219–71, is the first required reading on the building of the Central Pacific. See also Judah's pamphlet, *A Practical Plan for Building the Pacific Railroad* (1857). George T. Clark's *Leland Stanford* is less than critical, while Cerinda W. Evans's *Collis Potter Huntington* (2 vols., 1954) is unrelieved adulation. Better balanced are Norman Tutorow's *Leland Stanford* (1970) and David Lavender's *The Great Persuader* (1970), the latter a biography of Collis Huntington. Ward McAfee casts a broad net in *California's Railroad Era, 1850–1911* (1973). Oscar Lewis, *The Big Four* (1938), sees the magnitude of their achievements yet deplores some of the methods employed. Harry J. Carman and Charles H. Mueller, "The Contract and Finance Company and the Central Pacific Railroad," *Mississippi Valley Historical Review*, 14 (1927), 326–41, go about as far as the meager records permit.

17. Social Unrest

Doris M. Wright, "The Making of Cosmopolitan California," *CH*, 19 (1940), 323–43, and 20 (1941), 65–79, takes stock of the elements that had gone into the California population by 1870. Concerning rural population and its problems, see Paul S. Taylor, "Foundations of California Rural Society," *CH*, 24 (1945), 139–61; and Ezra S. Carr, *The Patrons of Husbandry on the Pacific Coast* (1875).

On the eve of completion of the Pacific Railway, Henry George issued a warning, "What the Railroad Will Bring Us," *Overland*, 1 (1858), 297–304. The rising resentment against the railroad is described in several of the titles in the section above, particularly in the latter part of Lewis, *The Big Four.* See also Stuart Daggett, *Chapters on the History of the Southern Pacific* (1922), and, as sidelights on the corporation's unpopularity, C. B. Glasscock, *Bandits and the Southern Pacific* (1929), and Wallace Smith,

Prodigal Sons: The Adventures of Christopher Evans and John Sontag (1951).

Mary R. Coolidge's *Chinese Immigration* (1909) is a standard reference on California's first Asians. Also valuable are Elmer Sandmeyer's *The Anti-Chinese Movement in California* (1939); Gunther Barth's *Bitter Strength* (1964); and Alexander Saxton's *The Indispensable Enemy: Labor and the Anti-Chinese Movement in California* (1971). Paul M. De Falla, "Lantern in the Western Sky," *SCQ*, 42 (1960), 57–88, 161–85; and William R. Locklear, "The Celestials and the Angels: A Study of the Anti-Chinese Movement in Los Angeles to 1882," *SCQ*, 42 (1960), 239–56, describe the Los Angeles Massacre.

Henry George contributed an article on "The Kearney Agitation in California" to *Popular Science Monthly*, 17 (1880), 433–54; James Bryce devoted a chapter to "Kearneyism in California," in his *The American Commonwealth* (2 vols., 1888). Ira B. Cross, *A History of the Labor Movement in California* (1935), and Frank B. Roney, *Irish Rebel and California Labor Leader: An Autobiography* (1931); R. A. Burchell, *The San Francisco Irish, 1848–1880* (1980); and James Walsh, *The San Francisco Irish, 1850–1976* (1978) touch on this political unrest.

For specifics on the new constitution, see Winfield J. Davis, *History of Political Conventions in California* (1893), and Carl Brent Swisher, *Motivation and Political Technique in the California Constitutional Convention, 1878–1879* (1930). Also valuable for this era and more is Robert Hine's *California Utopianism: Contemplations of Eden* (1981).

18. Southern California Development

The general setting is charted by J. J. Warner, Benjamin Hayes, and J. P. Widney, *An Historical Sketch of Los Angeles County* (1876); Sarah Bixby Smith, *Adobe Days* (1925); Ludwig L. Salvator, *Eine Blume aus dem goldenen Lande oder Los Angeles* (1878), translated by Marguerite Eyer Wilbur as *Los Angeles in the Sunny Seventies* (1929); John Albert Wilson, *History of Los Angeles County* (1880); and Joseph O'Flaherty, whose *An End and a Beginning* (1972) and *Those Powerful Years* (1978) cover greater Los

Angeles from 1850 to 1917. Richard F. Pourade gives an overview of San Diego in *The Glory Years* (1964); Remi A. Nadeau furnishes a more searching analysis in *City-makers: The Men Who Transformed Los Angeles from Village to Metropolis, 1868–1876* (1948). See also Albert Camarillo, *Chicanos in a Changing Society: From Mexican Pueblos to American Barrios in Santa Barbara and Southern California, 1848–1930* (1979); Richard Griswold del Castillo, *The Los Angeles Barrio, 1850–1890* (1979); Robert M. Fogelson, *The Fragmented Metropolis: Los Angeles, 1850–1930* (1967); Oscar O. Winther, "The Rise of Metropolitan Los Angeles, 1870–1900," *Huntington Library Quarterly*, 10 (1947), 391–405; Robert V. Hine, *William Andrew Spalding, Los Angeles Newspaperman* (1961) and his more offbeat *California's Utopian Colonies* (1953).

There are background references such as George W. Groh's *Gold Fever, Being a True Account, Both Horrifying and Hilarious, of the Art of Healing (so-called) During the California Gold Rush* (1966) and John E. Baur's "The Health Factor in the Gold Rush Era," *PHR*, 18 (1949), 97–108, which attest that California exerted an earlier attraction to health seekers. The principal authority on the health rush at its height is John E. Baur's *Health Seekers of Southern California, 1870–1900* (1959).

On railroad development, Quiett's *They Built the West* and Daggett's *Chapters in the History of the Southern Pacific* are supplemented by the works of Neill C. Wilson and Frank J. Taylor, *Southern Pacific: The Roaring Story of a Fighting Railroad* (1952); Glenn D. Bradley, *Story of the Santa Fe* (1920); James Marshall, *Santa Fe: The Railroad That Built an Empire* (1949); and L. L. Waters, *Steel Trails to Santa Fe* (1950).

The promotional literature that contributed to the boom may be sampled in California Immigrant Union, *All About California and the Inducements to Settle There* (1870); Jerome Madden, *The Lands of the Southern Pacific Railroad Company* (1876); Benjamin F. Taylor, *Between the Gates* (1878); William H. Bishop, *Old Mexico and Her Lost Provinces* (1883); T. S. Van Dyke, *Southern California* (1886); and Walter Lindley and J. P. Widney, *California of the South* (1888). Futher information is afforded by Newmark, *Sixty Years in Southern California*; Guinn, *Los Angeles and Its Environs*; Charles Dudley Warner, *Our*

Italy (1891); Laurance L. Hill, *La Reina: Los Angeles in Three Centuries* (1929); and W. W. Robinson, *Panorama: A Picture-History of Southern California* (1953).

Glenn S. Dumke, *The Boom of the Eighties in Southern California* (1944), and T. S. Van Dyke, *Millionaires of a Day* (1890), offer, respectively, a serious assessment and a hilarious lampoon. Walker, *A Literary History of Southern California*, takes stock of the cultural consequences.

Rahno Mabel McCurdy, *The History of the California Fruit Growers' Exchange* (1925), and Kelsey B. Gardner and A. W. McKay, *The California Fruit Growers Exchange System* (1950), tell the basic facts. The genius displayed in marketing is brought to light in Josephine Kingsbury Jacobs's "Sunkist Advertising" (UCLA dissertation, 1966). See also Charles C. Teague, *Fifty Years a Rancher* (1944); Sidney Burchell, *Jacob Peek, Orange Grower* (1915); Donald H. Pflueger, *Charles C. Chapman* (1976); H. E. Erdman, "The Development and Significance of California Cooperatives, 1900–1915," *Agricultural History*, 32 (1958), 179–84; and E. Kraemer and H. E. Erdman, *History of Cooperation in Marketing California Fresh Deciduous Fruits* (1933).

William H. Hall's *Irrigation in California* (1888) is an inventory of operative projects. Samuel C. Wiel, *Water Rights in the Western States* (3rd ed., 2 vols., 1911); Elwood Mead, *Irrigation Institutions* (1903); and W. E. Smythe, *The Conquest of Arid America* (1905), provide background. J. A. Alexander's *The Life of George Chaffey* (1928) is a brief biography of the leading irrigator of his time.

Regarding town and city development see John and LaRee Caughey, eds., *Los Angeles: Biography of a City* (1977); John D. Weaver, *Los Angeles: The Enormous Village, 1781–1981* (1980); David Clark, *Los Angeles: A City Apart* (1981); Andrew Rolle, *Los Angeles: From Pueblo to City of the Future* (1981); James M. Guinn, *A History of California and an Extended History of Los Angeles and Environs* (3 vols., 1915); H. L. Sherman, *History of Newport Beach* (1931); Mildred Yorba MacArthur, *Anaheim: The Mother Colony* (1959); H. F. Raup, *The German Colonization of Anaheim* (1932) and *San Bernardino: Settlement and Growth of a Pass-Site City* (1940); Merlin Stonehouse, *John Wesley North and the Reform Frontier* (1965); Donald H. Pflueger,

Glendora: The Annals of a Southern California Community (1951) and Covina: Sunflowers, Citrus, Subdivisions (1964).

19. Broadening the Economic Base

Sources on the Imperial Valley disaster include H. T. Cory, The Imperial Valley and the Salton Sea (1915); E. F. Howe and W. J. Hall, The Story of the First Decade in Imperial Valley (1910); Otis B. Tout, The First Thirty Years (1931); and George Kennan, The Salton Sea: An Account of Harriman's Fight with the Colorado River (2 vols., 1917). Robert L. Kelley, "Taming the Sacramento: Hamiltonianism in Action," PHR, 34 (1965), 21–49, outlines a major victory in reclamation scored by cooperative effort and federal aid. His Gold vs. Grain (1959) relates the controversy over hydraulic mining that made such a program necessary.

John R. Spears, Illustrated Sketches of Death Valley (1892); Ruth C. Woodman, The Story of the Pacific Coast Borax Company (1951); W. A. Chalfant, Death Valley, the Facts (1930); and Scherer, The Lion of the Vigilantes, provide glimpses of the borax mining. Concerning the oil industry, see Gerald T. White's Formative Years in the Far West (1962), which covers Standard Oil of California through 1919; Frank J. Taylor and Earl M. Welty's Black Bonanza (1950), on Union Oil; and Frank Latta's Black Gold in the Joaquin (1949). The flowering of other industries is touched upon by C. B. Glasscock, Lucky Baldwin (1935); H. Austin Adams, John D. Spreckels (1924); Gilson Gardner, Lusty Scripps (1932); William H. B. Kilner, Arthur Letts (1927); Robert O. Schad, "Henry E. Huntington," Huntington Library Bulletin, 1 (1931), 3–32; L. J. Rose, Jr., L. J. Rose of Sunny Slope, 1827–1899 (1959); Ruth Waldo Newhall, The Story of the Newhall Land and Farming Company (1958); and Spencer Crump, Ride the Big Red Cars (1962).

Remi A. Nadeau's The Water Seekers (1950) contains a good account of Los Angeles's Owens Valley project, but the most recent and complete analyses are Abraham Hoffman's Vision or Villany: Origins of the Owens Valley–Los Angeles Water Controversy (1981) and William L. Kahrl's Water and Power: The Conflict over Los Angeles's Water Supply in the Owens Valley (1982).

Mary Austin, The Land of Little Rain (1903), chronicles the valley before Los Angeles took a hand. Report of the Aqueduct Investigating Board (1912) tells of the inception of the project; Final Report of Construction of the Los Angeles Aqueduct (1916) describes the building. W. A. Chalfant, The Story of Inyo (1922); Morrow Mayo, Los Angeles (1933); and Carey McWilliams, Southern California Country (1946) comment scathingly on the methods of getting the water and distributing the benefits.

20. Culture Leaders

Reminiscences of end-of-the-century San Francisco are both numerous and glowing. The tone is set by Will Irwin's nostalgic essay, The City That Was (1906). Evelyn Wells's Champagne Days of San Francisco (1939) is an effective dramatization incorporating a multitude of authentic details. Oscar Lewis and Carroll D. Hall, Bonanza Inn, America's First Luxury Hotel (1939), throw a similar halo around the city's chief showplace, Ralston's Palace. Charles C. Dobie's San Francisco's Chinatown (1936) is a tribute to a most picturesque quarter; other writers have dwelt on the less distinctive but more notorious Barbary Coast, while more genteel memoirs are embodied in Amelia R. Neville's The Fantastic City (1932). Other sidelights are detailed by M. M. Marberry, The Golden Voice: A Biography of Isaac Kalloch (1947); Edgar M. Kahn, Cable Car Days in San Francisco (1940); Frank Parker, Anatomy of the San Francisco Cable Car (1946); Lucius Beebe and Charles Clegg, Cable Car Carnival (1951); and Edmond M. Gagey, The San Francisco Stage, a History (1950).

Arthur Miller's "Growth of Art in California," in Frank J. Taylor, Land of Homes (1929), 311–41; and Jeanne Van Nostrand's The First Hundred Years of Painting in California, 1775–1875 (1980) are instructive. Eugene Neuhaus's William Keith, the Man and the Artist (1938) is a sketch of the best known painter of the generation. Harold Kirker, California's Architectural Frontier (1960), discusses style and tradition in nineteenth-century design. A useful supplement is Porter Garnett's Stately Homes of California (1915).

Joseph Henry Jackson's Continent's End: A Collection of California Writing (1944) stresses the writers of this period, as does George Sterling's anthology of poetry, *Continent's End* (1925). Walker's *San Francisco's Literary Frontier* and *A Literary History of Southern California* appraise many of these writers as does his *The Seacoast of Bohemia* (1966). Although his third volume is incomplete, Vernon L. Parrington, *Main Currents in American Thought* (3 vols., 1927–30), comments at length on Norris, London, and George. Direct appraisal of the writings of this period is the best approach and, although first editions command a stiff premium, is feasible. Also useful is Kevin Starr's *Americans and the California Dream, 1850–1915* (1973).

For help on individual authors, see Gertrude Atherton, *Adventures of a Novelist* (1932); Mary Austin, *Earth Horizon* (1932); Franklin Walker, *Frank Norris* (1932); Ruth Odell, *Helen Hunt Jackson* (1939); Irving Stone, *Sailor on Horseback: The Biography of Jack London* (1938); Joan London, *Jack London and His Times* (1939); and Richard O'Conner, *Jack London* (1964). For perspective on Robert Louis Stevenson's California experiences, see J. C. Furnas, *Journey to Windward* (1951); Henry M. Bland, *Stevenson's California* (1924); Anne Roller Issler, *Stevenson at Silverado* (1939) and *Our Mountain Heritage, Silverado and Robert Louis Stevenson* (1950); Anne Fisher, *No More a Stranger* (1946); and James D. Hart, ed., *From Scotland to Silverado* (1966). Edwin R. Bingham's *Charles F. Lummis, Editor of the Southwest* (1955) and Dudley Gordon's *Charles F. Lummis, Crusader in Corduroy* (1972) are complementary studies.

John W. Caughey's *Hubert Howe Bancroft, Historian of the West* (1946) is a full-length study of an unusual man. Of the myriad works on George, Charles A. Barker's *Henry George* (1955) is superior; Henry George, Jr.'s *Life of Henry George* (1900) and Arthur N. Young's *The Single Tax Movement in the United States* (1916) supplement. Ambrose Bierce is on display in his *Collected Works* (12 vols., 1909–12), a badly planned and poorly edited set. Of numerous short appraisals, Wilson Follett's "Ambrose, Son of Marcus Aurelius," *Atlantic Monthly*, 140 (1937), 32–42, and Paul Fatout's *Ambrose Bierce, the Devil's Lexicographer* (1951) stand out. Chief item in a substantial body of writing on William Randolph Hearst is W. A. Swanberg's *Citizen Hearst* (1961), which suggests Orson Welles's remarkable film, *Citizen Kane* (1940). Useful also are John Tebbel's *The Life and Good Times of*

William Randolph Hearst (1952) and Lindsay Chaney and Michael Cieply's *The Hearsts* (1981).

Linnie M. Wolfe's biography, *Son of the Wilderness: The Life of John Muir* (1950), was preceded by her *John of the Mountains* (1938), drawing freely on his writings, which also have been given much currency in Sierra Club picture books. Holway R. Jones, *John Muir and the Sierra Club: The Battle for Yosemite* (1966), concentrates on the intersection of the man and the institution. The latest study in Stephen Fox's *John Muir and His Legacy: The American Conservation Movement* (1981).

Ferrier's books on education in California are supplemented for the south by Laurance L. Hill, *Six Collegiate Decades* (1929). David Starr Jordan's educational theories are set forth in his voluminous writings, especially *The Voice of the Scholar* (1903) and *The Days of a Man* (2 vols., 1922), as are Benjamin Ide Wheeler's in his *The Abundant Life* (1926). See also Verne A. Stadtman, *The University of California, 1868–1968* (1970); Edward M. Burns, *David Starr Jordan, Prophet of Freedom* (1953); and Benjamin P. Kurtz, *Charles Mills Gayley* (1943). For the California stay of Thorstein Veblen, see R. L. Duffus, *The Innocents at Cedro* (1944).

21. Political Housecleaning

R. Hal Williams, *The Democratic Party and California Politics, 1880–1896* (1973); Mansel G. Blackford, *The Politics of Business in California, 1890–1920* (1976); William Bullough, *The Blind Boss and His City* (1980); Judd Kahn, *Imperial San Francisco* (1979); Gilman Ostrander, *The Prohibition Movement in California* (1957); W. H. Hutchinson, *Oil, Land, and Politics: The California Career of Thomas Robert Bard* (2 vols., 1965); and Edith Dobie, *Political Career of Stephen M. White* (1927), dip into the politics of the era.

Complaints against the railroad are represented by James L. Brown, *The Mussel Slough Tragedy* (1958). Ward M. McAfee, *California's Railroad Era, 1850–1911* (1973), deals with the dissension and much more.

Charles D. Willard's *The Free Harbor Contest at Los Angeles* (1899) may be supplemented by Ella A. Ludwig, *History of the Harbor District of Los Angeles* (1928); Charles H. Matson, *The*

Story of Los Angeles Harbor (1935); and Anthony F. Turhollow, A History of the Los Angeles District, U.S. Army Corps of Engineers, 1898–1965 (1975).

Walton Bean's Boss Ruef's San Francisco (1952) is definitive on the San Francisco graft prosecution. Earlier references include Franklin Hichborn, "The System," as Uncovered by the San Francisco Graft Protection (1915); Fremont Older, My Own Story (1919); Evelyn Wells, Fremont Older (1936); Lincoln Steffens, Autobiography (2 vols., 1931); and Robert Davenport, "San Francisco Journalism in the Time of Fremont Older" (UCLA dissertation, 1969). Lately Thomas, A Debonair Scoundrel (1962), centers on Ruef. The best study on reform drives in southern California is Albert H. Clodius's "The Quest for Good Government in Los Angeles, 1890–1910" (Claremont dissertation, 1953).

For details on the San Francisco earthquake, see William Bronson, The Earth Shook, The Sky Burned (1959); Monica Sutherland, The Damndest Finest Ruins (1959); Robert Jacopi, Earthquake Country: How, Why and Where Earthquakes Strike in California (1964); Gordon Thomas and M. M. Witts, The San Francisco Earthquake (1971); and John C. Kennedy, The Great Earthquake and Fire, San Francisco, 1906 (1963).

For the Lincoln-Roosevelt League and its work, there is basic material in Franklin Hichborn's Story of the Session of the California Legislature of 1909 (1909) and similar volumes for 1911 and 1913. See also the files of the League's organs, The California Weekly, 1908–1910, and The California Outlook, 1911–1912. J. Gregg Layne's The Lincoln-Roosevelt League (1943) is important mainly for the documents quoted. Alice Rose's "The Rise of California Insurgency" (Stanford dissertation, 1942) is more fundamental. George E. Mowry's The California Progressives (1951) is a thorough analytical study. Discussion continues in Spencer C. Olin, Jr., California's Prodigal Sons (1968); Irving McKee, "The Background and Early Career of Hiram Johnson," PHR, 19 (1950), 17–30; James C. Findley, "Cross-filing and the Progressive Movement in California Politics," Western Political Quarterly, 12 (1961), 699–711; and Jackson K. Putnam, "The Persistence of Progressivism in the 1920's," PHR, 35 (1966), 395–411. Norris Hundley dis-

cusses a prominent woman progressive in "Katherine Philips Edson and the Fight for the California Minimum Wage, 1912–1923," PHR, 29 (1960), 271–86.

22. Race Prejudice and Labor Conflict

Roger Daniels, The Politics of Prejudice (1962), is a concise review of the anti-Japanese movement in California to 1924. Carey McWilliams, Prejudice: Japanese-Americans, Symbol of Racial Intolerance (1945); Yamato Ichihashi, Japanese in the United States (1932); T. Iyenaga and Kenoske Sato, Japan and the California Problem (1921); K. K. Kawakami, The Real Japanese Question (1921); and Thomas A. Bailey, Theodore Roosevelt and the Japanese-American Crisis (1934), may also be consulted. John Modell concentrates on Los Angeles in The Economics and Politics of Racial Accommodation: The Japanese of Los Angeles, 1900–1942 (1977). For broader coverage consult H. Brett Melendy, The Oriental Americans (1972), and Norris Hundley, ed., The Asian American (1976).

References on other minorities in farm labor include Facts about Filipino Immigration into California and Mexicans in California, issued by the California Department of Industrial Relations (1930); Bruno Lasker, Filipino Immigration to Continental United States and Hawaii (1931); Dhan Gopal Mukerji, Caste and Outcast (1923); Rajani Kanta Das, Hindustani Workers on the Pacific Coast (1923); Paul S. Taylor, Mexican Labor in the United States (1929); and Carey McWilliams, North from Mexico (1949) and Factories in the Field (1939).

California labor relations are seen overall in Cross, History of the Labor Movement in California and, more briefly, in Carey McWilliams, California: The Great Exception (1949), and David F. Selvin, A Place in the Sun (1981). For details on San Francisco-centered labor problems, see Robert E. L. Knight, Industrial Relations in the San Francisco Bay Area, 1900–1918 (1960); Bernard C. Cronin, Father Yorke and the Labor Movement in San Francisco, 1900–1910 (1943); Frederick L. Ryan, Industrial Relations in the San Francisco Building Trades (1936); Paul S. Taylor, The Sailors' Union of the Pacific (1923);

and Hyman G. Weintraub, *Andrew Furuseth, Emancipator of the Seamen* (1959). See also Philip Taft, *Labor Politics American Style: The California State Federation of Labor* (1968).

Grace Heilman Stimson, *Rise of the Labor Movement in Los Angeles* (1955), and Louis B. and Richard S. Perry, *A History of the Los Angeles Labor Movement, 1911–1941* (1963), provide comprehensive accounts. Supplementary works include Robert Gottlieb and Irene Wolf, *Thinking Big: The Story of the Los Angeles Times, Its Publishers and Their Influence on Southern California* (1977); Louis Adamic, *Dynamite* (1929); *The Forty Years War*, a *Los Angeles Times* brochure, October 1, 1929; William J. Burns, *The Masked War* (1913); Ortie McManigal, *The National Dynamite Plot* (1913); *Autobiography of Lincoln Steffens* (1931); and Clarence Darrow, *The Story of My Life* (1932).

Paul F. Brissenden, *The IWW, a Study of American Syndicalism* (1920); Patrick Renshaw, *The Wobblies* (1967); and Martin Dubofsky, *We Shall Be All: A History of the Industrial Workers of the World* (1969), survey the movement as a whole. Carleton Parker's *The Casual Laborer and Other Essays* (1920) and Cornelia S. Parker's *An American Idyll: Carleton H. Parker* (1919) are of interest. A careful study is Woodrow C. Whitten's *Criminal Syndicalism and the Law in California, 1919–1927* (1969). Hyman G. Weintraub, "The IWW in California, 1905–1931" (UCLA thesis, 1947), is thorough; thinly disguised as fiction, much of the story appears in Wallace Stegner's *The Preacher and the Slave* (1950). Robert H. Frost's *The Mooney Case* (1968) is the most complete follow-through on its subject. Other useful works are Curt Gentry's *Frame-up* (1967) and Ernest J. Hopkins's *What Happened in the Mooney Case* (1932). Eldredge F. Dowell, *A History of Criminal Syndicalism Legislation in the United States* (1939), trains the spotlight on a disgraceful injustice. See also Franklin Hichborn, *The Case of Charlotte Anita Whitney* (1920).

23. The Boom of the Twenties

Cleland and Hardy's *March of Industry* reaches into the twenties. Its tables and maps are a valuable adjunct. Also useful are the reports of the U.S. Bureau of the Census and such state documents as *California Crop Reports, Economic Resources and Extractive Industries of California,* and *California Mineral Production.* Julian Dana, *A. P. Giannini, Giant of the West* (1947), deals with a key figure, and Joe S. Bain, *Economics of the Pacific Coast Petroleum Industry* (3 vols., 1944–47), deals with a key industry. John O. Pohlmann, "Alphonzo E. Bell: A Biography," *SCQ*, 46 (1964), 197–217, 315–50, tells of a fortune made in oil and real estate. Other businesses are represented by Latta, *Black Gold in the San Joaquin*; Giles T. Brown, *Ships That Sail No More: Marine Transportation from San Diego to Puget Sound, 1910–1940* (1966); and Josephine Kingsbury Jacobs, "Sunkist Advertising" (UCLA dissertation, 1966). Anton Wagner's *Los Angeles: Werden, Leben und Gestalt der Zweimillionenstadt in Südkalifornien* (1935) is a geographer's analysis of the factors that contributed to the rise of the state's largest city.

The growing addiction to the automobile can be followed in *Touring Topics* and its successor *Westways*, particularly in the December, 1950, issue marking the fiftieth anniversary of the Automobile Club of Southern California. See also Ben Blow, *California Highways* (1920); Felix Riesenberg, Jr., *The Golden Road* (1962); Robert Fogelson, *Fragmented Metropolis* (1967); and Earl S. Pomeroy, *In Search of the Golden West: The Tourist in Western America* (1957).

Lewis Jacobs, *The Rise of the American Film: A Critical History* (1939), and Leo Rosten, *Hollywood, the Movie Colony, the Movie Makers* (1939), analyze economic growth, artistic development, and social impact. Later appraisals include Arthur Knight, *The Liveliest Art* (1957), and A. R. Fulton, *Motion Pictures: The Development of an Art from Silent Films to the Age of Television* (1960). Bosley Crowther writes authoritatively in *The Lion's Share* (1957), a history of Metro–Goldwyn–Mayer, and in *Hollywood Rajah: The Life and Times of Louis B. Mayer* (1960). There is a vast amount of writing about the movie makers. Among the most readable are Nathanael West's novel, *The Day of the Locust* (1939); F. Scott Fitzgerald's *The Last Tycoon* (1941); and Lillian Ross's *Picture* (1952), a *New Yorker* report on the filming of the *Red Badge of Courage*.

In McWilliams, *Southern California Country,* C. C. Julian and Aimee Semple McPherson are viewed as sociological phenomena. See also Guy

W. Finney, *The Great Los Angeles Bubble* (1925); Nancy Barr Mavity, *Sister Aimee* (1931); and the harsher view of Lately Thomas in *Storming Heaven* (1970) and *The Vanishing Evangelist* (1959).

24. The Great Depression

Dixon Wecter, *The Age of the Great Depression* (1948), portrays the nationwide impact of hard times after 1929. There is no comparable study for California, though Paul N. Woolf, *Economic Trends in California, 1929–1934* (1935); Leigh Athearn, *The California State Relief Administration, 1935–1939* (1939); and the California State Chamber of Commerce, *Economic Survey of California and Its Counties, 1942* (1943), inform on certain aspects. Carey McWilliams, *California: The Great Exception* (1949); Robert G. Cleland, in his historical summation, *California in Our Time, 1900–1940* (1947); and Oliver Carlson, more bitingly, in *A Mirror for Californians* (1941), offer analysis and commentary.

The labor problems of this decade are discussed by William M. Camp, *San Francisco, Port of Gold* (1947), and McWilliams, *California: The Great Exception*. The San Francisco general strike is examined by Paul Eliel, *The Waterfront and General Strikes* (1934); William F. Dunne, *The Great San Francisco General Strike* (1934); and Mike Quin, *The Big Strike* (1949). Another element of labor history is discussed by Manuel P. Servín, "The Pre–World War II Mexican American: An Interpretation," *CH*, 44 (1966), 325–32.

On the plight of the migrant farm workers, see Walter J. Stein, *California and the Dust Bowl Migration* (1973). A quick introduction is Dorothea Lange and Paul S. Taylor's *American Exodus* (1939; enlarged and reprinted, 1969). Varden Fuller's "The Supply of Agricultural Labor as a Factor in the Evolution of Farm Organization in California" (Berkeley dissertation, 1939) was published in a United States Senate Committee on Education and Labor report, *Violations of Free Speech and Rights of Labor*, part 54 (1940), 19, 777–819, 898. Other studies include Walter Goldschmidt, *As You Sow* (1947), a sociological analysis of two San Joaquin Valley communities; Carlton Beals, *The American Earth* (1939); Clarke Chambers, *California Farm Organizations, 1929–1941* (1952); and Carey McWil-

liams, *Factories in the Field* (1939). John Steinbeck communicated the message far more effectively in *In Dubious Battle* (1936) and *The Grapes of Wrath* (1939). For works on Mexican Americans, see Abraham Hoffman, *Unwanted Mexican Americans in the Great Depression* (1974); and Mercedes Carreras de Velasco, *Los mexicanos que devolvió la crisis, 1929–1932* (1974).

The cults and "isms" are admirably handled by McWilliams, *Southern California Country* (1946); Robert Hine, *California Utopianism: Contemplations of Eden* (1981); and by the Cleland and Carlson volumes cited above. See particularly Luther Whiteman and Samuel L. Lewis, *Glory Roads: The Psychological State of California* (1936); and *Out of the Frying Pan* (1939), Winston and Marian Moore's aptly titled book on Ham and Eggs. Upton Sinclair's *I, Governor of California and How I Ended Poverty* (1933) and *I, Candidate for Governor, and How I Got Licked* (1934) are key documents on Epic. A mainstay of the campaign, the *Epic News*, suddenly became a rarity. See also *The Autobiography of Upton Sinclair* (1962); George Creel, *Rebel at Large* (1947); Francis E. Townsend, *New Horizons: An Autobiography* (1943); Abraham Holtzman, *The Townsend Movement: A Political Study* (1963); and Jackson K. Putnam, *Old-Age Politics in California* (1970). Robert E. Burke's *Olson's New Deal for California* (1953) is an admirable study. The central issue in Frost's *The Mooney Case* continued important in California politics.

For a superb overview of California water resource development, see William Kahrl, ed., *The California Water Atlas* (1979). Remi A. Nadeau, *The Water Seekers* (1950), and Vincent Ostrom, *Water and Politics: A Study of Water Policies and Administration in the Development of Los Angeles* (1953), encompass the Boulder Canyon project. Norris Hundley focuses on the project's origins in "The Politics of Reclamation: California, the Federal Government, and the Origins of Boulder Canyon Act," *CH*, 52 (1973), 292–325. For the interstate preliminaries and conflicts, see Norris Hundley, *Water and the West: The Colorado River Compact and the Politics of Water in the American West* (1975), and on federal decision making, see Beverly R. Moeller, *Phil Swing and Boulder Dam* (1971). Frank Waters, *The Colorado* (1946), is particularly informing on the construction, which is also stressed by Ray L. Wilbur and Elwood Mead, *Construction of Hoov-*

er Dam (1935); George A. Pettitt, *So Boulder Dam Was Built* (1935); and Paul L. Kleinsorge, *The Boulder Canyon Project* (1941). International competition for the flow of the Colorado and some other border rivers as well is the subject of Norris Hundley's *Dividing the Waters: A Century of Controversy between the United States and Mexico* (1966). For details on the delivery system, see Metropolitan Water District, *The Colorado Aqueduct* (1939) and *The Great Aqueduct* (1941). For a sensitive treatment of environmental issues and more, see Philip L. Fradkin, *A River No More: The Colorado River and the West* (1981).

Robert De Roos, *The Thirsty Land: The Story of the Central Valley Project* (1948) is a popular prospectus but less elementary than *The Central Valley Project* (1942), compiled by the Writers' Program. Marion Clawson's *Acreage Limitation in the Central Valley* (1944), *The Effect of the Central Valley Project on the Agricultural and Industrial Economy and on the Social Character of California* (1945), and *History of Legislation and Policy Formation of the Central Valley Project* (1946) are expository and supportive of the policies of the Bureau of Reclamation. Senator Sheridan Downey's *They Would Rule the Valley* (1947) abominates the 160-acre limitation. For a contrasting view, see Paul S. Taylor, "Excess Land Law: Pressure versus Principle," *California Law Review*, 47 (1959), 499–541. Especially valuable is Clayton R. Koppes's "Public Water, Private Land: Origins of the Acreage Limitation Controversy, 1933–1953," *PHR*, 47 (1978), 607–36. For an overview of water use in California, see Erwin Cooper, *Aqueduct Empire* (1968).

25. A California Way of Life

Rediscovery of the environment is represented in guidebooks such as those by Aubrey Drury (1935; 1947) and the Federal Writer's Project (1939), the publications of the automobile clubs, and in photographic albums such as Edward Weston's *California and the West* (1940) and Ansel Adams's *The Sierra Nevada* (1938) and *My Camera in Yosemite Valley* (1949). In addition to natural history guidebooks published by the University of California Press and the Sierra Club, there are series devoted to regions, rivers, mountains, and lakes. Examples include Edwin Corle,

Desert Country (1941); Carey McWilliams, *Southern California Country* (1946); Anne B. Fisher, *The Salinas, Upside-down River* (1945); Roderick Peattie, *The Pacific Coast Ranges* (1946) and *The Sierra Nevada* (1947); and George and Bliss Hinkle, *Sierra-Nevada Lakes* (1949). François E. Matthes's *Geologic History of the Yosemite Valley* (1930), *The Incomparable Valley, a Geologic Interpretation of the Yosemite* (1950), and *Sequoia National Park, a Geological Album* (1950) go back to the geological beginnings. Carl P. Russell, *One Hundred Years in Yosemite* (1931; 1947), recites the human history. Also useful for this chapter and much more is Raymond Dasmann's *California's Changing Environment* (1981).

For information on architectural development, see Esther McCoy, *Five California Architects* (1960), and Reyner Banham, *Los Angeles: The Architecture of Four Ecologies* (1971).

Writings of this period can be sampled in George Sterling, ed., *Continent's End: An Anthology of Contemporary California Poets* (1925); Joseph Henry Jackson, ed., *Continent's End: A Collection of California Writing* (1944); J. H. Jackson, *The Western Gate: A San Francisco Reader* (1952); and in John and LaRee Caughey, eds., *California Heritage* (1971), 379–426, 435–59.

Edmund Wilson's *The Boys in the Back Room* (1941) is a rapid glance at several of the writers of this time. Appraisals of Steinbeck include Harry T. Moore, *The Novels of John Steinbeck* (1939), and Joseph Fontenrose, *John Steinbeck: An Introduction and Interpretation* (1964). Lawrence Clark Powell wrote the first book on Jeffers in 1932, *Robinson Jeffers, the Man and His Work* (revised 1940). Radcliffe Squires's *The Loyalties of Robinson Jeffers* (1956) and Melba Berry Bennett's *The Stone Mason of Tor House: The Life and Times of Robinson Jeffers* (1966) are supplemented by Ann N. Ridgeway, ed., *The Selected Letters of Robinson Jeffers* (1969) and *The Selected Poetry of Robinson Jeffers* (1938).

Educational developments in the twentieth century are succinctly presented by Irving Hendrick, *California Education: A Brief History* (1980). The astronomy story is detailed by G. Edward Pendray, *Men, Mirrors, and Stars* (1935), and David O. Woodbury, *The Glass Giant of Palomar* (1946). Palomar and other phases of scientific advancement are noted in McWilliams's

California: The Great Exception. There are hints in Oscar Lewis's *I Remember Christine* (1942) on the directions in historical scholarship and more concrete data in *New Spain and the Anglo-American West* (2 vols., 1932); *Greater America: Essays in Honor of Herbert Eugene Bolton* (1945); John Francis Bannon, *Herbert Eugene Bolton* (1978); and John W. Caughey, "Herbert Eugene Bolton," *American West*, 1 (1964), 36–39, 79.

26. Wartime Upsurge

McWilliams's *California: The Great Exception,* though broader in scope, is the closest approach to a survey of California during the war years. The reports of the Bureau of the Census and of various state agencies provide statistics. Particularly useful is one by the California State Chamber of Commerce, "Economic Survey of California and Its Counties," *California Blue Book, 1946*, pp. 409–772. Davis McEntire, *The Population of California* (1946), and Marion Clawson, "What It Means to Be a Californian," *CH*, 24 (1945), 139–61, deal with characteristics as well as numbers.

Katherine Archibald, *Wartime Shipyard* (1947); William G. Cunningham, *The Aircraft Industry: A Study in Industrial Location* (1951); John B. Rae, *Climb to Greatness: The American Aircraft Industry, 1920–1960* (1968); and Ewald T. Grether, *The Steel-using Industries of California* (1946), deal selectively with war industries.

Morton Grodzins, *Americans Betrayed* (1949), is an analysis of the motivation for the removal of the Japanese. Western Defense Command, *Japanese Evacuation from the West Coast* (1943), is General De Witt's apologia. In Kent Robert Greenfield, ed., *Command Decisions* (1960), Stetson Conn concentrates on the decision to evacuate. Effective summations are Roger Daniels, *Concentration Camps USA: Japanese Americans and World War II* (1971); Michi Weglyn, *Years of Infamy* (1976); Allan Bosworth, *America's Concentration Camps* (1967); Dillon S. Meyer, *Uprooted Americans* (1971); and Audrie Girdner and Anne Loftis, *The Great Betrayal* (1969). Carey McWilliams, *Prejudice: Japanese-Americans, Symbols of Racial Intolerance* (1944), and Bradford Smith, *Americans From Japan* (1948), are sharply critical. War Relocation Authority, *A Story of Human Conservation* (1946),

is the formal report of the administrators. Ansel Adams, *Born Free and Equal: The Story of Manzanar* (1944), and Miné Okubo, *Citizen 31660*, are pictorial, the latter by one of the evacuees. Other valuable firsthand accounts are John Modell, ed., *The Kikuchi Diary* (1973), and Jeanne Wakatsuki Houston and James Houston, *Farewell to Manzanar* (1973). The sociological consequences are meticulously reported by Dorothy S. Thomas and Richard Nishimoto, *The Spoilage* (1946); Thomas, with Charles Kikuchi and James Sakoda, *The Salvage* (1952); Jacobus TenBroek, Edward N. Barnhart, and Floyd W. Matson, *Prejudice, War and the Constitution* (1954); Leonard Bloom and Ruth Tiemer, *Removal and Return* (1949); Leonard Broom and John I. Kitsuse, *The Managed Casualty* (1956); and Leonard J. Arrington, *The Price of Prejudice* (1962). See Eugene V. Rostow, *The Sovereign Prerogative and the Quest for Law* (1962) for specifics on the law. Edward N. Barnhart, "Japanese Internees from Peru," *PHR*, 31 (1962), 169–78, deals with a neglected feature; and James Edmiston's novel *Home Again* (1955) personalizes the enormity of the injustice. In 1972 the California Historical Society memorialized the internment in *Executive Order 9066*, by Maisie and Richard Conrat, with illustrations by Dorothea Lange.

27. A Touch of Midas

A number of references cited in this chapter are also relevant to the content of the other chapters which concern California since World War II. Among them are books by Neil Morgan, *The California Syndrome* (1969); R. L. Duffus, *Queen Calafia's Island* (1965); Earl S. Pomeroy, *The Pacific Slope* (1965); Remi Nadeau, *California, the New Society* (1963) and *Los Angeles, from Mission to Modern City* (1960); Andrew Rolle, *Los Angeles* (1981); Edmund G. Brown and others, *California, the Dynamic State* (1966); and Carey McWilliams, *The California Revolution* (1968).

Reports of the Bureau of the Census are useful, as are the successive issues of *California Statistical Abstract*, by the California Economic Development Agency. Specialized studies include Warren S. Thompson, *Growth and Changes in California's Population* (1955); Margaret S. Gordon, *Employment and Expansion and Population*

Growth: The California Experience, 1900–1950 (1954); and Davis McEntire, The Labor Force in California, 1900–1950 (1952). Fortnight, launched in 1946, and Frontier (1949–67) are broadly informative.

Ernest A. Engelbert's Metropolitan California (1961) and a University of California publication, The Metropolitan Future (1965), may be supplemented by Winston W. Crouch and Beatrice Dinerman, Southern California Metropolis: A Study in Development of Government for a Metropolitan Area (1964); Richard Preston, The Changing Landscape of the San Fernando Valley between 1930 and 1964 (1966); Mel Scott, The San Francisco Bay Area: A Metropolis in Perspective (1959); Kingsley Davis and Eleanor Langlois, Future Demographic Growth of the San Francisco Bay Area (1959); Thomas J. Kent, Jr., City and Regional Planning for the Metropolitan San Francisco Bay Area (1963); Robert Cherny and William Issel, San Francisco: Presidio, Port and Pacific Metropolis (1981); John B. McGloin, San Francisco (1978); Lawrence Kinnaird, History of the Greater San Francisco Bay Region (3 vols., 1967); H. O. Stekler, Structure and Performance of the Aerospace Industry (1965); and John Anson Ford, Thirty Explosive Years in Los Angeles County (1961). Concerning water projects and their impact on urban and agricultural developments, see William Kahrl, ed., The California Water Atlas (1979); Norris Hundley, Water and the West (1975), Dividing the Waters (1966), and "Clio Nods: Arizona v. California and the Boulder Canyon Act—A Reassessment," Western Historical Quarterly, 3 (1972), 17–51; and Lawrence Jelinek, Harvest Empire (1979). H. Marshall Goodwin, Jr., "California's Growing Freeway System" (UCLA dissertation, 1969), provides a detailed account of almost every phase of freeway development.

28. Issues and Politics

A good summary of recent California politics is Jackson K. Putnam's Modern California Politics (1980). For the pre-1970s see also Gladwin Hill, Dancing Bear: An Inside Look at California Politics (1968). There are handbooks on California government and politics by Henry A. Turner and John A. Vieg; Winston W. Crouch, Dean E. McHenry, John Bollens, and Stanley Scott; and Bernard L. Hyink, Seyom Brown, and Ernest W. Thacker, all political scientists.

Leo Katcher, Earl Warren: A Political Biography (1967); Richard B. Harvey, Earl Warren: Governor of California (1969); and John D. Weaver, Warren: The Man, the Court, the Era (1967), offer salutes to a Californian who went on to a noteworthy term as Chief Justice of the United States. Lester Velie, "The Secret Boss of California," Collier's (August 13 and 20, 1949), and Carey McWilliams, in Nation (July 9, 1949), report the lobbying prowess of Art Samish. A firsthand report is Arthur H. Samish and Bob Thomas's The Secret Boss of California (1971). Trevor Ambrister, "The Octopus in the State House," Saturday Evening Post (Feb. 12, 1966), tells of Samish's tribe of successors. McWilliams, "Government by Whitaker and Baxter," Nation (April 14 and 21, and May 5, 1951), and Irwin Ross, "The Supersalesmen of California Politics: Whitaker and Baxter," Harper's, 219 (July 1959), inform on a potent agency.

Ernest R. Bartley, The Tidelands Oil Controversy (1953), discusses a matter pressed in court and in politics. Winston W. Crouch, The Initiative and Referendum in California (1950), measures the effectiveness of these techniques of direct democracy. The best treatment of its subject is Jackson K. Putnam's Old-Age Politics in California from Richardson to Reagan (1970).

Edward L. Barrett, Jr., The Tenney Committee (1961) is a judiciously restrained study. For analysis of the Hollywood Ten and what followed, see Gordon Kahn, Hollywood on Trial (1948), and John Cogley, Report on Blacklisting (2 vols., 1956). See John Caughey, "Farewell to California's 'Loyalty' Oath," PHR, 38 (1969), 123–28, on the exit of the test oath for all state employees. On the University's oath experience, see George R. Stewart, Jr., The Year of the Oath (1950); David P. Gardner, The California Oath Controversy (1967); and John W. Caughey, "A Battlefield Revisited," Law in Transition, 4 (1967), 172–78.

School segregation receives attention in Charles Wollenberg's All Deliberate Speed: Segregation and Exclusion in California Schools, 1855–1975 (1976) and Irving Hendrick's Public Policy Toward the Education of Non-White Minority Group Children in California, 1849–1970 (1975). The Berkeley pathway to school integration is charted by Neil Sullivan and Evelyn S.

Stewart in *Now Is the Time: Integration in the Berkeley Schools* (1969). Irving Hendrick covers another success story in *The Development of a School Integration Plan in Riverside, California* (1968). John and LaRee Caughey, *School Segregation on Our Doorstep: The Los Angeles Story* (1966) and *Segregation Blights Our Schools* (1967), and John Caughey, *To Kill a Child's Spirit* (1973), describe an effort largely unsuccessful. For an account of Richmond, California, see Lillian Rubin, *Busing and Backlash: White Against White in an Urban California School District* (1972).

In reference to related subjects, see David Hulburd, *This Happened in Pasadena* (1951); J. Allen Broyles, *The John Birch Society: Anatomy of a Protest* (1964); Thomas W. Storke, *I Write for Freedom* (1963), featuring his tiff with the Birch Society; Gerald Gottlieb, *Capital Punishment* (1967); and Edmund G. (Pat) Brown, "A Plea for Abolition of the Death Penalty," in John and LaRee Caughey, *Los Angeles: Biography of a City* (1976), pp. 417–22. *Open Forum* (1941 on), the periodical of the ACLU of Southern California, reports occasionally at length on violations of civil liberties and efforts in and out of court to prevent repetitions. On a controversial issue, see Raymond McHugh, *Land of the Free and Its Critics* (1967).

29. A Time of Confrontations

Though based on elaborate and well-financed hearings, the McCone Commission report, *Violence in the City* (1965), is a far from convincing analysis of the Los Angeles Riot. Also consult valuable supplements by Robert Conot, *Rivers of Blood, Years of Darkness* (1967); Jack Jones, *The Voice from Watts* (1967); Paul Bullock, ed., *Watts: The Aftermath* (1969); and Nathan Cohen, ed., *The Los Angeles Riots: A Sociopsychological Study* (1970). Budd Schulberg's *From the Ashes: Voices from Watts* (1967) is an anthology of writers in the workshop he organized in Watts after the riot. A broader viewpoint, though a succinct one, is Rudolph Lapp's *Afro-Americans in California* (1979).

In *The Holy Barbarians* (1959), Lawrence Lipton gives an avuncular view of the hippies. Albert T. Anderson and Bernice P. Biggs's *A Focus on Rebellion* (1962) is a documentary on

the San Francisco City Hall incident of May, 1960. A perceptive account of the Free Speech Movement at Berkeley is Seymour M. Lipset and Sheldon S. Wolin's *The Berkeley Student Revolt* (1965). The Muscatine Report, an approximate forecast of changes in educational program and governance, appeared under the title *Education at Berkeley* (1967). Art Seidenbaum's *Confrontation on Campus* (1969) is a revealing report compiled after indepth observing and interviewing at nine California campuses.

Leo Gebler, *Mexican Immigration to the United States* (1966); Leo Gebler et al., *The Mexican-American People* (1970); Norris Hundley, ed., *The Chicano* (1975); Lloyd S. Fisher, *The Harvest Labor Market in California* (1953); and Mark Reisler, *By the Sweat of Their Brow: Mexican Immigrant Labor in the United States, 1900–1940* (1976), contribute pertinent information. For works on the braceros, see Ernesto Galarza, *Merchants of Labor: The Mexican Bracero Story* (1964), and *Farm Workers and Agri-Business in California, 1947–1960* (1977); Truman E. Moore, *The Slaves We Rent* (1965); and Henry P. Anderson, *The Bracero Program in California* (1976). César Chávez's efforts on behalf of California harvest workers have been described in many newspaper and magazine stories. The principal book is John Gregory Dunne's *Delano: The Story of the California Grape Strike* (1967; 1971), but see also Ronald B. Taylor, *Chávez and the Farm Workers* (1975).

In *American Racism: Exploration of the Nature of Prejudice* (1970), a historian and a social psychologist, Roger Daniels and Harry H. L. Kitano, use California as an exhibit for a résumé of race prejudice operative up to and including the present generation.

Ronald Reagan has been a frequent subject in the local and national press and magazines and in Bill Boyarsky's *The Rise of Ronald Reagan* (1968); Lou Cannon's *Ronnie and Jesse: A Political Odyssey* (1969); and Joseph Lewis's *What Makes Reagan Run?* (1968).

30. New Challenges

Morgan, *The California Syndrome*; Brown, *California, the Dynamic State*; Nadeau, *California, the New Society*; Duffus, *Queen Calafia's Island*; and Hill, *Dancing Bear*, inventory many of the consequences of the hyperthyroid growth of the forties, fifties, and sixties. Consult Putnam, *Modern California Politics*; Robert Pack, *Jerry Brown: The Philosopher Prince* (1978); Ed Salzman, *Jerry Brown: High Priest and Low Politician* (1977); and John C. Bollens and G. Robert Williams, *Jerry Brown: In a Plain Brown Wrapper* (1978), on politics and Jerry Brown.

Mel Scott's *Partnership in the Arts: Public and Private Support of Cultural Activities in the San Francisco Bay Area* (1963); Arthur Bloomfield's *The San Francisco Opera, 1923–1961* (1961) and *The Arts in California* (1966) are introductory. Douglas Honnold, *Southern California Architecture, 1769–1956* (1956); Esther McCoy, *Five California Architects* (1960), *Richard Neutra* (1960), and *Modern California Houses: Case Study Houses, 1945–1962* (1962); Harold Gilliam and Phil Palmer, *The Face of San Francisco* (1960); and Reyner Banham, *Los Angeles: The Architecture of Four Ecologies* (1971), concentrate on one art form.

Irving Hendrick's *California Education: A Brief History* (1979); James C. Stone's *California's Commitment to Public Education* (1961); and Merton E. Hill's *The Junior College Movement in California, 1907–1948* (1949) extend into the recent past. Arthur G. Coons, *Crises in California Education* (1968), is mainly concerned with the master plan for higher education.

Eliot Porter, *The Place No One Knew: Glen Canyon on the Colorado* (1963); Philip Hyde and François Leydet, *The Last Redwoods* (1963); and Richard Kaufmann, *Gentle Wilderness: The Sierra Nevada* (1964), plead for conservation of natural beauties. *Cry California* (1965 on) is a periodical dedicated to the fight against pollution in all its forms. Raymond F. Dasmann, *The Destruction of California* (1965); Samuel E. Wood, *California, Going, Going . . .* (1962); Richard G. Lillard, *Eden in Jeopardy* (1966); and William Bronson, *How To Kill a Golden State* (1968), proclaim this same concern in their titles. The apocalyptic message that exploding population and runaway science are on the verge of sounding Doomsday for life on this planet is expounded in Rachel Carson's *Silent Spring* (1962) and Paul R. Ehrlich's *The Population Bomb* (1968). Consult James Krier and Emund Ersin, *Pollution and Policy: A Case Essay on California and Federal Experience with Motor Vehicle Air Pollution, 1940–1975* (1977), on a problem closer to home.

Index